Origins of African Plant Domestication

World Anthropology

General Editor

SOL TAX

Patrons

CLAUDE LÉVI-STRAUSS
MARGARET MEAD
LAILA SHUKRY EL HAMAMSY
M. N. SRINIVAS

MOUTON PUBLISHERS · THE HAGUE · PARIS
DISTRIBUTED IN THE USA AND CANADA BY ALDINE, CHICAGO

Origins of African Plant Domestication

Editors

JACK R. HARLAN
JAN M. J. DE WET
ANN B. L. STEMLER

MOUTON PUBLISHERS · THE HAGUE · PARIS
DISTRIBUTED IN THE USA AND CANADA BY ALDINE, CHICAGO

General Editor's Preface

Man's transition from hunting and gathering to deliberately growing food has been characterized by many scholars as his first step out of a "savage" existence. Thus it is that much attention has been focused by anthropologists on how and where that transition took place. Africa, for its diversity in agricultural techniques and crops, may be the ideal location for testing some of the theory generated by that attention. The papers in this book, updating our information on the domestication of plants in Africa, were mainly prepared for a conference just prior to, and separate from, the IXth ICAES. Professor Harlan was in the process of editing them for publication when I invited him to use a session of the IXth International Congress of Anthropological and Ethnological Sciences as a forum for their discussion. Thus they could be discussed together with those of a pre-Congress conference organized by Charles Reed on the more general problem of domestication; the Congress could obtain the considerable advantage of important information assembled previous to its meeting; and Harlan and his associates could profit from the presence of a major international assembly of scientists in related fields.

Like most contemporary sciences, anthropology is a product of the European tradition. Some argue that it is a product of colonialism, with one small and self-interested part of the species dominating the study of the whole. If we are to understand the species, our science needs substantial input from scholars who represent a variety of the world's cultures. It was a deliberate purpose of the IXth International Congress of Anthropological and Ethnological Sciences to provide impetus in this direction. The *World Anthropology* volumes, therefore, offer a first glimpse of a human science in which members from all societies have played an active role. Each of the books is designed to be self-contained; each is an attempt to update its particular sector of scientific knowledge and is written by specialists from all parts of the world. Each volume should be read and reviewed individually as a separate volume on its own given subject. The set as a whole will indicate what changes are in store for anthropology as scholars from the developing countries join in studying the species of which we are all a part.

The IXth Congress was planned from the beginning not only to include as many of the scholars from every part of the world as possible, but also with a view toward the eventual publication of the papers in high-quality volumes. At previous Congresses scholars were invited to bring papers which were then read out loud. They were necessarily limited in length; many were only summarized; there was little time for discussion; and the sparse discussion could only be in one language. The IXth Congress was an experiment aimed at changing this. Papers were written with the intention of exchanging them before the Congress, particularly in extensive pre-Congress sessions; they were not intended to be read aloud at the Congress, that time being devoted to discussions — discussions which were simultaneously and professionally translated into five languages. The method for eliciting the papers was structured to make as representative a sample as was allowable when scholarly creativity — hence self-selection — was critically important. Scholars were asked both to propose papers of their own and to suggest topics for sessions of the Congress which they might edit into volumes. All were then informed of the suggestions and encouraged to re-think their own papers and the topics. The process, therefore was a continuous one of feedback and exchange and it has continued to be so even after the Congress. The some two thousand papers comprising *World Anthropology* certainly then offer a substantial sample of world anthropology. It has been said that anthropology is at a turning point; if this is so, these volumes will be the historical direction-markers.

As might have been foreseen in the first post-colonial generation, the large majority of the Congress papers (82 percent) are the work of scholars identified with the industrialized world which fathered our traditional discipline and the institution of the Congress itself: Eastern Europe (15 percent); Western Europe (16 percent); North America (47 percent): Japan, South Africa, Australia, and New Zealand (4 percent). Only 18 percent of the papers are from developing areas: Africa (4 percent); Asia-Oceania (9 percent); Latin America (5 percent). Aside from the substantial representation from the U.S.S.R. and the nations of Eastern

Europe, a significant difference between this corpus of written material and that of other Congresses is the addition of the large proportion of contributions from Africa, Asia, and Latin America. "Only 18 percent" is two to four times as great a proportion as that of other Congresses; moreover, 18 percent of 2,000 papers is 360 papers, 10 times the number of "Third World" papers presented at previous Congresses. In fact, these 360 papers are more than the total of ALL papers published after the last International Congress of Anthropological and Ethnological Sciences which was held in the United States (Philadelphia, 1956).

The significance of the increase is not simply quantitative. The input of scholars from areas which have until recently been no more than subject matter for anthropology represents both feedback and also long-awaited theoretical contributions from the perspectives of very different cultural, social, and historical traditions. Many who attended the IXth Congress were convinced that anthropology would not be the same in the future. The fact that the next Congress (India, 1978) will be our first in the "Third World" may be symbolic of the change. Meanwhile, sober consideration of the present set of books will show how much, and just where and how, our discipline is being revolutionized.

Besides the volume on *Origins of agriculture* edited by Charles Reed, this book is most closely related to the several volumes of *World Anthropology* devoted to historical, archaeological, technological and African topics.

Chicago, Illinois   SOL TAX
March 29, 1976

Preface

The present volume evolved over a period of several years. The Crop Evolution Laboratory was established in the Agronomy Department of the University of Illinois in 1967. One of the researchers' major interests from the start was an inquiry into the origins of African crops. Little had been done in the area, especially with modern genetic and biosystematic techniques. Several collecting expeditions were conducted, materials were assembled, crosses were made, and genetic and morphological studies consummated. Early on, it became apparent that crops are artifacts, shaped and molded by human activities, and that it was as important to study the people, their cultures, and histories as it was to study the plants. The field was too vast and disorganized to be grasped by biological investigations alone. We could easily come to terms with our own ignorance of the subject, and it seemed likely that if we could pool the knowledge and expertise available we might not be as ignorant collectively as we were individually. This is the fundamental rationale for any symposium.

I approached the Wenner-Gren Foundation for a possible reaction. Letters went to and fro. One of the fro's I received in Addis Ababa, Ethiopia, and it was most encouraging. After much consideration, deliberation, and some agonizing over the choice of personnel, a select group met at Burg Wartenstein, in Austria, August 19–27, 1972. It was a remarkable conference. The setting was right; congeniality was superb; interaction among the participants was most productive. An amazing amount of African experience was represented, and the state of the art was fairly presented. We are all deeply grateful for the support of the Wenner-Gren Foundation, and the editors of this volume are enormously indebted to the participants who so freely gave of their time and expertise. We all have an emotional pull toward Africa and hope that this small volume will lead to a fuller understanding of African accomplishments and cultures.

The bias of the Western world, which is perhaps understandable, has generated a long and intensive study of the origins of the West. The Near East has become a perennial focus for investigations of the origin of agriculture, the rise of civilization, urbanism, literature, arts, politics, philosophy, and history. In the process, Africa has been largely forgotten. It has been forgotten or ignored that an indigenous African agriculture developed with a complete array of domesticated plants including cereals, pulses, oil crops, vegetables, fruits, spices, fibers, drugs, pharmaceuticals, ritual and ceremonial plants. Indigenous agriculture supported a widespread village farming economy and the high cultures of Nok, Ife, Ghana, Mali, Benin, various Sudanic kingdoms, and Zimbabwe. This volume examines the current evidence for the origins of African plant domestication.

Crop Evolution Laboratory   JACK R. HARLAN
University of Illinois, Urbana

Table of Contents

General Editor's Preface   V

Preface   IX

INTRODUCTION   3

Plant Domestication and Indigenous African Agriculture
    by *Jack R. Harlan, J. M. J. de Wet*, and *Ann Stemler*

SECTION ONE: BACKGROUND THEORY

A Note on the Problem of Basic Causes   23
    by *John E. Pfeiffer*

Archaeology and Domestication   29
    by *Eric Higgs*

SECTION TWO: BACKGROUND PALEOCLIMATES

Paleoecological Background in Connection with the Origin of
    Agriculture in Africa   43
    by *E. M. van Zinderen Bakker*

SECTION THREE: BACKGROUND ARCHAEOLOGY

Prehistoric Populations and Pressures Favoring Plant Domestica-
    tion in Africa   67
    by *J. Desmond Clark*

Early Crops in Africa: A Review of the Evidence   107
   by *Thurstan Shaw*
Early Food Production in Northern Africa as Seen from Southwestern Asia   155
   by *Philip E. L. Smith*

SECTION FOUR: REGIONAL ARCHAEOLOGICAL EVIDENCE

Archaeological Data on the Origins of Cultivation in the Southwestern Sahara and Their Implications for West Africa   187
   by *Patrick J. Munson*
The Kintampo Culture and Its Place in the Economic Prehistory
   of West Africa   211
   by *Colin Flight*
History of Crops and Peoples in North Cameroon to A.D. 1900   223
   by *Nicholas David*
The Use of Ground Grain During the Late Paleolithic of the
   Lower Nile Valley, Egypt   269
   by *Fred Wendorf* and *Romuald Schild*

SECTION FIVE: BOTANICAL AND ETHNOGRAPHIC EVIDENCE

The Origins and Migrations of Crops in Tropical Africa   291
   by *J. W. Purseglove*
Traditional Systems of Plant Food Production and the Origins
   of Agriculture in West Africa   311
   by *David R. Harris*
Social Anthropology and the Reconstruction of Prehistoric Land
   Use Systems in Tropical Africa: A Cautionary Case Study from
   Zambia   357
   by *Thayer Scudder*
The Origins and Domestication of Yams in Africa   383
   by *D. G. Coursey*
African Cereals: Eleusine, Fonio, Black Fonio, Teff, *Brachiaria
   paspalum Pennisetum*, and African Rice   409
   by *Roland Portères*
Variability in *Sorghum biocolor*   453
   by *J. M. J. de Wet, J. R. Harlan,* and *E. G. Price*

The Races of Sorghum in Africa   465
  by *Jack R. Harlan* and *Ann Stemler*

Biographical Notes   479

Index of Names   485

Index of Subjects   493

INTRODUCTION

Plant Domestication and Indigenous African Agriculture

JACK R. HARLAN, J. M. J. DE WET, and ANN STEMLER

For some decades now considerations of plant domestication and agricultural origins have been permeated by two fundamental concepts: the "revolutionary" nature of agriculture and "centers of origin." Neither concept appears to have much application to Africa and may have generated more in the way of mental blocks than enlightenment elsewhere. The idea of an agricultural revolution as elaborated by V. Gordon Childe for the Near East was basically applied to the social and cultural consequences of food-producing economies. Food production, as opposed to hunting and gathering, was considered to be so superior that, once invented, no one would dream of returning to the old ways. The new system would spread rapidly at the expense of the more "savage" tribes. Civilization could arise only from agricultural societies because everyone else was too busy eking out a living by hunting and gathering to have the time to develop the cultural traits of "civilization," such as writing, metallurgy, specialized crafts, standing armies, priestly castes, professional classes, and so on. It was the food-producing economy that lifted man from "barbarism."

Revolutionary attributes were also applied to domesticated plants. The idea of growing food plants on purpose was thought of as having been "discovered" by some prehistoric genius, and the idea had such obvious merit that it would be adopted readily and diffused widely from its center of origin. Indeed, it seemed to be widely accepted that the concept of food production versus food harvesting required such brilliant insight and superior knowledge that it could only have been thought of once or at most a few times. While the term "agricultural revolution" has been gradually losing favor, the revolutionary nature of plant and animal domestication permeates a good deal of current literature on the subject. As will become abundantly clear in this volume, plant husbandry is not a "Eureka!" type discovery (cf. John Pfeiffer, this volume). As we learn more about early agriculture it becomes more clear that it took a long time to develop and weld together the crops, technologies, and social practices necessary to build an effective agricultural system (cf. Higgs, this volume).

The center of origin concept, elaborated by the famous Russian geneticist Vavilov (1926), was first applied to individual crops. The geographic regions in which genetic variability was concentrated were supposed to correspond to the regions in which the crop originated. Vavilov did generalize to some extent in attempting to locate regions in which agriculture originated, but did not elaborate a great deal since his main interest was in sources of genetic variation for plant breeding. The geographer Sauer (1952) took the idea much further in postulating only a few or possibly one center for the origin of agriculture.

As more and more information has become available, the Vavilovian centers have become less clearly defined and centric concepts have been eroding. Zhukovsky, a colleague and follower of Vavilov, for example, enlarged the eight centers proposed by Vavilov until they fused over whole continents (Zhukovsky 1968). We suggest this modification is, indeed, closer to the real situation, but it weakens the center of origin idea. Our present understanding would hold that neither individual crops nor agricultural systems must necessarily originate in narrowly restricted geographic areas or centers. For our purpose, a more useful concept would be that of a temporally long, geographically widespread, and biologically intimate relationship between plants and man out of which domestication can proceed almost anywhere in temperate or tropical zones.

Massive data accumulated in the Near East point to what appears to be a center of agricultural innovation. The appearance may be an artifact due to the success of a particular agricultural complex. The complex was founded at first on barley and later on wheat, but what moved out of the nuclear area was a complete system including barley, emmer wheat, einkorn wheat, lentil, vetch, pea, chickpea, fava bean, rape, flax, vegetables, spices, tree and vine fruits, sheep, goats, cattle, and an array of agricultural techniques. The system spread, moving along the shores of the Mediterranean, up the Danube and down the Rhine, eastward to the Indus and North India, and southward across Arabia, the Yemen and into the Ethiopian plateau. It eventually reached China in the second half of the second millennium B.C.

In this sense we can demonstrate a Near Eastern center. But were the Europeans, the Indians, and the Ethiopians completely devoid of domesticated plants at the time? Did the Near Eastern complex compete successfully against hunter-gatherers, or was the expansion against less efficient or transitional agricultural economies? We cannot answer these questions at the present time, but African agriculture appears to be basically noncentric in character. Not only do we fail to detect a particular center for the origin of indigenous African agriculture, but some African crops do not seem to have "centers" either (cf. Harlan and Stemler, this volume).

To be sure, centers have been proposed for African agriculture. Vavilov cited Ethiopia and ignored all the other African domesticates not originating there. Chevalier (1938), Portères (1951), and Murdock (1959) claimed a center in West Africa, focused on the Bend of the Niger. Our own analyses of the situation would call for a much more diffused view (Harlan 1971). We grant that tef, noog, ensete, and possibly finger millet were probably domesticated in Ethiopia and that African rice was probably domesticated in the Bend of the Niger region. Yet yam, oil palm, and cowpea more likely originated as crops in the ecotone between forest and savanna; sorghum, voandzeia, and fonio are savanna crops, and pearl millet is a product of the Sahel. The basic pattern is diffuse or noncentric rather than centric.

When one looks at the end products of agricultural evolution — the fully domesticated plant or the full-blown agricultural economy — it is evident that there have been radical changes. But at the outset, there is no clear advantage to food production versus food harvesting; the primitive cultivar differs little if at all from the wild progenitor. Studies of origins must involve studying inital and transitional conditions.

Africa may turn out to be the most useful laboratory of all for developing a fuller understanding of plant domestication and agricultural origins. The African scene is rich in "transitional" and "intermediate" situations — that is to say, in situations which we consider to be analogous to past situations out of which plant domestication and fully fledged agricultural economies have developed. Our studies are just beginning; they are fragmentary and unsystematic. Yet we have done enough to see fascinating and tantalizing vistas ahead. A serious and systematic multidisciplinary study of Africa would be of interest in its own right, but might also give us a much more mature view of what might have gone on in the Near East, the Far East, Oceania, and the Americas. The steps in the evolutionary process appear to be more evident in Africa than elsewhere.

DOMESTICATION

Domestication is a process, not an event. The process can be carried out over various ranges of time and at different intensities. The process continues for every crop actively being cultivated and will continue for an indefinite period into the future. How far it can go, no one yet knows. If operated at a sufficient intensity for a sufficient period of time, dramatic changes in morphology and ecological adaptation can be expected. Among African crops, for example, some yams have lost the ability to flower and, consequently, cannot be disseminated in the wild. In wild cereal grasses the inflorescence fragments at maturity by the formation of abscission layers, and seeds are dispersed. In domesticated cereals the abscission layers are suppressed, and seeds are retained at maturity. With the loss of the natural mode of seed dispersal, fully domesticated cereals are no longer able to survive without the aid of man.

Morphological changes may accumulate to the point that the differences between the wild and the more specialized domesticated races are astonishing. The wild progenitor of pearl millet (*Pennisetum violaceum*) has many inflorescences, ten centimeters or less in length. The domesticated *mil des Peules* may have single heads over two meters in length. Wild sorghum has open lacy heads with small covered seeds, while some of the most specialized domesticated types have dense compact ball heads with large exposed seeds. Similar differences may accumulate in other domesticated plants.

The process of domestication is one of genetic manipulation through human activity. In the case of seed crops much of the manipulation is automatic and comes from planting harvested seed. As long as seed is only harvested and not planted, there is likely to be little or no genetic effect on wild populations. It is seldom possible to harvest as much as half the seed produced by wild populations and ample seed remains to maintain the stand. If there is any selection pressure at all, it will be in favor of such wild-type characteristics as shattering (spontaneous seed release because of formation of abscission layers), seed dormancy, and indeterminate growth with maturation over a long period of time. It is the seed that escapes the harvester that will contribute to the next generation.

As soon as man starts to plant what he has harvested, strong selection pressures are set up. Now there are two populations, one maintained by nature and one maintained by man, with selection going in opposite directions. Outside the realm of human activity, natural selection proceeds as before, favoring wide dispersal of propagules. In the cultivator's field, however, all modifications that augment the "harvestability" of plants have a selective advantage. Mutants in which abscission layers do not form and, hence, do not naturally disperse their seeds should appear in the population rather quickly and automatically. These mutants (quickly eliminated from wild populations) are most likely to be harvested by man and sown the next year. As we shall show by the example of Ethiopian oats, deliberate selection for the trait is not necessary. Nonshattering (nondispersal of seeds) is one of the first domestic characteristics to appear in seed crops, and it is one of the most critical and diagnostic in separating wild from domesticated races. The character is usually rather simply inherited; in most cases either one or two genes are involved.

More subtle, but equally important is a selection trend toward more uniform maturity. A wild sorghum plant, for example, has many main stems which are often branched so that a large number of inflorescences are produced over a period of several weeks. This is adaptive for a wild plant because seed production continues as long as conditions permit. Seed production over a period of weeks is a disadvantage to a domesticated plant since only a fraction of the seed that can be produced is available at a single time for harvest. As soon as people begin harvesting and sowing, it is the plants which produce the most grain at a single time (rather than those which produce seed for the longest time) that make the greatest genetic contribution to the next generation. When seeds gathered in a single harvest are sown the next year, selection is automatic towards plants with a single terminal seed head, as in domesticated sorghums.

The morphological changes as a result of this selection trend are perhaps even more spectacular in pearl millet than in sorghum. Some crops have been more affected morphologically than others in the process of domestication, but the the trend toward greater uniformity of maturity is consistent and automatic in all cereals and most other seed crops.

A trend toward larger seeds is also common, although not entirely universal. Some of the increase may simply come through the selection for fewer and larger inflorescences, but most of the change is probably due to seedling competition in the seed bed. The seedling that comes up first and grows the fastest is the most likely to contribute offspring to the next generation. Seedling vigor is closely related to seed size and energy storage in the endosperm. We also know that large seeds can emerge from deeper planting better than small seeds. The depth of planting under cultivation may, therefore, result in selection for larger seeds. Selection in the seed bed is very strong against prolonged dormancy. Most wild grasses produce at least some seeds so dormant that they will not sprout under natural conditions for several years. In domesticated races the dormant period is much reduced or eliminated altogether.

Other selection trends favor rather striking modifications in inflorescence morphology. These include "multiplication" and "condensation." By multiplication, we simply mean an increase in the number of panicle branches or row number of the spike. This may come about in the course of selection for fewer and larger inflorescences. By condensation we mean a shortening of panicle branches or internodes in the inflorescence. This results in compact heads and more convenient harvestable "packages."

Superimposed on the automatic selection pressures are those deliberately imposed by the cultivators. These may be in diverse directions and are likely to be biologically capricious, but can be genetically intense. Man selects for different colors, different flavors, for storage or nutritional quality, for culinary preference, and ease of processing in his equipment. Some sorghums are boiled like rice, some cracked for porridge, some ground to make flour for bread or dumplings. Different cultivars are used for different purposes.

A common procedure at harvest time is for the cultivator to go through his field and carefully select heads to be saved as stock seed for the next planting. The rest of the field is harvested for consumption. In this situation selection is total. The components of the population that contribute to the next generation are those chosen by the cultivator. The rest are eliminated from the gene pool. The fact that a cultivar makes good dumplings may confer no ecological advantage in the field, but the selection pressure may approach the absolute. It is this sort of human activity that has resulted in such a bewildering array of variation in most domesticated plants.

In this connection it should be pointed out that the part of the plant most used by man is the part most modified. In cereals it is the seeds and seedheads. In legumes it is the seeds and pods (or tuber in the case of the yampea). In yams it is the tuber, and in ensete the stem base. Fruits may be easily modified by selection. Some of the African *Solanum* species have fruits about as large and well developed as the American tomato, for example.

Among cereals and many other crops, weed races are produced as a by-product of domestication. These races are, in fact, continuously being formed through hybridization wherever wild and domesticated races are growing together. They can be very serious pests and cause substantial crop loss because they compete with crop plants for sunlight. They are usually identifiable by their intermediate morphologies and frequently mimic the local cultivated races in some particulars. The weed races may, in turn, interbreed with either or both parental types, and occasionally very complex populations are built up. As a rule, however, discontinuities are rather clear-cut. There are barriers of some sort to gene exchange and adaptation is either for the cultivated field or for a wild or segetal habitat. The genes that control the differences in adaptation and morphology are usually tightly linked on the chromosomes so that nonadaptive recombinations are infrequent.

While domestication is a process of genetic manipulation through human activity, cultivation consists of those activities concerned with caring for the plants. A cultivated food plant can be defined as a plant deliberately established by man with the expectation of a later harvest. We shall show, however, that there are various intermediate states from indifference to tolerance, to protection, to encouragement, to full cultivation and that precise definitions are not always possible.

As we have seen, the process of domestication may be carried on to the point that some races of the crop are completely dependent upon man for survival. This state can be termed full domestication, but as with cultivation there are many intermediate and transitional states. We shall illustrate some of them with African examples.

CEREALS

Wild grass seeds are commonly harvested for food in Africa today. Jardin (1967) lists over sixty species reported to have been collected within recent years. Among these, the weedy grass *Paspalum scrobiculatum* suggests an example of incipient domestication. The species is common in the wetter parts of the Old World tropics from Japan to Indonesia and westwards across tropical Africa. It is often abundant along paths, ditches, and low spots, especially under disturbance, and frequently infests rice fields in West Africa. Should the rice crop fail or do poorly, the cultivator is usually not too concerned because his rice field is likely to be choked with *Paspalum scrobiculatum* which he will harvest for food. The grass has not been domesticated in West Africa, but domesticated races have been developed in south India, probably through a long and intimate association with this useful weed. An intermediate state between "wild" and "domesticated" is illustrated by Ethiopian oats. These oats are related to the weedy tetraploid of the Mediterranean, *Avena barbata*, and were probably introduced as weeds of emmer and barley when the Near East agricultural complex arrived on the Ethiopian plateau. The oats are still weeds in the sense that they are not grown as a pure crop, but the Ethiopian cultivators do not object to them and make no effort to get rid of them. The oats have responded to this toleration by producing both nonshattering and semishattering races. The nonshattering races are harvested along with the emmer and barley, and the mixture is sown as harvested the next season. In the semishattering types, some of the seed falls to the ground infesting the soil, and some are harvested and planted. Here we have a plant that is not deliberately seeded with the expectation of a later harvest, but which has, nevertheless, responded by the production of nonshattering "domesticated" and semishattering "semidomesticated" races.

The Guinea millet (*Brachiaria deflexa*) is wild over large areas of tropical Africa and is harvested for food with some frequency. In the Futa Djalon region of Guinea a domesticated race is grown. Typically it is nonshattering and has much larger seeds than the wild races. The area of culture is very limited and no other domesticated races are known. The *Digitaria* millets are also endemic crops but not so limited in distribution as *Brachiaria* (cf. Portères, this volume).

If the process of domestication is discontinued before full domestication is achieved, the crop may revert partly toward the wild and become a spontaneous weed. African rice, *Oryza glaberrima*, is a crop rapidly declining in importance and acreage because of replacement by Asian rice. In some areas, the African rice lingers on only as a weed of Asian rice fields. Glaberrima rice is not fully nonshattering and sheds enough seed that it can perpetuate itself provided the fields are cultivated for rice production. The spontaneous glaberrimas are morphologically the same as the domesticated ones and are not to be confused with weed races that have developed during the course of domestication through genetic interaction between wild and cultivated races. The latter are identifiable morphologically and have been called *Oryza stapfii*.

Pearl millet is basically a fully domesticated plant, yet most West African populations of the crop contain a certain percentage of *shibra* or shattering types. These perpetuate themselves as weeds in the fields, and since the crop is cross-fertilizing, the genes for shattering are carried along genetically in the nonshattering forms. Again, these shatter types can be separated morphologically from the hybrid swarms produced when the wild progenitor crosses with the domesticated forms.

TREE AND TUBER CROPS

Intimate relationships between man and selected tree species are widespread in Africa. As with the cereals, we can arrange the examples in a series illustrating increasing degrees of manipulation and genetic response.

In many parts of the African savanna there is a close correlation between village sites past and present and the occurrence of the baobab (*Adansonia*). To what extent villages are located near baobabs by design or how frequently baobabs become established after the village is founded we do not know. The tree has multiple uses; the bark is used for fiber, the leaves are used as a pot herb, the fruits are eaten, and the large hollow boles are often used as cisterns to store water for the dry season. We have seen villages in Sudan that could not be occupied year around without baobab cisterns, since there is no surface water in the dry season. The baobab is not man dependent, but man can sometimes be baobab dependent.

Among some peoples *Moringa* sp. is an important part of the diet. In Konsoland, southern Ethiopia, the trees are grown in the villages near the houses. Again, to what extent they may be actually planted we do not know, but in that region they are confined to the villages. The leaves are used as a pot herb. While the trees are abundant and often quite large they are of little use for shade since the leaves are constantly being picked.

In the West African savanna the karité or shea butter tree (*Butyrospermum*) is protected and encouraged. The original arborescent flora probably contained a number of species, but selective cutting has been practiced for a long time. The karité is protected and every other species is cut for firewood, construction, or other uses. As a result vast areas are covered with a uniform orchard-like savanna of nearly pure stands of karité. The tree enjoys a nearly sacred status among the people who refuse to cut it or allow it to be destroyed. The trees are individually owned, and it is possible to transfer land without losing ownership of the trees growing on it. An edible oil is extracted from the fruit which is important in the diet of savanna peoples.

Extensive stands of *Acacia albida* may be built up by the same procedure. The acacia is not used by humans directly and does not enjoy
the same status as the karité, but it is protected because it is believed
that crops do better when grown between open stands of acacia trees.
Some research has been conducted that indicates the belief to be correct (Dancette and Poulain 1968). This species of *Acacia* has the peculiar property of shedding its leaves at the beginning of the rains and
remaining dormant through the rainy season. Therefore, it does not
compete with interplanted crops. The leaves are eaten by sheep and
goats which, in turn, deposit manure under the trees. Research has
shown that both the nitrogen balance and water regime are better under
acacia groves than without acacia although the reasons for the latter
are not too well understood. At any rate, human activities have brought
profound changes in the savanna flora without deliberately planting
trees with the expectation of a later harvest. *Parkia* spp., *Tamarindus*,
and the recently introduced mango are also protected trees of the
savanna. In general, useful plants are not destroyed in Africa and, consequently, are encouraged through protection.

The African oil palm, *Elaeis guineensis*, presents a more complex
transitional example. Since the plant does not tolerate deep shade, it is
thought that its original habitat was the margins of the wet forest zone.
The techniques of slash and burn agriculture have greatly expanded
habitats suitable for the oil palm. In the process of slashing and burning, oil palm is spared; and after repeated cycles of crop and bush
fallow, extensive stands may be built up without anyone deliberately
planting a seed. Such subspontaneous stands are often found well within the forest zones which would not be suitable for oil palm without
agricultural disturbance.

In oil palm there is a gene that profoundly affects the fruit. One
allele in homozygous condition produces the dura type which has a
thick shell and relatively little pulp. The other allele in homozygous
condition produces a pisifera type with lots of pulp but no kernel and,
consequently, is female sterile. The heterozygote (tenera) is intermediate
with a thin shell and good pulp yield. Presumably natural selection
would favor the dura allele, but the other two types are preferred by
the people for oil. The duras are more likely to be tapped for wine.
Repeated tapping kills the trees. So there may be genetic manipulation
of subspontaneous populations. More than this, a survey of oil palm
populations in Ivory Coast by Meunier (1968) revealed a strikingly
close correlation between the distribution of particular oil palm varieties, on the one hand, and of certain ethnic groups on the other. Because

the distributions are disjunct, it seems possible that migrating groups of people may have taken seeds for planting in their new homes. However, we still have no conclusive evidence for deliberate planting of the tree in traditional agriculture.

African yams are treated in detail by Coursey (this volume), but we would like to point out here that protection of yam plants was important in early stages of domestication. The loss of natural protective devices (thorns, poisons, fiberous tubers, etc.) is compatible with survival only to the extent that natural devices can be replaced by human protection. Ultimately, in some varieties of yams the capacity to produce seeds was lost, and such clones became completely dependent upon man not only for protection, but for propagation and survival.

Altogether, Africa provides such a series of transitional and intermediate stages in plant domestication that the process is fairly well revealed. More detailed studies should be very rewarding in providing a still clearer understanding. We shall now turn our attention to the consequences of plant domestication, examining very briefly the characteristics of the African agriculture that emerged from these processes.

GENERAL CHARACTERISTICS OF AFRICAN AGRICULTURE

1. We have already indicated our opinion that African agriculture is basically noncentric. We cannot point to any one region and say: "This is where it all began." In a very broad and general way the botanical and archaeological evidence agrees that most of the activity took place north of the equator and south of the Sahara. But, where was the Sahara during the critical time range? Abundant evidence is presented in this volume for profound changes of climate over the millennia during which plant domestication is likely to have been underway. (See in this volume van Zinderen Bakker; Clark; and Wendorf and Schild.) It will be shown that the Sahara was occupied by people who undoubtedly harvested plants and who might have been manipulating them. The occupation near lake sites continued well after the onset of desiccation (cf. Munson, this volume).

It has been argued that the Sahara was once the "center of origin" and that it was wiped out by desiccation (Chevalier 1938; Munson, this volume). As we shall see, the argument has merit for some crops and some techniques, but could hardly apply to yam, oil palm, ensete, noog, tef, cowpea, or finger millet. Traditional African agriculture is a mosaic of crops, traditions, and techniques which does not reveal a center, a nuclear area, or a single point of origin.

2. African agriculture is characterized by a rather unusual number of dominant crops. In Arabic *'aish* means "life," and in the Sudanic savanna the word is applied to sorghum — the staff of life, the source of sustenance. Life without sorghum is unthinkable. To the north in the Sahel, *'aish* means "pearl millet." Life itself depends on pearl millet, and pearl millet alone, in that ecological zone. To the west around the Bend of the Niger, the word may be applied to rice by some Arabic speakers. Certainly in West Africa, from Senegambia to central Ivory Coast, a meal without rice is considered no meal at all. The same intense dependence of a people on a single crop is found in the yam zone. Existence itself depends on yams. In different parts of the continent other dominant crops are ensete, tef, and fonio.

It seems that African agricultural systems tend to become heavily dependent upon single crops. The dependence on bananas in some parts of Uganda must have developed since the crop was introduced into Africa. The current dependence of some people on maize and others on cassava indicates that dependence on single crops does not take long to establish. Whatever the reasons may be, we suggest that the number of dominant crops has contributed to the mosaic pattern just referred to.

3. While we cannot point to one geographic region as a center of agricultural innovation, the adaptation of the major crops and their wild relatives suggests some ecological clustering as indicated below:
a. Forest — savanna ecotone: Oil palm (*Elaeis guineensis*), yam (*Dioscorea* sp.), cowpea (*Vigna unguiculata*), yampea (*Sphenostylis stenocarpa*), guinea millet (*Brachiaria deflexa*), black fonio (*Digitaria iburua*), Hausa potato (*Plectranthus esculentus*).
b. Savanna: Sorghum (*Sorghum bicolor*), pearl millet (*Pennisetum americanum*), voandzeia (*Voandzeia subterranea*), rice (*Oryza glaberrima*), cotton (*Gossypium herbaceum*), fonio (*Digitaria exilis*), roselle (*Hibiscus sabdariffa*), watermelon (*Citrulus lanatus*), karité (*Butyrospermum paradoxum*), parkia (*Parkia* sp.), sesame (*Sesamamum indicum*) (if African).
c. East African highlands: Tef (*Eragrostis tef*), noog (*Guizotia abyssinica*), ensete (*Ensente ventricosa*), finger millet (*Eleusine coracana*), chat (*Catha edulis*).

Most of the important crops grown in the forest zone appear to have been imported from the savanna or the forest-savanna ecotone. As we have indicated, the oil palm does not tolerate deep shade, and its original habitat was probably the forest-savanna ecotone. As will be elaborated by Coursey (this volume), yams with large tubers are native to the savanna, the tubers providing food storage which enables the plant to survive long dry seasons and periodic burning. The wild yams of the wet forest have less tuber development. Although African rice is now grown to the Guinea coast, it was domesticated from the annual *Oryza barthii* which is a savanna grass adapted to shallow water holes that dry up in the dry season. Only a few African crops are true forest species. They include coffee, cola, akee apple, and possibly a few others. The domesticated plants that provide food for peoples of the forest zone are almost all introductions from the savanna.

4.   The present savanna agriculture of West Africa is strongly influenced by *décrue* techniques. In French *crue* means "flood," and *décrue*, "the period when the flood waters recede." Lacking an appropriate English word, we adopt the French for convenience. There is not space here to elaborate fully on the remarkably sophisticated décrue agriculture that has evolved around the Bend of the Niger — Lake Faguibine area. The cultivators there have developed a number of options to help them deal with floods that are erratic in height and duration. The options include choice of crops, choice of cultivars, choice of seeding rates and hill spacing, time of sowing, and direct seeding versus transplanting. Cultivars are chosen for length of growing season, nutritional and storage qualities, adaptation to soil type, bird resistance, and ability to tolerate flooding before harvest. In some areas, sorghum and even pearl millet are harvested from a canoe because the waters rise before maturity. Some details are presented by Harlan and Pasquereau (1969).

A décrue crop must mature on moisture stored in the soil. Any device that will speed up the life cycle of décrue crops can be useful. One of the most common is transplanting, and sorghum is the crop most often handled in this way. Seedlings are established in a bed of sandy soil. As the waters recede and land becomes available, the seedlings are uprooted and placed individually in deep dibble holes provided by ramming a stake into the soil. The transplant dibble is 1.5 to 2 meters in length and the holes are often 30 to 40 centimeters deep. Transplanted sorghum is grown not only on lands vacated by floodwaters, but in low spots in the savanna where water stands during the rains. Burning off the vegetation at the end of the rains may be the only land preparation other than making the dibble holes. The practice permits the use of land that is too soggy and wet during the rains for sorghum. Under special circumstances, pearl millet may also be transplanted.

Although we have no proof, it seems likely that the original décrue techniques were learned along the margins of the Sahara or in what is now the Sahara itself. We have ample evidence of villages located at the margins of shallow lakes, now dried up, but which at the time of occupation would enlarge during the rains and shrink during the dry season. This, we suggest was the ideal situation for learning décrue techniques, now practiced under more demanding situations along the flood plains of the Niger, Senegal, Benue, and other West African rivers.

5.   African agriculture is a hoe and digging stick agriculture; the techniques of production, at least, are based on human labor. The plow and draft animals are hardly used in traditional agriculture except in Ethiopia and northern Sudan. Tsetse fly may be a contributing cause but can hardly explain the complete dependence on human energy in some areas. The labor expended is enormous. With incredible human effort the soil on millions of hectares is turned every year by hoes. In Senegambia a long-handled spade-like instrument is used to shape land and dig ditches for rice production. Mounding, ridging, and ditching are common in the wetter areas.

Other techniques also require a large expenditure of human energy. While grinding is common, the wooden mortar with pestle is the most universal equipment for reducing plant food materials for consumption. The sickle is used for harvesting rice and fonio in West Africa and for tef and small grains in Ethiopia, but little used elsewhere. Elaborate rock-walled terraces are or were constructed in widely separated regions on the continent.

6.   Several practices have evolved to sustain or improve soil fertility. Most of them are found in some form elsewhere, but a few are characteristically African. The most general is shifting agriculture, bush fallow or slash and burn. The African procedures differ little from those developed in Southeast Asia, Oceania, or the Americas. The most specialized of the slash and burn techniques is the *chitemene* practiced in East Africa. In this system, branches are lopped from trees over a wide area and carried to the plot to be burned in order to produce a hotter fire and more ash.

Mounding and ridging are very general in the wetter zones. Both mounds and ridges tend to concentrate top soil as well as provide drainage and aeration. Soil burning is practiced on the higher parts of the Ethiopian plateau. Here the soils are so cold that organic matter accumulates to the point that clods of soil can actually be ignited. The practice of burning makes phosphorus more available (Wehrmann and Johannes 1965).

The use of *Acacia* and livestock for soil improvement has already been mentioned. In West Africa some sedentary villagers often arrange for the more nomadic Fulani to pasture stock on their fields after harvest for the benefits derived from manure. A few groups stall feed cattle in order to accumulate manure for their fields.

Thus, we conclude that: (1) African agriculture has a number of unique characteristics which appear to be indigenous and are not likely to have been derived from the Near Eastern system; (2) that African agriculture is far from homogeneous and consists of a mosaic of crop and technique combinations occupying different regions; and (3) there is a suggestion of a southward movement with décrue techniques infiltrating the savanna from the Sahara and savanna crops moving into the forest. These matters are covered in more detail in this volume by Harris, Shaw, and Purseglove.

CAUSES

The question of causes is treated by several contributors to this volume — especially Pfeiffer, Higgs, and Smith. A number of points were also brought out in the discussions not covered in the papers. We can sum them up very easily by saying we really do not know what happened, but some factors were identified that were possibly preadaptive or that set the stage so that plant domestication could proceed. Other factors were suggested that might have triggered off the process.

Some factors that might be considered preadaptive are:

1. Protective attitudes toward plants. Useful plants are protected more or less throughout Africa and the attitude is often reinforced by ritual, belief, and "superstition."

2. Social systems that tend to favor larger group size and resist extreme fragmentation. This varies, of course, and some of the present hunter-gatherers seem to favor small groups to avoid quarrels. To the extent that larger group size is socially favored, agriculture may appear as an attractive option. Agriculture is a way to provide for large numbers of people living together in a small area.

3. Advanced hunting-gathering technologies may preadapt people for agriculture. Pottery, grinding equipment, sickles or reaping knives apparently were all available before we have evidence that plant domesti-

cates were actually being grown.

4. Productive habitats may provide opportunities for experimentation and innovation. The habitats identified in this connection were the shallow lakes of the Sahara before they dried up and the savanna-forest ecotone. The archaeological and ethnographic evidence suggests that good fishing was important to sedentism and stability.

Two demonstrable factors impinge on the African scene that might have triggered off domestication processes: the desiccation of the Sahara and the expansion of the Near Eastern agricultural system. As long as populations are comfortably in balance with their environments, radical innovations are not likely to occur although this may be a situation most fruitful for experimentation. As the lakes in the Sahara began to dry up, the hunting—fishing—herding—gathering people were forced to move southward into zones that might already have been rather intensely exploited by hunter-gatherers or even other agricultural economies. Contraction of the most favorable ecological zones might have applied stresses along the forest-savanna margins as well. The resulting imbalance may have stimulated more intense genetic manipulation of plant populations.

As to stimulus from the Near East, the evidence is equivocal to say the least. Livestock herding and pottery appear to have been widespread in the Sahara before they were found along the Nile. On the whole the stage seems to have been set in the Sahara and southward before clearly demonstrable connections with the Near East, but our evidence is too sketchy for definitive conclusions. The subject is treated in some detail in the papers by Clark and by Wendorf and Schild.

A third factor that could have been a triggering mechanism is simply a gradual increase in population density to the point that adjustments were required. The African savanna is exceptionally rich in food resources, and as long as population densities were low, there would always be room for people to exploit new ranges. Climatic stresses probably had little influence on basic hunting-gathering economies. With a rise in population density, however, stresses could become critical and a point of no return reached after which the man-plant relationship could only intensify. In due time man became as completely dependent on his crops as fully domesticated plants are dependent on man.

In this volume we have tried to assemble what evidence we could, and we have made the most reasonable interpretations we could. At this stage of our investigations, however, the evidence is so meager that we may find it necessary to revise our models radically as future studies provide new information.

REFERENCES

CHEVALIER, A.
1938   Le Sahara, centre d'origine de plantes cultivées. *Soc. Biogéographie Mém.* 6:307–322.

CHILDE, V. G.
1950   The urban revolution. *Town Planning Review* 21:3–17.

DANCETTE, C., J. F. POULAIN
1968   Influence de l'*Acacia albida* sur les facteurs pédoclimatiques et les rendements des cultures. *Sols Africains* 13:197–239.

HARLAN, J. R.
1971   Agricultural origins: centers and noncenters. *Science* 174:468–474.

HARLAN, J. R., JEAN PASQUEREAU
1969   Décrue agriculture in Mali. *Economic Botany* 23(1):70–74.

JARDIN, CLAUDE
1967   *List of foods used in Africa.* Rome: Food and Agriculture Organization.

MEUNIER, J.
1968   "Etude des palmeraies subspontanées d'*Elaeis guineensis* Jacq. en Cote d'Ivoire." Elève de seconde année à l'O.R.S.O.M. (Mimeo).

MURDOCK, G. P.
1959   *Africa, its peoples and their culture history.* New York: McGraw-Hill.

PORTÈRES, R.
1951   Géographie alimentaire, berceaux agricoles et migration des plantes cultivées en Afrique intertropicale. *C. R. Soc. Biogéogr.* 239:16–21.

SAUER, CARL ORTWIN
1952   Agricultural origins and dispersals. New York: American Geography Society.

VAVILOV, N. I.
1926   Studies on the origin of cultivated plants. *Bull. Appl. Bot. and Plant Breeding* 16(2):1–243. Leningrad.

WEHRMANN, J., L. W. JOHANNES
1965   Effect of "GUIE" on soil conditions and plant nutrition. *Sols Africains* 10:129–136.

ZHUKOVSKY, P. M.
1968   New centres of the origin and new gene centres of cultivated plants including specifically endemic micro-centres of species closely allied to cultivated species. *Bot. Zh.* 53:430–460.

SECTION ONE

Background Theory

A Note on the Problem of Basic Causes

JOHN E. PFEIFFER

After a soul-searching consideration of our convener's advice to discuss "something you know more about than anyone else," I decided to prepare a paper anyway — a paper involving a problem about which very little is known, namely, why agriculture arose where and when it did. More specifically, I shall discuss some of the implications of recent studies suggesting that hunter-gatherers do not necessarily lead insufferable lives, and that in a number of respects their way of life turns out to be rather more attractive than anything which has been developed since. This finding effectively changes the rules of the game as far as our efforts to understand the origins of agriculture are concerned. Among other things, it indicates that investigators can no longer afford to concentrate on the mechanisms of domestication to the almost complete exclusion of basic causes.

One theory about the origins of plant domestication, the happy-accident or "Eureka!" theory, is not yet as dead as it should be. (Indeed, various versions of it are still to be found in a number of contemporary textbooks.) It proposes that the idea of planting and cultivating seeds came by chance in a sudden flash of springtime insight to some prehistoric genius who noticed plants growing where she or he had never noticed them growing before, say, in disturbed soil in a rock shelter, near a place where wild seeds had been stored for the winter. The picture is straightforward and dramatic and, as such, has appealed to a number of investigators among the most distinguished being Darwin himself: "The first steps in cultivating would probably result ... from some such accident as the seeds of a fruit tree falling on a heap of refuse, and producing an unusually fine variety."

This theory, like a good many theories, is far more interesting for the assumptions it conceals than for anything it reveals about the beginnings of plant domestication. For one thing, it seriously underrates the capacities of our not-so-remote ancestors to observe and reason, as if it required an exceptional individual and exceptional circumstances to recognize what happens when seeds are planted, a phenomenon which was probably quite familiar to the Neanderthals and their predecessors. In line with the belittlement is the notion that hunting-gathering represents such a lowly and miserable way of making a living that people endured it solely by default as it were, because they knew no better — and that as soon as it dawned upon them that something better was possible, they naturally adopted it forthwith.

As brought out forcefully in the Wenner-Gren symposium on *Man the Hunter* in 1966, these assumptions have little basis in real life. Quantitative studies of contemporary hunter-gatherers suggest a number of good reasons why they have never turned to domestication. In one group of Kalahari Bushmen, for example, during the drought year of 1964 the individuals actually doing the work each spent about three hours a day obtaining food, not only for themselves, but also for their children and other nonworking dependents who, incidentally, made up more than a third of the group. Similar findings hold for many hunter-gatherer groups, and although severe emergencies may arise from time to time, it seems that more often than not the emergencies are rather less severe and less frequent than those due to crop failure among agriculturalists.

The effect of such evidence is to complicate an already complicated picture. When the gradual changeover from a predominantly hunting-gathering existence to agriculture was regarded, in effect, as doing what comes naturally, it made some sense to devote time primarily to detailed step-by-step studies of the process which led from the first moves toward domestication to cultivation on a full-scale basis.

Now in addition to that problem or complex of problems, investigators will have to deal head-on and systematically with the problem of why the change-over occurred in the first place. And it is definitely a distinct and separate problem in the sense that learning more and more about mechanisms can hardly be expected to provide fresh insights into basic causes. The forces which brought about the transition from hunting-gathering to agriculture were powerful, steady and increasing; they had to overcome powerful counterforces, tendencies built into the very structure of hunter-gatherer societies.

Agriculture generally means larger groups, larger settlements, and hunter-gatherers are often quite aware of the fact that the greater the size of the group, the greater the level of tension and conflict. The Bushman's reaction, as reported by Lee, is relevant in this connection: "We live in small groups, because we fear fights." Also, agriculture, at least in its large-scale and more intensive forms, generally means widening differences in social status, and most hunter-gatherer groups are essentially egalitarian and have developed ways of discouraging status distinctions.

So we may assume that agriculture arose, not automatically or "naturally," but as the result of strong selective pressures which favored the survival of people who could not survive any longer in a hunter-gatherer context. And wherever it arose it had to deal with the same fundamental resistances and, in all likelihood, was accepted only provisionally as a temporary measure required to preserve the hunting-gathering way of life. In other words, considered from a broad point of view, one region is probably as appropriate as another for investigating problems of origins, although each region may have its unique set of advantages and disadvantages.

To cite one example, a number of investigators are beginning to exploit the possibilities of ethnographic and archaeological research in Oceania. As a general rule, traveling from west to east across the Pacific amounts to moving forward in time, archaeologically speaking, because the easternmost islands tend to have been settled most recently. Australia and New Guinea were originally occupied 30,000 or more years ago, Hawaii only about 1,200 years ago. It would thus appear that some of the easternmost or most recently occupied islands might be of special interest in understanding why men turned increasingly to agriculture, because the original settlers of these islands are most likely to have been acquainted with a variety of both hunting-gathering and agricultural techniques.

Under such circumstances the tendency is almost invariably to lean in the main on hunting and gathering. This seems to have been the case in New Zealand, for instance, which was first occupied about a thousand years ago. Enormous quantities of moa bones have been found in some regions, notably along the eastern coast of South Island at estuarine sites, perhaps nesting areas where the birds returned season after season along ancient migration routes. Even during later periods, after the moas had been hunted into extinction, there is no sign of a sudden and massive shift to agriculture.

Research in other parts of New Zealand suggests the same general pattern. According to recent studies, there was a heavy reliance on shellfish in suitable coastal regions, and fern rhizomes, dried and stored, probably represented a more abundant source of food than any cultivated crop. Catchment analyses conducted in certain inland areas of North Island — analyses of the locations of hill-fort earthworks with respect to food-resource zones — indicate that the builders chose land favorable for hunting and gathering rather than prize agricultural land. A sign of increasing agriculture is the presence of sand and pebbles brought in in quantity and laid down for the growing of sweet potatoes. One area alone includes about 5,000 acres of such artificial soil, which generally appears relatively late in the archaeological record, often in protohistoric times.

The fact that people know about the elements of agricultural techniques is completely trivial as far as understanding causes is concerned (which, by the way, may provide a suitable perspective for the evaluation of diffussion theories). It has nothing to do with whether or not people will put their knowledge to use. Strong pressures are required for that to happen, and a rich assortment of arguments exists to identify the pressure and explain the changes that took place. One argument, which appeared not long ago in an undergraduate term paper, is quite representative in that it really explains nothing and illustrates some of the major problems involved in accounting for agricultural origins. It places the blame squarely on the invention of the bow and arrow, which made killing so efficient that man decimated herds of big game and was forced to turn more and more to plants, eventually to domesticated and cultivated plants. As a clincher, the student cites the record in Australia where agriculture never developed because the aborigines never had the bow and arrow.

This argument is no less vulnerable to destruction than most, but I present it for constructive reasons because, for all its shortcomings, it does contain a number of positive features which will have to be incorporated into solid theories when they appear. For one thing, it involves a subsistence crisis and faces up to the problem of timing, of explaining why agriculture arose when it did. Of course, it leaves another question of timing unanswered — namely, what forces favored the invention of the bow and arrow during a particular period — but unanswered questions, known as assumptions, are a feature common to theories in all branches of sciences.

As a further point worth noting, the argument also faces up to the fact that it may be as important to consider regions where agriculture did not arise as it is to consider the course of events in fertile crescents, hearths of domestication, and other nuclear areas. Indeed, nonorigins may turn out to be at least as significant as origins in identifying the major forces which determine whether or not agriculture will be applied on a large-scale, regular basis. In other words, the bow-and-arrow notion focuses attention on the null case — and, of all null cases, that of Australia perhaps requires the most explaining.

Although the continent had been settled originally more than 30,000 years before European contact times, no evidence exists for the practice of agriculture. Yet we know that in at least one region the aborigines not only knew about domestication and cultivation, but also on at least one occasion actually applied what they knew. This happened on Prince of Wales Island, just off Cape York in the Torres Strait where Australia is closest to New Guinea-Papua — less than a hundred miles away.

According to historical records, exceptionally heavy precipitation during the rainy season of 1849 ruined local supplies of wild yams which "ran all to leaves." So the people turned for help to a more northerly island, obtained domesticated yams wrapped in damp bark cloth, and planted and harvested the imported roots. But nothing more ever came of the emergency measure. As soon as wild yams became available again, the people resumed traditional gathering practices. Moreover, there does not seem to have been any interest in domesticating several other local wild plants which were being cultivated in New Guinea.

In the Darling River area of southeast Australia, aborigines used wild cereals such as *Panicum* and millets until the 1890's. Their practice was to harvest the grasses at a green stage before the seeds had matured to the point where they would fall off readily, pulling up masses of plants by the roots and piling them into stacks for later drying in the sun. The required research has not yet been carried out, but detailed studies of grasses and many other wild plants used regularly by the aborigines may reveal traits that were selected for, unconsciously or consciously. Perhaps this null case may turn out to be not quite so null after all.

In any event it is not at all obvious why in some places and not in others people turned increasingly to agriculture when they seem to have preferred hunting and gathering. Certainly it was neither an automatic and wholehearted acceptance of a "superior" way of life, nor a sudden discovery about the growing of plants. As indicated previously, diffusion theories explain nothing fundamental, because knowledge about agricultural techniques is not a crucial factor, in the sense that it does not by itself determine whether or not agriculture will be practiced.

The challenge is to identify the determining factors which forced people to change. We can expect that such pressures have left marks in the record, marks as distinctive as those left by the actual adoption of agricultural practices — specific changes in living patterns reflected perhaps by changes in the ratio of nonresidential or special-purpose sites to residential sites, the variety of special-purpose areas within residential sites, the frequencies of different bones found at different types of sites, and the dimensions of the catchment basin or region from which food is obtained. To a large extent the archaeology of agricultural origins is the archaeology of people living under subsistence stress, although stress is obviously not the whole story. (We must still account for the nonappearance of agriculture in arid and semiarid regions of Australia and elsewhere.)

A greater emphasis on basic causes might involve, among other things, more systematic and extensive efforts to develop quantitative models of the impact of different kinds and degrees of stress. The models could be used to indicate the probable effects of such factors as climatic change and population growth, and to suggest a number of distinctive patterns that might show up in the archaeological record. Considerations of this sort might well play a major role in the selection and most effective exploitation of sites relevant to the origin of African plant domesticates and, in a wide context, to the origin of plant domesticates elsewhere.

Archaeology and Domestication

ERIC HIGGS

From the archaeological point of view in order to devise a strategy for research into the origin of African domesticates, it would appear advisable to consider the problem in the light of information obtained from other continents. The proximity of western Asia, long considered the primary home of prehistoric agriculture, in any case renders this to some extent inevitable. On the other hand in order to place African domesticates in world perspective, what is known of early domesticates in the Americas as well as in eastern Asia should also be taken into consideration.

In the Old World it is generally held that plants and animals were first domesticated on the hilly flanks of the Fertile Crescent and from there the ideas and techniques of domestication and sometimes the domesticates themselves spread westwards into Europe, eastwards into Asia, and southwards into the African continent. Recent work, however, has indicated that this may be far too simple a picture. On current evidence the dog appears to have been domesticated at an earlier date in Europe (Star Carr) than in southwestern Asia.

There have also been convincing finds of dog remains with a Paleolithic industry (Magdalenian) at the Kniegrotte cave in Germany and with mammoth exploiters of Mezine in Russia (Pidoplichko 1969). Similarly, the earliest dates for domesticated cattle are from Greece (Argissa, Nea Nikomedeia, Knossos). With regard to the pig, the evidence from the Crimea suggests that domestication may have taken place there perhaps even earlier than in the Fertile Crescent (Tash Aïr), and there is an anomalous situation both there and in Greece where it is necessary to postulate a race of small wild pigs in order to explain their occurrence at a date which is too early to fit into the current hypothesis.

Less is known about plant remains in this connection, which is probably due to the difficulties of collecting them from archaeological sites, but recently pollen analytical studies have indicated that grain growing was probably as early as, or even earlier, in the Indus valley than it was in Mesopotamia (Singh 1971). In fact, the trend of new data is to widen steadily the area of supposed early domestication which, on the basis of our present data, appears to stretch from the Indus valley to Eastern Europe at the least.

In the New World plant domesticates seem to have arisen independently as early or almost as early as they did in the Old World. Of animal domesticates, the dog remains from Idaho (Lawrence 1967) antedate the earliest known dog remains from the Old World, circa 7000 B.C. The Idaho specimens were of a small animal with typical dog characteristics and it is presumed that domestication must have taken place at a much earlier date. As in the Old World, there is little evidence for innovating centers from which the ideas or technology of domestication disseminated. Species were apparently domesticated in a variety of ecological zones probably by transhumant as well as sedentary peoples.

In consequence, taking the evidence from the Americas as well as that from southwestern Asia and Eastern Europe, there seems little reason to continue to believe that domestication arose as a consequence of peculiar environmental circumstances in particular areas or that domestication in Africa had to await the development of agricultural techniques in southwestern Asia.

In the Americas, in southwestern Asia, and in China, there appears in the archaeological record to be one observable phenomenon which is common to all. That is the numerous-village stage. This had been called the effective agricultural stage, but this is an unfortunate name in that it implies that earlier agriculture was ineffective or at least less effective. This may have been the case as far as the development of civilization is concerned, but earlier agriculture was probably no less effective and no less important in the history of human development.

This so-called effective stage seems to have arisen partly as a result of the development of particular domesticates — maize in the Americas, rice and perhaps millet in China, and wheat and barley in southwestern Asia — and partly as a consequence of the integration of a number of domesticates into more complex and therefore more effective economies which utilized a broader spectrum of the available resources. Evidence from the Americas also shows that domesticates arose there thousands of years before the advent of numerous villages. The numerous-village

stage therefore did not arise immediately as a consequence of the inception of domestication, but as a culmination of a long-drawn-out
developmental process.

Taking the American evidence as a lead, if we are concerned with the
origins of plant domestication in Africa, then, as in southwestern Asia,
we are concerned with the relatively unexplored and shadowy period
which preceded the numerous-village stage, which preceded pottery,
and which, using European terminology, is artifactually Mesolithic or
Stone Age in character. As witness, of course, the steady growth in our
knowledge of what have been called "prepottery" Neolithic or aceramic
sites in Eastern Europe and southwestern Asia.

At this point it is as well to ask what objectives have guided our investigations into the origins of agriculture up to the present time. Much
work has been motivated by the desire to find out more about the
origins of civilizations. This has had some considerable success, as the
"numerous-village stage" can now be seen in certain areas as a step
towards civilization and, reasonably enough, research has been directed
towards those areas where civilization arose. But in consequence our
data relevant to agricultural origins, at least in the Old World, have
been heavily weighted by information gained from those areas. Furthermore they have been grossly weighted by data from "village sites," particularly pottery sites, and little or no attention has been paid to other
kinds of sites, particularly aceramic sites.

So far has this distortion gone that faunal assemblages, for example,
from aceramic sites are usually considered by paleontologists with
paleontological or climatic objectives in mind, and later sites are more
commonly analyzed by zoologists with domestication or prehistoric
economies in mind. Such zoological techniques are rarely, if ever,
applied to faunal assemblages, which are considered to be too early in
time to be significant to the study of the origins of domestication. The
hazards of such a dichotomy can be seen by referring to the work of
M. R. Jarman (1969) who has shown that morphological changes in
some domesticates which are usually attributed to domestication can
be traced back in time beyond the Holocene and into the Pleistocene;
and, furthermore, that similar changes can also be seen in carnivores
and insectivores, creatures which are not known to have been or are
not believed to have been domesticated.

In the design of a strategy to discuss the origin of plant domesticates,
we need not be unduly concerned with tracing the later steps towards
civilization. From the archaeological point of view, we are concerned

with human development and particularly the development of prehistoric economies. In order to understand those developments which
successfully lead on to yet further development such as civilizations,
it is also necessary to attempt to understand economic *culs-de-sac*
which had no great consequences wherever they may have occurred.
The fossil record of plant remains, which for obvious reasons is less
well-known than the animal record, badly needs supplementing by the
collection and study of plant remains from Paleolithic sites.

It is also true that, on the whole, much research has been directed
towards the study of those species which now provide the staple foods
of large populations today, to the neglect of those species which were
no doubt of great importance in their time but are now being superseded by more successful domesticates. Furthermore, there has been
a tacit assumption that where species have been domesticated, they
have remained domesticated and that those species which are known
only in a wild form today, have always been wild. The archaeological
evidence, however, is to the contrary.

Callen (1967) suggests that in the Americas domesticated foxtail
millet was superseded by maize; and we know that with animal domesticates, the onager was superseded in antiquity by the horse, and the elk
has repeatedly fallen in and out of domestication. It would seem necessary, therefore, in devising an overall strategy to take into account
species other than those which are now under domestication. Indeed,
recent attempts to do so have indicated that criteria of domestication in
current use, if applied to faunal assemblages consisting of animals
such as the red deer and the gazelle, suggest that they also were
"domesticated" (M. R. Jarman 1972; Legge 1972).

At this point it may be pertinent to ask how effective are our existing
techniques in determining whether or not the remains from archaeological sites are of domesticated or of wild plants and animals? In general
the detection of domesticates relies upon our ability to perceive
morphological CHANGES IN THE SPECIES CONCERNED WHICH CAN BE
ATTRIBUTED TO DOMESTICATION. Jarman and Wilkinson (1972) have
challenged the view that observed morphological changes such as size
changes in the postglacial, for example, can be attributed to domestication, and they suggest that they were more likely to have been due to
other natural selective processes.

Berry (1969), as a result of studies of laboratory rats, has pointed out
that domestication does not necessarily give rise to morphological
change, and H. N. Jarman (1972) has noted that the flourishing fields

of wild grain in the world's botanical institutes are evidence that this is also true of plants. Indeed, present interpretations of organic remains from archaeological sites support this view for Perkins (1964) who notes that morphologically unchanged sheep were being herded at Shanidar, and Helbaek (1966) concluded from the Beidha evidence that the inhabitants of that site were cultivating wild (i.e. morphologically unchanged) grain.

Clearly for those who postulate a beginning of agriculture in the Old World in southwestern Asia early in the postglacial period, the Beidha and the Shanidar data can be taken as evidence for the incipient domestication of sheep and barley at the expected time and in the expected place. In order to maintain this view, however, it must be argued that although morphological change had not taken place, it could not have been long delayed, a contention which is commonly based on the belief that isolation of the various species from the free-breeding pool would in itself have caused morphological change to have taken place very soon afterwards.

However, there are many objections to this view. To support it many examples are used where changes have followed isolation. Ehrlich and Raven (1969), however, suggest that observed changes attributed to isolation are more probably due to environmental changes. It also seems unlikely that complete isolation in primitive conditions would have been achieved, and there is plenty of evidence to indicate that with animals, at least, isolation was commonly considered to be disadvantageous. For example, with the Lapps and the Chukchi and many other peoples there is constant encouragement of the interbreeding of domesticated with wild populations. Here theory from the natural sciences conflicts with anthropological evidence, an example which we may do well to keep in mind and to which I shall refer later.

It is not difficult to imagine circumstances with plants where the development of a tough rachis would have been disadvantageous and discouraged if harvesting methods consisted of tapping the crop into baskets, a well-known harvesting method in primitive economies. Indeed, the development of the tough rachis may be due to no more than a change in harvesting methods, for example, the introduction of the sickle.

It is clear that morphological change may possibly indicate the presence of a domesticated plant, but the absence of it cannot be used to demonstrate that a plant was not domesticated, that is, that it was not under cultivation. It is unfortunate, therefore, that it has become the custom in the literature to regard the inhabitants of archaeological sites as farmers, if a morphological change has taken place in some of the species concerned, and hunter-gatherers if it has not.

If for the most part we cannot determine whether the plant remains from archaeological sites are of cultivated or uncultivated plants, then we may consider whether or not the artifactual evidence can help to distinguish between hunter-gatherers and farmers. Unfortunately it cannot. Very little is known of paleolithic tools, and possible hunting tools are exceedingly rare in all periods. Arrowheads are much more common with agricultural economies at Neolithic and Bronze Age sites. They are rare with supposed hunter-gatherers in the Stone Age.

Both digging sticks and grindstones, which are commonly taken to be indicators of agriculture, are used by hunter-gatherers, and grindstones are common in Paleolithic times. Even villages occur with the mammoth exploiters at Mezine in Russia (Pidoplichko 1969), and hunter-gatherer villages have been postulated at Suberde in Turkey (Perkins and Daly 1968) and Mallaha in Palestine. What is more, there are plenty of ethnological parallels to show that transhumant populations with mobile economies commonly build houses and villages for seasonal occupation, and it is probably even more difficult to establish with archaeological data all-the-year round occupation, than it is to establish seasonality.

If all our techniques cannot tell us whether or not plants were intentionally planted or sown in order that a crop should be gathered, we must admit that there are vistas of time over which domestication in one form or another could have taken place, and the hypothesis that there was a time when all men were in the loose relationship with plants and animals, which we now regard as typical of hunter-gatherers, may never have occurred. Indeed, as Carr-Saunders said of the social system, the origins of agriculture may well be as old as the Lower Paleolithic.

It is possible and indeed the author believes more profitable to look at agriculture not as a consequence of technological and cultural development, but as a continuously developing natural and selective process of unknown antiquity, an evolutionary rather than a revolutionary phenomenon.

Such a view has its advantages, in that it is then unnecessary to offer explanations of why an independent development of agriculture should have arisen in the New World, or why there should have been an especially inventive and innovating people in the early post-Glacial period in southwestern Asia, for whenever domestication or some similar man-plant relationship was an advantage, it is very possible it may have taken place in some form or another. As Jarman and Wilkinson (1972) have pointed out, there are many man-animal-plant relationships which cannot easily be classified as either domesticated or not domesticated, and they must also be taken into consideration.

Such an evolutionary view also fits the data which we have available to us. As far back as we are able to trace it, circa 11,000 years ago, right up to the present day, new species have continued to come under domestication, and old domesticates such as the onager, the elk, the gazelle, fat hen, gold of pleasure, pale persicaria in Denmark, and foxtail millet have been superseded by the development of more successful man-animal-plant relationships and more rewarding domesticates.

How many plant and animal species passed out of domestication in antiquity is not known, but Harris (1967) instances a number of domesticates which now need saving. With the world's animal protein shortage, such animals as the musk ox, the eland, and the red deer are recent domesticates designed to exploit some available resources to better advantage; the effective population pressure is not yet so great upon the staple carbohydrate foods. Such population pressures may be expected to have been just as great a force in antiquity as they are now: recurrent events related to the limited resources which were available with the technology of the time.

If such an evolutionary view is accepted, it provides a theoretical framework within which to work that replaces the former framework based on cultural and technological revolution that is now proving inadequate and unsatisfactory. Without such frameworks investigations are likely to lack purpose and direction. We need not, and in my opinion should not, confine our investigations to particular periods of time, to current domesticates, to particular kinds of sites, or to particular ecological zones, helpful as such restrictions may be to the solution of smaller and more specific problems.

Speaking as an archaeologist, our overriding interest should be the development of the study of prehistoric economies as a primary interest so that any particular form of economy or particular man-animal-plant relationship such as domestication can be seen in perspective. To do this we need to reconsider our current approach to the problems with which we are concerned. The main obstacle to further developments lies within the concerned disciplines themselves.

Each of the disciplines is largely confined to investigations conducted within the framework of its own discipline. It is a situation where each is of minimal value to the other. An effective interdisciplinary approach needs to begin at the concept level with common aims and objectives. The archaeologist has to be convinced that it is worth his while, in terms of cost and effort, to collect plant remains from his excavations.

A mere catalogue of species present as an appendix to an archaeological report hardly satisfies such a requirement, and many archaeologists are not thus convinced. On the other hand, the botanist has to be convinced that the laborious analysis of samples of plant remains from archaeological sites is worth his while. As most of our future information will probably come from archaeological sites, the overall field of enquiry might well be concerned with man-animal-plant relationships.

These have, in fact, been little studied. We know very little of their early effect upon the species concerned, and many of the basic hypotheses upon which we work remain largely untested. We do not even have the guidance of relevant good ethnological studies. It is not too late for such studies to begin and indeed the opportunities to do so with new domesticates are considerable.

SITE LOCATION

The development of site location studies in archaeology (Higgs, et al. 1967) may also begin to give us new information concerning the economies practiced from those sites and, therefore, of the relationship of prehistoric groups to other plant and animal speices in the biotope. The selection of a particular location for human habitation was commonly determined by the resources available for exploitation with the technology of the time. The concept of territory (Higgs, et al. 1967) applied to site distributions can indicate the clustering of sites in situations where particular staple foods may be exploited to the best advantage. Equally, the clustering of sites requires explanation, and this may well be relevant to particular man-animal-plant relationships.

The analysis of site territories gives a more precise evaluation of site potential than the more customary approach which endeavors to relate sites to climatic or vegetational zones. Such zones formed for classificatory purposes by other disciplines may have little or no relationship to archaeological data. In a sense the fact that a particular site location within a zone was selected for human habitation is probably an indication that it was atypical of the zone within which it was placed. Furthermore, the criteria upon which such zones are based are commonly of little importance to human affairs. It is apparent that agricultural zones, which may be more relevant to our purposes, commonly cross the vegetational and climatic zones of other disciplines.

Whatever may be the results of new approaches to the problems with which this symposium is concerned, an immediate improvement that can take place at the present time is in the collection and study of organic remains from archaeological sites. Apart from impressions on pottery, for the most part data has been collected from obvious concentrations in deposits. Such finds are rare and likely to remain so. In recent years water-flotation techniques have on occasion been used, and they have increased the quantity of data available to us. Nevertheless, the techniques are slow and cumbersome, and on the whole their use has also been confined to deposits which are thought to contain concentrations of organic remains.

Recently the development of froth flotation (H. N. Jarman, et al. 1972) has greatly increased the volume of deposits which in a given time can be examined for plant remains. Up to two cubic meters of deposit have been processed in one day by a single operator, and there is no reason why this should not be greatly extended by an increase in equipment. Briefly, air is forced through water to which has been added a wetting agent and a frothing liquid. The plant remains float off on the froth and are collected in sieves. The equipment is inexpensive and easily portable and can be operated by unskilled labor.

Field trials have shown that more plant remains are recovered from a site by this means than by any other method. Those heavier than water are commonly collected. Furthermore, the volume of deposits which can be examined is so much greater that investigations need not be confined to areas where the occupational discoloration of deposits suggests a possible concentration of organic remains. Indeed, plant remains have been recovered in quantity from the most unpromising deposits where no organic remains were suspected, and promising discolored areas were sometimes the least productive.

Other interesting results were that in the same occupational layer different areas and different features were associated with the remains of very different plants. Deposits taken from laid floors gave a very different result from deposits around hearths. Grain of small size which might have been taken for wild grain was found in association with many used (wild) seeds, and, from the same occupational layer, concentrations of large-sized grain were almost free from weeds.

Such information has given a useful indication of the harvesting, threshing, winnowing, and sifting techniques which were used in prehistoric times. However, perhaps the most promising development is in the wide variety of plant remains which have been recovered by this means from archaeological sites and the possibility of studying plant associations in prehistoric times. It may well be that the study of weeds and plant associations may become as informative as the study of individual crop plants.

To summarize, it is believed that it is important in forming a strategy for the study of the origin of African plant domesticates that we should be guided by the failures as well as the successes of more developed and comparative studies elsewhere. It is suggested that an overall theoretical framework should be formed to give purpose and direction to such studies, and it is suggested that such a framework can best be based on the study of prehistoric economies.

REFERENCES

BERRY, R. J.
    1969   "The genetical implications of domestication in animals," in *The domestication and exploitation of animals*. Edited by P. Ucko and G. Dimbleby, 207–217. London: Duckworth.
CALLEN, E. O.
    1967   The first New World cereal. *American Antiquity* 32.
EHRLICH, P. R., P. H. RAVEN
    1969   Differentiation of populations. *Science* 165.
HARRIS, D. R.
    1967   New light on plant domestication and the origins of agriculture: a review. *Geographical Review* 57(1):90–107.
HELBAEK, H.
    1966   "Pre-pottery Neolithic farming at Beidha," in *Five seasons at the Pre-pottery Neolithic village of Beidha in Jordan*. Edited by D. Kirkbride, 61–67. Special issue of *Palestine Exploration Quarterly* 98.
HIGGS, E. S., C. VITA-FINZI, D. R. HARRIS, A. E. FAGG
    1967   "The climate, environment and industries of Stone Age Greece." *Proceedings of the Prehistoric Society* 33.
JARMAN, H. N., A. J. LEGGE, J. A. CHARLES
    1972   "Retrieval of plant remains from archaeological sites by froth flotation," in *Papers in economic prehistory*. Edited by E. S. Higgs. Cambridge: Cambridge University Press.

JARMAN M. R.
1969 "The prehistory of Upper Pleistocene and recent cattle." *Proceedings of the Prehistoric Society* 35.
1972 "European deer economies and the advent of the Neolithic," in *Papers in economic prehistory.* Edited by E. S. Higgs. Cambridge: Cambridge University Press.
JARMAN, M. R., P. F. WILKINSON
1972 "Criteria of animal domestication," in *Papers in economic prehistory.* Edited by E. S. Higgs. London: Cambridge University Press.
LAWRENCE, B.
1967 Early domestic dogs. *Zeitschrift für Säugetierkunde* 32.
LEGGE, A. J.
1972 "Prehistoric exploitation of the gazelle in Palestine," in *Papers in economic prehistory.* Edited by E. S. Higgs. Cambridge: Cambridge University Press.
PERKINS, D., P. DALY
1968 A hunters' village in Turkey. *Scientific American* 219(5):97–106.
PIDOPLICHKO, I. G.
1969 *Late Palaeolithic dwellings of mammoth bones in the Ukraine.* Kiev: Academy of Sciences of the Ukraine.
SINGH, GURDIP
1971 The Indus Valley culture. *Oceania* 4:2.

SECTION TWO

Background Paleoclimates

Paleoecological Background in Connection with the Origin of Agriculture in Africa

E. M. VAN ZINDEREN BAKKER

As yet, little is known of the cultural history of mankind in Africa. The main reasons for our incomplete knowledge are certainly the vastness of the continent, the comparatively small number of research workers, and the conditions in most parts of Africa which are unfavorable for the preservation of organic material.

Seed agriculture in Africa began at very different periods in such widely separated regions as North Africa, the Sudan, and southern Africa. This difference in age is closely correlated with the abilities of prehistoric man, his origin, migrations, contacts, and certainly his physical and biological environment. In considering these we will not enlarge on the human aspect, but discuss only the climatological and botanical environment in which crop production could gradually have developed. This task is rendered difficult by the incomplete data we possess on many areas of Africa so that only general outlines can be described. The following points will be discussed: (1) the late Quaternary climatic evolution of Africa, and (2) environmental changes which occurred at the time of the possible origin of crop production.

The discussion will be centered on Africa south of the Tropic of Cancer, excluding the Cape region.

The present climatic pattern of the vast continent of Africa is controlled by a number of wind systems which can be briefly summed up as follows: The northern and southern extremities fall in the cyclonic belts and at present receive winter rain, while the central part of the continent is dominated by the equatorial rain system. The anomalous desert regions of the Sahara and the Horn of Africa prevent the tropical rain from following the sun northward as far as the Tropic of Cancer

(Flohn 1963).

The rain received by the central part of Africa comes mainly from the Atlantic Ocean from where the so-called "monsoon" penetrates the West African coast region, the Congo basin, and Central Africa as far as Ethiopia and East Africa. The southeastern trades and easterlies bring rain from the Indian Ocean to that part of Africa east of the Rift Valley.

Quaternary climatic changes in Africa have been studied from many different angles in recent years. The study of fossil dunes, periglacial phenomena, former lakes- and sea levels, and a wealth of paleontological material have shown that important environmental changes occurred in the recent past. Similar conclusions can be drawn from a study of the present-day pattern of biogeography. Although the contributions of pollen analysis in Africa are not as numerous as in Europe, the data provided by palynological studies are of fundamental importance for the understanding of the Quaternary paleoclimates. From this wealth of information only the dated events can be used for the setting up of chronological sequences (Coetzee 1967).

WORLDWIDE CHANGES IN TEMPERATURE DURING THE LATE QUATERNARY

The Bloemfontein Centre for Palynology has strongly supported the concept that during the Quaternary the temperature in Africa showed variations which were synchronous and parallel with those of the northern hemisphere. It has also been postulated that these variations were worldwide and had different amplitudes according to the latitudinal and altitudinal position of the area concerned (Coetzee 1967; van Zinderen Bakker 1969). The African equivalent of the last glacial of the northern hemisphere may be called the Kenya Glacial Period. In the East African mountains the decrease in temperature during the final cold phase of the last glaciation (synchronous with the Upper Pleniglacial of Europe) has been assessed to have been at least 5 to 8 degrees Centigrade (Flint 1959a; van Zinderen Bakker and Coetzee 1972; Morrison 1968; Hamilton 1972). African equivalents for the Denekamp Interstadial, the Upper Pleniglacial, the Late Glacial, and some Holocene subdivisions could be recognized.

The discovery of palearctic diatoms of Upper Pleniglacial, Late Glacial, and early Holocene age in the southern Sahara is of very great importance in this connection (Servant and Servant 1970, 1972). Similarly Wendorf (this volume) describes the occurrence of a diatom assemblage of cool temperate preference found in lake deposits near Isna in the Lower Nile Valley of an age of 12,700 to 12,000 B.P.

The variations in temperature described for Africa can be closely correlated with the paleotemperature curve of tropical South America (Coetzee 1967). In recent years proof for synchronous late Quaternary temperature variations has also become available from the sub-Antarctic islands (Schalke and van Zinderen Bakker 1971; van Zinderen Bakker 1973), Antarctica (Denton, Armstrong, and Stuiver 1971), and Greenland (Dansgaard, Johnsen, Clausen, and Langway 1971).

The analyses of the 1,390 meter ice core from Camp Century in North Greenland has provided impressive data on paleoclimatology (Dansgaard, et al. 1971). The assessment of the stable-isotope concentration in this core has provided information on temperature trends over the last 120,000 years. Although the results cannot be used as a temperature curve, they indicate periods of warming and cooling. Dansgaard, et al. (1971) could correlate these temperature variations in a very acceptable way with the American and European glacial chronology. The available evidence for parallel and synchronous changes in world temperature strongly suggests that the Camp Century curve can cautiously be recognized in the Late and Post Glacial section of the curve (Table 1).

It should be stressed that details, especially of the smaller fluctuations, cannot be expected to be found at every site as the influences of such small changes may not have been registered in the geological or paleontological record.

Table 1. Late and Post Glacial sections of the Camp Century Curve

Approximate years B.P.	Temperature	Equivalent of European pollen chronology
0 – 1000	cooler	
1000 – 2500	slightly warmer	
2500 – 3000	Cooler	
3000 – 3300	warmer	
3300 – 4100	cold	
4100 – 8000	warm	Atlanticum
	(maximum at 5000 and 6000 B.P.)	
9000 – 9800	colder	Preboreal
9800 – 10,200	warm	
10,200 – 11,000	cold	Younger Dryas
11,000 – 11,800	warm	Allerød
11,800 – 12,000	cold	Older Dryas
12,000 – 12,400	warmer	Bølling
> 12,400	very cold	Oldest Dryas Upper Pleniglacial

The energy budget of the earth and consequently the temperature variations are the primary factors determining world climate. The causal relationship between these entities is not yet fully understood, and the consequences of variations in world temperature can probably not always be explained with the actualistic principle. It is very often accepted that meridional contractions of the climatic belts occurred during colder periods. This led to acceleration of the wind system. A general rise in world temperature, on the other hand, would result in a widening of the tropical zone. Changes in the latitudinal position of the pressure systems and consequently of the direction and energy of the winds would have had a profound influence on the regional climates.

PLUVIALS AND INTERPLUVIALS

One of the very important consequences of global temperature changes has certainly been the variation in temperature of the tropical oceans (Emiliani 1971). The much lower temperature of the tropical Atlantic during glacial periods must have affected the evaporation rate and therefore the transport of humidity to all of the central parts of Africa. During warmer periods not only was much more water conveyed to the continent, but the tropical rainbelt expanded to higher latitudes and could bring rain to otherwise arid or semiarid regions. The meridional extension of the equatorial rain system also depends very much on the influence of the polar fronts of both hemispheres. The old hypothesis of "glacial pluvials" and "interglacial interpluvials" which should have affected the whole of the continent has now been changed completely for West and East Africa. The last glacial maximum was a dry period, while the end of the Late Glacial and the climatic optimum were marked by high precipitation.

It has been pointed out by Maley (1973) that in recent times rainfall and temperature in West Africa have been negatively correlated.

The former pluvial theory has to be abandoned for many reasons (Cooke 1958; Flint 1959b), one of which is that the last glacial maximum in the interior of South Africa was marked by higher humidity. This shows that the pluvials did not occur synchronously all over the continent.

STUDIES OF FOSSIL POLLEN

The fossil pollen sequences from Mount Kenya, the Cherangani, Kilimanjaro, and Uganda have provided valuable information on late

Quaternary stratigraphy and on environmental changes. During a time coeval with the European Upper Pleniglacial, the vegetation belts showed downward shifts of over 1,000 meters. These changes have primarily been interpreted as a consequence of a decrease in temperature of a magnitude of at least 5 to 8 degrees Centigrade (Coetzee 1967).

The fossil evidence for these temperature variations has not been accepted by Livingstone (1967), Morrison (1966), or Hedberg (1969). Livingstone is of the opinion that the pollen sequences of Ruwenzori show that plant successions on new volcanic deposits, and drier conditions were probably primarily responsible for simulating colder conditions. He also argues that the altitudinal vegetation belts did not shift up and down the mountains but that "certain taxa appeared to have behaved individually rather than as members of a migrating community" (Livingstone 1967). In his explanation of the fossil pollen sequence of the Muchoya swamp (southwestern Uganda) Morrison (1968) revised his opinion and used the temperature changes as proposed by Coetzee (1967). After an extensive study of the present production and dispersal of pollen of the mountain vegetation of Uganda, Hamilton (1972) reexamined the results of Livingstone and Hamilton. He refuted the explanations of Livingstone and arrived at conclusions very similar to those of Coetzee for Kenya.

The evidence on changes in temperature and humidity inferred from the pollen analytical studies of the East African mountains is combined in Table 2.

Table 2. Changes in temperature and humidity inferred from the pollen analytical studies of the East African mountains

Pollen zones Sacred Lake	Carbon 14 years B.P.	Temperature changes	Changes in humidity
Z	ca. 3000	probably cooler	on mountain drier (more misty)
Y	ca. 5000	warmer	very wet on mountain and probably wet on plateau
X	ca. 6000	cold oscillation	
W	ca. 8000	warm	becoming wetter on mountain
V	10,500		wetter on mountain, wet on plateau, moderately dry in Lake Victoria Basin
U	14,000	oscillating slightly warmer	becoming moist on plateau
T		cold	dry on mountain and plateau
	27,000		
S		cooler than at	
	33,350 ± 1020		
R	(GrN 4194)	present	

It is evident that the information on the East African plateau is still incomplete. The general conclusion which can be drawn is, however, that during Upper Pleniglacial times (zone T) the climate was cold and dry. These conditions changed during oscillations in Late Glacial times and became warm and wet between ca. 10,500 and 6000 B.P. After a cold spell the climate became warm and wet again. During the final 3,000 years the climate became cooler, but no definite information on the rainfall is yet available from pollen studies.

The pollen analytical studies done so far in southern Africa cover the Upper Pleistocene and part of the early Holocene and are only concerned with two sites: Florisbad and Aliwal North (van Zinderen Bakker 1957; Coetzee 1967). The deposits of both these sites, which occur round old volcanic springs, probably give typical information for the interior of the southern African plateau. The information can be correlated with geomorphological studies and especially with the age of lacustrine deposits of the Pleniglacial Alexandersfontein Lake west of Kimberley (van Zinderen Bakker and Butzer 1973).

The evidence for the central plateau of South Africa has been summarized in Table 3.

The conclusions which can be drawn from this still very incomplete data are that the general trend of the temperature changes can be correlated with similar variations recorded in East Africa, Europe and Greenland. The humidity curve is, however, negatively correlated with that of East Africa, as colder periods were humid and warmer periods dry in central South Africa. This strongly indicates that the southern subcontinent was exposed to a climatic system which was entirely different from that of East Africa.

LAKE LEVELS IN THE SOUTHERN SAHARA AND EAST AFRICA

An impressive range of data is now available on the former levels of lakes in this vast region during late Quaternary times (Butzer, Isaac, Richardson, and Washbourn-Kamay 1972; van Zinderen Bakker 1972). Important information on humidity has been inferred from a comparison of the levels of Lakes Chad, Rudolf, Afrera, Nakuru, Naivasha, Magadi, Victoria, and Katwa. The explanation of such changes in the water level of lakes in a tropical region can pose difficult problems. The crucial factors are rainfall and temperature, the latter being determinative for the former. Consistent changes in mean temperature have

Table 3.   Pollen analytical studies for the central plateau of South Africa

Lithology Florisbad	Pollen zones Aliwal North	Carbon 14 years B.P.	Temperature changes	Changes in humidity	Alexanders-fontein pan
	Z	9650 ± 150 (GrN-4012)	becoming warm	dry	
	Y		not as cold as zone W	wetter	
	X	11,650 ± 170 (I-2109) to 11,250 ± 180 (I-2110)	dry	warm	
	W	12,200 ± 180 (I-2107) to 11,650 ± 170 (I-2109)	not as cool as zone U	wetter	
	V	calculated 12,600 to 12,200	warm	dry	
	U	12,600 ± 110 (GrN-4011) 16,010 ± 185	cool	wetter	very high levels
"Peat III"		19,350 ± 650 (L-271D)	cool	wetter	
Sand			cooler	wetter	
"Peat II"		28,450 ± 2,200 (L-271C)	warm	oscillating, very arid to semiarid	
Clay					
"Peat I"		48,900 (GrN-4208)	warm	very dry, one wetter oscillation	
"Basal Peat"			warm	very dry	

a very important influence on the moisture content of the oceanic wind, on the depth to which the monsoonal front will penetrate the continent, and on the evaporation rate of large shallow lakes, such as Lake Chad.

It has been established that conditions were dry during the late Pleistocene in the vast region surrounding the lakes mentioned above, stretching from Mauretania to southern Ethiopia and hence to Lake Victoria (van Zinderen Bakker 1972). The lake levels in this enormous region subsequently rose at different times. Although these changes cannot yet be explained in detail, it is apparent that higher lake levels coincided with a period of gradual warming up. These subpluvial conditions have existed in the southern Sahara, the Sudan, Kenya, Egypt, and western Ethiopia (Butzer 1965, 1968, 1971) during the early and middle Holocene.

The lake levels which marked this subpluvial showed several high stands. At Lake Chad, Lake Rudolf, and Lake Victoria these high stands were interrupted by recessions between about 7500 and 6000 B.P.

An important change took place at about 4500 to 4000 B.P. in the Lake Chad region. The abrupt end of the Climatic Optimum coincided with a low level of Lake Chad. It is peculiar that the warmer episode just before 3000 B.P. (of the Camp Century Curve) again coincides with a higher level of the lake.

The results obtained by Munson (this volume) from the excavation of the interesting Dhar Tichitt site in south-central Mauritania fit extremely well with the latter part of the temperature variations of Camp Century and the sequence of levels of Lake Chad. The environmental evidence of this Neolithic site shows that a large lake probably dried up at about 4000 B.P. and that high lake levels were again reached at 3500 B.P. A dry period followed, just as at Lake Chad, at about 3000 B.P. This well dated sequence shows that the trend of these lake levels must have been indicative for the environmental changes which occurred in the southern Sahara during the last 4,000 years.

The more recent events are not known in enough detail to establish correlations betweeen the temperature curve and the lake levels. Maley (1973) has discussed the very interesting possibility that during the latter 3,000 years important changes in the polar influences on the equatorial climate were responsible for an inverted correlation between world temperature and lake levels. A lowering in temperature would then have caused a rise in the level of Lake Chad. He could demonstrate the validity of this model for historic times.

The results of the isotope determinations of Schiegl (1970) in the Lake Chad region show that the evaporation effect was strong during the last 4,000 years.

It is important to note that the climate of Egypt (Butzer 1965, 1968, 1971) and Israel (Horowitz 1971) was dry during subboreal times while the floods of the Nile, which received its water mainly from the western flank of the Egyptian highlands, were very low. According to the pollen analytical results, both the East African plateau as well as the surroundings of Pilkington Bay of Lake Victoria may have been drier. The latter could, however, have had a more seasonal rainfall (Kendall 1969).

VEGETATION CHANGES DURING THE LATE QUATERNARY

The general outline we now have of the climatic evolution of the late Quaternary of Africa only allows us to give a sketchy picture of former phytogeographic changes. It is evident that the endless variety of habitats which exist in Africa have undergone many unpredictable changes. It is, therefore, too early to make detailed maps of former vegetation. The recognition of the gaps in our knowledge does not, however, prevent us from realizing that considerable changes occurred in the biogeography. The ecotones, which are very wide in most parts of Africa, may have moved over vast areas as a consequence of a consistent change in temperature or rainfall. These variations caused migrations and mixing of formerly separated populations of plants and animals.

The colder periods were characterized by greater dryness in the tropical parts and greater humidity especially in central South Africa and the northern margin of the Sahara. In the tropical parts the appreciable decrease in rainfall was counterbalanced by lesser evaporation of soil moisture and free surface water, which has already been alluded to. As has been discussed, this aridity reigned during Upper Pleniglacial times from the central Sahara as far south as the plateau of Tanzania.

During the warmer periods and especially during the time of the climatic optimum of Europe, this extensive region received much more precipitation from the equatorial rain system. The vegetation zones are situated in a concentric fashion round the tropical rainforest center of the Congo and West Africa. These wide zones expanded and migrated further north, east and south into the surrounding deserts and semideserts. Such environmental changes must have been of enormous importance for the life and culture of prehistoric man and must have had a profound influence on his system of subsistence.

THE SOUTHERN SAHARA AND WEST AFRICA

Extensive geological research has shown that this vast region suffered very dry conditions during the extended last glacial maximum (Burke, Durotoye, and Whiteman 1971). Dunes invaded the dwindling Lake Chad during this cold period and the desert moved south to at least 13 degrees south latitude. The dry period of Lake Chad lasted from ca. 20,000 to 12,400 years ago. The central and southern Sahara must have formed a formidable barrier to migration of man, beasts, and plants, and only a limited portion of the flora and fauna could have survived in the more humid valleys of the high Saharan mountains. Geomorphological studies in Adamawa support the Lake Chad evidence (Hurault 1970).

The consequence of this aridity must have been that the enormous pattern of east-west arranged vegetation zones moved southward towards the coast. The xerophytic *Acacia* and *Commiphora* species from the Sahel invaded the Isoberlinia woodlands which in their turn took over the habitats of the moist woodland and the forest region. The tropical rainforest, which is at present divided into two areas separated by the dry Togo-Dahomey gap, during this excessive dry period must have been divided up into small remnants situated along the coast (van Zinderen Bakker 1967). It can be inferred from biogeographic and climatological evidence that these relics were situated at Cape Palmas, Cape Three Points, and the Niger Delta where the onshore westerlies always bring sufficient rain.

The rise in world temperature which started about 12,400 years ago had an enormous influence on the biogeography of West Africa. The consequence of this warming up was that the influence of the northern polar front diminished and that the South Atlantic anticyclone shifted further southward, so that the moisture-laden "monsoon" could gradually move further inland. At the same time, when the isotope curve of the Greenland ice cap showed signs of the warming up of the earth (Dansgaard, Johnsen, Clausen, and Langway 1971), when open woodland invaded the steppe of northern Greece (van der Hammen, Wymstra, and Zagwyn 1971), and the tundra of northern Europe was encroached upon by parkland during the Bølling Interstadial, Lake Chad started to rise. This close coincidence points to a narrow correlation which should be explained by climatologists. Lake Chad was apparently very sensitive to this changing climatic pattern, and the isotope curve of Camp Century (Dansgaard, Johnsen, Clausen, and Langway 1971) and the curve of the former levels of Lake Chad show a striking resemblance and remarkably exact coincidence in time, as has been pointed out already. The drier periods coincided with the European Older Dryas, the Younger Dryas, and the Friesland Stadials. These oscillations must have caused southward expansions and northward contractions of the desert so that the wide vegetation belts of West Africa were constantly moving in the same direction. Prehistoric man who lived in this region must have come under enormous stress during the arid periods. The disaster which recently struck men in the whole of the Sudan as far east as Ethiopia gives an image of similar events which happened long ago in this climatic coastland of the desert. The similarity of the climatic pattern points to identical causes.

The long humid subpluvial, which lasted with interruptions from about 12,400 to 4,500 years ago, is well known from the excellent work done by the French geologist Servant (Servant and Servant 1970) and the studies on fossil pollen by the team of van Campo Duplan (van Campo, Aymonin, Guinet and Rognon 1964; van Campo, Cohen, Guinet, and Rognon 1965; van Campo, Guinet, Cohen, and Dutil 1966, 1967). It has been difficult to assess the former vegetation of the Sahara and its mountains. The main problem has been that the allochtonous component of the fossil pollen spectra is not known. Important quantitative data on the pollen content of the atmosphere near Béni-Abbès are now becoming available from analyses carried out by Cour, Guinet, Cohen, and Duzer (Guinet 1972). The results will show whether the large number of collected airborne pollen grains has been produced by the sparse local vegetation or is of long-distance origin.

During the Holocene subpluvial the southern part of the Sahara seems to have been partly covered by an open Mediterranean vegetation, until the final desiccation set in at about 4000 B.P. Important work on the former vegetation of the Sahara mountains has been done by van Campo, et al. especially on the Hoggar. Preliminary results of pollen analytical investigations by Schulz (1972) in the Tibesti mountains indicate that, between 14,000 and 6000 B.P., an open grassland existed at the foot of these mountains, while *Acacia, Tamarix*, Combretaceae, and Salvadoraceae occurred along the wadis. This riverine forest extended into the mountains, where the slopes were covered with a Mediterranean *macchia* (*Cercis, Myrtus*, Oleaceae, etc.) which graded into a formation of deciduous trees (*Quercus*) at a higher altitude. The higher plateaux were probably covered by dry grassland with *Artemisia,* Chenopodiaceae, *Ephedra, Juniperus*, and some *Pinus*. The influence of long-distance dispersal on the pollen sedimentation has to be assessed in more detail, however, before this picture can be accepted with confidence.

Geomorphological research supported by radiocarbon dates shows that the monsoonal rain must have reached the southern flanks of Tibesti and the eastern slopes of the Aïr mountains. Rivers coming from these watersheds built up deltas of relatively fine sediments (Servant and Servant 1970, 1972). Pollen studies indicate that the surrounding vegetation contained Mediterranean and tropical elements, while Lake Chad, according to the cold water diatoms it contained in Lower Holocene deposits, cannot have had a high temperature.

Although the general trend of the environmental changes in West Africa is well known, detailed knowledge is lacking as so far no complete pollen cores have been studied. It would be very valuable for West African palynologists to undertake this task.

The Tropical Rainforest of Central Africa

It is not known whether the dry period of late Pleniglacial times also affected the tropical rain forest of the Congo basin although a retreat of the northern boundary of this forest and its West African continuation can be visualized (van Zinderen Bakker 1967). For the comparable Amazon rain forest, Vuilleumier (1971) postulated that during periods of a drier climate, synchronous with glaciations, the vast forest biome was fragmented into sections. These drastic changes are inferred from biogeographic data. The distribution of bird species in tropical South America points to the former existence of forest refuges which were isolated long enough to lead to speciation. If similar processes occurred in the African rain forest, this forest region cannot always have been inhospitable to human migration.

The East African Plateau

A wide variety of vegetation types is at present occupying the vast East African plateau. These range from desert and semidesert country around Lake Rudolf to woodlands around Lake Victoria and in the southern and southwestern parts of Tanzania. The dry *Acacia-Commiphora* grasslands, however, cover the greater part of the plateau. Montane and Afro-alpine communities with an entirely different ecology are found on the isolated high mountains of East Africa.

So far, little is known of the environmental changes which occurred on the plateau during late Quaternary times. The pollen analytical studies which were done on the high mountains cover the last 33,500 years and give an impressive record of changes in temperature, humidity, and vegetation which have happened since the Kalambo (European Denekamp) Interstadial of the Kenya Glaciation. It is not possible, however, to extrapolate these data to the plateau proper except on a very limited scale. In his extensive study on the interpretation of pollen diagrams from highland Uganda, Hamilton (1972) made a careful evaluation of the well-dispersed pollen types, such as *Celtis*-type, *Acalypha, Podocarpus*, and Urticaceae. Coetzee (1972) used the same method to reevaluate her pollen diagram from Sacred Lake on Mount Kenya. The conclusion which can be drawn from these studies has already been discussed.

The sequence of lake levels studied in East Africa, which have already been referred to, indicate changes in humidity which were broadly synchronous with those discussed for West Africa. These changes would probably have been important in the marginal areas where *Brachystegia* woodland and dry savanna grassland were in an unstable equilibrium. These environmental changes, however, would not have been very spectacular since we have no indications of a wide encroachment of the northern desert as in West Africa.

The palynological and limnological study of the Pilkington Bay of the Victoria basin by Kendall (1969) has revealed that the climate was dry before 12,500 years ago. The humidity then increased and reached a maximum between ca. 9500 and 6000 years B.P. after which time conditions became drier or the rainfall became more seasonal.

Kendall found that forest vegetation first appeared in the area after 12,000 B.P. After a decline it reached its optimum development soon after 10,000 years ago. Between 7000 and 6000 years B.P. the evergreen forest was replaced by semideciduous forest which remained dominant until 3000 B.P. It is very likely that human interference was responsible for changes in vegetation during the last 3,000 years.

In an extensive study of Lake Naivasha in the African Rift Valley, J. and A. Richardson (1972) came to the conclusion that the maximum rainfall (Gamblian Pluvial) occurred at the same time as at Pilkington Bay (viz. 9200 to 5650 B.P.). After that, conditions also became drier until 3000 B.P. The climate improved slightly during the last 3,000 years but was often somewhat drier than at present.

The Woodland Region of Central and East Africa

The *Brachystegia-Julbernardia* woodland, as a peritropical forest formation, covers the vast zone stretching south of the Congo basin and Lake Victoria, right across Central and East Africa from near the Atlantic coast to the coastal regions of Tanzania and Mozambique. Called *miombo* in northern Zambia, this woodland is, under certain conditions, a fire-climax vegetation. Another type of woodland, the *chipya*, is found mainly in the Chambeshi Valley and the Lake Bangweulu basin. *Chipya* means fierce fire which indicates the extensive influence by man on this vegetation type. The destruction man caused in the forests of this region has also been demonstrated by the disappearance of the luxuriant swamp forest or *mushitu* over vast areas.

These forest types have been studied particularly in Zambia by Lawton (1963, 1972) and in Katanga by Streel (1963), while Trapnell (1953) made a detailed survey of the agricultural method used at present in this region.

It appears that for a long time man has burnt down these forests for hunting purposes and even more for making his ash-gardens (*chitemene*) by lopping the trees and burning the stacks of wood. Flying over this part of Africa, the circular patches of these old *chitemenes* can be seen clearly over hundreds of kilometers. The destructive influence of this old method of agriculture on vegetation and soil cannot easily be over-estimated. If the *miombo* is not allowed twenty to thirty years to regenerate, it will not survive and will be replaced by open savanna and grassland. Lawton (1963) found that "much of the black soil of the top two feet of a chipya soil profile and the black ooze in the Bangweulu swamp deposits consists of finely divided pieces of carbon derived from burnt plant material." It would be very important to assess the age of these deposits by using the radiocarbon carbon 14 method.

These woodlands of Zambia have, according to taxonomic studies, developed as a result of the degeneration of a forest which had affinities with the moist tropical forest of West Africa and the humid montane forests of East and Central Africa (Lawton 1972). In his study on the biogeography of the African avifauna, Moreau (1966) concluded that a montane forest connection must have existed during the last glaciation between the Angolan forest relicts and the montane forests of the East Congo and Malawi. Lawton, however, concluded "that a lowland seasonally dry evergreen forest, containing many montane forest species, did exist until quite recently, probably 1,000–2,000 years ago" (1972: 256) in this region. This explanation would fit much better with our present knowledge of a humidity maximum during the early and middle Holocene in East and Central Africa.

The geomorphological studies of Alexandre (1971) of Katanga also suggest that this woodland region was covered by dry grassland during the colder last glacial maximum (Upper Pleniglacial). It is possible that the so-called "arid corridor," which has existed between southwestern Africa and the Horn of Africa through the present woodland region, was open to migration of species of these arid and semiarid regions during this cool and dry period (*Palaeoecology of Africa* 1966–1969).

Alexandre comes to the conclusion that after this dry phase a transitional period with dense forest may have occurred in the river valleys of Katanga, after which the present-day vegetation originated.

Still further south a geomorphological investigation by Flint and Bond (1968) indicates that after a dry period during which the long sand ridges were formed in the Wanki area (Rhodesia), a more humid and perhaps cooler climate encouraged the establishment of vegetation on the dunes. Unfortunately, these events have not yet been dated. If this interpretation is correct, the climate differed substantially from that further north in Central Africa and indicates conditions similar to those known from South Africa.

The South African Plateau

Important ecological changes occurred in the grassveld and Karroo vegetation of the central part of South Africa. At present a grassveld vegetation with tropical affinities occupies most of the Orange Free State. South of the Orange River, the semidesert Karroo vegetation occurs, while the high mountains of Lesotho are covered by alpine meadows. The Karroo vegetation is at present encroaching into the grasslands of the plateau and the mountains to the north and northeast of it, mostly as a consequence of farming practices. Under natural conditions the border between the grassland and the Karroo runs from Hope Town on the Orange River with a loop towards de Aar and Victoria West some 200 kilometers to the southwest of the river (Figure 1).

According to the data obtained from fossil pollen studies at Florisbad, the present grassveld at this site in the center of the Orange Free State was replaced by the undershrubs of the semidesert central Lower and central Upper Karroo before 29,000 B.P. Environmental changes of this magnitude point to shifts of vegetation over distances of hundreds of kilometers (minimum 200 to 500 kilometers). Extrapolating this data to northern regions, this climatic deterioration could have pushed the very dry Karroo vegetation into the northern Transvaal Province which is at present covered by woodland. The age of this change is not known, although this warm interstadial period could have been equivalent with the Riss-Würm Interglacial (Eemian).

The pollen diagrams of Florisbad (van Zinderen Bakker 1957) and Aliwal North (Coetzee 1967) indicate that between 28,450 ± 2,200 B.P. and 12,600 ± 110 B.P. the Karroo vegetation which occupied the central plateau gave way to a more humid grassveld. The many basins in the western region were then occupied by extensive deep lakes.

Aliwal North, where a pollen profile with an age of 12,600 B.P. to 9650 B.P. has been studied, is situated on the Orange River 200 kilometers south of Florisbad. During Late Glacial times, in the surroundings of this site there were frequent environmental changes. The warmer periods which were coeval with the Bølling, the Allerød, and the Preboreal of Europe were characterized by a northward movement of

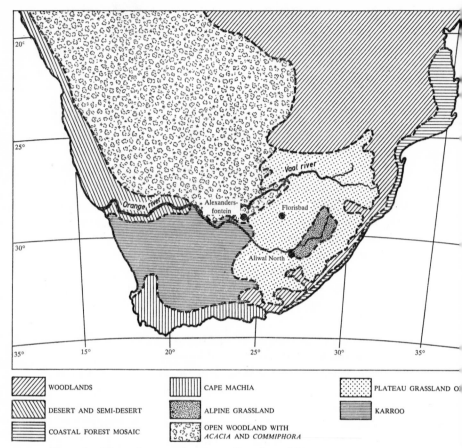

////	WOODLANDS	⫴⫴	CAPE MACHIA	⁙	PLATEAU GRASSLAND O⫶
\\\\	DESERT AND SEMI-DESERT	░	ALPINE GRASSLAND	▤	KARROO
▤	COASTAL FOREST MOSAIC	ᵒ⁰ᵒ	OPEN WOODLAND WITH *ACACIA* AND *COMMIPHORA*		

Figure 1.   The main vegetation types of southern Africa

the arid Karroo vegetation. The humid grassland, with some indicators of a lower temperature, occupied the region during the intervening periods. This grassveld may have been of alpine origin and could have moved from the high mountains of Lesotho to the plateau. This possibility is corroborated by the fact that during the last cold glacial maximum (coeval with the Upper Pleniglacial and Late Glacial) hardly any vegetation existed in the mountains of Lesotho above an altitude of 3,000 meters. The swamps which are found here, at present surrounded by alpine grassland, have a maximum radiocarbon age of 8,000 years. A decrease in temperature of 5.5 and 8 degrees Centigrade has been assessed by Harper (1969) on fossil periglacial evidence in Lesotho. This figure also lends circumstantial support to the hypothesis that the plateau of the Orange Free State was covered by a cold type of grassland during the last maximum of the Ice Age.

SUMMARY

The environmental changes which occurred in Africa during the last 30,000 years are discussed. The northern and southern extremities of the continent are not considered in this account. The conclusions are based on the results of pollen analysis, studies on former lake levels, and geomorphology. It appears that the changes which took place can be correlated with variations in temperature of a worldwide nature. The Camp Century isotope curve appears to give extremely interesting correlations with the events in Africa, especially with the humidity pattern. In the southern Sahara and West, East, and Central Africa, the last maximum of the Kenya glaciation (Upper Pleniglacial and the early Late Glacial of Europe) was marked by aridity. A prolonged subpluvial prevailed during the warmer period from ca. 12,500 to ca. 4,000 years ago. Several dry oscillations occurred which must have placed prehistoric man under heavy environmental stress. The opposite correlation between temperature and humidity existed on the central plateau of South Africa.

The consequences these climatic oscillations had on the distribution of the vegetation and, therefore, on the human environment are discussed in broad outline for the following regions: the southern Sahara and West Africa, the tropical rainforest of Central Africa, the East African plateau, the woodland region of Central and East Africa, and the South African plateau. The intensive human influence on the woodland biome is stressed.

REFERENCES

ALEXANDRE-PYRE, S.
    1971   Le plateau des Biano (Katanga): géomorphogie. *Acad. Foy. Sci. d'Outre-Mer., Sci. Nat. et Médic.* n.s. 18 (3).
BURKE, K., A. B. DUROTOYE, A. J. WHITEMAN
    1971   A dry phase south of the Sahara 20,000 years ago. *West African Journal of Archaeology* 1:1–8.
BUTZER, K. W.
    1965   "Physical conditions in Eastern Europe, Western Asia, and Egypt before the period of agricultural and urban settlement," in *The Cambridge ancient history*, 3–39.
    1968   "Climatic change in the arid zones of Africa during early to mid-Holocene times," in *Roy. Met. Soc. Symp. "World Climate from 8000 to 0 B.C.,"* 72—83.

1971   *Environment and archeology*, second edition. Chicago: Aldine-Atherton.

BUTZER, K. W., G. LL. ISAAC, J. L. RICHARDSON, C. WASHBOURN-KAMAY
1972   Radiocarbon dating of East African lake levels. *Science* 175:1069–1076.

COETZEE, J. A.
1967   Pollen analytical studies in East and Southern Africa. *Palaeoecology of Africa* 3:1–146.
1972   Appendix of "A re-appraisal of Late Quaternary climatic evidence from tropical Africa." *Palaeoecology of Africa* 7:74–77.

COOKE, H. B. S.
1958   Observations relating to Quaternary environments in East and Southern Africa. *Geology Society of South Africa*. Annexure 60.

DANSGAARD, W., S. J. JOHNSEN, H. CLAUSEN, C. C. LANGWAY JR.
1971   "Climatic record revealed by the Camp Century ice core," in *The Late Cenozoic glacial ages*. Edited by K. K. Turekian, 38–56. New Haven: Yale University Press.

DENTON, G. H., R. L. ARMSTRONG, M. STUIVER
1971   "The Late Cenozoic glacial history of Antarctica," in *The Late Cenozoic glacial ages*. Edited by K. K. Turekian, 267–306. New Haven: Yale University Press.

EMILIANI, C.
1971   "The amplitude of Pleistocene climatic cycles at low latitudes and the isotopic composition of glacial ice," in *The Late Cenozoic glacial ages*. Edited by K. K. Turekian, 183–197. New Haven: Yale University Press.

FLINT, R. F.
1959a   Pleistocene climates in Eastern and Southern Africa. *Bulletin of the Geology Society of America* 70:343–374.
1959b   On the basis of Pleistocene correlation in East Africa. *Geology Magazine* 96(4):265–284.

FLINT, R. F., G. BOND
1968   Pleistocene sand ridges and pans in western Rhodesia. *Bulletin of the Geology Society of America* 79:299–314.

FLOHN, H.
1963   Warum ist die Sahara trocken? *Zeitschrift für Meteorologie* 17 (9–12):316–320.

GUINET, PH.
1972   Activités "africaines" du laboratoire de palynologie de l'Ecole Pratique des Hautes Etudes. *Palaeoecology of Africa* 7:35–38.

HAMILTON, A. C.
1972   The interpretation of pollen diagrams from highland Uganda. *Palaeoecology of Africa* 7:45–149.

HARPER, G.
1969   Periglacial evidence in southern Africa during the Pleistocene Epoch. *Palaeoecology of Africa* 4:71–101.

HEDBERG, O.
1969   Evolution and speciation in a tropical high mountain flora. *Biology Journal of the Linnean Society* 1:135–148.

HOROWITZ, A.
1971   Climatic and vegetational developments in N.E. Israel during Upper Pleistocene-Holocene times. *Pollen et Spores* 13(2):255–278.

HURAULT, J.
1970   Les Lavaka de Banyo (Cameroun) témoins de paléoclimats. *Bull. Ass. Géogr. Française* 377–378:3–13.

KENDALL, R. L.
1969   An ecological history of the Lake Victoria Basin. *Ecological Monographs* 39:121–176.

LAWTON, R. M.
1963   Palaeoecological and ecological studies in the northern Provinɾe of Northern Rhodesia. *Kirkia* 3:46–77.
1972   A vegetation survey of northern Zambia. *Palaeoecology of Africa* 6:253–256.

LIVINGSTONE, D. A.
1967   Postglacial vegetation of the Ruwenzori Mountains in equatorial Africa. *Ecological Monographs* 37:25–52.

MALEY, J.
1973   Les variations climatiques dans le bassin du Tchad durant le dernier millénaire. *C. R. Acad. Sc. Paris.*

MOREAU, R. E.
1966   *The bird faunas of Africa and its islands.* New York, London: Academic Press.

MORRISON, M. E. S.
1966   "Low-latitude vegetation history with special reference to Africa," in *Royal Met. Soc. Symp. "World Climate from 8000 to 0 B.C.,"* 142–148.
1968   Vegetation and climate in the uplands of southwestern Uganda during the Later Pleistocene Period. 1. Muchoya Swamp, Kigezi District. *Journal of Ecology* 56(2):363–384.

Palaeoecology of Africa
1966–1969   "The arid corridor." *Palaeoecology of Africa* 1:188–189; 2:76–79; 3:139–144.

RICHARDSON, J. L., A. E. RICHARDSON
1972   History of an African Rift Lake and its climatic implications. *Ecological Monographs* 42:499–534.

SCHALKE, H. J. W. G., E. M. VAN ZINDEREN BAKKER SR.
1971   "History of the vegetation," in *Marion and Prince Edward Islands,* 89–97. Cape Town: Balkema.

SCHIEGL, W. E.
1970   "Natural deuterium in biogenic materials." Unpublished doctoral dissertation, Pretoria. (Mimeographed.)

SCHULTZ, E.
1972   Pollenanalytische Untersuchungen Pleistozäner und Holozäner

Sedimente des Tibesti-Gebirges (S. Sahara). *Palaeoecology of Africa*, 7:14–15.

SERVANT, M., S. SERVANT

1970   Les formations lacustres et les diatomées du Quaternaire récent du fond de la cuvette tchadienne. *Rev. Géogr. Phys. et Géol. Dyn.* (2)12(1):63–67.

1972   Nouvelles données pour une interprétation paléoclimatique de séries continentales du Bassin Tchadien (Pléistocène récent, Holocène). *Palaeoecology of Africa* 6:87–92.

STREEL, M.

1963   La végétation tropophylle des plaines alluviales de la Lufira Moyenne. *FULREAC, Univ. Liège.*

TRAPNELL, C. G.

1953   *The soils, vegetation and agriculture of north-eastern Rhodesia,* second edition. Lusaka: Government Printer.

VAN CAMPO, M., G. AYMONIN, PH. GUINET, P. ROGNON

1964   Contribution à l'étude du peuplement végétal quaternaire des montagnes sahariennes: l'Atakor. *Pollen et Spores* 6(1):169–194.

VAN CAMPO, M., J. COHEN, PH. GUINET, P. ROGNON

1965   Contribution à L'étude du peuplement végétal quaternaire des montagnes sahariennes, II: Flore contemporaine d'un gisement de mammifères tropicaux dans l'Atakor. *Pollen et Spores* 7(2)361–380.

VAN CAMPO, M., PH. GUINET, J. COHEN, P. DUTIL

1966   Nouvelle flore pollinique des alluvions pléistocènes d'un bassin versant sud du Hoggar. *C.R. Acad. Sci.* 263:487–490.

1967   Contribution à l'étude du peuplement végétal quaternaire des montagnes sahariennes, III: Flore de l'Oued Outoul (Hoggar). *Pollen et Spores* 9(1):109–120.

VAN DER HAMMEN, T., T. A. WYMSTRA, W. H. ZAGWYN

1971   "The floral record of the Late Cenozoic of Europe," in: *The Late Cenozoic glacial ages.* Edited by K. K. Turekian, 391–424. New Haven: Yale University Press.

VAN ZINDEREN BAKKER SR., E. M.

1957   A pollen analytical investigation of the Florisbad deposits (South Africa). *Proceedings of the Third Pan-African Congress of Prehistorians, Livingstone (1953)*, 56–67.

1967   "Upper Pleistocene and Holocene stratigraphy and ecology on the basis of vegetation changes in sub-Saharan Africa," in *Background to evolution in Africa.* Edited by W. W. Bishop and J. Desmond Clark, 125–147. Chicago: University Chicago Press.

1969   Quaternary pollen analytical studies in the southern hemisphere with special reference to the sub-Antarctic, *Palaeoecology of Africa* 5:175–212.

1972   Late Quaternary lacustrine phases in the southern Sahara and East Africa. *Palaeoecology of Africa* 6:15–27.

1973   The glaciation(s) of Marion Island (sub-Antarctic). *Palaeoecology of Africa* 8:161–178.

VAN ZINDEREN BAKKER SR., E. M., K. W. BUTZER
  1973 Quaternary environmental changes in southern Africa. *Soil Science* 116(3):234–246.
VAN ZINDEREN BAKKER SR., E. M., J. A. COETZEE
  1972 A re-appraisal of Late Quaternary climatic evidence from tropical Africa. *Palaeoecology of Africa* 7:151–174.
VUILLEUMIER, B. S.
  1971 Pleistocene changes in the fauna and flora of South America. *Science* 173:771–780.

SECTION THREE

Background Archaeology

Prehistoric Populations and Pressures Favoring Plant Domestication in Africa

J. DESMOND CLARK

The causes underlying cultural change are usually to be found in a number of interconnected phenomena. When the relationship between these remains the same, cultural changes generally proceed slowly and with no major disruption of the traditional way of life. A population may be said to be in equilibrium with its environment when the demographic situation remains stable; the supply of food resources is both abundant, varied, and of good quality; the water resources remain unreduced; and the technology is adequate to deal with the level of exploitation. That is to say, when exploitation is insufficient to upset the balance of plant/animal/human relationships withio the ecosystem, unless, for some reason, there was a radical drop in population. Partial isolation, self-sufficiency, complete flexibility in group size, and a low level of population density at the hunting-gathering level minimize competition and, thus, the disruption of the status quo.

When the relationship between one or more of these factors is altered, either by nature or by man, the equilibrium is upset and a time of cultural instability and readjustment begins. Long range climatic changes towards desiccation cause diminution or disappearance of water supplies or of animal and plant resources, affecting the availability of

I wish to express my very best thanks to Elizabeth Colson, Glynn Isaac, Robert Rodden, Andrew Smith, and Monica Wilson for suggestions and criticisms on the draft paper, and to Richard Klein, Stuart Marks, Colette Roubet, Philip Smith, and Gerald Wickens for their advice and for so generously supplying and giving me permission to quote unpublished data. Discussions with Jack Harlan, Fred Wendorf, Patrick Munson, Thurstan Shaw, and several other colleagues have considerably clarified the ideas expressed in the paper. Douglas B. Cargo drew the text figures. To all of these and to my wife, my indebtedness is most gratefully acknowledged.

preferred species and the overall quality and quantity of the food supply. Similar effects can be produced by human misuse of land by destructive exploitation techniques — disruption of vegetation and plant and animal habitats, either by indiscriminate or uncontrolled burning or by overstocking. Population increase may lead inevitably to more extensive use of the traditional resources, experimentation with new ones, and, ultimately, to competition for their use, while the technology must also be improved and adapted by invention to make possible the readjustment at the new level. Besides these changes in technical efficiency, readjustment often necessitates a change of settlement location, a shift or change in the food base, and increased communication by the introduction and establishment of long and short distance contacts with other groups by population movement, carrying with it the diffusion of improved traits of behavior and equipment. The competence and speed with which this readjustment is carried out depends upon the availability and suitability of the innovations and the flexibility and degree of receptivity of the traditional group.

If, therefore, change is, as we believe, more likely to take place under pressures such as those mentioned above, it will be of interest for comprehending the causes underlying the domestication of the African food plants to examine the relationships between some of the prehistoric populations and their environments, as these can be traced in the archaeological record, and to consider some of the cultural and other developments that might have led to their domestication. Also, since archaeology suggests that domestication of plants and animals are mutually associated phenomena, I shall consider, where appropriate, the more easily identifiable evidence for stock raising.

DOMESTICATION IN NORTH AFRICA

An impressive series of radiocarbon dates from the Middle East and the eastern Mediterranean, the oldest reaching back to ca. 7000 B.C., provides unquestionable evidence for the antiquity of dry farming in these subhumid, subtropical regions (J. G. D. Clark 1965). Moreover, indications exist of the earlier manipulation of plant and animal resources by groups of specialized hunter-gatherers in some parts of southwestern Asia that are as early as the ninth millennium B.C. (P. E. L. Smith 1971). As yet, no part of the African continent has provided evidence for domestication that is as early as this. The oldest excavated farming settlements are in the Nile Valley and have comparatively late dates in the fifth and

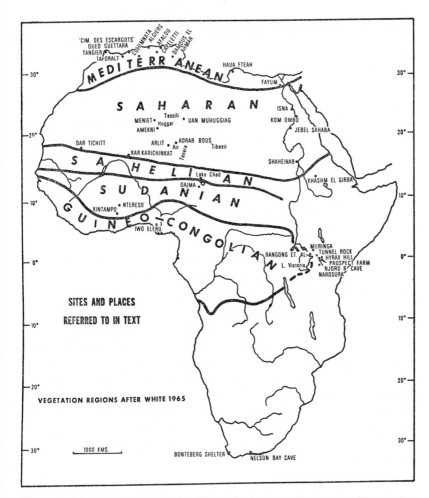

Figure 1.   Map to show the sites and localities mentioned in the text. The vegetation regions are taken from White (1965)

fourth millennia. At these sites (see Figure 1) in Lower and Upper Egypt, emmer wheat and barley were cultivated and sheep/goats, pigs, and cattle were a regular source of protein.[1] All of these are proven or believed domesticates in southwestern Asia, and their presence at the Neolithic Egyptian settlements is taken as proof of their diffusion, together with fully developed food-producing techniques, into northeastern Africa sometime during or anterior to the fifth millennium B.C. (Kantor 1965; Trigger 1968).

---

[1]   At the Egyptian Neolithic sites, these species are believed to be domestic but no definite study has yet been made.

In recent years, however, an increasing amount of evidence is becoming available to show that the human populations living in the Nile Valley, from Nubia northwards, were already more intensively exploiting both plant and animal resources from 13,000 B.C. or before — at a time, that is to say, at least as early as were some of the hunting-gathering groups in southwestern Asia (Wendorf 1968; Reed 1960; Irwin, Wheat, and Irwin 1968; P. E. L. Smith 1966). They were exploiting the river, the riverine bush, the floodplain, and the arid steppe — fishing, fowling, hunting, and harvesting the wild grain and seed plants. For example, the late Pleistocene inhabitants of the Kom Ombo plain, north of Aswan, made use of at least three fish, one reptile, twenty-two bird, and fourteen mammal species. At least one of the occupation sites at which these food resources occur appears to have been lived in the year round and is dated to ca. 12,500 B.C. (Churcher and Smith 1972). Some of the Kom Ombo and other sites in Upper Egypt and Nubia contain numbers of grinding stones and also, in several cases, backed bladelets with "sickle gloss" on the cutting edges.

The large cemeteries that date from this time are an indication of the size and comparative permanence of the communities, while the apparently mutually exclusive industrial traditions suggest that the valley occupants were now sufficiently diverse culturally to constitute a number of ethnically distinct populations. The more intensive use being made of the resources appears, however, to have resulted in competition between these "tribal" communities, if this is the interpretation that can be given to the high percentage of individuals buried in the Jebel Sahaba cemeteries who had met a violent end (Wendorf 1968: 954–95; Clark 1971a).

At this time during the Deir el-Fakhuri event of cooler, moister conditions (Wendorf, et al. 1970), the Nile Valley can be seen as the most favorable habitat for human settlement anywhere in northeastern Africa, to the extent that it attracted populations with technologies based on the prismatic blade (M. G. Smith 1965; Wendorf 1968) who came into contact with and in part replaced the traditional technology based on flakes removed by the Levallois technique. I have elsewhere sought to show that this was a time of population growth and expansion in the Nile Valley, as it was also in southwestern Asia, though demographic density is not easy to prove with any conclusiveness in prehistoric contexts (Clark 1971a). However, if this was so (as I believe it may have been), it is small wonder that the pressures attendant upon this increased density, and no doubt increased settlement size also, would have had the result of intensifying the use of the plant and animal food sources and making for a more efficient social organization. This led to both an increasing resistance to and an aptitude for encroachment upon the traditional territories of others, if the alternative to being overrun was to be forced into the eastern or western deserts where, although the resources may have been adequate, they could not have occurred in the abundance or variety with which they were available on the Nile. The extensive bush burning, for which there is evidence over a distance of 200 kilometers in Upper Egypt, is likely to have been the result of human interference and dates to the middle of the eleventh millennium (Wendorf, et al. 1970: 1166).

If this assumption and interpretation of the ecological evidence are, in general, correct, then it is difficult to understand why a similar manipulation of plant and animal resources leading to incipient domestication was not taking place in the Nile between 12,000 and 5000 B.C. at the same time as these processes made their appearance in Asia. Part of the problem in answering this question lies in our minimal knowledge of settlement sites falling within this time range. The few that have been investigated are all small and, from the limited technical range of the tool assemblages, would seem to have been special purpose camps for fishing and limited hunting (Vermeersch 1970; Wendorf, et al. 1970; Wendt 1966) rather than the main settlements. If no autochthonous step towards incipient cultivation was indeed ever taken, this could have been due in part to the adequacy of the wild grasses used for food but they were generally also unsuitable for and lacked a response to cultivation. Although pollen data from the Nile for the early Holocene are almost nonexistent, the plant communities are unlikely to have been very greatly different from those existing there today, if the exotic forms are excluded. There is evidence that *Echinochloa* and *Eragrostis* may both have been collected and eaten and other grasses and plants besides, but in no case can any of them yet be shown to have been domesticated[2] (Clark 1971a). Better evidence perhaps exists to show that experiments in taming wild cattle, hartebeest, gazelle, oryx, and other large animals, together with several waterbirds, were already well established by pre-Dynastic times (Clark 1971a) and continued, for reasons of religious ceremony and ritual, from a remote past well into Dynastic times (H. Smith 1969).

It may therefore be postulated that even if the active exploitation

---

[2] Pollen associated with sites at Isna (Complex G) and dating to 10,740–10,000 B.C. has produced a large-grass cereal-pollen tentatively identified as barley (Wendorf and Schild, this volume) so that if wild barley was present in the Nile Valley at this time, it could have been domesticated there independently.

that was taking place on the Nile during the early Holocene did not lead to full domestication of any species before the appearance there of the Asian cereals and domestic animals, it nonetheless resulted in pre-adapted communities that were very ready to accept food production and the changed social relationships and obligations that this implied (Clark 1971a). The only alternative to such a premise is that the earliest Neolithic cultivators were immigrants from Asia who imposed their food-producing economy on the peoples they found there. Despite earlier claims to the contrary, this hypothesis is at variance with the existing archaeological and biological evidence (Trigger 1968; Berry, et al. 1967). In view, also, of the general resistance to change inherent in all human populations at the simpler social and economic levels, the apparent speed with which the Nile inhabitants seem to have accepted a Neolithic economy, must surely indicate a long period of preadaptation prior to 5000 B.C.

For the rest of the continent, chronological documentation of the change from hunting and gathering to full food production has barely begun, even on the most general level. In part, this is because it is only in recent years that archaeologists there, previously and sometimes still involved with the intricacies of typology, have come to appreciate the possibilities for interpreting economic behavior from food waste. There is only one piece of well-documented, direct evidence for early domestic stock in North Africa. This comes from the Haua Fteah Cave in Cyrenaica (Higgs 1967) and dates to the interface between the sixth and fifth millennia; domestic sheep/goats are attested but the evidence from the cattle bones is inconclusive. The cultural equipment of the Neolithic community there is still essentially the traditional one to which, however, certain new tool forms have been added. These are surely introductions associated with the additional activities connected with Neolithic behavior, and although grinding stones are present, there is no direct evidence for cultivation of grains or other plants.

In the Maghreb, so-called "sickles," comprised of slotted bone handles with inset microliths, have been found with epi-Paleolithic and Neolithic occurrences, notably with the Columnata of the Algerian plateau (Camps-Fabrer 1965), while long blades with sickle gloss occur also with the "typical Capsian" in Tunisia (Camps 1974: 170). Upper and lower grindstones are generally associated with the flaked stone and bone artifacts at most of these epi-Paleolithic and Neolithic sites in the Maghreb, but there is no certain knowledge as to whether these artifacts were used with anything other than wild species. The earliest, regional, epi-Paleolithic, small blade-using communities there (Ibero-Maurusian) date to ca. 14,000 B.P. and possessed an economy based upon specialized hunting, collecting, and fishing activities which show a preference for the large mammals of the Ethiopian fauna and for the grinding of grains and seeds. This economic pattern has not a little in common with the contemporary traditions in the Nile Valley where the ecology would have been very similar. There is, besides, the same evidence for larger, semipermanent settlements (e.g. the cemeteries at Afalou Bou Rhumel, Taforalt, and Columnata, where between fifty and one hundred individuals have been recorded), while the similarities between some of the small-blade industries suggest that the pattern of economic exploitation was basically similar. Comparable ecosystems and similarities of economy and food preferences probably underlie the likenesses seen by one investigator (Anderson 1968) between the Nubian and the Afalou/ Mechta populations, thus obviating any need to presuppose long distance migratory movement at this time. The chief difference lay in the fact that the Nile was a particularly rich environment where, due to the confining desert, the main movements among the population must have been either north or south within the valley itself, while the North African Mediterranean zone, though in general less rich ecologically, readily permitted movement in every direction except across the sea to the north.

After 5000 B.C., pottery, pressure-flaked projectile points, and ground stone tools, make a gradual appearance in the stratigraphic record of the excavated sites (e.g. Gar Cahal and Tangier [Achakar], Oued Guettara, and "Cimetière des Escargots" on the coast, and Jebel Marhsel, Damous el Ahmar, and Djebel Bou Zabaoine in the traditional Capsian region [Roubet 1968]). Domestic sheep and goat are present at all levels at the Capéletti Cave (4580 ±250 to 2396 ±200 B.C.) in Batna where they comprise nine-tenths of the total fauna; cattle are also present but less certainly domesticated (Roubet, personal communication). Sheep/goat remains are reported to be common in the earlier Neolithic levels of the Khril Cave at Tangier and are so common in Neolithic horizons, generally in the littoral zone, that it has been suggested that they were domestic. Similarly, goats and sheep (identified with *Ovis africana*) are reported from the Grande Roche Cave at Algiers (Camps 1974: 275), though I know of no associated radiocarbon dates other than those from Haua Fteah and Capéletti. It is likely, however, that by shortly after 5000 B.C. sheep/goats and somewhat later, perhaps, domestic cattle became generally distributed throughout North Africa.

It is important to stress that the equipment of these "Neolithic" pastoral peoples is essentially the traditional one using various hafted microlithic forms to which are added several new elements, just as is the case in Cyrenaica and Egypt. These tool kits indicate, therefore, that the change to food production was not accompanied by any basic change in the ethnic population and that it was the economy that underwent a gradual process of alteration as expediency or pressures demanded. The acquisition of livestock provided a readily available source of protein over the lean months, and since, at any rate, small stock would have necessitated no drastic change in the general behavior pattern, its adoption is more readily understandable. It is, however, apparent that a large part of the meat supply of most of these Neolithic communities came from hunted wild animals. To this end the dog, said to be present in the earliest levels of the Neolithic of the Mediterranean littoral (Camps 1974: 337) would have considerably increased the returns from communal hunting.

THE SAHARAN EVIDENCE FOR DOMESTICATION

The same situation is becoming increasingly better documented from the Sahara where, between ca. 12,000 and 4000 B.P., climatic conditions within the desert supported many favorable open habitats of grassland and cooler Mediterranean flora (Rossignol and Maley 1969) and shallow lakes and swampy depressions where the large Ethiopian fauna were to be found in great abundance. These were exploited by populations of hunters and fishers who were occupants of one of the most favorable ecosystems in the whole continent at this time. This was the traditional kind of environment in which man had evolved, and for some two million years it had been his preferred habitat. Geomorphological studies in the Chad Basin (Servant, et al. 1969) show that an arid phase ended there about 12,000 years ago and was followed by one of lacustrine deposition which continued with drier intervals until ca. 2000 B.P. In northern Tibesti alluvial sedimentation was taking place between 12,000 and 7,000 B.P. in river channels (Hagedorn and Jakel 1969) and in crater lakes (Maley, et al. 1970), and lacustrine sediments in the Ténéré desert have been dated to the same period of time (Faure, et al. 1963). Lakes and swamps are similarly attested at Adrar Bous, dated between ca. 7500 and ca. 4000 B.P. (Williams i.p.) and in the Hoggar swampy depressions filled with calcareous sediments are dated between 12,000 and 8000 B.P. and extended as far to the north as the Erg Chech west of the Tademai't plateau (Conrad 1969: 257–274).

This climatic amelioration to warmer, more humid conditions after the cooler, drier period of the late Upper Pleistocene is recorded also in southwestern Asia from pollen studies in Turkey (Wright 1968), Iran (Van Zeist 1969), and northern Syria (Niklewski and Van Zeist 1970) where steppe gave way to forest. In East Africa a period of rising and high lake levels is recorded in the Gregory Rift and dated beween 12,000 and 5600 B.P. (Butzer, Isaac, et al. 1972). A similar fluctuation for the same period is recorded for Lake Victoria (Kendall 1969) and for Lake Rudolph (Butzer 1971), and the evidence from the Nubian Nile after 12,000 B.P. is also in accord with this (Butzer and Hansen 1968).

Although they are, as yet, imperfectly known, certain stone tool assemblages based on the use of prismatic blades and some specialized projectile points, from the foothills of the Saharan Atlas and the more central and eastern parts of the desert, display affinities with epi-Paleolithic industries from the Maghreb and Nubia and show that, around 6000 B.C., a very similar economy based on hunting and grain collecting existed there (Clark i.p.). Lakeside settlements with a micro-lithic technology and bone equipment including harpoons — with which not only the fish and other aquatic fauna, including hippo, but also the large land mammals were exploited — superseded the epi-Paleolithic at Adrar Bous sometime prior to 5000 B.C. (A. Smith i.p.b) and other settlements occurring throughout the central and southern Sahara as far as Senegal are of a generally comparable age. Similar "early Neolithic" hunting communities occupied the Hoggar and Mouydir where fish were a regular source of food and large mammals were hunted, including the giant buffalo. The lowest occupation levels at one of these sites (Amek-ni) has dates in the seventh millennium (Camps 1969). However, al-though pottery was a regular part of the equipment of these groups, there is not the least direct evidence as yet to suggest that any of them were food producers.

Direct evidence for domestication in the Sahara is at present confined to only a few sites and, so far as stock is concerned, relates mostly to cattle: in the Acacus Mountains (4000 B.C.) (Mori 1965); at Adrar Bous (3800 B.C.) (Carter and Clark i.p.); at Dar Tichitt[3] (from 1500 B.C.) (Munson 1968, 1970); at Arlit (3200 B.C); Tilemsi valley (2000 to 1360 B.C.) (A. Smith, personal communication; i.p.b); and at Meniet (3450 B.C.) where the *Bos* remains are believed to be from domestic animals (Hugot 1963). Further abundant evidence for pastoral cattle herders is provided by the rock art which dates mostly to the fifth and fourth

---

[3] Goat and cattle both present.

millennia. At one of the Acacus cave sites, paintings covered by later, dated sediments suggest that cattle herders were present in the eastern Tassili as early as 5000 B.C., and some areas (e.g. Dar Tichitt) were able to support cattle until the latter half of the first millennium. At Adrar Bous, Dar Tichitt, and Karkarichinkat in the Tilemsi valley, a large proportion, or most, of the meat consumed was from domestic cattle.

The pastoral way of life of the Neolithic Saharan herdsmen can be reconstructed in part from settlement excavations, distribution plots, and edge-wear studies in addition to analysis of the behavioral and technological characteristics depicted in the rock art, and of ethnographic trait complexes among existing Saharan populations, such as the Tuareg (Lhote 1955, 1958; Nicolaisen 1963) and Tebu (Chapelle 1958). The cattle complex, hunting, and ritual are all emphasised in the rock art.

A range of dated evidence from sediments, pollens, diatoms, and changing salinity values shows that the desiccation of the Sahara was a gradual process, no doubt hastened by bad land usage and overstocking which, however, does not appear to have become a serious threat to the traditional economy before 2000 B.C., after which time the advance of aridity became more rapid. There is probably no other part of the continent in which climatic controls have had such a significant effect on the lifeways of the human inhabitants. Since, at the best of times, the Sahara appears never to have been anything other than semiarid, it would always have favored a social pattern based upon a high degree of mobility and seasonal transhumance — a premise that is supported by the indications for long distance trade or barter in amazonite and other exchange items (Mauny 1956) as well as by certain generalized traits exhibited by the stone and bone artifact types and pottery traditions over vast areas of the central and eastern parts of the desert as far as the Nile (Arkell 1962). Nevertheless, although intergroup contacts can be expected to have encouraged communication and exchange, detailed studies of the regional industries show much local differentiation, such as is to be found among communities developing in semi-isolation (Hays 1971).

I have discussed some of the evidence for animal husbandry here since I believe it to be crucial for understanding the relationships and the differences between the Saharan and Sudanic populations.

There is no certain direct evidence for the cultivation of cereal grasses in the Sahara before the very end of the second millennium B.C. when various collected wild grases gave way to the almost exclusive use of *Pennisetum* and *Brachiaria* millets after 1100 B.C. at Dar Tichitt in Mauretania (Munson 1970). This is based on grain impressions in pottery, and Jacques-Felix has undertaken a similar study for the Neolithic of the Ténéré Desert from Adrar Bous, dating between ca. 4000 and 2000 B.C.; unfortunately, in this case the results were not so rewarding. There is little evidence for the xerophytic plants associated with the Dar Tichitt complex, except for one impression of *Cenchrus*; instead, swamp grasses and reedy plants (fragments of *Rhytachne* and *Echinochloa stagnina*) are common. Interesting, but unfortunately only isolated, identifications are one impression of *Brachiaria brizantha*, one good impresson of a cultivated sorghum (cf. *S. durra*), and one unidentified cereal (Jacques-Felix, personal communication). Claims for cereal cultivation in and to the north of the Hoggar have also been made on the basis of two pollens from Meniet[4] (Hugot 1963) and for *Pennisetum* pollen in a sixth millennium context at Amekni (Camps 1969). Fruits of *Celtis* and *Zizyphus* (preferred fruits of the present-day Saharan populations and sometimes found stored in pots in Neolithic contexts) appear to have been regularly collected and are found at several sites. At Adrar Bous and other localities in the Ténéré, several associated small stone piles are probably the bases of silos similar to those still made by the Hoggar Tuareg today; they belong with the Ténérian Neolithic.

Some of the most significant and common artifacts found at all these Sahara Neolithic sites are upper and lower grinding stones, frequently made of rock not local to the site. There can be no doubt that these were used for grinding grains and seeds, but there is, as yet, no solid substantiation for any claim that they were used with cultivated cereals prior to the end of the second millennium. The importance of wild grasses to the peoples of the Sahel belt and the Tuareg and Teda has received careful documentation from a number of observers (Barth 1857; Nicolaisen 1963; Gast 1968; Chapelle 1958; Bernus 1967), and the indications are that, even today in the desert, a single family in a good year might collect as much as 1,000 kilograms from three or four preferred varieties (Nicolaisen 1963: 179–181). Although nowadays the Tuareg and Teda have to supplement these gathered stocks with imported cultivated grain or that grown in oases, the ecological conditions pertaining during the early Holocene can be expected to have provided sufficiently large harvests from wild species (e.g. *Panicum, Echinochloa, Eragrostis, Cenchrus, Aristida, Pennisetum,* and *Sorghum*) to have precluded the necessity of turning to cultivation before obliged

---

[4] Both finds are now considered inconclusive evidence for domestication (Maley, personal communication).

to do so by the more rapid onset of desiccation. The single scene in the Tassili rock art, claimed to represent women harvesting grain (Lhote 1958), could equally well refer to wild as to cultivated species.

The Saharan populations of the fifth and fourth millennia B.C., therefore, were pastoralists and collectors, so far as we can tell by the evidence we have today. The evidence indicates that domestic stock — sheep/goats (especially in the northern parts of the desert) and cattle — were acquired by many, though not all, of the Neolithic populations from 5000 B.C. onwards. If the assumption is correct that cultivation was not practiced until some three thousand years later, it is necessary to inquire why stock herding preceded cultivation there since both occur together in the valley of the Nile. Furthermore, it is necessary to know from where this domestic stock came, why it was adopted in the first instance, and, finally, what were the circumstances which led to certain wild, sub-Saharan grasses being brought under cultivation.

POSSIBLE CAUSES OF THE ADOPTION OF STOCK RAISING AND AGRICULTURE IN THE DESERT AND NORTHERN SAVANNAS

Pastoral nomadism is generally considered to be a special offshoot of agriculture, useful because it made possible the more extensive use of dry, ecologically unfavorable habitats, and today there are no nomads who are not economically dependent upon agriculture (Johnson 1969). If this is so, then the most likely place for the Sahara populations to have acquired their stock initially was the Nile Valley.[5] Alternatively, the suggestion has been put forward that cattle were domesticated in the Sahara independently from the indigenous *Bos ibericus* (Mori 1965),[6] on the principle that concentration on the hunting of *Bos*, regular association, and gradual manipulation led to taming and eventually to full domestication along the lines that Thurnwald (1937) has suggested. Most probably there was more than one source for the original stock which was supplemented by the capturing and taming of wild individuals to increase herds, using for this techniques well shown in the pre-Dynastic and Dynastic art of Egypt and seen in the ethnography of

[5] It has also been suggested that cattle might have been introduced into the Maghreb independently from Europe (Higgs 1967).
[6] Now more generally considered to represent the female of the North African *Bos primigenius*. A Smith (i.p.b.) indicates, however, that the measurements of Pomel's *B. ibericus* material all fall below the figures for the European female *B. primigenius*, suggesting the possibility that more than one taxon may be present.

the present Sahara populations (Clark 1971a).[7]

It is, however, by no means clear why the Sahara communities should have turned to stock raising in the first instance. In view of the abundance of large mammals available for hunting and the resources of the rivers and lakes, there can hardly have been any shortage of meat; since projectile points are among the commonest artifacts found on these sites, hunting appears to have remained a preferred activity to the end. If the favorable ecology of the early Holocene had resulted in an increase in population density,[8] or if the acceptance of stock, especially cattle, permitted such an increase to take place, then, in order to maintain the population at the existing level and to compensate for the increase, it can be seen how ever greater reliance would have to be placed on stock raising and the important new food source provided by the milk. So far as cattle were concerned, however, and these are undoubtedly the most important stock to Saharan pastoralists, another explanation could be offered. Cattle were accepted because they represented a source of wealth, a means of establishing individual group identity, and more efficient social organization of larger groupings — in fact, the primary role played by cattle among most pastoral nomads and mixed farmers in Africa today. The answer most probably lies, in part, in all these possibilities and more besides; but the last suggestion is the most convincing where wild food supplies were still abundant, and it can better explain the subsequent events following upon desiccation after 2000 B.C.

During the first millennium B.C. part of the population of the Ténéré moved westward into the cooler and previously little used uplands of the Aïr which today still support Sahelian flora and fauna and contain little evidence of human occupation before the late Neolithic. It may be expected that the population remaining in the Sahara became more concentrated, as at Dar Tichitt, before being further dispersed and disrupted by invasions of Libyco-Berbers from the north. Around 2000 B.C., C-group cattle-herding nomads from the western desert invaded and settled in Nubia (Arkell 1961: 46-50) and the later Libyan invasions of Egypt during the Nineteenth Dynasty between 1300 and 1210 B.C. are most probably related movements to escape the increasing arid-

---

[7] At Tiout on the Algerian plateau is a representation in the "Bubalus style" of a *Bos primigenius* and several figures of hunters who have secured one hind leg with what appear to be ropes in a manner similar to that shown in early representations of capturing wild cattle in Egypt (Camps n.d.).

[8] The overall increase in the number of sites in the Sahara dating from this time, as compared with that from both earlier and later times, may provide some measure of support for this contention.

ity in the desert. When traditional seasonal movements began to be disrupted all over the southern Sahara, it can be postulated[9] that some of the nomadic groups there followed their retreating food sources southwards and moved down the drying river systems, such as the Tilemsi, into the present Sahel and Sudan belts after 2000 B.C., and so came into permanent contact with the aboriginal populations of these ecosystems. Archaeologically, the Sahel[10] and Sudan zones are an entirely different technological province, indicating a fundamentally different way of life in the grasslands, bush, and open deciduous forests stretching from Senegal to the Red Sea. The Sahel provided the grazing and the permanent water as well as the stands of wild grasses that have remained such a very important source of regular food for the population there up to the present day, to the extent that they can obviate or considerably limit the amount of millet it is necessary to purchase (Bernus n.d.). Many of these grasses (*Panicum* spp., *Echinochloa, Eragrostis, Sorghum virgatum,* and *Oryza barthii*) grow around and in the bottoms of the temporarily inundated depressions and are harvested at the end of the rains and in the beginning of the dry season between September and December. *Cenchrus bifloris* (cram-cram) is harvested throughout the dry season from November to March.

Paleoecological evidence suggests that some of these would have been available to the central Saharan Neolithic pastoralists between 5000 and 2000 B.C. In Senegal, Mali, Nigeria, and the Sudan, fixed dune systems covered with vegetation are evidence that the southern boundary of the desert extended as far as four degrees south of the present limit (Grove and Warren 1968) during the period from 22,000 to 12,000 B.P. Some of the evidence for the shift in the opposite direction has already been cited, but to this must be added the evidence for the former greatly extended Lake Chad graded to the 320 meter strandline, dating between 10,000 and 6000 B.P., and having a surface area fluctuating between 10,000 and 25,000 square kilometers (Grove and Warren 1968), indicative of the generally increased amount of runoff within the Tibesti and Sahel-Sudan zones at this time. Another indication of the former more northerly extension of the savanna belt lies in the discovery of a pericarp of the oil palm (*Elaeis guineensis*) at Esh Shaheinab and of *Acacia nilotica, Celtis, Grewia,* and a waterlily

---

[9] Davies describes the Saharan form of arrowheads and bone equipment found at such sites as Ntereso and Kintampo which as a result of this contact may have spread deeply into the savanna zone (Davies 1964, 1966).
[10] The more humid zone receiving 130 to 150 millimeters of rainfall annually, north and south of the 15° line of north latitude.

which were found at Karkarichinkat (A. Smith 1974). A recent attempt to map the Saharan rainfall isohyets (Hobler and Hester 1969) shows that the plant and animal resources now found in the Sahelian belt probably extended to 20 to 22 degrees north latitude, covering most of the more southerly and a large portion of the central parts of the desert. There would, therefore, appear to have been little or no incentive for the Neolithic pastoralists to have turned to cultivation, as the ethnographic situation in the present Sahel belt shows that they may be considered as having been living in equilibrium with the environment until increasing desiccation or population increase forced a change. This, we have suggested, was after 2000 B.C. though manipulation and experiment in the northern savannas are likely to have begun perhaps a millennium earlier.

Besides the wild grasses referred to above should also be included the wild ancestors of *Pennisetum americanum, Sorghum bicolor,* and *Oryza glaberrima* which Harlan has shown were most probably first domesticated within the Sahel zone — *Pennisetum* in west and central Africa to the east and west of Lake Chad; *Sorghum* east of Chad across the upper Nile almost to Ethiopia; and rice in the Niger Delta. It seems most probable, therefore, that, as desertification advanced, the belt between 20 and 15 degrees north (which includes southern Mauretania, the Niger Bend, the Aïr, and the northern part of the Mega Chad Lake centered on the Bodele depression, as well as the Qoz of Khordofan eastwards to the Nile at Khartoum and east again to the Atbara) was the crucial area for the domestication of these African cereals.

Unfortunately, most of this area, archaeologically, is among the least known in the continent, so that the stages whereby the domestication came about are also unknown except at Dar Tichitt where increasing desiccation may be seen as the most significant contribution to the cultivation of *Pennisetum*. Physical anthropology (Chamla 1968) shows that the Neolithic pastoralists of the Sahara were partly Negroid, partly Mediterranean. Whether or not the ethnic affinities of most of those that moved south were with the Negro populations into whose territories they came, it seems most probable that the relationship established south of the desert between hunter-fishers, who had already begun to manipulate their plant resources, and the slowly infiltrating pastoralists would, in general, have been one of symbiosis rather than of competition or conflict, except, perhaps, where the immigrant nomads and their herds encroached on grain collecting preserves[11] of the inhabitants.

---

[11] It is unrealistic to suppose competition in hunting because of the comparatively small number of large animals killed in a year by both hunter/gatherers (Marshall

There were no natural boundaries to restrict movement such as on the Nile, other than the forest and the tsetse belt to the south, so that a situation encouraging mutual exchange of produce may be envisaged — not unlike that found today among the Hausa, where for meat, milk, and butter they depend upon the pastoral Fulani who, in turn, purchase Hausa products (millet, sorghum, rice, and subsidiary crops) and manure their fields by grazing their stock on them (M. Smith 1965).[12]

The overall increased population densities following the movement of pastoralists into regions where some specialized hunting-gathering groups may have already reached optimum density and the deterioration of some resources and the advent of new ones attendant upon the intensification of aridity can be expected to have resulted in increasing experimentation to maintain the population levels, to preserve tenure, and so prevent displacement. The areas that are most likely to have seen the greatest concentration of population are probably the regions north of the Senegal River, the Niger Bend, the Chad Basin, and the Nile Valley north and south of Khartoum. The archaeological data for these areas in this time period, between 3000 and 2000 B.C., are minimal except in the Nile where ca. 3200 B.C., the inhabitants of the riverside site of Esh Shaheinab (Khartoum Neolithic) possessed domestic goats and, less certainly, sheep, and hunted and fished extensively though there is no direct evidence for cultivated crops (Arkell 1953).

In the Khashm el Girba area of the Atbara, southwest of Kassala, Khartoum Neolithic sites have been located while the succeeding Butana Industry, studied by Shiner (1971), is characterized by large mound sites, one with an estimated 30,000 cubic meters of midden and with a general date of 2400 B.C. Besides pottery, there were many pitted

---

1960; Lee 1969) and subsistence farmers (S. A. Marks i.p.) and the great richness of the Sahel and Sudan zones in large and small mammals as well as the resources of the lakes and rivers.

12   The winter transhumance of the southern Tuareg today covers approximately 200 kilometers northwards of permanent wells lying north and west of Niamey, and the Daza of Borku cover approximately the same distance southwards in summer and northwards in winter from their "home base" (Johnson 1969: 144–157). The seasonal range of the Wodaabe Fulani of Bornu and southern Niger varies between 100 and 300 kilometers from the permanent well areas. During the main part of the wet season, their herds of cattle are concentrated in the Sahel and northern savanna, free from tsetse fly; and they move southwards again in the dry season as the grazing and water become progressively exhausted from north to south (Dupire 1962: 63–82). The historical migrations covered appreciably greater distances, and it is reasonable to presume that those prehistoric movements that took place as desertification in the Sahara became more severe could have brought some of the pastoral groups to penetrate deeply into the savanna, possibly as far as the limit of the tsetse belt.

grindstones, stone rings, ground stone axes, choppers, and a variety of microlithic tools and scrapers; the depth and permanence of the site and the nature of some of the material culture suggest the likelihood that part of the staple food sources came from cultivation, presumably of sorghum. Clearly, the Butana Industry sites warrant large-scale excavation.

In the Tilemsi valley at Karkarichinkat, north of Gao, Andrew Smith has recently completed excavations at the two occupation mounds that date within the second millennium B.C., on the basis of six radiocarbon dates (1360 ±110–2000 ±90 B.C.). The midden areas are extensive but not deep, and contrary to expectations, the inhabitants derived most of their protein from domestic cattle except in the fishing season. *Celtis* and *Balanites* are represented, but no remains of domesticated plants have been recovered. A dwarf goat is represented by a metapodial at another Neolithic site at Arlit on the western edge of the Aïr and dated to the fourth millennium B.C. (A. Smith, personal communication).

A study of the ethnographic literature, in particular that concerned with behavior in times of food scarcity, might throw some light on the processes whereby domestication came about. Seeds collected and brought back to semipermanent seasonal camps, where some always became scattered, would have provided the opportunity for hybridization. The enriched soil of the midden refuse and the proximity to, or inclusion within, seasonally inundated depressions or floodplains (as most of the known sites were) can be expected to have produced a richer yield. Nicolaisen records seeing, regularly, self-sown plots of millet and sorghum round deserted Tuareg camps in the Aïr where many seeds are lost in the process of preparing them for food (Nicolaisen 1963: 184). These self-sown plots were not made use of by the Tuareg; but it is not difficult to see how a population living in an ever more impoverished environment would turn to harvesting such spontaneous yields and thence to intentionally sowing and reaping, if this could be done with no great time and labor, especially since *Pennisetum* and *Sorghum* mature rapidly and two, sometimes three, crops a year can be obtained under favorable conditions.[13]

The usual methods of harvesting the West African wild grass grains

---

[13] Some peoples will sow and harvest a crop, not for their own consumption, but for exchange with adjacent groups as, for example, do the Fur in Darfur who have grown wheat under irrigation to barter, since before the 1790's though they themselves eat *Pennisetum* and *Sorghum*. The Fur also guard against total crop failure by planting unselected seed that produces grain maturing over a period of time (G. E. Wickens, personal communication), possibly a practice also of the earliest African cultivators.

— by hand, sweeping with a basket through the open stands, or sweeping after the seeds have fallen to the ground — favors the natural method of dispersal in the wild and is less likely to produce genetic changes than if the complete head were collected. If, however, birds and insects became major competitors with man, as they often did in the African savanna, some groups may have taken to harvesting the complete head while it was still not fully ripe. An even more cogent reason — hunger — makes the Kel Tamasheq in the West African Sahel reap wild grain while it is still ripening. They obtain three harvests from the wild *Panicum* spp.: the first is cut with a knife while the grain is still ripening; the main harvest, after ripening, is obtained by beating the heads over a basket; and the third by sweeping the grains after they have fallen to the ground (S. Smith i.p.). Again, the Sorko, a hunting-gathering-fishing group of Bozo in the inland delta of the Niger, gather wild millet while it is still growing in the water by cutting part of the stem and head with a sickle (Ligers 1964: 36). This kind of activity could have brought about some reduction in the ease with which seed was naturally dispersed, and further selection would result once seed began to be sown. Again, the harvesting of wild grains late in the season will naturally favor plants with a hard rachis, and if a regular routine of harvesting and sowing is practiced, cultigens will be developed comparatively quickly (de Wet, this volume; personal communication).

A very important factor in the growth of seed-cropping techniques leading to cultivation would be, as Boserup has emphasized (1965), the frequency with which the land can be cropped and the amount of time that has to be spent in preparing and harvesting, away from more pleasurable pursuits such as hunting. Whereas wild grain collecting is generally done by women, the preparation of "fields," especially where grasses with spreading roots have to be eliminated, is often arduous and can be expected to have required at least some male participation. This, for example, is the case today among the Nuer where men and women equally prepare the gardens for two crops of millet and sorghum a year and weed them, often three to five times. No wonder that cultivation is regarded as an unfortunate necessity by these cattle-orientated people who grow sufficient only to provide one of several elements that together make up the total food supply and use the same field, situated on the slope zone between the village and the seasonally flooded plain, until it becomes exhausted after five to ten years (Evans-Pritchard 1940: 76–81). Among the Rahanwein in southern Somalia, who cultivate sorghum in cotton soils, both men and women share responsibility,

but, after planting, the fields receive only brief attention before harvesting, the greater part of the inhabitants of the village being away in the
grazing lands. Among the cattle-herding Jie of northern Uganda,
sorghum is cultivated on light soils and is the sole responsibility of the
women (Gulliver 1965).

In fact, it is probably safe to generalize and say that in Africa, among
basically cattle-orientated societies that practice some form of cultivation, this is looked upon as an unfortunate necessity; as little time as
possible is devoted to it by the men, and wherever possible, most of the
time and labor expended on agricultural work are relegated to the
women. Pastoral groups, like the Fulani, will generally only engage in
cultivation and become semi- or fully sedentary when their stock is lost
through disease or other cause, but they will return to the nomadic way
of life if and when the opportunity should occur. In such circumstances
as we have envisaged in the northward extended Sahel zone in the first
two millennia B.C., it seems more likely, therefore, that the initial steps
to cultivation began among the indigenous hunting-collecting-fishing
populations with whom the cattle nomads came into contact than
among the stock owners themselves. Most probably, therefore, the most
crucial zone for seed crop domestication south of the Sahara is the
former extension and present Sahel belt stretching from Senegal to the
Red Sea. The significant time was probably during the period between
3000 and 1000 B.C.; and the development of domesticates followed
from experiment and necessity, compounded by the pressure from increased human and animal densities, leading to intensification of efforts
to sustain existing population levels and to keep pace with further
increases by intensive conservation of dwindling food resources and
adoption of new ones in the face of the total disappearance of others
(e.g. fish) due to desertification (see Figure 2).

DOMESTICATION IN THE SAVANNA AND FOREST ZONES

Both Harris (1972) and Boserup (1965) suggest that it was most likely
that agriculture first developed in forest and woodland habitats where
a system of long fallow based upon cutting and burning provided a very
adequate return for a minimal number of man-days spent in agricultural pursuits. Harris further identifies the ecotones between forest and
woodland and grassland as the most favorable zones for the beginning
of cultivation, since these are areas of maximum local and seasonal
variability and availability of plant and animal species relating to both

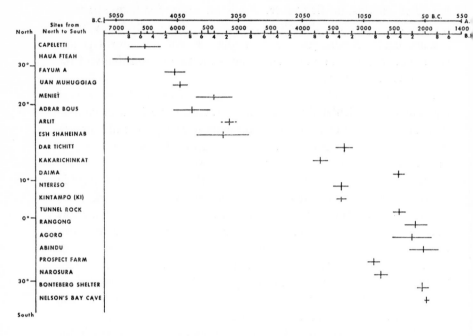

Figure 2.   Chronology of the spread of domestic stock in Africa

Arranged geographically with the most northern site at the top and the southern-most at the bottom. Radiocarbon dates from twenty-one sites associated with cattle and/or sheep/goat remains; shown to one standard deviation and based on the Libby half-life of 5,568 years.

Mean values have been used for the following sites, the number of dates in each case being recorded in brackets: Fayum A (4); Adrar Bous (2); Dar Tichitt (3); Kakarinchinkat (6); Ntereso (3); Kintampo (3); Prospect Farm (2); Tunnel Rock (2); Narosura (3).

The very few available dates for cultivated plant remains suggest that domes-tication south of the Sahara is likely to be closely associated with and sometimes follows the appearance of domestic stock — e.g. *Pennisetum* at Dar Tichitt; *Sorghum* — *S.* sp. at Niani, Guinea dating to 750 ± 100 A.D.; *S. caudatum* at Daima in ninth century A.D.; *Sorghum bicolor* race bicolor at Qasr Ibrim dating to Meroitic times [ca. 300 B.C.–350 A.D.] and Sorghum in eight century A.D. context with *Penni-setum, Eleusine, Vigna, Voandzeia* at Inyanga, Rhodesia; *Vigna* at Kintampo; *Lagenaria* at Njoro River Cave, ca. 1000 B.C.; barley, chickpea, and legumes from southwest Asia at Lalibela Cave, Begemeder, Ethiopia, 520 ± 80 B.C. (See de Wet, Harlan, and Price, this volume; Shaw, this volume.)

the major ecosystems. Animal and human communities in the savanna regions of Africa make preferred use of such localities (cf. S. A. Marks). However, Vita-Finzi and Higgs (1970) suggest that if regular trans-humance was practiced, they may not have been as important for pre-historic hunter-gathering groups as is generally thought. On the whole, tropical Africa provides, within a comparatively limited area, several distinct micro-environments, each of which is utilized as seasonal move-ments of game or availability of plant foods dictate; in drier ecosystems their exploitation is often dependent upon a regular system of trans-humance.

The diversity of the African plant domesticates and the limited regions over which many of them are used (Harlan 1971) with the exception of sorghum, bulrush millet, and, to a lesser extent, finger millet, show them to have been mostly domesticated in the zone south of the desert (or where the desert was ±3000 B.C.) where open bush and grass give place to woodland and where the woodland interfingers with the rainforest: that is to say in the Sahel and southern Sudan belts and the high plateau of Ethiopia. Up to about 3000 B.C. or later, the occupants of both zones appear to have been food gatherers with a technology that made use of microliths and some heavier, percussion flaked equipment. Some time after that date these groups began to acquire pottery and ground stone tools[14] which might, but does not necessarily, indicate a change in the economic base. Informative sites dating to these two millennia B.C. are not common and have been col-lectively discussed elsewhere (Clark 1967; Davies 1964).

The best evidence comes from the central Ghana site of Kintampo. This shows that small cattle and a dwarf goat were present by 1250 B.C.[15] (Carter and Flight 1972), with the possibility also of cultivation or, at least manipulation of oil palm and cow peas (Flight 1970 and this volume). The Bornu mound settlement site of Daima shows further evidence for cattle, sheep, and goats in the middle of the first millenni-um B.C. (Connah 1968; B. M. Fagan, personal communication), and other mound sites also suggest farming communities here in the second millennium (Connah 1971). The record of cattle at Kintampo in what is now the tsetse fly belt is important since it suggests that the tsetse was not present at this time. Thus either cattle or other livestock could be seasonally introduced, as in many parts of West Africa today, or else could live permanently far to the south of the present limits of this belt;

[14] Also trapezes with "sickle" gloss at Iwo Eleru (Shaw 1969).
[15] A dwarf goat is also recorded by the same authors from Ntereso 1630 B.C. ±130–1320 B.C. ±100.

the degree of immunity of the N'dama and West African Shorthorn breeds was, therefore, probably acquired during or after this time. Here again, the available evidence suggests the first two millennia B.C. as the time when fundamental economic changes were taking place in the West African savanna zone.

The African savanna is one of the richest ecosystems in the world for human exploitation, and there can be no doubt that it offers infinitely greater potential than either the grasslands or the forest. The long lists of wild plant foods given by Dalziel (1937), Schnell (1957), and Busson, et al. (1965) show the variability, nutritional value, and seasonal range available to hunter-gatherers. If to these are added the various edible insects and the great variety of game as shown, for example, in the distribution maps of Dorst and Dandelot (1970), it is difficult to see, given the reciprocal access to resources, that the need for a recourse to cultivation should ever have arisen. The carrying capacity of the savanna for food-gatherers is surely considerably higher than that of the Kalahari, the Ituri forests, or the Eyassi Rift which support such populations today. There is not, however, such a great difference between average size of the communities — desert, rainforest, and dry savanna dwelling groups, each of which fluctuates considerably with the seasons and with the inclinations of the individual families that compose it.[16] If, as has been shown, the effect of hunting-gathering groups, so far as depletion of the plant and animal resources in these very different habitats is concerned, is negligible (as it also is for the game even among sedentary Bantu in Zambia [S. A. Marks i.p.]), then it is unreasonable to expect that population density can have increased sufficiently over that which could be supported by hunting and gathering to have become the sole factor in inducing the inhabitants to turn to cultivation. The hunting life is the preferred life (Laughlin 1968); and one of the attractions it held was the opportunity to join together for limited periods, to share resources over poor seasons (Lee 1972a), or for reasons of exchange and general intercommunication but to be free to disperse again whenever desirable (Lee 1972b). Once plants were brought under cultivation and became the main source of nourishment, regular settlement also became a virtual necessity, and a more rigid structuring of society with less reciprocity and community of use between groups was bound to follow.[17]

---

[16]   Estimates for !Kung Bushmen range between sixteen and ninety-four individuals (Lee 1968: 31), for Mbuti Pygmy net hunters twenty-eight to one hundred twenty (estimating a nuclear family at a minimum of four individuals) (Turnbull 1968: 134) and for Hadza one to a hundred (Woodburn 1968: 105).

[17]   The Tiv, occupying the orchard bush in west-central Nigeria, with an annual rainfall of 1000 to 1500 millimeters, have developed a well-structured economy

In such a rich, natural environment, therefore, some other pressures or incentives, in addition to any deriving from increased population, can be expected to have induced groups to adopt an agricultural way of life.

Change from hunting-gathering to agriculture is unlikely while equilibrium existed within the habitat for there would then be no incentive to move out of the traditional territory. Spatial distributions between groups can be expected to have allowed absorption of normal population growth at this subsistence level; but when this was upset by a combination of factors — population growth, changes in the environment, or movement into the area by other groups possessing a different and superior technology — then changes might be expected. Settlement size does not appear to have increased significantly until after 1000 B.C. If population growth alone was, in fact, insufficient at the hunting-gathering level to bring about these changes, then it is necessary to look to the addition of one or more of those other factors in the record. The example of the Sandawe of central Tanzania provides one possible explanation of why agriculture was first adopted. The Sandawe, studied recently by Newman (1970) occupy a semi-arid, woodland-savanna environment with less than 30 inches of rain a year. They are traditionally hunters and gatherers and it is clear that they have only comparatively recently (within the last 300 years or so) taken to cultivation and acquiring livestock. The degree of disorganized, haphazard, and uninformed practices in relation to their crops (usually millet and sorghum) and livestock are in sharp contrast to the organization of the other groups, both agriculturalists and herders, with whom the Sandawe are in contact. They appear to have taken to cultivation before the acquisition of livestock which is, as is general in the region, a symbol of wealth. Traditionally, they are considered to have done this following a severe famine when some Sandawe began to settle among the agricultural Turu. Livestock were acquired from contacts with the pastoral Barabaig, and the relationship between the Sandawe and these and other tribal groups is, in general, good. Clearly the adjustment to an agricultural economy was a gradual adaptation and assimilation following from the infiltration and complementary relationships with the new-

---

based on the cultivation by all adult members of the society of grain crops (*Pennisetum* and *Sorghum*) from the north and yams and other root crops from the south. Livestock are confined to goats, some sheep, and a few tsetse resistant dwarf cattle. As a result of this diversified agricultural system, the hunger period has been reduced to a minimum or eliminated (Bohannan 1965). Such economies can be expected to have developed only after a large labor force became available for clearing and weeding in zones of reliable rainfall unfavorable to cattle-herding.

comers. If, at the same time, population density increased, there would be ever greater pressure to cultivate more in order to keep pace with the higher level and maintain it in spite of uncertain rainfall and the likelihood of famine.

Perhaps even more relevant is the case of the Ik on the Uganda-Sudan-Kenya border who are being encroached upon by pastoralists (Turnbull 1968, 1972). The Ik are both marginal cultivators and hunter-gatherers who, because of the uncertain and inhospitable nature of their mostly arid environment and the regularity of crop failures, maintain a fluid social pattern and band composition, related to the time in the not distant past when they were solely food-gatherers. Owing to the largely migratory habits of the game and the locally confined plant foods, the Ik bands move over a wide area during the half year that is devoted to hunting and collecting; the rest of the time is spent in agriculture. Competition with encroaching pastoralists is an important factor in encouraging millet cultivation as a means of ensuring maintenance of tenure over their traditional territory. Crops fail about one year in five, and the Ik then exist almost entirely by hunting and gathering. The change from hunting-gathering to cultivation among the Ik is, as it was among the historic Hottentots, contingent upon circumstances and not "once-for-all." (S. Marks 1972). This may be considered a general pattern until input for crop production increased to the extent that output from harvested crops became adequate to meet the new needs in all, other than exceptional, years, thus obviating the necessity for regularly supplementing the food supply to a major degree by hunting and collecting. Processes leading to an economy based primarily on cultivation might operate sometimes through incentives following from mutual dependence between the incipient cultivator-hunters and pastoral nomads, or sometimes from competition as when, for example, reciprocal use of resources between groups is denied or reduced by overcropping (including hunting out the game), disease, or other factors.

The symbiotic relationship that exists among some Kalahari Bushmen and the Tswana, or among the Mbuti and the forest Negro groups, may reflect the kind of early relationships we have postulated between immigrant pastoral peoples and hunter-gatherers, more especially the position of the Mbuti Pygmies. Once mutual interdependence and exchange relationships had been established, then a more compelling reason would exist for the development of cultivation in the ecotones where these contacts would most frequently have taken place. The intimate knowledge of the wild plants in regular use would have favored the basis for selection of those best adapted to manipulative reproduction and planting. This presupposes the sacrifice on the part of the males of leisure hours and time spent in hunting, but the system of long fallow in forest and woodlands necessitates the devotion of only a comparatively small amount of time by both sexes to agricultural pursuits, as Boserup (1965) demonstrates. The average time spent on agricultural work among the Bemba of northern Zambia, living in *Brachystegia* woodland, is one to two hours a day, including the clearing of land (Boserup 1965: 45). In Nigeria, the time spent on clearing the land for yam cultivation averages fifty to sixty man-days per hectare, and in orchard bush, collective teams can prepare fields in less than twelve eight-hour man-days per hectare. Just under half a hectare of yams is said to support a family of five for a year, while the yield of cereal crops per half hectare (one acre) is barely sufficient for two persons for a year. On the basis of input versus output, therefore, selection is likely to favor the woodland-forest ecotones.

From the analogies that have been cited, it can be expected that the change to fully food-producing communities must have been both gradual and irregular. The transformation of some more favorably situated and receptive groups would have been completed sooner than that of others; while for some there never was the incentive or pressure to effect the change. Impetus to more efficient cultivation and social organization can be expected in particular as the tsetse fly belt expanded in the savanna after ca. 1200 B.C. and many groups lost both the stock they had acquired through diffusion and their individual identity through acculturation.[18] The Goula by Lake Iro in southeastern Chad now keep only goats and chickens, due to tsetse, and have developed an efficient system of cultivation and a diet based upon millet and sorghum

[18]   A comparison of present distribution of cattle in the West African savanna and forest with the distribution of cattle bones from dated archaeological horizons should go a long way to help document the fluctuating limits of the tsetse belt after 2000 B.C. When tsetse are dispersed during the rains, the effects of the fly are less than when they are concentrated on the dry season water resources. The minimal effect in the rainforest, Nash suggests (1969: 169–173), is because of their greater dispersal there due to more general availability of water and wild hosts. While both of these remained readily available and bush cleared for cultivation had not advanced beyond that of small isolated gardens on a system of long fallow, the effects of fly must be considered to have been less disastrous for man or beast than they became later. Attempts to reconstruct the prehistoric fluctuations of the fly belt need to take into account the extent of contractions of the forest zone during the last part of the Upper Pleistocene, the extent to which this belt may have expanded under the warmer and more humid conditions of the early Holocene, and how extensive was its subsequent contraction as this "subpluvial" or "wet phase" came to an end. A few well-sited pollen profiles would be of great assistance in this connection.

supplemented by hunting, fishing, and the collection of wild plant foods (Pairault 1966: 25 ff.). In savanna with a rainfall of 760 millimeters (30 inches), falling over a six month period, the Goula are able to plant and reap two to three crops of millet a year, the labor being shared by both sexes. Since their habitat is rich in large mammals and fish, the men spend most of the dry season exploiting these resources; in former times, hippo and giraffe in particular were selected. The millet-sorghum crop is clearly essential to the Goula for maintaining their tenure on their traditional territory. Without the products of fishing and hunting, however, the crop is in itself insufficient to support the village populations, just as with the Nuer, cultivation, fishing and herding, together, provide the basis for the diet and the economy. Again, the reason why more cereals are not planted to produce a surplus, thus obviating the need for supplementary food sources, must be sought, as Boserup has pointed out, in the inadequacy of the additional return in output relative to the additional input in labor and man-hours, and the complementary reduction of leisure and time spent on more favored pursuits.

The chief occupation and means of livelihood of the Bozo in the inland delta of the Niger is catching and selling fish, supplemented by cultivation. One group, the Sorko, still live solely by fishing, supplemented by hunting and collecting; they grow only very small plots of *Digitaria* (fonio) which they use only for ceremonial purposes (Ligers 1964: 39). The Sorko economy provides an interesting model that might be applied to some of the later prehistoric groups in the Sahel-Sudan. During the dry season some fifteen pastoral Fulani and three Tamasheq clans migrate into the delta with their stock — cattle, sheep, and goats. Relations with the sedentary population, many of whom move downstream with the fish as the river level drops, are reasonably good, and the pastoralists are one of the main markets for the fish (Imperato 1972). If, however, increasing desiccation caused the lakes and streams to dry up, as did almost all those in the present Sahel and southern Sahara, a major food source — the fish and hippo — and the main items of trade would have been removed. For the populations living off these resources to maintain their territory and traditional rights of usage, they would need to find some other staple for food and barter that could take the place of fish; such a potential surely existed in the wild grain harvest.

The only alternative would have been to migrate, but the northward expansion of the tropical rainforest during the early Holocene hyperthermal and later increasing desiccation advancing from the north can be expected to have compressed the savanna zone resulting in some relative crowding of population and so to have placed some restriction on resettlement of peoples migrating southwards after 2000 B.C. This would have been an added incentive for such groups to remain where they were.

Initially, it might have been the spontaneous maturing of spilled grain round the homesteads and the regular reaping of this that could have encouraged the first experiments in sowing a crop. The Sorko grow their fonio surreptitiously. Their plots are only some 2 by 2 meters and are always located on old settlement sites (Ligers 1964: 39). Possibly the first prehistoric groups to cultivate in the Sahel and Sudan may have gone about it in a similar manner. As yields were increased, grains would have largely become the basic staple that fishing formerly provided. Once maintaining and increasing grain yields became a necessity, unrestricted grazing of stock was no longer permissible, and the maturing stands would have had to be protected. Unless harvests were late and poor grazing to the north caused the nomads to arrive early, relations are likely to have remained friendly as they do in general in the Sudan zone today (Horowitz 1972).

By the degree of dependence still placed on hunting, fishing, and collecting, the examples cited above suggest that the beginnings of cultivation and the development of local cultigens, though both a long and a gradual process, is unlikely to have been of very great antiquity in sub-Saharan Africa. Had it been very ancient, it might be expected that wild products would have been reduced to an insignificant proportion of the diet as more frequent cropping was carried out, more and more land was cleared, and more elaborate systems of cultivation were developed to produce the returns necessary to support the labor force of a community which would then need to have been sufficiently large to require a more or less total commitment to agriculture.

The course of events within the Ethiopian region may well have followed a similar pattern to that in the West African-Sudan belt, although the climatic changes that accompanied the desiccation of the Sahara would have been felt to a lesser degree on the Ethiopian plateau. This region of rapid altitudinal changes in vegetational zones can be expected to have favored experimentation as such altitudinal variability appears to have done in the Middle East. If the inhabitants of the mid-third millennium mound settlements on the Atbara were, indeed, cultivators of sorghum and stock herders, then even though communication between the plains and the plateau may have been sporadic and casual, it can be expected to have led to experimentation with local species on the plateau and the introduction of cattle, sheep, and goats. In this way, teff, ensete, and the number of other local cultigens in use in Ethiopia can be expected to have been developed prior to the introduction of wheat, barley, and plow culture which more probably relates to the time of the Himyaritic migrations in the mid-first millennium B.C.[19] Available archaeological evidence is, unfortunately, either inconclusive (Arkell 1954) or late (Dombrowski 1970).[20]

More reliably, archaeology shows that transformation from gathering to farming had not been completed in the southern and East African savanna until the first part of the first millennium A.D., and the transition is most likely to be related to immigration and stimulus diffusion introducing the local populations to crops and livestock. Two races of cattle were present in "Punt" by 1500 B.C., and those depicted in the rock art groups in Ethiopia are hardly likely to be later than the mid-first millennium B.C. Cattle-herding groups, who still hunted extensively, are attested at several first millennium sites in the East African Gregory Rift, and most probably were there by the middle of the second millennium (G. Ll. Isaac, personal communication). Although direct evidence for plant domesticates of any kind has not yet been found, the stone bowls associated with these groups were most probably used for preparing food which could have been a cultivated grain (Clark 1972).

Sheep/goats and cattle are present also by the first half of the first

---

[19]   From its historical connections and distribution, Simoons (1960: 99–104) suggests that teff (*Eragrostis teff*) may have first been domesticated from *E. pilosa* in northern Ethiopia. Cultivation of ensete (*Ensete edule*) by planting lateral shoots is related to habitats between 5,000 and 10,000 feet and forms a monoculture among the Gurage and other peoples of southern Ethiopia (1960: 89–99). Its cultivation can be presumed to have an antiquity equal to that of teff. Although it was domesticated only in Ethiopia, the plant has a wider distribution in the higher altitude and high rainfall plant communities of central, eastern, and southern Africa (in west central and southeastern Sudan, the highlands of the western Rift, the Lake Victoria basin, Kalambo Falls and the montane forests of Malawi at least as far south as Mlanje Mountain; no doubt also in many other localities besides). It may be suspected, therefore, that it was a food source for other hunter-gathering groups besides those in Ethiopia. The circumstances and manner in which ensete was brought under cultivation may have been not unlike those described by Simoons (1960: 92–96) in use in the few surviving areas of ensete culture in the Semien in northern Ethiopia where wild ensete is collected and planted near the villages. Even though the suggestion that ensete was the cultivated plant of the pre-Dynastic Egyptians finds little favor with Egyptologists, further research into this possibility would certainly be advantageous. Similarly a comparison of the distribution of wild ensete and that of the banana-based cultures of central and eastern Africa, whose traditional organization, ritual, and ceremony focused on the cultivation of the banana are clearly very ancient, might help to show whether this East Indian domesticate could, indeed, be a replacement for an older, similar crop such as ensete.

[20]   Lalibela Cave, Begemeder — 520 B.C. ±80.

millennium B.C. at sites in the Lake Victoria basin (Gabel 1969).[21] Ehret (1967, 1968), using historical linguistics, has suggested that sheep, goats, and cattle were introduced into southern Africa by a people speaking central Sudanic languages, and that it was from these groups that the Bantu-speaking people acquired their stock around the beginning of the present era. Possibly the "Stone Bowl Cultures" are evidence of this migration of Sudanic speakers. Whether or not it was from these groups that some of the Khoisan peoples in the drier parts of southwestern Africa acquired stock, pottery, and the trait of making stone bowls is not known. Pottery has now been shown to have reached the southern African coast at a surprisingly early time — by 2050 ±95 B.P. at the Bonteberg Shelter, Cape Province (Grindley, et al. 1970) and by 1935 B.P. at Nelson's Bay Cave, Plettenberg Bay (R. H. Klein, personal communication). Klein also informs me that he has identified sheep in association with the pottery at the first site and that he expects it to be present also at the second. Representations of sheep in the rock art of southern Africa are rare but appear to be associated with people of non-Bushman stock (Cooke 1965); however, the art provides no evidence that these people were cultivators and, in view of the general disinclination on the part of nomadic peoples to engage in cultivation, it is more probable that the products of their stock raising, hunting, and collecting were sufficient for their needs. However, the negative evidence that the historic Hottentots had acquired no traits relating to cultivation, except possibly for *Cannabis indica*, can hardly be regarded as conclusive proof that the group from whom they obtained their stock did not do some cultivation.

Sheep/goats and, less certainly, cattle are present at several of the early Iron Age sites in southern Africa dating between 0 and 500 A.D.; the direct evidence of plant remains suggests that the full range of indigenous food plants traditional to southern Africa was already present. It is generally held that the Bantu-speaking peoples developed within the southern parts of the Congo (Zaïre) Basin (Oliver 1966). In that case it seems probable that the explosion which spread these languages over the greater part of eastern and southern Africa may have resulted from the increased opportunities for developing socially and politically more closely structured societies which the acquisition of livestock and seed crops afforded to groups who, for a millennium or more before that, had been manipulating the plant foods of their forest/ savanna ecotone to a point where they were nearly, or perhaps fully,

---

[21] *Bos* at Rangong, Agora, and Abindo; sheep/goats also at Rangong rock shelters.

vegecultural communities. The acquisition of stock for prestige purposes and the related, but not necessarily contemporary, diffusion of metallurgy and the Asian food plants may, together, have provided the economic base that was the means of relieving the overpopulation in the forest zone and the main incentive for expansion into eastern and southern Africa.

Evidence for experiment leading to cultivation in the savanna and forest belts of eastern and central Africa is minimal; but the indications ca. 1000 B.C. for extensive burning of forest and bush and for changes in sedimentation rates in Zaïre, northern Angola, and Zambia, as well as for nonclimatically induced changes in pollen spectra in the Lake Victoria basin and at Ishiba Ngandu in northern Zambia, suggest that some fundamental alteration in human behavior began to make itself felt from that time (Clark 1971b; Livingstone 1971). In the Congo Basin, in the savanna overlooking the gallery forest, some occupation sites dating after 12,000 B.C. cover several hundred square meters and show that conditions favorable for large seasonal concentrations of population were probably already in existence by that date. In view of the original center postulated by Harlan and Stemler (this volume) for the kafir race of sorghum and of the way in which the pollen diagrams from Uganda and Zambia correlate with this, it seems possible that this paleoecological evidence, slight as it is, might relate to the initial stage in the domestication of this crop by communities living in the ecotone between forest and savanna. Again, as with the transition to full farming subsistence in the Nile Valley, it is necessary to suppose some prior adaptation and manipulation such as deliberate conservation of fruit trees or regular burning to encourage new growth and to concentrate game, so leading to vegeculture in favorable, streamside and basin localities as well as to more efficient communal hunting and trapping.

CONCLUSIONS

Summarizing the main points of the theoretical model put forward in this paper, it is suggested that:

1. The change from gathering to cultivation was unlikely to have taken place where the human population was in a state of equilibrium with its environment.

2. Increases in population density, while providing the incentive for more intensive exploitation methods, are unlikely alone to have been the factor that triggered this transition, because of the great richness of

the African savanna and forest ecosystems with inexhaustible resources and room for expansion, where the densities were no greater than could be supported at the hunting-gathering level.

3.   The circumstances whereby cultivated species of African plants were developed are integrally related to the introduction of domestic stock, in particular cattle, to the peoples of the Sahel and Sudan belts south of the Sahara (Figure 2).

4.   These circumstances are connected with the developing desiccation of the Sahara, in particular after 2000 B.C. when nomadic stock herders, who were also collectors of wild grains, moved southward, penetrating the savanna and establishing a symbiotic relationship with the indigenous populations they found there.

5.   These hunting-collecting-fishing populations were already pre-adapted, like the earlier populations of the Nile Valley, to select for cultivation the most satisfactory genera and species once the necessity to do so arose. The initial steps in manipulation may have begun as early as 12,000 B.C. in some regions, but would have been greatly intensified by the severe depletion or disappearance of fish supplies in the northern Sahel in the second millennium B.C.

6.   Where the carrying capacity of the northern savanna proved inadequate for supporting the newly increased densities, exchange relationships leading to mutual dependence and perhaps some competition led, firstly, to more intense exploitation and later to deliberate conservation of the favored food plants, in particular the millets, sorghum, and dry rice.

7.   Selective harvesting by removing the whole inflorescence while still not fully ripe and the intentional broadcasting of seed may have been intensified also through the loss of stock following the northward expansion of the tsetse belt after 1000 B.C. Incipient cultivation now placed increasing dependence on crops, in particular millet, sorghum, and rice, so leading to more efficient and intensive methods of cultivation as more land was taken into use; at the same time some pastoralists also began to form semi- and later fully sedentary cultivating communities.

8.   The transition from collecting to regular cultivating possibly took place between 3000 and 1000 B.C. in the Sahel and northern Sudan zones which in 3000 B.C. were displaced some 4° to 5° to the north and during this time retreated southward towards their present geographical positions.

9.   Proof of the validity of this and other models will lie in systematic team studies of selected localities in former and existing ecotones as

well as in the main ecosystems. The sequential changes in settlement patterns, technology, plant and animal remains, and pollen profiles may permit identification of subsistence behavior and the reconstruction of the economy for comparison with the results made possible by catchment analysis studies.

REFERENCES

ANDERSON, J. E.
1968   "Late Palaeolithic skeletal remains from Nubia," in *The prehistory of Nubia*, volume two. Edited by F. Wendorf, 996–1040. Dallas: Southern Methodist University Press.

ARKELL, A. J.
1953   *Esh Shaheinab, an account of the excavation of a Neolithic occupation site*. Oxford: Oxford University Press.
1954   Four occupation sites at Agordat. *Kush* 2:33–62.
1961   *A history of the Sudan to 1821*. London: Athlone.
1962   "The distribution in central Africa of one early Neolithic ware (Dotted Wavy Line pottery) and its possible connection with the beginning of pottery," in *Actes du IVe Congrès Panafricain de Préhistoire et de l'Etude du Quaternaire*. Edited by G. Mortelmans and J. Nenquin, 283–287. Section three, Pré et Protohistoire. Mus. roy. de l'Afrique central, Ann. Sér. 8° Sci. Hum. 40. Tervuren.

BARTH, H.
1857   *Travels and discoveries in north and central Africa, 1849–1855*. New York. (Reprinted 1965 by International Scholarly Book Service, Portland.)

BERNUS, E.
1967   Cueillette et exploitation des ressources spontanées du Sahel nigérien. *Cahier ORSTOM, Sér. Sci Hum.* 4(1).
n.d.   "Graines sauvages récoltées par les Tuaregs Sahéliens," in *Encyclopédie Berbère*, Cahiers 3 (édition provisoire). Edited by G. Camps. Aix en Provence.

BERRY, A. C., R. J. BERRY, P. J. UCKO
1967   Genetical change in ancient Egypt. *Man* 2(4):551–568.

BOHANNAN, P.
1965   "The Tiv of Nigeria," in *Peoples of Africa*. Edited by J. L. Gibbs, 513–546. New York: Holt, Rinehart and Winston.

BOSERUP, E.
1965   *The conditions of agricultural growth: the economics of agrarian change under population pressure*. Chicago: Aldine.

BUSSON, F., P. JAEGER, P. LUNVEN, M. PINTA
1965   *Plantes alimentaires de l'ouest africain*. Marseilles: Leconte.

BUTZER, K. W.
1971 "Recent history of an Ethiopian delta." Department of Geography, University of Chicago, Research Paper 16.

BUTZER, K. W., C. L. HANSEN
1968 *Desert and river in Nubia.* Madison: University of Wisconsin Press.

BUTZER, K. W., G. LL. ISAAC, J. L. RICHARDSON, C. WASHBOURN-KAMAU
1972 Radiocarbon dating of East African lake levels. *Science* 175: 1069–1076.

CAMPS, G.
1969 *Amekni: Néolithique ancien du Hoggar.* CRAPE. Mém. 10. Arts et Métiers Graphiques. Paris: Flammarion.
1974 *Les civilisations préhistoriques de l'Afrique du Nord et du Sahara.* Paris: Doin.
n.d. *Beginnings of pastoralism and cultivation in North Africa and the Sahara.* Cambridge History of Africa, volume one. In preparation.

CAMPS-FABRER, H.
1965 *Matière et art mobilier dans la préhistoire nord-africaine et saharienne.* CRAPE. Mém. 5. Arts et Métiers Graphiques. Paris: Flammarion.

CARTER, P. L., J. D. CLARK
i.p. "Adrar Bous and African cattle," in *Actes du VIIe Congrès Panafricain de Préhistoire et de l'Etude du Quaternaire, Addis Ababa, 1971.*

CARTER, P. L., C. FLIGHT
1972 A report on the fauna from the sites of Ntereso and Kintampo rockshelter 6 in Ghana with evidence for the practice of animal husbandry during the 2nd millennium B.C. *Man* 7(2):277–282.

CHAMLA, M. C.
1968 *Les populations anciennes du Sahara et des régions limitrophes.* CRAPE, Mém. 9. Arts et Métiers Graphiques. Paris: Flammarion.

CHAPELLE, J.
1958 *Nomades noirs du Sahara.* Recherches en sciences humaines 10. Paris: Plon.

CHURCHER, C. S., P. E. L. SMITH
1972 Kom Ombo: preliminary report on the fauna of late Palaeolithic sites in Upper Egypt. *Science* 177:259–261.

CLARK, J. D.
1967 "The problem of neolithic culture in sub-Saharan Africa," in *Background to evolution in Africa.* Edited by W. W. Bishop and J. D. Clark, 600-627. Chicago: University of Chicago Press.
1971a "A re-examination of the evidence for agricultural origins in the Nile Valley," in *Proceedings of the Prehistoric Society* 37:34–79.
1971b "Opportunities for collaboration between archaeologists, ethnographers and linguists." in *Language and history in Africa.* Edited by D. Dalby, 1–19. London: Frank Cass.
1972 "Mobility and settlement patterns in sub-Saharan Africa: a comparison of late prehistoric hunter/gatherers and early agricultural

occupation units," in *Man, settlement and urbanisation.* Edited by P. J. Ucko and G. W. Dimbleby. London: Duckworth.

i.p.   "Epi-Palaeolithic aggregates from Greboun Wadi, Aïr and Adrar Bous, northwestern Ténéré, Republic of Niger," in *Actes du VIIe Congrès Panafricain de Préhistoire et de l'Etude du Quaternaire, Addis Ababa, 1971.*

CLARK, J. G. D.

1965   Radiocarbon dating and the spread of farming economy. *Antiquity* 39(153):45–48.

CONNAH, G.

1968   Radiocarbon dates for Benin city and further dates for Daima, N.E. Nigeria. *Journal of the Historical Society of Nigeria* 4:313–320.

1971   Recent contributions to Bornu chronology. *West African Journal of Archaeology* 1:55–60.

CONRAD, G.

1969   *L'Evolution continentale post-Hercynienne du Sahara algérien.* Centre Rech. des Zones arides Sér. Géol. 10. Paris: CNRS.

COOKE, C. K.

1965   Evidence of human migrations from the rock art of Southern Rhodesia. *Africa* 35(3).

DALZIEL, J. M.

1937   *The useful plants of west tropical Africa.* London.

DAVIES, O.

1964   *The Quaternary in the coastlands of Guinea.* Glasgow: Jackson.

1966   "The invasion of Ghana from the south in the early Iron Age," in *Actas del Ve Congresso Panafricano de Prehistoria y de Estudio del Cuaternario.* Edited by L. D. Cuscoy, 2:27–42. Tenerife.

DOMBROWSKI, J.

1970   Preliminary report on excavations in Lalibela and Natchabeit caves, Begemeder. *Ann. d'Ethiopie* 8:21–9.

DORST, J., P. DANDELOT

1970   *A field guide to the larger mammals of Africa.* London: Collins.

DUPIRE, M.

1962   *Peuls Nomades.* Univ. de Paris. Trav. et Mém. de l'Inst. d'Ethnologie 64. Paris.

EHRET, C.

1967   Cattle keeping and milking in eastern and southern African history: the linguistic evidence. *Journal of African History* 8(1):1–18.

1968   Sheep and central Sudanic peoples in southern Africa. *Journal of African History* 9(2):213–221.

EVANS–PRITCHARD, E. E.

1940   *The Nuer: a description of the modes of livelihood and political institutions of a Nilotic people.* Oxford: Oxford University Press.

FAURE, H., E. MANGUIN, R. NYDAL

1963   Formations lacustres du Quaternaire supérieur du Niger oriental: diatomites et âges absolus. *Bull. Bur. Rech. Géol. Min.* 3:41–63. Dakar.

FLIGHT, C.
   1968   Kintampo, 1967. *West African Archaeological Newsletter* 8:15–19.
   1970   "Excavations at Kintampo," in Report on Third Conference of
           West African archaeologists. Edited by D. Calvocorassi. *West
           African Archaeological Newsletter* 12:71–73.

GABEL, C.
   1969   Six rockshelters on the northern Kavirondo shore of Lake Vic-
           toria. *African History Series* 2(2). Boston.

GAST, M.
   1968   *Alimentation des populations de l'Ahaggar: étude ethnographique.*
           CRAPE Mém. 8. Arts et Métiers Graphiques. Paris: Flammarion.

GRINDLEY, J. R., E. SPEED, T. MAGGS
   1970   The age of the Bonteberg Shelter deposits, Cape Province. *South
           African Archaelogical Bulletin* 25(97):24.

GROVE, A. T., A. WARREN
   1968   Quaternary land forms and climate on the south side of the
           Sahara. *Geography Journal* 134(2):194–208.

GULLIVER, P. H.
   1965   "The Jie of Uganda," in *Peoples of Africa.* Edited by J. L. Gibbs,
           57–196. New York: Holt, Rinehart and Winston.

HAGEDORN, H., D. JAKEL
   1969   Bemerkungen zur quartären Entwicklung des Reliefs in Tibesti-
           Gebirge (Tchad). *Bull ASEQUA* 23:25–42. Dakar.

HARLAN, J. R.
   1971   Agricultural origins: centers and non-centers. *Science* 174:468–
           474.

HARRIS, D. R.
   1972   The origins of agriculture in the tropics. *American Scientist* 60(2):
           180–193.

HAYS, T. R.
   1971   "The Sudanese Neolithic: a critical analysis." Unpublished doc-
           toral dissertation, Southern Methodist University, Dallas.

HIGGS, E. S.
   1967   "The Neolithic: domestic animals," in *The Haua Fteah (Cyre-
           naica) and the Stone Age of the southeast Mediterranean.* Edited
           by C. B. M. McBurney, 313–319. Cambridge: Cambridge Uni-
           versity Press.

HOBLER, P. M., J. J. HESTER
   1969   Prehistory and environment in the Libyan desert. *South African
           Archaeological Bulletin* 23(92):120–130.

HOROWITZ, M. M.
   1972   "Ethnic boundary maintenance among pastoralists and farmers in
           the western Sudan (Niger)," in *Perspectives on nomadism.* Edited
           by W. Irons and N. Dyson-Hudson, 105–114. Leiden: E. J. Brill.

HUGOT, H. J.
   1963   *Recherches préhistoriques dans l'Ahaggar nord-occidental, 1950–
           1957.* CRAPE. Mém. 1. Arts et Métiers Graphiques. Paris: Flam-
           marion.

IMPERATO, P. J.
    1972   Nomads of the Niger. *Natural History* 81(10):61–68.
IRWIN, H. T., J. B. WHEAT, L. F. IRWIN
    1968   *University of Colorado investigations of Palaeolithic and Epi-Palaeolithic sites in the Sudan, Africa.* University of Utah Anthropology Papers 90, Nubian Series 3.
JOHNSON, D. L.
    1969   *The nature of nomadism.* Department of Geography, University of Chicago, Research Paper 118. Chicago.
KANTOR, H.
    1965   "The relative chronology of Egypt and its foreign correlations before the Late Bronze Age," in *Chronologies in Old World archaeology.* Edited by R. W. Ehrich, 1–46. Chicago: University of Chicago Press.
KENDALL, R. L.
    1969   An ecological history of the Lake Victoria basin. *Ecology Monographs* 39:121–176.
LAUGHLIN, W. S.
    1968   "Hunting: an integrating biobehaviour system and its evolutionary importance," in *Man the hunter.* Edited by R. B. Lee and I. DeVore, 304–320. Chicago: Aldine.
LEE, R. B.
    1968   "What hunters do for a living, or How to make out on scarce resources," in *Man the hunter.* Edited by R. B. Lee and I. DeVore, 30–43. Chicago: Aldine.
    1969   "!Kung Bushman subsistence: an input-output analysis," in *Environment and cultural behaviour.* Edited by A. P. Vayda, 47–79. Garden City, N.Y.: Natural History Press.
    1972a !Kung spatial organisation: an ecological and historical perspective. *Human Ecology* 1(2):125–147.
    1972b "Work effort group structure and land use in contemporary hunter-gatherers," in *Man, settlement and urbanisation.* Edited by P. J. Ucko, R. Tringham, and G. W. Dimbleby, 177–186. London: Duckworth.
LHOTE, H.
    1955   *Les Touaregs du Hoggar (Ahaggar)* (second, revised edition). Paris: Payot.
    1958   *A la découverte des fresques du Tassili.* Grenoble: Arthaud.
LIGERS, Z.
    1964   *Les Sorko (Bozo) Maîtres du Niger.* Etude Ethnographique 1. C.N.R.S.
LIVINGSTONE, D. A.
    1971   A 22,000-year pollen record from the plateau of Zambia. *Limnology and Oceanography* 16(2):349–356.
MALEY, J., J. COHEN, H. FAURE, P. ROGNON, P. M. VINCENT
    1970   Quelques formations lacustres et fluviatiles associées à différentes phases du volcanisme au Tibesti (nord du Tchad). *Cahiers ORSTOM Ser. Geol.* 2:127–152.

MARKS, S.
1972 Khoisan resistance to the Dutch in the seventeenth and eighteenth centuries. *Journal of African History* 13(1):55–80.

MARKS, S. A.
i.p. "Large mammals and a brave people: study of hunting and the role of the hunter among the valley Bisa of Zarbia."

MARSHALL, L
1960 !Kung Bushman bands. *Africa* 30(4):325–355.

MAUNY, R.
1956 Perles ouest africaines en Amazonite. *Bull. IFAN 18 Sér. B* (1–2): 140–147.

MORI, F.
1965 *Tadrart Acacus: arte rupestre e culture del Sahara preistorico.* Turin: 9. Einaudi.

MUNSON, P. J.
1968 Recent archaeological research in the Dar Tichitt region of south central Mauretania. *West African Archaeological Newsletter* 10: 6–13.
1970 Corrections and additional comments concerning the "Tichitt Tradition." *West African Archaeological Newsletter* 12:47–48.

NASH, T. A. M.
1969 *Africa's bane: the tsetse fly.* London: Collins.

NEWMAN, J. L.
1970 *The ecological basis for subsistence change among the Sandawe of Tanzania.* Washington.

NICOLAISEN, J.
1963 *Ecology and culture of the pastoral Tuareg.* Nationalmuseets Skrifter: Ethnografisk Rœkke 9. Copenhagen.

NIKLEWSKI, J., W. VAN ZEIST
1970 A late Quaternary pollen diagram from northwestern Syria. *Acta Bot. Neerl.* 19(5)737–754.

OLIVER, R.
1966 The problem of the Bantu expansion. *Journal of African History* 7(3):361–377.

PAIRAULT, C.
1966 *Boum-le-Grand: village d'Iro.* Univ. de Paris. Trav. et Mém. Inst. d'Ethnologie 73. Paris.

REED, C. A.
1960 The Yale University prehistoric expedition to Nubia 1962–1965. *Discovery* 1(2):16–23. New Haven: Yale University Press.

ROSSIGNOL, M., J. MALEY
1969 "L'activité hors de France des palynologues et paléobotanistes français du Quaternaire," in *Etudes françaises sur le Quaternaire VIIIe Congrès de l'INQUA,* 265–274. Paris.

ROUBET, C.
1968 *Le gisement du Damous el Ahmar et sa place dans le Néolithique de tradition capsienne.* CRAPE. Travaux. Arts et Métiers Graphiques. Paris: Flammarion.

SCHNELL, R.
1957   *Plantes alimentaires et vie agricole de l'Afrique noire.* Paris: Larose.

SERVANT, M., S. SERVANT, G. DELIBRIAS
1969   Chronologie du Quaternaire récent des basses régions du Tchad. *C.R.Ac.Sc.* 269:1603–1606. Paris.

SHAW, T.
1969   "The Late Stone Age in the Nigerian forest," in *Actes du Premier Colloque International d'Archéologie africaine (Fort Lamy, 1966),* 364–373. Fort Lamy.

SHINER, J. L.
1971   *The prehistory and geology of northern Sudan,* two volumes. Report of the National Science Foundation, Washington. Dallas: Southern Methodist University Press.

SIMOONS, F. J.
1960   *Northwest Ethiopia: peoples and economy.* Madison: University of Wisconsin Press.

SMITH, A. B.
1974   "A comparative study of Saharan and Sahelian assemblbages from Adrar Bous and Kakarichinkat." Unpublished doctoral dissertation, University of California, Berkeley.
i.p.a   "A microlithic industry from Adrar Bous, Ténéré desert, Niger," in *Actes du VIIe Congrès panafricain de Préhistoire et de l'Etude du Quaternaire, Addis Ababa, 1971.*
i.p.b   "Domesticated cattle in the Sahara and their introduction into West Africa," in *West African culture dynamics: archaeological and historical perspectives.* Edited by B. K. Swartz, Jr., and R. A. Dumett. World Anthropology. The Hague: Mouton.

SMITH, H. S.
1969   "Animal domestication and animal cult in dynastic Egypt," in *The domestication and exploitation of plants and animals.* Edited by P. J. Ucko and G. W. Dimbleby, 307–316. London: Duckworth.

SMITH, M. G.
1965   "The Hausa of northern Nigeria," in *Peoples of Africa.* Edited by J. L. Gibbs, 119–156. New York: Holt, Rinehart and Winston.

SMITH, P. E. L.
1966   "The late Palaeolithic of northeast Africa in the light of recent research," in *Recent studies in paleo-anthropology.* Edited by J. D. Clark and F. C. Howell. *American Anthropologist* 68(2):326–355.
1971   Iran, 9000–4000 B.C.: the Neolithic. *Expedition* 13(3–4):6–13.

SMITH, S. E.
i.p.   "The environmental adaptation of nomads in the West African Sahel: a key to understanding prehistoric pastoralists," in *West African culture dynamics: archaeological and historical perspectives* Edited by B. K. Swartz, Jr., and R. A. Dumett. World Anthropology. The Hague: Mouton.

THURNWALD, R.
1937   *L'Economie primitive.* Paris: Payot.
TRIGGER, B. G.
1968   *Beyond history: the methods of prehistory.* New York: Holt, Rinehart and Winston.
TURNBULL, C. M.
1968   "The importance of flux in Iwo hunting societies," in *Man the hunter.* Edited by R. B. Lee and I. DeVore, 132–137. Chicago: Aldine.
1972   *The mountain people.* New York: Simon and Schuster.
VAN ZEIST, W.
1969   "Reflections on prehistoric environments in the Near East," in *The domestication and exploitation of plants and animals.* Edited by P. J. Ucko and G. W. Dimbleby, 35–46, London: Duckworth.
VERMEERSCH, P.
1970   L'Elkabien. *Chronique d'Egypte* 45(89):45–68.
VITA-FINZI, C., E. S. HIGGS
1970   Prehistoric economy in the Mount Carmel area of Palestine: site catchment analysis. *Proceedings of the Prehistoric Society* 36:1–37.
WENDORF, F.
1968   *The prehistory of Nubia,* two volumes. Dallas: Southern Methodist University Press.
WENDORF, F., R. SAID, R. SCHILD
1970   Egyptian prehistory: some new concepts. *Science* 169:1161–1171.
WENDT, W. E.
1966   Two prehistoric sites in Egyptian Nubia. *Postilla* 102:1–46.
WHITE, F.
1965   The savanna woodlands of the Zambian and Sudanian domains. *Webbia* 19(2):651–81.
WILLIAMS, M. A. J.
i.p.   "Upper Quaternary stratigraphy of Adrar Bous, Republic of Niger, south central Sahara," in *Actes du VIIe Congrès Panafricain de Préhistoire et de l'Etude du Quaternaire, Addis Ababa, 1971.* In press.
WOODBURN, J.
1968   "Stability and flexibility in Hadza residential groupings," in *Man the hunter.* Edited by R. B. Lee and I. DeVore, 103–110. Chicago: Aldine.
WRIGHT, H. E.
1968   Natural environment of early food production north of Mesopotamia. *Science* 161:334–339.

Early Crops in Africa:
A Review of the Evidence

THURSTAN SHAW

In the present state of our knowledge any consideration of the beginnings and development of agriculture in Africa must largely be a survey of our ignorance and a reasoned essay in speculation. What is needed to advance the subject is more firm evidence. The debate on the age of tropical "vegeculture," for example, "has raged for some decades without much in the way of concrete evidence being put forward" (Harlan 1969: 313). This paper will only have been worthwhile if it asks the right questions and serves to stimulate efforts to win that solid evidence.

Reviews of the data have been published fairly recently (Mauny 1967; J. D. Clark 1967; Davies, et al. 1968). While there is no point in duplicating these, there is a need to look critically at the quality of the evidence; but a paper of this length cannot pretend to be exhaustive.

EVIDENCE

In considering the beginnings and development of food production in Africa, it is necessary first to consider the types of evidence which are available to us concerning this, and to realize that different kinds of data have different levels of reliability when it comes to assessing from them the balance of probabilities concerning what actually happened.

These different kinds of evidence have already been well categorized

I wish to acknowledge a great deal of assistance in the preparation of this paper from a large number of colleagues who were very generous in supplying and checking data.

(Seddon 1968: 489):
1. Direct archaeological evidence — the remains of domesticated plants and animals in context;
2. Indirect archaeological evidence — all other material discovered in an archaeological context that, by its nature, suggests the presence of agriculture and a food-producing economy;
3. Evidence from botanical, ethnographic, and linguistic studies.

Pieces of indirect evidence may be of different weight: an iron hoe excavated in a dated archaeological context is of much greater worth and reliability than a grindstone or a "digging-stick weight," since such stones can be used for nonagricultural purposes. Caution has to be exercised in using the indirect evidence, and this has also been well emphasized (Seddon 1968: 489):

The indirect evidence of material artifacts without the proof of cultivated plants and permanent settlement or of domestic stock is often misleading, and "the short list of technological traits that occur only in association with agricultural economics (prepared by Meighan, et al. 1958) demonstrates the difficulty of judging subsistence from indirect sources..." (Gabel 1960: 438).

A warning against the uncritical use of the indirect type of evidence to infer agriculture is provided by a list of traits commonly associated with agriculture but which are also possessed by some societies without domesticated plants or animals (Alexander 1969: 124).

As will appear below, Africa lags behind Europe, western Asia, and the New World in relation to archaeological research and in knowledge about the beginnings of food production. Not only is there less actual evidence bearing specifically upon this particular subject, but in very few areas have those cultural sequences and chronological frameworks been established through which it is alone possible to trace the patterns of origin and growth of agricultural and stock-raising practices.

This was true until recently even of Egypt and the Nile Valley, where one might have expected a clear and firm picture; yet the lack of this in the crucial period is one of the conclusions which emerged from all the contributions to a review of pre-Dynastic development (Arkell and Ucko 1965). In some areas of Africa, too, radiocarbon datings are from one or two determinations, the reliability of which is less than for series and constellations of dates. One must also remember the need for adjustment of radiocarbon ages to real ages in the light of the most accurately determined half-life of carbon 14 instead of the conventionally adopted one (Deevey, et al. 1963: v) and in the light of fluctuations revealed by bristle-cone pine dendrochronology (Stuiver and Suess 1966; Reed 1966; Neustupny 1970; Olsson 1971), although for our present purpose relative ages are more important than absolute ones.

THEORY

This lack of evidence in Africa, compared with other parts of the world where much more is known about agricultural origins, means also that we have a number of theoretical models open to our choice — since different models, rather than a single one, have been shown to give the best fit to the evidence in different parts of the world.

The concept of the "Neolithic Revolution" was introduced by Gordon Childe in terms of simple diffusion; and a fairly straightforward pattern of diffusion still seems to be taken as the dominant mechanism for the beginning of farming in Europe (G. Clark 1965) although it is felt that necessary predisposing conditions must have been present for it to find acceptance (G. Clark 1969: 62, 67–69). Similarly, Balout has described the spread of food production in the Sahara as a matter of simple diffusion. "The Neolithic current moved from East to West" (1965). It must be remembered, too, that diffusion may be cultural diffusion only or a movement of peoples — or a mixture of both. Certainly it seems that in the Sahara there were complex movements going on in Neolithic times. Appropriately, Hugot concludes a chapter on the Neolithic in the Hoggar by applying Cartailhac's earlier dictum to the Sahara "*Lorsqu'on parle du Néolithique comme d'une seule entité on ... semble oublier qu'il n'y a pas un mais des Néolithiques*" (Hugot 1963: 168). Lastly, the diffusion idea may only be a preferred hypothesis, "arising out of a legend rather than out of the data itself" (Higgs and Jarman 1969: 36).

On the other hand, the demonstration of independent centers of agricultural invention in the New World (MacNeish 1965) and probably in eastern Asia (Gorman 1969; Solheim 1969; Chang 1970: 182) has clearly shown that the idea of food production did not have a single origin in the world. If at least three independent centers have been demonstrated, it opens up the possibility of there having been more.

Furthermore, additions to the evidence from southwestern Asia have changed the picture of a single, comparatively small nuclear place of origin for agricultural invention to one of a much larger area (and a much longer span of time) in which conditions were right for innovations. Such innovations may have been made in different places within the general area and these may have interacted with each other (Higgs and Jarman 1969). But it seems that the most fertile advances in our understanding at the moment come neither from environmental determinism by itself, nor from cultural determinism — the idea that food production is initiated when human culture has "advanced" to a point capable of it. Rather, the concept of an interaction of the two processes, "cultural ecology," or what has been called the "Binford-Flannery" model, seems most productive of understanding of the process (Flannery 1965, 1969; Wright 1971).

Perhaps it is helpful to think of a brush-fire model of diffusion in in which there is a main area where the fire spreads and a number of rather haphazard little patches of fire, separated in space from the main fire and set off by flying sparks: i.e. the concept of a rapidly transmitted idea, or more probably a rapidly moving small group of people (or even one individual), the traces of whose movements are too small to show on the archaeological record; they only reappear to produce a separated occurrence of the diffused trait when they land somewhere where the ecology is right or the socioeconomic receptivity of the existing society is right, or both. From a very broad summary of the distribution of the early food-producing communities, it looks as if they are ecologically, perhaps partly by choice, restricted to hill country on the edges of substantial uplands. Perhaps this relates to very local diversification of the environment in broken country, so that: (1) necessary control of water is obtained by choice of suitable site; (2) the diversified environment means that various different natural resources are comparatively close at hand and do not involve wide-ranging migration to catch up with them at the right time of year; (3) the country gives a much better chance of defending the immovable crop assets against passing or marauding gatherers. If this sort of ecological restraint (in addition, of course, to the environmental restraint on the crops) did operate strongly, then a brush-fire effect might be very marked.

Lastly, we have to bear in mind the mechanism of stimulus diffusion, in which culture contact with an idea or a principle serves to trigger off the development of an analogous practice rather than the importation of the practice itself (Chang 1970: 183).

All these mechanisms may have been operative in different parts of Africa at different times in relation to food production, and we must keep an open mind to see which model fits a particular set of data best. One needs to apply to Africa what has been said about the advent and spread of food production in other parts of the world:

These changes have to be seen in terms of both innovation and historical contact, so that we ask ourselves, on one hand, why certain food-collectors began to experiment with plant and animal domestication in Western Asia or Latin America; and on the other hand, why intrusive agricultural econ-omies did not immediately replace hunting and gathering in Europe and the U.S. once they were introduced (Gabel 1960: 438).

In the light of the above — our present lack of data and the choice of theoretical models open to us — it is better to proceed not by trying to pursue the course of abstracted entities such as "agriculture," "vege-culture," or "arboriculture," but first by examining the evidence for domesticated plants crop by crop. After having done this, we may be in a position to see what it all adds up to in terms of subsistence patterns and food-winning economies, considered in relation to the ecology of the area. This is the point at which we should bring in all the botanical, ethnographical, linguistic, and geographical data, so that we can con-sider food production practices in terms of response to environment and as a part of a total cultural pattern. Because of the speculative and now discredited nature of some botanical or ethnographical theories about the origins of food production in Africa (e.g. Murdock 1959; Vavilov 1951), there was a healthy reaction to place more reliability on archaeological types of evidence (Seddon 1968; Harlan and de Wet 1973): this in turn produced a counter-reaction supporting "a total geographical orientation, emphasizing ecology" (Yarnell 1968) and a statement of the theoretical problems involved (Seddon 1969). Thus the two types of evidence should not be regarded as conflicting but as complementary, controlling each other. Also complementary to the need to obtain "hard facts" in the African situation is the need em-phasized in this paper, to interpret the data in the light of generaliza-tions derived from cultural change elsewhere (Harris 1971, 1972).

A review of our ignorance of this whole question in Africa also points up the need for those ecological studies which have been com-bined so profitably with archaeological evidence in southwest Asia and Mesoamerica to give new insights into the probable mechanics of the process, and the need also for harder evidence on climatic and vege-tational changes in different areas of Africa, derived and substantiated from those areas and not merely inferred by extrapolation from else-where.

DIRECT ARCHAEOLOGICAL EVIDENCE

Direct evidence for food of botanical origin includes the finding in datable archaeological contexts of actual remains of seed, fruit, root, or tree crops; their pollen; or impressions of them in such material as pottery. The preservation of actual remains is largely a matter of lucky accident, thanks to aridity, carbonization, charring, or waterlogging, either of the material itself or in human and animal coprolites; the increasing use of the technique of flotation in excavations (Struever 1968; Jarman, et al. 1972) should help to recover more evidence of this kind. This applies particularly to seed crops; tubers and root crops are liable to remain much more elusive. African palynology has a long way to go to catch up with that of temperate regions, but some progress is being made (Assemien 1971; Bonnefille 1971a, 1971b; Bronckers 1967; Coetzee 1965; Guers 1970; Guinet 1968; Livingstone 1964; Livingstone and Kendall 1969; Lobreau, et al. 1969; Maley 1970; Miège 1965; Quezel 1960; Quezel and Martinez 1958, 1961, 1962; Smith 1964; Sowunmi 1968; van Campo 1957, 1958, 1960; van Campo, et al. 1959, 1960, 1964, 1965; van Zinderen Bakker 1965–1969, 1967a, 1967b). Studying seed impressions on pottery has already paid dividends in the Sahara area of Africa (Munson 1968, 1970; J. D. Clark 1971a) and could almost certainly be applied with profit to other areas, although it is not always rewarded (Fagan 1967: 62).

Direct evidence for the early cultivation of crops in Africa is surprisingly small in total, and it falls into two groups, separated widely in time and space. (Sites mentioned below are shown in Map 1, p. 120.)

The first group of data comes from Egypt and the Sahara, extending from the sixth to the fourth millennium B.C. At Amekni in the Hoggar two pollen grains of a cultivated cereal were dated to between 6100 and 4850 B.C. and identified as *Pennisetum* (pearl millet, bulrush millet), together with other pollen which might be *Triticum* (wheat) (Camps 1969: 188, 1971) — but one has to be cautious concerning pollen identifications of cereals, as the Gramineae are notoriously difficult in this respect. Remains of emmer wheat (*Triticum dicoccum*), barley (*Hordeum*), and flax (*Linum*) from Fayum A where radiocarbondated to the later part of the fifth millennium B.C. (Caton-Thompson and Gardner 1934: 34, 46–49; Seddon 1968: 490; Wendorf, et al. 1970: 1168). Pollen at Meniet in the Hoggar dated to the mid-fourth millennium B.C. has been interpreted on account of its size (40 microns) to be a type of cultivated grass (Hugot 1968: 485), but its domesticated status is now less certain since the finding of wild Sahara grasses with pollen grains up to 50 microns (J. D. Clark 1971a). Emmer wheat and barley (and castor oil seeds *Ricinus communis*, but these are probably wild) from the Badarian of Egypt are said to date to at least the first half of the fourth millennium B.C. (Arkell and Ucko 1965: 150); Hugot (1963) quotes a radiocarbon date of 3160 B.C. (Gro-22), but this is not certainly identified with any horizon and so cannot be an indication of the age of the settlement. Emmer wheat and barley, with radiocarbon dates from 4380 B.C. to 2740 B.C., came from the unsatisfactory site of Merimde where the excavator may have "confused a very early culture with later ones" (Baumgartel 1955, 1965). This likelihood is perhaps made greater by the presence of club wheat (*Triticum compactum*) "not known till much later anywhere in the Near East except at certain Lower Egyptian sites" (Helbaek 1955); on the other hand, the dates of 3670, 3760, 3820 and 3850 B.C. were actually on charred grains (Deevey, et al. 1965: 175). The predynastic cemetery at El Mahasna produced "grain" (Ayrton and Loat 1911: 18), and the cereal from the predynastic grain kilns of Abydos was identified as wheat (*Triticum vulgare*) (Peet and Loat 1913: 1–7). The dates (2430 and 2340 B.C.) for the "A Group" site of Afyeh (Deevey, et al. 1963: 279) in Egyptian Nubia which produced abundant charred wheat and barley were later than expected (Lal 1963). To the above mentioned should be added the carbonized fragment of the pericarp of the oil palm, *Elaeis guineensis*, found in the excavation of Shaheinab in the Sudan with a mean radiocarbon date of 3300 B.C., "brought from West Africa or the Congo for its food value, although it is conceivable that ecological conditions at this time were suitable for wild growth locally" (Arkell 1953: 105; Arkell and Ucko 1965: 149).

The last pieces of evidence in the first group are somewhat later in time than the former, but they are extremely important. At Adrar Bous in the Aïr region of the Sahara, pottery impressions have yielded a single grain of *Brachiaria* dated to ca. 4000 B.C. and one of cultivated *Sorghum* dated to 2000 B.C. (J. D. Clark 1971a). Second, in settlements in the Dhar Tichitt region of Mauretania, spanning from the mid-second to the mid-first millennium B.C. and divided into seven phases, impressions on pottery revealed the use of the grain of a number of desert grasses. In the first three phases there were many seeds of *Cenchrus bifloris* (bur grass) — still collected to some extent as a famine food — and a single grain of *Pennisetum* sp., but it was impossible to tell whether it was wild or cultivated. In the fourth phase, *Brachiaria deflexa* and *Panicum laetum* also appear, with *Pennisetum* rising to 3 percent. In the fifth and sixth through seventh phases, *Pennisetum* impressions jump to 60 percent and 80 percent respectively and have definite characteristics of cultivated grains, with *Panicum turgidum* also appearing in the last phase (Munson 1968, 1970). At first sight it looks as if the Tichitt communities were experimenting with the local grass seeds and finally hit on *Pennisetum* as the best, and as if this was an independent discovery of how best to exploit the environment; on the other hand perhaps the interpretation of the evidence most likely to be correct favors an introduction of cultivated *Pennisetum* into the Tichitt area from somewhere else during the fifth phase.

The second group of evidence all comes, with two exceptions, from the interior of southeastern Africa and extends forward in time from the middle of the first millennium A.D. The exceptions both concern sorghum (*Sorghum bicolor*; Guinea corn, great millet): the first from the late first millennium A.D. (Gif-1292, A.D. 750 ± 100; Kl-293, A.D. 860 ± 65) at Niani, Republic of Guinea (Filipowiak, et al. 1968: 617, 645); and the second from a ninth to tenth century A.D. level at Daima, northeastern Nigeria (Connah 1967: 25).

In eastern Africa, Engaruka, with radiocarbon dates ranging from the fourth to the nineteenth century A.D., has produced carbonized sorghum at all levels, sufficiently well preserved for it to be possible to identify the types represented (Sassoon 1967, 1971). In the area of southeastern Africa we begin with "what are tentatively identified as a squash seed and a possible bean" from Chundu (Zambia), believed from its pottery types to belong to the period from the sixth to the eighth centuries A.D. (Vogel 1969). Inyanga ruins, belonging to the eighth century A.D. or before, produced carbonized remains of *Sorghum* sp., *Pennisetum typhoides, Eleusine coracana* (finger millet), *Voandzeia subterranea* (groundnut, peanut), *Vigna unguiculata* (=*Vigna sinensis,* cowpea),[1] *Citrullus vulgaris* (Kaffir melon), and *Ricinus communis* (Summers 1958: 175–177). Charred seeds of *Sorghum* sp. and possibly a seed of *Pennisetum typhoides* come from Mwamasapwa in Malawi, a site considered to belong to the ninth century A.D. on the similarity of its beads to the Leopard's Kopje industry of Rhodesia (Robinson 1966: 180). Seeds of *Sorghum* sp. come from Isamu Pati and Kalundu of the Kalomo tradition of Zambia dated to the period from the ninth to the eleventh centuries A.D. (Fagan 1967: 62). The site of Mapungubwe produced carbonized remains of *Sorghum* sp., *Sclerocarpa caffra*

---

[1]   The cowpea has been called *V. unguiculata* or *V. sinensis* almost indiscriminately according to the nationality of the writer, the British preferring one, Americans the other. It is now proposed to call the wild form *V. unguiculata* and the domesticated *V. sinensis* (Purseglove, this volume).

Plate 1. A shaped stick found at Nok, Nigeria, radiocarbon dated to ± 120–875 A.D. This has been described
by Fagg (1965:23) as "a stout and well-carved pounding
stick . . . found waterlogged and partly carbonised close to
a heavy axe-handle in a similar condition." Scale in centimeters. (Photograph by kind permission of Mrs. Angela
Rackham and the Nigerian Department of Antiquities.)

Plate 2.　An enlargement of a portion of the shaped stick shown in Plate 1. Scale in centimeters. (Photograph by kind permission of Mrs. Angela Rackham and the Nigerian Department of Antiquities.)

("marula," a wild nut), *Pseudocadia zambesiaca* (an indigenous tree), *Citrullus* sp. (melon), *Vigna unguiculata*, and *Grewia* sp. ("Kruis bessie" — unlikely to have been cultivated) (Fouché 1937: 31); the site has hitherto been regarded as late fourteenth century but it may be up to 300 years earlier on account of the isotopic fractionation of the sorghum whose remains provided the radiocarbon samples (van der Merwe 1971). The site of Ingombe Ilede, where the gold burials are now dated to the fourteenth to fifteenth centuries (Phillipson and Fagan 1969), produced carbonized seeds of *Sorghum* sp. in levels four and five and a leaf impression of sorghum with burial II/3; but as date R-908 (A.D. 680 ± 40) was actually obtained from a specimen of charred sorghum, this gives a seventh century date for sorghum from the earlier period at the site (Fagan, et al. 1969: 81, 85). Klipriviersberg produced three seeds of *Sorghum* sp. (Mason 1967); many thousands of seeds or grains of *Sorghum* sp. were recovered during the 1971 excavations at the Olifantspoort Iron Age site, 60 miles west of Klipriviersberg, and dated to the period from the sixteenth to the nineteenth centuries A.D. (Mason 1971); seventeenth to eighteenth century levels of the Inyanga ruins complex produced maize (*Zea mays*) (Summers 1958: 175–177). In connection with the probability that agriculture was in fact practiced at Bambandyanalo at the beginning of the eleventh century A.D., in spite of its denial by the excavator, it has been pointed out that on many sites "abundant domestic animal remains make it easy to overstress the importance of stockbreeding, even to the exclusion of agriculture" (Fagan 1964: 343).

In addition to the above, there are various pieces of relevant direct evidence, although they do not provide any unambiguous proof of domestication. At the K6 rockshelter near Kintampo, in Ghana, seed husks of *Celtis* sp. (African nettle tree, African false elm) were found in the Punpun phase dated to before 1400 B.C. In the succeeding Kintampo culture levels vegetable remains include husks of *Elaeis guineensis* and cowpea; but the latter are small compared with those now grown in the area, and it is not possible to say whether they are wild or cultivated (Flight 1970: 72). There have been many finds of *Celtis* sp. in archaeological contexts (Hugot 1968: 486) but no evidence of domestication. It is unlikely that the *atili* seeds (*Canarium schweinfurthii*) associated with Nok culture finds indicate its formal cultivation (Fagg 1959: 289). The remains of calabashes, *Lagenaria vulgaris*, were found at the Njoro River Cave among remains of the Stone Bowl people dated to the beginning of the first millennium B.C. (Leakey and Leakey 1960: 38), and possibly at another Stone Bowl site at Ilkek

(Brown 1966: 66). In Malawi *Vigna unguiculata* is reported from Nkope, layer one (dating herefore to ca. A.D. 115 ± 100) (Robinson 1970: 171).

Conclusions from Direct Archaeological Evidence

What emerges from the above, as so often in an area where archaeological work is uneven, is more a pattern of our present knowledge and ignorance than of what actually happened in the development of food production in the African continent. It is perhaps not so surprising that we are entirely without direct evidence in the whole of the humid area of the Congo basin and the West African rain forest, where archaeological work is difficult and acid and corrosive soils militate against preservation, but it is very regrettable that we are without direct evidence concerning early crops from Ethiopia, the Horn, and East Africa.

It is clear that wheat and barley were introduced into Egypt from Asia probably not later than the sixth millennium B.C. Whether the fact that dates for cultivated cereals in the central Sahara are earlier than in Egypt represents a true state of affairs is open to question. It is widely believed that the sites of the earliest agriculturalists in the Nile delta and in Middle Egypt are buried beneath meters of later silt (Butzer 1965); the same reason used to be given for the apparent absence of late Paleolithic industries in Upper Egypt and Nubia, an absence now shown to be illusory (Wendorf, et al. 1970: 116). As indicated above, present evidence is ambiguous about the early presence of domesticated wheat and *Pennisetum* in the Hoggar; and at present we are not sure whether, during the northward expansion of the tropical monsoon rains, *Sorghum, Pennisetum,* and *Eleusine* were included in the predominantly Mediterranean-type flora of the Hoggar and the central Sahara during the Holocene up to the final desiccation, or whether they were confined to the Sahel-Sudan belt as nowadays. This raises a fundamental issue concerning the domestication of the tropical grasses; for another thing which emerges from the foregoing survey of the direct evidence from Africa is that by the later part of the first millennium A.D., *Sorghum* was established as a domesticated crop in western and southeastern Africa, and probably *Pennisetum* and *Eleusine* as well. The issue is whether the tropical grasses became domesticated as a result of: (1) local interaction with the environment without outside stimulus, (2) experimentation with local resources as the result of the stimulus of the idea of food production received from outside, (3) attempts to grow wheat and barley and these being supplanted by their own weeds (Darlington 1969: 68–69); but tropical weeds in fields of wheat and barley, which must be grown in the cool season, are regarded as unlikely (Harlan 1971a).

It has been suggested that impressions on pots excavated at Ntereso, in Ghana, are of *Pennisetum*; but the stratigraphy, associations, and the claimed dating of the second millennium B.C. are somewhat in a "suspense account" at the moment (Davies 1968: 481; Shaw 1969a: 228).

Returning to our review of the direct evidence in sub-Saharan Africa, we notice that before the end of the first millennium A.D. there are records of cucurbits, beans, and African groundnuts. As with the millets, their domestication undoubtedly goes back much further than the dates of our earliest evidence.

We have already noted wide geographical and chronological gaps in the record provided by direct evidence; there is one important botanical gap as well — we have no archaeological evidence for the use of yams and other tubers at all. Nor, because of the very nature of these crops, is the prospect of getting such evidence very hopeful, although perhaps one day some recognizable charred yam may be recovered in a significantly dated archaeological context. Pollen evidence is likely to be either lacking or equivocal since the domesticated varieties tend not to flower (Shaw 1968: 501). Nor is the equipment for preparing tuberous crops as likely to provide indirect evidence as that for preparing grain crops since wooden pestles and mortars replace stones; not only is their evidence ambiguous, since pestles and mortars are also used for grain-crop food-preparation, but, above all, chances of preservation are low — although not nonexistent (See Plates 1 and 2. Fagg 1965: 23). Since the indigenous domestication of certain yams was probably one of the most important events in the development of agriculture in West Africa, we have to rely for information about this on our third type of evidence — the botanical, ethnographical, and linguistic.

INDIRECT ARCHAEOLOGICAL EVIDENCE

Before we can settle the question as to whether *Pennisetum* was separately domesticated in the Tichitt area in the Hoggar (as discussed in the direct archaeological evidence) we need more facts. However, there is some interesting indirect evidence relating to this whole question, and it takes us back to an earlier period than any we have yet considered. On the evidence of grinding stones and other circumstantial evidence, it has been claimed that "near the end of the Nubian Final Stone Age, techniques were developed to permit the use of the wild grain which grew along the Nile, and thus to make possible the exploitation of a new and rich source of food" (Wendorf 1968: 1056). It is suggested that this practice goes back along the Nubian Nile at least to the twelfth millennium B.C., and thus appears to be an entirely indigenous response to the problems of winning food from the local environment. However, this theory is considered by some to rest on very slender evidence (Arkell 1969: 488). The question that has to be asked is: if this utilization of grain occurred earlier in the Nile Valley than anywhere in southwestern Asia, why did it not lead to settled villages and to domestication? The answer given lies in those changes of climate which meant that the wild grasses on which those communities were dependent became less and less abundant (Wendorf 1968: 1059) — although one school of thought would argue that this in itself should have provided the very stimulus for domestication. However, perhaps these Nubian sites are not, in fact, earlier than the earliest grain-using sites in southwest Asia, since sites with grinding stones have been found in the southern Negev dated to around 15,000 B.C. (Wendorf 1971). With the slightly moister climate of the sixth millennium, there is again evidence of a similar kind in the silt areas of the Dungul region for the specialized gathering and milling of wild grass seeds, especially perhaps *Panicum turgidum*, which has now retreated to the highlands of Tibesti (Hobler and Hester 1969). These authors suggest that in the Dungul area there may have been an independent evolution from intensive food gathering to food production, and that it was from here that ideas of food production were introduced up and down the Nile Valley; they reinforce their argument from the dissimilarity between the food-producing cultures of the Fayum and Khartoum on the one hand and those of southwestern Asia on the other. However, two things go against this argument: the fact that the earlier intensive exploitation of wild grains in Nubia did not lead to food production; and the fact that wheat must have been imported into Africa from Asia. From the 1968–1969 season at Jebel Uweinat, no direct evidence was obtained; however "the ecology (and also the presence of *Panicum turgidum* in great quantity, close to the Neolithic and older sites) would suggest a stage of vegeculture. It appears that Uweinat was more isolated than previously thought, but could be regarded as an area where tropical grasses might have become domesticated as a result of local interaction with the environment without outside stimulus" (van Noten 1971).

Of course there is a great deal more indirect evidence, much too much to enumerate in a paper of this length. Increased archaeological knowledge has shown us not only the unreliability of former simple definitions of the "Neolithic," in which it was implied that food production could be inferred from the presence of certain technological traits such as pottery and ground stone axes, but also that "agriculture" is not a unity — i.e. that food production has many forms and that we have to be more precise. Grinding stones can be used for grinding other things beside food, such as pigments, and we know that they were; nevertheless, ethnographic parallels suggest the possibility of dual use and that true quern forms only result from the persistent heavy grinding of grain, not from pigment grinding alone (Wendorf, et al. 1970). In spite of the need for such caution, the finding of tool-kits, admittedly with many regional variants and facies, belonging to what is usually referred to as the Neolithic of North Africa and the Sahara, is useful presumptive evidence for filling in many of the gaps left by the exiguous records of direct evidence. In Upper Egypt there are sites dated to the eleventh millennium B.C. which yield grindstones and abundant pieces with lustrous edges believed by some to be sickles, and a pollen profile associated with one of these sites has a sudden increase in the frequency of a large grass pollen which the palynologist is "95 percent sure is barley" (Wendorf 1971). The Terminal Paleolithic of the Fayum dated to the sixth millennium B.C. has abundant grindstones, but no direct data so far on food production (Wendorf 1971).

The stone mullers which appear about 4800 B.C. in the Haua Ftea record are suggestive of grain milling (McBurney 1967: 298); and the increased number, size, and wealth of Naqada I settlements between 3800 B.C. and 3600 B.C. have been interpreted as indicating a growth in the importance of agriculture over Badarian times (Kaiser 1957; Arkell and Ucko 1965: 153). Clay models of garlic appear in pre-Dynastic cemeteries in Egypt (Ayrton and Loat 1911: 18–29).

Although there are no radiocarbon dates for Early Khartoum, it looks as if pottery is earlier in the area stretching from there through Ennedi right across the Sahara into western Algeria than it is anywhere in the Nile Valley from Nubia to the Fayum, since in the latter pottery does not appear before 4000 B.C. (Wendorf 1971), whereas for the Sahara sites there is now a collection of dates from the fifth and sixth millennia B.C. (Camps 1969: 260ff.).

When we move south of the Sahara, we are in a much more difficult

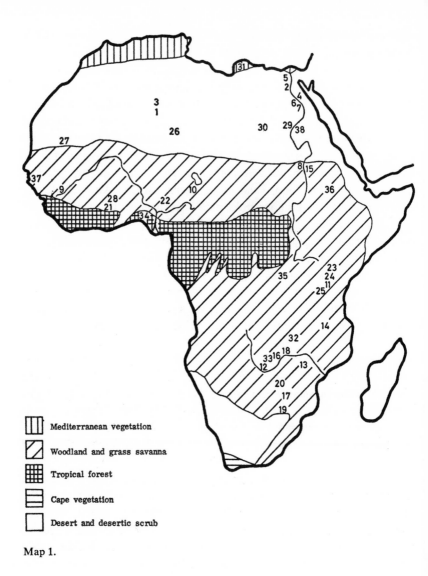

Mediterranean vegetation

Woodland and grass savanna

Tropical forest

Cape vegetation

Desert and desertic scrub

Map 1.

Key: Sites mentioned in the text

Numerical list	Alphabetical list	
1. Amekni	Abydos	6
2. Fayum	Adrar Bous	26
3. Meniet	Afyeh	38
4. Badari	Amekni	1
5. Merimde	Badari	4
6. Abydos, El Mahasna	Bambandyanalo	17
7. Naqada	Casamance	37
8. Shaheinab	Chundu	12
9. Niani	Daima	10
10. Daima	Dhar Tichitt	27
11. Engaruka	Dungul	29
12. Chundu	Early Khartoum	15
13. Inyanga	El Mahasna	6
14. Mwamasapwa, Nkope, Phopo Hill	Elmenteita	24
15, Early Khartoum	Engaruka	11
16. Kalundu, Isamu Pati	Fayum	2
17. Mapungubwe, Bambandyanalo	Haua Fteah	31
18. Ingombe Ilede	Hyrax Hill	24
19. Klipriviersberg, Olifantspoort	Ilkek	24
20. Khami	Ingombe Ilede	18
21. Kintampo	Inyanga	13
22. Nok	Isamu Pati	16
23. Njoro River Cave	Ishango	35
24. Ilkek, Hyrax Hill, Elmenteita, Nakuru	Iwo Eleru	34
25. Ngorongoro	Jebel Uweinat	30
26. Adrar Bous	Kalundu	16
27. Dhar Tichitt	Kapwirimbwe	32
28. Ntereso	Khami	20
29. Dungul	Kintampo	21
30. Jebel Uweinat	Klipriviersberg	19
31. Haua Fteah	Kumadzulo	33
32. Kapwirimbwe	Lalibela and Natchabiet Caves	36
33. Kumadzulo	Mapungubwe	17
34. Iwo Eleru	Meniet	3
35. Ishango	Merimde	5
36. Lalibela and Natchabiet Caves	Mwamasapwa	14
37. Casamance	Naqada	7
38. Afyeh	Nakuru	24
	Ngorongoro	25
	Niani	9
	Njoro River Cave	23
	Nkope	14
	Nok	22
	Ntereso	28
	Olifantspoort	19
	Phopo Hill	14
	Shaheinab	8

position with regard to handling our indirect evidence. One cannot always be sure that stone implements classified as hoes on the basis of their morphology were in fact used for tillage, whether as hoes or as digging stick blades (Hugot 1968: 484); and one questions whether it is justifiable on the basis of such tools alone, mostly collected as surface finds, to create a "culture" and give it a date and a name (Davies 1964: 203–230). Perhaps some edge-damage studies could throw light on the question.

The Nachikufan Industry of the woodland savannas of Zambia and Malawi, extending from about 8000 B.C. to A.D. 1600, has bored stones that could have been used as digging stick weights, but could equally well have been used in the making of some sort of animal trap; there are also edge-ground stone axes (J. D. Clark 1970: 177–178). Stone axes with their cutting edges made by grinding have been invented independently in more than one part of the world, and it is possible that this may have happened in subequatorial Africa, although some of the forms found in East Africa bear a resemblance to the Egyptian lugged axe (Leakey 1943; Brown 1969; van Noten 1969). It has been suggested that the infilling of the valleys with the deep deposits containing remains of the Nok culture in Nigeria was the result, not of climatic change, but of sheet and gulley erosion following extensive clearing of the vegetation cover by agriculturists during the later part of the first millennium B.C. (Shaw 1964: 455); and the same thing has been suggested for northeast Angola (J. D. Clark 1968: 146–148).

The presence of grindstones and quern fragments has been taken as "demonstrating" the practice of agriculture at the northern Malawi site of Phopo Hill, dated to the third to fifth centuries A.D. (Robinson and Sandelowsky 1968: 134), but it can only be classified among the indirect evidence. The stone rubbers at Ngorongoro (Leakey 1966; Sassoon 1968a, 1968b) were probably used for grinding ochre because they have red ochre ingrained in their surfaces; the bowls do not look as if they were used for grinding or pounding — one was blackened inside. It may be possible to establish that certain types of querns are associated with agriculture: deep dish-querns are only found on agricultural settlements in south-central Africa (J. D. Clark 1971a); in southern Zambia, lightweight, flat ones, similar to late Stone Age types, continue until late in the early Iron Age sequence, while deep querns are probably to be associated with maize cultivation (Vogel 1971).

An interesting piece of pollen-analytical evidence comes from cores taken from Lake Victoria, which indicate that about three thousand years ago, there was a sharp decline of forest species with a corresponding rise in grass pollens, while another genus (*Acalypha*), which is an early-stage pioneer in the regeneration of forest after gardens have been abandoned, also increases in abundance (J. D. Clark 1970: 206). This is suggestive of agriculture, especially in view of the plausible date; but it cannot be taken as conclusive, since elsewhere a decline in tree pollen and an increase in the ratio of grasses to trees cannot be due to agricultural practice, e.g. in the Hoxne Interglacial of eastern England (West and McBurney 1954: 135). The earliest recognizable iron hoes come from Zambian sites: Kapwirimbwe dated to the fifth century A.D. (tang only) (Phillipson 1968), Kumadzulo dated to the sixth-seventh centuries (Vogel 1969), and Chundu dated to the early eighth century (Vogel 1970).

The indirect evidence for a specialized form of agriculture at Engaruka (in northern Tanzania) is still rather tantalizing, in spite of recent work there. Two radiocarbon dates from the terrace sites on the hillside belong to the first millennium A.D., but it has not been possible to link the system of fields and enclosures to the hillside terrace-platforms; contrary to what was formerly supposed, careful examination has thrown doubt on whether the fields were irrigated, except close to the stream (Sassoon 1967).

There may be a possible new line of evidence for millet agriculture from an elevated carbon 13 content in skeletal material, due to the constant eating of isotopically fractionated material (van der Merwe 1971).

From the archaeological evidence that we have, it is clear that the millets became important in sub-Saharan Africa, but we do not know for how long this had been the case in different areas before we first actually meet them at the end of the first millennium A.D. Was some form of domesticated millet in use in sub-Saharan Africa for 500 or for 5000 years before that? At this point we have to take our first look at our third type of evidence — the botanical, ethnographic, and linguistic.

BOTANICAL AND ETHNOGRAPHIC EVIDENCE

Millets

Botanical evidence has been adduced to show that there is a coincidence of the greatest variability of the wild and cultivated sorghums in the area south of the Sahara, north of 10 degrees south and east of 25 degrees east, and on the basis of Vavilovian theory the implication was that it is in this area that we must look for the origin of the crop (Doggett 1965: 58), most probably in the northern part of it (Hemardinquer, et al. 1967; Harlan 1968), and perhaps specifically in Ethiopia (Doggett 1970: 2). On the other hand, "comparative morphological studies indicated that sorghum was probably ennobled independently in at least three African regions, from three morphologically different prototypes" — in the Ethiopian region, tropical West Africa north of the rain forest, and southeast Africa (de Wet and Huckabay 1967: 800). At one time it was thought that linguistic evidence precluded any belief that sorghum reached India earlier than the first millennium B.C., or at most 1500 B.C. (Watt 1893: 6, 291; Doggett 1970: 7); and Allchin quotes it as a latecomer in India, not appearing until the opening of the Christian era (Allchin 1969: 325). However, other evidence has been adduced to claim that it had already reached India by the mid-second millennium B.C. (Marshall 1931: Plate LXXXVII, Photo 5; Vishnu-Mittre 1968). It seems more likely that it reached India initially as ships' provisions in early seaborne traffic than that it traveled all the way overland (Doggett 1970: 7). (The introduction of the cultivated kapok tree [*Ceiba pentandra* (L.) Gaertn. var. *pentandra*] from West Africa to southern Asia seems to have been a much later development for which the Arabs were responsible [Baker 1965].) Sorghum reached Mesopotamia and the Middle East from India and only arrived in Egypt in Roman Byzantine times, so it did not travel from tropical Africa to the Middle East through Egypt (Doggett 1965: 61). Thus, in the area of northeast Africa specified, we have to think of late Stone Age people as growing emmer wheat and developing some of the local plants, including *Eleusine*, teff (*Eragrostis abyssinica*), and sorghum, for use in the areas less well suited to wheat (Doggett 1965: 59); but it can be argued that crops such as ensete (African banana, false banana) and teff must have been domesticated before the introduction of wheat and barley to Ethiopia or else they never would have been cultivated. *Eleusine coracana* was formerly thought to be of Indian origin (de Candolle 1884; Burkill 1935; Werth 1937; Portères 1951, this volume), but recent work suggests that it originated as a domesticated plant in Africa (Kennedy-O'Byrne 1957; Mehra 1962, 1963a, 1963b) and was transmitted to India by way of the Sabaean Lane (Anderson 1960). The whereabouts of the wild ancestors of *Pennisetum* and its first domestication has long remained something of a mystery (Harlan 1968), but its story may well be the same as that of *Eleusine coracana*. Doggett now sees both *Eleusine* and *Pennisetum*, as well as *Sorghum*, as originating in the Ethiopian area and being transmitted thence to India by sea (1970: 2, 7). On the other hand, Rachie's investigations, while they suggest to him that Ethiopia was indeed the center of origin for cultivated *Sorghum* and *Pennisetum* (with the possibility of a second center for *Pennisetum* towards the western end of the Sudan zone), do not provide the same evidence for *Eleusine* — for which there are many wild varieties in southwest Uganda and adjacent regions (Rachie 1971). *Pennisetum* has been recorded in Rajasthan and Gujarat in northwest India during the second half of the second millennium B.C., and *Eleusine* in the middle of that millennium from Mysore (Vishnu-Mittre 1968). Most of the millets grown in Bantu Africa today are said to be of eastern varieties, and agronomists stress their difference from the western (Grundeman 1968: 2, 4). *Digitaria exilis* ("fonio," "hungry rice") is not known wild but is cultivated as a secondary cereal throughout the savanna zone from northern Nigeria to the Atlantic. The same is true, except on a much smaller scale and in a much more restricted area, for *D. iburua* (Dalziel 1955: 526) which was perhaps domesticated in the Aïr region, with a secondary center in the Atakora mountains (Portères, this volume). J. D. Clark (1971b: 67–70) has recently reviewed the ethnographic evidence on the use for food of the grain of the grasses of the Sahara, the Sudan zone, and the Nile Valley.

It seems, then, that late Stone Age peoples of northeastern Africa, south of Egypt, were cultivating sorghum, but we have little evidence about its spread from here to other parts of Africa. Gloss-edged trapezoids, looking very much as if they are parts of a composite sickle, make their appearance (along with pottery and ground stone axes) in the Iwo Eleru sequence of Nigeria after about 3000 B.C.; but sickles are not suitable, and not normally used for cutting sorghum, and the trapezoids may have been used in a composite implement adapted to the purpose or for gathering wild or other cultivated grasses (Shaw 1969b: 369; n.d.). The same can be said of possible obsidian sickle blades found in a burial mound of the Stone Bowl culture in the Ngorongoro Crater of Tanzania, dated to the second half of the first millennium B.C. (Sassoon 1968a, 1968b). The stone bowls of this culture also may or may not have been associated with agricultural practices.

It is tempting to think that the makers of "Uelian" stone axes were agriculturalists, living on the northeastern border of the rain forest, but in fact we know nothing else at all about this "culture," neither its date nor the character of the rest of its material equipment (van Noten 1968).

Apart from the foregoing rather ambiguous pieces of indirect evidence, and the fact that the teeth of the skeleton from the Rop rock-shelter in Nigeria, radiocarbon-dated to 25 B.C. ± 120 are said to be those of an agriculturist (Gaherty 1968), we have very little idea how the practice of millet cultivation may have spread among people with a Late Stone Age technology in the savannas of West Africa, Central Africa (i.e. the Central African Republic) and parts of East Africa. Nevertheless, although we know so little as yet about the details, we can feel reasonably confident that some such spread did occur. The Kotoko living south of Lake Chad regard *Pennisetum* as their oldest kind of food grain (Lebeuf 1969). It is assumed that the first known iron-users in sub-Saharan Africa, the Nok people of the second half of the first millennium B.C. in Nigeria, were agriculturists; two terracottas represent fluted pumpkins (*Telfairia occidentalis*) (Fagg 1956: 289, 1086).

In most of Africa south of the equator, the archaeological record usually shows an iron technology succeeding late Stone Age industries of a type believed to be indicative of a hunting, fishing, and gathering economy (sometimes highly specialized and perhaps semisedentary, e.g. Ishango [Heinzelin 1957]), rather than of a food-producing one. Hence the idea has developed that in most of subequatorial Africa, a knowledge of iron technology and of food production were diffused together — and that the agents of this diffusion were speakers of Bantu languages (Oliver 1966a, 1966b). This idea of Oliver's was an attempt to put together the results of linguistic work done by Greenberg (1955) and Guthrie (1962) and Murdock's suggestion that the expansion of the Bantu-speaking peoples was the result of their possession of superior food resources (Murdock 1959: 290–291). Greenberg had decided that Bantu languages belonged to the western Sudanic family and that the more easterly peoples of this language group, as a result of the general southward trend, had moved into the Congo basin and thence into the rest of Bantu-speaking Africa. Guthrie, on the other hand, as a result of his linguistic studies, saw the Katanga and an east-west oval area around it as the center of dispersion. Oliver married the two pieces of linguistic research by postulating a small band of proto-Bantu speakers moving rapidly through the Congo forest from a primary dispersal center in southeast Nigeria and Cameroon to a secondary center in Katanga.

This is an attractive hypothesis, but there are a number of difficulties about it which have been enumerated (Posnansky 1968); in particular, in relation to the subject under discussion, the proto-Bantu, making their

quick dash through the forest, are supposed to have been millet-grow-
ers and might have found this difficult in a different ecosystem (Shaw
1969a: 229), whereas the pattern of distribution of *Eleusine* might be
regarded as favoring a route around the forest along its northern and
eastern margins (Portères 1951).

Anthropological evidence confirms the general pattern of movement,
but gives no preference for a north-south route through the forest or a
clockwise movement around it, and tells us nothing about the sources
of subsistence of the travelers (Hiernaux 1968). The key to a through-
the-forest route may be the Nana-Ekeia-Sanga waterway, leading from
forest-savanna mosaic in Cameroon and western Central African Republic to the similar zone of the Middle Congo, a distance of less
than 500 miles; trading contacts of a later date along this route suggest that it may have been in use earlier (Vansina 1970). Study of
the early Iron Age in the pre-Bantu homeland area of Cameroon has
suggested an agricultural economy tied to the river valleys (David
1971); the area of land for expansion (or even of maintenance, if soils
become exhausted or weeds of cultivation become too difficult to cope
with [Carneiro 1961: 57]), would in this case have been limited and
have tended to push settlement up the valleys of the upper Logone-
Chari system, whose headwaters rise comparatively close to those of
the Nana and Lobaye — rivers which run south into the Congo. What
is of importance is that, extending in a rather broken fashion from the
area of Kinshasa through northeastern and eastern Angola into Katanga
and adjacent parts of Zambia, there is a great stretch of grassland
which was at one time a puzzle to geographers but which has been
explained as the result of early agricultural activities (Gray 1962: 184);
and it will be noted that this is largely Guthrie's nuclear area for
Bantu expansion. It now seems likely that both the northern group of
early Iron Age industries in East Africa (Dimple Base, Kwale, Sanda-
weland), as well as the southern group (Kamadzulo, Ziwa, Gokomere
etc.) in the Zambia-Rhodesia area, are, on the basis of their pottery,
derivatives of a co-tradition from another area, rather than that they
influenced each other directly in a north and south direction (Huffman
1970). This other area could well be Guthrie's nuclear area.

Some doubts have been expressed about the idea that it was Bantu
speakers who spread both a knowledge of iron and of agriculture
throughout subequatorial Africa. Not many people now subscribe to
the idea of earlier writers (Johnston 1913: 413; Wrigley 1960) that it
was the possession of the iron hunting spear which gave such superiori-
ty to its possessors as to enable small parties of them to establish their

language and their leadership over others by being fabulous hunters and meat providers. There is some evidence that iron technology may have been introduced into subequatorial Africa by more than one route — one from West Africa and one by an eastern route from north of the Great Lakes (Summers 1958; Posnansky 1968: 11); that the earliest iron-using peoples in southern Africa were not all Negroes (Gardner 1963; Posnansky 1968); that agriculture was first introduced into Bantu Africa "prior to the adoption of metallurgical techniques" (Grundeman 1968: 4); and that later Bantu expansion into East Africa came into an area already partly occupied by food-producing societies, especially in the central Rift Valley of Kenya (Posnansky 1968). We cannot even be sure that the presence of Negroes definitely implies agriculture, as the example of the foraging Hadza shows (Posnansky 1968: 9). However, recent radiocarbon dates for East Africa, Zambia, Rhodesia, and down into Swaziland "serve to emphasize the basic contemporaneity of the introduction of the early Iron Age throughout the area of its distribution" (Phillipson 1970: 5) which means the first few centuries of the first millennium A.D. The archaeologist who in 1964 wrote "Iron Age technology and economic practices spread into southern Africa faster than either the language or the physical type associated with them in the first place" (Fagan 1964: 359) is not now inclined to think that this is true of southern Africa to any great extent (Fagan 1971); and in this area the accumulated evidence indicates that Iron Age culture was introduced as a fully integrated system, incorporating food-production, metallurgy, and a tribal organization with very little participation by previously stone-using culture bearers (Vogel 1971).

Tuberous Crops

Hitherto, nothing has been said about tuberous crops — for the simple reason that we have no direct or indirect archaeological evidence about them at all — so we have to rely on our third type of evidence for one of the most important classes of cultigens in Africa. We do not have to concern ourselves with cassava, sweet potatoes, or *Xanthosoma* (coco-yam with sagittate leaf) which are introductions to Africa from the New World since its discovery, nor with *Colocasia* (coco-yam with peltate leaf, or taro), one of the introductions from Asia (Coursey 1967: 7); it has been suggested (Dalziel 1955: 481; Allan 1967: 226) that *Colocasia* was indigenous to Ghana, but other opinion favors its having reached West Africa from Asia via the Nile

Valley (Burkill 1938; Purseglove 1972). Just as it is likely that many tropical grasses were at one time grown for their grain, so it is likely that a number of African tubers were formerly much more widely cultivated than now and have come to be displaced by more successful ones; *Plectranthus esculentus* (*Coleus dysentericus, C. dazo*; Hausa potato; Kafir potato) serves a case in point (Busson, et al. 1965: 405). Latest opinion considers that *Plectranthus* was cultivated from the wild independently in the upper Niger Valley, in Hausaland, and in the Central African Republic (Portères, this volume). The yam bean (*Sphenostylis stenocarpa*) is widely cultivated in tropical Africa, both for the seed and for the tuber (Dalziel 1955: 262; Busson, et al. 1965: 245–248).

The important cultigen is the yam, whose name has an interesting history (Burkill 1938). What has tended to obscure the history of this genus in Africa is that until recent years it was believed that the use and domestication of the indigenous African yams, *Dioscorea cayenensis* and *D. rotundata* were only brought about by the stimulus of the introduction of the Asian forms, *D. alata* and *D. esculenta* (Forde 1953: 211; Gray 1962: 183), although the latter is quite a recent introduction (Morgan 1962: 236; Lawton 1966). Alternatively, as a result of thinking in terms of "the introduction of agriculture," it was envisaged that the African yams were only developed when the idea of cultivation reached the "natural" yam-growing areas of West Africa (Morgan 1962: 238), following the domestication of *Oryza glaberrima* (African rice; see below). Even the poorer indigenous *D. dumetorum* is grown in West Africa as much as the Asiatic *D. esculenta* (Coursey 1967: 8).

Murdock (1959: 222–223) speculated that the Asiatic food plants entered Africa via the Ethiopian lowlands, traveling westward along what he erroneously called "the yam belt" (Morgan 1962: 235), thus enabling the western Sudanic peoples to expand southwards into the forest. Oliver has criticized this concept (1966b: 356), and the Asian food crops are generally believed to have reached Africa from Indonesia via Madagascar or the adjacent part of the east coast, in the first three centuries of the first millennium A.D. (Gray 1962: 182) or somewhat later.

Currently, it seems a more acceptable idea that yam cultivation may be very ancient in West Africa (as it was in Southeast Asia); and it has been suggested, indeed, that the Sangoan pick may have been a tool for grubbing up wild species from which practice natural vegetative reproduction, localized around living places, might result (Davies 1968: 479–481). In addition, it is a characteristic of the yam that it can regenerate after the removal of the tuber if not too much damage is done to the vine and roots. Thus very early collectors and gatherers might have become accustomed to the idea of returning to the same spot for a source of food, and from this practice it is a small step to a kind of proto-agriculture in which care is taken not to damage the plant in removing the tuber in order to safeguard a future food supply (Coursey 1967: 12). The use of wild yams has been recorded among hunter-gatherers in the Congo (Burkill 1939) as well as their use in time of scarcity among farmers in Nigeria (Okiy 1960: 118) and the Chokwe in Angola (J. D. Clark 1963: 194). In support of an early domestication of yams in Africa, Coursey points to the prohibition in certain areas on the use of iron tools for the digging of yams in New Yam festivals which strongly suggests that yam cultivation antedates the commencement of the Iron Age (Coursey 1967: 10). The Idoma and some Ibo prefer to use a wooden spade for digging yams, but the reason given is that an iron implement is likely to injure the yam (Armstrong 1971). It has been suggested that yam-growing was a development resulting from the stimulus of cereal cultivators to the north rather than as having an independent origin (Alexander and Coursey 1969: 421). But the opposite possibility has to be borne in mind — that yam-growing along the northern forest margins was older than cereal cultivation and that it was yam-growers who developed the use of local grasses encountered as weeds in their yam patches. In Asia it seems that root- and tuber-growing in the southeast were older than cereal growing in northern China, and that it was the root- and tuber-growers of southern China who domesticated rice — although they may have had some stimulus from northern cereal growers (Ho 1969; Chang 1970: 183). Posnansky has suggested (1969: 106) that West African yam cultivation began between 2500 and 1500 B.C.

One might perhaps apply the Binford-Flannery model here: the savanna was the "optimal" habitat for the hunting and gathering population and the forest a "less favorable" habitat, which received the groups which hived off from the savanna population when this became necessary if the savanna was to maintain its capacity to carry its population density. Even if this was not the sole factor involved, it is just in these marginal forest areas that the African yams and the oil palm must have been developed, first as protected, and then as planted sources of food supply (Binford 1968; Flannery 1969). Theoretical reasons have been given for supposing that once both seed agriculture and tuber agriculture have been established, the former will be more expansive than the latter (Harris 1971, 1972).

The advent of holoendemic and hyperendemic malaria in West Africa, with the attendant establishment of the sickle-cell gene in the human populations of the area, appears to be associated with the introduction of agricultural practices (Livingstone 1958; Wiesenfeld 1967). A period of at least 1,500 years is estimated to be required to obtain the high percentages of the sickle-cell trait found at present in many West African populations (Wiesenfeld 1968).

Tree Crops

The demonstration that after 3000 B.C. the West African forest was occupied by late Stone Age people who had pottery, ground stone axes, and stone tools that could well have been used as hoes or as blades for digging sticks may be of the greatest importance in suggesting that they systematically exploited tuberous crops; they probably also made use of the fruit of the oil palm. This can be regarded as a specialized form of "gathering" at first; the crossing of the line to "vegeculture" and "arboriculture," beginning with the mere protection of wild trees, could have been hardly perceptible. An important step in the exploitation and domestication of the yams must have been the devising of the wooden pestle and mortar which so greatly facilitates the human consumption of fibrous starchy foods, particularly by infants, and which therefore may be an invention as important for tropical African agriculture as the plow was elsewhere. Is it a coincidence that the densest populations in sub-Saharan Africa are in southern Nigeria where the combination of yam cultivation and the exploitation of the oil palm, providing complementary food values, has been most highly developed? Within this area all these factors are seen to their greatest extent among the Ibo, who are "the most enthusiastic yam cultivators in the world" (Coursey 1967: 198) and who have converted the greater part of their rain forest into oil palm bush. Thus, there is probably a quite simple explanation for the density of population in Iboland — the antiquity and effectiveness of yam cultivation and the exploitation of the oil palm. It is probably significant, too, that Ibo cultural origins, associated with yam cultivation and a yam festival, seem to have been in northwest Iboland on the Anambra river, on the northern forest margins (Onwuejeogwu 1971); and here, also, is a grassland fringe indicative of early agricultural clearings (Gray 1962: 184; Allison 1962: 243).

We need to learn more about the early protection and "domestica-

tion" of the oil palm, since it is not native to the primeval West African
rain forest, requiring more light to grow than this allows and the fruit
needing the heat of full insolation to germinate, and yet needing plenty
of groundwater (Hartley 1967: 4); wherever it is now found in the
forest area, it indicates human settlement at some time (Allison 1962:
246; van Meer 1971). Presumably, therefore, the oil palm also must
have been first developed along forest margins and in gallery forests
in the savanna. We have already noted among the direct archaeological
evidence a pericarp of oil palm at Shaheinab, and Raymond (1961:
69) has suggested that there may have been a trade in palm oil in the
Nile Valley "some 3000 years B.C.," but this was on the basis of an
analysis of a large jar of fat from an Abydos tomb carried out nearly
eighty years ago (Friedel 1897). In the Ivory Coast the exploitation of
the oil palm is considered to be ancient, and a correlation has been
observed between certain varieties and certain human population
groups (Meunier 1969, 1972).

Other tree crops have been protected and developed, such as *Butyrospermum paradoxum*, the shea butter tree (Dalziel 1955: 350–354;
Davies 1968: 480; Hugot 1968: 486); *Cola acuminata* and *C. nitida*,
the kola nut (Dalziel 1955: 100–104); and *Adansonia digitata*, the
baobab. The latter occurs throughout the drier parts of tropical Africa
and has many uses (Dalziel 1955: 112–115; Owen 1968, 1970). It is
usually assumed to be indigenous to Africa (Baker 1965: 193), and its
introduction to India in the fourteenth century A.D. has been associated
with the arrival of African slaves (Burton-Page 1969). However, one
botanist (Jackson 1970) considers that it was spread over the African
continent by the activities of Arab traders from the East African coast
(Madagascar being its "center"), but a radiocarbon dating of wood
from a 45 foot baobab near Lake Kariba of 1010 ± 100 B.P. might
be thought to militate against this idea (Swart 1963). If the baobab
has to be thought of as being diffused by man from the Madagascar
area, perhaps it was spread by the same agency that spread the bananas.
Its presence in wooded savanna commonly indicates the site of a
former village (Allison 1962: 248; Davies 1968: 480); and north of
Nouakchott in Mauritania they are regarded as relicts, but whether
they are associated with cultivation is unproven (Hugot 1968: 487).
In Nigeria a number of indigenous fruits are still used as food: wild
mango (*Irvingia* spp.), African breadfruit or African rice tree (*Treculia
africana* Decne), fan palm (*Borassus aethiopicum*), native pear (*Dacryodes edulis*), *Allanblackia floribunda*, and *Parkia clapertoniana* (Redhead 1971).

"Centers of Origin"

Vavilov did pioneer work in the interwar period on the botanical evidence concerning centers of domestication for cultivated plants, but he did not investigate the African yams. He was convinced that he had "established the independence of Ethiopia in its cultivated flora and had proven beyond doubt the existence here (including the hill country of Eritrea) of an independent center of origin of the world's cultivated plants" (Vavilov 1951: 37). This view was based to a considerable extent, it seems, on the existence in this area of an amazing wealth of forms of wheats and barleys — now thought to be the result not of primary domestication there, but of the introduction and hybridization of a variety of already cultivated forms — and perhaps of a new environment exerting selective pressures. Thus Vavilov made Abyssinia one of his eight major centers in the world for the origin of domesticated plants, also attributing to this area the origin, among others, of *Sorghum* sp., *Eragrostis abyssinica*, *Eleusine coracana*, *Pennisetum spicatum*, *Vigna unguiculata*, *Ricinus communis*, and *Hibiscus esculentus* (okra) (Vavilov 1951: 38). It is now considered that wheat and barley cultivation and the use of the plow were introduced into Ethiopia by the ancient Cushitic inhabitants who were in a good position in northern Ethiopia to have contacts with countries at the northern end of the Red Sea (Simoons 1965). A research project designed to gain data from Ethiopia on its role in the development of African agriculture has so far not found sites with sufficient time depths to give us what we are seeking, as the caves at Lalibela and Natchabiet do not go back beyond 500 B.C.; they show the presence at that date of barley and chickpea (*Cicer arietinum*), which need not surprise us (Dombrowski 1969).

Murdock posited an ancient center of plant domestication in his "nuclear Mande area" around the headwaters of the Niger. He based his argument primarily on linguistic distributions, but claimed "modest support from archaeologists, on the basis of admittedly fragmentary evidence from the very few relevant excavations reported to date" (but none of which are cited) "and from botanists who have identified the ranges of wild species from which the domesticated forms have presumably been ennobled." However, the latter type of evidence offered by Murdock did not stand up well to examination by a botanist. Baker (1962) examined Murdock's list and on botanical grounds considered that *Hibiscus sabdariffa* (roselle), *Sesamum indicum* (sesame), and *Gossypium herbaceum* (cotton) could equally well have been domesticated in Asia, and if they were domesticated in Africa, it need not have been in the western Sudan. (A consideration of cotton is intentionally omitted from this study since its domestication has not been for purposes of human consumption; the subject is complex, and expert opinion about it has changed frequently in recent years. It is now believed that cotton was domesticated in Asia and introduced to Egypt in Meroitic times [Arkell 1971] although there were wild cottons in Africa the seeds of which were collected for stockfeed in Egyptian Nubia by the middle of the third millennium B.C. [Chowdhury and Buth 1970].) Similarly Baker considered there was insufficient evidence to regard the following members of Murdock's list as only domesticated in the western Sudan: *Sorghum vulgare, Pennisetum typhoideum, Coleus dazo* and *Coleus dysentericus, Vigna unguiculata, Sphenostylis stenocarpa, Citrullus vulgaris, Cucumeropsis edulis* and *C. mannii, Lagenaria siceraria, Tamarindus indica, Hibiscus esculentus,* and *Hibiscus cannabinus.* "If the first domestication of these species in the Nuclear Mande area is, after all, unproven" says Baker, "we are left with only a fraction of the original list." (Evidence has since been adduced to suggest that the cowpea [*Vigna sinensis, Vigna unguiculata*] was domesticated in West Africa, most likely in Nigeria [Faris 1963]; it has been grown for centuries both in Africa and in India [Ames 1939; Anderson 1952].) Baker divides the remaining species into two groups: the first group of species is "Sudanic" but virtually restricted to West Africa, and it was the existence of such "endemics" that Murdock considered provided the strongest botanical evidence for a domestication center in the nuclear Mande area — *Butyrospermum parkii (paradoxum),* shea butter tree (really a wild tree given protection) *Telfairia occidentalis* (fluted pumpkin, wild and cultivated), *Kerstingiella geocarpa* (a groundnut), and *Digitaria exilis* (fonio), very close to the wild *D. longiflora.* With the exception of *Kerstingiella geocarpa,* these species are either undifferentiated from wild plants still occurring in the area or else show a close and obvious relationship, and could have been added from the local environment after agricultural ideas had been introduced from elsewhere. *Kerstingiella geocarpa,* however, is the only species in its genus, and when Baker was writing, it was unknown wild (both it and *Voandzeia subterranea* have since been found wild near the Nigeria-Cameroon border [Hepper 1963]; he regarded it as Murdock's best bit of evidence — together with *Oryza glaberrima,* although the center of origin of this form of rice is believed to have been in the inland delta of the Niger, not its headwaters area (Portères 1962: 237). (Inferential evidence has been adduced for the growing of rice in the

Casamance region of Senegal by the beginning of the first millennium A.D. [Linares de Sapir 1971: 43].) In the second group are savanna and woodland species which are "Guinean" rather than "Sudanic" in distribution: *Blighia sapida* (Akee apple), *Cola acuminata* and *C. nitida*, *Elaeis guineensis*, and *Dioscorea* spp. Baker observed that the species occur wild as well as planted, that one could not be sure of any great antiquity for them as domesticates, and that these Guinea species could not be held to contribute any evidence in favor of the nuclear Mande domestication center.

A great deal of botanical work on centers of plant domestication in sub-Saharan Africa has been done by Portères (1962). His interest has been predominantly with grain crops, which perhaps makes him under-estimate the importance and potential of the forest products; and some of his inferences appear to be based more on doubtful anthropological and archaeological ideas than on botanical evidence — such as his assertion that food production in the forest is a recent innovation, the invention of former cereal-growing savanna peoples forced into the forest by steppe nomads. His examination of the botanical evidence led Portères to posit some eight centers of crop domestication in Africa, four in West Africa and one each in Central Africa (Cameroon-Central African Republic), the Upper Nile, Abyssinia, and East Africa. In West Africa, Portères sees the middle Niger area as originating *Oryza glaberrima*, *Pennisetum cinereum*, five species of sorghum, *Kerstingiella geocarpa*, and as a secondary center for the development of *Coleus dazo* and *Coleus dysentericus*; the Senegambian area as a secondary center for *Oryza glaberrima* and as producing *Sorghum gambicum*, *Digitaria exilis*, and four species of *Pennisetum*; the Chad region as originating the cultivation of *Dioscorea cayenensis, D. rotundata, D. dumetorum, D. bulbifera*, and four other species of yams, as well as the oil palm, *Elaeis guineensis*, and the fluted pumpkin, *Telfairia occidentalis*. In the upper Nile area Portères places the origin of *Sorghum durra* and three other species, four species of *Pennisetum*, and three species of *Sesamum*, while the debt to Abyssinia is especially for teff (*Eragrostis abyssinica*), *Eleusine coracana*, and the African banana, *Musa ensete* (*Ensete edulis*), while it is also regarded as a secondary center for wheats and barleys. The Central African area is regarded as the primary center for *Coleus dazo, C. dysentericus*, and *Voandzeia subterranea* and in part for *Elaeis guineensis*; and the East African center for five species of *Pennisetum* and three of sorghum.

It should be pointed out that to call ensete "the African banana" is somewhat misleading, and in one way the name "false banana" is more appropriate, as it is a banana-like plant but one which bears no edible fruit. Nevertheless the stem and especially the root are edible and provide the staple diet for the ensete cultivators of southwestern Ethiopia (Shack 1966: 1). Ensete is distributed throughout West Africa, the Congo basin, and East Africa (Simmonds 1962: 25), but it is only in Ethiopia that it has been domesticated. When such ensete cultivation began seems to be quite unknown, but the Sidama peoples of southern Ethiopia are thought to have been responsible. The claimed evidence for ensete cultivation in ancient Egypt, although firmly believed in by some (e.g. Laurent-Tackholm 1951; Arkell 1971), is regarded as inconclusive (Simoons 1965).

Unfortunately for archaeologists — or perhaps fortunately, if ultimately it brings us nearer the truth and stops us wandering down misleading byways — the whole principle that a proliferation of variant forms indicates a "center of origin" now seems called into question; as has recently been written, referring to Vavilov: "Slowly over the years almost all the points made in his centers of origin theory have been refuted . . . This is not to say that Vavilovian theory was not an important contribution . . . Yet, when the evidence is properly qualified and corrected there is little left of the original theory except that crops are more variable some places than others" (Harlan and de Wet 1973; Baker 1971; Harlan 1971b). This must cast some doubt on the basis for Portères's centers of plant domestication. On the other hand, perhaps we shall gain from the application to Africa of the newly-understood principle of "disruptive selection." For example, this may account for there being no known wild ancestor of "fonio" (*Digitaria exilis*) the nearest being *D. longiflora* (Dalziel 1955: 526).

LINGUISTIC EVIDENCE

Linguistics is obviously an important source of evidence for the history of food production in Africa, although, unfortunately, the study of comparative linguistics has not yet reached a state where there is general agreement on interpretations. For example, it is difficult to know how much reliance to place upon the time depths proposed by the exponents of glottochronology. Nevertheless, it is interesting that one of them sees people in southern Nigeria cultivating yams, cotton, and beans and making palm wine 6,000 years ago (Armstrong 1964: 136).

The introduction of the Asiatic food crops in the first three centuries A.D., or a little later, into Madagascar and the adjacent parts of the mainland has already been mentioned above. One of the most important groups of these consists of the bananas and plantains, although Dalziel (1955: 468) speculated that the plantain was introduced into Africa "probably through Egypt in ancient times." The banana and the plantain were formerly called respectively *Musa sapientum* and *Musa paradisiaca* (or *M. sapientum* var. *paradisiaca*), but the Latin nomenclature is in such confusion that it is regarded as better "to disregard all Latin names" (Simmonds 1959: 54). Other important Asiatic crops are the Asiatic yam, *Dioscorea alata*, and probably the cocoyam, *Colocasia esculentum*, (although Dalziel says [1955: 481] it "was cultivated in Egypt and India from remote antiquity"; see also the discussion of tuberous crops). Just how these Asiatic cultigens spread from the East African coast must be a very interesting story, but we know little about it at the moment. It would have been much easier for *Musa* spp., being vegetatively propagated and requiring considerable moisture, to have spread up the Zambezi Valley and via the East African lakes to the other suitable areas of Africa, rather than by any other route. It would have been more difficult to get these species inland from the African coast around Mombasa, and even more difficult still to bring them along the arid Sabaean Lane into the Nile Valley. However this is the route favored by Sauer (1952: 36), who states that root stocks can be thoroughly dried out and left exposed for months before replanting. Simmonds also states (1962: 31) that the Eumusas are tolerant of considerable drought, ranging far out into the seasonal climates of the monsoon lands. Unfortunately, scientific archaeology in Madagascar is in its infancy, and about all we know archaeologically of its early history is that the southern part of the island was inhabited by the end of the first millennium A.D. (Verin 1966: 124). Deschamps has supposed that the Malayo-Polynesians who colonized Madagascar only did so after first reaching the East African coast (Deschamps 1960: 26). The spread of the Asiatic crops on the mainland could have been rapid because they quickly came into contact with African, probably Bantu-speaking, food producers, who may have only taken to food production comparatively recently; or the introduction of these crops and their growers could itself have been an important stimulus to the adoption of food-producing practices. However this may be, when we come to southern Nigeria, where the Asiatic crops penetrated at some point, it is interesting that linguistic evidence independently splits the crops presently grown into three groups: the crops cultivated prior to the Asiatic introductions; the Asiatic introductions; and the latest comers, such as maize and cassava, introduced after the European discovery of America (Williamson 1970). Thus, the following are the food plant names which are sufficiently well correlated with the different genetic language group as to suggest an origin in Proto-Niger-Congo, i.e. at least 4,000 years ago: raffia palm (*Raphia hookerii*), oil palm (*Elaeis guineensis*), yam (*Dioscorea cayenensis* and *D. rotundata*), and kola nut (*Cola acuminata* and *C. nitida*). The second group, which it will be observed contains the Asiatic introductions, have names which are not so neatly correlated with genetic language groups but which do not cross language boundaries in such a way as to suggest recent borrowing: cocoyam (*Colocasia esculentum*), plantain (*Musa sapientum* var. *paradisiaca*), banana (*Musa sapientum*) and water yam (*Dioscorea alata*). It should be noted, however, that Blakney (1963) thinks that the *Ko* root for plantain or banana is so widespread that it really belongs to the earlier Proto-Niger-Congo group. The third group of names are those with very little correlation with the language groupings: instead the names are spread over wide areas which can sometimes be associated with trade routes and give an idea of the direction from which the plant was introduced; bitterleaf (*Vernonia amygdalina* and *V. colorata*), is probably a recent introduction to the Niger Delta from Iboland; okra (*Hibiscus esculentus*) is indigenous to Africa but again probably a recent introduction from Iboland; the different names in the delta for groundnut (*Arachis hypogaea*) and maize (*Zea mays*) correlate with the trading centers of Port Harcourt, Onitsha, and Warri; the names for cassava (*Manihot esculenta*), rice (*Oryza sativa*), orange (*Citrus aurantium*), lime (*Citrus aurantifolia*), and coconut (*Cocos nucifera*) are derived from Portuguese; while those for onion (*Allium cepa*) are either from Portuguese or from Arabic through Hausa.

Many local plants in different parts of Africa which are not staple food providers have been used for making sauces, soups, or condiments. One of the most interesting is *Aframomum melegueta*, named "Melegueta pepper" by the Portuguese, the derivation of "Melegueta" being obscure; currently in English it is commonly corrupted to "alligator pepper." "Melegueta" is probably a derivative of the Tamil *milaga* [pepper], but the earliest thirteenth century references in Europe probably refer to a plant from India different from *Afromomum melegueta* (Mauny 1953: 708). Because Melegueta pepper was called "grains of paradise" in the sixteenth century, the coast of Liberia came to the called the "Grain Coast" — a somewhat misleading term to anyone thinking it referred to cereals (Dalziel 1955: 471).

CONCLUSIONS AND QUESTIONS

What conclusions can be drawn from the foregoing review of the evidence from botanical sources for the intentional production of food in Africa? It would be possible from it to attempt yet another synthesis concerning "the spread of agriculture in Africa," "centers of origin," "nuclear areas for diffusion," and so on, even if such a synthesis would be somewhat cautious. However, in accord with the attitude outlined at the beginning of this paper, it may be better to realize that we are left with more questions than answers and to list these questions in order that research workers may pay attention to them and look for the evidence that will throw light upon them. There are two theoretical questions that require further attention:

1. What can justifiably be inferred concerning historical processes of domestication from a study of present distributions of wild and domesticated crop varieties?
2. Since it has become evident from this paper that direct archaeological evidence is scarce, and likely to remain relatively so, are we to confine ourselves to the minimum firm ground provided by this evidence and say that we cannot venture further? Surely this would be a counsel of despair; rather, we have to consider in more detail what can be proved by also considering all the indirect evidence, both archaeological and other, and what methodology we should employ. We need to start with theoretical frameworks for processes of change towards husbandry and food production and ask ourselves what types of archaeological evidence we might get in order to give confirmation or negation of our hypotheses.

If we get information on the likely economy of critically situated sites securely tied in to a chronological framework over the relevant time span, we shall be obtaining data to contribute to the solving of the more generalized problems. A number of specific questions are listed below; in considering them we need to be asking all the time what ecological factors have been involved in the emergence of food production in different micro-environments in Africa, and what lessons can be learnt from surviving agricultural practices?

1. What was the relationship between early cereal growers in Egypt and in the Saharan highlands?
2. How well founded is the claim that cereal growing was earlier in the Saharan highlands than in the Nile Valley?
3. Was experimentation with tropical wild grasses an independent process or was there a stimulus from wheat and barley growers

further north?

4. If it is agreed that *Sorghum* and *Pennisetum* are of African origin and that they had been transmitted to India by the middle of the second millennium B.C., what evidence can we find, and going back how far, for the domestication process in the areas of Africa where this is likely to have taken place?

5. What archaeological evidence can be found in Africa (perhaps in Uganda) on the domestication at an early date of *Eleusine*?

6. A greater knowledge of contacts between East Africa, Arabia, and India in the three millennia up to ca. A.D. 1000 would give us greater confidence in speaking about crop movements between them.

7. Was the cultivation of yams in the West African yam area independent of influence from cereal growers in the savanna, or did it only develop under the influence of agricultural practices from the north?

8. Could independently-attained yam cultivation along the forest margins have led to the cultivation of local wild grasses?

9. Can we locate more precisely the areas of initial exploitation and protection of the oil palm?

10. What is the precise relationship in subequatorial Africa between the spread of agricultural practices, the spread of iron technology, and the spread of Bantu speech?

11. Did the Asian food crops introduced into East Africa in the first few centuries A.D. merely become added to the repertoire of existing agriculturists, or did they serve to initiate the practice of agriculture itself in the area of introduction?

If in the course of the next ten years we can find evidence to throw light on some of these questions and give more precise chronology to what we already know, we shall certainly have advanced our knowledge concerning the history of African food production. There is not space here to go into the best strategy of framing research so as to obtain these results, but it is to be hoped that there will not only be research programs designed to tackle some of these questions, but also that no opportunity will be lost in other programs to watch out for data which might contribute.

REFERENCES

ALEXANDER, JOHN
1969 "The indirect evidence for domestication," in *The domestication and exploitation of plants and animals*. Edited by P. J. Ucko and G. W. Dimbleby, 123–129. London: Duckworth.

ALEXANDER, JOHN, D. G. COURSEY
1969 "The origins of yam cultivation," in *The domestication and exploitation of plants and animals*. Edited by P. J. Ucko and G. W. Dimbleby, 405-425. London: Duckworth.

ALLAN, W.
1967 *The African husbandman*. London.

ALLCHIN, F. R.
1969 "Early cultivated plants in India and Pakistan," in *The domestication and exploitation of plants and animals*. Edited by P. J. Ucko and G. W. Dimbleby, 323–329. London: Duckworth.

ALLISON, P. A.
1962 Historical inferences to be drawn from the effect of human settlement on the vegetation of Africa. *Journal of African History* 3(2):241–249.

AMES, O.
1939 *Economic annuals and human cultures*. Cambridge, Massachusetts: Botanical Museum of Harvard.

ANDERSON, E.
1952 *Plants, man and life*. Boston. (Revised edition published 1967 by University of California Press.)
1960 "The evolution of domestication," in *Evolution after Darwin*, volume two. Edited by Sol Tax, 67. Chicago: University of Chicago Press.

ARKELL, A. J.
1953 *Shaheinab*. Oxford: Oxford University Press.
1969 Review of Wendorf's "The prehistory of Nubia . . . ." *Journal of African History* 10(3):487–489.
1971 Comment on "Origins of food production in southwestern Asia" by G. A. Wright. *Current Anthropology* 12:471–472.

ARKELL, A. J., P. J. UCKO
1965 Review of predynastic development in the Nile Valley. *Current Anthropology* 6:145–156.

ARMSTRONG, ROBERT G.
1964 "The use of linguistic and ethnographic data in the study of Idoma and Yoruba history," in *The historian in tropical Africa*. Edited by J. Vansina, R. Mauny, and L. V. Thomas, 127–144. London: Oxford University Press.
1971 Personal communication.

ASSEMIEN, P.
1971 *Etude comparative des flores actuelles et quaternaires récentes de quelques paysages végétaux*. C.N.R.S. Centre de Documentation 5868. Paris.

AYRTON, EDWARD R., W. L. S. LOAT
1911   *Predynastic cemetery at El Mahasna.* London.

BAKER, H. G.
1962   Comments on the thesis that there was a major centre of plant domestication near the headwaters of the River Niger. *Journal of African History* 3(2):229–233

1965   "The evolution of the cultivated kapok tree: a probable West African product," in *Ecology and economic development in tropical Africa.* Edited by D. Brokensha, 185–216. Institute for International Studies, University of California, Berkeley. Research Series 9.

1971   Commentary on Section Three, in *Man across the seas.* Edited by C. L. Riley, J. C. Kelley, C. W. Penington, and R. L. Rands, 428–444.Austin, Texas: University of Texas Press.

BALOUT, L.
1965   Comment on "Review of predynastic development in the Nile Valley" by A. J. Arkell and P. J. Ucko. *Current Anthropology* 6(2):156.

BAUMGARTEL, ELISE J.
1955   *The cultures of prehistoric Egypt,* volume one, (revised edition). Oxford: Oxford University Press.

1965   What do we know about the excavations at Merimde? *Journal of American Oriental Society* 85(4):502–511.

BINFORD, L. R.
1968   "Post-Pleistocene adaptations," in *New perspectives in archaeology.* Edited by L. R. Binford and S. R. Binford, 313–341. Chicago: Aldine.

BISHOP, W. W., J. DESMOND CLARK, *editors*
1967   *Background to evolution in Africa.* Chicago: University of Chicago Press.

BLAKNEY, C. P.
1963   *On "banana" and "iron"; linguistic footprints in African history.* Hartford Studies in Linguistics 13. Hartford.

BONNEFILLE, R.
1971a   Atlas des pollens d'Ethiopie. *Adansonia* (2) 11(3):463–518.

1971b   Atlas des pollens d'Ethiopie. Principales espèces des forêts de montagne. *Pollen et Spores* 13(1):15–72.

BRONCKERS, F.
1967   Palynologie africaine VII. *Bull. de* l'I.F.A.N. 29(A):471–520.

BROWN, JEAN
1966   The excavation of a group of burial mounds at Ilkek near Gilgil, Kenya. *Azania* 1:59–77.

1969   Some polished axes from East Africa. *Azania* 4:160–166.

BURKILL, I. H.
1935   *A dictionary of economic products of the Malay Peninsula.* London: Crown Agents for the Colonies.

1938   The contact of the Portuguese with African food-plants, which gave such words as"yam" to European languages. *Proceedings of the Linnean Society* 3 Feb. 1938.

1939   Notes on the genus *Dioscorea* in the Belgian Congo. *Bulletin du Jardin Botanique de Bruxelles* 15:345–392.

BURTON-PAGE, J.

1969   "The problem of the introduction of *Adansonia digitata* into India," in *The domestication and exploitation of plants and animals.* Edited by P. J. Ucko and G. W. Dimbleby, 331–335. London: Duckworth.

BUSSON, F., P. JAEGER, P. LUNVEN, M. PINTA

1965   *Plantes alimentaires de l'ouest africain.* Marseilles: Leconte.

BUTZER, KARL W.

1965   Comment on "Review of predynastic development in the Nile Valley." *Current Anthropology* 6(2):157–158.

CAMPS, GABRIEL

1969   *Amekni: Néolithique ancien du Hoggar.* CRAPE. Mém. 10. Arts et métiers graphiques. Paris: Flammarion.

1971   Personal communication.

CARNEIRO, ROBERT L.

1961   "Slash and burn cultivation among the Kuikuru and its implications for cultural development in the Amazon basin," in *The evolution of horticultural systems in native South America: causes and consequences.* Edited by Johannes Wilkers, 47–67. Caracas: Sociedad de Ciencias Naturales La Salle.

CATON-THOMPSON, GERTRUDE, E. W. GARDNER

1934   *The desert Fayum.* London: Oxford University Press.

CHANG, KWANG-CHIN

1970   The beginnings of agriculture in the Far East. *Antiquity* 44:175–185.

CHOWDHURY, K. A., G. M. BUTH

1970   4,500 year old seeds suggest that true cotton is indigenous to Nubia. *Nature* 227:85–86.

CLARK, GRAHAME

1965   Radiocarbon dating and the spread of farming economy. *Antiquity* 39(153):45–48.

1969   *World prehistory: a new outline* (second edition). Cambridge: Cambridge Universiy Press.

CLARK, J. DESMOND

1963   *Prehistoric cultures of north-east Angola and their significance in tropical Africa.* Lisbon: Diamantes.

1967   "The problem of Neolithic culture in sub-Saharan Africa," in *Background to evolution in Africa.* Edited by W. W. Bishop and J. Desmond Clark, 601–627. Chicago: University of Chicago Press.

1968   *Further palaeo-anthropological studies in northern Lunda.* Lisbon.

1970   *The prehistory of Africa.* London: Thames and Hudson.

1971a   Personal communication.

1971b   Evidence for agricultural origins in the Nile Valley. *Proceedings of the Prehistoric Society* 37(2):34–79.

COETZEE, J. A.
1965 The morphology of *Acacia* pollen. *South African Journal of Science* 52(1):23–27.

CONNAH, GRAHAM
1967 Progress report on archaeological work in Bornu 1964–1966. *Northern History Research Scheme, Second Interim Report:* 20–31. Zaria.

COURSEY, D. G.
1967 *Yams.* London: Longmans.

DALZIEL, J. M.
1955 *The useful plants of west tropical Africa* (second reprint). London.

DARLINGTON, C. D.
1969 "The silent millennia in the origin of agriculture," in *The domestication and exploitation of plants and animals.* Edited by P. J. Ucko and G. W. Dimbleby, 67–72. London: Duckworth.

DAVID, N.
1971 Personal communication.

DAVIES, O.
1964 *The Quaternary in the coastlands of Guinea.* Glasgow: Jackson.
1968 The origins of agriculture in West Africa. *Current Anthropology* 9(5):479–482.

DAVIES, O., H. J. HUGOT, DAVID SEDDON
1968 The origins of African agriculture. *Current Anthropology* 9(5): 479–509.

DE CANDOLLE, A.
1884 Origin of cultivated plants. London: Kegan Paul. (Second edition 1959. London: Hafner's.)

DE HEINZELIN DE BRAUCOURT, J.
1957 *Les fouilles d'Ishango,* volume two. Brussels: Institut des parcs nationaux du Congo belge.

DE WET, J. M. J., P. HUCKABAY
1967 The origin of *Sorghum bicolor.* Distribution and domestication. *Evolution* 21(4): 787–802.

DEEVEY, EDWARD S., RICHARD FOSTER FLINT, IRVING ROUSE
1963 Editorial statement. *Radiocarbon* 5:v.
1965 *Radiocarbon measurements comprehensive index 1950–1965.* New Haven: American Journal of Science. Haven.

DESCHAMPS, M.
1960 Histoire de Madagascar. *Col. Mondes d'Outre-Mer.* Paris: Berger-Levrault.

DOGGETT, H.
1965 "The development of the cultivated sorghums," in *Essays in crop plant evolution.* Edited by Sir Joseph Hutchinson, 50–69. Cambridge: Cambridge University Press.
1970 *Sorghum.* London: Longmans.

DOMBROWSKI, JOANNE
1969 Preliminary report on excavation in Lalibela and Natchabiet Caves, Begemeder. *Annales d'Ethiopie* 8:21–29.

FAGAN, BRIAN
1964 The Greefswald sequence: Bambandyanalo and Mapungubwe. *Journal of African History* 5(3):337–361.
1967 *Iron Age cultures in Zambia*, volume one, London: Chatto and Windus.
1971 Personal communication.

FAGAN, BRIAN, D. W. PHILLIPSON, S. G. H. DANIELS
1969 *Iron Age cultures in Zambia*, volume two. London: Chatto and Windus.

FAGG, B. E. B.
1956 The Nok culture. *West African Review* 27:1083–1087.
1959 The Nok culture in prehistory. *Journal of the Historical Society of Nigeria* 1(4):288–293.
1965 Carbon dates for Nigeria. *Man* 65:22–23.

FARIS, D. G.
1963 "Evidence for the West African origin of *Vigna sinensis* (L.) Savi." Unpublished doctoral dissertation, University of California.

FILIPOWIAK, W., S. JASNOSZ, R. WOLAGIEWICS
1968 Polskogwinejskie badaria archaeologiczne w Niani w 1968 r (Les recherches archéologiques polonoguinéennes à Niani en 1968). *Materiaty Zachodniopomorskie* 14:575–648.

FLANNERY, KENT
1965 The ecology of early food production in Mesopotamia. *Science* 147:1247–1255.
1969 "Origins and ecological effects of early domestication in Iran and the Near East," in *The domestication and exploitation of plants and animals*. Edited by P. J. Ucko and G. W. Dimbleby, 72–100. London: Duckworth.

FLIGHT, COLIN
1970 Excavations at Kintampo. *West African Archaeological Newsletter* 12:71–73.

FORDE, DARYLL
1953 The cultural map of West Africa: successive adaptations to tropical forests and grasslands. *Transactions of the New York Academy of Sciences*, Series II, 15(5):206–219.

FOUCHÉ, LEO, *editor*
1937 *Mapungubwe*. Cambridge: Cambridge University Press.

FRIEDEL, M. C.
1897 Sur des matières grasses trouvées dans les tombes egyptiennes d'Abydos. *C. R. Acad. Sci.* 124:648–653.

GABEL, CREIGHTON
1960 Seminar on economic types in pre-urban cultures of temperate woodland, arid and tropical areas. *Current Anthropology* 1:437–438.

GAHERTY, GEOFFREY
   1968   The human skeleton from Rop rockshelter. *West African Archaeological Newsletter* 9:18–19.

GARDNER, GUY A.
   1963   *Mapungubwe,* volume two. Pretoria.

GORMAN, CHESTER
   1969   Hoabinhian: a pebble-tool complex with early plant associations in southeast Asia. *Proceedings of the Prehistoric Society* 35:355–358.

GRAY, RICHARD
   1962   A report on the conference. Third Conference on African History and Archaeology. *Journal of African History* 3(2):175–191.

GREENBERG, J. H.
   1955   *Studies in African linguistic classification.* New Haven.

GRUNDEMAN, TULLI
   1968   Wenner-Gren conference on Bantu origins. *Bulletin of the African Studies Association of the United Kingdom* 13:1–9.

GUERS, J.
   1970   Palynologie africaine X. *Bull. de l'I.F.A.N.* 32(A):312–365.

GUINET, P. H.
   1968   Palynologie africaine VIII. *Bull. de l'I.F.A.N.* 30(A):Pls. 151–166.

GUTHRIE, MALCOLM
   1962   Some developments in the prehistory of the Bantu languages. *Journal of African History* 3:273–282.

HARLAN, JACK R.
   1969   Ethiopia: a centre of diversity. *Economic Botany* 23(4):309–314.
   1971a Personal communication.
   1971b Agricultural origins: centers and noncenters. *Science* 174:468–474.

HARLAN, JACK R., J. M. J. DE WET
   1973   "On the quality of the evidence for origin and dispersal of cultivated plants." *Current Anthropology* 14(1–2): 51–62.

HARRIS, DAVID R.
   1971   "The prehistory of tropical agriculture: an ethnoecological model." Paper presented to the Research Seminar on Archaeology and Related Subjects, Shefffield, December, 1971. (Mimeographed.)
   1972   The origins of agriculture in the tropics. *American Scientist* 60(2): 180–193.

HARTLEY, C. W. S.
   1967   *The oil palm.* London: Longmans.

HELBAEK, H.
   1955   Ancient Egyptian wheats. *Proceedings of the Prehistoric Society* 21:93–95.

HEMARDINQUER, JEAN-JACQUES, MICHAEL KENT, W. C. L. RANDLES
   1967   *Sorgho. Documentation géographique et historique.* Paris: Centre de Recherches Historiques de l'Ecole Pratique des Hautes Etudes.

HEPPER, F. N.
   1963   The Bambara groundnut (*Voandzeia subterranea*) and Kersting's groundnut (*Kerstingiella geocarpa*) wild in West Africa. *Kew Bulletin* 16(3):395–407.

HIERNAUX, JEAN
1968 Bantu expansion: the evidence from physical anthropology confronted with linguistic and archaeological evidence. *Journal of African History* 9(4):505–515.

HIGGS, E. S., M. R. JARMAN
1969 The origins of agriculture: a reconsideration. *Antiquity* 43(169): 31–41.

HO, P. T.
1969 The loess and the origin of Chinese agriculture. *American Historical Review* 75:1–36.

HOBLER, PHILIP M., JAMES J. HESTER
1969 Prehistory and environment in the Libyan Desert. *South African Archaeological Bulletin* 33:120–130.

HUFFMAN, THOMAS N.
1970 The Early Iron Age and the spread of the Bantu. *South African Archaeological Bulletin* 25(1):3–21.

HUGOT, H. J.
1963 *Recherches préhistoriques dans l'Ahaggar nord-occidental 1950– 1957.* Mémoires du CRAPE 1. Arts et Métiers Graphiques. Paris: Flammarion.
1968 The origins of agriculture: Sahara. *Current Anthropology* 9(5): 483–488.

HUTCHINSON, SIR JOSEPH, *editor*
1965 *Essays in crop plan evolution.* Cambridge: Cambridge University Press.

JACKSON, G.
1970 Personal communication.

JARMAN, H. N., A. J. LEGGE, J. A. CHARLES
1972 "Retrieval of plant remains from archaeological sites by froth flotation," in *Papers in economic prehistory.* Edited by E. S. Higgs. Cambridge: Cambridge University Press.

JOHNSTON, SIR H. H.
1913 A survey of the ethnography of Africa: and the former racial and tribal migrations in that continent. *Journal of the Royal Anthropology Institute* 43:375–421.

KAISER, W.
1957 Zur inneren Chronologie der Naqadakultur. *Archaeologia Geographica* 6:69–77.

KENNEDY-O'BYRNE, J.
1957 Notes on African grasses XXIX — a new species of *Eleusine* from tropical and South Africa. *Kew Bulletin* 11:65–72.

LAL, B. B.
1963 The only Asian expedition in threatened Nubia, work by an Indian mission at Afyeh and Tumas. *Illustrated London News.* 242: 579–581.

LAURENT-TACKHOLM, V.
1951 The plants of Naqada. *Annales du Service des Antiquités de l'Egypte* 51:299–312.

LAWTON, J. R. S.
  1966   Personal communication.
LEAKEY, M. D.
  1943   Notes on the ground and polished stone axes of East Africa. *Journal of the East Africa and Uganda Natural History Society* 17(3 and 4):182–195.
  1966   Excavation of burial mounds in Ngorongoro crater. *Tanzania Notes and Records* 66:123–135.
LEAKEY, M. D., L. S. B. LEAKEY
  1960   *Excavations at the Njoro river cave.* Oxford: Oxford University Press.
LEBEUF, A. M. D.
  1969   *Les principautés Kotoko.* Paris: CNRS.
LINARES DE SAPIR, OLGA
  1971   Shell middens of Lower Casamance and problems of Diola proto-history. *West African Journal of Archaeology* 1:23–54.
LIVINGSTONE, D. A.
  1964   Post-glacial and post-pluvial profiles from tropical Africa. *Abstracts of the 10th International Botanical Congress.* Edinburgh.
LIVINGSTONE, D. A., R. L. KENDALL
  1969   Stratigraphic studies of East African lakes. *Mitt. Internat. Verein. Limnol.* 17:147–153.
LIVINGSTONE, FRANK B.
  1958   Anthropological implications of sickle cell gene distribution in West Africa. *American Anthropologist* 60:533–562.
LOBREAU, D., J. GUERS, P. ASSEMIEN, G. BOU, P. H. GUINET, L. POTIER
  1969   Palynologie africaine IX. *Bull. de l'I.F.A.N.* 31(A):411–460, pls. 167–190.
MC BURNEY, C. B. M.
  1967   *The Haua Fteah.* Cambridge: Cambridge University Press.
MAC NEISH, R. S.
  1965   The origins of American agriculture. *Antiquity* 39:87–94.
MALEY, J.
  1970   Contribution à l'étude du bassin tchadien. Atlas du pollens du Tchad. *Bull. Jard. Bot. Nat. Belgique* 40(1):29–48.
MARSHALL, SIR. J.
  1931   *Mohenjo-Daro and the Indus Valley civilisation.* London: Probst-hain.
MASON, R. J.
  1967   Prehistory as a science of change. *Occ. Pap. Archaeol. Res. Unit. Univ. Wit.* 1.
  1971   Personal communication.
MAUNY, RAYMOND
  1953   Notes historiques autour des principales plantes cultivées d'Afrique occidentale. *Bull de l'I.F.A.N.* 15(2):684–730.
  1967   "L'Afrique et les orgines de la domestication," in *Background to evolution in Africa.* Edited by W. W. Bishop and J. Desmond Clark, 583–599. Chicago: University of Chicago Press.

MEHRA, K. L.
1962 Natural hybridization between *Eleusine coracana* and *E. africana* in Uganda. *Journal of the Indian Botanical Society* 41(4):531–539.
1963a Consideration on the African origin of *Eleusine coracana* (L) Gaertn. *Current Science:* 7:300–301.
1963b Differentiation of the cultivated and wild *Eleusine* species. *Phyton* 20(2):189–198.

MEIGHAN, C. W., D. M. PRENDERGAST, B. K. SWARTZ, JR., M. D. WISSLER
1958 Ecological interpretation in archaeology, part two. *American Antiquity* 24:131–150.

MEUNIER, J.
1969 Etude des populations naturelles d'*Elaeis guineensis* en Côte d'Ivoire. *Oléagineux* 24(4):195–201.
1972 Personal communication.

MIÈGE, J.
1965 L'appui de la palynologie dans la distinction des espèces africaines de *Dioscorea. Webbia* 19:491.

MORGAN, W. B.
1962 The forest and agriculture in West Africa. *Journal of African History* 3(2):235–239.

MUNSON, PATRICK J.
1968 Recent archaeological research in the Dhar Tichitt region of south-central Mauretania. *West African Archaeological Newsletter* 10:6–13.
1970 Corrections and additional comments concerning the "Tichitt Tradition." *West African Archaeological Newsletter* 12:47–48.

MURDOCK, G. P.
1959 *Africa: its peoples and their culture history*. New York: McGraw-Hill.

NEUSTUPNY, EVZEN
1970 A new epoch in radiocarbon dating. *Antiquity* 44(173):38–45.

OKIY, G. E. C.
1960 Indigenous Nigerian food-plants. *Journal of the West African Science Association* 6(2):117–121.

OLIVER, ROLAND
1966a Bantu genesis. *African Affairs* 65:245–258.
1966b The problem of the Bantu expansion. *Journal of African History* 7(3):361–377.

OLSSON, INGRID U., *editor*
1971 *Radiocarbon variations and absolute chronology*. New York: John Wiley and Sons.

ONWUEJEOGWU, M. A.
1971 The culture history of an Anambra civilisation: Nri culture. *African Notes*. Ibadan.

OWEN, J.
1968 Water storage properties of *Adansonia digitata* (Baobab). *West African Archaeological Newsletter* 9:55–56.

1970   The medico-social and cultural significance of *Adansonia digitata* (Baobab) in African communities. *African Notes* 6(1):24–36. Ibadan.

PEET, T. ERIC, W. L. S. LOAT
1913   *The cemeteries of Abydos*, part three. London: H. Milford.

PHILLIPSON, D. W.
1968   The early Iron Age site at Kapwirimbwe, Lusaka. *Azania* 3:87–105.
1970   Notes on the late prehistoric radiocarbon chronology of eastern southern Africa. *Journal of African History* 11(1):1–5.

PHILLIPSON, D. W., BRIAN FAGAN
1969   The date of the Ingombe Ilede burials. *Journal of African History* 10(2)L 199–204.

PORTÈRES, ROLAND
1951   *Eleusine coracana* Gaertner. *Bull. de l'I.F.A.N.* 13:1–78.
1962   Berceaux agricoles primaires sur le continent africain. *Journal of African History* 3(2):195–210.

POSNANSKY, M.
1968   Bantu genesis — archaeological reflexions. *Journal of African History* 9(1):1–11.
1969   Yams and the origins of West African agriculture. *Odu* 1:101–107.

QUEZEL, P.
1960   Flore et palynologie sahariennes. *Bull. de l'I.F.A.N.* 22(A):353–360.

QUEZEL, P., C. MARTINEZ
1958   Étude palynologique de deux diatomites du Borkou. *Bull. Soc. Hist. Nat. Afrique Nord* 49:230–244.
1961   Le dernier interpluvial au Sahara central. Essai de chronologie palynologique et paléoclimatique. *Libyca* 6/7:211–227.
1962   "Premiers résultats de l'analyse palynologique de sédiments recuillis au Sahara méridional à l'occasion de la Mission Berliet Ténéré Tchad," in *Missions Berliet Ténéré-Tchad*. Edited by H. J. Hugot, 313–327. Arts et Métiers Graphiques. Paris: Flammarion.

RACHIE, K. O.
1971   Personal communication.

RAYMOND, W. D.
1961   The oil palm industry. *Tropical Science* 3:69–89.

REDHEAD, J. F.
1971   Personal communication.

REED, CHARLES A.
1966   Interpretation of the radiocarbon determinations. *Postilla* 102:42–46.

ROBINSON, K. R.
1966   A preliminary report on the recent archaeology of Ngonde, northern Malawi. *Journal of African History* 7(2):169–188.
1970   *The Iron Age of the southern lake area of Malawi*. Publication 8, Department of Antiquities of Malawi.

ROBINSON, K. R., B. SANDELOWSKY
1968   The Iron Age of northern Malawi: recent work. *Azania* 3:107–146.

SASSOON, HAMO
1967   New views on Engaruka, northern Tanzania. *Journal of African History* 7(2):201–217.
1968a Excavation of a burial mound in Ngorongoro Crater. *Tanzania Zamani* 3:2.
1968b Excavation of a burial mound in Ngorongoro Crater. *Tanzania Notes and Records* 69:15–32.
1971   Excavations at Engaruka, an Iron Age archaeological site in Tanzania. *National Geographic Society Research Reports. 1965 Projects*, 221–230.

SAUER, CARL O.
1952   *Agricultural origins and dispersals.* New York: American Geographical Society.

SEDDON, DAVID
1968   The origins and development of agriculture in East and southern Africa. *Current Anthropology* 9(5):489–494.
1969   Comment on "On early evidence of agriculture in southern Zambia" by J. O. Vogel. *Current Anthropology* 10(5):524–525.

SHACK, WILLIAM A.
1966   *The Gurage. A people of the Ensete culture.* London: Oxford University Press.

SHAW, THURSTAN
1964   Field research in Nigerian archaeology. *Journal of the Historical Society of Nigeria* 2(4):449–464.
1968   Commen on "Origins of African agriculture" by O. Davies, H. Hugot, and D. Seddon. *Current Anthropology* 9(5):500–501.
1969a On radiocarbon chronology of the Iron Age in sub-Saharan Africa. *Current Anthropology* 10(2–3):226–231.
1969b The late Stone Age in the Nigerian forest. *Actes du Premier Collogue International d'Archéologie Africaine* 364–373. Fort Lamy.

SIMMONDS, N. W.
1959   *Bananas.* London: Longmans.
1962   *The evolution of the bananas.* London: Longmans.

SIMOONS, FREDERICK J.
1965   Some questions on the economic prehistory of Ethiopia. *Journal of African History* 6(1):1–12.

SMITH, F. G.
1964   Some pollen grains in the Caesalpinaceae of East Africa. *Pollen et Spores* 6(1):85–98.

SOLHEIM II, WILHELM G.
1969   Reworking southeast Asian prehistory. *Paideuma* 15:125–139.

SOWUNMI, M. A.
1968   Pollen morphology in the Palmae, with special reference to trends in aperture development. *Rev. Paleobotanique et Palynologie* 7:45–53.

STRUEVER, STUART
1968   Flotation techniques for the recovery of small-scale archaeological remains. *American Antiquity* 33(3):353–362.

STUIVER, MINZE, HANS E. SUESS
1966   On the relationship between radiocarbon dates and true sample ages. *Radiocarbon* 8:534–540.

SUMMERS, R.
1958   *Inyanga*. Cambridge: Cambridge University Press.
1969   Personal communication.

SWART, E. R.
1963   Age of the baobab tree. *Nature* 198:708.

UCKO, P. J., G. W. DIMBLEBY *editors*
1969   *The domestication and exploitation of plants and animals*. London: Duckworth.

VAN CAMPO, M.
1957   Palynologie africaine I. *Bull. de l'I.F.A.N.* 19(A):659–678.
1958   Palynologie africaine II. *Bull. de l'I.F.A.N.* 20(A):753–760.
1960   Palynologie africaine IV. *Bull. de l'I.F.A.N.* 22(A):1165–1199.

VAN CAMPO, M. L. BERTHRAND, F. BRONCKERS, B. DE KEYSER, PH. GUINET, F. ROLAND-HEYDACKER
1964   Palynologie africaine V. *Bull. de l'I.F.A.N.* 26(A):1037–1070.

VAN CAMPO, M., F. BRONCKERS, P. GUINET
1965   Palynologie africaine VII. *Bull. de l'I.F.A.N.* 27(A):795–842.

VAN CAMPO, M., R. COQUE
1960   Palynologie et géomorphologie dans le sud tunisien. *Pollen et Spores* 2:275–284.

VAN CAMPO, M., NICOLAS HALLE
1959   Palynologie africaine III. *Bull. de l'I.F.A.N.* 21(A):808–899.

VAN DER MERWE, N. J.
1971   Personal communication.

VAN MEER, P. P. C.
1971   Personal communication.

VAN NOTEN, FRANCIS
1968   *The Uelian. A culture with a neolithic aspect, Uele — Basin (N.E. Congo Republic)*. Tervuren.
1969   A ground axe from Burundi. *Azania* 4:166–167.
1971   Personal communication.

VANSINA, J.
1970   Personal communication.

VAN ZINDEREN BAKKER, E. M.
1965–1969   *Palaeoecology of Africa* 1–5. Cape Town.
1967a   "Upper Pleistocene and Holocene stratigraphy and ecology on the basis of vegetation changes in sub-Saharan Africa," in *Background to evolution in Africa*. Edited by W. W. Bishop and J. D. Clark, 125–146. Chicago: University of Chicago Press.
1967b   "Palynology and stratigraphy in sub-Saharan Africa," in *Background to evolution in Africa*. Edited by Walter W. Bishop and J. Desmond Clark, 371–374, Chicago: University of Chicago Press.

VAVILOV, H.
1951   The origin, variation, immunity and breeding of cultivated plants. *Chronica Botanica* 13(1949–1950):1–364.

VERIN, P.
1966   L'Archéologie à Madagascar. *Azania* 1:119–137.

VISHNU-MITTRE
1968   Protohistoric records of agriculture in India. *Transactions of the Bose Research Institute* 31(3):87–106.

VOGEL, JOSEPH O.
1969   On early evidence of agriculture in southern Zambia. *Current Anthropology* 10(5):524.
1970   Early Iron Age tools from Chundu Farm, Zambia. *Azania*. 5:173–178.
1971   Personal communication.

WATT, G.
1893   *Dictionary of the economic products of India.* London and Calcutta: W. H. Allen.

WENDORF, FRED
1968   "Summary of Nubian prehistory," in *The prehistory of Nubia*, volume 2. Edited by F. Wendorf, 1041–1059. Dallas: Southern Methodist University Press.

WENDORF, F., R. SAID, R. SCHILD
1970   Egyptian prehistory: some new concepts. *Science* 169:1161–1171.
1971   Personal communication.

WERTH, E.
1937   Zur Geographie und Geschichte der Hirsen. *Angewandte Botanik* 19:42–88.

WEST, R. G., C. N. B. MC BURNEY
1954   The Quaternary deposits at Hoxne, Suffolk, and their archaeology. *Proceedings of the Prehistorical Society* 20(2):131–154.

WIESENFELD, STEPHEN L.
1967   Sickle-cell trait in human and cultural evolution. *Science* 157: 1134–1140.
1968   African agricultural patterns and the sickle cell. *Science* 160:1475.

WILLIAMSON, KAY
1970   Some food plant names in the Niger Delta. *International Journal of American Linguistics* 36:156–167.

WRIGHT, GARY A.
1971   Origins of food production in southwestern Asia: a survey of ideas. *Current Anthropology* 12(4–5):447–477.

WRIGLEY, CHRISTOPHER
1960   Speculations on the economic prehistory of Africa. *Journal of African History* 1(2):189–193.

YARNELL, RICHARD A.
1968   Comment on "Origins of African agriculture" by O. Davies, H. Hugot, and D. Seddon. *Current Anthropology* 9(5):502.

Early Food Production in Northern Africa as Seen from Southwestern Asia

PHILIP E. L. SMITH

I interpret the purpose of this volume in the broadest sense as involving the origins not simply of the plants that were indigenously domesticated in Africa, but also of those early cultigens that were not native to Africa but became important after their introduction to the continent. This interpretation allows me to discuss northern Africa, including the Sahara and the lower Nile Valley, with an easier mind; otherwise, it must be admitted, a prehistorian dealing with this region would at the present time have few concrete data to contribute to the discussion.

The theme of this paper is the relationship of the early agriculture of northern Africa to that of southwestern Asia and, by inference, the Mediterranean world. I do not attempt to deal with the relations between northern Africa and the regions south of the Sahara because of my lack of familiarity with the latter areas. These relations have already been well summarized by Clark (1967, 1970, this volume). I have written from the perspective of a prehistorian whose fieldwork in recent years has been divided between the late Paleolithic of the Nile Valley in Egypt and the early village and food-producing cultures of southwestern Asia, especially of Iran. From this vantage point it may be helpful to examine the problems of early food production, and particularly the early cultigens, of northern Africa from a somewhat different perspective than that of a pure Africanist. There does, after all, seem to be a strong though not unanimous feeling among prehistorians working in northern Africa that much or perhaps even all of the "Neolithic" of the region was inspired in one way or another by that of southwestern Asia. In addition, many of the concepts used to characterize or define the Neolithic of northern Africa have been borrowed from those developed for the most part in southwestern Asia — at least insofar as those archaeologists who consider food production to be the hallmark of Neolithic life are concerned. But some of the concepts developed in southwestern Asia have been changing under the stimulus of research carried out in recent years, especially in the last decade or so. With this in mind, this may be a good opportunity to look at northern Africa from the outside and to see whether this perspective I have spoken of provides any new or useful insights into the problems treated in this volume. When compared with southwestern Asia, it is evident that we know relatively little about the origins of the plant and animal domesticates that were used in prehistoric northern Africa, nor about their cultural contexts and the nature of the human societies that were based to various degrees on these domesticates. In southwestern Asia we have learned a great deal since World War II, thanks to intensive collaboration between archaeologists and natural scientists, and we have also become aware of some of the fallacies in our previous thinking. Perhaps in northern Africa we might keep some of these errors in mind in order to avoid repeating them.

A prehistorian from another region who examines the present status of the Neolithic in northern Africa is bound to be struck by a number of weaknesses in the approaches typically used in the past, and by the near-absence of certain kinds of essential information. The poor quality of many of the older excavations, and the resulting low confidence that can be placed on the results, are misfortunes that are of course not restricted to northern Africa; many of the former investigations in southwestern Asia are also nearly useless to us today. More peculiar is the almost complete absence of reliable paleobotanical and paleozoological studies of archaeologically recovered materials. Very few attempts have been made to study the faunal remains of the possible domesticates along the lines developed by Perkins, Flannery, Ducos, Lawrence, Reed and others in southwestern Asia; Higgs' analysis of the Haua Fteah remains from Cyrenaica (McBurney 1967) is exceptional in northern Africa. Where plant foods are concerned, there is very little solid evidence in the form of carbonized seeds, impressions on mud and pottery, pollen, and so on except for Egypt and, most recently, Mauretania. The rock art gives no real clues about the use of plant foods in spite of some claims for depictions of cultivation in the Sahara (Lhote 1958; but see Monod 1963: 186); this is in sharp contrast to the information the rock art has yielded about the status of animal domestication in the Sahara. One is also struck by the enormous emphasis traditionally placed, particularly in the Sahara and the Maghreb, on artifact classification and on the chronological ordering of sites, as contrasted with the low level of interest by the archaeologists in such aspects as settlement patterning and internal community structuring. More important, there seems to have been little expression of interest by most prehistorians in the principles of ecological adaptations, i.e. how man utilized the landscape and resources and accommodated his technology to the exploitation of the local environments. It is very uncommon to find much attention given to such matters as the nature of the floral and faunal remains apart from their roles as climatic indicators. There have been few attempts to estimate the prehistoric demography as reflected in the archaeological sites, or to calculate the carrying capacities of given zones through time. Similarly, little interest is expressed in the food values (proteins and calories) which are suggested by the remains of vertebrates and mollusks found in abundance in many of the sites, although such analyses have often yielded interesting results in other parts of the world. The problem of seasonality of site or regional occupations, and the complementarity of sites with regard to the variation in food resources of a region, have been virtually ignored. The kinds of intensive studies of restricted zones through time using a multidisciplinary approach such as Braidwood and others pioneered in southwestern Asia are all but unknown (Braidwood and Howe 1960). Finally, the near-absence of explicitly formulated theoretical frameworks has undoubtedly been operative in holding back an understanding of the nature of early cultivation and domestication in northern Africa. The archaeological models of change and adaptation used in the past have been extremely simplistic ones usually based on rather naïve concepts of diffusion of traits, on vague centrifugal or centripetal movements of populations, on the consequences of poorly documented environmental and especially climatic changes, and on preconceived notions of "retardation" with respect to other regions. Another problem concerns the definition of archaeological units — the "cultures" or civilizations, industries, traditions, and so forth; the confusion caused by the creation of such vaguely defined groupings as the Neolithic of Capsian Tradition and the Neolithic of Sudanese Tradition is a result of this kind of thinking. It is true that there have been attempts to define more localized Neolithic cultures, for example Camps-Fabrer (1966), but there is little consistency in the taxonomy used and one can even suggest that efforts like these, whether in northern Africa or in southwestern Asia, are counterproductive today.

Too often, preconceived ideas rather than any real awareness of how human groups behave in situations of stress or abundance have been the implicit basis for archaeological interpretations of the data; the once popular desiccation hypothesis, with its alleged explanation of the development of agriculture in the Nile Valley or in the oases, is one instance of this. Similarly, as long as archaeologists are interested only in grand diffusionary schemes or in establishing cultural zones, very little understanding of the real mechanisms involved will be attained. Archaeological data in northern Africa have been collected, set in chronological and spatial order, and sometimes correlated in rudimentary form with environmental data, but there has been little progress beyond this point. What is needed is a framework or frameworks that will help us form hypotheses against which the data may be examined and that will in some cases lead to an understanding of the processes involved with the problems we wish to tackle. In southwestern Asia, and in other archaeological regions of the world, something like this approach is beginning to emerge and to give good results.

I deliberately choose to avoid a discussion of the validity of the term "Neolithic" as used in northern Africa. After two decades or more of debate, prehistorians working in southwestern Asia seem to have learned to live with the term although admitting the unsatisfactory nature of the expression. Nearly all working in that area consider food production to be the most distinguishing feature of what is termed the Neolithic. The situation is somewhat different in northern Africa, particularly in the Francophone countries, where far more weight is usually given to the presence of certain classes of artifacts (but see Bailloud [1969] for a viewpoint stressing the economic and subsistence aspects of the Neolithic of the Sahara). Certainly it is an internally consistent opinion in purely archaeological terms that food producing is merely one of a number of traits characterizing the Neolithic, and one that is apparently no more significant and perhaps less so than such traits as pottery, polished stone, or bifacially flaked arrowheads (e.g. Camps 1969: 204–205); after all, the preceding Paleolithic cultural stages are traditionally defined by technical and artifactual criteria rather than by criteria based on subsistence activities. Nevertheless, however well the forewarned archaeologist may adapt to this state of affairs, it is bound to be confusing for the unsuspecting specialist from other disciplines when he finds that the existing classification permits a grouping of many non-food-producing sites in the Neolithic and many food producing ones in the Epipaleolithic. This situation is reflected in most of the major syntheses of North African prehistory that have been produced up to now (Balout 1955; Vaufrey 1955, 1969).

SOME RECENT DEVELOPMENTS IN SOUTHWESTERN ASIA

I will touch only briefly on the most important changes that have come about in the thinking of those prehistorians working on the problems of early cultivation and domestication in southwestern Asia. Most readers, whether from prehistory or from other disciplines, will be aware of the extent to which Braidwood's original "hilly flanks" natural-habitat-zone hypothesis has been modified in recent years by its author (Braidwood 1965, 1967). Equally significant is the fact that it has once again become respectable to regard the initial development of food production in the area (or at least that part that is visible in the archaeological record after about 12,000 B.C.) as being linked in some way to the changes in climate and environment documented by Wright (1968) and van Zeist (1969) in the Zagros Mountains of Iran; this does not, however, involve a return to the old "triggering" hypothesis, but indicates a willingness to add one further variable to the study of the problem. The concept of a level of incipient cultivation and domestication, which was never easily defined or demonstrated, has become even more elusive (Braidwood 1965; Flannery 1965); some prefer to abandon entirely what they consider a somewhat deterministic or teleological concept. Indeed, the more or less unilinear sequence of levels or stages in subsistence originally proposed by Braidwood as a heuristic device or model against which to plan fieldwork must now be considerably revised or renovated in the light of recent discoveries, as he insists (Braidwood and Braidwood 1969).

Another point increasingly emphasized in recent years (Flannery 1972; Smith 1972a) is that food production, sedentary life and village life are three variables that are not necessarily interdependent, since any one of the three can exist apart from the others and does in some cases. The linkages between three other old favorites in the traditional definition of the Neolithic — pottery, sedentism, and food production — are still unclear but do not seem to be inevitable or necessarily close ones in southwestern Asia or elsewhere. There is increasing caution in assuming that certain morphological changes in animal remains or in age-sex ratios necessarily demonstrate domestication (for example, see Higgs and Jarman 1969), and this caution may be extended to floral remains. There is some suspicion that the "classical" plant domesticates (wheat and barley) may have played lesser roles in the beginning of food production in southwestern Asia, and that some plants, now considered weeds, may formerly have been important cultigens. In addition, there is a growing awareness that the modern distribution of the wild forms of the present domesticates is not always a completely reliable reflection of their distribution at, say, 10,000 B.C. Food production is increasingly seen as a process that probably had its "origins" not in a particular zone but in a number of zones of southwestern Asia from the Mediterranean coast to at least the highlands of Anatolia, Iraq, and Iran, with some degree of specialization by region in the earlier phases according to the potential domesticates available. In addition, doubts are occasionally expressed as to whether southwestern Asia was, in fact, as important and as early a center for the development of domestication as it has traditionally been considered to be.

Another change that has come about recently is the introduction of more sophisticated or at least more complex explanatory models to replace older ones. The new models are generally based on economic, ecological, and demographic approaches and in some instances utilize concepts borrowed from general systems theory (Hole, Flannery, and Neely 1969). Whatever their ultimate value, these models do succeed better in accommodating, for example, the increasing evidence that various human groups with different subsistence bases and different types of land use coexisted in certain regions, or that a single group performed different subsistence activities under different settlement arrangements according to seasonal or other requirements. There is also increasing affirmation that within given regions the subsistence adaptations were not always in the direction of straightforward intensification of food producing through time but that there may have been cases of "reversion" to forms involving less intensive land use, for example, from partly sedentary cultivation to seminomadic herding (Contenson 1971; Smith, Young, and Cuyler 1972).

In the past archaeologists have probably made their greatest contributions to the study of the origins of man's domesticated food sources by recovering the primary botanical and zoological remains from their sites and by establishing the chronological frameworks and the direction of diffusion through space of the domesticates. Less frequently emphasized, perhaps, are the attempts by archaeologists, geographers, and others to establish the conditions (social, demographic, technological, and ecological) in which we might expect humans to alter their relationships to plants and animals living in "natural" circumstances. It may be useful to discuss northern Africa in the light of the approaches tentatively put forward in southwestern Asia in the last few years.

One such approach stems from the growing realization that the "origins" of the processes lumped under the term "food production" should be sought in situations where the homeostatic relationship between food resources and productivity was changing. This may occur when the human population increases in numbers while natural resources remain unchanged, or when local resources diminish without a corresponding immediate change in human population. Societies may react in various ways when disequilibrium occurs: by emigration; by reduction in group size through the use of internal population control; by predation against neighbors; by the development of new extractive techniques or power sources; by an increase in the work input of food extraction; by an emphasis on food resources that had traditionally been insignificant in the diet; or by the development of more efficient forms of social organization for carrying out subsistence-related activities (Smith 1972b). It is in such contexts, it is suggested, that we should look for the origins of food production and the beginning of what is familiarly called domestication.

It has become almost commonplace among prehistorians interested in explaining the origins of food production in southwestern Asia, and elsewhere, to suggest that the causes might usefully be seen in the context of human population pressure straining against natural food resources. This is certainly not a novel or heretical proposition — Lord Kames had said essentially the same thing in the eighteenth century (Slotkin 1965: 424), and a number of philosophers, geographers, and anthropologists have since made the same observation. In recent years it has been offered as at least part of the explanation for early food production in southwestern Asia (see Binford 1968; Flannery 1969; Wright 1971; Smith, Young, and Cuyler 1972), while Clark (1970: 170; 1971) has made a somewhat similar suggestion in his discussions of the approximations of intensive cereal utilization in the late Paleolithic of the Nile Valley in Upper Egypt and Nubia. The approaches suggested by these authors are not identical, and it is true that sometimes the magic term "population pressure" is used in a vague way without defining clearly how this pressure operates in given situations. Nevertheless, these approaches do seem to clarify some of the events and processes better than the traditional explanatory models have. In general, it is postulated that an increase in human population occurred in southwestern Asia in the early Holocene or late Pleistocene, and although the causes of this increase are not agreed on, the presence of abundant supplies of wild grains or aquatic resources (or both) following favorable post-Pleistocene environmental changes is usually offered as part of the explanation. Increased sedentism based on these more plentiful resources may have further accelerated population growth through a closer spacing of births, a higher rate of infant survival, and perhaps lower rates of adult mortality, and disequilibrium ensued. Partly as a means of reducing the work input required in collecting from scattered stands of wild plant foods, land use was intensified by gradually introducing some plants from their natural habitats into others nearer the settlements. Simultaneously, human interference through intensive collecting may have significantly altered the reproductive patterns of the plants. It is in this context of growing demographic pressure that cultivation of certain plants might have come about — on the margins of the optimal growth zones, according to some writers, though this point is debatable. From then on human manipulation would be directed towards progressive restriction of the spectrum of utilized plants in favor of certain species such as pulses, wheats, and barleys. Animal domestication may have paralleled this process, perhaps (Flannery 1969) as a way of diversifying subsistence and reducing risks resulting from crop failures.

Pristine food-producing situations are, in the beginning, probably best seen as regional variants of a whole series of adaptive shifts in subsistence (Adams 1966: 40); from originally insignificant adaptations they gradually became the dominant ones in some regions and tended to eliminate the other forms of adaptation. Southwestern Asia was certainly one such region, and one where important social and economic changes followed very rapidly the establishment of food production as a viable way of life. Regardless of where or when the first food production began — and it may well have occurred in other parts of the world as early as, or perhaps earlier than, in southwestern Asia — the archaeological evidence now available strongly suggests that the first integration of domestic plants and animals to form a peasant complex occurred in the land area between the eastern Mediterranean and the Indus Valley. In many other regions the food-producing adaptation was probably stalled for a much longer time, or even displaced by a renewed emphasis on foraging. Since northern Africa, or at least that part outside the Nile Valley, may be an example of an area that remained at a rudimentary level of food production for many millennia, it is worth asking what factors determined the process in each case. Why, instead of a long-term equilibrium being established in southwestern Asia and elsewhere on the subsistence level sometimes called incipient cultivation and domestication, did food production in these particular regions become increasingly intensive and technologically complex? From the viewpoint of culture history, this is, of course, an even more important question than that of the origins of the domesticates themselves. Indeed, discovering the origins of the animal or plant domesticates no more "explains" the development of societies based on food production than the adoption of ground life by certain early apes explains human locomotion (see Washburn [1968] for a discussion of this last point); in each case we must distinguish between causation and essential prerequisites.

One suggested answer to the question posed above is based on an economic argument and maintains that the types of agricultural land use practiced are intimately related to the supply of labor available (Boserup 1965; Smith 1972b; Smith, Young, and Cuyler 1972). Less intensive types of land use, such as long-fallow cultivation, are more productive per man-hour of work (though not per unit of land) than more intensive forms. Consequently there is normally a resistance to intensification where the work input is considered to be disproportionate to the additional production theoretically possible. (This approach assumes, of course, the absence of a prehistoric work ethic which would value economic labor activity for its own sake.) But increasing population, when it reaches the point of density where the critical carrying capacity of the land is approached with the existing technology, may induce more intensive agriculture through greater investments of work and shorter fallow intervals between crops; the alternatives are a decline in production and living standards, an increase in group mobility, or a reduction in numbers. Changes in agricultural equipment and techniques, such as the adoption of hoes, plows, draught animals, fertilizers, and simple irrigation may also be introduced with the gradual intensification of agriculture. The end result in southwestern Asia, as in some other parts of the world, was highly intensive agriculture in some zones, very complex societies with urban bases, and a gradual transformation of the less intensively organized societies under the influence of the stronger and more centralized ones.

A study of the circumstances in northern Africa may serve as a useful check of this hypothesis, and indeed the data from this area may eventually throw nearly as much light on the economic processes by which food production developed as does the evidence from other areas of the world where more complex societies eventually emerged. In northern Africa (apart, of course, from the Nile Valley in Egypt) the societies apparently did remain at the simple subsistence level for a very long time after food production was known on the continent. In some ways this is reminiscent of the situation in Mesoamerica, where sedentary village life and complex societies did not develop for some five millennia after plant cultivation began.

Why did the typical southwest Asian pattern of development not take place in northern Africa at an early date, and why, even after it became established in Egypt in the fifth millennium B.C., did it not take hold more intensively in other parts of the region? After all, it is tempting to see northern Africa as largely an extension of the lands east of the Mediterranean. Both regions are characterized mainly by winter rainfall regimes and a continuum of climatic zones ranging from very arid to reasonably well-watered. The vegetation patterns are comparable, and both have extensive desert and subdesert areas. At the end of the Pleistocene and in the early Holocene, roughly the same grade of industrial technology and style of lithic artifacts were present among the various hunting-gathering-fishing groups in each region. The human physical types also seem comparable, at least in the Capsian zone of the Maghreb and in the Levant area, suggesting perhaps some degree of gene exchange between the two regions, possibly along the Mediterranean littoral.

Thus one might reasonably expect to see the typical southwest Asian pattern of subsistence, based on food production, with its associated forms of settlement and technology, extended easily and rapidly into northern Africa. But in fact it comes as something of a surprise to note how few close resemblances there are with southwestern Asia, even in the Nile Valley. While southwestern Asia itself is by no means a homogeneous culture area, during the Neolithic, nevertheless, there were some pervading characteristics that seem to link most of it from the Mediterranean to Turkestan. Among these are: the emphasis on wheat, barley, and pulses and on goats, sheep, pigs, and cattle as domesticates; sizeable clusters of buildings that apparently were in many cases sedentary villages; certain architectural forms, especially in the use of rectangular mud-walled, brick-walled, and stone houses; and the frequent use of obsidian and other items which were distributed widely from a few resource centers. Seen from this perspective, northern Africa at first calls to mind some of the areas of southwestern Asia where, for various reasons, certain of the paraphernalia of the food producers were adopted but food production itself, if practiced, was not an important part of the subsistence activity. Examples are the Caspian shorelands, the Negev and Sinai Deserts, and perhaps much of the Iranian plateau and Arabia. But simply to catalogue northern Africa as a "marginal" zone in relation to southwestern Asia (Monod 1963: 209–210) is to beg the question. These "explanations," like such terminology as sub-Neolithic or proto-Neolithic, impede rather than assist understanding. It is more profitable to look at the question of just what food production involves, and then to examine the contexts of the evolution and diffusion of early food production in southwestern Asia itself.

Food production, obviously, is not automatically adopted when non-food producers come into contact with food producers, even when environmental conditions are favorable for agriculture. It is more likely that there is an inherent resistance to such change among peoples who are already reasonably well-off, and a similar reluctance to intensify food production if it is already practiced on a simple level. The reason for this has been suggested earlier in this paper: food producing often (perhaps usually) involves a greater input of labor and energy per unit of production than does foraging.[1] Nor, as Flannery (1969) points out, is it safe to assume that the earliest food producers of southwestern Asia had a more stable or reliable subsistence basis, ate better, or were better nourished than the preceding hunters and gatherers; dry farming in areas of erratic rainfall is highly unpredictable from one year to another. The real economic advantage of food production is that progressively greater applications of labor can extract larger quantities of food per unit of land — at least up to a point which is far beyond the point of diminishing returns in most non-food-producing areas, with the exception of areas with permanent fishing grounds. This is especially true in zones of good cultivable land where intensification of agriculture is possible. In contrast, among most hunters and gatherers, greater work input either does not result in correspondingly greater productivity, or does so on a short-term basis at the risk of seriously depleting the natural resources.

It follows, then, that we should not expect to see elementary food production expand or intensify unless circumstances make it economically necessary or advantageous to the groups concerned. Even in southwestern Asia, there is increasing reason to believe that food production (which can really be identified with certainty only about 7000 B.C. and after) failed to spread in some regions until rather late, and it seems likely that there were cases of reversion to foraging at times. But, as mentioned earlier, one of the strongest forces promoting a shift to cultivation and domestication is the pressure of population on available resources, while continuing pressure of this sort tends to encourage greater intensification of food production and, ultimately, a social and economic commitment to this pattern.

[1]   Lévi-Strauss (1966: 126) has pointed out that "until recently anthropologists have neglected to study the elasticity of the yields of crops and the relationship between yield and the amount of work involved" in spite of its importance for understanding social and other aspects of the societies concerned. Prehistoric archaeologists have also failed to give this point much attention.

It is against this background that we should look at the Holocene events in northern Africa, taking into account three important variables: changes in the physical environment, the effects of increased sedentism, and the roles of work input and relative productivity. It is possible that environmental conditions in this region in early Holocene times changed sufficiently to promote not only a more intense occupation of the region but also a greater degree of sedentism than had been the rule previously. After ca. 9000 B.C. sites are more numerous than in the period of desiccation that went back to ca. 20,000 B.C., when the somewhat infrequent sites of the Aterian represent by and large the equivalent of the Upper Paleolithic elsewhere. The postulated increased sedentism after ca. 9000 B.C. (when the lithic assemblages usually show a technique based on blades) may have been only on a seasonal basis, of course, supported by more adequate resources of food through fishing, hunting, and intensive collecting of wild plants. As long as population pressures remained low, there would be little incentive for the local groups to develop food production or to adopt it even when they were aware of its existence elsewhere. The populations of the Nile Valley, perhaps those of some of the Libyan Desert oases, probably those of some of the lacustrine areas of the central and southern Sahara (the Ténéréen and other groupings), and possibly of the better-watered parts of the Maghreb, come to mind as examples of populations who may have somewhat reduced their mobility and intensified their collecting patterns, although apparently not to the point of requiring mud, brick, or stone dwellings.

The archaeological data available at the present time in northern Africa can be interpreted in a way that supports this hypothesis, although they do not yet demonstrate with any certainty that plant domestication had already occurred. Indeed, perhaps archaeologists have traditionally been focusing on the wrong aspect in studying the events and processes of the periods of early food production, in this region and elsewhere. It may have been sedentism, which theoretically permits larger and more stable communities with more complex forms of social behavior and cultural organization, and not food production *per se* that was the attractive feature of life in certain regions in early post-Pleistocene times and one of the prime movers toward food production (Hawkes 1969; Smith 1972a; also Suttles 1951, for an ethnographic illustration of the significance of sedentism in the adoption of a crop by recent collectors and fishermen). In other words, where a high degree of sedentism could be supported by means other than food production, as seems to have been the case in the Syrian site of Mureybit ca. 8000 B.C. (van Loon, et al. 1968), it probably was; food production may, at the beginning, have been simply a means of conserving the accustomed sedentary pattern, the standard of living, and the "social capital" in the face of increasing difficulties. Where plant domestication did not take place locally in spite of intensive use of wild plant foods, we can suspect that there was no serious disequilibrium between population and resources, or that there was a low degree of sedentism, or that there was a combination of both variables.

This viewpoint enables us to look at some of the available archaeological data and interpretations in a different light. Thus Wendorf (1968) has postulated a reliance on wild plant foods among some late Pleistocene groups in the lower Nile Valley of Nubia and has suggested that the trend toward incipient cultivation was aborted when a climatic change to drier conditions caused the wild grains to become less abundant before a full development of dependence on them was achieved. Hester and Hobler (1969) have offered a similar explanation based on increased desiccation for the disappearance of the supposed "incipient cultivation" of their Libyan Culture in the Libyan Desert ca. 6000 B.C. Even earlier Vignard (1923) had made essentially the same interpretation of the presence of grinding stones in the late Paleolithic Sebilian of Upper Egypt. But perhaps we should see the abandonment of the hypothetical grain foods principally in terms of the apparent absence of any significant degree of community sedentism based on intensive collecting in the Nile Valley and nearby oases at this time; that is, as the wild plants were reduced in their natural habitats under the postulated environmental stresses, there was little incentive to manipulate or encourage them (as we would expect if the classical "desiccation theory" were accepted) in order to conserve a pattern of sedentary or partly sedentary life. Instead, other kinds of adaptation to the new conditions were probably worked out, for groups continued to occupy the banks of the Nile with various degrees of emphasis on hunting and fishing. Just why there was no significant sedentism and no permanently occupied villages in the area at the time (assuming that this is true) is, of course, a different problem, and one which it is not necessary to solve here; perhaps the wild cereals or seeds were too sparse at any time to promote population concentrations or sedentism. Whether there was a similar pattern of exploitation of wild plants in the rest of northern Africa, with the same consequences, is still unknown. We shall come back to this later.

DIFFUSION FROM SOUTHWESTERN ASIA TO NORTHERN AFRICA

Direct movements of food-producing people from southwestern Asia to northern Africa, if they occurred, must almost certainly have taken place via the Sinai Peninsula into northern Egypt. Movement by boat across the southern Red Sea to Egypt is possible but not likely. Unfortunately, we know too little of the prehistory of the Arabian Peninsula (apart from the Persian Gulf area) before ca. 1300 B.C. to reject completely the possibility of diffusion of domesticates to the Horn of Africa at an early date, but the present (largely negative) evidence does not offer much to support this route. A direct route from the general Palestinian region is still the best bet; hence an examination of the early food-producing situation in this region will be helpful in following the argument I offer here.

Sometime between about 9000 B.C. and 8000 B.C., modern ecological conditions were probably established throughout southwestern Asia, and by 7000 B.C. there is satisfactory evidence for domestication of plants and animals and for communities based in part at least on food production. The information before ca. 7000 B.C. is still somewhat sketchy and less reliable, though evidence for some kind of manipulation of reproduction of plants and animals from the ninth millennium or even earlier is to be expected.[2] Einkorn was probably domesticated in southeastern Anatolia, emmer perhaps in the Palestine-Syria area or in the zone from southern Anatolia to northern Iraq, while barley may have been domesticated anywhere in the less humid regions of the Fertile Crescent belt (Zohary 1969). By about 7000 B.C. at Jericho and Beidha in Jordan, einkorn and emmer were apparently domesticated, and perhaps other cereals as well (Renfrew 1969). These two sites are roughly 400 kilometers from the Nile Valley and one might, in all good faith, expect an overflow into Africa about this time, particularly if we agree that seed agriculture, especially under long-fallow conditions, is unstable and expansive (Harris 1972, this volume). But in

---

[2]   Probably the sheep at Zawi Chemi Shanidar, northern Iraq, dating to approximately 8700 B.C., represent the earliest indication of control in the direction of domestication known so far in southwestern Asia (Perkins 1964); not all specialists have accepted this evidence, however. Recent unofficial reports mention the discovery of cereal grains in the Zarzian of the Zagros mountains of Iraq, presumably dating to somewhere between ca. 10,000 B.C. and 20,000 B.C. Cereals are also reported from excavations in the late Paleolithic Kebaran at Nahal Oren, Israel, and wheat may be involved although it is not yet clear whether it can be considered "domesticated" or wild (T. Noy, personal communication).

fact there is no good evidence of such a rapid expansion into Africa. So far we have no archaeological indication of southwest Asian domesticates before the sheep or goats at Haua Fteah in Cyrenaica dated ca. 4800 B.C. (Higgs, in McBurney 1967) or even later, around 4500 B.C. to 4000 B.C. in the form of domesticated emmer and barley in Fayum A sites of Lower Egypt (Caton-Thompson and Gardner 1934; Wendorf, et al. 1970). It seems that the southwest Asian domesticates took nearly as long to reach Egypt as to diffuse to Britain.

Perhaps this lag is not so surprising when we look at the situation more closely. The adjacent region in southwestern Asia (Palestine and perhaps southern Syria) was not itself highly developed agriculturally between the eighth and fifth millennia, possibly, in part, because the suggested rich resources of wild cereals described by Zohary (1969) and others restrained the spread of more intensive cultivation (see also Perrot 1968); in the Upper Jordan basin of Israel, where today wild wheat and barley grow in abundance, no agriculture can be demonstrated with certainty before the fifth millennium. In Palestine there may also have been a heavy reliance on deer and gazelles and a special economic relationship with these species (Vita-Finzi and Higgs 1970). The apparent absence of efforts towards cultivation suggests that population pressure on resources was low; therefore, migration of food producers in need of agricultural land into northern Africa, whether through Palestine or via the Transjordanian plateau to the Red Sea, was unimportant until a late date.[3] Another factor to consider is that in semiarid Palestine between ca. 6000 and 4500 B.C. there may have been a partial hiatus in occupation when many sites were abandoned (Mellaart 1967); if this was due to increasing desiccation interacting with the low physical relief of the area, as some writers think (Perrot 1968), then the movement across several hundred kilometers of semi-desert or desert terrain into northern Egypt and northern Africa (which were apparently experiencing a phase of hyperarid climate during at least part of this time) might have faced further obstacles.[4] At any

[3] Direct evidence of movement from southwestern Asia into Egypt is rare, and the Sinai and Negev Deserts offer no archaeological indications so far. However, some of the arrowheads found on the surface in the Fayum by Caton-Thompson and Gardner (1934: I, 22; II, Plate 51) suggest that there may have been links with the "Tahunian" (roughly, the pre-pottery Neolithic) of Palestine, possibly between 7500 and 6000 B.C. But movement into Egypt by food collectors and hunters at this time and earlier in the Holocene is quite probable, and this may explain the "Natufian" of Helwan near Cairo. The delta would probably have been capable of absorbing many newcomers, especially fishermen, who may have been displaced from Palestine by the increasing population postulated there.

[4] But not all prehistorians accept Perrot's argument for an important hiatus in the

rate, the first known Egyptian sites possessing domesticated cereals of southwest Asian type seem to occur at almost precisely the moment one would expect if an eastern origin is postulated, that is, after about 5000 B.C. when at least Upper Egypt and Nubia enjoyed somewhat less arid conditions. Possibly, as Clark (1971) suggests, there was already a Nilotic preadaptation in the general direction of domestication using local plant and animal resources, but this is not yet clear. The earliest that have been dated so far are the Fayum A sites in the depression west of Cairo and the site of basal Merimde on the edge of the delta, dated to the last half of the fifth millennium or slightly later. However, it is quite possible even earlier food-producing sites with southwest Asian domesticates will be found in the first half of that millennium. The Fayum A people evidently cultivated wheat and barley, but the status of the sheep and goat remains found there is uncertain; however, the chances are that they were domesticated. Both the Fayum A sites and Merimde probably reflect the local development or modification of the southwest Asian pattern of an economy based on animal and cereal cultivation. The Fayum A sites seem to lack solid architecture, however, while at Merimde only the bases of the walls of the village were built of mud; the upper parts of the houses may have been built of less permanent materials, like those of the closely succeeding Badarian groups in Upper Egypt. In other words, the typical southwest Asian architectural techniques were not taken over completely.

Seen from southwestern Asia, the late diffusion of food production out of that region into northeastern Africa is, thus, quite understandable. It is a mistake to consider southwestern Asia during early Holocene times as a cornucopia poised at the entrance to Africa and overflowing with food producers and domesticates; an intermittently leaky faucet might be a better metaphor. This interpretation suggests, in addition, that in spite of the views of many prehistorians including

---

occupation of Palestine, arguing that some of the ceramic phases that Perrot would place after 5000 B.C. are actually older. Whether the hiatus can be demonstrated or not, the evidence for more severe climatic conditions is convincing (see Servant, et al. 1969; van Zinderen Bakker, this volume; Butzer 1971) since the data from Upper Egypt and Nubia are probably applicable to Lower Egypt as well. In passing, one wonders what influence the climatic conditions might have had on linguistic groups in Africa and southwestern Asia. Greenberg has been quoted (Trigger 1968: 74) as suggesting that the original separation of the Afroasiatic languages may have occurred in the period between 6000 and 5500 B.C. Perhaps before ca. 6000 B.C. there was continuity between the two regions, and the break in contact may have led to the divergence of ancient Egyptian and the Semitic languages (e.g. Akkadian) of Asia.

Vaufrey (1969), Balout (1955), Mauny (1967), and Clark (1967), we should not look, after all, with too much expectancy towards the Neolithic and Predynastic of Egypt and the lower Nile Valley as the sources of the early plant domestication postulated in the Sahara and in the Maghreb. For one thing, the cultigens and perhaps the idea of domestication and cultivation may have arrived too recently in Egypt, probably not long before 4500 B.C. For another, the availability of good soils in the valley combined with the rich natural riverine resources may have slowed down the tendency towards intensification of local agriculture and so absorbed much of the pressures toward diffusion of cultivators westward. The movement of food producers, once the domesticates had been introduced from outside, was probably up the Nile Valley rather than along the Mediterranean fringe or across the Libyan Desert. However, connections between the Sudanese Nile cultures and those of the southern Sahara were probable, judging by the distribution of unburnished dotted wavy-line pottery from Khartoum to the Ahaggar (Arkell 1972).

But it is by no means unlikely that animal and plant domesticates that were ultimately of southwest Asian origin reached the Maghreb, the north African littoral, and even the Sahara without diffusing through northeastern Africa. Recent discoveries of Neolithic settlements in Crete, Corsica, southern France, and the western Mediterranean as early as ca. 6000 to 5000 B.C., as well as radiocarbon determinations from a Neolithic site with impressed pottery in western Algeria ca. 4700 B.C. (Camps 1971; Guilaine and Calvet 1970), suggest that maritime movements of farmers were taking place and that the Maghreb, at least, was in a position to be influenced from centers other than Egypt.[5] Indeed, the Neolithic of Haua Fteah in Cyrenaica, apparently possessing domesticated sheep or goats ca. 4800 B.C., may have been derived from the west (the Maghreb) rather than from the east (McBurney 1967: 310).

INDIGENEOUS DOMESTICATION IN NORTHERN AFRICA?

The question of indigenous domestication of some plants and animals

---

[5] Possibly it was by this mechanism that the *Panicum miliaceum* (proso-millet) which may ultimately be of African origin (Renfrew 1969) reached Greece, where it is believed to occur in the preceramic site of Argissa-Maghula ca. 6000 to 5000 B.C. Its first known occurrence in southwestern Asia is several thousand years later. The Maghrebian agriculture may have been based on barley rather than Wheat, which was first known in Roman times, whereas the Carthaginians already grew barley (Portères, personal communication).

in Africa has been discussed by a number of writers in recent years (e.g., Lhote 1964; Camps 1968). Insofar as northern Africa and plants are concerned, I do not think the archaeological evidence available at present allows any clear resolution of this problem. The main difficulty consists of the curious absence, west of Egypt, of reliable proof of any kind of domesticated plant before the late second millennium B.C., when impressions of millet and other grass seeds occur on the pottery of sites in the Dhar Tichitt region of south-central Mauretania (Munson 1968, 1970, this volume). Earlier than this there seem to be only the suggestions from the Ahaggar of pollen of *Pennisetum* at Amekni between 6100 and 4800 B.C., and of a "cultivated grass" at Meniet in the fourth millennium B.C. (Camps 1969; Hugot 1968). However, this evidence is far from acceptable as it stands at present. The size of pollen grains can be treacherous clues to domestication status, and we cannot be entirely sure that the charcoal at Amekni dates the occupations, rather than being long-lived trees that may have been burned as fuel (see Clark 1971: 54). All examples of carbonized seeds found so far belong to wild forms, particularly of *Celtis*. The indirect evidence, such as milling stones, mortars, and gloss on flint "sickle" blades, is not in itself convincing proof of food production, as prehistorians working in southwestern Asia have learned the hard way.

Nevertheless, in spite of this absence of direct botanical data, I am inclined to believe that if the argument outlined above for the context of early plant cultivation and domestication in general is valid, then an independent origin for some domesticated plants in northern Africa is by no means unlikely. Whether wheat or barley was domesticated from local wild forms is unknown. The ancestry of wild barley, *H. spontaneum,* found today in Cyrenaica seems undecided (Zohary 1969: 54), and there seems to be no known occurrence of wild wheat in spite of Vavilov's claims for emmer in Algeria. But we must remember that more careful work in Neolithic and even Capsian sites in the Maghreb and northern Sahara, particularly in the *ramadiyas* [mounds], using modern flotation techniques, might provide us with some surprises in this respect. The same is true for the Nile Valley, where cereals now found growing wild in more northern latitudes may have been present in the somewhat cooler and moister periods of the late Pleistocene and may have been utilized by some of the Nilotic people. Similarly, in the early Holocene plants now growing only south of Nubia and the Sahara, including sorghum, may have been growing further north.

It is not difficult to suppose that in Holocene times, and probably even earlier, wild grasses and fruits were significant elements in the diets of many hunting, collecting, and fishing groups in northern Africa. With the growth of population in circumscribed areas with generalized natural ecosystems and high diversity of wild species (Harris 1969), there might be efforts to cultivate some of the local plants in order to maintain, at the very least, the traditional standards of living and patterns of settlement. The great numbers of Capsian sites recently surveyed in some parts of the Maghreb, for example, in eastern Algeria south of Tebessa, may reflect a considerable density of population of late hunters-gatherers; in one such area of about 100 square kilometers, at least forty-five new sites were found (D. Grébénart, personal communication), and Vaufrey (1955: 324) reported other high concentrations of Capsian and Neolithic sites. Indeed, Balout has suggested (1955: 431) that the late Capsian groups enjoyed a sedentary life based on plant collecting if not on a rudimentary form of agriculture. While we know relatively little as yet about the precise rainfall and temperature conditions in northern Africa during the earlier Holocene, the reconstructions of Saharan rainfall isohyets for the period after ca. 6000 B.C. offered by Hester and Hobler (1969: Figure 154) are suggestive; see also the summary of van Zinderen Bakker (this volume). It is likely that once cultivation had begun, dry farming was possible in some regions, particularly in the Maghreb; and perhaps mud-flat cultivation and simple irrigation techniques characterized the agriculture near the lakes and streams of the Sahara. This may have taken place without stimulation of any kind from southwestern Asia. It is against this background that we should view the recent claims for the intensive collecting of wild grains in the Nile Valley of Egypt and Nubia in late Pleistocene times (Wendorf, et al. 1970; Clark 1971), for the "incipient cultivation" by floodwater farming of unknown plants in the Libyan Culture at Dungul Oasis west of the Nile in Egypt ca. 6000 B.C. (Hester and Hobler 1969), and for the alleged cultivation of cereals in the Sahara at Amekni and Amiet as well.[6]

---

[6] The suggestion recently made by several writers (e.g. Harlan 1971) that perhaps the early grain-grinding technique of the late Paleolithic Egyptian cultures was exported to southwestern Asia to stimulate the food producing revolution there, and that later the idea of domestication was introduced from Asia to Africa, is an intriguing one. However, it is not yet clear that the grinding stones in the Nile Valley are earlier than those known in southwestern Asia. In the latter region some are known in Upper Paleolithic times although their precise ages are not always certain; but one in Israel is almost unquestionably older than 20,000 B.C. In Europe they are well known in Upper and even in Middle Paleolithic contexts, and they are probably much more numerous than the published reports indicate. It is difficult to accept that the food producing "revolution" of southwestern Asia was dependent on the importation of a technique which is hardly a complex one and

One possibility is that the original emphasis on food production in the Sahara and the Maghreb was on plant foods, including some domesticated local forms, and that animal husbandry was introduced, probably from outside, to reduce the risks and to act as insurance for survival in bad years. Certainly goats, sheep, and pigs are likely to have been northern African imports that were derived from southwestern Asia or Europe; there is less certainty about cattle, for which local domestication from wild forms is a possibility. In any case, domesticated cattle were probably present in the Sahara by the fifth millennium B.C., if not earlier; and domesticated sheep apparently were known in the northern Sahara of Algeria by about 4000 B.C. As aridity increased and plant foods became less abundant, and even the possibilities of wet-farming and fishing decreased with the shrinking of lakes and streams, the emphasis may have shifted to nomadic herding, particularly of cattle, as a means of maintaining an equilibrium between population size and reduced resources. This would agree with the admittedly ambiguous evidence that cultivation was short-lived in the Sahara and soon gave way to a nomadic pastoral economy (Hugot 1968) but it need not mean that cultivation was abandoned entirely. Cultivation may never have gone past the long-fallow stage except in areas where mud-flat agriculture was feasible. Perhaps supplementary is a better adjective than incipient to describe the kind of early cultivation practised in most of northern Africa west of the Nile, and the overall trend in subsistence evolution was from the hunter-cultivator to the herdsman-collector with whom cultivation was a marginal activity.

A tentative reconstruction of the development of food production in northern Africa, which undoubtedly errs grossly on the side of oversimplification, is as follows. An economy based on hunting, fishing, and the cultivation of some still unidentified African plant foods (millet or sorghum?) may be older in the Sahel zone and in the southern Sahara than any food production in the Nile Valley, Cyrenaica or the Maghreb, or in the savanna zone to the south. The priority of this "Neolithic of Sudanese Tradition" is not yet settled. The very early seventh millennium radiocarbon dates need to be verified and the "Neolithic of Capsian Tradition" sites may produce dates that are of comparable

---

which was probably already known in that region. In any case, few prehistorians today would be content to see the causal factors in the development of food production in an exclusively technological framework. A reliance on technological or climatic "triggers" tends to deflect attention from more fundamental aspects of the explanation of prehistoric behavior.

ages (e.g. the sites of Ain Naga in the Maghreb and El Bayed in the Sahara, both apparently in the sixth millennium B.C. [Roubet 1969]). By about 5000 B.C. food producing had become established on the Maghreb littoral in western Algeria and Morocco, perhaps as a result of maritime contacts with the Mediterranean islands and Europe. It may have been in this way that domesticated sheep and cattle were adopted by some Neolithic of Capsian Tradition groups by at least 4000 B.C. Cyrenaica seems to have had some domesticated animals at about the same time. The role of cultivated plants is obscure. Finally, societies that were committed to food production seem to be later developments in Egypt, apparently not until the fifth millennium B.C. and probably (but not certainly) derived directly from southwestern Asia.

CONCLUSIONS

It is clear that many of the interpretations offered here for northern Africa are based on very incomplete or ambiguous archaeological evidence. This reflects, to a large extent, the kind of research orientation that has been the rule in past investigations in this area. More adequate studies of settlements in northern Africa are obviously needed to produce better evidence than is now available for the earlier Holocene. In these investigations a good deal of priority should be given to the question of the periodicity and duration of site occupations, and the matter of the probable density of occupations in relation to the estimated carrying capacities of given regions. This is not an easy task anywhere, but archaeologists in other parts of the world are gradually developing techniques for extracting this kind of information (e.g. Zubrow 1971). In any case, it remains the only way to confirm or invalidate specific interpretations based on general principles such as are offered in this paper.

In this research special attention should be paid to sites containing pottery, for this may have a particular significance. In our zeal in recent years to emphasize that not all food producers had pottery,[7] and

---

[7] I suspect that the division between aceramic and ceramic (or pottery and pre-pottery) Neolithic is less real than many think, at least where southwestern Asia is concerned. In many cases it simply reflects differences in the rate of preservation of the pottery in the sites. Simple or sun-baked vessels can disappear rapidly unless preserved by unusual circumstances such as a conflagration (see Smith [1972c] for a probable instance from Ganj Dareh, Iran). Pottery is now known in some parts of southwestern Asia by 7000 B.C. and very likely goes back even further.

that some nonfood producers did have it, we have perhaps missed the real point. It seems likely that pottery tends to be associated with the kind of living conditions that usually, though not always, accompany agriculture, or the kind of conditions that sometimes lead to the adoption of agriculture. Small quantities of pottery may only indicate that vessels were little needed and may have been obtained from other pottery-making groups in the same region. But where more than small quantities of pottery occur, we can legitimately suspect a degree of sedentary life beyond that of mobile hunters and collectors. (The same argument can of course be made for grinding or pounding stones: small quantities may mean little in indicating plant food utilization or sedentism, but large quantities in a site may be more significant.) Therefore when we find quantities of pottery in an apparently nonfood producing context, several interpretations are available. Food producing may have been present although direct proof is lacking. Or it may mean that the local natural resources were sufficient to maintain some permanency of settlement that required improved methods of storage and food processing. As far as northern Africa is concerned, the significance of the suggestion is this: the presence of pottery provides a hint that something interesting was going on, either by way of contacts between groups with different economic bases, or in situations where a degree of community sedentism made pottery useful. In any case, we should not simply dismiss the presence of pottery as a nonsignificant trait in identifying the mode of subsistence. The existence of pottery in a number of the Saharan and Maghrebian sites by the middle of the sixth millennium B.C. and, possibly, even earlier (Bailloud 1969; Camps 1969; Mori 1965) — that is, about a thousand years earlier than its first known occurrence in the Nile Valley of Nubia and Egypt, if the available radiocarbon determinations are accepted at face value — may further support the hypothesis that food production in the Sahara began earlier than that in the Nile Valley and that the latter region was not, after all, an important contributor to the processes of early food production in the rest of northern Africa.

After the fifth millennium B.C. in Egypt, the southwest Asian pattern of plant domestication replaced the hypothetical earlier one based on the use of local wild plants, if the latter had survived so late. The local pattern of indigenous animal utilization may have lasted longer, until Dynastic times. Perhaps the southwest Asian cereals were better suited to winter rainfall regimes; and possibly, as Braidwood has suggested (1962), it was necessary to await the development in Mesopotamia of cultivated plant strains that would tolerate hot, dry alluvial conditions while still yielding abundant crops. As already mentioned here, there is not much evidence that Egypt was a very important agent for the diffusion westward of this subsistence pattern or of the settlement and architectural forms that usually accompany it in southwestern Asia. It is likely that in the southern Sahara the older, indigenous African pattern continued, where it was not replaced by an emphasis on herding, since these plants were better adapted to conditions of summer rainfall.[8] In the Maghreb and the northern Sahara, we might anticipate a continuation of whatever local plants had been used, a replacement by cultigens from southwestern Asia, or a combination of both adaptations. This reconstruction is thus in agreement with Harlan's concept (1971) of centers and noncenters for plant domestication.

Whether, in fact, there was in northern Africa a cultivation or even an intensive utilization of millets, sorghums, and other local African plants at an early period, as I have supposed here, will no doubt be discovered some day by archaeologists working in this region. From the viewpoint of archaeologists who favor the kind of processual model outlined here and who are currently working on the problems of early plant cultivation and domestication in the relatively well-known region of southwestern Asia, there is nothing at all surprising in the idea of a wholly independent domestication of some plant foods in Africa. On the contrary, in fact, if the basic argument concerning the relationship between productivity and work input is valid in southwestern Asia, it should be applicable to other regions as well.

I doubt that the majority of prehistorians now studying the origins of early food production in southwestern Asia would insist strongly on the priority or the uniqueness of the area. After all, the people most responsible for the diffusionist position which would derive all food production in the Old World from southwestern Asia, such as the proponents of the *ex oriente lux* hypothesis in the last century and Childe in the present one, were not themselves seriously involved in excavating there. The reason that in the past archaeologists and others have placed so much emphasis on the diffusion of agriculture from a single or a very few "centers of origin" is, I believe, not hard to understand. It was based on the assumption that agriculture and food production in general were very complicated forms of adaptation which came about by a lucky set of circumstances or by a rare stroke of insight, and that it was

---

[8] Thus it is significant that no wheat or barley appears among the impressions on the pottery in the Dhar Tichitt sites in Mauretania, even as late as the second and first millennia B.C. (Munson 1968, 1970). The implication is that they were not grown locally and that "African" plants formed the basis of the vegetal diet.

unlikely to be repeated frequently. Hence the emphasis on finding the place or places where the revolution occurred and then plotting the spread through space.

On the other hand, if one starts with a quite different assumption — that food production in an elementary form is a very normal and frequent adaptation under certain circumstances and one that might be expected to occur at many different times and places — then we can put the research emphasis where it belongs: on establishing the conditions under which simple food prouction does and does not originate, and does or does not develop into more complex and intensive forms. Seen in this perspective, the necessity to search for the initial stimulation for African food production outside that continent loses much of its urgency. I do not mean that a good deal of prehistoric African agriculture was not influenced by that of southwestern Asia; I think, in fact, that it was — or at least this is, at the present time, the most economical way of explaining some of the archaeological, botanical, and zoological data in Africa. But my central point is that once we free ourselves of the need to look outside a given region for the stimulus to the earliest steps towards food production, we are also freed from having to face certain false problems.

REFERENCES

ADAMS, ROBERT MC C.
  1966 *The evolution of urban society: early Mesopotamia and pre-Hispanic Mexico*. Chicago: Aldine.
ARKELL, A. J.
  1972 Dotted wavy-line pottery in African prehistory. *Antiquity* 46: 221–222.
BAILLOUD, GÉRALD
  1969 "L'évolution des styles céramiques en Ennedi (République du Tchad)," in *Actes du Premier Colloque International d'Archéologie Africaine, Fort-Lamy, 11-15 Déc. 1966*. Institut National Tchadien pour les Sciences Humaines, Études et Documents Tchadiens, Mémoire 1:31–45.
BALOUT, LIONEL
  1955 *Préhistoire de l'Afrique du nord*. Arts et Métiers Graphiques. Paris: Flammarion.
BINFORD, LEWIS R.
  1968 "Post-Pleistocene adaptations," in *New perspectives in archaeology*. Edited by S. R. Binford and L. R. Binford, 313–344. Chicago: Aldine.

BOSERUP, ESTER
1965   *The conditions of agricultural growth: The economics of agrarian change under population pressure.* London: George Allen and Unwin.

BRAIDWOOD, LINDA, ROBERT J. BRAIDWOOD
1969   Current thoughts on the beginnings of food production in southwestern Asia. *Mélanges Université St.-Joseph* 45(8):149–155. Beirut.

BRAIDWOOD, ROBERT J.
1962   "The earliest village communities of southwestern Asia reconsidered," in *Atti del VI Congresso Internazionale delle Scienze Preistoriche e Proto-istoriche*, volume one, 115–126. Relazioni Generali.
1965   The biography of a research project. *Chicago Today* 2 (3).
1967   *Prehistoric men* (seventh edition). Glenview, Illinois: Scott, Foresman.

BRAIDWOOD, ROBERT J., BRUCE HOWE
1960   *Prehistoric investigations in Iraqi Kurdistan.* Oriental Institute Studies in Ancient Oriental Civilization 31. Chicago.

BUTZER, KARL W.
1971   "The significance of agricultural dispersal into Europe and northern Africa," in *Prehistoric agriculture.* Edited by S. Struever, 313–334. Garden City, New York: Natural History Press.

CAMPS, GABRIEL
1968   Tableau chronologique de la préhistoire récente du nord de l'Afrique. Première synthèse des datations absolues. *Bulletin de la Société Préhistorique Française* 65(2):609–622.
1969   *Amekni: Néolithique ancien du Hoggar.* Mémoires du CRAPE 10. Arts et Métiers Graphiques. Paris: Flammarion.
1971   A propos du Néolithique ancien de la Méditerranée occidentale. *Bulletin de la Société Préhistorique Française* 68, CRSM fasc. 2:48–50.

CAMPS-FABRER, HENRIETTE
1966   *Matière et art mobilier dans la préhistoire nord-africaine et Saharienne.* Mémoires du CRAPE 5. Arts et Métiers Graphiques. Paris: Flammarion.

CATON-THOMPSON, G., E. W. GARDNER
1934   *The desert Fayum*, two volumes. London: Royal Anthropological Institute.

CLARK, J. DESMOND
1967   "The problem of Neolithic culture in subsaharan Africa," in *Background to evolution in Africa.* Edited by W. W. Bishop and J. D. Clark, 601–627. Chicago: University of Chicago Press.
1970   *The prehistory of Africa.* London: Thames and Hudson.
1971   A re-examination of the evidence for agricultural origins in the Nile Valley. *Proceedings of the Prehistoric Society* 37:34–79.

CONTENSON, HENRI DE
1971   Tell Ramad, a village of Syria of the 7th and 6th millennia B.C. *Archaeology* 24(3):278–285.

FLANNERY, KENT V.

1965   The ecology of early food production in Mesopotamia. *Science* 147:1247–1256.

1969   "Origins and ecological effects of early domestication in Iran and the Near East," in *The domestication and exploitation of plants and animals*. Edited by P. J. Ucko and G. W. Dimbleby, 73–100. London: Duckworth.

1972   "The origins of the village as a settlement type in Mesoamerica and the Near East: a comparative study," in *Man, settlement and urbanism*. Edited by P. J. Ucko, R. Tringham, and G. W. Dimbleby, 23–53. London: Duckworth.

GUILAINE, J., A. CALVET

1970   Nouveaux points de chronologie absolue pour le Néolithique ancien de la Méditerranée occidentale. *L'Anthropologie* 74(1–2): 85–92.

HARLAN, JACK R.

1971   Agricultural origins: centers and noncenters. *Science* 174:468–474.

HARRIS, DAVID R.

1969   "Agricultural systems, ecosystems and the origins of agriculture," in *The domestication and exploitation of plants and animals*. Edited by P. J. Ucko and G. W. Dimbleby, 3-15. London: Duckworth.

1972   The origins of agriculture in the tropics. *American Scientist* 60 (2):180–193.

HAWKES, J. G.

1969   "The ecological background of plant domestication," in *The domestication and exploitation of plants and animals*. Edited by P. J. Ucko and G. W. Dimbleby, 17–29. London: Duckworth.

HESTER, JAMES J., PHILIP M. HOBLER

1969   *Prehistoric settlement patterns in the Libyan Desert*. University of Utah Anthropological Papers 92, Nubian Series 4. Salt Lake City.

HIGGS, E. S., M. R. JARMAN

1969   The origins of agriculture: a reconsideration. *Antiquity* 43:31–41.

HOLE, F., K. V. FLANNERY, J. A. NEELY

1969   *Prehistory and human ecology in the Deh Luran Plain: an early village sequence from Khuzistan, Iran*. Memoirs of the Museum of Anthropology 1, University of Michigan. Ann Arbor.

HUGOT, H. J.

1968   The origins of agriculture: Sahara. *Current Anthropology* 19(5): 483–488.

LÉVI-STRAUSS, CLAUDE

1966   Anthropology: its achievement and future. *Current Anthropology* 7(2):124–127.

LHOTE, HENRI

1958   *A la découverte der fresques du Tassili*. Paris: B. Arthaud.

1964   "Faits nouveaux concernant la chronologie relative et absolue des gravures et peintures pariétales du Sud Oranais et du Sahara," in *Prehistoric art of the western Mediterranean and the Sahara*.

Edited by L. Pericot Garcia and E. Ripoll Perelló, 191–214. Viking Fund Publications in Anthropology 39. New York.

MAUNY, RAYMOND
1967 "L'Afrique et les origines de la domestication," in *Background to evolution in Africa*. Edited by W. W. Bishop and J. D. Clark, 583–599. Chicago: University of Chicago Press.

MC BURNEY, C. B. M.
1967 *The Hauna Fteah (Cyrenaica) and the Stone Age of the south-east Mediterranean*. Cambridge: University Press.

MELLAART, J.
1967 "The earliest settlements in Western Asia from the ninth to the end of the fifth millennium B.C.," in *The Cambridge ancient history* (revised edtion), volume 1, Chapter 7, fascicle 59.

MONOD, THÉODORE
1963 "The late Tertiary and Pleistocene in the Sahara and adjacent southerly regions," in *African ecology and human evolution*. Edited by F. C. Howell and F. Bourlière, 117–229. Viking Fund Publications in Anthropology 36. New York.

MORI, FABRIZIO
1965 *Tadrart Acacus. Arte rupestre e culture del Sahara preistòrico*. Turin: G. Einaudi.

MUNSON, PATRICK J.
1968 Recent archaeological research in the Dhar Tichitt region of south-central Mauretania. *West African Archaeological Newsletter* 10:6–13.
1970 Corrections and additional comments concerning the "Tichitt Tradition." *West African Archaeological Newsletter* 12:47–48.

PERKINS, DEXTER
1964 Prehistoric fauna from Shanidar, Iraq. *Science* 144:1565–1566.

PERROT, JEAN
1968 La préhistoire palestinienne. *Supplément au dictionnaire de la Bible* 8: cols. 286–446.

RENFREW, JANE H.
1969 "The archaeological evidence for the domestication of plants: methods and problems," in *The domestication and exploitation of plants and animals*. Edited by P. J. Ucko and G. W. Dimbleby, 149–172. London: Duckworth.

ROUBET, COLETTE
1969 Intérêt des datations absolues obtenues pour le Néolithique de tradition capsienne. *Libyca* 17:245–265.

SERVANT, M., S. SERVANT, G. DELIBRIAS
1969 *Chronologie du Quaternaire récent des basses régions du Tchad*. C.R. Académie des Sciences de Paris 269, série D:1603–1606.

SLOTKIN, J. S.
1965 *Readings in early anthropology*. Viking Fund Publications in Anthropology 40. New York.

SMITH, PHILIP E. L.
1972a *The consequences of food production*. Addison-Wesley Module in Anthropology 31. Reading, Massachusetts.

1972b Changes in population pressure in archaeological explanation. *World Archaeology* 4(1):5–18.

1972c Survey of excavations in Iran during 1970–71. Ganj Dareh Tepe. *Iran, Journal of the British Institute of Persian Studies* 10:165–168.

SMITH, PHILIP E. L., T. YOUNG, T. CUYLER, JR.

1972 "The evolution of early agriculture and culture in Greater Mesopotamia: a trial model," in *Population growth: anthropological implications*. Edited by B. J. Spooner, 1–59. Cambridge: Massachusetts Institute of Technology Press.

SUTTLES, WAYNE

1951 The early diffusion of the potato among the Coast Salish. *Southwestern Journal of Anthropology* 7(3):272–288.

TRIGGER, BRUCE G.

1968 *Beyond history: the methods of prehistory*. New York: Holt, Rinehart and Winston.

VAN LOON, MAURITS, *et al.*

1968 The Oriental Institute excavations at Mureybit, Syria: preliminary report on the 1965 campaign, part one: architectural and general finds. *Journal of Near Eastern Studies* 27:265–290.

VAN ZEIST, W.

1969 "Reflections on prehistoric environments in the Near East," in *The domestication and exploitation of plants and animals*. Edited by P. J. Ucko and G. W. Dimbleby, 35–46. London: Duckworth.

VAUFREY, RAYMOND

1955 *Préhistoire de l'Afrique*, volume one: *Le Maghreb*. Publications de l'Institut des Hautes Études de Tunis, volume four. Paris.

1969 *Préhistoire de l'Afrique*, volume two: *Au nord et à l'est de la Grande Forêt*. Publications de l'Université de Tunis, volume four. Tunis.

VIGNARD, EDMOND

1923 Une nouvelle industrie lithique, le "Sébilien." *Bulletin de l'Institut Français d'Archéologie Orientale* 22:1–76, pl. 24.

VITA-FINZI, C., E. S. HIGGS

1970 Prehistoric economy in the Mount Carmel area of Palestine. Site catchment analysis. *Proceedings of the Prehistoric Society* 36:1–37.

WASHBURN, S. L.

1968 "One hundred years of biological anthropology," in *One hundred years of anthropology*. Edited by J. O. Brew, 97–115. Cambridge: Harvard University Press.

WENDORF, FRED, *editor*

1968 *The prehistory of Nubia*, two volumes. Dallas: Southern Methodist University Press.

WENDORF, F., R. SAID, R. SCHILD

1970 Egyptian prehistory: some new concepts. *Science* 169:1161–1171.

WRIGHT, H. E., JR.

1968 Natural environment of early food production north of Mesopotamia. *Science* 161:334–339.

WRIGHT, GARY A.
  1971   Origins of food production in southwestern Asia: a survey of
         ideas. *Current Anthropology* 12(4-5):447–477.
ZOHARY, DANIEL
  1969   "The progenitors of wheat and barley in relation to domestication
         and agricultural dispersal in the Old World," in *The domestica-
         tion and exploitation of plants and animals.* Edited by P. J. Ucko
         and G. W. Dimbleby, 47–66. London: Duckworth.
ZUBROW, EZRA B.
  1971   Carrying capacity and dynamic equilibrium in the prehistoric
         southwest. *American Antiquity* 36(2):127–138.

SECTION FOUR

Regional Archaeological Evidence

Archaeological Data on the Origins of Cultivation in the Southwestern Sahara and Their Implications for West Africa

PATRICK J. MUNSON

Since 1959 perhaps no single subject has more occupied the attention of West African cultural historians and ethnobotanists than the question of the origins of plant cultivation in this area. Most of this interest and controversy have resulted, directly or indirectly, from a hypothesis presented by Murdock (1959: 64–70). In the total absence of relevant archaeological and paleobotanical data from this area, Murdock relied upon modern ethnographic, linguistic, and ethnobotanical material to construct an argument that some twenty-five food and fiber plants, including such seed crops as bulrush millet (*Pennisetum typhoideum*), sorghum (*Sorghum vulgare*), fonio (*Digitaria exilis*), and African rice (*Oryza glaberrima*), had been brought under domestication, independent of external influences, in the Sudanic zone around the headwaters of the Niger River and that this had occurred around 4500 B.C.

Chevalier (1938), some two decades previously and on the basis of plant geography, had presented a somewhat similar hypothesis. He argued that during a wetter period at an unspecified period in the past sorghum, bulrush millet, African rice, *Eleusine, Echinochloa, Panicum, Dactyloctenium*, cotton, the jujube (*Zizyphus* spp.), and possibly the date palm were all originally domesticated at the southern edge of the Sahara. Vignier (1945) presented a rather similar argument for the domestication of sorghum. Using plant geography, ethnographic data, and some indirect archaeological considerations, Portères (1950, 1951a) argued for the domestication of African rice in the central delta of the Niger prior to 1500 B.C.

It is the "Murdockian Hypothesis," however, which has commanded the greatest attention, at least among Anglophone scholars; and although at least one ethnobotanist seems to have accepted Murdock's position almost in its entirety (Anderson 1967: 175), the great majority of botanists and archaeologists have raised very serious objections (e.g. Wrigley 1960; Baker 1962; Clark 1962). These counter-arguments, however, shared one basic weakness with Murdock's position, as well as with the earlier and somewhat similar hypotheses put forward by the French plant geographers. They are all based primarily on modern botanical distributions and to a lesser extent on modern ethnographic material, rather than on direct archaeological data, which until the last few years had been nonexistent, at least as directly relevant to this question and for this area.

During the winter months of 1966–1967 and 1967–1968, a program of archaeological research was carried out by the author which had as one of its major objectives the testing of the hypothesis that there was an early, independent center of origin of seed-crop agriculture in the general West African Sudanic-Sahelian zone. Several significant altera- tions were made, however, in the hypothesis as presented by Murdock. The first alteration took into account the fact that archaeological re- search in the Near East and in Mexico had adequately demonstrated that seed-crop agriculture emerged not around the relatively lush oases and river valleys, but rather in marginal areas which were steppe or semi- desert in climate; only subsequently did agriculture move into the oasis- valley areas. The headwaters of the Niger, being near the southern and wetter margin of the Sudanic zone, would not compare environmentally with known seed-crop hearths. Second, there has been increasing evi- dence that from ca. 5500–5000 B.C. to ca. 2500–2000 B.C., during the so-called Neolithic Wet Period, the Sahara enjoyed significantly more precipitation than it does at present; and if comparable changes in annual rainfall had occurred in areas farther south, the Niger headwaters region during this period may well have been rainforest.

Accordingly, the modified hypothesis to be tested was that if seed- crop cultivation did emerge at a relatively early date in the general West African area, this occurrence would have been in the steppe (or Sahelian) zone; and if it had occurred early enough to qualify as an independent hearth, its emergence would have coincided with a period of increased rainfall which would have pushed the Sahelian zone northward into areas that are now Saharan, or near-Saharan, in climate.

The region chosen to test this hypothesis was the Dhar Tichitt region of south-central Mauritania, a region which today has a mean annual rainfall of about 100 millimeters and thus straddles the boundary between Sahara and Sahel as defined. This area had several qualifications for this kind of program. Numerous dry lake beds which occur in this region showed evidence of existing as freshwater lakes in the not too distant past, and their existence would have considerably modified the overall environment. The area presently is also at or near the northern boundary of distribution of a number of wild grasses that are related to several of the African cultigens, namely *Pennisetum*, *Digitaria*, *Sorghum*, and *Echinochloa*, thus perhaps qualifying as a "nuclear zone" as defined by Braidwood (1963: 106). Several brief archaeological surveys in this region (e.g. Mauny 1950) had recorded the existence of large, well-preserved, stone-masonry, "Neolithic" villages in this area, thus suggesting a relatively high level of cultural achievement here in the past presumably based upon effective food production. And finally, pottery collected from the surfaces of some of these sites and stored at the Institut Fondamental d'Afrique Noire were found to bear numerous and clear grain and chaff impressions.

THE ARCHAEOLOGICAL SEQUENCE OF DHAR TICHITT

The Later Stone Age occupation that was discovered and investigated in this area can conveniently be divided into a sequence of eight phases. The earliest sites from the Akreijit Phase are not numerous. They are small, thin, and nonarchitectural and are located just behind the highest

Table 1.　Date, sibsistence, and environment of the Tichitt Phases

Date B.C.	Phase	Subsistence	Environment
400– 700	Akjinjeir	Herding, cultivation, limited collecting and hunting	Invasion of desertic species, rainfall less than x1.5
700– 900	Arriane		Lakes gone, decreasing rainfall
900–1000	Chebka	Herding, cultivation, collecting, limited hunting	
1000–1100	Naghez	Herding, collecting, limited hunting and fishing, incipient cultivation?	Shrinking lakes, decreasing rainfall
1100–1200	Nkhal	Herding, fishing, limited collecting and hunting	Large lakes, rainfall greater than x1.75
1200–1400	Goungou		
1400–1500	Khimiya		
Hiatus			Very dry
2000?	Akreijit	Hunting, fishing, limited collecting	Large lakes, rainfall greater than x2.0

of the three beach ridges of the now extinct freshwater lakes. Associated artifacts include ground stone axes and gouges, chipped stone geometric microliths (none of which show evidence of use as sickle blades), projectile points, scrapers, a few small milling stones, and pottery decorated with stamped and incised patterns similar to ceramics found over a considerable portion of the western Sahara. Rock art of the so-called Ethiopian Megafauna Style, heavily emphasizing giraffes and other Sahelian-Sudanic wild animals, is apparently associated. Unfortunately, no sites with subsurface deposits could be found. No bone was preserved on the sites, nor did the pottery bear recognizable grain impressions. The consequence is that we have little "hard" data on the subsistence pattern of the peoples of this phase. The total emphasis on wild animals in the apparently associated rock art and the high incidence of projectile points on the sites, however, suggest some considerable emphasis on hunting. Furthermore, the sites' locations, immediately adjacent to the lakes, suggest at least some utilization of aquatic resources probably including fish; and the presence of the small milling stones, albeit in limited numbers, argues for at least some utilization of hard seeds. The absence of depictions of domesticated animals in the rock art and the scarcity of milling stones, on the other hand, argues against the presence of food production. A single radiocarbon determination on aquatic shells collected from near the surface of the beach which was apparently contemporary with this phase yielded the surprisingly late date of 1750 B.C. ± 130 (GX-1890). Although this date is earlier than determinations for the following phase, it must still be viewed with suspicion since comparable data, both archaeological and environmental, from elsewhere in the western Sahara would suggest a date at least several hundred years earlier.

Following the Akreijit Phase, there is a hiatus in the cultural chronology which coincides with a period of extreme dryness — perhaps as dry as today or even drier. The lakes at this time shrank drastically, possibly almost drying up completely; and the human population of the area either followed the receding shorelines of the lakes (and their sites, if they exist, have been buried by the silts of a subsequent rise in lake levels) or the people migrated southward into more hospitable regions. There is some slight archaeological support for this latter possibility in the form of artifactual similarities from sites near Nioro, just south of the Mauritania-Mali border (Vaufrey 1947) and from the rockshelter of Kourounkorokalé near Bamako, Mali (Szumowski 1956).

As dated by several satisfactory radiocarbon determinations, another period of increased rainfall commenced about 1500 B.C. or slightly earlier, and the lake basins again partially refilled. The area was then reoccupied by peoples who, on artifactual grounds, seem to have been the descendants of the earlier Akreijit Phase or a culturally closely related group. This second phase, named the Khimiya Phase, and the two following phases, Goungou and Nkhal, represent a cultural continuum which, dated by six radiocarbon determinations, spans the period from just before 1500 B.C. to about 1100 B.C. Each of these phases can readily be separated from the others on the basis of changing artifactual styles. Also site locations vary with time: sites of the Khimiya Phase are located on low dunes immediately behind the beach of the middle of the three lake stages; Goungou Phase sites are located directly on the middle beach; and Nkhal Phase sites are situated directly on the lowest of the three beaches. Despite these differences, however, subsistence patterns, for which considerable data exist for interpretation, are essentially identical for each.

Domesticated cattle and goats, as evidenced by numerous bones and as identified by Turnbull (i.p.), are present in numbers from the beginning; their appearance and adoption in the general region obviously occurred during the hiatus between the Akreijit and Khimiya phases (i.e. some time prior to 1500 B.C., but probably not earlier than about 2000 B.C.). The numerous fish bones on and in the sites indicate that fishing was an important activity. Hunting also played some role, but since bones of wild animals occur at a much lower percentage than do bones of domesticated animals, it appears that this was a relatively minor part of the subsistence pattern. Of greatest importance for purposes of the problem at hand, however, are the relatively abundant recovered plant remains, both in the form of mineralized hackberry seeds (*Celtis integrifolia*) and identifiable impressions of grains and chaff upon the pottery (Jacques-Félix i.p.).

A total of sixty-seven identifiable impressions were discovered on the ceramics which were recovered from sites of these phases. Of these, 66 (99 percent) are seed coverings of the grass "kram-kram" (*Cenchrus biflorus*), a species which, because of the burry nature of the seed head, has probably never been considered a candidate for cultivation. Where it occurs in the wild state today, however, it is widely collected, particularly as a famine food (e.g. Chapelle 1957: 192; Dalziel 1937: 522). The remaining impression (1 percent) is of the genus *Pennisetum*, which is of particular interest since this is the same genus as the modern cultigen bulrush millet. Unfortunately, however, it has not been possible to determine if this impression represents a wild or domesticated form. There are, however, a number of reasons for arguing that the peoples of these phases were not cultivators: the very low percentage of even potential cultigens, the fact that wild species of *Pennisetum* exist even today just south of the Tichitt region, the limited occurrence and small size of associated milling stones, and the paucity (relative to subsequent phases) of grain impressions.

The following Naghez Phase, dated by three radiocarbon determinations to about 1100 to 1000 B.C., clearly derived from the preceding Nkhal Phase. It does, however, represent a point of inflection from preceding patterns in at least several respects. Villages, like the villages of the ancestoral Nkhal Phase, are still located on or just behind the lowest of the three beaches, but the sites for the first time are of stone-masonry construction. Furthermore, and rather surprisingly, they are quite large; the site of Glaib Tijat is 500 meters square, and the site of Naghez is approximately 1200 meters long by 300 meters wide.

Although the sites of this phase are still located adjacent to the lake basins, all indications are that the lakes had almost dried up again by this time. Consequently the fish potential was much reduced and emphasis on fishing was much more limited than in preceding phases. Apparently as a substitute for this diminishing resource, the peoples turned to a heavier emphasis on plant foods as indicated by the greatly increased numbers of milling stones (which are also quite large at this time, and which take a variety of shapes), by the increased numbers of associated small collecting stations, by the increased numbers of grain impressions on the pottery, and by the greater variety of species represented by these impressions. Herding of cattle and goats continued in its apparently rather significant role, and limited hunting continued to be practiced.

A few hackberry seeds were recovered, which certainly represent collecting, and of the thirty-two identifiable grain and chaff impressions found on the pottery, twenty-four (75 percent) are of the wild *Cenchrus biflorus*. *Panicum laetum*, another wild seed plant widely collected today as a food source, makes its appearance in limited numbers (9 percent), as does *Brachiaria deflexa* (12 percent); and *Pennisetum* sp. increases slightly (3 percent). Here again it has not been possible to determine if the *Pennisetum* represents a wild or cultivated variety; but in view of the increased attention the peoples of this phase were giving to plant foods, the possibility of cultivation of this species, albeit only to a very limited degree, would seem to be enhanced. Furthermore, the *Brachiaria deflexa* might be of some interest in this regard; although seeds of this plant are today fairly commonly collected in the wild state and despite the fact that the Naghez Phase specimens seem in no way

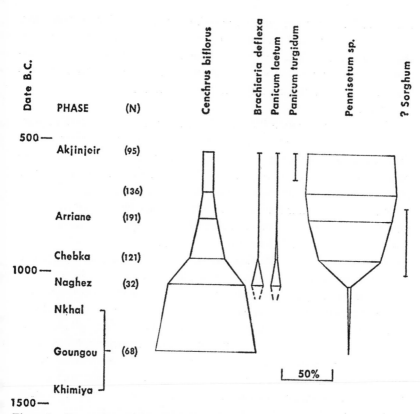

Figure 1. Percentages of identified grain impressions per phase

different from modern wild varieties, there is, nevertheless, one contemporary record for the cultivation of this species in West Africa (Portères 1951b). Whatever the status of *Pennisetum* and *Brachiaria deflexa* (as wild or domesticated) in this phase, the much higher incidence of the definitely wild *Cenchrus biflorus*, plus *Panicum laetum* and *Celtis*, both also wild, indicates that most plant foods were still derived from collecting.

The following Chebka Phase, dated by two radiocarbon determinations to the period from about 1000 B.C. to 900 B.C., represents still another point of inflection because *Pennisetum*, much of it now showing definite characteristics of a domesticated variety, "jumps" to a position of 61 percent of the 121 identifiable grain impressions for this phase. This happens despite the fact (or perhaps BECAUSE of the fact) that all indications are that the climate of the region was becoming even drier. Some collecting continued to be practiced and apparently still played a rather significant role since *Cenchrus biflorus* occurs as 34 percent of the total. However, it is the *Pennisetum*, much or all of it cultivated, which formed the bulk of the plant food. Also noteworthy is the fact that *Brachiaria deflexa* persists (although at a much reduced percentage), and one impression was found which might be sorghum. Herding also continued to play an important role, and limited hunting was still practiced.

Villages of the Chebka Phase, although similar in construction, plan, and size to the villages of the preceding Naghez Phase, differ in that they are about four times more numerous (reflecting, one might suspect, an increase in population resulting from the increased potential from an almost fully-food-producing subsistence pattern). Sites are also no longer placed immediately adjacent to the lake basins, but rather are placed along the lip of the sheer, 200 meter high escarpment which transects this region. Movement away from the margins of the lake basins is explained by the fact that the lakes had ceased to exist as permanent features by this time. The placement of the villages at the top of the escarpment, however, is best explained in terms of defense, an explanation much strengthened by the presence of many clearly defensive structures associated with these villages; each village is entirely encircled by a high, thick masonry wall and each approach to the village is lined with masonry "archer's redoubts." All indications are, however, that the warfare that was occurring was of an internal nature, probably village against village, and very possibly representing conflict over the limited arable land which exists in this region.

The subject of arable land leads us, at this time, to a consideration of how cultivation was practiced in this area. Today, with mean annual rainfall only about 100 millimeters and surface deposits consisting of little more than sand and rock, cultivation is, at best, extremely marginal and is limited to a few hand-watered gardens. From studies based on the wild plant and animal remains associated with the Chebka Phase, it can be inferred, however, that mean annual rainfall at that time was probably somewhere between 150 to 175 millimeters. Today in the vicinity of Tidjikja, some 200 kilometers to the west of Tichitt, where annual rainfall averages about 155 millimeters, fairly intensive cultivation is practiced utilizing the *décrue* system, a system whereby a low dam is placed across a shallow wadi, and after a pool collects during the brief rainy season, crops are planted in the moist soil at the margins (Toupet 1958: 87). It seems unlikely, however, that an identical practice was employed prehistorically in the Tichitt area since there is no evidence of the necessary dams. But a variation of the *décrue* system is also found today in the central valley of the Niger. Here, natural basins in the floodplain are filled yearly by the flooding of the river, and as the trapped water evaporates, crops are planted in the moist, newly exposed silt deposits (Drouhin 1944; Harlan and Pasquereau 1969). The internally drained lake basins in the Tichitt area would have filled in a comparable manner during the rainy season particularly if rainfall was greater than today; and because the lake beds had only recently been exposed after centuries of existence as lake bottoms, it seems likely that they would have been blanketed with deep, rich silt deposits.

Returning to the archaeological sequence, the Arriane Phase, which derived from the Chebka Phase, can be dated by extrapolation from radiocarbon determinations for preceding and following phases to about 900 to 700 B.C. The evidences of warfare which were so common in the preceding phase are now gone, indicating that the sources of conflict had somehow been resolved. Villages are somewhat smaller but are much more numerous, reflecting still greater increases in population. Evidence of cultivation involving *Pennisetum* and possibly very limited amounts of sorghum (and perhaps also *Brachiaria deflexa*) are even more numerous; of the 141 identifiable impressions found on the pottery recovered from sites of this phase 82 percent are *Pennisetum*. Herding also continued in its important role, and collecting of wild plant foods and hunting were still practiced to limited extents.

The terminal Neolithic phase of this region, Akjinjeir, is dated by two radiocarbon determinations to the period from about 700 B.C. to 400 B.C. With a sample of 231 identifiable impressions from the associated pottery, *Pennisetum* climbs still further to about 90 percent, despite the fact that the peoples of this phase were experiencing considerable stress from two quarters. For the first time since the end of the Akreijit Phase, we find evidence of true Saharan species (addax, jerboa, *Panicum turgidum*) indicating that mean annual rainfall had probably dropped below 150 millimeters. And there is considerable archaeological evidence that the area at this time was invaded by very mobile, horse-riding Libyco-Berbers from North Africa who were equipped with metal weapons. Under the combined weight of these two pressures the presence of Neolithic cultivators in this region came to an end about 400 B.C.

THE ORIGIN OF CULTIVATION IN THE TICHITT AREA

For our purposes here the major concern is with the middle portion of the Tichitt sequence, from the Nkhal Phase dating just prior to 1100 B.C. (with no evidence of cultivation and only limited collecting of wild seeds), to the Naghez Phase dating from ca. 1100 B.C. to 1000 B.C. (with intensive seed collecting and possibly some incipient seed cultivation), and to the Chebka Phase dating ca. 1000 B.C. to 900 B.C. (with abundant evidence of rather intensive cultivation of *Pennisetum*). The question now is what was the source of this complex: (1) Was it basically an *in situ* development, perhaps without benefit of external stimulation? (2) Was it the result of diffusion of the idea and the species of cultivation from a still earlier (and possibly independent) agricultural hearth to the south of the Tichitt region? (3) Was it the result of diffusion of ideas and crops westward across the Sudanic zone from an earlier hearth or center of dispersal in the general Ethiopian area? (4) Or was it the result of diffusion of the idea and perhaps the domesticated plants from earlier agricultural groups dwelling to the north or northeast?

Independent, In-place Development?   If one disregards the absolute chronology for the Tichitt sequence, it would appear to represent a "classical" pattern of agricultural emergence, the peoples progressively changing from a limited collecting system utilizing only a small range of wild species, to intensive collecting and experimentation with a large number of wild species, and finally to the selection of one or perhaps several of the more promising of these species to be brought under full domestication; and all of these events occurring during a period of demonstrated environmental deterioration. The problems in this picture emerge, however, when one places this sequence of events within a dated chronology. First, the date of ca. 1100 to 1000 B.C. for the initial appearance of cultivation makes it extremely difficult to argue that this was an invention totally independent of external influences since cultivation was present at least 3500 years earlier in northeastern Africa. Furthermore, domesticated cattle and goats had appeared in the Tichitt area at least 500 years prior to the first evidence of cultivation, and these species were unquestionably domesticated initially in the Near East. Second, in the two independent seed-crop hearths of the world which have been adequately investigated, the Near East and Mexico, the cultural transition from collecting through incipient cultivation to intensive cultivation, plus the botanical transition from a totally wild species to a fully domesticated form, is measured in millennia, whereas in the Tichitt sequence this transition seems to have occurred in only a little over one century. Perhaps the Near Eastern and Mexican situations do not represent a universal pattern; and some of my botanist colleagues inform me that a morphological transition, such as that seen in the prehistoric Tichitt *Pennisetum*, might very possibly have occurred in a hundred years (a century, after all, does represent a hundred generations for an annual). Nevertheless, one might legitimately feel uncomfortable in arguing for this sequence to represent an independent development.

Diffusion from an Earlier Hearth to the South?   Those who are enamored, wholly or in part, of Murdock's hypothesis of an early center of origin of seed-crop agriculture in the West African savanna zone will perhaps be tempted to see the Tichitt seed-crop complex as deriving from earlier developments to the south. Since 1959, a few scattered pieces of archaeological data have accumulated for West Africa which bear directly on this problem. The earliest, but by no means conclusive, hint of cereal cultivation comes from Iwo Eleru rockshelter in southwestern Nigeria where microlithic trapezoids with silica gloss (indicating their use as sickle blades) were recovered in levels dating only shortly after 3000 B.C. (Daniels 1969: 27). Unfortunately, however, sickle blades like milling stones, digging stick weights, and hoes, although sometimes associated with cultivation, are not confined to use as agricultural implements.

The next two earliest suggestions of cultivation in this area both come from Ghana. Davies (1968: 481) has found "what are almost certainly impressions of *Pennisetum* cobs" on shards from the northern Ghana site of Ntereso, and this site has three radiocarbon determinations ranging from 1240 B.C. ± 120 to 1630 B.C. ± 130. Assuming that these impressions do represent *Pennisetum* and that it is a domesticated variety, this would then precede the Tichitt material. However, in previous articles we find that not only are the radiocarbon determinations contrary to the stratigraphy of the site, but also that there was iron in some of the levels (Davies 1967a: 116; 1967b: 238–239) which, if it is not intrusive, would suggest a date of ca. 500 B.C. at the earliest. Equally nebulous, but for different reasons, is material from the Kintampo rockshelter in central Ghana, where Flight (1970) recovered carbonized remains of oil palm (*Elaeis guineensis*) and cowpeas (*Vigna* sp.) in levels dating after 1400 B.C. but prior to the introduction of iron. Both of these species are domesticated today, but it has not been possible to determine if the early Kintampo materials represent cultigens.

The earliest definite evidence of plant cultivation in West Africa, excluding the Tichitt material, comes from the site of Daima in north-eastern Nigeria and is surprisingly late. Here, in levels radiocarbon dated to about A.D. 500, "actual carbonised grains (of sorghum) were discovered" (Connah 1969: 34). Lower levels of this site (which extend back to ca. 500 B.C.) produced no evidence of cultivation. If the archaeological absence of cultigens in these lower levels is "real," and not simply the result of preservation factors and/or recovery techniques, and if the lower levels of the site do not result from specialized and/or seasonal occupations, then the absence of cultigens in this area until a very late period would seem highly significant.

In view of the relative paucity of archaeological research directed toward recovery of data bearing upon Later Stone Age subsistence patterns in West Africa, however, the negative evidence for early cultivation is far from conclusive. But, given the absence of evidence for cultivation prior to ca. 1100 to 1000 B.C. in the relatively well-investigated Dhar Tichitt sites, and given the validity of my initial postulate that seed-crop cultivation would appear earlier in areas environmentally marginal to West Africa, I do not now find it at all surprising that cultivation in West Africa proper does not seem to have begun much earlier than about 1000 B.C.

The reasons for this position involve in large part the consideration of WHY peoples become food producers in any case, and, even more specifically, why the first steps in this direction were more likely to occur in environmentally marginal areas. The most convincing explanation has recently been presented by Binford (1968) who has modified certain aspects of Childe's propinquity theory (1951: 23–25) and incorporated White's (1959: 284) concept of equilibrium systems. The argument is that in areas with large resources of wild foods, peoples at a hunting and gathering level of subsistence would establish an equilibrium system with their resources, and:

If we recognize that an equilibrium system can be established so that populations are homostatically regulated below the carrying capacity of the local food supply, it follows that there is no necessary adaptive pressure continually favoring means of increasing the food supply (Binford 1968: 327).

Therefore, in seeking the origins of food production (or any other change in subsistence), it is concluded that "we are forced to look for those conditions which might bring about disequilibrium and bring about selective advantage for increased productivity" (Binford 1968: 328). He then goes on to suggest two ways in which disequilibrium might have occurred: (1) a change in the physical environment which reduced the available food resources, or (2) an increase in population density which strained the carrying capacity.

... it is in the context of such situations of stress in environments ... that we would expect to find conditions favoring the development of plant and animal domestication. Such situations would be characterized by disequilibrium between population and resources which, in turn, would offer selective advantage to increases in the efficacy of subsistence technology (Binford 1968: 332).

In neither the Tichitt area, nor West Africa in general, do we have evidence of increased population densities preceding the establishment of food production. But, at least in the Tichitt area, there were two well-documented episodes of environmental deterioration. Prior to the first of these, during the high-lake-level period, the peoples of the Akreijit Phase had apparently established an equilibrium at a hunting-fishing-limited collecting level of subsistence. It was only during the period following, beginning around (?) 2000 B.C. with a reduction in rainfall and the resultant near-disappearance of the Tichitt lakes, that a new element of subsistence was added: the people adopted herding of cattle and goats (probably via pastoral peoples who had been forced out of the central Sahara by the same environmental factors). With a return to moister conditions around 1500 B.C. a new equilibrium was established, now based on herding, fishing, limited collecting, and limited hunting; and the population stabilized at a higher density. By about 1100 B.C., however, the lakes began drying up once again, thus reducing (and eventually eliminating) the fish potential. Hence a new disequilibrium resulted, and if the people were to maintain themselves at the same density in this area, a new food source had to be substituted for the fish. The solution was the adoption of cultivation of seed plants.

The relevance here to cultivation farther south in the West African savanna is twofold. If cultivation had been present in West Africa during the earlier of these two periods of environmental stress, why did the peoples of the Tichitt region not adopt it at that time? They did adopt herding, and there is evidence of contacts with the more southern regions. Second, and more important, if the above model is a valid explanation for changes in subsistence patterns, what would have been the motivation for peoples to the south to have changed earlier? It would have been in the environmentally marginal areas, such as southern Mauritania, that stress would have appeared earliest and with the greatest intensity. In short, I would argue that the source of seed-crop cultivation in the Sudanic zone of West Africa was from cultivators (or at least the idea of cultivation) expanding into that area from the drier, more sensitive margins.

Was It Diffusion from an Earlier Hearth in Ethiopia?   This possibility would seem to be considerably stronger than either of the other two just considered. Numerous botanists have argued for many years that Ethiopia was a major center of origin and/or dispersal for many African seed crops, including finger millet (*Eleusine coracana*), teff (*Eragrostis abyssinica*), sorghum, and bulrush millet (Snowden 1936; Vavilov 1949–1950; Wrigley 1960; Portères 1962; Doggett 1965; Simoons 1965). Furthermore, at least some antiquity for seed-crop cultivation can be demonstrated for this region. There is fairly good historical evidence for the cultivation of teff, and probably millet, sorghum, wheat, and barley, in the northern Ethiopian highlands prior to 1000 B.C. (Simoons 1965: 9), and both archaeological and linguistic evidence from India suggests that finger millet, sorghum, and possibly bulrush millet had spread to that area, presumably from Ethiopia, prior to 1500 B.C. (Allchin 1969: 325; Doggett 1965: 61–62; Portères 1962: 204). Furthermore, Portères (1962: 205) and Wrigley (1960: 193), on the basis of Egyptian archaeology and cotton genetics respectively, have argued for the presence of cultivation in this area prior to 3000 B.C.

Assuming a fair antiquity for seed-crop cultivation in Ethiopia (the question of its origin in this area is essentially irrelevant in regard to West Africa), the next question is, did it spread across what someone has called "the easiest of all corridors," the savanna zone bordering the southern edge of the Sahara, and if so, when? It would seem entirely possible that it did spread by this route, moving relatively slowly and taking perhaps 2000 years to complete its "journey" to the western margins. However, the only piece of archaeological evidence that might be brought to bear upon this hypothesis does not lend support; the site of Daima, located near the Sudanic-Sahelian boundary in northeastern Nigeria and about equidistant between Ethiopia and Tichitt, produced evidence of cultivation only in levels dated some 1500 years later than its appearance on the western margins. A single excavated site, of course, can hardly be considered conclusive; but still there is another possibility for the source of the prehistoric Tichitt cultigens, and it is one for which there is (at least yet) no detracting evidence.

Was the Tichitt Cultigen Complex Diffused from the North or Northeast? Direct archaeological evidence for cultivation in the Sahara proper is, at best, only slightly better than that for sub-Saharan Africa, but such evidence as exists suggests an initial date for cultivation much earlier than anywhere to the south (with the possible exception of Ethiopia). Perhaps indirectly relevant as well, however, is the presence of Near Eastern plant domesticates in Egypt by about 4500 B.C. and the presence of Near Eastern domesticated animals in the northeastern quarter of the Sahara perhaps as early as (or earlier than) 5000 B.C.

The earliest evidence for cultivation in the Sahara comes from the site of Ameki in the Hoggar (near the center of the Sahara) where Camps (1969: 186–188) recovered two pollen grains which, because of their size and shape, seem to represent a domesticated variety of *Pennisetum*. The zone from which these pollen grains were recovered is bracketed by radiocarbon determinations from about 6100 B.C. to 4850 B.C. Somewhat comparable although later evidence comes from the site of Méniet, also in the Hoggar, from which Pons and Quézel (1957: 27, 35) identified two pollen grains which appear to represent a cultivated cereal, and this site has been radiocarbon dated to about 3500 B.C. Hugot (1968: 485) not only accepts the Méniet pollen as indicative of cultivation in this area at this date, but also goes on to suggest that it represents the cultivation of wheat.

Additional but much less conclusive evidence for seed-crop cultivation in this area comes from the rockshelter of Sefar — located in the Tassili and radiocarbon dated about 3100 B.C. — where paintings seem to depict cultivation (Lhote 1959: 118), and from some linguistic evidence which suggests a considerable antiquity for the cultivation of sorghum in the central Sahara (Camps 1960: 79).

Assuming that seed-crop cultivation was being practiced, at least to some extent, in the central Sahara prior to 3000 B.C., two other questions arise which have some relevance to the origins of cultivation in the Tichitt area and areas farther south in West Africa: one question regards both the intensity and extent of cultivation in this region; the other concerns the origin of both the idea and the crops.

Today, in the higher plateaus and mountainous regions of the Sahara, as well as around the scattered oases, a fairly wide range of seed crops is cultivated, including bulrush millet, sorghum, wheat, and barley (Nicolaisen 1963: 184; Gast and Adrian 1965). The intensity of cultivation today, however, is often not great; the Taureg of Aïr and Tassili-n-Ajjer, for example, simply sow seeds upon the moist beds of wadis following the rainy season and then leave the area until harvesting time (Nicolaisen 1963: 184). The important aspect for our concern, however, is not the intensity but rather the simple presence of cultivation in this area today. If it can be practiced here in modern climates it could also have been possible at any period in the past when rainfall was as high as today and in periods of increased rainfall it would have been easier and could have been more widespread.

The other question regards the origin of this central Saharan crop complex. The majority opinion, and the one perhaps easiest to defend, is that it represents stimulus-diffusion from the Near East via Egypt. Near Eastern domesticated crops were demonstrably present in Egypt by 4500 B.C., and Near Eastern domesticated animals were introduced into the central Sahara at a very early date, perhaps prior to 5000 B.C. Thus the "lines of communication" were present. Furthermore, with only slightly wetter conditions (which certainly existed in the central Sahara between 5000 B.C. and 3000 B.C.), it seems likely that wild *Pennisetum*, as well as perhaps wild *Sorghum*, would have been present at least in the higher, better watered regions of the central Sahara. Therefore, the peoples of this region, possessing knowledge of cultivation but confronted with the difficulty of growing the winter-rainfall adapted, Near Eastern crops in this summer-rainfall zone, began experimenting with such wild, summer-rainfall adapted, local species as *Pennisetum*.

Neat as this picture is, however, there is still another hypothesis for the origin of Saharan cultivation which at least deserves serious consideration. In the vicinity of the Dungal and Dineigil oases in southwestern Egypt, Hobler and Hester (1969) have discovered a pre-ceramic complex with numerous milling stones and sickle blades, and this complex dates at least as early as 6000 B.C. and may extend back as early as 8300 B.C. The associated artifacts, plus the fact that this complex is restricted to the vicinity of now-dry silt basins, argue that these peoples were at least intensive seed collectors and possibly that they were incipient seed-crop cultivators. This position is considerably strengthened by the results of recent research in the Nubian region of the Nile, only a few hundred kilometers to the south, in a context dating perhaps as early as 13,000 B.C., which has revealed the existence of a complex with numerous sickle blades and milling stones, plus associated spores of smut and fungi which today are most commonly associated with wheat (Wendorf 1968: 935–946). Probably no one would argue that this early Nubian complex represents cultivation, even incipient cultivation. However, it clearly represents a heavy orientation toward wild seeds as a source of food, which can be considered a prerequisite to actual cultivation, and this complex predates by at least 3000 years evidence for comparable activities in the Near East.

In viewing this evidence, Hobler and Hester (1969) and Hester (1968) have suggested that incipient cultivation, including perhaps wheat, sorghum, and millet, may have been present in this Nubia-southwestern Egypt region as early as (or earlier than) 6000 B.C. and then go on to suggest a route of dispersal of this complex to other areas of the Sahara. The plateaus and mountains of Darfur, Ennedi, Tibesti, Tassili, Hoggar, Aïr, and Adrar des Iforas form a broad arc from the southeastern Sahara to the central Sahara and then down to the southwestern Sahara. Gebel Oweinat and Gilf Kebir in extreme southwestern Egypt represent a northeastward extension of these highlands. Today, these higher areas receive considerably greater precipitation than do other portions of the Sahara, and most present cultivation of the Sahara is confined to these regions. Hester and Hobler then argue that developments in cultivation which arose in the Dungal-Dineigil-Nubian region jumped the few hundred kilometers which separate these areas from Gebel Oweinat and Gilf Kebir and from there spread through this highland "Saharan Fertile Crescent."

Whether the crops of the Sahara were domesticated independently in the eastern Sahara or as a result of stimulus-diffusion from the northeast, the most relevant aspect in regard to West Africa is that the tip of the southwestern horn of this "fertile crescent" is Adrar des Iforas. Only a few hundred kilometers away the great bend of the Niger, just east of Timbuktu, is connected to this area by the valley of the Tilemsi. Timbuktu, in turn, lies less than 400 kilometers east-southeast of the southeastern edge of Dhar Tichitt-Oualata. Consequently, any pressure in the central Sahara, either in terms of environmental deterioration or population density, could well have forced cultivators in that region southwestward into Adrar des Iforas and beyond into the central Niger region; and from that area there would be no major geographical problem for ideas and plants to be transmitted to the Tichitt region.

In this regard, it would be extremely interesting to have some data on the subsistence patterns of the peoples at sites such as Karkarichinkat-Sud (Mauny 1955), located in Adrar des Iforas and recently radiocarbon dated to 1360 B.C. $\pm$ 110 (Fagan 1969: 150), or of late prehistoric groups in the vicinity of Timbuktu. My guess is that as one moves eastward from Tichitt to Timbuktu, and then northeastward from Timbuktu, the earliest date for the occurrence of seed-crop cultivation (particularly *Pennisetum*) will become progressively earlier, and conversely, as one moves south and southwestward from Timbuktu (or southward from Tichitt) the date of initial occurrence will become progressively later.

SUMMARY

Archaeological research in the Dhar Tichitt region of south-central Mauritania has revealed the existence of an eight phase Later Stone Age sequence. Subsistence data from this well dated sequence not only shed considerable light on the question of late prehistoric food production in this specific vicinity, but also serve as the basis for testing previous hypotheses and presenting new ones dealing with the origins of seed-crop cultivation in the general West African Sahelian-Sudanic zone.

The late prehistoric sequence in the Dhar Tichitt region begins with the Akreijit Phase, coinciding with a substantially wetter period with extensive lakes and probably dating prior to 2000 B.C. Subsistence data for this phase are limited, but suggest an orientation toward hunting, fishing, and limited plant collection and a total absence of food production. Following a sizable hiatus in the cultural sequence, which coincides with a very dry episode, the sequence resumes about 1500 B.C. with the Khimiya Phase, sites of which are located around the refilled lake basins. The abundant data for this phase suggest a subsistence pattern based upon extensive herding (cattle and goats) and fishing combined with limited hunting and seed collecting (with almost total collecting emphasis on the wild grass *Cenchrus biflorus*). The following Goungou and Nkhal phases show a continuation of this pattern, but by about 1100 B.C. the lakes once more began to dry up, reducing and eventually eliminating the fish potential. In apparent response to this environmental stress, the peoples at this time (the Naghez Phase) turned to intensive collecting of a wide range of wild seeds including *Cenchrus biflorus*, *Panicum laetum*, *Brachiaria deflexa*, and *Pennisetum* sp. There is at least a possibility that some limited cultivation of *Pennisetum*, as well as possibly *Brachiaria deflexa*, was beginning to be practiced at this time, but as yet this cannot be demonstrated with certainty. In the following Chebka Phase, however, beginning by or only shortly after 1000 B.C., *Pennisetum* increases to over 60 percent of the recovered and identifiable food-plant remains, and much of this shows definite characteristics of a domesticated variety. One grain impression very tentatively identified as *Sorghum* was also found associated with this phase, and *Brachiaria deflexa* continued to be present.

The following Arriane Phase reflects an intensification of this agricultural pattern, as does the still later, terminal Neolithic Akjinjeir Phase which came to an end, at least in this specific region, about 400 B.C. under combined pressures from desiccation and an invasion of horse-mounted raiders from North Africa.

In view of the lateness of appearance of cultivation in this area (ca. 1000 B.C.) and since the cultural transition from limited seed collecting to intensive seed-crop cultivation encompassed little more than a century, the hypothesis that this represents an independent, *in situ* development of plant domestication can probably be rejected. Furthermore, if our model explaining why food production was developed or adopted is valid, the hypothesis that there was an earlier agricultural hearth to the south in the savanna zone of West Africa can also be rejected. This position is strengthened by the absence of archaeological evidence for cultivation in that area at a period earlier than its appearance in the Tichitt area.

The possibility of Ethiopia being an early center of domestication and of the dispersal of cultivated plants from that area ultimately to the Tichitt-West Africa region is also examined. Although this hypothesis suffers no serious flaws in terms of available evidence, there is, nevertheless, still another model which seems more satisfactory. There is some evidence for seed-crop cultivation, including *Pennisetum*, in the highlands of the central Sahara prior to 3000 B.C. Its ultimate origins are probably very early, possibly independent seed-crop domestication in the eastern Sahara or stimulus-diffusion from earlier developments in the Near East via Egypt. Pressure in the central Sahara, either from population increases resulting from this increased food base and/or environmental deterioration, might well have pushed some of these cultivators southwestward into such southern Saharan highland areas as Aïr and Adrar des Iforas, and from there down such corridors as the Tilemsi Valley into the central valley of the Niger in the vicinity of Timbuktu. From that point there would be no geographical barriers to both the ideas and the already domesticated plants moving to anywhere in the Sahelian-Sudanic zone of western Africa.

REFERENCES

ALLCHIN, F. R.
1969   "Early cultivated plants in India and Pakistan," in *The domestication and exploitation of plants and animals*. Edited by Peter J. Ucko and G. W. Dimbleby, 323–329. Chicago: Aldine.

ANDERSON, EDGAR
1967   "The bearing of botanical evidence on African culture history," in *Reconstructing African history*. Edited by Creighton Gabel and Norman R. Bennett, 169–180. Boston: Boston University Press.

BAKER, H. G.
1962   Comments on the thesis that there was a major centre of plant domestication near the headwaters of the river Niger. *Journal of African History* 3(2):229–233.

BINFORD, LEWIS R.
1968   "Post-Pleistocene adaptations," in *New perspectives in archeology*. Edited by Sally R. Binford and Lewis R. Binford, 313–344. Chicago: Aldine.

BRAIDWOOD, ROBERT J.
1963   *Prehistoric men* (sixth edition). Anthropology Popular Series 37. Chicago: Chicago Natural History Museum.

CAMPS, GABRIEL
1960   Aux origines de la Berbérie: Massinissa ou les débuts de l'histoire. *Libyca (sér. Archéologie-Épigraphie)* 8(1):1–320.
1969   *Amekni: Néolithique ancien du Hoggar*. Mémoire du Centre de Recherches Anthropologiques, Préhistoriques et Ethnographiques 10. Arts et Métiers Graphiques. Paris: Flammarion.

CHAPELLE, JEAN
1957   *Nomades noires du Sahara*. Paris: Librairie Plon.

CHEVALIER, A.
1938   Le Sahara, centre d'origine de plantes cultivées. *Mémoires de la Société de Biogéographie* 6:307–322.

CHILDE, V. GORDON
1951   *Man makes himself*. New York: Mentor.

CLARK, J. DESMOND
1962   The spread of food production in sub-Saharan Africa. *Journal of African History* 3(2):211–228.

CONNAH, GRAHAM
1969   "The coming of iron: Nok and Daima," in *Lectures on Nigerian prehistory and archaeology*. Edited by Thurstan Shaw, 30–36. Ibadan: Ibadan University Press.

DALZIEL, J. M.
1937   *The useful plants of west tropical Africa*. London: Whitefrairs Press.

DANIELS, S. G. H.
1969   "The Middle and Late Stone Age," in *Lectures on Nigerian prehistory and archaeology*. Edited by Thurstan Shaw, 23–29. Ibadan: Ibadan University Press.

DAVIES, OLIVER
  1967a Timber-construction and wood-carving in West Africa in the second millennium B.C. *Man* n.s. 2(1):115–118.
  1967b *West Africa before the Europeans*. London: Methuen.
  1968 The origins of agriculture in West Africa. *Current Anthropology* 9(5):479–482.

DOGGETT, H.
  1965 "The development of the cultivated sorghums," in *Essays on crop plant evolution*. Edited by Sir Joseph Hutchinson, 50–69. Cambridge: Cambridge University Press.

DROUHIN, M. G.
  1944 Le Niger central: ses possibilités agricoles et économiques. *Bulletin de la Société de Géographie et d'Archéologie d'Oran* 65:7–34.

FAGAN, BRIAN M.
  1969 Radiocarbon dates for sub-Saharan Africa VI. *Journal of African History* 10(1):149–169.

FLIGHT, COLIN
  1970 Excavations at Kintampo. *West African Archaeological Newsletter* 12:71–72.

GAST, MORCEAU, JEAN ADRIAN
  1965 Mils et sorgho en Ahaggar: étude ethnologique et nutritionnelle. *Mémoire du Centre de Recherches Anthropologiques, Préhistoriques et Ethnographiques* 4. Algiers.

HARLAN, JACK R., JEAN PASQUEREAU
  1969 Décrue agriculture in Mali. *Economic Botany* 23(1):70–74.

HESTER, JAMES J.
  1968 Comments on "The origin of African agriculture." *Current Anthropology* 9(5):497–498.

HOBLER, PHILIP M., JAMES J. HESTER
  1969 Prehistory and environment in the Libyan desert. *South African Archaeological Journal* 23(92):120–130.

HUGOT, H. J.
  1968 The origins of agriculture: Sahara. *Current Anthropology* 9(5): 483–488.

JACQUES-FÉLIX, H.
  i.p. Grain impressions. Appendix K in *The Tichitt tradition: a late prehistoric occupation of the southwestern Sahara*. Patrick J. Munson. Bloomington: Indiana University Press.

LHOTE, HENRI
  1959 *The search for the Tassili frescoes*. New York: E. P. Dutton.

MAUNY, RAYMOND
  1950 Villages néolithiques de la falaise (dhar) Tichitt-Oualata. *Notes Africaines* 50:35–43.
  1955 Les gisements néolithiques de Karkarichinkat (Tilemsi, Soudan Français). *Actes du IIe Congrès Panafricain de Préhistoire* (1952): 616–629. Algiers.

MURDOCK, GEORGE P.
  1959   *Africa: its peoples and their culture history.* New York: McGraw-
          Hill.

NICOLAISEN, JOHANNES
  1963   *Ecology and culture of the pastoral Taureg.* Nationalmuseets
          Skrifter, Etnografisk Rœkke 9. Copenhagen: National Museum.

PONS, A., P. QUÉZEL
  1957   Première étude palynologique de quelques paléosols sahariens.
          Travaux de l'Institut de Recherches Sahariennes. 16(2):15–40.

PORTÈRES, ROLAND
  1950   Vieilles agricultures de l'Afrique intertropicale: centres d'origine
          et de diversification variétale primaire et berceaux d'agriculture
          antérieurs au XVIe siècle. *L'Agronomie Tropicale* 5(9–10):489–
          507.
  1951a   Géographie alimentaire, berceaux agricoles et migrations des
          plantes cultivées en Afrique intertropicale. *Compte Rendu Som-
          maire des Séances de la Société de Biogéographie* 239:16–21.
  1951b   Une céréale mineure cultivée dans l'Ouest africain (*Brachiaria
          deflexa* C. E. Hubbard var. *sativa* nov. var.). *L'Agronomie Tro-
          picale* 6(1–2):38–42.
  1962   Berceaux agricoles primaires sur le continent africain. *Journal of
          African History* 3(2):195–210.

SIMOONS, FREDERICK J.
  1965   Some questions on the economic prehistory of Ethiopia. *Journal
          of African History* 6(1):1–12.

SNOWDEN, J. D.
  1936   *The cultivated races of sorghum.* London: Adlard and Sons.

SZUMOWSKI, G.
  1956   Fouilles de l'abri sous roche de Kourounkorokalé (Soudan Fran-
          çais). *Bulletin de l'Institut Français d'Afrique Noire (sér. B)* 18:
          462–508.

TOUPET, CH.
  1958   La vallée de la Tamourt en Naaj. Tagant. Problèmes d'aménage-
          ment. *Bulletin de l'Institut Français d'Afrique Noire (sér. B) 20*
          (1–2): 68–110.

TURNBULL, PRISCILLA F.
  i.p.   Mammalian fauna. Appendix L in *The Tichitt tradition: a late
          prehistoric occupation of the southwestern Sahara.* Patrick J.
          Munson. Bloomington: Indiana University Press.

VAUFREY, RAYMOND
  1947   Le néolithique para-toumbien, une civilization agricole primitive
          du Soudan. *La Revue Scientifique* 85(3267):205–232.

VAVILOV, N. I.
  1949–1950   The origin, variation, immunity and breeding of cultivated
          plants. *Chronica Botanica* 13(1–6):1–364.

VIGNIER, P.
1945   Les sorghos à grains et leur culture au Soudan Français. *Revue Int. de Botanique Appliquée et d'Agriculture Tropicale* 25:163–230.

WENDORF, FRED
1968   "Late Paleolithic sites in Egyptian Nubia," in *The prehistory of Nubia,* volume 2. Edited by Fred Wendorf, 791–953. Dallas: Fort Burgwin Research Center and Southern Methodist University Press.

WHITE, LESLIE A.
1959   *The evolution of culture.* New York: McGraw-Hill.

WRIGLEY, CHRISTOPHER
1960   Speculations on the economic prehistory of Africa. *Journal of African History* 1(2):189–203.

The Kintampo Culture and Its Place in the Economic Prehistory of West Africa

COLIN FLIGHT

The Kintampo culture is the only prehistoric culture in Ghana to have been at all adequately defined (cf. Flight n.d.). It has sometimes been called the Kintampo Neolithic, but the name Kintampo culture has priority (Davies 1962) and is preferable in any case. In spite of the recommendations of Bishop and Clark (1967), I do not propose to start calling cultures "industrial complexes."

Rather less than twenty sites are known which can be assigned with confidence to the Kintampo culture. Some were discovered by the Geological Survey many years ago: the first two sites to be recorded were found in 1916, one near Jema and the other near Tolundipe (Kitson 1916). However, the majority have been discovered within the last twenty years, mostly by Davies, who was responsible for recognizing and initially defining the culture (Davies 1962, 1964, 1967).

Some sites have been excavated (these I later mention individually), but the collections we have to work with are mostly small, consisting, at best, of a few dozen pieces picked up off the surface. As far as it is possible to tell, however, the sites all seem to be very similar in content. The Kintampo culture is apparently so distinctive, so unlike any other prehistoric culture in Ghana, that sites belonging to it can be recognized easily. Only when the collection is very small does doubt sometimes arise.

In order to qualify for inclusion in the Kintampo culture, a site ought to possess all or most of the following characteristics: a good number (say three or more) of the enigmatic objects which Davies describes as terracotta cigars, but which I would prefer to call stone rasps (certainly they are not of terracotta); polished stone axe blades; polished stone bracelets; grooved stones made either from broken rasps or else from sandstone; grinding and pounding stones; pottery of a distinctive style (but shards exposed on the surface are often too badly weathered to be diagnostic); and chunks of burnt daub which sometimes bear the impression of wooden poles.

Even twelve years ago, before any of the sites had been excavated, enough was known about the Kintampo culture for it to seem likely, on indirect evidence, that the economy was one of village farming. Thus it was possible to cite evidence for durable structures of some kind (the burnt daub), for trade in essential equipment as well as luxuries (the axe blades and bracelets), for land clearance (the axe blades again), and perhaps for the processing of seeds (the grinding stones). Until recently, however, there was no direct evidence either for cultivated crops or for domestic animals.

The distribution map (Map 1) needs to be read with care, but it does show more than just the distribution of archaeological effort. A few of the blank spaces may well be filled in by future work (sites are surely awaiting discovery, for example, on the other side of the Ghana-Ivory Coast border), but some of the patterning in the map can probably be relied on.

A clear distinction can be made, in terms of geography at least, between upland and lowland sites; it remains to be seen whether there is any corresponding difference in material culture. The upland sites occur in relatively dense concentrations: one in the Banda hills and another on the high ground around Kintampo, not far from the edge of the forest. The lowland sites occur more sparsely in the open woodland of the inner Volta Basin, and most of them are in riverain locations.

Rather surprisingly, the Kintampo culture also turns up in the Accra plains, a long way further south. The site excavated by Davies (1964: 244) at Christians Village was unstratified, and it seems to me that the material from it is very mixed. However, there are many stone rasps, and some of the pottery can also be ascribed to the Kintampo culture on grounds of fabric and decoration. Another site may possibly exist at Somanya where a few rasp fragments have been collected. It is likely that this gap in the distribution will sooner or later be bridged. Access to the Afram plains is difficult, and they are almost unknown archaeologically. One large fragment of a stone rasp, presented to the Department of Archaeology at Legon some years ago, was reported to have been found near the remote village of Adiemmra; this is as yet the only hint we have of a Kintampo culture site in that region.

On the other hand, the absence of sites in the forest is very probably

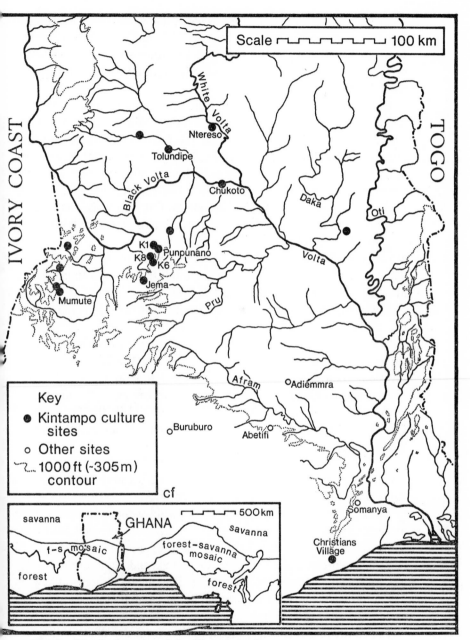

Map 1.   Distribution map of the Kintampo culture.

genuine. Some rasp fragments admittedly do occur — for instance, there is one from an eighteenth-century site at Mampongten, and a few were found at a site on the University campus at Kumasi (Nunoo 1969).

Such finds serve only to confirm what is known from evidence else-where, that stray fragments do turn up occasionally on later sites, and sometimes well outside the range of the Kintampo culture. (By the same token, of course, we should not rely much on that single fragment from Adiemmra.)

In broad outline, therefore, the distribution pattern is as follows. Kintampo culture sites do not occur, as far as we know, in the forest. There are many sites on the edge of the forest, concentrated on high ground, and a few further north, mostly near rivers. Further north again there are none. The Kintampo culture is thus confined within the zone described by some (e.g. J. D. Clark 1967: Map 5) as forest-savanna mosaic; but when that is said, the question at once arises whether it may not be thoroughly misleading to superimpose the distribution map of a prehistoric culture on a map of the modern vegetation. Can we afford to ignore the possibility of environmental change? For the time being, and with some qualifications, I think that we can (but this is a question I shall need to return to later).

It was suggested at one time by Davies that the Kintampo culture began in about 500 B.C. The argument was never convincing, but criticism seems superfluous now that we know from the evidence of radiocarbon dates that the conclusion was mistaken. The Kintampo culture turns out to have been much earlier than was supposed.

We know nothing for certain of the contemporaneous cultures which, presumably, must have existed in the forest and in the far north of Ghana. Perhaps we may guess that they were of an undistinguished "later Stone Age" character.

Two of the lowland sites had been excavated before I began work at Kintampo, and I will comment briefly on both.

A site at Chukoto on the Black Volta was investigated by Mathewson in 1965 as part of the program of rescue excavation carried out by the Volta Basin Research Project. Chukoto gave us, for the first time, a large and representative collection of pottery and stone artifacts from a site belonging without argument to the Kintampo culture (Mathewson 1967). Organic material, unfortunately, was not preserved, and even the pottery is in bad condition.

The controversial site at Ntereso, not far from the White Volta, was excavated by Davies in 1961 and 1962. Most of the differences which were claimed to exist between this and other "typical" sites of the Kintampo culture have disappeared, perhaps predictably, now that the Kintampo culture is better known. Ntereso has become famous for the iron objects which were allegedly found in association with the Kintampo culture material. I say nothing of these, since Davies (1969) has asked for time to reconsider. It is my opinion that only the stone arrowheads, unique to this site as far as we know and thoroughly Saharan in appearance, require some special explanation. Ntereso is nonetheless an important site. Organic material was well preserved. Shells and fish bones occur in quantity, proving the economic importance of aquatic resources that was already implied by the location of the site on a low ridge overlooking the river and by the occurrence of bone harpoons and fish-hooks. The animal bones are mostly from wild species — from antelopes especially — but dwarf goats are represented as well (Carter and Flight 1972). More relevant is the claim that ears of *Pennisetum* were used as roulettes for decorating some of the pottery. This identification does not seem to have been authenticated by a specialist, however, and I would rather reserve judgement. None of the pottery from my own excavations is decorated in this way, as far as I can tell. Three radiocarbon dates suggest that the Ntereso site was occupied around 1300 B.C. These dates are in good agreement with those obtained more recently from sites near Kintampo itself, in spite of being very much earlier than Davies had expected.[1]

The research which I carried out around Kintampo in 1967 and 1968 was intended to determine more satisfactorily the date and character of the Kintampo culture in the area where it had first been recognized. This is very different terrain from that in which the lowland sites occur — a dissected sandstone plateau bounded on the west by a steep and sometimes precipitous scarp. Rainfall is higher here, the dry season shorter, the vegetation lusher. We concentrated our attention entirely on the many caves and rock shelters in the hope of finding organic material better preserved than is generally the case on open sites. The Kintampo culture had not been found in a rock shelter before, but some of the sites already known in the area — like Jema, the first ever to be discovered, or Punpunano, the first to be discovered by Davies — were in close proximity to sandstone inselbergs. This encouraged the hope that some use might have been made of the available rock shelters. In the event, our hopes were justified. At several of the shelters which we investigated, there had indeed been occupation by Kintampo culture communities. Preservation was bad, but in others it was excellent. We were thus able to make some progress in defining the date and char-

---

[1] I may add that an upland site belonging to the Banda hills group has been discovered and excavated by Joanne Dombrowski since this paper was written.

acter of the culture and in placing it for the first time in a local cultural-
stratigraphic sequence.

Work began with the excavation — by Philip Rahtz in 1966 and
myself on a smaller scale in 1967 — of a rock shelter (K1) 10 kilometers north of Kintampo (this should soon be published [Rahtz and
Flight n.d.]). During 1967 I also made trial excavations at three other
shelters (K2-4) in the same inselberg as K1; at three shelters (K5-7) in
an inselberg 4 kilometers to the south of Kintampo; and finally at a
shelter (K8) in a cliff 1 kilometer to the west. In 1968 I returned to
K6, which had produced by far the most promising results, and enlarged the original excavation. For much of this second season I had
the help of Peter Schmidt, then of Northwestern, now of Brown University. (Some account of the work has been given in interim reports:
Flight [n.d., 1968]; cf. Calvocoressi [1970: 71–3]; Willett [1971:
352–3].)

The cultural sequence, as far as it can be pieced together at present,
is described in the forthcoming K1 report. Here I am concerned only
with what happen to be the two best documented parts of the sequence
— the Kintampo culture itself and the immediately preceding but altogether different Punpun phase. For the break between the two, a date
of 1450 to 1400 B.C. is likely on the evidence of six radiocarbon dates,
and neither seems to be of more than a few centuries' duration.

Occurrences of the Punpun phase (to which I referred initially as the
"Buobini culture") have been found at three sites in the Kintampo
area, but nowhere else. The distinctive pottery turned up first in small
quantities at K1, and quite substantial middens were excavated later
at K6 and K8. These middens are full of snail shells, seed husks of
Celtis sp., and animal bones from a wide variety of species. Here we
seem to be dealing with the camp sites occupied at least during the
wet season — for that is when the snails appear and the hackberries
ripen — by groups of hunter-gatherers; I believe that this population
was then displaced by the immigrant communities which are represented in the archaeological record by the Kintampo culture. I have no
special liking for hypotheses of invasion, but in this case the differences
are so pronounced in almost every respect that no other explanation
seems possible.

The Kintampo culture is present at the same three sites overlying the
Punpun phase occurrences and also at two others (K4 and K7). It is only
at K6, however, that the material is both abundant and well preserved.
A study of the pottery suggests that the Kintampo culture in this area
can be divided into two phases, but the distinguishing characteristics

need not be considered here. Solid structures were being built at K6 during the second phase at least. Unluckily none were found in the excavated area, but large quantities of burnt daub had been dumped repeatedly in this part of the shelter in the later stages of the Kintampo culture occupation.

The evidence from K6 throws light on two main aspects of the economy; one is trade, the other subsistence.

The importance of trade is worth emphasizing. Except for grinding stones, which may have been made from local rock, all of the stone equipment must have been imported. Axe blades occur by the hundred, many being made of Birrimian rocks, the nearest outcrops of which are in the Banda hills. Traffic in stone rasps and bracelets can also be inferred, though it is not possible yet to pinpoint the sources. I suspect that a small proportion of the pottery was traded as well. One surprising find was a shell of the brackish-water species *Tympanotonus fuscatus* which must somehow have travelled northwards from the coast, perhaps beginning its journey at one of the Kintampo culture sites in the Accra plains.

The evidence relating to subsistence is of more immediate interest. Animal bones were disappointingly few, but Carter has identified as many of them as possible and arrived at some valuable conclusions (Carter and Flight 1972). Domestic animals are certainly present — dwarf goats and a small breed of cattle as well. The remaining bones are mostly from various antelopes. These were presumably hunted, except perhaps for the tiny nocturnal species, the Royal Antelope (*Neotragus pygmaeus*), which would, I suppose, more probably have been caught in traps. Snail shells occur, though not in the same large quantities as in the Punpun phase middens. For the recovery of carbonized vegetable remains we used the flotation technique described by Struever (1968). No detailed study of this material has yet been made, but cowpeas (*Vigna unguiculata*) and seed husks from the oil palm (*Elaeis guineensis*) are both easily identified and very common. Also recognized were a few seed husks from the tree *Canarium schweinfurthii*, which has edible fruit. *Celtis* husks, being largely composed of carbonate, come out in the heavy fraction. They are much less common than in the Punpun phase.

The question of possible cultivation hardly arises except in the case of *Vigna*. With regard to *Celtis, Canarium,* and (probably) *Elaeis*, it is to be presumed that the trees grew wild. There is no proof that the cowpeas were cultivated, but in view of their abundance I regard it as likely that they were. Whether they were domesticated in the sense of having pods which did not burst when ripe is unknown.[2]

Evidence for the cultivation of cereals is still only indirect and circumstantial. It might reasonably be argued, however, that indirect evidence carries greater weight in this environment than it would, say, in the southern Sahara. I would go so far as to suggest that it is pedantic, knowing what we do about the Kintampo culture, to insist on waiting for direct evidence. Of course I regret not being able to prove that cereals were grown; but it irks me more that I cannot say which cereals they were. If I were asked to guess, my first choice would be sorghum.

There is no direct evidence to show that yams were cultivated or even that they were used as food, likely though this would seem. It is a serious question, however, whether yams can be expected to survive at all in a recognizable form.

Clearly the evidence is not as complete as might be wished. In spite of that I think we are justified in some conclusions which do not altogether fit the conventional picture of later African prehistory.

I am convinced by Munson's work in Mauritania (Munson, this volume) that environmental change is an important factor in the prehistory of the southern Sahara during the last few thousand years B.C. Further south I see no reason to think that it had much effect. The evidence from K6 is roughly what we might expect of a village farming site placed in a forest-savanna setting not greatly different from the modern environment. We can point to the Royal Antelope, for example, as proof of forest not far away; but the existence of more open vegetation, too, is implied by the presence of other antelopes, as well as by the occurrence of oil palms and cowpeas. What attracted human settlement was, I suppose, precisely this ecological diversity. Forest and savanna do not merge; they become interspersed. Thus it seems to me that the evidence from Kintampo is consistent with the conclusion reached by Morgan and Moss (1965: 293) who say, with reference to the forest-savanna mosaic, "Diversity is not the product of human intervention; it is an inherent property of the pattern."

It is also significant, I think, that this is an area where today both yams and cereals are grown. According to the conventional view of the origins of African agriculture, such a combination of crops would be

---

[2] A careless remark of mine to the effect that the cowpeas are small has been quoted by Calvocoressi (1970: 72). This, though true, need not be significant: it may be simply due to shrinkage during carbonization.

regarded as a secondary development, resulting from an overlap between the two primary complexes — a vegecultural complex in the
forest, and a seed-agricultural complex in the savanna. Even if it were
true, however, this would not be a sufficient explanation. It does not
explain WHY people should choose to grow yams and cereals in combination: it suggests how the opportunity to do so might have arisen, but it
does not explain why the opportunity should ever have been taken.
The combination ought instead to be seen as an attempt to solve the
problems posed by one specific environment — as a strategy which
aims to achieve the maximum yield with the minimum risk.[3] This particular solution will only work where in most years there is neither too
much rain for cereals, nor too little for yams; and those limits coincide
very nearly with the limits of the forest-savanna mosaic. It is within
this zone, in Ghana and perhaps elsewhere, that the earliest village-
farming settlements we know of are found. I am led to suggest that the
yam-cereal combination may not be a secondary development at all,
but the primary form of agriculture in sub-Saharan Africa. The K6
evidence is admittedly inconclusive, but it points in the right direction.
Yams have not been recognized, but at least we have proof of the oil
palm; cereals have not been identified, but at least we have found the
cowpeas.

I doubt whether any close relationship exists between the Kintampo
culture and the various aspects of "late Neolithic" in the southern
Sahara. It would be easy to exaggerate the significance of the arrowheads from Ntereso. They are, as I have said, anomalous: they require
some special explanation. Perhaps it is not coincidental that they occur
only at one of the most northerly Kintampo culture sites.

In summary, then, I visualize the Kintampo culture spreading eastwards along the edge of the forest as small groups of people move on
in search of land. They bring with them their cattle and goats; they
make clearings where they can build their villages and plant their
crops; they hunt, they set traps, they gather snails and fruit from the
forest; they trade with their neighbors. Mostly they settle in upland
areas where patches of forest are juxtaposed with patches of savanna.
Other groups move northwards into more open country which is less

---

[3] I originally referred at this point to an article by Gould (1963), believing it to be
an empirical study (cf. Haggett 1965: 173–4; D. L. Clarke 1968: 492–6). Having read
the article again, I realize that I was mistaken. Gould makes it quite clear that his
example is imaginary, intended only to illustrate the application of game theory
to a problem in geography. I apologize for adding to the confusion, but still think
that my argument is valid.

attractive on the whole, but where by way of compensation they can fish in the rivers and collect shellfish during the dry season.

The Kintampo culture is already developed when it makes its appearance around Kintampo in 1400 B.C. or a little earlier. It had taken shape elsewhere, perhaps in the Banda hills, but I think more probably further west, perhaps in Ivory Coast. In Ghana it seems to represent a rather brief episode, not lasting for more than a few hundred years at most. What happened afterwards is obscure. Were it not for the evidence of a few shards from K1, it could be thought that the area was entirely uninhabited during the first millennium B.C. Possibly the Kintampo culture survived in some form, but not in the rock shelters where we were looking for it.

This is a paper written mainly for archaeologists. I hope that they may find the information of value and the ideas of interest. But any botanist who has read this far, now that he sees the end approaching, will realize that there is little in it for him. Not much has been added to the stock of archaeobotanical evidence — evidence which is at the same time archaeological and botanical — relating to the history of crop cultivation in Africa. Shaw (this volume) has drawn up a list of all the direct evidence available to us; the list is embarrassingly short. And yet, by looking for sites where preservation is good and by using the very efficient recovery techniques which have now been developed, the evidence we need should not be hard to come by.

REFERENCES

BISHOP, W. W., J. D. CLARK, *editors*
   1967   *Background to evolution in Africa.* Chicago: University of Chicago Press.
CALVOCORESSI, D.
   1970   Report on the Third Conference of West African Archaeologists. *West African Archaeological Newsletter* 12:53–90.
CARTER, P. L., C. FLIGHT
   1972   A report on the fauna from the sites of Ntereso and Kintampo rock shelter six in Ghana, with evidence for the practice of animal husbandry in the second millennium B.C. *Man* n.s. 7:277–282.
CLARK, J. D. *editor*
   1967   *Atlas of Africain prehistory.* Chicago: University of Chicago Press.
CLARKE, D. L.
   1968   *Analytical archaeology.* London: Methuen.

DAVIES, O.
1962   "Neolithic cultures of Ghana," in *Actes du IVe Congrès Panafricain de Préhistoire*, volume 3. Edited by G. Mortelmans and J. Nenquin, 291–301. Tervuren: Musée royal de l'Afrique centrale.
1964   *The Quaternary in the coastlands of Guinea*. Glasgow: Jackson.
1967   *West Africa before the Europeans*. London: Methuen.
1969   On radiocarbon chronology of the Iron Age in sub-Saharan Africa. *Current Anthropology* 10:230.

FLIGHT, C.
1968   Kintampo 1967. *West African Archaeological Newsletter* 8:15–20.
n.d.   "The prehistoric sequence in the Kintampo area of Ghana," in *Actes du VIe Congrès Panafricain de Préhistoire*. Edited by H. Hugot.

GOULD, P. R.
1963   Man against his environment: a game theoretic framework. *Annals of the Association of American Geographers* 53:290–297.

HAGGETT, P.
1965   *Locational analysis in human geography*. London: Arnold.

KITSON, A. E.
1916   The Gold Coast: some considerations of its structure, people and natural history. *Journal of the Royal Geographical Society* 48: 369–392.

MATHEWSON, R. D.
1967   "Chukoto," in *Archaeology in the Volta Basin, 1963–1966*. Edited by R. N. York, R. D. Mathewson, D. Calvocoressi, and C. Flight, 26–27. Legon: Volta Basin Research Project and Department of Archaeology.

MORGAN W. B., R. P. MOSS
1965   Savanna and forest in western Nigeria. *Africa* 35:286–293.

NUNOO, R. B.
1969   "Buruburo factory excavations," in *Actes du Premier Colloque Internaional d'Archéologie Africaine*. Edited by Y. Coppens, 321–333. Fort-Lamy: Institut National Tchadien pour les Sciences Humaines.

RAHTZ, P. A., C. FLIGHT
n.d.   A quern factory near Kintampo, Ghana. *West African Journal of Archaeology* 4.

STRUEVER, S.
1968   Flotation techniques for the recovery of small-scale archaeological remains. *American Antiquity* 33:353–362.

WILLETT, F.
1971   A survey of recent results in the radiocarbon chronology of western and northern Africa. *Journal of African History* 12:339–370.

History of Crops and Peoples in North Cameroon to A.D. 1900

NICHOLAS DAVID

My aims are:
1. to summarize the few archaeological data available on the environment and prehistory of the Neolithic and later peoples and on the cultivated plants of North Cameroon;
2. to attempt, by a combination of linguistic, historical, and distributional approaches, to relate the archaeology of the area to its ethnohistory;
3. to present a tentative periodization of the establishment of crop plants in North Cameroon and suggest some features that may differentiate the Neolithic economies of the Chad and Benue basins; and
4. to point out some implications of relevance for the culture history of West and Central Africa.

North Cameroon extends from Lake Chad to the southern boundary of Adamawa department at 6° north latitude. The administrative departments correspond fairly closely with geographical regions and have been retained as the basis of the following brief description of the area (see Map 1).[1]

The Upper Benue Basin Archaeological Project was supported by the National Science Foundation (GS–2236), by Ford Foundation Archaeological Traineeships, and by the University Museum (University of Pennsylvania). In the writing of this paper I owe a particular debt of gratitude to George Jackson, with whom for a happy month I tramped around the Benue valley and in the process assimilated a little African botany. He is not to be held responsible for my mistakes. I thank Philip Burnham for his many useful comments on an earlier draft and for generously allowing me to make use of his Gbaya data in advance of publication.
[1] In the absence of a satisfactory regional geography of Cameroon, this description is a patchwork of Billard's *Essai de géographie physique* (1963), Segalen's (1957) and Letouzey's (1958) sections on soils and phytogeography in the *Atlas du*

The CHAD-LOGONE region (15,871 square kilometers) in the north and northeast comprises the Departments of Logone and Chari and Mayo (River) Danaï. In the Logone-Chari delta and on either side of the former river, which is at this point the eastern border of Cameroon, stretch seasonally inundated plains and marshes and higher patches of sandy soils that slope imperceptibly from 330 meters above sea level northward to Lake Chad at 282 meters. The rainy season (June-September) is short and, as elsewhere in the area, evaporation greatly exceeds precipitation, which varies considerably from year to year. Average rainfall in the south is 900 millimeters, falling to about 400 millimeters in the extreme north. The average annual temperature at Fort-Foureau is 28° Centigrade. During the long dry season the mean of the maxima [MM] rises to 36° in April (42° at Yagoua), while in December the mean of the minima [Mm] falls to 20° (10° at Yagoua). South of the lake there are leached, sandy, ferruginous soils, locally hydromorphic or halomorphic; the central part of the region is blanketed by black tropical clays and silts, halomorphic in the north. South and west of Yagoua the soils are again sandy and ferruginous. Thorny acacia scrub grows on sandy soils above the level of the floods; tall grass savanna with *Echinochloa pyramidalis, Vetiveria nigritana, Oryza barthii*, and *Hyparrhenia sect. rufa* covers the inundated plains. The population density (1969) is 9.4 per square kilometer in the north, 32.0 in the south (17.4 overall).

The MANDARA region (Department of Margui-Wandala; 7,433 square kilometers) is a raised block of Precambrian anatexites and ancient granites that have been pierced by igneous rocks. The plateau is at an altitude of 700-800 meters, with peaks rising to 1,450 meters. In the deeply incised valleys, streams and torrents run irregularly during the rains and are dry for much of the year. The rainy season (i.e., months with 100+ millimeters rainfall) lasts from May to September with 967 millimeters average precipitation at Mokolo in the center of the plateau. March and April MM are between 41° and 42° Centigrade, but the nights are chilly in December and January (Mm = 8° Centigrade). The tropical ferruginous (fersiallitic) soils of the area are immature and, where not terraced by man, much subject to erosion. Sudan and

Cameroun, and the latter author's *Etude phytogéographique*, also the *Carte géologique de Cameroun*, published by the Direction des Mines et de la Géologie (1956), the Synthèse Régional pour la préparation du 3e Plan, 1971–76, put out by the Service Régional de l'Economie et du Plan, Région Administrative du Nord-Cameroun (1969), data kindly supplied by M. Letouzey and by the Direction de la Météorologie, Climatologie et Statistiques of the Ministère des Transports, and information culled from monographs and other sources cited below.

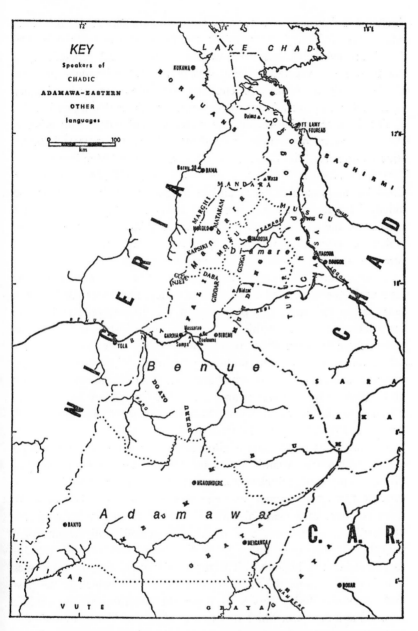

Map 1. North Cameroon: regions, towns, main sites, and peoples (omitting the Shuwa Arab pastoralists of the extreme north and the Fulani)

Sudano-Sahelian dry savanna woodland with abundant *Isoberlinia doka* and grasses including *Andropogon schirensis, Hyparrhenia rufa,* and *Loudetia acuminata,* has been widely destroyed and replaced by a "domesticated" vegetation with *Acacia albida, Adansonia digitata, Celtis integrifolia, Ficus* spp., etc. The population density is 44.0 per square kilometer overall, but reaches over four times that figure locally.

The three remaining regions are effectively coincident with administrative departments and are named after them. The DIAMARÉ (9,695 square kilometers) lies between the Chad-Logone and Mandara regions. The plain averages 400 meters above sea level and forms part of the Chad basin. Around Maroua and in tongues extending south to the indented border with Chad, northeast along the Mayo Tsanaga, and east along the Mayo Boula are the *harde* [black tropical clays] on which are grown durra races of sorghum; in the northwest and west are foothills and outliers of the Mandara mountains. In the southwest, bands of embrechites, gneiss, and mica-schists extend across the low Logone-Benue watershed to the Benue valley; anatexites and granites reappear to the east. The pedology of the lithomorphic and sandy ferruginous soils reflects this geological diversity, while the climate is intermediate between those of the neighboring regions. Maroua receives an average of 850 millimeters rainfall. The vegetation, tree savanna and light savanna woodland, has been transformed by man and degraded by cultivation and use as pasture. There is a definite advance to the south of thorny Sahelian elements. The population density is 37.3 per square kilometer.

The BENUE (61,754 square kilometers) and ADAMAWA regions lie mainly within the Atlantic drainage. The former region is roughly divisible into two geological zones. The Benue river flows in a geosyncline filled with cretaceous rocks that extend some distance away from the river at a mean altitude of about 200 meters. Around this "trough" the ancient rocks reappear as a granitic and metamorphic peneplain broken up by inselbergs and outlying massifs of the Mandara and Adamawa highlands. The main tributaries, and the only ones that flow throughout the year, are the Mayo Kébi (which in the past and sometimes today serves to drain the overflow of the middle Logone) and the Faro, which flows north along the Alantika mountains to meet the Benue near the Nigerian border. During the rains (May-September), Garoua, the capital of North Cameroon, receives an average 980 millimeters of precipitation. The average annual temperature is 28° Centigrade, the MM 40° in March-April, the Mm 17° in December-January. Tropical ferruginous soils, often eroded and little affected

by leaching, cover almost the entire region with the exception of the
Benue and Kébi floodplains around and below their confluence, where
there are black tropical clays and rich modern alluvium. The region
falls within the Sudan savanna zone, varying from tree savanna to
savanna woodland and open dry forest. The grass cover tends to consist
mainly of *Hyparrhenia* spp.; characteristic woody plants include *I.
doka, Monotes kerstingii,* and *Uapaca togoensis* on the slopes and in
the valleys bordering the Adamawa. Towards the north the forests are
characterized by *Boswellia odorata, Sclerocarya birrea,* and *Prosopis
africana,* but have for the most part been transformed into savanna
bush with *Combretum* and *Terminalia* species and *Anogeissus leiocarpus.* North of the Benue, *Boswellia* and *Ficus* spp. *Prosopis, Sterculia setigera,* and *Acacia* spp. become more abundant. The population
density is only 4.95 per square kilometer.

The ADAMAWA plateau (64,000 square kilometers), at an average
altitude of 1,200 meters, with folded mountain ranges up to 2,450
meters, was formed by the uplifting of the Precambrian and granitic
basal complex. Effusive igneous rocks, predominantly basalts, lie in a
broad arc to the north of N'gaoundéré. The region is significantly
cooler and wetter than those to the north. The rainy season lasts from
April to October. At N'gaoundéré the average precipitation is 1,574
millimeters, average temperature 22° Centigrade, the MM only 29° in
March, the Mm 16° in January. The pedology ranges from the poor
ferralitic soils of the northeast to thin, immature, mountain soils in
the west. The remainder of the region is characterized by complex
red ferralitic savanna soils. Plantains grow in the derived savannas of the
southern margins of the plateau (Letouzey's *"Zone péri- ou postforest-
ière"*). Elsewhere, with the exception of some mountain communities
and gallery forests, there is Sudan-Guinea grassland and shrub savanna
with *Daniella oliveri* and *Lophira lanceolata.* The grass cover varies
according to the intensity of its use as pasture, *Andropogon* spp., *H.
rufa,* and *Panicum phragmitoides* becoming progressively degraded on
eroded soils and replaced by *Urelytrum thyrsioides, Sporobolus pyramidalis,* and *Chloris pycnothrix.* On bare areas with some protection
from fire, woody species may grow up to form thickets. Population
densities, averaging 3.8 per square kilometer, are the lowest in North
Cameroon.

The peoples and crops of the Tikar plain, administered as part of
North Cameroon but in other ways more closely related to the south
and west, are excluded from this study.

THE HOLOCENE ENVIRONMENTAL SEQUENCE

The Bame-Limani-Bongor ridge is an old shoreline formed between about 8000 and 1500 B.C. during stays of Lake Paleo-Chad at the 320 meter contour (Pullan 1969). Following a drop in the lake level to 300 meters, the lake divided into two parts, connected by the Bahr-el-Ghazal. From that time the level of the lake in the Chadian "Pays-Bas" dropped more rapidly than that of Lake Chad. Neolithic sites in the Pays-Bas are clustered around the 320 meter contour but extend down to about 250 meters, whereas Lake Chad still stands at 282 meters (Schneider 1967). Thus, for much of the Holocene, the northern part of our area was denied to human habitation.

Hervieu (1969) has offered a tentative sequence for the area between the northern Adamawa and the borders of the Chad basin, and has correlated his work with that of Pias (1967, 1968) on the southern Chad sequence. Hurault (1970) has studied the processes of gully erosion around Banyo in the Adamawa. In Table 1, I attempt to bring these sources together. The dates are taken from the Lake Chad sequence (Schneider 1967; Servant and Servant 1970; van Zinderen Bakker, this volume). A radiocarbon date of 8150 ± 230 B.C. (Gif-871) from a vertisol in the middle terrace of the Kébi (Hervieu 1969: 17) would suggest that this was forming after the period of desert invasion during the first rise and subsequent recession of Lake Chad. Table 1 should be considered — at best — as a working hypothesis.[2]

As van Zinderen Bakker has demonstrated, our knowledge of the later Holocene geoclimatic sequence is rapidly improving, but vegetation patterns cannot yet be reconstructed. The fall in the level of Lake Chad that occurred at about 2000 B.C. may have been the result either of lowered rainfall or of higher temperatures and the consequent increased evaporation. Both alternatives, with their contrasting implications for the environment and for man, must still be entertained. The climatic changes of the time were, however, minor in comparison with those of the Late Glacial, and any shifts of vegetation belts are likely to have been correspondingly less marked. In this connection it is note-

---

[2]   Dates of 18,000 and 15,000 B.P. are cited by Marliac (1971, volume 2: 6) for paleosols identified by Hervieu as "Douroumien" and considered by him to be of the Middle Quaternary. If these dates are confirmed, substantial modifications, at least of the early part of the sequence, will be required.

It should also be noted that the arid period represented in the Chad sequence from ca. 2550 to 1550 B.C. is not recognizable in the Adamawa, and that, conversely, the dry period commencing there at about the beginning of our era is not recorded in the north. Can the Banyo dates be misleading?

Table 1. A tentative outline, with approximate dates, of the Late Pleistocene and Holocene sequences of North Cameroon. After Hervieu (1969), van Zinderen Bakker (1972), and Servant and Servant-Vildary (1972).

Dates	Phases	Inferred climate	Regions — Adamawa (Banyo)	Regions — N. Adamawa, Benue Mandara	Lake Chad	Dates
A.D. 1900	Actuel	Tropical semihumid	Savanna grassland. Forest destroyed by man; Partial regeneration of forest	Modern erosion and recent alluvium	282 meter lake. Minor fluctuations	A.D. 1900
A.D./B.C.			Arid: open savanna		Lake above present level	
1500 B.C.	Sub-actuel	Recurrence of dry conditions		Low (1–2 meters) terraces	Lower lake levels	1500 B.C.
2500 B.C.			Humid		High lake 320 meters (?)	2500 B.C.
5000 B.C.			Forest		Minor recession	5000 B.C.
5500 B.C.		Tropical and more humid		Badlands erosion	320 meters lake. Formation of Bama ridge	5500 B.C.
8000 B.C.					Recession	8000 B.C.
						9000 B.C.
10,000 B.C.	Later Bossoumian	Semi-arid	Open savanna	Middle (4–8 meters) terraces and glacis accumulation and sheet erosion	Rising lake	10,400 B.C.
22,000 B.C.					Desert	
					Invasion	22,000 B.C.

worthy that Hurault does not see the destruction of the Adamawa forest taking place until the last millennium B.C., by which time human intervention is by no means an impossibility.

A further obstacle to the reconstruction of vegetation patterns is our ignorance of the plant communities that would occur in the area today were it not for centuries of clearing and firing by man and the grazing and trampling of his cattle. Are edapho-climatic factors sufficient for the interpretation of man-land relationships in prehistory? Or must the modern flora be understood in climato-anthropo-edaphic terms (in which case both zonal shifts and the creation of quite new types of plant communities must be envisaged)? The work of Sillans (1958) on the ecology, origins, and development of the savannas of the Central African Republic is of the greatest relevance in this context. Sillans argues that the Central African savannas between 6° and 10° north latitude are an anthropogenic subclimax replacing, except in certain specialized habitats (as, for example, marshes and gallery forests), dense dry forest with tall trees forming a more or less closed canopy and with a virtual absence of grass cover. Clearing and cutting of the forest for cultivation are primarily responsible for savannization.

L'homme par la RÉPÉTITION PLURISÉCULAIRE DE SES TECHNIQUES CULTURALES PRIMITIVES, a détruit d'immenses étendues boisées dont la régéneration post-culturale MALGRÉ LES FEUX semble avoir donné vraisemblablement naissance à toutes les formations savanisées oubanguiennes (Sillans 1958).

Fire acts to retard forest regrowth, but cannot alone degrade the forest and create savanna.

L'inexistence des stades de dégradation nous apparaît manifeste maintenant que nous croyons connaître le vrai processus évolutif des formations végé-tales centrafricaines: FORÊT → CULTURES → SAVANE → FORÊT. Insistons sur L'ORIGINE POSTCULTURALE des savanes .... l'évolution actuelle de la végé-tation est commandée par les cultures, il en fut, de tous temps, la même chose. Depuis l'arrivée de premiers agriculteurs, l'évolution générale de la végétation oubanguienne tend vers le type savane, mais ces savanes, à leur tour, tendent manifestement vers le recrû forestier (Sillans 1958: 258–259).

For Cameroon, Letouzey constantly emphasizes the effects of shifting agriculture, pasturage, and the cutting of trees for lumber and fuel, showing how these modify both the physiognomy and the species composition of the regional floras. He has shown how, in the zone of derived savanna around the forest and on the Adamawa plateau, fire alone cannot prevent forest regrowth and recolonization (1968: 231–232). On the Sudano-Sahelian boundary, the 2,000 hectare Gokoro forest, 30 kilometers north-northeast of Mokolo, has been protected for some forty years from clearing and, theoretically, from use as pasture. During this period thorny scrub with some Sudanic elements has developed into more or less closed canopy forest. Grasses are being progressively displaced by various *Dioscorea* species, ferns, and tangles of *Acacia ataxacantha*. Fires lick around the margins but appear no longer able to penetrate. Although species will change, dense dry forest is already reestablished (Letouzey 1968: 317–318; personal communication 1973).

If these conclusions be accepted, they must radically influence our interpretation of the prehistory of large parts of the Central and West African savanna zone. For, in comparison with savanna ecosystems, dense dry forest must be of far less potential to men at the hunter-gatherer or Neolithic technological level. A probable greater variety of plant foods would not compensate for the lack of exploitable protein; game, and especially the preferred herd ungulates, would be scarce, and the forest itself would be irreducible without stone axes; with them the process would still proceed only slowly. Sillans (1958: 246) describes a relict stand as composed of a large number of tree species, tall and straight trunked in contrast to their often stunted and gnarled savanna habitus. Beneath the canopy there is a thick, impenetrable undergrowth of bushes and lianas. Before the introduction of iron technology the dry forest would appear singularly unattractive to human settlement.

It is unclear whether Sillans's conclusions can be extended north of the tenth parallel to the Sahel-Sudan zone of thorn scrub with its reduced grass cover that disappears during the long dry season. From Nigeria and Cameroon there is, however, historical evidence concerning recent vegetation changes in regions that are comparable in latitude and rainfall. The "Great Forest" covering 6,000 square miles of Bornu was destroyed in less than fifty years after large-scale immigration began (Stenning 1959: 26–27). Savanna has replaced forest in several other places south of Lake Chad that had been visited by the early explorers (e.g. Denham, et al. 1828, volume 2: 11, 24; Barth 1857, volume 3: 161). Lestringant (1964: 22) quotes Diziain and old native informants on the retreat of the forest in Giddar territory on the Benue-Diamaré border. He concludes, "Il importe donc d'avoir toujours à l'esprit que l'ensemble du pays, chaine du Mandara et bas-plateau, ont dû, voici plusieurs siècles, bénéficier d'un manteau forestier continu et épais."

These examples support Sillans by establishing both the presence of forest north of 10° north latitude in our area and that the manner in which it was destroyed was by clearing and burning, not by firing alone — with the implication that such clearance could not occur before the introduction of food production. Other authorities, including Aubreville (1949) and Trochain (in his preface to Sillans 1958: xi), consider that fire is capable of degrading forest. The Central African savannas should, in their view, be considered as a fire subclimax. They could thus predate the origins of agriculture.

Edapho-climatic savannas unquestionably exist; the problem of savanna origins must be approached area by area and by ecologists, archaeologists, and botanists working in concert. Nevertheless there is broad agreement that were it not for the intervention of man, the present savanna zone of the Central African Republic and neighboring regions of Chad and Cameroon would have a closed rather than an open vegetation cover. The same would hold under similar climatic conditions in the past, while the zone of present savanna ASPECT, although likely to be of botanically different composition, would be some distance north of the tenth parallel, and, for edapho-climatic reasons, narrow from north to south and more in the nature of a transition between thorn scrub and dry forest than of a vegetation belt. If, as suggested above, climatic changes over the past 5,000 years have been of limited amplitude, then, if Sillans is correct, we might expect a shifting contrast between the northern and southern parts of our area. The Chad basin would be under either dry forest and savanna or thorn scrub and savanna, and in such times attractive to hunter-gatherers, cultivators, and pastoralists; dense dry forest is likely to have been more constant in the Benue basin and to have offered little inducement to settlement unless to farmers equipped with iron tools.

ARCHAEOLOGY: THE STONE AGE

Nothing is known of late Stone Age populations in the area until the Neolithic. The Bornu 38 site (11°32′ North 13°40′ East), situated just within the Bama ridge, has given four dates ranging from 1880 ± 160 B.C. to 640 ± 170 B.C. (Libby half-life; laboratory numbers N-793 and N-796). These are the earliest dates for the Neolithic south of Lake Chad and agree well with dates from Bornu 70 and Daima (Connah 1970, and reported in Calvocoressi 1970). The earliest Chadian dates are 425 ± 150 B.C. (Gif-742) and 200 ± 135 B.C. (DaK-10) from Mdaga and 120 ± 180 B.C. (Gif-435) from Amkoundjo; both sites are located near Fort Lamy at about 290 meters above sea level (Lebeuf 1969: 8). The early occupants of Daima, the only site to have been published even in part (*Illustrated London News* 1967; Connah 1966, 1967), had cattle and were fishermen; there is no direct evidence of Neolithic agriculture. As the lake fell, the peoples of the area followed the retreating shoreline. No doubt there are many Iron Age mounds in the Chad-Logone region that have Neolithic components, but none have yet been excavated.

Several Neolithic axe factories from the mountains around Maroua have been described by Hervieu (1968) and Marliac (1971). Similar sites are known from Hossere (Mt.) Balda on the Limani-Bongor ridge and, within the ridge, from H. Waza. Although all are undated surface collections, Hervieu originally attributed some of them to the lower Paleolithic on grounds of tool morphology and the virtual absence of polished stone tools. The archaic features are, however, characteristic of workshop materials and can be duplicated in the assemblages of several concentrations of stone tools excavated by Marliac and Quechon along 1,250 meters of the low terrace of the Mayo Tsanaga at Maroua. These are of undoubted Neolithic age. Although some fragments of pottery were found, decorated mainly by punctations, the Mayo Tsanaga sites do not appear to be settlements but again factory or workshop areas. The lithic assemblages are composed largely of waste flakes and axe roughouts at varying stages of manufacture. Very rare pieces are ground or "semipolished" (Marliac 1971, volume 1). On the basis of Hervieu's suggested chronology, the low terrace is likely to have formed between the fourth and the second millennia B.C. Marliac (letter of May 15, 1972) has kindly allowed me to cite a recently processed radiocarbon determination from one of the excavations. The date of A.D. 230 ± 90 (Gif-2232) is later than expected but still within the Neolithic period.

The discovery of ground and polished stone axes, which are lithologically similar to those from Maroua found in other parts of the Diamaré and in the Mandara region, suggests that Maroua pieces were widely distributed in an unfinished state. Other sources of raw material were also exploited (Hervieu 1968).

At Bidzar, a village south of Maroua, Buisson (1933) discovered simple abstract engravings on marble blocks. They are as yet undated and may be Neolithic or of the Iron Age.

There are no Neolithic sites with indisputable evidence of food production in the Benue region. A small cave at Sumpa (9°18′ North, 13°31′ East), located thirteen kilometers east of Garoua in a sandstone and conglomerate massif immediately west of the Benue-Kébi confluence, was excavated by Frank Bartell of the Upper Benue Basin

Archaeological Project (UBBAP). He found 180 centimeters of deposits, the upper eighty centimeters somewhat disturbed by burrowing animals and the lower meter consisting largely of slabs fallen from the cave roof and rotting *in situ*. In, among, and just above the rockfall and below Iron Age levels were traces of an occupation that can best be designated Mesoneolithic. The assemblage included numerous quartz microliths, a little pottery with punctations, and three upper grindstones. Two fragments of iron are likely to be intrusive. The microliths have not yet been studied but appear similar to the series from the upper (ceramic) level at Rop rock shelter in Nigeria (Rosenfeld 1972). Duiker has been identified from this level, but there were no identifiable vegetable remains.[3] Dating of the Sumpa cave series is problematic. A radiocarbon date in the sixteenth century A.D. for Mesoneolithic level 3 is certainly too young, and others for Iron Age level 1 and 2 are reversed. The samples were in all probability contaminated by recent use of the cave as a stable. A thermoluminescent determination made on a shard found beneath the rock fall of 6310 ± 400 B.C. is almost certainly too old, but it does suggest a considerable antiquity for the Mesoneolithic occupation.

A few undated pieces of Neolithic technology have been reported further to the south and from the Adamawa (Alimen and Lecoq 1953; Pervès 1945; Jauze 1944).

THE IRON AGE

With the coming of iron, the northern and probably also the southern parts of the Chad-Logone region became relatively densely populated. Lebeuf's *Carte archéologique des abords du Lac Tchad* (1969) lists only eighteen Cameroonian sites outside this region as against 331 within it. Only a minute proportion of the latter have been excavated and all of those were done before 1939. The sites, villages and town mounds, are attributed to the Sao; however, previous conceptions of the Sao phenomenon, as set forth for example in Lebeuf and Masson-Detourbet's *La civilisation du Tchad* (1950), require drastic modification due to recent excavations and dates from Nigeria and Chad that have raised major questions regarding the regional sequences and periodization (cf. Lebeuf 1962: postface; 1969). Direct evidence of agriculture comes as yet only from Daima, where sorghum of the caudatum race was

---

[3]   Dr. Brian Fagan (University of California, Santa Barbara) has kindly undertaken the analysis of the faunal remains recovered by the UBBAP.

found in levels of the nine and tenth centuries A.D. (Connah 1967: 25; de Wet, et al. (this volume).

The most southerly mounds of any size on the left bank of the Logone are two at Pouss (10°51' North, 15°4' East); one of them was tested by the UBBAP. It began to form late in the first millennium A.D. While there are similarities, the pottery differs markedly from that of Sao sites to the north (cf. Griaule and Lebeuf 1948, 1950, 1951; Lebeuf 1962), and there is no reason to designate the inhabitants as Sao. Sedge nutlets (*Fimbrystylis* sp.) dated about A.D. 1200 have been identified from the site, and, according to George Jackson (letter of May 2, 1972), they were with other grains and suggest that WILD grass seeds were collected from wet areas.[4] South of Pouss, one and sometimes two levels of pottery are visible in the bank of the Logone and extend with few breaks at least as far south as Yagoua. The Iron Age inhabitants would seem to have lived as the Massa today, in long villages strung out along the levees.

Thirty-nine Iron Age sites, mounds, and mound complexes have been recorded by the UBBAP around the Benue-Kébi confluence, from Garoua in the west, up the Kébi as far as Bibémi (and probably beyond), and up the Benue to Douloumi Lake. An open site of some antiquity was found further up the Benue at Lagdo. Five small mounds were discovered in the Benue-Faro confluence area, and another at Ndinkere on the Faro. Surface scatters of pottery have been collected from other sites in the region, but until typological analyses are completed, it would be unwise to suggest even approximate dates.[5] Some may well be as late as the Fulani incursion and conquest in the late eighteenth and early nineteenth centuries.

Excavations at Bé (9°18' North, 13°40' East) on the Mayo Kébi, one of the largest of the mound complexes, revealed over seven meters of occupation deposits. Two major phases (which can be further sub-

---

[4] All provisional identifications of plant remains recovered by the UBBAP are by George Jackson (Botany Department, University of Ibadan), who also worked with the project on the ecology of the Benue-Kébi confluence area.

Dates for sites excavated by the project are based on radiocarbon readings calculated according to the 5,730 year half-life and corrected for changes in the atmospheric inventory of radiocarbon. They should thus correspond as closely as possible to calendar dates. They were run by Dr. E. K. Ralph and Mrs. Barbara Lawn of the Museum Applied Science Center for Archaeology (University of Pennsylvania). Thermoluminescent determinations were made by Mark Han of the same institution. A full listing and brief discussion of all the absolute dates is to appear in a summary article by Colin Flight in the *Journal of African History*.

[5] Frank Bartell is presently working up the pottery. His completed analysis will first appear as a Ph.D. dissertation (University of Pennsylvania).

divided) are recognized on the evidence of the sequence of well-preserved structures. The first is characterized by round huts with beaten
earth floors, and lasted from the first occupation of the mound in the
ninth century to about A.D. 1300. In the second phase, which continued
until the Fulani conquest of the Nyamnyam inhabitants in 1839,
tessellated potsherd pavements, identical to those first reported from
Nassarao I (David 1967, 1968; and reported in Calvocoressi 1970:
69–70) and to modern examples made by the Fali (Lebeuf 1961: 84),
make their appearance. The oldest date for the Iron Age in the Benue
region is from a village mound at Douloumi Lake (9°12′ North, 13°39′
East), where the earliest levels are of the sixth century A.D. As at Bé,
two major structural phases are represented. Carbonized vegetable
remains were recovered by flotation from these two sites and from the
Iron Age levels at Sumpa cave. They are provisionally identified in
Table 2.

Table 2. Carbonized vegetable remains

Plant remains	Date in centuries A.D.		
	Bé	Douloumi	Sumpa
Sorghum	11–12	9	–
Eleusine	9–10	–	17–18?
Setaria	13–14	–	–

The Setaria is unlikely to be a cultigen. As at Pouss, it forms part of a
collection of wild grasses from wet places such as those that adjoin
the site.

The ancient peoples of the Benue-Kébi confluence lived in permanent, nucleated villages on or very near light, sandy, terrace soils
that they would have cultivated, and in close proximity to rivers and
lakes that they exploited intensively for fish. Domestic sheep/goats and
cattle are represented in the sequences and were probably present
throughout the Iron Age. The culture differs from that of the Sao in
its pottery, in burial customs, and in the absence of figurine material.
Neither is the pottery very like that of Pouss, where figurines were
also lacking.

Gauthier (1972) has excavated at Fali and pre-Fali cemeteries in the
massifs north of the Benue, and has shown parallels in urn-burial
practices between Ngoutchoumi-Dolu Koptu necropolis and a site in
the Mayo Kébi valley northwest of Bibémi. Anthropomorphic figurines
are present in the upland sites. A late sixteenth to early nineteenth
century time range is suggested.

Nothing is known of the prehistoric Iron Age of the Mandara, Diamaré, or Adamawa. Across the border in the Central African Republic, Vidal (1969) has discovered a group of about a hundred megalithic structures. The sites are contained within a rectangle 130 kilometers long and about 30 kilometers broad, running southeastward from Mount Ngaewi on the Cameroon border to Bouar and beyond. They lie along the Chad-Congo watershed and are often situated near headwaters. Little is known about the builders; a few shards, a smoking pipe, iron slag, and an iron bracelet were found in the megaliths and are believed contemporary. Two structures have been dated, one to 5490 ± 170 B.C. (Gif-1636) and another to A.D. 30 ± 100 (Gif-1637) (Willett 1971: 353). The precise association of the dated material and the structures is unclear. It would appear improbable that megaliths were being built in that area in the sixth millennium B.C. and equally unlikely that the tradition persisted for over 5,000 years.

SPECULATIONS

Although there is a strong presumption of agriculture among the Neolithic peoples around Lake Chad, there is still no proof; further to the south even the indirect evidence is unconvincing. Grindstones and rubbers have not been found *in situ* at the Maroua workshop sites, while miscellaneous pieces found elsewhere may be of Iron Age date. Only the rubbers from Sumpa are in stratigraphic context, but their date — although likely to be early — is unknown. So much is firm fact; the rest is speculation, but I hope useful.

Our prediction of a technologically and environmentally determined contrast between the northern and southern parts of the area is supported by the available evidence, such as it is. Thorough survey work throughout the area will provide confirmation or disproof. The full Neolithic appears to have been limited to the Chad basin and not to have extended south to the Benue drainage. The Diamaré and Mandara regions may at certain times during this period have had an open vegetation cover of thorn scrub and savanna and offered a more favorable habitat to peoples with a mixed farming, stock-breeding, and fishing economy than the dense dry forest, which I suppose to have covered the Benue region and, until very late, the Adamawa.

Except perhaps in the far north, the Iron Age of North Cameroon is unlikely to have begun before the fifth or sixth century A.D., after which there was an intensification of settlement in the Chad-Logone region and a local extension south into the Benue. Shortly afterwards, according to our direct evidence, cultivation of sorghum and finger millet was taking place in the latter region. The heavy soils, vertisols, and silts of the floodplains were probably not cleared at this time. There is historical evidence that the Fulani under Ardo Bakari, ruler of Garoua 1855-1867, were the first to clear the Benue plain in order to plant dry season durra sorghums (Bassoro 1965: 67). Maistre (1895: 244), passing through some thirty years later, described the valley much as it is today, "*peu boisée et au sol fendillé.*" The nucleated Iron Age settlements are unlikely to have been a response to external political pressure, at least until the rise of the Jukun kingdom of Kororofa in the first half of the second millennium A.D. It may be that the mound dwellers desired to reserve the maximum area of light, sandy soils for cultivation — rational, "economizing" behavior if the region was indeed forested at the time. Over the centuries clearance for fields and pasture would have worked the transformation to savanna. The process may be reflected in the archaeology of Bé by the appearance of several small mounds, at least two of which have pottery pavements near their base, and a reduction in the area of occupation on the largest mounds.

LINGUISTICS AND ETHNOHISTORY

In this section I shall consider the linguistic affiliations of North Cameroonian peoples in conjunction with ethnohistoric data on their origins and migrations. The linguistic classification, which is that of Greenberg (1963), has not only a very real intrinsic value for the reconstruction of culture history, but also serves as an antidote to the sometimes quite wild theorizing of the ethnohistorians. The latter have been for the most part early travellers, colonial administrators, or ethnologists without special training in ethnohistoric techniques. Moreover they have usually been concerned with only one group at a time, and are prone to attribute its origin to a distant area without proper consideration of whether this makes sense in the context of the distant area in question. It should also be borne in mind that many of the historical documents on which they rely, for example those brought together by Palmer in his *Sudanese memoirs* (1928), were written at about the same time as antiquaries in England were assiduously tracing the Britons back to Troy — and they should be as critically received. Thus, while myths and legends indubitably reflect cultural values and contacts, they cannot be accepted as history in the absence of supporting evidence. As Meek (1931: 24) once put it, "Any imaginative Muslim who can write is capable of manufacturing history for the benefit of the unlettered."

Over the past millennium North Cameroonian peoples have been the continual prey of powerful neighbors to the north, west, and east. These predations culminated in the eighteenth and nineteenth centuries with the influx and subsequent conquests of the Fulani, which drastically modified tribal distributions in the Adamawa and lowland Cameroon, except in the Chad-Logone region, which was suffering its own vicissitudes at the time and had, since the seventeenth century, been penetrated by ever-increasing numbers of Shuwa Arab pastoralists. The majority of ethnolinguistic groups are today an amalgam of units that have undergone episodes of fusion and acculturation under exterior pressures.

Les brassages et les influences réciproques entre ethnies de niveau technique équivalent sont anciens, ce qui rend difficile de caractériser les cultures traditionelles en présence et fournit un découpage géographique distinct selon les critères que l'on retient,

wrote de Garine (1964: 22) of the Massa and their neighbors, but it is generally true. Tribal culture is a momentary constellation of traits; the Fali of A.D. 1600 were no doubt very different from those studied by Lebeuf (1961: 20–44).

The peoples of the Chad-Logone region are speakers of Chadic languages, representing three of the nine groups recognized by Greenberg. These are: group 2 — Kotoko dialects in the north; group 7 — Musgu in the center; group 8 — Massa in the south. No other languages of these groups are spoken by geographically distant populations.

The traditions of the Kotoko and of their ancestors, the Sao, have been extensively studied over many years by several scholars (Griaule and Lebeuf 1948, 1950, 1951; Lebeuf and Masson-Detourbet 1950; Lebeuf 1962, 1969). The term "Sao" has been widely applied since antiquity in the general sense of *"les hommes d'autrefois"*; early traditions, such as that which situates Sao at Bilma in the seventh century A.D., must be regarded with suspicion. Ibn Hawqal mentions "fetishists" south of Lake Chad between the Komadugu Yobe (on the Nigeria-Niger border) and the Chari rivers in A.D. 930. Various groups seem to have moved into the area at about this time, and, after coalescing with earlier inhabitants, to have become the Sao-Kotoko. Most, driven by the rising power of Kanem, would have come from the north; others are thought to have migrated westward from Moïto and Lake Fitri (Lebeuf 1969: 19). Over the next centuries the Sao peoples were harried and enslaved by the Sefawa and, following the loss of Kanem c. 1380 A.D. and the removal of the dynasty to Bornu, forced into a contracting territory around the southern margins of the lake. Some Sao moved south to Logone Birni, Logone Gana, and other fortified mound towns; other remnants may have gone toward the Mandara, although traditions reflecting immigration to this and the Benue regions have received no archaeological support. By the death of *Mai* Idris Alooma in 1617 many Kotoko chiefs had accepted the suzerainty of Bornu. From then until the arrival of the French in 1900, their lands were ravaged and depopulated by wars and slave raiding by the forces of Bornu, Baghirmi, Wadai, and lastly by the banners of Rabeh.

A legend reported by Lebeuf and Masson-Detourbet (1950: 33) locates Musgu at Minntour (Nigeria) south of the lake in the eighth century A.D. However this may be (and it is indeed likely that, after the fourteenth or fifteenth century, they were caught up in a general southward movement up the Logone and Chari), the Musgu would appear long established at about 11° north latitude between the Chari and Logone and locally further west. From the sixteenth century they were irregular vassals of Bornu and, as such, conducted slave raids to the south. More recently they were shifting slowly west to escape Baghirmian depredations (Lembezat 1961: 66–67). Their expansion along the Logone would have been one factor in the shunting of the Massa up and down the river. The latter, after establishing themselves by the assimilation of earlier inhabitants in the south of the region at an unknown date, were forced north of Pouss by the Tupuri, only to retreat upstream under northern pressure. From the eighteenth century, their return to the Yagoua area was accelerated by constant slave raiding (de Garine 1964: 22).

Nevertheless, in spite of various intrusions and a myriad local movements, the linguistic and ethnohistorical evidence suggests that these three peoples are autochthonous to the lake shores and *"pays amphibie"* of the lower Logone and Chari.

The Mandara peoples are also speakers of Chadic languages; the mountaineers are all, except the Matakam and Mofu (and conceivably the unclassified Bana), speakers of Bata-Marghi languages (group 3), which extends across the Nigerian border (Marghi) and south to the Benue and Faro (Bata). The Mandara north of the mountains are placed in group 6 with the Gamergu. Their dynasty claims a northern origin, but there is no reason to suppose that the bulk of the population are not indigenous to the northern fringes of the Mandara range. Since the sixteenth century, they have been heavily influenced by Bornu and were their allies against the Fulani in the early 1800's.

The mountains have long been considered a refuge area. Several peoples have traditions of eastern origins; the Matakam and Mofu extended down to the Diamaré plains before the Fulani incursion (Lembezat 1961: 12). Nonetheless the weight of the evidence is in favor of a respectable antiquity in the region of its present peoples, perhaps augmented by Sao and other refugees.

The Gisiga and Daba of the Diamaré are both classed in Chadic group 4 together with their erstwhile neighbors the Matakam and Mofu. There are now Daba groups in the Mandara, Diamaré, and Benue regions, the result of a recent history described by Lembezat as *"assez confuse et 'bousculée'."* They are considered here as a people of the Diamaré on account of their close relationship to the Gisiga (Lembezat 1961: 151–152), although the information on their crops was gathered at Mousgoy, over the border in the Benue region. Neither Daba nor Gisiga has been intensively studied, but they are known to have embraced a much larger portion of the plain in the past and to have been harassed by the Fulani.

The southern part of the region is occupied by the Mundang and the Tupuri, speakers of closely related Adamawa dialects of group 2. Greenberg classified the Tupuri as Chadic, but his Tupuri are in fact the Kera, a neighboring people closely similar in many aspects of culture, who live over the Chad border south of Lake Tikem (de Garine 1973; Claus Schubert, oral communication 1973). The Kera are speakers of Chadic group 9, which includes Somrai and a number of other languages that have their center of distribution far to the east in southern Chad. This might suggest, in the light of the very little that is known of the earlier culture history of that area, that the Kera were displaced and became separated from their linguistic congeners by the westward movement early in this millennium of Sudanic speakers, amongst whom were the Baghirmi.

The Tupuri claim to be autochthonous. Once extending up the Logone as far as Pouss, now Musgu territory, they have over the past five (?) centuries retracted south and west to the borders of the Chad-Logone and Diamaré regions. The Mundang, relatively recent immigrants into the Diamaré from a base on the upper reaches of the Kébi around Léré in Chad, claim, like so many other peoples, an eastern origin. Their linguistic affiliation is more suggestive of a local or ultimately southern derivation.

In the north of the Benue region on its border with the Diamaré, live the Giddar, Chadic speakers classed by themselves in group 5. Lestringant (1964: 79–80) insists upon the composite origin of the Giddar and neighboring peoples, but does not suggest migrations from afar. In the northwest along the Benue and up the Faro, the Bata and related tribelets, who moved into the region from the Mandara mountains in the eighteenth century, have replaced Chamba and other groups (Kirk-Greene 1958: 17–18, 168–169). They are a Chadic intrusion into an otherwise Adamawa-speaking area.

Until the Fulani conquests of the early nineteenth century, the Benue valley was the frontier between speakers of Chadic and Adamawa languages. The Adamawa speakers are now either assimilated or confined to the massifs north of the Adamawa and to the Alantika mountains. Outside our area they extend westward down the Nigerian Benue to 11° East. In the massifs northeast of Garoua, the Fali are a reconstitution of divers groups, including some Bata, and speak the only language of Adamawa subgroup 11. Lebeuf (1961) has demonstrated their mixed northern and southern characteristics, but it is hard to accept his suggestion that they were driven from the Kébi, a tributary of the Niger, in the fifteenth or early sixteenth century and thence via the Mandara to their present habitat.

The remnant populations, Mambay, Laka, and others on the Mayo Kébi and to the east of the Benue, are classed together with the Mundang and the Mbum in Adamawa subgroup 6. West of the Benue, the Durru, Do Ayo or Namchi, and numerous smaller groups are placed in subgroup 4, which is confined to this area. The ethnohistory of these fragmented tribelets is little understood; it is possible that the Ngewe, Nyamnyam, Oblo, Puri, and Duli, who lived around the Benue-Kébi confluence and who claimed an origin on the Logone (Mohammadou Eldridge, oral communication), may be identifiable with the mound dwellers of the second structural phase. If this is so, their migration might conceivably be correlated with the movements of the Tupuri and Mundang in the fourteenth and later centuries. Their linguistic affiliation is uncertain. The western part of the region must have been considerably influenced by the slaving and trading of the Jukun kingdom of Kororofa, which flourished on the middle Benue from perhaps as early as the thirteenth century until its destruction by the Fulani in the nineteenth (Kirk-Greene 1958: 16). Kororofa was at the height of its power in the seventeenth century and its contacts with the Cameroon hinterland extended through the Benue to the Mbum of the Adamawa (Meek 1931: 39–40).

The Mbum have lived in the Adamawa and adjoining portions of the Central African Republic for a very considerable period, during which some groups have split off and amalgamated with others to the south-west to form the Tikar, Bamum, and Vute, all speakers of Bantoid languages of Benue-Congo (Eldridge 1971: 213 ff.). The Mbum language is related to Mundang and those of other peoples of the eastern Benue region. It is hard to credit the traditions reported by Eldridge (1971: 146–173) that they derive ultimately from the Yemen or the Nile. The Gbaya, southern and eastern neighbors of the Mbum, are the only Cameroonian representatives of the Eastern branch of Adamawa-Eastern, and are recent immigrants. Previously located in the Central African Republic north and west of the Ubangi river, they have been moving northwest throughout the nineteenth century, up the Mambere valley to Cameroon (Burnham 1972: chapter 3 and appendix A). Under pressure from the Yangere at their backs, their immigration was facilitated by the disarray of the Mbum under Fulani attack, and possibly by the supposed emigration southwards from the Meiganga area of the "Pahouin" group of Bantu (Alexandre 1965).

SUMMARY

The bulk of the ethnohistoric literature on North Cameroonian peoples emphasizes their peregrinations (cf. Lembezat 1961 for a summary of the dispersed information available). In recent years Eldridge has been performing invaluable work in collecting and compiling oral traditions, but their synthesis is incomplete. In its absence I have taken the view that traditions that have neither been subjected to modern critical analysis nor supported by archaeological data must, in cases of conflict, yield to the evidence of linguistics.[6] This is not to deny the very great value of oral tradition in revealing the direction and importance of culture contacts and influences within, between, and beyond the regions under consideration.

With exceptions noted above, the linguistic distributions suggest that population blocks have remained areally stable, although with shifting borders and internal movements, for a period sufficiently long for differentiation to have occurred at group and subgroup levels. This is most marked in the case of the Chadic subfamily of Afro-Asiatic. The peoples of the Chad basin form part of a broad belt of Chadic-

[6] Greenberg has unfortunately not disclosed the genetic relationships BETWEEN subfamilies and groups of languages. Thus, if the Kotoko group turns out to be more closely allied to group 9 (Kera, Somrai, etc.) than to the Musgu group, our reading of the ethnohistory will require much revision.

speaking peoples that extends far to the east and west of North Cameroon. They have been subjected to influences mainly from the north,
but also from the west and east, for at least a thousand years. The inhabitants of the Benue basin and Adamawa plateau are again a section
of a chain of Adamawa-Eastern speakers that reaches from the Azande
in the east across to the Nigerian Benue. These regions have been less
impinged upon from without.

We have to date no evidence that might indicate that speakers of
early Benue-Congo languages such as pre-Bantu or proto-Bantu were
ever occupants of our area. On the contrary, it would appear that the
main linguistic groupings have been implanted since very ancient times.

THE CROPS

The distribution of cultivated plants by peoples can now be considered
against the archaeological and ethnohistorical background sketched
above, with a view to determining crop histories through age-and-area
reconstruction (Kroeber 1948: 561–571).

Few tribes have received more than summary treatment by ethnographers, and fewer yet of the ethnographers have had any botanical
competence, or even, like Barth, carried a copy of Hooker's *Flora
Nigritia* in their pockets. Jaques-Felix's summary (1940) of crops
grown at particular villages of various peoples is a valuable resource,
especially for the Mandara region, but his listings are unlikely to be exhaustive. Other botanists, admirably precise on the crops, occasionally
fail to make it clear who is growing them. I have been able to collect
only limited and imperfect information, but at least one tribe of each
region and of each linguistic grouping is represented, albeit often un-
satisfactorily, and in two cases data are available for two time horizons.
For the sake of comparison I have included material from southeast
Bornu, collected by Denham, Barth, and Nachtigal before 1900, from
the Jukun, and from the Sara and the Gulla of Lake Iro in Chad. The
Gulla are placed by Murdock (1959: 136) in his Sara cluster, but the
ethnography (Pairault 1966) leaves it uncertain whether the Gulla of
Iro are in fact closely related to the Sara (Sudanic speakers) or whether
they are a Bua (Adamawa-Eastern) people.

Plants known to have been introduced since 1900, or of which the
cultivation is said to be *"récente"* or *"ne fait pas partie de l'agriculture
traditionelle,"* are excluded from Table 3. Neither data nor available
space permit the listing and discussion of protected species and semi-

domesticates. These include the very common trees, baobab, desert date, nettle tree, tamarind, etc. The useful plants that are commonly protected in and around Fulani villages in the Garoua area are noted in the appendix to this paper. Detailed botanical study of these plants, their distribution and history, would be of certain value to the culture historian.

In consulting Table 3 it should be remembered that the omission of a plant from the listings may only mean that it has not been reported.

Sorghum bicolor, present in the area by the ninth century A.D., and, inferentially, long before, is the staple of the Chadic speakers.[7] Early maturing sorghums of the caudatum race and subraces show the greatest variety and were the only sorghums cultivated by those Adamawa-Eastern speakers not in close contact with Chadic groups. Later maturing sorghums mainly of the guinea and caudatum races and subraces are grown by most Chadic speakers and in Bornu, while bicolor race sorghums are only reported for the Tupuri and Gulla, among whom there are many subraces. The severely limited data are in accordance with Harlan and Stemler's view (this volume) that sorghums of caudatum race were developed from bicolor in the area extending eastward from Lake Chad. The date of the probable replacement of the early forms is uncertain, as is that of the arrival of guinea sorghums from the west. If my reading of the Kera immigration is correct, then it is conceivable that they reintroduced some bicolor strains from the east between A.D. 1000 and A.D. 1500, perhaps bringing with them the technique of transplanting caudatum sorghums. Transplanted sorghums of the durra race and subraces were introduced from Bornu to the Kotoko and western Musgu (Barth 1857, volume 3: 186). Elsewhere they became established through Fulani agency, and until recently the Tupuri were alone in accepting them.

A sweet-stemmed guinea-bicolar sorghum (*S. mellitum* Snowden) is grown by the Gulla, and it may be this form that is known to the Fulani as *"lakkawal"* [the sorghum of the Lakka], which suggests that it was

---

[7] Identifications of sorghums by species and variety are given only for the Massa, Gulla, and Tupuri. I received help in identification from the agricultural research station at Guétalé, but this extended only to the classification of the main groups. These identifications, of course, preceded Harlan and de Wet's (1972) new classification by race and subrace, which I have attempted to follow, referring where necessary to Doggett's modification of the Snowden key (Doggett 1970: 41–48).

The reader is referred to Purseglove (1968, 1972) and Coursey (1967) for the authorities for binomial names given in the text. Authorities are rarely cited in the sources, in which the names given are now in many cases incorrect. I have standardized to Purseglove and Coursey wherever possible, and in cases of doubt have allowed the author's term to stand or placed it in inverted commas.

Table 3. The distribution of crops by peoples. Crops KNOWN to have been introduced after 1900 have been excluded*

PLANT NAME Binomial	Vernacular	S.E. Bornuans	Kotoko	Musgu	Massa	Sara	Gulla of Iro	Tupuri	Mundang	Daba	Matakam	Mofu	Kapsiki	Gude	Bana	Njei	Giddar	Fali	Fulani (1900)	Fulani (1970)	Do Ayo	Durru	Mbum	Gbaya (1914)	Gbaya (1968)	Jukun
		(Chad-Logone)	←	→				(Diamaré)			(Mandara)	←				→	(Benue)	←				→	(Adamawa)	←	→	
CEREALS																										
Sorghum bicolor	Sorghum	+	+	+	+	+	+	+	+	+	+	+	+	+	+	+	+	+	+	+	+	+	+	+	+	+
	Early maturing sorghums, mainly red-grained and of caudatum race and subraces	+	?		+	+	+	+	+	+	+	+	+	+	+	+	+	+	+	+		+				?
	Later maturing sorghums, mainly of the guinea, but including caudatum and bicolor races and subraces	+					+	+																		
	Transplanted sorghums, mainly of caudatum race and subraces				+	+		+											+	+						
	Transplanted sorghums, mainly of durra race and subraces	+	+					+			+ +	+ +														
Pennisetum americanum	Bulrush and pearl millet	+	+ +	+	+ + +	+ +	+						+ +	+ +	+ +	+ +	+ +	+ +	+	+	+	+ +	+ +			+
Eleusine corocana	Finger millet								+		+	+					+									
Digitaria exilis	Fonio									+																+
Oryza sp.	Rice																							+	+	+
O. sativa	Asian rice		+ +	+															+	+						
O. glaberrima	African rice																					+ +				
Zea mays	Maize	+ + +						+	+	+	+	+	+	+	+	+	+	+	+ +	+	+		+	+	+	+
Triticum sp.	Wheat																									
Hordeum vulgare	Barley																									
ROOT CROPS																										
Dioscorea sp.	Yam												+	+	+	+	+	+	+	+	+	+	+ +	+	+ +	+
D. bulbifera	Potato yam						+ +																+	+ +		
D. dumetorum	Bitter yam																						+	+		
D. praehensilis	Bush yam				+																	+				
D. abyssinica	—																						+			

D. rotundata   Guinea yam
D. cayenensis   Yellow yam
D. alata   Winged yam
Coleus dysentericus and/or Plectranthus esculentus   Hausa potato and/or rizga
Colocasia esculenta   Taro
Xanthosoma sagittifolium   Yautia
Ipomoea batatas   Sweet potato
Manihot esculenta   Manioc
Cyperus esculentus   Tiger nut

PULSES

Vigna unguiculata   Cowpea
V. sinensis
Cajanus cajan   Pigeon pea
Voandzeia subterranea   Earthpea
Arachis hypogaea   Groundnut

OIL-YIELDING

Sesamum indicum   Sesame
S. radiatum   —
Ricinus communis   Castor
Jatropha curcas   Physic nut

VEGETABLES

Abelmoschus esculentus   Okra
Hibiscus sabdariffa   Guinea sorrel
H. cannabinus   Hemp-leaved hibiscus
Ceratotheca sesamoides   —
Corchorus olitorius   Jew's mallow
Solanum melongena   Eggplant
S. incanum   Bitter tomato
S. aethiopicum   —
Lycopersicum esculentum   Tomato
Capsicum spp.   Guinea peppers
Allium spp.   Onions, etc.
Physalis peruviana   —

Table 3. (Continued)

PLANT NAME		PEOPLE																									
			Chad-Logoe					Diamaré			Mandara						Benue						Adamawa			
Binomial	Vernacular	S.E. Bornuans	Kotoko	Musgu	Massa	Sara	Gulla of Iro	Tupuri	Mundang	Daba	Matakam	Mofu	Kapsiki	Gude	Bana	Njei	Giddar	Fali	Fulani (1900)	Fulani (1970)	Do Ayo	Durru	Mbum	Gbaya (1914)	Gbaya (1968)	Jukun
CUCURBITS																										
—	Cucurbit	+	?	+		++	++	++			++	+	+	+	+	+	++	+++	++	++	+	+	+++	+++	+	++
Lagenaria siceraria	Gourd				++																					
Citrullus lanatus	Watermelon							+																+	?	
Cucumeropsis edulis	—																+	+	?	++						
Momordica balsamina	} Balsam apple																									
M. charantia	} Bitter gourd																									
Cucurbita pepo	Pumpkin																									
C. maxima	Pumpkin																									
FRUITS																										
Musa paradisiaca	Plantain and Banana	+			+																			+	+	+
Citrus aurantiifolia	Lime																	+	+++	+++						
Phoenix dactylifera	Date																									
Carica papaya	Pawpaw																									
Passiflora foetida	Stinking passion flower																									
OTHER																										
Tephrosia vogelii	Fish poison bean	+++	+++	+	+	++	++	++	+	+	++	+	+	++	+	++	+++	+++	++++	++++	+	++	++	++	+	+++
Gossypium spp.	Cotton																							+	+	
Nicotiana spp.	Tobacco																									
Indigofera arrecta	Indigo																									
Lawsonia inermis	Henna																									

* Main sources:

General: Pelé and Le Berre 1966; Lembezat 1961.
Bornuans: Denham, et al. 1828; Barth 1857; Nachtigal 1881.
Kotoko: Barth 1857; Nachtigal 1881; Jacques-Felix 1940.
Musgu: Jacques-Felix 1940.
Massa: Diziain 1954; de Garine 1964.
Sara: Chevalier 1907; Cabot 1965.
Gulla ... Pairault 1966.

Matakam: Jacques-Felix 1940; Boulet 1966.
Mofu: Jacques-Felix 1940; Vaillant 1947.
Kapsiki, Gude, Bana, Njei, Giddar: Jacques-Felix 1940.
Fali: Jacques-Felix 1940; Malzy 1956; Lebeuf 1961.
Fulani of Bé: N. David fieldnotes.
Do Ayo: Lembezat 1961.
Durru: Jacques-Felix 1940; Hata 1973.

introduced from the east. The Fulani and other peoples grow *S. bicolor* var. *colorans* to obtain a red dye.

Pennisetum americanum, bulrush and pearl millet, is a less important but widespread crop. Five varieties are grown by the Massa and four by the Matakam. *Eleusine corocana*, finger millet, provisionally identified in the Benue in the ninth and tenth centuries A.D. and still grown there by the Fali, is second only to sorghum among the Mukhtele of the northern Mandara (Juillerat 1971: 26). It is grown by all the Mandara peoples listed and also by the pagans of Dikwa emirate in the former British Cameroons (White 1943). Further to the east, it attains the status of a staple among some Kabalai, Gambai, and other riverine peoples of the middle Logone (Cabot 1965: 103–104). Fonio, *Digitaria exilis*, is reported from the Massa and Mundang, and from the Mofu (Vaillant 1947).

The bulrush millets, domesticated to the north of our area, have long been cultivated in association with sorghum for variety and as insurance against a poor rainy season. The distribution of finger millet suggests that it was once more widely and extensively cultivated, but has been largely replaced (by guinea and, subsequently, durra sorghums?), except where it has been retained on account of its adaptability to a wide range of soil and moisture conditions. The rarity of fonio might indicate that it, too, was an early cultigen that subsequently dropped out of cultivation or, more probably, that it is a later introduction from the west.

The failure of the peoples living around Lake Chad to domesticate the wild African rice of the region is another indication of the antiquity of sorghum and millet as cereal staples. Wild rice was collected in the nineteenth century and is still collected in times of scarcity by the Massa (*Oryza barthii* ex *breviligulata*) and the Fali, but the Kotoko only brought the local varieties under cultivation in the very late nineteenth or early twentieth centuries, perhaps to supplement the supplies of Asiatic rice that were imported from Hausaland (Denham, et al. 1828, volume 2: 159). At the time of Barth's visit, rice was grown only in the western parts of Nigerian Adamawa, where there were close contacts with Hausa (Barth 1857, volume 2: 481).[8] The cultivation of African rice (identified by Professor S. Nakao, Osaka Prefectural University, Japan) by the Durru of the Benue is exceptional for this region (Hata 1973: 98).

[8] The rice of the Matakam is not identified as to species, but it is most unlikely to be *O. glabberima* because their neighbors, the Mofu, grow the "Fulani variety" (Vaillant 1947: 88).

Maize (*Zea mays*) was already an important crop in Bornu in the late eighteenth century (Miracle 1965: 42), but its introduction to the Massa is described as recent, suggesting that Bornu was a less important source of dissemination than Kororofa. The Jukun, who may have received it from Calabar, passed it on to the Adamawa speakers probably in the first half of the eighteenth century (Meek 1931: 39). Maize, the most important cereal on the Adamawa plateau, may have passed from there to the Gbaya, reaching northern Gabon only in the later nineteenth century (Miracle 1965: 46). An alternative route or simultaneous diffusion of maize to the Gbaya could have come from the east via the Congo and the savannas of the Central African Republic (Tisserant 1953: 226).

Barth (1857, volume 2: 314) states that wheat (*Triticum* sp.) and onions (*Allium cepa*) reached Bornu across the Sahara about a hundred years before his visit. Denham's mention of barley (*Hordeum vulgare*; Denham, et al. 1828, volume 1: 216) is confirmed by Dalziel (1937: 529). Neither was ever grown on a large scale in Bornu. The Fulani used to grow small quantities of wheat, which was used for ceremonial breaking of the fast, in watered plots. *Echinochloa colona* Link was raised in small quantities by the Banda and Gbaya of the Central African Republic to aid in the fermentation of beer (Tisserant 1953: 241). This practice has not been reported from Cameroon. The floating millet cultivated by the Massa under the name of *ourlaga* is likely to be *Echinochloa stagnina* while the Mundang are said to have grown small quantities of *Setaria pallidifusca* (Portères, oral communication).

Yams, for long a staple of the Adamawa speakers south of the Benue and much less important to the north, have been progressively replaced by sorghum, maize, and manioc. Pelé and Le Berre (1966) accord the Dioscoreaceae only a paragraph in their compendium of Cameroonian food plants. With the exception of the Durru, there are no firm identifications of the Guinea yam (*D. rotundata*). The yellow yam (*D. cayenensis*) and the winged yam (*D. alata*), nineteenth century introductions to the savannas of the Central African Republic from the southwest (Tisserant 1953: 229), were probably not in North Cameroon any earlier. *D. minutiflora*, found only among the Gbaya and native to the wetter parts of West Africa (Coursey 1965: 57), may be another late arrival. *D. abyssinica*, native to Ethiopia and cultivated by the Durru, is perhaps the only species to have been transmitted from east to west along Murdock's "yam belt." The widely distributed potato yam (*D. bulbifera*) and bitter yam (*D. dumetorum* [Kunth] Pax. and/or *latifolia* Benth.) may, on the other hand, have come under cultivation very early. *D. sansibarensis* Pax (= *D. macroura* Harms), which went out of cultivation only very recently in the Central African Republic (Tisserant 1953: 229) and is still grown by the Banen of South Cameroon (Dugast 1944: 43), should no doubt be added to this list. Jaques-Felix (1948) gives a Mbum name for *D. liebrechtiana* (= *cayenensis?*) and Gbaya terms for *D. "gribinguiensis"* and *D. lecardi* without stating specifically that they are cultivated.

The yams grown north of the Benue are identified to species only in one instance, the bush yam (*D. praehensilis*) of the Massa. Raised only in minute quantities, sometimes even a single plant in a compound garden, they would repay study as possible relicts of an earlier phase of plant husbandry in a forest-savanna ecotone.

The spotty distribution of the Hausa potato (*Coleus dysentericus*) and apparent absence of rizga (*Plectranthus esculentus = Coleus dazo*) are best explained as the result of replacement. Both are grown to the east and west, and were attributed by Portères (1962: 207) to his central African cradle of agriculture. Professor Portères has stated that he tends to agree with Harlan (1971: 470) on an origin of the Hausa potato further to the west between Guinea and Togo, although he has not excluded the possibility of independent domestication in more than one area. Yautia (*Xanthosoma sagittifolium*), recorded only from three Mandara peoples, the Durru, the Mbum, and the Gbaya of 1968, must be a colonial introduction as its Mbum name, *Agô nasara* implies. It has only been known to the Banen since around 1910 (Dugast 1944: 13). Taro (*Colocasia esculenta*) is not commonly cultivated in our area. According to Burkill (1938: 95), it was transmitted to West Africa either from Egypt and North Africa across the Sahara by Arabs and Berbers, or from the east coast "by infiltration along equatorial parts." Except perhaps in the extreme north, it is unlikely to have been established in Cameroon until after 1600. Sweet potatos (*Ipomoea batatas*) are often known by corruptions of Hausa or Fulani names and are an introduction of the Fulani period. Their arrival in Bornu may be quite precisely dated between 1850 and 1880 (compare Barth 1857, volume 2: 315 and Nachtigal 1881: 533). Cassava or manioc (*Manihot esculenta*) was grown by the Fulani of Yola in 1850 (Barth 1857, volume 2: 436), but had not yet reached the Adamawa plateau (Barth 1857, volume 2: 505). In the later nineteenth century it diffused rapidly from the southeast and west, and by the 1880's had replaced the yam as a staple except among the Durru (Mission Ponel, Relevé de Carnet d'Itineraire de Bania à N'gaoundéré, 31 Dec. 1892–17 Feb. 1893. Min. d'Outre-Mer, Paris; Archives Gabon-Congo III, 14; Passarge

1895: 464).

Tiger nuts (*Cyperus esculentus*), known from ancient Egypt (Dalziel 1937: 517), are grown in the Diamaré, Mandara, and Benue regions and are primarily associated with Chadic speakers. In Bornu they appear to be escapes; Barth (1857, volume 2: 381, volume 3: 31, 262) saw them dug up wild and says that there was also extensive use of their rhizomes for perfume (and/or of *C. articulatus*?). Their introduction must predate, perhaps very considerably, Islamic times.

Pulses are frequently mentioned by authors, but rarely by their binomial name. The earthpea (*Voandzeia subterranea*) is ubiquitous and was until recently more important than the groundnut (*Arachis hypogaea*), for the presence of which there is no certain evidence before the Fulani period.[9] The distributional and botanical evidence is in accordance with the theory that the earthpea was domesticated near the Benue on the Cameroon-Nigeria border (Harlan 1971: 471). On the other hand, I can find no report suggesting that the geocarpa bean (*Kerstingiella geocarpa*), also believed to have been domesticated in that region, has ever been cultivated in the area. Although not — or no longer — grown in the Central African Republic, a subspontaneous form, named *K. tisserantii* by Pellegrin, occurs in sandy places in the hills north of Bamberi (Tisserant 1953: 235). Several varieties of cowpea (*Vigna unguiculata* and/or *sinensis*) are grown; it is ubiquitous and a very old cultigen.

The botanical and distributional evidence also favors a high antiquity for the cultivation of sesame (*Sesamum indicum*) in Cameroon. Sesame was a traditional oil-yielding plant before the advent of the groundnut, and is considered by Portères (1962: 206–207) to have been domesticated between Lake Chad and Ethiopia. *Sesamum radiatum*, from the same general area, is curiously only reported from the Mbum. The oils of the castor plant (*Ricinus communis*) and physic nut (*Jatropha curcas*) are widely used in tropical Africa for specialized purposes, and the latter is often grown as a hedge plant (Dalziel 1937: 160–163, 147–148). The castor plant, while utilized in the north of the area, is cultivated only in the south and by the Sara and tribes of the Central African Republic to the east. Of Ethiopian origin, it must have spread early along the savanna zone. I have no information on the physic nut, which is of New World origin.

---

[9]   Groundnuts are not called by corruptions of Fulani or Hausa names. They may have reached Bornu quite early. Barth (1857, volume 5: 334 ff., 447) reports that they had reached Baghirmi in his day, and Maistre (1895: 176, 273) remarked that the Sara were already growing them in quantity in the late nineteenth century.

In contrast to the majority of plants discussed above, which are commonly field crops, vegetables are usually produced in small gardens within and adjacent to the compound, on termite mounds, or in other special microenvironments. Some twenty years ago, Anderson (1952: 136–150) pointed out the significance of such plots for experiments in cultivation. Harris (1973: 400) has gone further, postulating that "fixed plot horticulture preceded swidden cultivation." Unfortunately, on account of their biotic complexity and minor economic importance, gardens have received little attention. Of twenty-six vegetable species for which I have information, no less than fourteen are reported only from the Gbaya,[10] although many of these same species are collected by the Fulani of Bé and no doubt most other peoples. Philip Burnham has described to me how Gbaya will avoid chopping down useful leafy plants during swidden clearing, and may transplant them to their temporary garden plots. Such semidomestication would not "provide a genetic environment ideally suited to the emergence of domesticated variants through the selection and fixation of desirable characteristics" (Harris 1973: 400) because selection, even unconscious, does not seem to occur. Plants are simply moved over short distances to more convenient locations, are replaced or not, as the case may be, from year to year, and are not taken along if the village is moved. Thus, although these plants may have a very long history of exploitation by man, they have not been ennobled.

So many wild and protected herbs, shrubs, and trees produce edible, even delicious, leaves, that the only vegetables to have come under

[10]   Tessman (1934: 51–52) lists the following plants by their binomial and/or vernacular names, the latter translated here by reference to unpublished vocabularies prepared by. P. Burnham and P. Vidal:

Tessman	Burnham (B) and Vidal (V)
mbǫ̱ndǫ̱	*Justicia insularis* (B)
Amaranthus caudatus	Native terms given include *A. viridis* (V).
sá̱yṵmbá	*Gynandropsis gynandra* (V)
Composite (liló)	– – – – – –
Composite (mbuli, mbui-zam)	– – – – – –
"*Abelmoschus moschatus*"	
(? = *Hibiscus moschatus* L.)	
Polygonum species (mbaṅga-ta̱na)	– – – – – –
"*Ocimum basilicum*"	
(? = *O. americanum* L.)	
Solanum "*dinklagei*" (sǫ̱óle)	*S. nigrum* (B)
Solanum species (ngagō)	*S. nodiflorum* (B) or *S.* "*distichum*" (V) (? = *S. indicum* L. var *distichum* Thonning)
Asterocantha longifolia	*Vernonia cinerea* (V), presumably used medicinally.
gba-wuo	

According to Burnham's list, *Amaranthus* cf. *hybridus* and *Urena lobata* are also semidomesticates.

regular cultivation are those with other qualities. The bitter tomato (*Solanum incanum*) and okra (*Abelmoschus* [*Hibiscus*] *esculentus*) have sizable fruit; *Ceratotheca sesamoides* gives a mucilage that is used by the Fulani in plastering their walls; the *Hibiscus* species provide fiber. Guinea sorrel (*H. sabdariffa*) is a widely distributed and probably old domesticate with several cultivars. The hemp-leaved hibiscus (*H. cannabinus*) must be attributed to the Fulani period on the grounds that so many of its local names are corruptions of the Fulani *gabay*. Jew's mallow (*Corchorus olitorius*) appears to be an old cultigen, perhaps originally introduced as a fiber plant and now subspontaneous in much of North Cameroon. It was brought to Africa from the East in the first centuries A.D./B.C. (Murdock 1959: 207). Capsicum pepper (*Capsicum annuum* and *C. frutescens*) and *Allium* species were introduced relatively recently, the latter across the Sahara, the former probably by the Fulani (as many local names suggest), but also via Bornu, whence it was traded to Baghirmi in the 1850's (Barth 1857, volume 3: 383). Birds may also have acted as agents of dispersal. Among the complex family of cucurbits, the extraordinarily wide distribution within and beyond Africa of the gourd (*Lagenaria siceraria*) and watermelon (*Citrullus lanatus*) argues for their very great age as cultigens. The botany of the multitude of local cultivars is little understood (Pelé and Le Berre 1966: 6).

Although many native fruits were collected, none were ever regularly cultivated. The pawpaw (*Carica papaya*), of New World origin and yet of fundamental importance in Fali mythology, probably entered the area from Kororofa at the same time as maize. Tobacco may derive from the same source or have been introduced by the northern route. The plantain (*Musa paradisiaca*), which will not grow north of the southern Adamawa, and the banana (*M. paradisiaca* variety *sapientium*) seem to have diffused very late from the south. The lime (*Citrus aurantiifolia*) and date palm (*Phoenix dactylifera*) are Islamic imports spread by the Fulani.

Cotton (*Gossypium* spp.), grown as a perennial, is said to have been introduced into Kanem-Bornu between the tenth and the sixteenth centuries (Urvoy 1949: 19). Although never grown on a large scale outside those areas where demand for woven clothing was stimulated by Islam, it was not limited to them. The Sara grew small quantities in 1900 (Chevalier 1907: 267), and, although barkcloth made of the bark of figs or the roots of *Chlorophera excelsa* Benth. and Hook. was the preferred material in the Central African Republic, Tisserant (1953: 249) considers cotton to be a very old savanna cultigen.[11] Indigo (*In-*

[11]   Courtet and Chevalier give the following as species of cotton found in Bornu,

digofera arrecta) had been carried into Kotoko territory and to Baghirmi from Bornu, often by immigrant Kanuri dyers, before the first European contact (Denham, et al. 1828, volume 2: 19–20). The Fulani were responsible for its extension to the central and southern parts of the area, and also for the introduction of henna (*Lawsonia inermis*), not mentioned by the early visitors to Bornu.

CONCLUSIONS: CROPS AND CULTURE HISTORY

The data on crop history are presented in summary form in Table 4. The table suggests that there were two main periods during which crop plants became established in North Cameroon: the Neolithic and Fulani periods. In the course of the intervening centuries, crops from East Africa and India and West African yams reached the area, but, except for finger millet, there is no direct evidence as to the date of their arrival. The question of pre-Islamic diffusion between central and eastern Africa (including the northeast) urgently requires investigation. Our polarized view of the process is almost certainly misleading, reflecting our ignorance of events within the long course of the Neolithic and of the agricultural economy of the Iron Age before A.D. 1600. The influx of New World crops after this date, even if less revolutionary than in the forests, nevertheless transformed many aspects of savanna agriculture; nor should the accompanying diffusion of plants with a longer history of cultivation in Africa be forgotten. In thinking of the past we are perhaps overinclined to forget that "traditional" agriculture, even as described by early travellers, is a recent development. The supposedly conservative African cultivator has a remarkable record of innovation.

The crops listed as Neolithic are of three classes:
1. those for which botanical and in some cases archaeological evidence suggests domestication in or near North Cameroon (*bicolor* sorghums, *caudatum* sorghums, earthpeas),
2. those for which archaeological and/or botanical evidence would seem to indicate an early introduction from outside the immediate area (*guinea* sorghums, bulrush millet), and

---

Baghirmi, and Chad in the early years of this century (Chevalier 1907: 731–732):

Gossypium hirsutum	— from Nigeria
G. arboreum	— from Egypt
G. barbadense	— via the Congo to the Sara
G. anomalum	— wild south of Kanem, along the Bahr-el-Ghazal, and in the Dar-el-Hadjer.

Table 4.   The establishment of cultivated plants in North Cameroon: an attempted periodization

Neolithic	Early Iron Age	Kanem-Kororofa	Kororofa-Bornu	Fulani	
?B.C.	A.D. 500	1000	1600	1750	1900
(*Bicolor* sorghums)		Cotton N	Maize W	Durra sorghums N	
Caudatum sorghums			Pawpaw W	Asian rice	
Pennisetum N			Tobacco W	African rice	
Earthpea				Wheat	
Sesame E				Barley	
Cowpea				Winged yam S	
Gourd			Pigeon pea	Yellow yam S	
Watermelon				Manioc S/W	
Guinea sorghums W	Finger millet E			Sweet potato W	
Bitter yam	Rizga			Hemp-leaved Hibiscus W	
Potato yam	Castor plant E			*Musa* cultivars S	
Bush yam	Jew's Mallow E			*Allium* spp. N	
Guinea sorrel	Tiger nut N/E			Lime N	
C. sesamoides	Guinea yam W		Taro N/E	Date palm N/W	
Bitter tomato	White yam W		Indigo N	Henna W	
	D. abyssinica E		Ground-nut W	Pumpkin W	
	Fonio		D. minutiflora	Tomato N	

*   Plants are placed in the column suggested by the weight of the various lines of evidence. When the period cannot be specified with confidence, the vertical lines indicate the likely time range, i.e. groundnuts were probably established between 1600 and 1750, but perhaps not until the Fulani period.

The northern (mainly trans-Saharan Islamic), southern (from South Cameroon), eastern (along the Sudan zone), and western (from Nigeria) origins of introduced cultigens are indicated.

3. residuals, that is to say plants that are at home in the savanna zone, are widely cultivated (although often little ennobled), and for which there is no relevant botanical or archaeological evidence.

A fourth category, unlisted, should include crops that have fallen out of cultivation (e.g. most *bicolor* sorghums, and perhaps the geocarpa bean and *Dioscorea sansibarensis*). Without supposing that the list approximates a complete inventory of Neolithic cultigens, it may, in combination with other lines of evidence, be taken to suggest marked differences between Neolithic economies in the northern and southern parts of our area.

It can be inferred that the peoples of the Chad basin practiced a mixed economy of stock breeding and fishing combined with the cultivation of cereal staples and a variety of subsidiary crops. Hunting made some contribution to the diet, as almost certainly did the gathering of wild seeds (although according to Barth [1857, volume 2: 312, volume 3: 29–30, 161, 274, 447] it was not the settled "black natives" but the pastoral Shuwa Arabs who exploited this resource). In the Benue basin there are few traces of Neolithic technology — let alone economy — and it is arguable whether food production was practiced south of the river before the Iron Age. Cereals were introduced from the north, while the Benue and Adamawa regions are marginal to the West African yam belt and are unlikely to have played a major role in yam domestication (Coursey 1967: 22–25). The inhabitants, widespread although thinly scattered, must have relied far less on food production and on fishing than the northerners, and more on hunting and gathering (cf. Sillans 1953) together with some plant husbandry. Their crops are likely to have included the earthpea, maybe their only significant achievement in domestication, and some of the more widely distributed yams. Because, as discussed above, there is no evidence of large-scale population replacements or immigration before the seventeenth and eighteenth centuries A.D., the practitioners of these contrasting economies may be provisionally identified as speakers of languages ancestral respectively to Chadic and Adamawa-Eastern.

I have attempted here to follow Murdock's (1959) example in making as systematic a use as possible of the evidence of crops for the reconstruction of culture history. The difficulties encountered in applying his approach even on a small scale help to explain the failure — howbeit stimulating and productive — of those sections of his continental synthesis that treat early developments in agriculture (Baker 1962; Portères 1962). The results of the present study are of relevance primarily to Cameroonian history, but because the United Republic occupies a strategic position near the center of the continent, they may have wider implications.

The presence of the Chadic subfamily of Afro-Asiatic languages in sub-Saharan Africa is best explained by the hypothesis that the ancestral language originated in the southern Sahara, perhaps through the contact of its Neolithic pastoral population with peoples of the south (Olderogge 1956). With desertification in the last two to three millennia B.C., there would have been a tendency for some of these peoples to migrate southward, attempting thus to maintain their environmental adaptation. It is at this point that knowledge of the vegetation patterns of the day becomes crucial to an understanding of the processes of domestication. If there lay to the south the inexhaustible resources of the savanna, then, as Clark discusses in his paper (this volume), why were they unable to maintain their broad spectrum economy? If on the other hand they were hemmed into a narrow zone of scrub and savanna between the advancing desert and a less rapidly retreating forest, economic experimentation or specialization under population pressure becomes immediately comprehensible. In either case, competition for fishing rights along the few perennial rivers and retreating lakes is a probability. With the restriction of at least the fishing and perhaps also of the pastoral components, greater reliance would have been placed on other sectors of the economy. Specialization and the development of new exploitative techniques would have followed as responses to this difficult period. We cannot tell whether any differentiation of the Chadic languages occurred during the period of residence in the Sahara, but it would seem a strong possibility that the linguistic spread over much of its present wide distribution formed part and parcel of (1) the diffusion of a complex of successful economic adaptations to the peoples of the Sahel and North Sudan zones, and (2) a southward expansion of the complex and assimilation of forest hunter-gatherers as the edges of the dry forest were eroded by clearing and firing.

According to Murdock (1959: 232), "the incidence and distribution of cultivated plants among the Eastern Nigritic [i.e. Adamawa-Eastern] peoples illuminate their culture history with exceptional clarity." Nothing, alas, could be farther from the truth; agreed that their present distribution suggests an overall, long-term movement eastward, agreed that this may have been stimulated by diffusion of Sudanic agriculture later supplemented by plants of the Malaysian complex, nevertheless the culture history of the Central African Republic and of the neighbor countries, in which these languages are found, is less well understood than that of any area of comparable size in the whole of Africa. There is no information about the date of their early movements, which may have commenced in the Neolithic or quite late in the Iron Age, nor about their character; we do not know whether the spread of the languages was the product of migration or of diffusion of language along with a new economy or with iron technology. Any combination of dates and of these or other processes is possible.

North Cameroon may yet be implicated in the puzzle of Bantu origins, but no support has been found for the prevailing view that the Ur- or pre-Bantu homeland is to be sought in or to the east of our area (Johnston 1913: 391; Guthrie 1962: 281; Oliver 1966). The evidence, negative though it is, rather favors Greenberg's position, firmly restated in a recent article, "that the ultimate origin of Bantu should be approximately in the middle Benue area of Nigeria" (Greenberg 1972: 192).

There is a strong argument here for a concentration of archaeological research in Cameroon in Letouzey's (1959) *"Zone péri- ou post-forestière,"* the man-made savannas still occupied by some Bantoid-speaking peoples (see above) that stretch south of the Adamawa from the Tikar plain across to Batouri.

None of these problems will be solved until much more archaeological and paleoecological information becomes available. The archaeological gaps are obvious enough but the contribution of archaeologists will very largely depend upon the success of paleoecologists in reconstructing past ecosystems.

Any human settlement has effects on its immediate environment. The present distribution of species on the quaternary terraces of the Mayo Kébi is a human artifact (see Appendix). There are few trees that are not encouraged or protected for their economic value, scarcely a shrub that is not in some way exploited, and the herbs are for the most part either weedy colonizers of the fields or used for thatch, matting, or fodder. (Two grasses are even said to have been introduced by the Nyamnyam.) The flotation technique, especially in its improved form (Higgs, this volume), can be expected to provide the archaeologist with direct evidence of cultigens AND of other plants growing in the environs of his sites. Interpretation of these data depends upon identification, and secondly upon the "ethnoecological" expertise necessary to infer from fragmentary evidence a complete system of man-land interrelationships. The difficulty of this task can be appreciated when we remember that "primitive" African agriculture has not been practiced these last two hundred years.

A fundamental requirement for future culture-historical studies and research into crop plant evolution is a better knowledge of the Holocene environmental sequence and vegetation patterns. Prolonged swidden cultivation, especially if combined with stock breeding and the driving of game with fire, profoundly modifies plant communities, not only in the immediate vicinity of settlements. Some modifications may be irreversible. Human agency is arguably paramount in the creation of the central African savannas from dense dry forest. Dry forest and savanna must require quite different adaptive strategies on the part of peoples with and without agriculture and with or without iron. Unless these strategies can be defined and recognized where and when they occur archaeologically, there is little hope of significant progress. And finally I would ask the botanists to tell us what might have been the effects of savannization on the distribution of the wild ancestors of African domesticates and semi-domesticates. Is it not possible that ignorance of man-made vegetational changes that may in many areas go back no further than the middle Iron Age is distorting not only our views of culture history but also of crop plant evolution?

APPENDIX

Useful plants found in and near settled Fulani villages in the Benue-Kébi confluence area of North Cameroon, a partial listing

Binomial name	Vernacular name	Use
Amaranthus spinosus L.	Spiny amaranth	Pot-herb
Asteroclina species		Pot-herb
Brachiaria ramosa (L.) Stapf		Horse fodder
Cleome hirsuta Sch. and Thonn.		Pot-herb
C. ciliata Sch. and Thonn.		Pot-herb
Cyperus cf. *articulatus*		Rhizomes burnt for fragrance
Dactyloctenium aegyptium Beauv.	Comb-fringe grass	Horse fodder
Echinochloa species		Horse fodder
Gynandropsis gynandra (L.) Briq.		Pot-herb
Hemarthria altissima (Poir.) Stapf and Hubbard		Thatch
Hyparrhenia species		Thatch
Pennisetum pedicellatum Trin.		Thatch
Polygonum species		Ashes as salt substitute
Trachypogon species		Thatch
Vetiveria nigritana Stapf		Zana matting
Adansonia digitata L.	Baobab	Multiple
Annona senegalensis Pers.	Wild custard apple	Fruit
Acacia albida Del.	Winter thorn	Fodder (dry season)
A. arabica Willd.	Egyptian thorn	Glue
A. polyacantha Willd. subsp. *campylacantha* (Hochst *ex* A. Rich.) Brenan	Catechu tree	Fence posts
A. senegal Willd.		Fodder, glue
Balanites aegyptiaca Del.	Desert date	Multiple
Bombax costatum Pellegr. and Vuillet	Red-flowered silk cotton tree	Mattress stuffing
Butyrospermum paradoxum (Gaertn. f.) Hepper subspecies *parkii* (G. Don)	Shea tree	Fruit
Capparis corymbosa Lam.		Arrow poison (root)
Cassia tora L.	Foetid cassia	Pot-herb
Ceiba pentandra Gaertn.	Silk cotton tree	Mattress stuffing
Celtis integrifolia Lam.	Nettle tree	Fruit, pot-herb
Commiphora kerstingii Engl.	African myrrh	Fodder, fence posts
Corchorus olitorius L.	Jew's mallow	Pot-herb
C. tridens L.		Pot-herb
Euphorbia unispina N.E. Br.		Arrow poison (sap)
Ficus gnaphalocarpa A. Rich.		Fruit, fodder

APPENDIX (continued)

Binomial name	Vernacular name	Use
F. iteophylla Miq.		Fruit
F. platyphylla Del.	Gutta-percha tree	Fruit, fodder
F. polita Vahl		Fruit
Gardenia erubescens Stapf and Hutch.		Fence posts
Grewia tenax (Forsk.) Fiori		Wood for bows
G. mollis Juss.		Spice (bark)
Haematostaphis barteri Hook f.	Blood plum	Fruit
Hyphaene thebaica Mart.	Dum palm	Fruit, matting
Jatropha curcas L.	Physic nut	Hedge plant
Khaya senegalensis A. Juss.	Dry zone mahogany	Canoe wood
Kigelia africana Benth.	Sausage tree	Fence posts
Manihot glaziovii Muell Arg.	Ceara rubber	Glue, ornamental
Moringa oleifera Lam.	Horse-radish tree	Drink (leaves)
Parkinsonia aculeata L.	Jerusalem thorn	Ornamental
Parkia clappertoniana Keay	Locust bean tree	Flavoring (seeds)
Prosopis africana Taub.		Smiths' charcoal
Ricinus communis L.	Castor plant	Oil
Securinega virosa (Roxb. *ex* Willd.) Baill.		Withies for beds and traps
Sterculia setigera Del.		String
Tamarindus indica L.	Tamarind	Drink (fruit pulp)
Vitex doniana Sweet		Fruit, wood for canoes
Ximenia americana L.	Wild olive	Fruit
Zizyphus mauritiana Lam.	Jujube tree	Fruit, wood for bows
Z. mucronata Willd.	Buffalo thorn	Fruit

REFERENCES

ALEXANDRE, P.
1965   Proto-histoire du groupe beti-bulu-fang: essai de synthèse provisoire. *Cahiers d'Etudes Africaines* 5(4):503–560.

ALIMEN, H., P. LECOQ
1953   Une curieuse roche "gravée" des Monts Alantika. *Bull. Soc. Préhist. Française* 50:345–351.

ANDERSON, E.
1952   *Plants, man, and life.* Boston: Little, Brown.

AUBREVILLE, A.
1949   *Climats, forêts et désertification de l'Afrique tropicale.* Paris: Soc. Edit. Gégraphiques, Maritimes, et Coloniales.

BAKER, H. G.
1962   Comments on the thesis that there was a major centre of plant domestication near the headwaters of the River Niger. *Journal of African History* 3(2):229–233.

BARTH, H.
1857   Travels and discoveries in north and central Africa: being a journal of an expedition undertaken under the auspices of H.B.M.'s Government in the years 1849–1855, five volumes. London: Longman, Brown, Green, Longman, and Roberts.

BASSORO, M. H.
1965   Un manuscrit peul sur l'histoire de Garoua. Abbia 8:45–76. Yaoundé.

BILLARD, P.
1963   Le Cameroun Fédérale, volume one: Essai de géographie physique. Lyon: Imprimerie des Beaux Arts.

BOULET, J.
1966   "Magoumaz: étude d'un terroir de montagne de pays mafa." Yaoundé: ORSTOM. Mimeographed.

BUISSON, E. M.
1933   Matériaux pour servir à la préhistoire du Cameroun. Bull. Soc. Préhist. Française 30:335–348.

BURKILL, I. H.
1938   The contact of the Portuguese with African food-plants which gave words such as "yam" to European languages. Proceedings of the Linnean Society 150:84–95.

BURNHAM, P. C.
1972   "Residential organisation and social change among the Gbaya of Meiganga, Cameroon." Unpublished doctoral dissertation, University of California, Los Angeles.

CABOT, J.
1965   Le bassin du Moyen Logone. Paris: ORSTOM.

CALVOCORESSI, D.
1970   Report on the 3rd conference of West African archaeologists. West African Archaeological Newsletter 12:53–90.

CHEVALIER, A.
1907   Mission Chari-Lac Tchad 1902–1904. L'Afrique centrale française: récit du voyage de la mission. Paris: A. Chellamel.

CONNAH, G.
1966   Summary of research in Benin City and in Bornu. West African Archaeological Newsletter 5:22–25.
1967   Progress report on archaeological work in Bornu 1964–1966. Northern History Research Scheme, 2nd Interim Report, 20–31. Zaria.
1970   Precursors of Daima? West African Archaeological Newsletter 12:91–92.

COURSEY, D. C.
1967   Yams. London: Longmans.

DALZIEL, J. MC E.
1937   The useful plants of west tropical Africa. London: Crown Agents.

DAVID, N.
1967   An archaeological reconnaissance in Cameroon and the Iron Age site of Nassarao I, near Garoua. VI. Cong. Panaf. Préhist. Ét. Quat. Dakar.

1968   Archaeological reconnaissance in Cameroon. *Expedition* 10(3): 21–31.

DE GARINE, I.
1964   *Les Massa du Cameroun: vie économique et sociale.* Paris: Presses Universitaires de France.
1973   "Traditions orales et cultures au Mayo Kebbi (Tchad)," in *L'homme, hier et aujourd'hui: recueil d'études en hommage à André Leroi-Gourhan*, 421–433. Paris: Editions Cujas.

DENHAM, MAJOR D., CAPTAIN CLAPPERTON, DR. OUDNEY
1828   *Narrative of travels and discoveries in northern and central Africa in the years 1822, 1823, and 1824*, (third edition), two volumes. London: John Murray.

DIZIAIN, R.
1954   Densité de la population, démographie, économie rurale dans les subdivisions de Guider-Kaélé et Yagoua (Nord-Cameroun). Yaoundé: I.R.CAM. Mimeographed.

DOGGETT, H.
1970   *Sorghum.* London: Longmans.

DUGAST, R.
1944   L'agriculture chez les Ndiki de population Banen. *Bull. Soc. Études Camerounaises* 8:9–104.

ELDRIDGE, M.
1971   "Traditions d'origine des peuples du centre et de l'ouest du Cameroun." Yaoundé: Ministère de l'Education, de la Culture et de la Formation Professionelle. Mimeographed.

GAUTHIER, J. G.
1972   La civilisation Sao: recherches archéologiques en pays Fali (Nord-Cameroun). *Archéologia* 49:45–56.

GREENBERG, J. H.
1963   The languages of Africa. *International Journal of African Linguistics* 29(1, pt. 2). Publication 25 of the Indiana Research Center in Anthropology, Folklore and Linguistics.
1972   Linguistic evidence regarding Bantu origins. *Journal of African History* 13(2):189–216.

GRIAULE, N., J.-P. LEBEUF
1948   Fouilles dans la région du Tchad, I. *Journal de la Société des Africanistes* 18(1):1–116.
1950   Fouilles dans la région du Tchad, II, *Journal de la Société des Africanistes* 20:1–151.
1951   Fouilles dans la région du Tchad, III. *Journal de la Société des Africanistes* 21:1–95.

GUILLARD, J.
1965   *Golonpoui: analyse des conditions de modernisation d'un village du Nord-Cameroun.* Paris, The Hague: Mouton.

GUTHRIE, M.
1962   Some developments in the prehistory of the Bantu languages. *Journal of African History* 3(2):273–282.

HARLAN, J. R.
1971 Agricultural origins: centers and noncenters. *Science* 174(4008): 468–474.

HARLAN, J. R., J. M. J. DE WET
1972 A simplified classification of cultivated sorghum. *Crop Science* 12:172–176.

HARRIS, D. R.
1973 "The prehistory of tropical agriculture: an ethnoecological model," in *The explanation of culture change: models in prehistory.* Edited by C. Renfrew, 391–417. London: Duckworth.

HATA, N.
1973 The swidden crops and the planting pattern of Dourou agriculture in North Cameroon. *Kyoto University African Studies* 8:93–115.

HERVIEU, J.
1968 "Contribution à l'étude des industries lithiques du Nord-Cameroun. Mise au point et données nouvelles." Yaoundé: ORSTOM. Mimeographed.
1969 "Le quaternaire du Nord-Cameroun. Schéma d'évolution géomorphologique et relations avec la pédogenèse." Yaoundé: ORSTOM. Mimeographed.

HURAULT, J.
1970 Les lavaka de Banyo (Cameroun): témoins de paléoclimats. *Bull. Ass. Géog. Française* 377–378:3–13.

Illustrated London News
1967 "Classic excavation in north-east Nigeria." *Illustrated London News*, section number 2276, October 14.

JACQUES-FELIX, H.
1940 L'agriculture des noirs au Cameroun. Enquêtes sur les plantes cultivées, sur les outils agricoles et sur les greniers. *Rev. Bot. Appliq. et Agric. Trop.* 20:815–838.
1948 Ignames sauvages et cultivées du Cameroun. *Bull. Soc. Études Camerounaises* 21–22:13–18.

JAUZE, J. B.
1944 Contribution à l'étude de l'archéologie du Cameroun. *Bull. Soc. Études Camerounaises* 8:105–123.

JOHNSTON, SIR H. H.
1913 A survey of the ethnography of Africa: and the former racial and tribal migrations in that continent. *Journal of the Royal Anthropology Institute* 43:375–421.

JUILLERAT, B.
1971 *Les bases de l'organisation sociale chez les Mouktélé (Nord-Cameroun). Structures lignagères et mariage.* Mém. Inst. Ethnol. 8. Université de Paris.

KIRK-GREENE, A. H. M.
1958 *Adamawa past and present: an historical introduction to the development of a North Cameroons province.* London: Oxford University Press for the International African Institute.

KROEBER, A. L.
1948   *Anthropology* (revised edition). London: G. C. Harrap.

LEBEUF, A. M. D.
1959   *Les populations du Tchad (nord du 10e parallèle)*. Paris: Presses Universitaires de France.

LEBEUF, J.-P.
1961   *L'habitation des Fali, montagnards du Cameroun septentrionale: technologie, sociologie, mythologie, symbolisme*. Paris: Hachette.
1962   *Archéologie tchadienne: les Sao du Cameroun et du Tchad*. (Postface 1969.) Paris: Hermann.
1969   *Carte archéologique des abords du Lac Tchad (Cameroun, Nigeria, Tchad.)* Paris: Ed. du C.N.R.S.

LEBEUF, J.-P., A. MASSON-DETOURBET
1950   *La civilisation du Tchad*. Paris: Payot.

LEMBEZAT, B.
1961   *Les populations paiennes du Nord-Cameroun et de l'Adamawa*. Paris: Presses Universitaires de France.

LESTRINGANT, J.
1964   "Le pays du Guider au Cameroun: essai d'histoire régionale." Paris: CNRS. Mimeographed.

LETOUZEY, R.
1959   "Phytogéographie camerounaise," in *Atlas du Cameroun*. Imprimerie Nationale. Separatum 6 pages, map.
1968   *Etude phytogéographique du Cameroun*. Encyclopédie biologique LXIX. Paris: Eds. P. Lechevalier.

MAISTRE, C.
1895   *A travers l'Afrique centrale du Congo au Niger*. Paris: Hachette.

MALZY, P.
1956   Les Fali du Tinguelin. *Bull. Soc. Études Camerounaises* 51:3–37.

MARLIAC, A.
1971   *La préhistoire du Cameroun*, two volumes. Yaoundé: ORSTOM. Mimeographed.

MEEK, C. K.
1931   *A Sudanese kingdom*. London: Kegan Paul, Trench, Trubner.

MIRACLE, M. P.
1965   The introduction and spread of maize in Africa. *Journal of African History* 6(1):39–56.

MURDOCK, G. P.
1959   *Africa: its peoples and their culture history*. New York, Toronto, London: McGraw-Hill.

NACHTIGAL, G.
1881   *Sahara und Sudan. Ergebnisse sechsjähriger Reisen in Afrika*, volume two. Berlin: Weidmannsche Buchhandlung, Verlagshandlung Paul Parey.

OLDEROGGE, D. A.
1956   The origin of the Hausa language. *Vth Int. Cong. Anth. Ethnol. Sci.* Separatum 28 pages.

OLIVER, R.
1966   The problem of the Bantu expansion. *Journal of African History* 7(3):361–376.

PAIRAULT, C.
1966   *Boum-le-grand, village d'Iro.* Trav. et Mém. Inst. Ethnol. 73. Université de Paris.

PALMER, H. R.
1928   *Sudanese memoirs.* Lagos: Government Printers.

PASSARGE, S.
1895   *Adamaua. Bericht über die Expedition des deutschen Kamerun-Komitees in den Jahren 1893/4.* Berlin: Geographische Verlags-handlung Dietrich Riemer (Hoefer and Vohsen).

PELÉ, J., S. LE BERRE
1966   "Les aliments d'origine végétale au Cameroun." Yaoundé: OR-STOM. Mimeographed.

PERVÈS, M.
1945   Notes de préhistoire africaine: Hoggar-Sahara occidentale-Cameroun. *Bull. Soc. Préhist. Française* 42:216–220.

PIAS, J.
1967   Quatre deltas successifs du Chari au Quaternaire (Républiques du Tchad et du Cameroun). *C. R. Hebdom. Acad, Sci. Paris* 264 (série D): 2357–2360.
1968   *Contribution à l'étude des formations sedimentaires tertiaires et quaternaires dans la cuvette tchadienne et des sols qui en derivent.* Thèse Sc. ORSTOM (not consulted).

PORTÈRES, R.
1962   Berceaux agricoles primaires sur le continent africain. *Journal of African History* 3(2):195–210.

PULLAN, R. A.
1969   Geomorphology and pedological investigations in the south-central part of the Chad basin, Nigeria. *Palaeoecology of Africa* 4:49–51.

PURSEGLOVE, J. W.
1968   *Tropical crops: dicotyledons 1 and 2,* two volumes. London: Longmans.
1972   *Tropical crops: monocotyledons 1 and 2,* two volumes. London: Longmans.

ROSENFELD, A.
1972   The microlithic industries of Rop rock shelter. *West African Journal of Archaeology* 2:17–28.

SCHNEIDER, J.-L.
1967   Evolution du dernier lacustre et peuplements préhistoriques aux pays-bas du Tchad. *Bull. de Liaison. Ass. Sénégalaise pour l'Etude du Quaternaire de l'Ouest Africain.* 14–15:18–23.

SEGALEN, P.
1957   Les sols du Cameroun. *Atlas du Cameroun.* Imprimerie Nationale. Separatum 6 pages, map.

SERVANT, M., S. SERVANT
1970   Les formations lacustres et les diatomées du Quaternaire récent

du fond de la cuvette tchadienne. *Rev. Géog. Phy. Géol. Dynam.* (2)12(1):63–76.

SERVANT, M., S. SERVANT-VILDARY
1972 Nouvelles données pour une interprétation paléoclimatique de séries continentales du Bassin Tchadien (Pléistocène récent, Holocène). *Palaeoecology of Africa* 6:87–92.

SILLANS, R.
1953 Sur quelques plantes alimentaires spontanées de l'Afrique centrale. *Bull. Inst. Ét. Centrafricaines* 5–6:77–100.

1958 *Les savanes de l'Afrique centrale. Essai sur la physionomie, la structure et le dynamisme des formations ligneuses des régions sèches de la République Centrafricaine.* Encyclopédie Biologique LV. Paris: Eds. P. Lechevalier.

STENNING, D. J.
1959 *Savannah nomads.* London: Oxford University Press for the International African Institute.

TESSMAN, G.
1934 *Die Baja: ein Negerstamm im mittleren Sudan. Teil I. Materielle und seelische Kultur.* Stuttgart: Strecker and Schroeder.

TISSERANT, R. P. CH.
1953 L'agriculture dans les savanes de l'Oubangui. *Bull. Inst. Ét. Cen-. trafr.* 5–6:209–274.

URVOY, Y.
1949 *Histoire de l'empire de Bournou.* Mém. IFAN 7. Paris: Larose.

VAILLANT, A.
1947 Une enquête agricole chez les Mofu de Wazam. *Bull. Soc. Études Camerounaises* 17–18:41–98.

VAN ZINDEREN-BAKKER, E. M.
1972 Late quaternary lacustrine phases in the southern Sahara and East Africa. *Palaeoecology of Africa* 6:15–27.

VIDAL, P.
1969 *La civilisation de Bouar: prospections et fouilles.* Recherches Oubanguiennes 1. Paris: Firman-Didot Études.

WHITE, S.
1943 L'économie rurale des montagnes Kirdis de l'Emirat de Dikoa au Cameroun sous mandat britannique. *Bull. Soc. Études Camerounaises* 3:77–86.

WILLETT, F.
1971 A survey of recent results in the radiocarbon chronology of western and northern Africa. *Journal of African History* 12(3):339–370.

The Use of Ground Grain During the Late Paleolithic of the Lower Nile Valley, Egypt

FRED WENDORF and ROMUALD SCHILD

Only in the last ten years has there been even the minimum evidence available to permit an evaluation of the role of the Nile Valley in the development and spread of food production in Africa. The evidence is still far from satisfactory, but there is now a reasonably firm outline of the late Paleolithic cultural developments along the Nile and some clues which suggest that this area may have been one of the important contributors to the initial developments which preceded the emergence of food production in the Old World. Until this recently obtained data became available, most of the scholars who were interested in the beginning of food production came to the conclusion that the Nile Valley could not have contributed significantly to these developments, at least not initially (Movius 1953: 175). First of all, the limited data available on the prehistory of the lower Nile Valley suggested that it was a culturally conservative *cul-de-sac* and, therefore, hardly likely to have inspired such a significant new technology as domestication of plants or animals. Second, it was believed that the initial steps toward food production, at least for the cereals, must have occurred in the area where wild wheat and barley — generally held to be the first cultigens — grow today (Braidwood 1958). Thus, the upland area around the Tigris and Euphrates rivers was seen as the most likely area for this to have taken place. There is still a great deal of appeal to these concepts,

The research projects which yielded much of the previously unpublished data described in this paper were jointly sponsored by Southern Methodist University, the Polish Academy of Sciences, and the Egyptian Geological Survey. Financial support was provided by National Science Foundation Grant GS-1886 and Smithsonian Institution Grant Number 2423.

particularly if domestication of wheat and barley did not occur until
around 7000 B.C., by which time, on the basis of pollen evidence, there
is reason to believe that the present patterns of plant distributions had
been established. If plant domestication occurred a few thousand years
earlier, however, then there is a good likelihood that the distribution
of wild wheat and barley may have been significantly different and
could have included parts of the Nile Valley.

The excavations in Nubia and, subsequently, along the Nile, have
shown that the Nile Valley, far from being a cultural *cul-de-sac*, was
fully as advanced as adjacent areas and participated at an early date in
most of the significant technological and typological developments of
the Upper and Terminal Paleolithic, including that of blade technology
and composite tools (Wendorf 1968). It is not surprising, then, to discover that several Final Paleolithic groups in the Nile Valley also were
intimately involved in the initial steps which may have led to food
production, either there or elsewhere. The evidence for such involve-
ment consists of:

1.   Numerous grinding stones and lustrous-edged pieces (probably

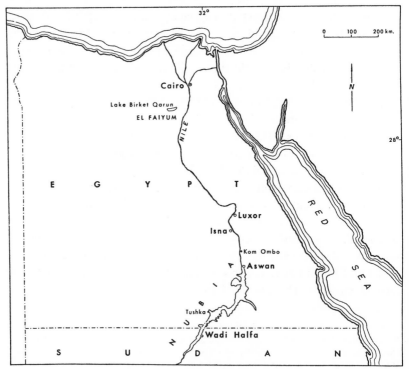

Figure 1.   Map of Egypt showing location of sites at Tushka, Kom Ombo and Isna

sickles) from several late Paleolithic sites scattered along the Nile Valley from the Sudanese frontier to Middle Egypt (Figure 1) and confidently dated well before 10,000 B.C., and as early as 12,500 B.C.;

2.   Biological data which confirm the presence along the Nile Valley at this time of a *graminae* suitable for exploitation — the evidence being the occurrence within the sediments containing the archaeological materials of cells from an unidentified large grass, spores from typical wheat flag and smut fungi, and pollen tentatively identified as barley;

3.   A significant but short-lived demographic change in at least one area which closely coincides with the initial appearance there of the grinding stones and sickle blades.

The reader will note that this list does not mention any domestic grain or animals. The omission is deliberate for remains of neither domestic grains nor animals have been found in any context within the valley with an age greater than 4000 to 4500 B.C. Furthermore, it seems likely, on the basis of demographic studies and economic analyses, and in spite of a pollen diagram which might be interpreted as indicative of deliberate planting of barley by man around 10,500 B.C., that domestic plants and animals were not present in the Nile Valley until introduced from elsewhere, presumably southwestern Asia, along with pottery, permanent architecture, and other typical "Neolithic" elements around 4000 B.C.

In spite of these limitations, the role of the late Paleolithic inhabitants of the Nile Valley was highly significant in the ultimate development of food production — at least insofar as grains are concerned. Also at the present time, these Nilotic communities offer one of the best-known examples of the social and economic changes which occurred when man first began utilizing ground grain as an important source of food.

Since the collecting and grinding of grain are such widespread human activities and even occur among some of the most primitive modern hunting and gathering societies, it might be assumed that it is a very old practice, perhaps occurring in the earlier Paleolithic. However, the evidence is to the contrary. While a rare, occasional grinding stone has been recovered from a few Paleolithic sites in Europe and the Near East, in most instances these rare grinding stones are directly associated with ground pigment; and it is highly likely that this was their exclusive function. In the Near East, for example, a total of about six such grinding stones are known — three of them from the site of Ein Aqev in Israel, dated between 15,000 and 16,000 B.C., where they occur with abundant red ocher (S. Marks, personal communication). The others are single examples from scattered sites. In any event, the crucial adaptation was not the discovery of how to grind, for this could well be a very old technique, but the application of this technique to the preparation of grain for food. While we cannot state with certainty that this technique was unknown in the earlier Paleolithic, it clearly was of little consequence then, for even if Paleolithic man was aware that ground grass seeds could be utilized for food and occasionally took advantage of this knowledge, he made such little use of it that it had no economic significance.

A very different situation is evident along the Nile when the first grinding stones appear, perhaps slightly before 12,500 B.C. Here, almost immediately, the exploitation of ground grain as a source of food became an important economic activity, to judge by the numbers of grinding stones present; and furthermore, this new activity seemingly spread rapidly among groups with diverse cultural traditions. Since it did spread so rapidly, one might suspect that when additional sites are excavated in the adjacent Near East and perhaps in the central Sahara (particularly those dating between 12,000 and 10,000 B.C.) many of these sites will also yield evidence for intensive use of ground grain at a time level comparable with its presence along the Nile.

In evaluating the Nilotic evidence in these terms, it may be useful to consider the data in their proper stratigraphic and chronological framework. In this connection the deposits of interest to us are the series of fluvial silts, sands, gravels, aeolian sands, and lacustrine sediments which record the history of the Nile during the last 15,000 to 20,000 years. This portion of the sequence begins with a series of silts and interfingering aeolian dunes assigned to the Ballana-Masmas aggradation (the discussion here follows the scheme proposed in an unpublished manuscript by the present authors and is modified slightly from that previously published). These silts and dunes record a maximum aggradation of the Nile ranging from 25 meters above the modern floodplain in Sudanese Nubia to around 4 meters at Isna. A number of radiocarbon determinations place the end of this event around 15,000 B.C. The climate in Egypt during this period appears to have been closely similar to that which prevailed there during historical times and today. Seemingly, there was little vegetation beyond the floodplain; and dunes, driven by prevailing westerly winds, were extremely active along the west side of the valley.

A number of archaeological sites have been excavated which were occupied during this period. The lithic materials associated with these sites indicate that the lower Nile Valley was occupied by several groups, each characterized by distinct technological and typological attributes which appear to be too different to be reflections of specialized activities by the same cultural units. All of these groups had a mixed economy based on large mammal hunting, primarily *Bos*, hartebeest, hippopotamus, and gazelle, together with fishing (mostly the large Nile catfish) and shellfish gathering. None of the sites have yielded any evidence of grinding stones, sickle blades, or other indications of the use of ground grain for food.

Following the episode of maximum Nile aggradation represented by the Ballana silts and interfingering dunes, the level of the Nile fell significantly (more than 16 meters in Nubia and more than 2 meters at Isna). This interval of lower Nile levels has been named the Deir El-Fakhuri and is believed to represent a period of about 3,000 years, from 15,000 to 12,000 B.C. Wadi deposits and fossil soils are the major physical records of the Deir El-Fakhuri interval, but they are too limited to be of much assistance for reconstructing the environment during this time. Both the soils and wadi deposits, however, suggest slightly more rainfall than today. Archaeological assemblages dated within this period occur at several localities in Nubia at Kom Ombo and in Upper Egypt. These indicate a mixed hunting and fishing economy as in the sites occupied during the preceding Ballana-Masmas aggradation. Also, none of the sites contain any evidence for the exploitation of ground grain for food.

Following the Deir El-Fakhuri interval, the level of the Nile again rose, beginning, according to the radiocarbon dates, shortly before 12,000 B.C. In the dune areas along the west bank of the river, the effects of this rise were initially reflected in the appearance of numerous small ephemeral ponds, separated from the river by a barrier of dunes along the edge of the floodplain, but probably drawing water from the river by seepage. Lacustrine clays, silts, and diatomites were deposited in these ponds. Eventually the river rose sufficiently to break through the dune barrier which had protected the ponds, and at this point a thick series of Nile silts was laid over the pond sediments. This period of aggradation is known as the Sahaba-Darau, and it coincides with the introduction all along the Nile, from Sudan to Upper Egypt, of a complex of new technological features which strongly indicate that for the first time the ground grain was being intensively utilized as a source of food.

These new economic activities should be viewed against what may have been only modest but significant and favorable changes in the environment. Diatom and pollen analyses from the pond deposits representing the initial phase of the Sahaba-Darau aggradation indicate that summer temperatures were somewhat cooler at this time. These lower temperatures presumably reduced evaporation and possibly enabled the ponds to survive much longer than they would today. At the same time there seems to have been greater local rainfall, for wadi gravels frequently interfinger with the Sahaba-Darau silts, particularly in the lower part of the unit. The total pollen spectra from these ponds also indicate the presence of an arid grassland beyond the floodplain, a situation which markedly contrasts with the virtually total absence of vegetation in this same area today and probably during the preceding Ballana-Masmas interval.

During the final part of the Sahaba-Darau aggradation, there is no evidence of interfingering wadi deposits, suggesting that local rainfall was again reduced. Also, along the west bank which apparently had been stabilized slightly earlier by the grassland vegetation, active dunes again developed in several areas at this time. Dune formation, however, was by no means comparable to that which occurred during the final phase of the Ballana-Masmas deposition.

The massive Sahaba-Darau silts reached an elevation of around 24 meters above the modern floodplain at Wadi Halfa and 8 meters above the floodplain at Isna. One distinctive event which occurred near the end of the Sahaba-Darau aggradation was a widespread fire (or possibly several nearly contemporary fires) which swept the marshy aquatic and floodplain vegetation for a distance of at least 150 kilometers, from Isna in the south to Dishna in the north. The burned layer of silt which resulted from the fire is a useful chrono-stratigraphic marker. A radiocarbon date indicates the fire or fires occurred around 10,500 B.C.

The end of the Sahaba-Darau saw a series of exceptionally high floods, some of which were more than 10 meters above the top of the main Sahaba-Darau silt aggradation. These floods have been dated between 10,500 and 9,700 B.C., but their climatic and environmental significance is not clearly understood.

After the maximum of the Sahaba-Darau aggradation around 9600 B.C., the level of the Nile again fell, and this was followed by another major episode of aggradation, the Arkin, dated between 9200 and 7400 B.C. The Arkin reached a maximum elevation of 10 meters above the modern floodplain in Nubia. Climatic data for this interval are limited, but there was extensive hunting of the savanna-type megafauna by some groups, which may indicate some persistence of the arid grasslands adjacent to the river.

A series of microaggradations and declines marks the general reces-

Plate 1. View of Tushka Site. Low mounds in middle distance are remnants of interdune ponds exposed by deflation. Note severe desert conditions which prevail today

Plate 2. Grinding stones from Tushka. From Wendorf (1968: 942)

sion from the maximum of the Arkin aggradation. These pauses or microaggradations are dated at several sites with maxima at 5700 B.C., 5100 B.C., and 3600 B.C. It is perhaps of climatic significance that all of the sites of this period yield evidence which suggests that only limited hunting of the savanna-type animals was possible. Fish and hippopotamus apparently were the important sources of food.

EARLY GRAIN UTILIZATION IN EGYPT: THE EVIDENCE

Evidence for the initial utilization of ground grain occurs along the Nile at about the same time in three widely separated areas. This spacial separation is not indicative of three separate centers of development, but only reflects where extensive exposures of deposits of this period have been preserved and studied. It is probable that the grain utilization phenomena was virtually continuous along the entire valley in Egypt and extended an unknown distance southward into Sudan. The three areas where the evidence has been preserved are at Tushka, near Abu Simbel in the south; at Kom Ombo, below Aswan, about 200 kilometers to the north; and at Isna, still farther north near Luxor. All three areas are located in the valley proper and share the additional similarity of being in situations where the floodplain was unusually wide. Two of the localities are also within or adjacent to extensive fossil dune fields.

The Tushkan Sites

The series of closely adjacent sites given this name is located on the west bank of the Nile near the now inundated Nubian village of Tushka and a short distance downstream from the famous temple of Abu Simbel (Figure 1). The sites were situated at the head of a wide fossil embayment filled with silts of the Sahaba-Darau aggradation (Albritton 1968). Along the shore of the embayment at 22 meters above the modern floodplain, the Sahaba silts fringed against the remnants of an extensive dune field. At some time prior to the maximum of the Sahaba aggradation, ponds developed in the topographic lows between the dunes particularly in the area adjacent to the embayment. These ponds were ephemeral but seemed to have survived for reasonably long periods — at least long enough for diatomite to occur in the larger ones. The stratigraphic evidence indicates that both the ponds and the human occupations occurred before the maximum of the Sahaba.

The shore of the Tushka embayment and the adjacent dunes were repeatedly occupied by late Paleolithic groups (Wendorf 1968: 864–946). The artifacts clustered into several discrete concentrations, each apparently representing a different occupation. These concentrations were not large, ranging from 10 to 20 meters in diameter, which suggests that the social groups probably were small (Plate 1). The stone tools left by these groups were predominantly microlithic (less than 3 centimeters in length), and generally the tools were made on simple flakes. Three subgroups of typological assemblages were recognized, but these differed only in frequencies of certain tool categories. These subgroups may have chronological significance, but it is also likely that they reflect specialized activities the nature of which could not be identified.

Five conflicting radiocarbon dates were obtained from these sites at Tushka, the earliest at 12,550 B.C. ± 490 years (WSU–315), and the latest at 400 B.C. ± 300 years (WSU–415a). One is justified in being suspicious of all these dates since they are so inconsistent, but the earliest date has the advantage of being in agreement with the stratigraphic evidence which places the occupation of the site prior to the Sahaba-Darau maximum, an event for which there are numerous radiocarbon dates elsewhere along the Nile at before 10,000 B.C. A reasonable date for the occupation at Tushka would be between 12,500 and 10,500 B.C., and certainly before 10,000 B.C.

The Tushkan communities were sustained by a mixed economy. Fishing was extremely important, and the presence of the nearby embayment may have been the major factor in the repeated occupation of this locality for the deeper swales in this embayment would have been particularly attractive for fishing after the annual summer floods. Hunting the large savanna-type animals such as *Bos*, hartebeest, and gazelle was also important, judging by the quantities of their remains which occurred there; but there was a third important economic activity: the collecting and grinding of grain. The use of grain is suggested by new categories of artifacts not previously present in Nubia. These are lustrous-edged pieces and grinding stones. The grinding stones are numerous and include both the shallow basin milling stones and the upper grinders or handstones (Plate 2). All of the grinding stones were roughly shaped by pecking, and most of them showed extensive wear. Some had been resharpened by pecking. A considerable investment in time and effort had been expended both in their manufacture and in their subsequent use. Some had traces of pigment still present, and these clearly had at some point been employed for grinding paint. However, this could hardly have been their primary function since the grinding stones are both too numerous and too heavily worn.

The lustrous edged pieces are usually microlithic flakes with one steeply retouched and thick convex edge (Figure 2, a through d). The lustrous edge is unretouched, and the sheen usually diffuses back from the edge diagonally across the piece. The pattern of wear, together with the occasional traces of adhesive still evident, suggest that they were mounted by inserting the thick edge at a slight angle into some sort of shaft (probably of wood) and held in place with pitch or other adhesive (Figure 2, e).

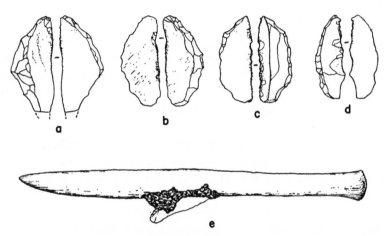

Figure 2.   Pieces with lustrous edges from Tushka and reconstruction of probable method of hafting. Stipple indicates area of sheen. Hatching on "b" indicates area covered by traces of adhesive. The hafting technique is reconstructed from an actual flint-edged sickle found near Lucerne, Switzerland, and illustrated by Semenov (1964: 118). (From Wendorf 1968: 943)

Experiments have shown that diffused gloss or sheen, such as observed on these pieces from Tushka, is produced by repeated use in cutting grain or similar flexible substances containing silica (Curwen 1935; Semenov 1964: 113–122). A great deal more needs to be done, however, before this gloss can be distinguished with any certainty from that which might be produced from cutting cane, wood, or leather. It is significant, however, that none of the literally thousands of artifacts excavated from earlier sites in Nubia yielded any evidence of similar lustrous edges while, on the other hand, it does occur on tools at several other sites which are contemporary and/or slightly later than those at Tushka, and always in association with grinding stones.

The precise identity of the grain which was utilized at Tushka could not be established, but microscopic examination of the sediments from one of the interdune ponds disclosed a few pollen grains of a large wheat-like grass, together with cell structures of an unidentified large Gramineae and wheat and bunt spores. Unfortunately, none of these features were distinctive of any specific grass — wild or domestic — but they did indicate the presence in the immediate vicinity of some kind of large grass, the seeds from which might have been collected with the aid of a stone sickle and pulverized on a grinding stone.

Sites at Gebel Silsilla, Kom Ombo

The Kom Ombo plain is a broad reentrant or embayment located on the east bank of the Nile about 30 kilometers north of Aswan. The Pleistocene geology of this area has been studied in detail by Butzer and Hansen (1968). One locality here, known as Gebel Silsilla 2B, Area I, yielded numerous grinding stones associated with an archaeological assemblage buried within deposits filling an old channel of the Nile (Reed 1966: 22). These channel-fill deposits are believed to be the equivalent to the Sahaba formation elsewhere in Nubia. There are two radiocarbon dates with this occupation: 11,610 B.C. ± 120 years (Y-1447) and 11,120 B.C. ± 120 years (Y–1375). The dates are consistent with the stratigraphic evidence and support the suggested correlation with the Sahaba-Darau aggradation. The Gebel Silsilla settlement was small (the remaining portion was about 78 square meters) and thus also similar to those at Tushka (J. Phillips [personal communication] and Butzer and Hansen [1968: 170], report a very large settlement; however, here they were referring to the area covered by material deflated from later deposits and unrelated to the *in situ* living floor).

Detailed descriptions of the Silsilla materials have not yet been published, but according to J. Phillips (personal communication), who is in the process of analyzing the collection, the assemblage is closely similar to the Afian industry recovered from several sites near Thomas Afia village near Isna, Egypt. The materials include a high frequency of arch-backed and truncated semigeometric lithic pieces which may represent an incipient state in the development of compound tools.

No lustrous-edged pieces were reported, but the grinding stones from Gebel Silsilla are closely similar to those from Tushka. Many of these grinding stones also display traces of pigment, and a function for this purpose rather than grain grinding has been suggested (Butzer and Hansen 1968: 170). This interpretation is rejected here on the grounds that grinding stones are too numerous, are far too heavily worn, and thus represent such an investment of effort that an important economic function is much more likely. Incidentally, it is useful to note that an examination of similar grinding stones from Egyptian sites of undoubted Neolithic age and from several prehistoric pueblos in the American Southwest discloses that in both instances a majority of these grinding stones also display traces of pigment.

The settlements of the closely similar Affian industry near Isna are also small and compact concentrations and are believed to represent small social groups. Unlike the Gebel Silsilla settlement, however, the Afian sites did not yield grinding stones or lustrous-edged pieces. The Afian sites are not dated, but they occur in deposits related to the early phase of the Sahaba-Darau aggradation and thus may be either slightly earlier than or approximately contemporary with the Gebel Silsilla occupation. The absence of grinding stones, therefore, might be due either to an occupation prior to the appearance of the grinding stone technology or, equally plausible, to a seasonal occupation or specialized activity where grinding stones were not utilized.

Other Isnan Sites

The first clear-cut demographic change which might be attributed to the new technology occurs slightly later at Isna. In the same area where the Afian sites without grinding stones are recorded, but slighly later in the stratigraphic sequence, there are numerous other sites containing artifacts of another and quite different lithic industry named the Isnan. The Isnan sites occur in the upper part of the interdune pond deposits (which have been correlated with the middle phase of the Sahaba-Darau aggradation) and in the overlying upper Sahaba silts, the final phase of that event. Some of the sites were occupied just before and others just after the widespread fire which swept the Nile Valley in this area.

Sites of the Isnan industry appear suddenly in the area, have no known local progenitors, and represent over half of the known sites of ALL ages in this region. The settlements are also several times larger than any of the previous Paleolithic communities, suggesting either repeated reoccupation of all localities (for which there is no evidence, such as internal clustering) or, more likely, the presence of much larger social groups. It is also significant that none of the Isnan sites have yielded fish remains, an important element in earlier sites as well as in those occupied a few thousand years later during the Terminal Paleolithic. These data suggest a sudden demographic explosion accompanied by significant changes in the economic base.

Unlike the earlier small Afian sites, the Isnan sites contain grinding stones, some with deeply worn basins, and numerous blades and flakes with pronounced lustrous edges, indistinguishable from the sickle sheen found on Neolithic stone sickles (Figure 3). Under a microscope these lustrous-edged pieces show pronounced traces of use very typical for sickles. They are, in fact, identical with traces found on large sickle blades from the Funnel Beaker sites in central Europe. The traces of use appear on shining surfaces as very dense lines at a very acute angle toward the edge. They are reminiscent of a paint brush stroke on a surface covered by thick oil paint. The attacking angle suggests parallel hafting in a straight simple way and a kind of use similar to unidirectional sawing or parallel unidirectional long strokes. Some of those sickles which are on naturally or partially backed large flakes might have been used without any mounting at all.

Lustrous edges occur on up to 15 percent of all tools found *in situ* at these Isnan sites. This remarkably high frequency suggests a significant emphasis on the reaping of grain.

A trench in one of the Isnan sites, which was studied in detail, revealed a series of Nile and pond deposits overlying a cemented dune assigned to the Ballana formation. Above the fossil dune is a thin layer of diatomaceous pond silts interfingering with beach sands. A sample of carbonaceous sand at the base of this unit yielded a radiocarbon date of 10,740 B.C. ± 240 years (I–3421). This series of pond deposits is, in turn, covered by sediments of a maximal phase of a Nile siltation. This upper silt bears a pronounced burned layer, and the top of this unit is confidently assigned to the upper part of the Sahaba-Darau aggradation, which dated around or slightly before 10,000 B.C. The entire pond section, therefore, was deposited between 10,700 and 10,000 B.C.

The diatomaceous pond deposits under the Sahaba silts yielded a rich diatom flora, the composition of which suggests a shallow, ephemeral, and highly alkaline environment. The diatom assemblage also included three species which may have slight tropical preference. This contrasts markedly with a Holocene assemblage from the Fayum depression where tropical forms were well represented (Abdel Aleem 1958).

Several pollen samples were taken from the exposed profile and

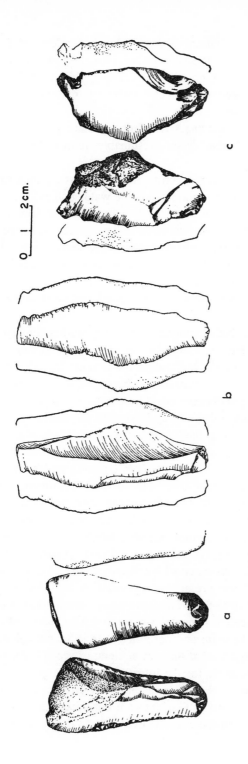

Figure 3.   Lustrous-edged pieces from Isnan sites. Stipple indicates area of sheen

analyzed by M. J. Dabrowski of the Polish Academy of Sciences. The final results are not yet available; however, in a preliminary statement (personal communication 1970) Dr. Dabrowski reported the following:
1.   The diatomaceous sediments yielded a fair amount of pollen grains, all of them in a fossil state.
2.   The pollen assemblages from all the diatomaceous layers include an amount of boreal types presumably representing long distance transport.
3.   None of the pollen spectra included aquatic plants suggesting an absence of permanent or long-standing water bodies.
4.   The remaining elements suggest a grassland environment.
5.   Scattered throughout the pond sediments were low frequencies of a large grass cereal-type pollen grain. These cereal-type grains become suddenly numerous (about 10 to 15 per cent of the total pollen) near the top of the sequence.
6.   Dr. Dabrowski tentatively identified the large cereal-like pollen as barley.

Dr. Dabrowski also suggested that the sudden fluorescence of the cereal-type pollen may indicate the rapid introduction of the grains through human activity and recalls the changes in pollen spectra which occurred in northern Europe at the beginning of the Neolithic. He also observed that such changes might have occurred as a result of collecting wild grains. Such collection and possible protection from other weed plants would promote the increment and spread of selected plants and account for the sudden fluorescence of barley in the pollen profile.

The identity of the barley needs to be confirmed by additional analyses, but if these grains have been correctly identified, then the range of the plant during the late Pleistocene must be extended into North Africa and southward for a considerable distance up the Nile Valley.

Of significance is the fact that simultaneous with the sudden increase in cereal-type pollen, the new Isnan industry appears in this area, and a large settlement associated with this industry was established some 300 meters away. There are at least two possible explanations for this coincidence: first, that there may have been a minor shift in climate or in the local microenvironmental situation which made conditions more favorable for the grain and permitted it to suddenly colonize the area, and this in turn attracted the new settlers; or second, the people somehow were responsible for the introduction of the grain, either through transport to the locality after reaping it elsewhere or by bringing it to the area and planting it. Our data are not adequate for an appropriate evaluation between these alternatives.

Post-Sahaba Data

Unfortunately, there is a marked reduction in the quantity of data on prehistoric developments in Central Egypt after the maximum of the Sahaba-Darau aggradation until the final phase of the Terminal Paleolithic. Only one site dating immediately after the Sahaba-Darau is known. It is located near El Kilh where it occurs associated with a recessional beach cut into the Sahaba-Darau silts. A sample of Unio shell from the site yielded a date of 9610 B.C. ± 180 years (I–3760) (Wendorf, Said, and Schild 1970b: 69). The lithic assemblage at this site has a number of similarities with the earlier Isnan industry, and indeed, this assemblage may be a later phase of that industry. Ground grain was also still an important source of food because several extensively worn grinding stones and lustrous-edged pieces were present; but fish — absent from the earlier Isnan communities — also occurs, together with bones from large savanna-type animals such as *Bos* and hartebeest. This site is small, however, suggesting the possibility that the larger communities, which were indicated during the final phase of the Sahaba-Darau aggradation, did not survive the environmental changes which accompanied the succeeding recession of the Nile.

Our next information comes from a cluster of sites in Nubia dated about 7400 B.C., approximately 2,000 years later than the one at El Kilh. This site cluster, known as DIW-1, contained thirteen small oval concentrations, each of which was believed to represent separate seasonal encampments by a small group (Schild, Chmiekwska, and Wieckowska 1968: 687). The associated microlithic flake industry, the Arkinian, is apparently unrelated to the preceding complexes in that area, and a North African or Saharan source was postulated. The Arkinian sites also yielded a few grinding stones and one or two pieces with lustrous edges; but neither ground grain nor fishing could have been important, at least during the season represented by the sites, for judging by the quantities of bones from large savanna-type animals, hunting was far more significant.

At a slightly later date, between 6500 and 3500 B.C., our data are more satisfactory. Several sites occupied during this time range have been excavated. They are:

1. In Sudanese Nubia a sequence of six sites representing the Shamarkian industry and located in the same area where the Arkinian concentrations occur (Schild, Chmiekwska, and Wieckowska 1968). These sites have several radiocarbon dates ranging from 5900 to 3200 B.C.
2. Downstream a short distance in Egyptian Nubia, at Catfish Cave,

a similar occupation occurs which is dated by radiocarbon at around 5100 B.C. (Wendt 1966).

3. Still farther downstream in central Egypt at El Kab, on the east bank opposite El Kilh, is another site with two superimposed occupations (Vermeersch 1970). The lithic assemblages in both levels are closely similar and indistinguishable from the Shamarkian in Nubia. Radiocarbon dates indicate an age for these occupations between 6400 and 6000 B.C.

4. The Fayum in northern Egypt where several Terminal Paleolithic concentrations have been excavated and dated by radiocarbon between 6000 and 5000 B.C. (Said, et al. 1972).

The Qarunian industry with the Fayum sites is different from that at the Shamarkian sites at El Kab and in Nubia, but all of them clearly belong within the same general industrial complex and share a number of resemblances with Capsian and similar contemporary materials in the Maghreb and along the North African coast. These Egyptian and Nubian sites also share another common feature. Except for the very latest Shamarkian communities, they represent short-lived occupations by small groups. Evidently the larger communities suggested for the Isna did not recur.

Both the Shamarkian sites in Nubia and the Qarunian sites in the Fayum also contain occasional grinding stones and lustrous-edged pieces, but they are never numerous. Only limited faunal materials were recovered from most of the Nubian sites, but fishing was very important at both Catfish Cave and in the Fayum; and large mammal hunting — while present — was definitely not important anywhere. Furthermore, it seems likely that during this period ground grain either must have had very limited importance or, by chance, none of the excavated sites were occupied during the season when grain was utilized. The latter is not very likely not only in terms of sampling theory, but also because the best time for fishing (shortly after the Nile floods in late summer) is the same period when many of the grasses suitable for exploitation reach maturity.

Around 4000 B.C. (or perhaps a few hundred years earlier) new communities appear along the Nile in central Egypt. These sites are often very large and contain well-made pottery, both domestic plants (wheat and barley) and animals (sheep and/or goats), and a lithic assemblage which is distinctly different in both technology and typology from that of the immediately preceding Terminal Paleolithic (Caton-Thompson and Gardner 1934; Said, et al. n.d.). These new sites appear to represent a true Neolithic society, and because no transitional period seems to be present, it is assumed they came to the Nile Valley from beyond its borders. Some have suggested southwestern Asia as a likely source (Kantor 1965).

A different situation is evident upstream along the Nile in Nubia where the local population does not appear to have been replaced as in central Egypt, and the Shamarkian lithic industry persists. The later sites of this industry are, however, much larger, more permanent, and contain pottery. The excavations did not yield any evidence for domestic plants or animals, but a new economic base is indicated (Schild, Chmiekwska, and Wieckowska 1968: 748).

DISCUSSION

It seems probable that the Nilotic evidence discussed above may have considerable bearing on understanding the trend which food production may well have taken elsewhere in Africa. First of all, it is evident that the key ideas necessary for large-scale exploitation of grain as a source of food, particularly such ideas as how grain can efficiently be gathered through the use of a sickle and how large quantities of it can be made edible through cracking or crushing with milling stones, were known in Africa (at least in the Nile Valley) as early as anywhere else. Wherever these techniques were first discovered or developed, once known, they likely spread rapidly over a broad area and might have been utilized on any suitable grain. This would be an ideal time for some utilization of ground grain to occur also in the Sahara or along the grassland fringe either to the north or south of the desert.

Although utilization of grain occurs surprisingly early in the Nile Valley, there is no evidence of food production (i.e. domestic plants or animals) anywhere along the Nile until around 4000 B.C. A possible exception to this statement may be indicated at Isna, around 10,500 B.C., but this seems highly unlikely at the moment and certainly needs additional confirmation before it can be seriously considered.

The response to the new economic resource of ground grain is partially recorded in the community patterns of this period. The earliest evidence for grain utilization along the Nile is found in southern Egypt at Tushka if the radiocarbon date there is correct. These sites display no evident change in settlement size or character from those of preceding periods although communities are more numerous. The first suggestion of a change in settlement type is seen at Isna where very large sites may indicate a shift in the size of social groups after grain

grinding becomes an important economic activity. This shift of settlement type and social group size at Isna occurs around 10,500 B.C., or
perhaps 2000 years after the first recorded utilization of grain. The
grain here has been tentatively identified as barley. In addition to
changes in settlement size, there also seems to have been a shift away
from fishing as an important source of food. The decline in fishing
could well have been the result of competition resulting from the use
of grain. The most favorable time for fishing and harvesting of grain
is in late summer and early fall, immediately after the Nile flood.

It is perhaps significant that these evident increases in the dependence
on ground grain seem to coincide with a minor climatic change which
would tend to favor the wild grasses which were being collected. This
may also explain why the social changes indicated for the end of this
period did not survive the climatic changes which apparently accompanied the decline of the Nile after the Sahaba-Darau maximum. The
barley or other grasses being exploited may have been less abundant
as a result of the less favorable climate. By 9000 B.C. there is no
evidence for large communities although the small sites of this period
were at least partially dependent on ground grain. From 7500 B.C. until
around 4000 B.C., some use of ground grain is indicated, but it definitely has a minor role in the economy. Unfortunately, there is very little
information available on the environment of the Nile Valley during this
crucial period, but there is the temptation to relate directly the decline
in dependence on ground grain with the shifts in climate which presumably occurred here at the end of the Pleistocene and the subsequent
emergence of the modern vegetation distribution along the Nile. If
general climatic factors were the cause, it then seems highly likely that
patterns of grain utilization elsewhere in Africa, if established during
the earlier more favorable phase, might have been similarly restricted
during this time.

Finally, the absence of any evidence for true Neolithic communities
with domestic animals and plants, pottery, and large permanent settlements anywhere in the Nile Valley prior to 4000 B.C. must be considered in our evaluation of those presumably Neolithic ceramic sites
in the Sahara which have been dated at before 6000 B.C. (Camps 1968).
If food production and pottery were indeed present in the Sahara at that
time, then Neolithic traditions either somehow bypassed the Nile Valley
and were introduced into Africa through another route, or they were
independently invented in North Africa.

REFERENCES

ABDEL ALEEM, ANWAR
1958 Taxonomic and paleoecological investigation of the diatom-flora of the extinct Fayum Lake (Upper Egypt). University of Alexandria, *Bulletin* 2:217–244.

ALBRITTON, CLAUDE C.
1968 "Geology of the Tushka site: 8905," in *The prehistory of Nubia*. Edited by Fred Wendorf, 856–864. Fort Burgwin Research Center and Southern Methodist University.

BRAIDWOOD, ROBERT J.
1958 Near Eastern prehistory. *Science* 127:1419–1430.

BUTZER, K. W., C. L. HANSEN
1968 *Desert and river in Nubia: geomorphology and prehistoric environments at the Aswan Reservoir.* Madison: University of Wisconsin Press.

CAMPS, GABRIEL
1968 Tableau chronologique de la préhistoire récente du Nord de l'Afrique. *Bulletin de la Société Préhistorique Française* 65:609–622.

CATON-THOMPSON, GERTRUDE, E. W. GARDNER
1934 *The desert Fayum.* London: Oxford University Press.

CURWEN, E. CECIL
1935 Agriculture and the flint sickle in Palestine. *Antiquity* 9:62–66.

DE HEINZELIN, JEAN
1968 "Geological history of the Nile Valley in Nubia," in *The prehistory of Nubia*. Edited by Fred Wendorf, 19–55. Fort Burgwin Research Center and Southern Methodist University.

DE HEINZELIN, JEAN, R. PAEPE
1965 "The geological history of the Nile Valley in Sudanese Nubia," in *Contributions to the prehistory of Nubia*. Edited by Fred Wendorf, 29–56. Fort Burgwin Research Center and Southern Methodist University.

KANTOR, HÉLÈNE J.
1965 "The relative chronology of Egypt and its foreign correlations before the late Bronze Age," in *Chronologies in Old World archaeology*. Edited by Robert W. Ehrich, 1–31. Chicago: University of Chicago Press.

MOVIUS, H. L.
1953 The Mausterian cave of Teshik Tash, southeastern Uzbekistan, central Asia. *American School of Prehistoric Research Bulletin, Harvard University* 17:11–71.

REED, CHARLES A.
1966 The Yale University prehistoric expedition to Nubia, 1962–1965. *Discovery* 1(2):16–23.

SAID, RUSHDI, BAHAY ISSAWAY
1965 "Preliminary results of a geological expedition to Lower Nubia and to Kurkur and Dungul Oases, Egypt," in *Contributions to the prehistory of Nubia*. Edited by Fred Wendorf, 1–28. Fort Burgwin Research Center and Southern Methodist University.

SAID, RUSHDI, FRED WENDORF, ROMUALD SCHILD
    1970   The geology and prehistory of the Nile Valley in Upper Egypt. *Archaeologia Polona* 12:43–60.
SAID, RUSHDI, CLAUDE C. ALBRITTON, FRED WENDORF, ROMUALD SCHILD, MICHAL KOBUSIEWICZ
    1972   Remarks on the Holocene geology and archaeology of northern Fayum Desert. *Archaeologia Polona* 13.
SCHILD, ROMUALD, MARIA CHMIEKWSKA, HANNA WIECKOWSKA
    1968   "The Arkinian and Shamarkian industries," in *The prehistory of Nubia*. Edited by Fred Wendorf, 651–767. Fort Burgwin Research Center and Southern Methodist University.
SEMENOV, S. A.
    1964   *Prehistoric technology*. London: Cory.
SMITH, PHILIP E. L.
    1966   "The Late Paleolithic of northeast Africa in the light of recent research," in *Studies in paleoanthropology*. Edited by J. D. Clark and F. C. Howell. *American Anthropologist* 68(2)2:325–355.
VERMEERSCH, P.
    1970   Une nouvelle industrie epigéolithique à Elkab en Haute Egypte. *Chronique d'Egypte* 45(89):45–67.
WENDORF, FRED
    1968   *The prehistory of Nubia,* two volumes and atlas. Fort Burgwin Research Center and Southern Methodist University.
WENDORF, FRED, RUSHDI SAID
    1967   Paleolithic remains in Upper Egypt. *Nature* 215:244–247.
WENDORF, FRED, RUSHDI SAID, ROMUALD SCHILD
    1970   Late Paleolithic sites in Upper Egypt. *Archaeologia Polona* 12: 19–42.
    1970a Egyptian prehistory: some new concepts. *Science* 169:1161–1171.
    1970b "Problems of dating the late Paleolithic Age in Egypt," in *Radiocarbon variations and absolute chronology*. Edited by I. U. Olsson. Nobel Symposium XII. Upsala.
WENDT, W. E.
    1966   Two prehistoric archaeological sites in Egyptian Nubia. *Postilla* 102:1–46.
WRIGHT, H. E. JR.
    1961   Pleistocene glaciation in Kurdistan. *Eiszeitalter und Gegenwart* 12:131–164.

Botanical and Ethnographic Evidence

The Origins and Migrations of Crops in Tropical Africa

J. W. PURSEGLOVE

Our knowledge of tropical Africa is mostly very recent. Guiljelmo Blaeuw's map from the mid-seventeenth century shows the Nile rising in two lakes at 10 degrees south. Swift, in 1733, writes:

So geographers, in Afric-maps,
With savage-pictures fill their gaps;
And o'er unhabitable downs
Place elephants for want of towns.

Speke, the first European to visit Uganda, did not reach there until 1862. For the most part, the first written record is in the accounts of the early explorers. To decide on the place of domestication and subsequent migrations of African crops is fraught with difficulties.

Burkill (1953) considers that cultivation in Africa at large began much later than in Asia. The hunting and food-gathering phase may well have continued longer in Africa than in some other continents, particularly where there was a plentiful supply of game. The number of plants domesticated in Africa is usually considered less than elsewhere. Burkill (1953) states: "It is recognised that Africa has been comparatively ineffective in plant ennoblement," a view also held by Vavilov. Nevertheless, perusal of Appendix 1 will show that the number is larger than is often realized.

Man has only cultivated crops for less than one percent of the time spent as a hunter and food gatherer. Some 300,000 species of flowering plants occur on this planet, but surprisingly few of them, belonging to a limited number of families, have been domesticated. Although man may collect the grains of wild grasses in times of shortage, and must have done so regularly in many regions before he became a cultivator very few have been domesticated. Only five species constitute the major cereals of the world — wheat, rice, maize, sorghum and barley; and there are up to twenty other species of lesser importance, some of them very minor, out of some 10,000 species of Gramineae. Almost all the cultivated cereals were domesticated at least 2,000 years ago and most of them were widely spread before then. The cultivated cereals exhibit wide genetic, morphological, and physiological variation which permitted the development of high-yielding improved cultivars that have nonshattering rachises, simultaneous ripening, large grains which are more easily threshed, and with a wide ecological amplitude and plasticity. Having obtained species suited to a particular environment, there was little need to domesticate any more.

Most crops, with their attendant weeds, are grown in the disturbed habitats created by cultivation. Many of the crops are unable to survive under natural wild conditions and have lost any effective means of natural dispersal. Some of the domesticates occurred as weeds of the first crops. Some plants were cultivated in earlier times and purposeful planting was later abandoned. If the progenitor of a crop has a wide distribution, it may be taken into cultivation in more than one place and does not necessarily have to diffuse outwards from a single center of domestication.

During and since the domestication, introgression has occurred between related species and wild forms. Polyploids are frequent among crop species. Crops are widely spread in a variety of habitats; and their variability and plasticity, together with man's selection — both unconscious and conscious — permit rapid evolutionary change. The nature of the original introduction, often from a limited portion of the gene pool, will determine the future progeny of an area; and the crop is subject to disruptive selection and genetic drift.

Greenway (1944–1945) is a useful source of information on East African food crops and further information on many of the crops will be found in Purseglove (1968, 1972).

CROPS DOMESTICATED IN AFRICA (see Appendix 1)

Vavilov (1951) gives only one center of origin in Africa, namely Ethiopia. It should be recognized that Vavilov's famous centers may be centers of cultivation, migration, and selection, and not necessarily of origin. Certainly, plants were domesticated in Africa outside Ethiopia, and West Africa is obviously an important center of domestication. As far as I can ascertain, there is no really reliable evidence as to where and when the first cultivation of crops began in tropical Africa. Harlan and Stemler in their paper at this symposium consider that "agriculture originated in Africa south of the Sahara and north of the equator." In the same paper, Harlan and Stemler suggest that sorghum was domesticated on the east side of the continent and was taken at an early date, before 1000 B.C., to West Africa. Van Zinderen Bakker in his paper (this volume) considers that the southern parts of the Sahara were wetter before 500 B.C. when final desiccation set in, so conditions would be more favorable for the spread of crops. In another paper, de Wet, Harlan and Price say that "the most likely area for early sorghum cultivation seems to be a broad band across the northern savanna from Sudan to Mauritania."

Doggett (1965, 1970) considers that sorghum was domesticated from wild sorghum some 5,000 years ago in the northeastern quadrant of Africa by disruptive selection by a people of Caucasoid origin who migrated into Ethiopia through southwestern Asia. They brought with them emmer *(Triticum dicoccum)* and durum wheat *(T. durum),* and barley *(Hordeum vulgare),* which had been cultivated in the Iraqi-Kurdistan area since about 7000 B.C. It is suggested that these people, with a tradition of cereal culture, domesticated sorghum, which permitted them to move into habitats less favorable for wheat. Doggett also believes that sorghum was taken early to West Africa. Bulrush millet, *Pennisetum americanum,* which was domesticated in the Sahel zone of West Africa, was brought back in the opposite direction.

Plants which were domesticated within Ethiopia include: tef, *Eragrostis tef;* ensete, *Ensete ventricosa;* niger seed, *Guitzotia abyssinica;* khat, *Catha edulis.* None of these crops have achieved any importance in Africa outside their country of origin.

West Africa was an important center of domestication. Those crops which originated in the savanna include: bulrush millet, *Pennisetum americanum;* hungry rice, *Digitaria exilis, D. iburua* and *Brachiaria deflexa;* Bambara and Kersting's groundnuts, *Voandzeia subterranea* and *Kerstingiella geocarpa;* shea butter, *Butyrospermum paradoxum;* Hausa potato, *Plectranthus esculentus;* and locust bean, *Parkia filicoidea.* Those crops which originated in the forest zone or on its edge, and were grown with vegeculture include: yams, *Dioscorea cayenensis* and *D. rotundata;* oil palm, *Elaeis guineensis;* yam bean, *Sphenostylis stenocarpa;* West African coffees, *Coffea liberica, C. excelsa* and *C. stenophylla;* kola, *Cola* spp.; kapok, *Ceiba pentandra;* roselle, *Hibiscus sabdariffa;* akee, *Blighia sapida;* and grains of paradise, *Aframomum melegueta.* African rice, *Oryza glaberrima,* originated in West Africa, where it is grown in the southwestern rice zone and in the flood plains of the savanna zone.

Other important crops which originated in tropical Africa, but for which it is impossible to define the area of domestication with any certainty although eastern Africa is likely for some of them, include: finger millet, *Eleusine coracana*; cowpea, *Vigna unguiculata*; pigeon pea, *Cajanas cajan*; sesame, *Sesamum indicum*; castor, *Ricinus communis*; gourd, *Lagenaria siceraria*; water melon, *Citrullus lanatus*; melon, *Cucumis melo*; robusta coffee, *Coffea canephora*; kenaf, *Hibiscus cannabinus*; okra, *Hibiscus esculentus*; and tamarind, *Tamarindus indica.*

The Nile sudd formed a fairly effective barrier between Egypt and the South, as did the central African rain forests for many of the crops of the northern savannas. The drier climates so hemmed in this humid area of forests that its ennobled plants were mostly retained within it until shipping carried them across the Atlantic. The area of the central African lakes formed a useful passage between north and south for sorghum and other crops.

Egypt had established some contact with countries to the south by the twelfth Dynasty, but Harlan (1969) considers it unlikely that the Egyptians ever reached the highlands of Ethiopia "with either military or political persuasion."

There was early movement of crops from the Sudan and/or Ethiopia southwards into East Africa (Harlan and Stemler suggest a date of more than 3,000 years ago for sorghum), and later it continued further south. It was sorghum that permitted the explosive expansion of the Bantu into the savanna regions of eastern and southern Africa.

MOVEMENT OF CROPS BETWEEN AFRICA AND ASIA
(see Appendix 2)

The most accessible routes out of Ethiopia to the north were those leading to the Red Sea coasts and then along the Sabaean lane. About 1000 B.C. the Sabaean kingdom, with its capital in the Yemen, became the maritime power in the Red Sea. There was the meeting between Solomon and the Queen of Sheba whose son is regarded as the founder of the Royal Dynasty of Ethiopia, which has lasted nearly three thousand years.

Crops such as sorghum, finger millet, and bulrush millet had reached

India about 3,000 years ago across the southern end of the Red Sea along the Sabaean lane. The Sabaeans continued to dominate the maritime trade between East Africa and India until 100 B.C. India became an important center of variability when many crops, among which were pigeon peas, sesame, and cowpeas, were taken over. Later, from about 2,000 years ago, there were direct contacts between East Africa and India. Ethiopian conquests of Arabia in the fourth and sixth centuries A.D. resulted in the movement of crops, probably taking peas to Ethiopia and arabica coffee to Arabia. From the seventh century A.D. waves of migration occurred from Persia and Arabia to the East African coast. Fortified towns were established from Cape Guardafui to Mozambique which caused further crop movements, probably including the introduction of sugarcane, citrus, mango, and pomegranate to East Africa. Yemenite Arabs had a colony in Zanzibar from the eighth to the eleventh century A.D. and also visited the Magunga coast of the Malagasy Republic.

There was little movement into the African interior except along the slave routes, which in Eastern Africa became demarcated with poor quality mangoes and resulted in the spread of some crops. Greenway (1944–1945) recalls that Vasco da Gama was offered sugarcane, oranges, and lemons by the Sheikh of Mombasa on April 9, 1498. Very few of these Asian crops reached West Africa until such crops as coconuts, mangoes, and citrus were taken there by the Portuguese after 1500.

People of Malaysian-Indonesian descent arrived in the Malagasy Republic during the first millennium A.D., and probably by the fifth century or even earlier. It is likely that they brought with them bananas, *Musa* cvs., which later spread to Africa where they became of the greatest importance as the staple food of the Baganda and others. They spread into the heart of the continent via the Zambezi valley and the great lakes and then across the Congo to West Africa, where they were found by the earliest Portuguese explorers. Simmonds (1962) considers that this is the most likely route as dispersal via northern India, Arabia, and the Horn of Africa is unlikely because of adverse climatic conditions. These Indonesian migrants also probably brought with them rice, *Oryza sativa*, and the greater yam, *Dioscorea alata*.

INTRODUCTION OF NEW WORLD CROPS (see Appendix 3)

I am convinced that it is NOT necessary to invoke the aid of man to bring about the movement of crops between the New and the Old

World, and vice versa, in pre-Columbian times. This does not preclude the spread of plants between the hemispheres by natural means. The only crops which occurred in both the New and Old Worlds before 1492 were the gourd *(Lagenaria siceraria),* the sweet potato *(Ipomoea batatas),* which had reached Polynesia from tropical America, and the possible presence of coconuts on the west coast of Panama. We must also account for the probable presence of African diploid cotton in South America to cross with a New World diploid to produce the New World tetraploid cottons. All these subjects have been discussed at length by Purseglove (1963, 1965, 1968, 1972), and I do not intend to deal with them here.

The Portuguese were mainly responsible for the early introduction of New World crops into Africa. They also had early contact with Ethiopia. Many of these first introductions were to become widespread, some of them becoming the staple foods over wide areas, and they have had a profound effect on African agriculture. They are: maize, *Zea mays*; common bean, *Phaseolus vulgaris*; groundnut, *Arachis hypogaea*; sweet potato, *Ipomoea batatas*; cassava, *Manihot esculenta*; pumpkins, *Cucurbita* spp.; chillies, *Capsicum annuum* and *C. frutescens*; and tobacco, *Nicotiana tabacum.*

In many areas where the climate was suitable, maize has replaced sorghum and millets as the staple food; cassava and sweet potato have increased at the expense of yams and have become extremely important throughout the whole of tropical Africa. The increase in cassava has probably been greater on a world basis than any other crop during the present century. *Phaseolus vulgaris* has become the dominant pulse crop and groundnuts, the dominant oil seed, throughout large areas of tropical Africa.

Some of the later introductions were to become important export crops, such as cocoa, sisal, and the New World cottons. Africa is now the principal producer of the first two, illustrating the strange fact that most of the world's important economic crops are now produced in the greatest amount far from their centers of origin.

BRIEF DETAILS OF SELECTED CROPS

Below are brief notes on the origin and distribution of selected crops, but space prohibits fuller discussion or the inclusion of all the crops mentioned in this study.

SORGHUM *(Sorghum bicolor)* Some details have already been given and Harlan and de Wet are dealing with it in detail.

BULRUSH MILLET *(Pennisetum americanum)* The nomenclature of this crop is very similar for that which existed for *Sorghum.* Stapf and Hubbard recognized eighteen subspecies, with the greatest number in West Africa. As all the subspecies are interfertile, I prefer to limit the cultivated bulrush millets to one species, *Pennisetum americanum,* which was probably domesticated in the Sahel zone of West Africa, a view also held by Chevalier (1934). The crop spread along the southern borders of the Sahara to the Sudan, and later to East and Central Africa. It was taken early to India along with sorghum and finger millet.

FINGER MILLET *(Eleusine coracana)* This is an important staple in East and Central Africa. It appears to have been derived from a large-grained mutant of the tetraploid *E. africana* on the East African plateau, probably in the region of Uganda. The Afro-Asian cultivars with shorter glumes and visible grains were evolved from the crop (Mehra 1963), and it is these that were carried to India. In the citemene or ash culture of the crop in Zambia, eight to ten acres of woodland are cut down and burned on one acre to provide the ash in which the crop is grown. This system permits a population density of about eight per square mile.

HUNGRY RICE *(Digitaria exilis)* This crop is often considered to be the oldest indigenous West African cereal, and is still confined to this area.

COWPEAS *(Vigna unguiculata)* The wild species, *V. unguiculata,* is indigenous to tropical Africa and gave rise to the catjung cowpea; there are some cultivars in Africa, but it is commoner with more cultivars in Asia. The common cowpea, which is sometimes placed in a separate species, *V. sinensis,* has most cultivars in Africa and is an important potherb as well as a pulse. Burkill (1953) states that the cowpea passed over the Sabaean line and reached Sumeria about 2300 B.C.

PIGEON PEA *(Cajanus cajan)* This crop probably originated in Africa, where wild subspecies have been recorded, but was taken at an early time to India, where the greatest variability now occurs.

BAMBARA and KERSTING'S GROUNDNUTS *(Voandzeia subterranea* and *Kerstingiella geocarpa)* Both these pulses have been found wild in

West Africa where they must have been domesticated. The former is now found spasmodically throughout tropical Africa and is of some importance in Zambia.

SESAME *(Sesamum indicum)*   Weiss (1971) states that sesame is probably the most ancient oilseed known and used by man. It appears to have been domesticated in Africa where there are a number of wild subspecies, possibly in Ethiopia or the Sudan. The crop was taken at an early date to India where a secondary center of diversity developed. It eventually reached China, probably by the Silk Road.

CASTOR *(Ricinus communis)*   The plant occurs wild in various parts of eastern Africa, including Ethiopia, and must have been domesticated somewhere within this region. It was cultivated in ancient Egypt and has been found in tombs dating ca. 4000 B.C. According to Burkill (1953), linguistic evidence shows that castor was spread throughout India before the Aryans came. It was probably taken into cultivation in more than one area.

OIL PALM *(Elaeis guineensis)*   It is undoubtedly of West African origin, where it occurs wild in riverine forests and freshwater swamps. The palm cannot survive in dense or primeval forests. Most of the semiwild oil palms in West Africa grow in palm bush or palm groves as the result of man's activities. It was carried to East Africa and reached the Malagasy Republic, where *E. madagascariensis* is undoubtedly a form of *E. guineensis.*

YAMS *(Dioscorea* spp.)   *D. rotundata,* sometimes regarded as a subspecies of *D. cayenensis,* is the most important cultivated species in West Africa. It was domesticated in areas with a longer dry season than *D. cayenensis,* which is more suited to humid forest conditions. The Asian *D. alata* was probably taken to West Africa by the Portuguese, although an earlier introduction is postulated for Madagascar and East Africa. It never achieved any major importance in Africa. Further details are given by Coursey.

GOURD *(Lagenaria siceraria)*   The bottle gourd is one of the most ancient and widespread of cultivated plants in both the Old and New Worlds. The hard shells were widely used as domestic utensils long before the invention of ceramics. It is considered of African origin, but has been found in tropical America in horizons of ca. 5000 B.C.

It could easily have been dispersed from Africa to the New World by ocean currents (Purseglove 1968). It must have reached Asia at a very early date; the Aryans had gourds about 2000 B.C. Gourds were known in the Mediterranean in classical times, and they had reached China not later than the first century A.D.

ARABICA COFFEE *(Coffea arabica)*   This small understory tree grows wild in the forests of the Ethiopian massif between 1500 and 2000 meters in altitude. It was also cultivated, but was used for chewing and not as a beverage. It was probably introduced into Arabia during the Ethiopian conquests about the sixth century A.D. The discovery of brewing coffee was made in Arabia about the fifteenth century. Some eighty percent of the world's coffee is now produced in the New World, where much of the coffee originated from one plant. Coffee is the second most valuable commodity in world trade, surpassed only by petroleum and its products.

ROBUSTA COFFEE *(Coffea canephora)*   This coffee has become important economically only during the present century. Before this, it was grown by the Baganda and related tribes for chewing and use in the blood-brotherhood ceremony. The tree occurs wild in the forests from West Africa to Uganda.

COTTON *(Gossypium herbaceum)*   The race *africanum* (A genome), which occurs wild in southern Africa, is regarded as one of the parents of the tetraploid New World cottons (Purseglove 1968). In Egyptian Nubia, Chowdhury and Buth (1971) have found cotton seed, dated ca. 2500 B.C., which was being fed to stock, that shows the early stages of evolution from wild to lint-bearing *Gossypium*. Nicholson (1960) suggests that A genome cotton was gradually evolved in southern Ethiopia as an ancestral cultivated stock.

KAPOK *(Ceiba pentandra* var. *pentandra)*   Baker (1965) considers that the cultivated kapok of West Africa with indehiscent fruits is a natural hybrid between var. *caribaea,* which drifted to West Africa from tropical America by natural means, and var. *guineensis,* a West African savanna form. Var. *pentandra* was taken to Asia and reached Java about the tenth century A.D.

PEAS *(Pisum sativum)*   The field pea, a native of southwestern Asia and sometimes placed in the species *P. arvense,* was introduced into

Ethiopia early, probably about the middle of the first millennium A.D. It had reached Kigezi in southwestern Uganda, Rwanda, and Burundi long before the arrival of the first European explorers and is a staple pulse (Purseglove 1946). Here it is broadcast in mountain grassland or resting land after fallow, hoed once, and no further cultivation is given. Yields are low, but introduced cultivars give no yield at all under these conditions. It is a valuable crop in the rotation before the sorghum is planted and is one of the main sources of protein.

COCONUT *(Cocos nucifera)*   Coconuts had certainly reached East Africa before the first Europeans and were recorded at Malindi by Vasco da Gama in 1498 (Furtado 1964). They did not reach West Africa until taken by the Portuguese. The origin and distribution have been the subject of much speculation; a full account is given in Purseglove (1972).

SUGARCANE *(Saccharum cvs)*   I now believe that the thin canes, *S. barberi,* originated from *S. spontaneum* in northern India. The thick or noble canes, *S. officinarum,* developed from *S. robustum* in New Guinea and need not have been introduced into India until a later date (Purseglove 1972). Most modern commercial canes are of hybrid origin. Sugarcane had reached East Africa before 1498. Apart from a few large estates, many Africans grow small clumps, preferably of noble canes, for chewing.

DASHEEN, COCOYAM *(Colocasia esculenta* var. *esculenta)*   Much confusion exists in the nomenclature of the cocoyams. This variety, which has peltate leaves and a single large corm, originated in Southeast Asia and was spread at an early date to India. It had reached the eastern Mediterranean in classical times and spread across Africa to the Guinea coast. It is the principal taro of the Pacific. It should not be confused with *Xanthosoma sagittifolium,* also known as cocoyam in West Africa, which has sagittate leaves and is a recent introduction from the New World. It is popular in Ghana as it provides a good nurse-crop for cocoa and makes a good *fufu.*

MAIZE *(Zea mays)*   Maize, which originated in Mexico and was widespread in the New World in pre-Columbian days, was introduced into Africa soon after 1500. Portères (1955) considers that flint maize was introduced into West Africa across the Sahara by Arab traders and that flour types from Brazil were taken to the coast by the Portuguese, who also introduced maize into East Africa. There are references to maize in Zanzibar in 1643, but it does not appear to have reached Uganda by 1862. In many parts of Africa, maize became a major staple food only during the present century (Miracle 1966).

COMMON BEAN *(Phaseolus vulgaris)*   Kaplan (1965) suggests that multiple domestication took place within Middle America. Beans were introduced to the coastal areas of Africa by the Portuguese. They have been established as a food crop for a long period, as is evidenced by the wealth of distinctive cultivars and local names in such remote areas as Bufumbira in southwestern Kigezi, Uganda. *P. lunatus* was probably a later introduction into Africa and does better in wetter climates than *P. vulgaris.*

SWEET POTATO *(Ipomoea batatas)*   This crop probably originated in Mexico and was spread throughout tropical America in pre-Columbian times. It had also been taken to Polynesia, and I have attempted elsewhere to explain its method of getting there (Purseglove 1968). I do not believe that the crop reached Africa until taken there by the Portuguese.

CASSAVA *(Manihot esculenta)*   Cassava was probably domesticated in both Central America and northeastern Brazil; in 1492 it had reached its present limits of cultivation in the New World to 25 degrees north and south. Jones (1959) states that it was taken to São Tomé, Fernando Po, and to Warri and the mouth of the Congo River in the second half of the sixteenth century. The French introduced it into Mauritius in 1736. It has mainly spread into the interior of tropical Africa during the present century, being encouraged by the suzerain powers as a reserve against famine and locust attack. Africa now has more cassava than all the rest of the world.

CHILLIES *(Capsicum* spp.)   The chillies or red pepper, with fruits borne singly, belong to *C. annuum*; and the small, more pungent bird chillies, with two or more fruits borne together, to *C. frutescens.* The latter species has become naturalized in many parts of Africa. One of the main reasons for the discovery of the New World was an attempt to reach the spice islands of the East. The new "pepper" was seized upon by Columbus, and the ease with which the seeds, of long viability, can be transported assisted in its rapid spread throughout the tropics and subtropics, including Africa.

TOBACCO *(Nicotiana tabacum)*   Tobacco, which originated in South America, was widely spread in the Americas in pre-Columbian times. It took quite some time to reach Europe and thereafter was spread rapidly by the Portuguese and Spaniards. It probably reached tropical Africa in the first decade of the seventeenth century and was widely used by the time of the early explorers. Plants which contribute to man's pleasure are often dispersed more quickly and freely than some of the staple foods.

SUMMARY

Our knowledge of crops in tropical Africa is very recent. They can be divided into:

1.   Crops originating and domesticated in Africa with major centers in Ethiopia and West Africa. There was early movement of crops between east and west along the fringe of the Sahara, with subsequent movements to central and southern Africa.

2.   Crops originating mainly in Asia and introduced into Africa. This first movement into and out of Africa was along the Sabaean lane. From the second half of the first millennium A.D. Persians and Arabs established fortifications on the East African coast and introduced more crops. Indonesians brought crops from Southeast Asia to the Malagasy Republic.

3.   Crops introduced from the New World in post-Columbian times, some of which were to become important staples replacing traditional African crops.

Brief details are given on selected crops.

APPENDIX 1

Crops originating in Africa

Scientific name	Common name	Family	Area of probable domestication
CEREALS			
Sorghum bicolor (L.) Moench	Sorghum	Gramineae	Ethiopia
Pennisetum americanum (L.) K. Schum.	Bulrush millet	Gramineae	W. Africa
Eleusine coracana (L.) Gaertn.	Finger millet	Gramineae	E. Africa
Eragrostis tef (Zucc.) Trotter	Teff	Gramineae	Ethiopia
Oryza glaberrima Steud.	West Africa rice	Gramineae	W. Africa
Digitaria exilis Stapf	Hungry rice	Gramineae	W. Africa

cientific name	Common name	Family	Area of probable domestication
. iburua Stapf	Hungry rice	Gramineae	W. Africa
rachiaria deflexa C. E.Hubbard		Gramineae	W. Africa
ULSE CROPS			
igna unguiculata (L.) Walp.	Cowpea	Leguminosae	Tropical Africa
ajanas cajan (L.) Millsp.	Pigeon pea	Leguminosae	? Tropical Africa
oandzeia subterranea (L.) Thouars	Bambara groundnut	Leguminosae	W. Africa
erstingiella geocarpa Harms.	Kersting's groundnut	Leguminosae	W. Africa
IL SEEDS			
esamum indicum L.	Sesame	Pedaliaceae	? Eastern Africa
uizotia abyssinica (L. f.) Cass.	Niger seed	Compositae	Ethiopia
icinus communis L.	Castor	Euphorbiaceae	Eastern Africa
eratotheca sesamoides Endl.		Pedaliaceae	Tropical Africa
olygala butyracea Heck.	Black beniseed	Polygalaceae	W. Africa
yptis spicigera Lam.		Labiatae	Tropical Africa
rassica juncea (L.) Czern. & Cass.	Indian mustard	Cruciferae	? Ethiopia
laeis guineensis Jacq.	Oil palm	Palmae	W. Africa
utyrospermum paradoxum (Gaertn. f.) Hepper	Shea butter	Sapotaceae	W. Africa
OOT CROPS			
ioscorea cayenensis Lam.	Yellow Guinea yam	Dioscoreaceae	W. Africa
. rotundata Poir.	White Guinea yam	Dioscoreaceae	W. Africa
lectranthus esculentus N.E. Br.	Hausa potato	Labiatae	? W. Africa
henostylis stenocarpa Harms	Yam bean	Leguminosae	? W. Africa
UCURBITS			
agenaria siceraria (Molina) Standl.	Gourd	Cucurbitaceae	Tropical Africa
itrullus lanatus (Thunb.) Mansf.	Watermelon	Cucurbitaceae	Tropical Africa
ucumis melo L.	Melon	Cucurbitaceae	Tropical Africa
. anguria L.	W. Indian gherkin	Cucurbitaceae	Tropical Africa
elfairia pedata Hook. f.	Oyster nut	Cucurbitaceae	E. Africa

Scientific name	Common name	Family	Area of prob able domes-tication
BEVERAGES AND STIMULANTS			
Coffea arabica L.	Arabica coffee	Rubiaceae	Ethiopia
	Robusta coffee	Rubiaceae	Uganda and
C. canephora Pierre ex Froehner	Liberica coffee	Rubiaceae	Congo
C. liberica Bull ex Hiern		Rubiaceae	W. Africa
C. excelsa A. Chev.		Rubiaceae	W. Africa
C. stenophylla G. Don	Kola	Sterculiaceae	W. Africa
Cola spp.	Khat	Celastraceae	W. Africa
Catha edulis Forsk.			Ethiopia
FIBERS			
Gossypium herbaceum L.	Diploid cotton	Malvaceae	Tropical Africa
Ceiba pentandra (L.) Gaertn. var. pentandra	Kapok	Bombacaceae	W. Africa
Hibiscus cannabinus L.	Kenaf	Malvaceae	Tropical Africa
VEGETABLES			
Hibiscus esculentus L. = *Abel-moschus esculentus* (L.) Moench	Okra	Malvaceae	Tropical or E. Africa
H. sabdariffa L.	Roselle	Malvaceae	W. Africa
Amaranthus spp.	Spinach	Amaranthaceae	Tropical Africa
Cleome spp.	Spider-flower	Capparidaceae	Tropical Africa
FRUITS			
Tamarindus indicas L.	Tamarind	Leguminosae	E. Africa
Adansonia digitata L.	Baobab	Bombacaceae	Tropical
Parkia filicoidea Welw. ex Oliv.	Locust bean	Leguminosae	Africa
Blighea sapida Koenig	Akee	Sapindaceae	W. Africa
			W. Africa
Balanites aegyptica Del	Desert date	Simarubaceae	Tropical Africa
Zizyphus mauritiana Lam.	Jujube	Rhamnaceae	Tropical Africa
Solanum macrocarpon L.		Solanaceae	E. Africa
S. aethiopicum L.		Solanaceae	E. Africa
MISCELLANEOUS			
Ensete ventricosa (Welw.) Cheesm.	Ensete	Musaceae	Ethiopia
Aframomum maligueta (Rosc.) K. Schum.	Grains of paradise	Zingiberaceae	W. Africa
Ficus natalensis Hochst. and other spp.	Bark cloth	Moraceae	E. Africa

cientific name	Common name	Family	Area of probable domestication
idigofera arrecta Hochst. ex A. Rich.	Indigo	Leguminosae	Tropical Africa
orassus aethiopicum Mart.	Fan palm	Palmae	Tropical Africa
aphea spp.	Raffia palms	Palmae	
uphorbia tirucalli L.	Pipe-stem euphorbia	Euphorbiaceae	W. Africa E. Africa

PPENDIX 2

ne crops grown in Africa of Asiatic origin

entific name	Common name	Family	Probable country of origin and route
RODUCED BEFORE 1500 A.D.			
icum dicoccum Schubl.	Emmer wheat	Gramineae	S.W. Asia early to Ethiopia
urum Desf.	Durum wheat	Gramineae	S.W. Asia early to Ethiopia
estivum L.	Bread wheat	Gramineae	S.W. Asia later to Africa
rdeum vulgare L.	Barley	Gramineae	S.W. Asia early to Ethiopia
im sativum L.	Pea	Leguminosae	S.W. Asia to Ethiopia
sa cvs AA, AAA, AAB	Bananas	Musaceae	Malaysia to Madagascar and Africa
os nucifera L.	Coconut	Palmae	Pacific to East Africa
charum cvs	Sugarcane	Gramineae	S.E. Asia to E. Africa
ocasia esculenta Schott	Dasheen	Araceae	S.E. Asia to most of Africa
us spp.	Orange, lemon, etc.	Rutaceae	S.E. Asia to E. Africa
igifera indica L.	Mango	Anacardiaceae	India to E. Africa
inum melongena L.	Eggplant	Solanaceae	S.E. Asia to E. Africa
innabis sativa L.	Hemp	Cannabinaceae	S.W. Asia to Africa
za sativa L.	Rice	Gramineae	Asia to E. Africa
ca catechu L.	Betel nut	Palmae	India to Zanzibar

Appendix 2.   (Continued)

Scientific name	Common name	Family	Probable country of origin and rou‌
Piper betle.	Betel pepper	Piperaceae	India to E. African coas‌
Zingiber officinale Rosc.	Ginger	Zingiberaceae	S.E. Asia to E. Africa
Curcuma domestica Val.	Turmeric	Zingiberaceae	S.E. Asia to E. and W. Afri‌
Allium cepa L.	Onion	Alliaceae	S.W. Asia to Tropical Africa
Dioscorea alata L.	Greater yam	Dioscoreaceae	S.E. Asia via Madagascar
Carthamus tinctorius L.	Safflower	Compositae	S.W. Asia to Ethiopia
Cicer arietinum L.	Chick pea	Leguminosae	S.W. Asia to Ethiopia
Lens esculenta Moench	Lentil	Leguminosae	S.W. Asia to Ethiopia
SOME LATER INTRODUCTIONS			
Eugenia caryophyllus (Sprengel) Bullock & Harrison	Clove	Myrtaceae	Moluccas to Zanzibar vi‌ Réunion
Camellia sinensis (L.) O. Kuntze	Tea	Theaceae	S.E. Asia to E. Africa
Aleurites montana (Lour.) Wils.	Tung	Euphorbiaceae	S. China to Malawi
Glycine max (L.) Merr.	Soya bean	Leguminosae	China to E. Africa

APPENDIX 3

Some crops grown in Africa of New World origin introduced after 1500 A.D.

Scientific name	Common name	Family	Probable country of or‌ and route
MAINLY EARLY COLONIAL (MAINLY PORTUGUESE)			
Zea mays L.	Maize	Gramineae	Mexico to m‌ of Africa
Arachis hypogaea L.	Groundnut	Leguminosae	S. America; e‌ to W. Afric‌
Phaseolus vulgaris L.	Common bean	Leguminosae	C. America to‌ most of Africa

ientific name	Common name	Family	Probable country of origin and route
lunatus L.	Lima bean	Leguminosae	C. and S. America; to W. Africa
ɔmoea batatas (L.) Lam.	Sweet potato	Convolvulaceae	Mexico to most of Africa
anihot esculenta Crantz	Cassava	Euphorbiaceae	S. America; early to W. Africa
ɩpsicum annuum L.	Chillies and sweet pepper	Solanaceae	C. America; early to W. Africa
frutescens L.	Bird pepper	Solanaceae	C. America to Tropical Africa
ɩcurbita spp.	Pumpkins	Cucurbitaceae	C. America to most of Africa
ɩcotiana tabacum L.	Tobacco	Solanaceae	S. America to most of Africa
ɩacardium occidentale L.	Cashew	Anacardiaceae	Brazil, via India
ɩanas comosus (L.) Merr.	Pineapple	Bromeliaceae	S. America to Tropical Africa
ɩdium guajava L.	Guava	Myrtaceae	Tropical America to Tropical Africa
ɩrica papaya L.	Papaya	Caricaceae	C. America to Tropical Africa

*STLY LATE COLONIAL

ɩnthosoma sagittifolium (L.) Šchott	Tannia	Araceae	Tropical America to W. Africa
ɩanum tuberosum L.	Potato	Solanaceae	S. America to E. Africa
ɩsea americana Mill.	Avocado	Lauraceae	C. America to Tropical Africa
ɩeobroma cacao L.	Cocoa	Sterculiaceae	S. America, first to W. Africa
ɩsiflora edulis Sims	Passion fruit	Passifloraceae	Brazil to most of Africa
ɩcopersicon esculentum Mill.	Tomato	Solanaceae	S. America to most of Africa Mexico to

Appendix 3.   (Cotinued)

Scientific name	Common name	Family	Probable country of origin and rou*
Agave sisalana Perrine	Sisal	Agavaceae	Mexico to E. Africa
Gossypium hirsutum L.	Upland cotton	Malvaceae	N. America to Tropical Africa
G. barbadense L.	Sea Island cotton	Malvaceae	N. America to Sudan and Egypt

REFERENCES

BAKER, H. G.
   1965   "The evolution of the cultivated kapok tree: a probable West African product," in *Ecology and economic development in Tropical Africa*. Edited by D. Brokensha, 185–216. Berkeley: University of California Press.

BURKILL, I. H.
   1953   Habits of man and the origins of the cultivated plants of the Old World. *Proceedings of the Linnean Society, London* 164:12–42.

CHEVALIER, A.
   1934   Étude sur les prairies de l'Ouest Africain. *Rev. Bot. Appl. et Agric. Tropicale* 14:17–48.

CHOWDHURY, K. A., G. M. BUTH
   1971   Cotton seeds from the neolithic in Egyptian Nubia and the origin of Old World cotton. *Biol. J. Linn. Soc.* 3:303–312.

DOGGETT, H.
   1965   "The development of the cultivated sorghums," in *Crop plant evolution*. Edited by Sir Joseph Hutchinson, 50–69. Cambridge: The University Press.
   1970   *Sorghum*. London: Longmans.

FURTADO, C. X.
   1964   The origin of the word "Cocos." *Gardens' Bulletin, Singapore* 20:295–312.

GREENWAY, P. J.
   1944–1945   Origins of some East African food plant. *East African Agricultural Journal* 10:34–39, 115–119, 177–180, 251–256; 11: 56–63.

HARLAN, J. R.
   1969   Ethiopia: a center of diversity. *Economic Botany* 23:309–314.

JONES, W. O.
   1959   *Manioc in Africa*. Stanford, Calif.: Stanford University Press.

KAPLAN, L.
   1965   Archaeology and domestication in American *Phaseolus* (beans). *Economic Botany* 19:358–368.

MEHRA, K. L.
1963 Differentiation of the cultivated and wild *Eleusine* series. *Phyton* 20:189–198.

MIRACLE, M. P.
1966 *Maize in tropical Africa.* Madison: University of Wisconsin Press.

NICHOLSON, G. E.
1960 The production, history, uses and relationships of cotton (*Gossypium* spp.) in Ethiopia. *Economic Botany* 14:3–36.

PORTÈRES, R.
1955 L'Introduction de maïs en Afrique. *J. Agric. Trop. et Bot. Appl.* 5–6.

PURSEGLOVE, J. W.
1946 Land use in the overpopulated areas of Kabale, Kigezi District, Uganda. *East African Agricultural Journal* 12:3–10.
1963 Some problems of the origin and distribution of tropical crops. *Genet. Agraria* 17:104–122.
1965 "The spread of tropical crops," in *The genetics of colonizing species.* Edited by H. G. Baker and G. L. Stebbins, 375–389. New York: Academic Press.
1968 *Tropical crops: Dicotyledons 1 and 2,* two volumes. London: Longmans.
1972 *Tropical crops: Monocotyledons 1 and 2,* two volumes. London: Longmans.

SIMMONDS, N. W.
1962 *The evolution of the bananas.* London: Longmans.

VAVILOV, N. I.
1951 *The origin, variation, immunity and breeding of cultivated plants.* Waltham: Chronica Botanica.

WEISS, E. A.
1971 *Castor, sesame and safflower.* London: Leonard Hill.

Traditional Systems of Plant Food Production and the Origins of Agriculture in West Africa

DAVID R. HARRIS

Enhanced understanding of the origins of plant domestication and the earliest development of agriculture, in Africa as elsewhere, remains dependent ultimately on the accumulation of factual evidence relating to precisely known locations and time periods. But the intellectual approach each investigator adopts, whether explicitly or implicitly, necessarily conditions his recognition, selection, and interpretation of the factual evidence. To search for "the facts" alone, without reference to any preconceived ideas, is neither feasible nor desirable; and the history of science suggests that major advances in understanding are more likely to be achieved when evidence is sought to test explicitly formulated hypotheses than when relatively random "fact gathering" is undertaken.

The advantages of a hypothetico-deductive approach are likely to be greatest at an early stage in the development of a field of knowledge when factual evidence is limited and there is still divergence of opinion as to the most significant research objectives. Understanding of the origins of plant domestication and agriculture in Africa is still at such a stage. Faced with a paucity of data and a lack of agreement on research priorities and methods, the need for explicitly formulated hypotheses which may be tested by direct investigation is acute. It is the aim of this paper to focus attention on one major question in this field — that of the spatial and temporal relationships between traditional seed-cultural and vegecultural systems of food production — and in so doing to propose a hypothesis on the origins of agriculture in West Africa[1] which is susceptible, in part at least, to testing by direct archaeological

---

[1] The area regarded as comprising West Africa is indicated in Figure 1.

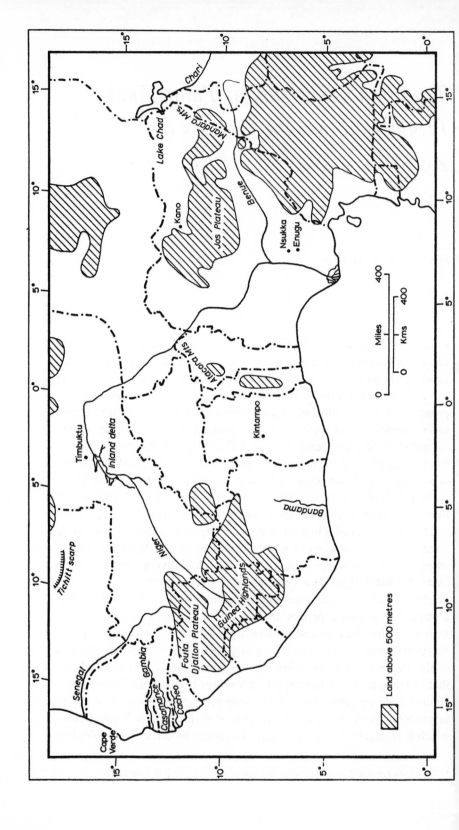

investigation, and which may have relevance to other parts of the continent.

A classification of traditional West African plant food-producing systems, based both on duration of cultivation and crop association, is first suggested. The relative antiquity of these systems is then considered in order to isolate those that were established in pre- or early-European times. The ecological attributes of seed-cultural and vegecultural systems are then discussed, and in conclusion the hypothesis on the origins of agriculture in West Africa is summarized.

TRADITIONAL SYSTEMS OF PLANT FOOD PRODUCTION

Paleotechnic systems of food production[2] as practiced in the traditional world, like their neotechnic equivalents in the modern world, may be classified in a variety of ways according to the purposes for which they are studied. One approach is to regard them as man-modified ecosystems and to analyse them in terms of concepts borrowed from the study of natural ecosystems, such as species diversity, productivity, and homeostasis. If this is done, it becomes apparent, for example, that whereas neotechnic systems such as plantation agriculture and commercial grain farming represent highly simplified ecosystems in which species diversity is deliberately kept low for economic gain, most paleotechnic systems are biotically more complex and frequently incorporate diverse assemblages of plants in polycultural patterns of structural and functional interdependence (Harris 1969: 4–7). The tendency for traditional systems to exhibit greater ecological complexity than modern systems is clearly evident in West Africa where a striking contrast exists between the small, biotically more uniform areas where cash crops such as cacao, rubber, bananas, and oil palm are raised on modern plantations, and the much more widespread and biotically diverse pattern of subsistence and semisubsistence agriculture. However, within the subsistence sector of the economy there is also considerable variation in species diversity from one traditional system to another as is emphasized in the subsequent discussion of crop associations.

A second criterion by which paleotechnic systems can usefully be classified is temporal continuity of land use. The length of time a unit of land is occupied by food-producing plants provides a valuable key

[2] In this paper attention is restricted to food plants and the role of domestic livestock in food production in West Africa is referred to only casually.

to the comparative study of agricultural systems and also directs attention to associated patterns of settlement and levels of population. This criterion is adopted here to define the major categories of classification. It suggests a range of systems from those in which land is cultivated in staple crops for shorter periods than it is fallowed to those in which cultivation is continuous or "permanent." Within this broad spectrum, which incorporates the familiar dichotomy between land-extensive and land-intensive methods of production, systems defined more precisely by crop associations can then find their place. Thus the major categories range from long-term fallowing or swidden systems, through short-term fallowing systems in which the average period of cultivation exceeds that of fallow, to various systems of continuous cultivation. The latter maintain productivity by obtaining their supply of nutrients mainly either from the direct addition of fertilizing substances to the soil or the control of water supplies which import and release soluble and suspended nutrients. Systems of continuous cultivation can accordingly be subdivided into "edaphic" and "hydraulic" systems.

All four of these major categories of paleotechnic agriculture are represented among the traditional food-producing systems of West Africa; but their spatial distribution is very uneven, and their economic and social significance varies widely. Long-term fallowing systems are more widespread than any other type of cultivation, and they continue to provide basic subsistence for most rural populations. However, under the impact of increasing populations and developing cash economies, they are giving way progressively to more land-intensive and cash-crop-oriented systems of production. The distribution and characteristic crop associations of the main traditional systems are briefly described in the following subsections. The succeeding section considers their relative antiquity.

Long-Term Fallowing Systems

The essential characteristic of swidden or shifting cultivation, which has been succinctly defined as "any continuing agricultural system in which impermanent clearings are cropped for shorter periods in years than they are fallowed" (Conklin 1963: 1), is the relatively frequent shifting of the fields or plots. Field shifting is commonly prompted by declining soil fertility and/or weed invasion, and it takes the place of crop rotation or the use of fertilizers in fixed-field systems as a means of maintaining productivity. The periodic shifting of settlements is not a necessary corollary of swidden cultivation although the relocation of villages and hamlets is not uncommon among shifting cultivators (Harris 1972a).

It is unnecessary to examine the general attributes of this familiar system of cultivation, such as the characteristically small size of cleared plots; the use of fire as well as axes and other hand tools in clearance; the cyclical pattern of cropping, abandonment, regeneration, and re-cultivation; and the low densities of population that it usually supports. It is the pattern of variation that it exhibits in West Africa that merits attention. It is practiced as a basic system of subsistence food produc-tion throughout the area, from the humid tropical coastlands to the semiarid savannas and arid shrublands of the interior; but within this vast area many regional and local subtypes can be distinguished. Among these are the systems involving clearance and regeneration of closed forest, open woodland or bush, and savanna grasslands. These three subtypes correlate broadly with the moisture regions and vegetational zones that lie approximately parallel to the coast (Figures 2 and 3); and they also correspond, from forest to savanna, with the increasingly large average size of plots and with decreasing input of ash-derived nutrients as a result of the reduced amounts of organic matter available for burning.

Other subtypes may be recognized on the basis of tillage techniques, for example: those depending on hoe and/or digging-stick, which char-acterize most of the forest zone; and those that incorporate plows and draught animals and are restricted to parts of the more northerly savanna and shrub zone. For the purposes of this paper, however, the most significant subtypes to distinguish are those based on dominant crops. Here the primary distinction is that between the seed-cultural systems which predominate in the subhumid and semiarid lands of the interior — the crop associations of which tend to be dominated by sorghum and millets — and the vegecultural systems of the southerly forest zone which depend primarily on yams, manioc, cocoyams, and plantain bananas. This division greatly oversimplifies a complex situa-tion, particularly in relation to the importance of seed crops such as rice and maize in parts of the forest zone and of manioc far into the interior, but it remains of fundamental significance in West African agriculture.

VEGECULTURAL SYSTEMS   The area in which vegetatively reproduced crops dominate traditional agriculture is shown in Figure 4. It corre-sponds quite closely to the forest zone in the east, but in the west

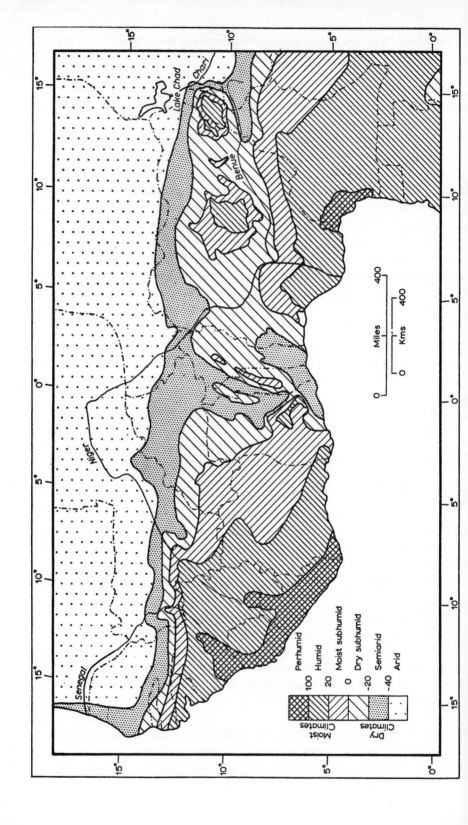

Perhumid
Humid
Moist subhumid
Dry subhumid
Semiarid
Arid

100
20
0
-20
-40

Moist
Climates

Dry
Climates

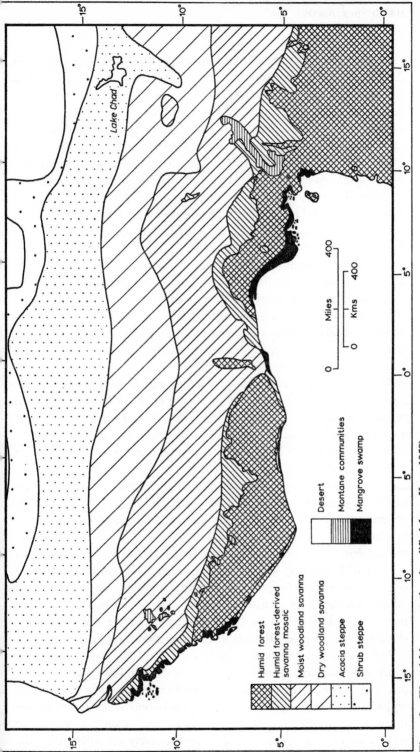

Figure 3. West Africa: vegetation (modified from Keay 1959)

Humid forest

Humid forest-derived
savanna mosaic

Moist woodland savanna

Dry woodland savanna

Acacia steppe

Shrub steppe

Desert

Montane communities

Mangrove swamp

Lake Chad

Miles

Kms

0   400

0   400

vegeculture gives way rather abruptly to rice-dominated seed culture in the vicinity of the Bandama River in present-day Ivory Coast. Within the zone of vegeculture yams occupy a greater area than any other staple crop, although manioc, which dominates in limited areas and is frequently codominant with yams elsewhere, is almost as widely cultivated. Cocoyams are the third most widespread root crop, being grown usually in association with yams and manioc but also as an understory crop with plantains. The latter constitute the fourth major vegetatively reproduced staple, and they are grown throughout the more humid parts of the coastal forest zone, although they are dominant in two areas only: in southeastern Ivory Coast and southern Ghana, and towards the Congo (Figure 4).

Within the vegecultural zone swidden systems differ widely in the relative emphasis on particular crops, in planting sequences, and in the duration of fallow periods. However certain regularities can be discerned. Over most of the zone, systems are characterized by crop combinations in which yams and manioc are dominant and fallow periods relatively long (five to fifteen years). Secondary crops are mainly seed plants such as maize, which is typically the most important, and vegetable crops such as okra, beans, cucurbits, and melons. Cocoyams are also commonly raised as an additional root crop. This system of mixed planting, whereby species with differing growth habits and root systems are raised in close association, ensures effective vertical and lateral exploitation of available light, warmth, moisture, and nutrients. Although they appear chaotic to observers accustomed to the clean-field monocultures of neotechnic agriculture, such polycultural swidden plots achieve high temporary levels of productivity on soils of generally low nutrient status. Also, by screening the soil from the direct effects of insolation and raindrop impact for much of the year, they minimize soil erosion. Soil stability may also be enhanced by the widespread practice of heaping up soil mounds in which yams, manioc, and other crops are planted. The principal benefits, however, that this practice affords are the concentration of humus and ash around the growing plants; improved tilth for root development; and, in low-lying areas subject to waterlogging, the raising of crops above soil-saturation level.

There is much ecological merit in such polycultural swidden plots, which simulate more closely than other agricultural systems the structure and dynamics of the tropical forest ecosystem they temporarily replace; but they preserve ecological stability only if the fallow period remains sufficiently long. If, as a result of population increase or for other reasons, the fallow period is progressively curtailed, then the

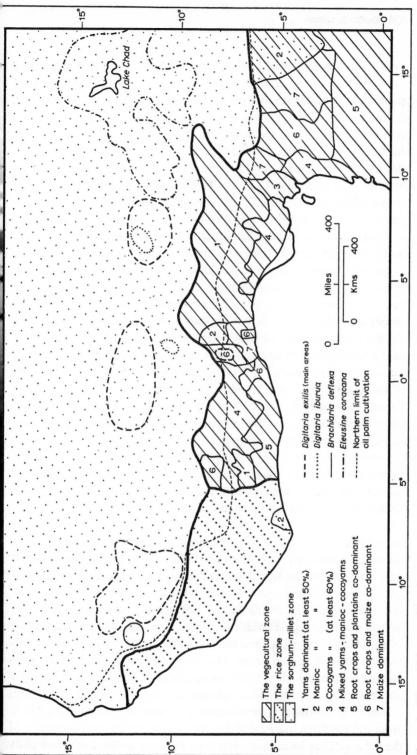

Figure 4. West Africa: traditional crop zones and subareas of crop dominance (based on Johnston 1958: 59, 70, 81; Portères 1955a)

The vegecultural zone
The rice zone
The sorghum-millet zone

1 Yams dominant (at least 50%)
2 Manioc   "   "
3 Cocoyams "   (at least 60%)
4 Mixed yams - manioc - cocoyams
5 Root crops and plantains co-dominant
6 Root crops and maize co-dominant
7 Maize dominant

– – – *Digitaria exilis* (main areas)
· · · · · *Digitaria iburua*
——— *Brachiaria deflexa*
–·–·– *Eleusine coracana*
– – – – Northern limit of
        oil palm cultivation

Lake Chad

Miles

0   400
0   Kms   400

system loses its ecological equilibrium. In West Africa this has occurred most dramatically in southeastern Nigeria, where in some parts rural population densities are exceedingly high and the average fallow period, following one to two years of cultivation, has been reduced to three to four years or even less. Under these conditions there is insufficient time for forest to regenerate, and the vegetation cover has been progressively degraded until closed forest has been extensively replaced by woodland savanna and grassland savanna. These dominantly herbaceous plant communities provide insufficient woody growth to yield an adequate supply of ash on burning, and they become vulnerable to soil erosion.

Apart from the widely distributed swidden systems in which yams and manioc, often associated with maize, are the dominant crops, there is one other vegecultural crop combination which is sufficiently distinctive to merit separate consideration. This is the association of plantains and cocoyams. Both crops require abundant atmospheric and soil moisture, and their distribution as staples correlates quite closely with the discontinuous zone of humid rain forest west and east of the semi-arid coastal plains in southeastern Ghana, Togo, and Dahomey. They do not, however, extend as staple crops beyond the western boundary of the vegecultural zone in Ivory Coast despite the continuation into Liberia of humid rain forest. Plantains and cocoyams are also ecologically complementary in that the cocoyams, which are shade-tolerant as well as moisture-demanding, are grown as understory plants beneath the canopy layer formed by the plantains. Swidden cycles that incorporate these crops as staples tend to be of longer duration than those focusing on yams or manioc, with individual plots sometimes cultivated for four to five years before abandonment to long periods of fallow.

SEED-CULTURAL SYSTEMS   The region in which seed-reproduced crops dominate traditional agriculture is shown in Figure 4. For the most part it lies within the woodland, savanna, and shrub zones of the sub-humid, semiarid, and arid interior; but it also extends in the form of rice culture into the humid forest zone west of the Bandama River. Within this huge region swidden cultivation remains the dominant mode of agriculture, but more land-intensive and continuous systems of cultivation exist in certain areas. The most widespread subtype of seed-cultural swidden is that based on sorghum and millets, but subtypes dominated by rice and maize respectively are also widely distributed.

The sorghum-millet systems extend over most of interior West Africa from the northern margins of the forest zone to the southern edge of the Sahara. They incorporate less crop diversity within individual plots than do the vegecultural systems of the forest zone, but associated secondary crops are still numerous. Most of the latter are seed crops, such as groundnuts, beans, and rice, with manioc as the only prominent root crop. Internal differentiation within this area in terms of crop dominance relates broadly to the decreasing availability of moisture from south to north. In the southern subhumid zone, from the margins of the forest approximately to the isohyet of 1,000 millimeters mean annual rainfall, sorghum is the principal staple; in the semiarid savanna zone, which extends roughly from the 1,000 millimeters to the 600 millimeters isohyet, sorghum and millets are codominant. In the arid north millets progressively supplant sorghum, which reaches its limit of nonirrigated cultivation at approximately the 400 millimeter isohyet, while millets continue to be grown without irrigation to the absolute limits of dry farming at about the 275 millimeter isohyet (Miège 1954: 41).

Planting sequences and crop combinations vary less over this large area than they do in the southern vegecultural zone. Most of the cultivated land tends to be devoted to one or more of the staple grains with relatively small areas under secondary crops, and the planting in the same plot of different species of complementary life-form is also less highly developed. The dominantly herbaceous seed-crop associations do not provide as complete and perennial a canopy of vegetation to protect the soil from weathering and erosion, and soil mounding is much less frequently practiced. The length of the fallow period is extremely variable in areas of sorghum-millet swidden, but in general it tends to be shorter than in vegecultural systems. This tendency corresponds broadly to Boserup's distinction (1965: 15) between bush-fallow and forest-fallow systems with respectively shorter and longer fallow periods. However, on account of the relatively low rural population densities that characterize most of the West African interior, there are fewer cases of the fallow period being shortened so drastically as to induce ecological breakdown of the system and its replacement by more land-intensive methods of production than in the vegecultural zone of forest fallow.

The second most extensive seed-crop zone is that which is dominated by rice (Figure 4). It occupies most of the humid forest zone from the Bandama River in Ivory Coast west through Liberia, Sierra Leone, Guinea, and Portuguese Guinea, and almost to the Casamance River in southern Senegal. Throughout this area rice is cultivated primarily as a "dry" or upland crop by swidden methods, but "wet" or lowland rice is also cultivated along parts of the coast by techniques of water management. This specialized development of intensive rice irrigation is considered later in the subsection on hydraulic systems.

As a subsistence crop, upland rice is by no means restricted to the western rice zone, but it is only there that it attains widespread dominance as a staple. Among certain ethnic groups, notably the Kissi of the forest zone in Guinea, Sierra Leone, and Liberia, most economic, social, and ceremonial activities focus upon its cultivation (Paulme 1954). Both the indigenous "red" rice and the "white" rice introduced from eastern Asia are grown in nonirrigated clearings, frequently in association with other seed crops and with manioc. Fallow periods in the rice zone are very variable, but rice is seldom cultivated as the staple for more than two years in succession, and it is often associated with progressive forest degradation and soil erosion, particularly when grown on steep slopes.

The third subtype of seed-cultural swidden is that dominated by maize. There is no large continuous zone, comparable to the sorghum-millet and rice zones, in which maize is the dominant staple. Maize does dominate swidden systems locally, and it is also cultivated very widely in West Africa as a secondary crop. There are two areas in which maize attains dominance or codominance as a staple (Figure 4). The more westerly of these coincides closely with the subhumid and semiarid coastal enclave between the western and eastern blocks of humid forest, but the larger eastern area does not correlate with drier climates (Figures 2 and 3). Throughout its area of dominance maize is cultivated as the only important cereal within systems otherwise oriented strongly towards root-crop cultivation. It is commonly interplanted with yams, cocoyams, and manioc, and it is often the first food crop to be harvested, thus fulfilling a valuable function in the planting sequence by providing roasting cobs during the period of food shortage which often precedes the main harvest. Swiddens in which maize is the dominant crop are normally cultivated for one or two years in succession before being turned over more completely to root crops or abandoned to long fallow. Like upland rice, maize makes relatively heavy demands on the soil, and its cultivation as a primary crop often leads rapidly to low yields, to marked reductions in soil fertility, and sometimes to soil erosion. The tendency of maize to be more demanding of the soil than sorghum or millets is reflected in the fact that in the subhumid and semiarid interior it is only a minor constituent of swidden systems, being more usually raised on small village plots which are permanently or semipermanently cultivated with the aid of animal manure and other organic wastes.

Short-Term Fallowing Systems

In the absence of comprehensive data on variations in the relative lengths of cropping and fallow periods, it is not possible even to outline the regional occurrence in West Africa of short-term fallowing systems. Over the greater part of the region long-term fallowing still prevails. However, in many areas, and usually as a response to increased population and/or the inception of cash cropping, the average duration of fallow has been reduced so far that it no longer exceeds the average period of cropping by a sufficient margin to allow adequate regeneration of the vegetation cover. In southeastern Nigeria, for example, where rural population densities are among the highest in Africa, the fallow period following one to two years in which yams are the staple crop has been widely reduced to three to four years; and comparable reductions can be observed in some of the more densely peopled parts of the interior, as among the Tiv of the Benue valley (Vermeer 1970).

Edaphic Systems of Continuous Cultivation

The dividing line between short-term fallowing and continuous systems is necessarily somewhat arbitrary, but the distinction serves to focus attention on the degree to which agricultural productivity is maintained by means other than fallowing. In West Africa continuous cultivation is very limited in areal extent, but it exists in several distinctive forms. Three major types of edaphic systems, which depend mainly on the direct addition of fertilizing substances to the soil, may be distinguished: crop-rotational fixed-field systems; fixed-plot horticulture or compound farming; and specialized tree cropping.

CROP-ROTATIONAL FIXED-FIELD SYSTEMS When crop rotation is combined with the regular use of organic fertilizers, the continuous cropping of fixed fields becomes possible. The principal source of fertilizer may be either vegetable matter derived from agricultural and household wastes or animal manure, and in West Africa both sources are traditionally used to sustain limited areas of continuous cultivation. In the vegecultural zone of southeastern Nigeria small hillslope areas have been modeled into terrace complexes that provide pockets of deep, nearly level soil in which the staple crops are grown according to a systematic rotation. Some of these terrace systems are now abandoned and fossilized beneath a grass cover, as are those near Nsukka, but in the Maku area, south of Enugu, terrace cultivation is still actively practiced, the principal crops being rotated on contiguous groups of terraces (Floyd 1964). The organic fertilizers used consist mainly of composted vegetable wastes from kitchen and compound, together with grasses and tree leaves collected from nearby forest areas. Terrace farming has also been traditionally practiced by seed-crop agriculturalists in certain upland areas of the interior, for example: in parts of the Guinea Highlands, around the margins of the Jos Plateau (Netting 1968); and in the Mandara Mountains where an elaborate system of terracing was developed which depends on the heavy use of animal manure and household waste and on the rotation of crops to build up and maintain soil fertility (White 1941).

Terrace farming is not the only traditional crop-rotational fixed-field system which depends on organic fertilizers to reduce or eliminate the need for fallowing. Around the margins of the larger cities of the semiarid interior, where cattle and other livestock are an important part of the local agricultural economy, continuous intensive cultivation is practiced based upon simple crop rotations and the use of manure. This system of peri-urban farming is most highly developed around Kano and other cities of northern Nigeria, where a rudimentary system of mixed farming has arisen in response to high rural population densities, readily accessible supplies of ground water, and easily tilled soils. (Buchanan and Pugh 1955: 111–113). The principal crops are sorghum, millets, and groundnuts; and all available types of organic fertilizer are used to enrich the fields. However, neither peri-urban farming nor terrace farming can strictly be regarded as systems of mixed farming in that they do not achieve balanced production of crops and livestock, including the growing of fodder crops solely for consumption by the animals. In that sense of the term, mixed farming does not occur as a traditional system indigenous to West Africa, although attempts have been made during and since the Colonial period to develop modern mixed farming in some of the tsetse-free areas of the interior.

FIXED-PLOT HORTICULTURE   The continuous or long-term cultivation of small "garden" plots in the immediate vicinity of settlements is a widespread phenomenon in the tropics, and it is highly developed in West Africa, where it is sometimes referred to as compound farming (Floyd 1969: 180–182). Such plots incorporate a wide variety of seed-reproduced and vegetatively reproduced tree, shrub, and herbaceous crops, and fertility is maintained by the frequent application of organic wastes from houses and compound yards. These wastes often contain human excreta and animal manure derived from poultry, goats, sheep, and to a lesser extent cattle, as well as vegetable residues. Many different crops are planted in close proximity and in seasonal sequence, the whole plot often forming a multi-layered plant community. Polycultural plots are particularly characteristic of the vegecultural zone where the smaller, economically valuable trees and shrubs, such as plantain and kola, are grown beneath a discontinuous canopy of oil palms and are themselves undercultivated with a mixture of root and vegetable crops. Garden plots in seed-cultural areas, especially those in the drier interior, tend to be less complex both biotically and structurally, but they still contribute essential and varied foodstuffs to the household economy.

In many parts of the more densely populated areas, particularly in southeastern Nigeria, this tradition of intensive horticulture has been developed and extended beyond the immediate vicinity of the compounds into peripheral areas which were previously cultivated by swidden methods. Here the collection and application of organic fertilizer is more highly developed; goats, sheep, and poultry are confined and fed, at least temporarily, in enclosures and their droppings are composted with vegetable wastes before being applied to the garden plots. This extended and intensified form of fixed-plot horticulture is extremely labor-intensive, but it is highly productive and contributes significantly to the sustenance of rural populations, especially in areas where densities exceed 1,000 per square mile.

SPECIALIZED TREE CROPPING   Tree crops are widely grown in West Africa on a small scale in association with both continuous and fallowing systems of cultivation, but certain species are also exploited more intensively. Specialized tree cropping takes two forms: modern commercial cultivation of recently introduced species, such as cacao and Para rubber, and of indigenous species, such as oil palm, which are raised both as minor cash crops and on plantations; and the tending and cultivation for subsistence of native species, principally oil palm and kola nut. Modern commercial developments do not concern us, but traditional subsistence tree cropping invites comment. It is important as a specialized activity only in and along the margins of the forest zone and it is concerned primarily with the oil palm.

Oil palm occurs wild and semiwild throughout the forest zone and is cultivated sporadically from Senegal to Cameroon (Figure 4). It is valued principally for the oil which is extracted from the pericarp of the fruit by maceration. The oil is used for illumination and a variety of other purposes, but mainly to cook starchy foods, especially those derived from the root crops of the vegecultural zone. The oil palm also provides nuts, the kernels of which yield a different type of oil; sap which is tapped to make an intoxicating wine; fiber; fuel; and thatching materials from its leaves. It is propagated with difficulty from seed, but most stands consist of self-regenerating semiwild groves which have developed from wild trees preserved by swidden cultivators during clearance and sometimes replanted in clusters, often near settlements. The oil palm has thus multiplied both naturally and artificially in the forest zone and become the focus of a specialized though casual system of tree cropping. It is not naturally abundant in areas of closed forest, flourishing best in open situations with much sunlight; and its spread has paralleled the progressive replacement of closed-canopy forest by woodland and bush savanna which has resulted from intensified cultivation.

In traditional West African economies no other tree crop attains an importance equivalent to the oil palm, but kola is quite extensively cultivated in the forest zone as a specialized tree crop, valued for its nuts which contain caffeine and are chewed as a stimulant. Useful products are collected from a variety of other trees in the forest zone, such as seeds from indigenous species of coffee and fruit from the akee tree; but this mode of exploitation does not always involve cultivation. Similarly, in the savanna and desert lands of the interior, several tree species are quite intensively exploited without entering into regular cultivation. Notable among these are the shea butter tree, which is valued as a source of oil in the savanna zone beyond the limit of culti- vation of the oil palm, and the locust bean tree which provides edible fruit and seeds. The exploitation of such trees commonly involves indi- vidual ownership, protection, tending, and sometimes also planting; but it constitutes no more than a rudimentary form of specialized tree cropping.

Hydraulic Systems of Continuous Cultivation

In the development of techniques for the maintenance of agricultural productivity by means other than fallowing, the manipulation of water supplies represents an alternative strategy to the addition of fertilizing substances direct to the soil. Hydraulic and edaphic systems are not always mutually exclusive, but it is useful to distinguish between them as they rely primarily on contrasted methods of maintaining productivity. In hydraulic systems the provision and regulation of water supplies, which contribute nutrients in solution and suspension, are vital in ensuring continuity of production, whereas in edaphic systems the supply of fertilizers to the soil tends to be critical. In West Africa hydraulic systems, like the edaphic systems, have been developed only to a limited extent, but several distinct types of hydraulic cultivation exist as traditional food-producing systems. Three major types may be recognized on the basis of water exploitation techniques and crop associations: small-scale hand irrigation; flood-water farming; and swamp-rice cultivation.

SMALL-SCALE HAND IRRIGATION   In parts of the interior, particularly in the vicinity of the larger towns along the southern margin of the Sahara, small streamside plots, devoted principally to vegetable crops such as onions, are hand-irrigated by bucket, scoop, and *shaduf*. Production is limited by pronounced seasonal variations in streamflow, and the small output of this labor-intensive system of irrigation goes mainly to supply the nearby urban markets.

FLOOD-WATER FARMING   The practice of raising cereals and vegetable crops on seasonally flooded land is widespread throughout the arid and semiarid zones. Done on a small scale, the crops usually are sown after natural flooding has sufficiently saturated riparian soils for a harvest to be obtained without the addition of more water by artificial means.

However, along major river and lake systems of the interior, such as the Senegal, the Niger, and Lake Chad, traditional systems of flood-water farming exist on a larger scale. They have reached their maximum development along the Niger, particularly in the area of the "inland delta" in present-day Mali. Here a complex system of seed-cultural flood-water farming has been developed which successfully exploits both the rising and falling phases (*crue* and *décrue*) of the seasonal flood regime. The principal crop planted before the flood is lowland or wet rice. Varieties are selected according to the anticipated depth of the flood waters, the shorter stemmed forms being planted in the higher fields and the "floating" varieties, the stems of which lengthen as the flood waters slowly rise, being planted in the lower fields subject to deeper flooding. The rice is harvested as the flood waters recede, and in the lower areas floating rice is harvested from canoes (Dalziel 1937: 533).

Agricultural exploitation of the *décrue* focuses on millet and sorghum rather than rice, and it involves a more complex sequence of planting and harvest. *Décrue* agriculture is most extensively developed as a traditional system in the lacustrine sector of the upper Niger, southwest of Timbuktu (Harlan and Pasquereau 1969). Here — on moist soils exposed as the water level falls — pearl millet and durra and Guinea corn sorghums are sown in a sequence adjusted to the gradual recession of the flood, and harvesting takes place before or when the flood waters next begin to rise.

SWAMP-RICE CULTIVATION   Like flood-water farming, the cultivation of swamp rice involves hydraulic management but not irrigation as such. Most swamp rice is grown within the rice zone itself, but there are also small areas of flood-plain cultivation in the vegecultural zone and in the interior. Freshwater swamps are usually cultivated, but along the southwestern coast rice is grown in tidal swamps which formerly supported mangrove.

THE RELATIVE ANTIQUITY OF PLANT FOOD-PRODUCING SYSTEMS

Having outlined the major traditional plant food-producing systems and crop associations of West Africa, we may next turn to the question of their relative antiquity. In the absence of detailed archaeological and historical data on the evolution of agricultural techniques, this problem is best approached through an examination of the evidence for crop introductions. For each of the three major agricultural zones, Table 1 summarizes data on introductions to West Africa in order to isolate the indigenous — and generally more ancient — crop associations of the region.

The Vegecultural Zone

In Table 2, the crops listed in Table 1 as principally associated with the vegecultural zone are rearranged according to their status as African or introduced domesticates and then subdivided into West African and other African species, and pre-Colonial and Colonial introductions. Although uncertainty attaches to the area of origin and time of introduction of many species, this table brings into focus the elements in the

Table 1. Food plants principally associated with the three traditional crop zones of West Africa (Sources: Baker 1962; Coursey 1967; Dalziel 1937; de Wet and Harlan 1971; Harlan 1971; Irvine 1961; Portères 1950, 1955a; Purseglove 1968, 1972; Schnell 1957)

ecies	English name	Continent or region of origin	Probable period of introduction to West Africa
	THE VEGECULTURAL ZONE		
oot crops			
Dioscorea rotundata Poir	White Guinea yam	W. Africa	
D. cayenensis Lam.	Yellow Guinea yam	W. Africa	
D. praehensilis Benth.	Bush or forest yam	W. Africa	
D. colocasiifolia Pax.	False water yam	W. Africa	
D. dumetorum (Kunth) Pax.	Bitter or cluster yam	Africa	
D. bulbifera L.(= *D. latifolia*)	Potato or aerial yam	Africa	
D. esculenta (Lour.) Burk.	Lesser yam	S.E. Asia	Colonial
D. alata L.	Greater or water yam	S.E. Asia	Colonial?
Plectranthus esculentus N.E.Br. (= *Coleus dazo*)	Hausa or Kafir potato	W.? Africa	
Plenostemom rotundifolius (Poir.) J. K. Morton (= *Coleus dysentricus?*)	Piasa	W.? Africa	
Sphenostylis stenocarpa Harms	Yam pea or bean	W.? Africa	
Colocasia esculenta (L.) Schott	Cocoyam or taro	S.E. Asia	Pre-Colonial
Xanthosoma sagittifolium (L.) Schott	Cocoyam or tannia	S. America	Late Colonial
Manihot esculenta Crantz	Manioc or cassava	Tropical America	Early Colonial
Ipomoea batatas (L.) Lam	Sweet potato	Tropical America	Early Colonial
ereal crops			
Zea mays L.	Maize	Tropical America	Early Colonial?
ree crops			
Elaeis guineensis Jacq.	Oil palm	W. Africa	
Blighia sapida Koenig	Akee	W. Africa	
Cola nitida (Vent.) Schott & Endl.	Gbanja kola	W. Africa	
C. acuminata (P. Beauv.) Schott & Endl.	Abata kola	W. and C. Africa	
C. verticillata (Thonn.) Stapf ex A. Chev.	Owé kola	W. and C. Africa	
C. anomala K. Schum.	Bamenda kola	W. Africa	
Coffea liberica Bull ex Hiern	Liberica coffee	W. Africa	
C. excelsa A. Chev.	—	W. Africa	
C. stenophylla G. Don	—	W. Africa	
C. canephora Pierre ex Froehner	Robusta coffee	C. Africa	
C. arabica L.	Arabica coffee	Ethiopia	Colonial

Species	English name	Continent or region of origin	Probable period of introduction to West Africa
Musa paradisiaca L. var. *normalis* Kuntze	Plantain	S.E. Asia	Pre-Colonial
M. paradisiaca L. var. *sapientum* Kuntze	Banana	S.E. Asia	Colonial
Cocos nucifera L.	Coconut	Asia	Pre-Colonial
Anacardium occidentale L.	Cashew	Tropical America	Colonial
Carica papaya L.	Papaya or pawpaw	Middle America	Colonial
Theobroma cacao L.	Cacao or cocoa	Tropical America	Early Colonial

Other crops

Hibiscus esculentus L. (= *Abelmoschus esculentus*)	Okra or gombo	Tropical Africa	
H. sabdariffa L.	Roselle	W.? Africa	
Telfairia occidentalis Hook. f.	Fluted gourd	Tropical Africa	
Lagenaria siceraria (Molina) Standl.	Bottle gourd	Tropical Africa	
Saccharum officinarum L.	Sugar cane	S.E. Asia	Pre-Colonial?
Solanum melongena L.	Egg plant	S. Asia	Pre-Colonial
Capsicum annuum L.	Chili or sweet pepper	Middle America	Colonial
Lycopersicon esculentum Mill. var. *cerasiforme* (Dun.) Alef.	Cherry tomato	S. America	Colonial
Phaseolus vulgaris L.	Common or haricot bean	Tropical America	Early Colonial
P. lunatus L.	Lima bean	Tropical America	Colonial
Ananas comosus (L.) Merr.	Pineapple	S. America	Colonial
Cucurbita pepo L.	Edible pumpkin or marrow	Middle America	Colonial

THE RICE ZONE

Cereal crops

*Oryza glaberrima Steud.	African rice	W. Africa	
*O. sativa L.	Asian rice	Tropical Asia	Early Colonial

Tree crops

Citrus aurantifolia (Christm.) Swing.	Lime	S.E. Asia	Pre-Colonial?
C. limon (L.) Burm. f.	Lemon	Tropical Asia	Pre-Colonial?
C. sinensis (L.) Osbeck	Sweet orange	S.E. Asia	Colonial
C. aurantium L.	Bitter orange	S.E. Asia	Colonial?
Persea americana Mill.	Avocado	Middle America	Late Colonial

Species	English name	Continent or region of origin	Probable period of introduction to West Africa
Other crops			
Aframomum melegueta (Roscoe) K. Schum.	Melegueta pepper or Grains of Paradise	W. Africa	

THE SORGHUM-MILLET ZONE

Cereal crops			
Digitaria exilis Stapf	Fonio or hungry rice	W. Africa	
D. iburua Stapf	Black fonio	W. Africa	
Brachiaria deflexa C. E. Hubbard	—	W. Africa	
Sorghum bicolor (L.) Moench	Sorghum	Tropical Africa	
var. *bicolor* (Guinea race)	Guinea corn	W. or E. Africa	
var. *bicolor* (Durra race)	Durra sorghum	N. Tropical Africa	
Pennisetum americanum (L.) K. Schum.	Pearl millet	N. Tropical Africa	
Eleusine coracana (L.) Gaertn.	Finger millet	Ethiopia/ E. Africa?	
Hordeum vulgare L.	Barley	S.W. Asia	Pre-Colonial
Triticum aestivum L.	Bread wheat	S.W. Asia	Pre-Colonial
T. durum Desf.	Durum wheat	S.W. Asia	Pre-Colonial
Tree crops			
Butyrospermum paradoxum (Gaertn. f.) Hepper subsp. *parkii* (G. Don) Hepper	Shea butter tree	W. Africa	
Parkia filicoidea Welw. ex Oliv.	Locust bean	Tropical Africa	
Tamarindus indica L.	Tamarind	Tropical Africa	
Mangifera indica L.	Mango	S. Asia	Early Colonial
Other crops			
Voandzeia subterranea (L.) Thou.	Bambara groundnut	W. Africa	
Kerstingiella geocarpa Harms	Kersting's groundnut	W. Africa	
Vigna unguiculata (L.) Walp.	Cowpea	Tropical Africa	
Cajanus cajan (L.) Milsp.	Pigeon pea	Africa?	
Polygala butyracea Heck.	Black beniseed	W. Africa	
Sesamum indicum L.	Sesame or beniseed	Africa?	
Citrullus lanatus (Thunb.) Mansf. (= *Colocynthis citrullus*)	Watermelon	Tropical Africa	

Species	English name	Continent or region of origin	Probable period of introduction to West Africa
Allium cepa L.	Onion	W. Asia	Pre-Colonial?
A. ascalonicum L.	Shallot	W. Asia?	Pre-Colonial?
Arachis hypogaea L.	Groundnut or peanut	S. America	Early Colonial
Canavalia ensiformis (L.) DC.	Jack bean	Middle America	Colonial?
Capsicum frutescens L.	Chili or bird pepper	Tropical America	Colonial

* = staple crops.

Table 2.   African and alien plants associated with the three traditional crop zones of West Africa

Indigenous to Africa		Introduced to West Africa	
West Africa	Elsewhere in Africa	Pre-Colonial	Colonial

THE VEGECULTURAL ZONE

Root crops

*African yams		*Taro	Greater yam?
Hausa potato			Lesser yam
Piasa?			*Manioc
Yam pea?			Sweet potato
			*Tannia

Cereal crops

			Maize?

Tree crops

*Oil palm		*Plantain	Banana
Akee		Coconut	Papaya
*Kola			Cacao
W. African coffees			Arabica coffee

Other crops

Roselle?	Okra	Egg plant	Common bean
	Fluted gourd	Sugar cane?	Lima bean
	Bottle gourd?		Sweet chili pepper
			Cherry tomato
			Marrow
			Pineapple

THE RICE ZONE

Cereal crops

*African rice			*Asian rice

West Africa	Elsewhere in Africa	Pre-Colonial	Colonial
Tree crops			
		Lime?	Sweet orange
		Lemon	Bitter orange?
			Avocado
Other crops			
Melegueta pepper			
	THE SORGHUM-MILLET ZONE		
Cereal crops			
*Fonio	*Guinea corn sorghum	Barley	
Black fonio	*Durra sorghum	Bread wheat	
Brachiaria deflexa	*Pearl millet	Durum wheat	
	Finger millet		
Tree crops			
Shea butter tree	Locust bean		Mango
	Tamarind		
Other crops			
*Bambara groundnut	*Cowpea	Onion?	*Groundnut
Kersting's groundnut	*Pigeon pea?	Shallot?	Jack bean?
Black beniseed	*Sesame?		Bird chili pepper
	Watermelon		

* = staple crops.

crop associations of the vegecultural zone that appear to be indigenous to West Africa.

The major contribution of American species introduced since the beginning of Colonial times is clearly apparent. They include vegetables, fruits, and pulses, which have added valuable nutritional variety to local diets, and, most importantly, the American root crops — manioc, tannia, and sweet potato — which have extended the ecological diversity and range of the root-crop complex. Of these, manioc has made the greatest contribution as a staple food, and its spectacular spread and widespread adoption in tropical Africa since the sixteenth century have been closely studied (Jones 1953, 1959). Tannia has also been readily adopted because it grows well as an understory species and, particularly in Ghana, because it provides shade for young cacao seedlings. It was not introduced to West Africa until the mid-nineteenth century, but is now regarded as superior to the other cocoyam — taro — which, according to Burkill (1938), reached West Africa from its Southeast Asian homeland about the beginning of the Christian era. Two other vegetatively reproduced crops of Southeast Asian origin —

the greater yam and the plantain banana — may also have reached West Africa well before the Colonial period. But the case for a pre-Colonial introduction of the greater yam rests on weak circumstantial evidence, and the Portuguese may have carried the plant to West Africa by sea some time after 1498 (Alexander and Coursey 1969: 418). The plantain, on the other hand, probably reached West Africa at an early date as a result of transcontinental diffusion from the East African coast (McMaster 1962; Simmonds 1962: 143–146). The introduction of the edible banana, on a large scale at least, does not appear to have taken place until the nineteenth century. With the exception of the lesser yam, all the remaining Asian introductions listed — sugarcane, coconut, and eggplant — were probably introduced to West Africa before the arrival of the Europeans.

Uncertainty and controversy surround the question of when and how maize was introduced into West Africa. It would be out of place to attempt a summary here of the conflicting arguments (Jeffreys 1957, 1963; Miracle 1963, 1965, 1966: 87–93; Willett 1962). Despite a recent attempt by Jeffreys (1971) to marshall the evidence in favor of the pre-Columbian introduction of maize, the most tenable hypothesis remains that of a very early Colonial introduction by the Portuguese direct to the west coast and possibly also an independent introduction from Spain via the Mediterranean and Egypt, followed by transmission across the Sahara by Arab traders (Portères 1955b).

When the veneer of historically introduced crops is thus stripped off, a group of plants remains, all of which appear to be indigenous to Africa and most of which — including the staple root and tree crops — are probably West African in origin. In this group the vegetatively reproduced root crops, chiefly the West African yams, appear overwhelmingly important as providers of vegetable food, and the oil palm likewise is preeminently important among the limited number of indigenous seed-reproduced plants. The minor crop plants provide useful supplementary foodstuffs — fruits, vegetables, and stimulants — but none makes a major contribution to the bulk food supply. The question therefore arises as to whether the root-crop/oil-palm association represents an indigenous, primarily vegecultural system established in West Africa in ancient times.

A strong inferential case for the local domestication of yams in prehistoric times has been developed by Coursey in recent years (Coursey 1967: 22–25, 197–203; this volume; Alexander and Coursey 1969; Coursey and Coursey 1971). Two aspects of the question, namely the location and antiquity of yam domestication, will be briefly examined here. It can be argued on general grounds that the yams, like other tropical root crops with underground organs specialized for food storage, are naturally adapted to survive dry seasons and to grow quickly to maturity during rainy periods. They are unlikely to have been abundant as wild plants in areas of humid forest and short dry season, and the selection by man of shallow-rooting forms with larger tubers probably occurred in areas with more pronounced dry seasons. In West Africa yam domestication is most likely to have taken place within the zone where the dry season normally lasts between two and a half and five months (Figure 5) and where the natural vegetation — before man-derived savannas were widely developed — probably consisted of semi-evergreen and deciduous forests which would have provided a suitable niche for yam vines adapted to growth under a light tree canopy. In view of the possible significance of ecotone situations in the earliest phases of plant domestication (Harris 1969: 9), we may surmise that forest-edge locations played a primary role, if the West African yams were first domesticated by foragers who remained principally dependent on varied wild foods. However, in the absence of specific evidence, precise locations for the origins of yam domestication cannot be suggested with assurance, although the Courseys (1971: 479, note) have speculated that the process may have begun in the semiarid "Dahomey Gap" which occupies a central position within the present yam zone (Figures 2 and 4).

It is still more difficult to establish the antiquity of yam cultivation in West Africa. No direct archaeological evidence of root crops has been recovered, but there is considerable indirect evidence, both archaeological and ethnographic, to suggest that the systematic utilization of yams dates back several millennia. Whether or not Davies's interpretations of prehistoric artifacts found in West Africa as tools for digging up wild and cultivating domesticated yams are acceptable, his suggestion of a "protoagricultural" stage of food procurement based on the collection and planting of tubers (Davies 1960, 1967: 205–216; 1968: 479–481) is well in accord with botanical and ethnographic inferences. Among these are: the presence in West Africa of several wild species of yam closely related to the indigenous cultivated forms; the fact that yams can continue to grow and produce more tubers after removal of the first crop provided the roots and vine are not damaged, which suggests the possibility of a phase of regular harvesting having preceded cultivation proper; the existence in Africa of forager populations who collect and replant wild yams (Chevalier 1936 as noted by Coursey and Coursey 1971: 477); and the great agricultural and ceremonial im-

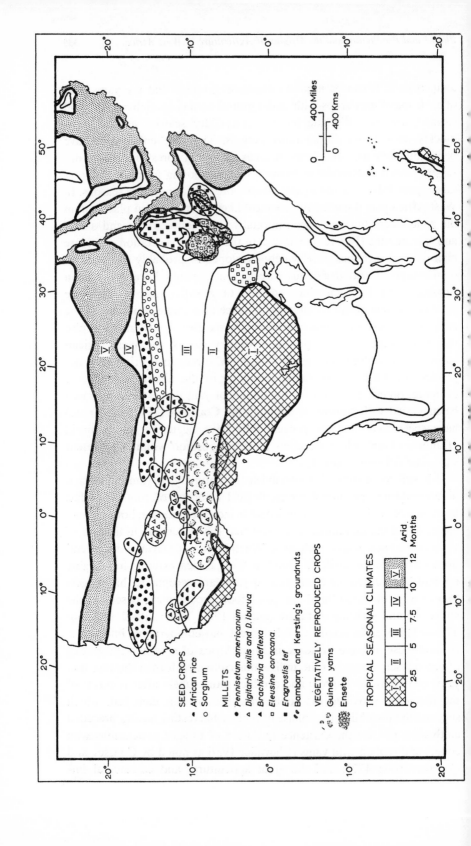

SEED CROPS
● African rice
○ Sorghum

MILLETS
● Pennisetum americanum
▲ Digitaria exilis and D. iburua
▲ Brachiaria deflexa
□ Eleusine coracana
■ Eragrostis tef
❝ Bambara and Kersting's groundnuts

VEGETATIVELY REPRODUCED CROPS
❝ ❝ Guinea yams
░░░ Ensete

TROPICAL SEASONAL CLIMATES

Ⅰ	Ⅱ	Ⅲ	Ⅳ	Ⅴ	Arid
0	2.5	5	7.5	10	12 Months

portance of the indigenous as opposed to the Asian yams in West Africa, including the prohibition on the use of iron tools for the digging of tubers to be used in New Yam festivals (Coursey 1967: 10, 197–203; Coursey and Coursey 1971).

The possibility of the origins of yam domestication going back several millennia in West Africa and of a long period of semicultivation having preceded full vegeculture there is indeed in accordance with the suggestion (Harris 1972b) that an initial phase of protocultivation by ecosystem-manipulation was a general phenomenon in the evolution of agriculture in the tropics. It also focuses attention on the important distinction — which is often lost sight of — between the origins of domestication (in the sense of human intervention in the breeding system of a plant or animal population) and of organized agriculture. It is quite probable that the beginnings of the domestication of yams, as of many other crops, lie deep in the Paleolithic period, but even so the central question remains of when and how their protocultivation gave way to a system of specialized vegeculture. In West Africa three possibilities suggest themselves. First, vegeculture based primarily on yams may have developed independently of external influence along the inland margins of the humid forest zone several millennia ago. Second, yam-based vegeculture may have arisen from the third millennium B.C. onwards, in response to cultural interaction between seed-crop agriculturalists from the dry interior and foragers in the forest and savanna zones who were already using wild yams but not cultivating them (Alexander and Coursey 1969: 421; Coursey and Coursey 1971: 477). Third, it is possible that the systematic cultivation of Guinea yams did not get under way until Asian yams and other vegetatively reproduced crops of Asian origin had reached West Africa. This last possibility was envisaged by Sauer (1952: 34–36) but, as has already been pointed out, the evidence suggests a relatively late introduction of the Asian yams after indigenous yams had been brought into cultivation. As yet, however, there is insufficient evidence to indicate which of the first two hypotheses may be the more tenable.

Little can be said, too, about the domestication of the minor root crops that form part of the West African vegecultural complex. They are probably of West African origin (Harlan 1971: 470; Purseglove, this volume), although Dalziel (1937: 262, 459–460) gives Ethiopia as a possible homeland of piasa and yam pea, and Portères (1962: 206–207) attributes Hausa potato and piasa primarily to Central Africa with a secondary center of development in West Africa. When and where these root crops first entered cultivation is entirely unknown, and they invite speculation as to whether they represent ancient cultigens, eclipsed by the rise to preeminence of staple root or seed crops such as yams and sorghum, or whether they are later additions to the West African roster of cultivated plants which have never attained more than marginal importance as food crops.

While the Guinea yams are the single most important indigenous food crop of the vegecultural zone, the oil palm is second only in importance to them. By providing edible oil and vitamin A, it complements the carbohydrate-rich root crops, and it gives high yields with minimal cultivation. It has been relatively little altered from the wild state and is therefore sometimes regarded as only semidomesticated, but it has been extensively multiplied and spread by man through the West African forest zone. Unfortunately little is known of its origin and early exploitation, but there is no serious doubt that it is native to West Africa. Like other palms it flourishes best in open situations, and it is thought not be be native to the closed-canopy humid forest, its most natural habitat being the forest fringe, especially along rivers (Hartley 1967: 2–4). Its present distribution throughout the forest zone is a result mainly of selective swidden clearance, and in regions such as southeastern Nigeria, where it is intensively exploited, oil palm bush has completely replaced forest over wide areas.

There is almost no direct evidence for the antiquity of oil palm exploitation in West Africa, but seed husks of wild or cultivated palms have been recovered from deposits in a rock shelter near Kintampo in central Ghana which are dated to about 1400 B.C. (Flight 1970: 72, this volume). This evidence is too slender to demonstrate conclusively that oil palm was anciently cultivated in West Africa, but it does strengthen the presumption of antiquity that derives from the status of the oil palm in traditional food-producing economies of the region. The chances of archaeological recovery are, however, much greater for the oil palm than for yams and other root crops, and future investigation can be expected to throw direct light on the question of its antiquity.

From this review of some of the inference and evidence that relate to the early exploitation of root and tree crops associated with the vegecultural zone, it is possible to hypothesize about the origins of food-producing systems in this part of West Africa. It may be suggested that from a very early time, reaching back into the Paleolithic, forager groups — occupying the more open forest and woodland areas and perhaps living mainly along stream courses and in other ecologically transitional areas — evolved techniques for the tending and harvesting of certain valued trees and tuberous plants which amounted to a form of protocultivation. This is likely to have occurred in the subhumid zone of the interior where the dry season lasts more than two and a half months in the year rather than in the humid forest zone, although allowance must be made for possible shifts in the position of these zones as a consequence of "pluvial" and "post-pluvial" climatic change if the time scale is extended that far back.

As part of this pattern of foraging and protocultivation, we can envisage a gradual transition from the exploitation of wild plants in their natural habitats to the tending of plants redistributed casually near camp sites and eventually deliberately planted. This gradual process is particularly easy to envisage in the case of yams and other vegetatively reproduced plants which sprout readily from discarded parts. It is possible that at an early stage root crops and oil palm were found to be both nutritionally and ecologically complementary and that they became closely associated in a pattern of protocultivation. Major dependence on wild foods, both animal and vegetable, no doubt persisted a long time, but gradually, as domestication proceeded and preferred forms of yams and other plants were selected, dependence on the products of cultivation increased, and the range of wild foods gathered was reduced. Certain forest species which provided special wants, such as kola and the West African coffees, also became the object of selection and eventual cultivation.

It is difficult to hypothesize about the type or types of food-producing systems that may first have crystallized out of this tradition of foraging and protocultivation, but both swidden and fixed-plot horticulture can be regarded as prototypes for the earliest systems of cultivation. I have argued elsewhere that in terms of the general evolution of agriculture in the tropics, the cultivation of fixed-plots or "gardens" in the immediate vicinity of dwellings is likely usually to have preceded the development of swidden systems, because small domestic plots afford the cultivator easier opportunity than swidden clearings to tend and harvest individual plants at optimum times, to ward off animal and human predators, and to fertilize the soil, whether intentionally or not, with domestic refuse (Harris 1973: 399–401). By comparison, swidden plots demand more expenditure of time and energy in clearance and cultivation, as well as in traveling to and from them. Cultivation close to dwellings also implies the transfer of potential cultigens from their natural habitats to the man-modified habitats of the settlement area. This would tend to reduce natural selective pressures and to increase the chances of survival of less well-adapted variants with recessive characters, such as those with imperfect seed-dispersal mechanisms, which would then become available for human selection. It may also lead to greater spatial separation from parent populations and, as Heiser has stressed (1969: 229), reduce opportunities for free intercrossing with wild relatives, thus allowing the more rapid fixation of characteristics valuable to man. Temporary swidden clearings located at some distance from the settlement in less modified habitats would not have isolated potential cultigens so effectively from their wild relatives, nor, it may be argued, would such plots have been deliberately cleared, planted, and harvested until the concept of cultivation was itself well established and some cultigens of evidently superior value to wild plants were available.

Thus, the tending of small domestic gardens close to dwellings, rather than long-term fallowing, is more likely to represent man's earliest system of cultivation in the tropics. However, this argument has greater force in relation to vegetatively reproduced plants and seed-reproduced climbers, shrubs, and trees, which have relatively long life cycles and provide multiple fruit from each plant, than it does to annual cereals and other short-lived crops which require many plants to make up a worthwhile harvest. Domestic plots would have provided ideal sites for the close and continuing attention to individual plants and clones that the domestication of the former type of crop presupposes, whereas the latter could be more appropriately cultivated in larger plots specifically cleared for the purpose. Swidden may have provided a means of large-scale cultivation of plants of relatively short life cycle which were gradually becoming established as staple crops, and expansion from domestic to swidden plots may have been precipitated or accentuated by population increase and intergroup warfare. In the vegecultural zone of West Africa, therefore, the swidden cultivation of yams may only have become a dominant mode of food production following a long period of small-scale experimental cultivation of domestic plots during which the yams, as well as oil palm and perhaps other plants, such as okra, roselle, fluted gourd, and kola, were domesticated and incorporated into a pattern of deliberate food production.

The Rice Zone

Table 2 suggests the relative antiquity of the few cultigens that are principally associated with the rice zone in West Africa. Many of the crops ascribed to the other zones are also cultivated in the rice zone, but they do not attain comparable importance there. Cultigens of American origin are less significant than in the vegecultural zone; the only one that is chiefly associated with the rice zone is avocado, which appears not to have been introduced to Africa until the late nineteenth century (Purseglove 1968: 193). The citrus fruits from Asia represent a more important group of tree crops. Some of the cultivated species were introduced to Africa in pre-Colonial times, but whether any of them reached West Africa before the Europeans remains uncertain. The lime is the most widespread, and it and the lemon may have been introduced to the interior by the Arabs. Sweet and bitter oranges were probably introduced to the coastal zone by the Portuguese (Dalziel 1937: 305–306).

Rice, which gives traditional agriculture in this zone its distinctive character, has a dual origin. The "white" rices belong to the Asiatic species *Oryza sativa*, whereas the "red" rices of the species *O. glaberrima* are native to West Africa. The question of when and where Asiatic rice was introduced to West Africa has been examined by Portères (1950: 492–493, 1962: 200–201), Dresch (1949: 297–298), and Mohr (1969: 33–35) who conclude that it did not reach West Africa until the early Colonial period, although it was introduced to the East African coast by the Arabs prior to A.D. 1000. The Portuguese are thought to have brought Asiatic rice to the West African coast early in the sixteenth century, and Portères suggests that it spread into the rice zone from two principal areas of entry: one between the Casamance and Cacheo Rivers along the present boundary between Senegal and Portuguese Guinea, and the other in present-day Sierra Leone and adjacent parts of Guinea and Liberia.

It is clear, however, that prior to the arrival of Asiatic rice, the cultivation of African rice was well established, both within the rice zone and in western parts of the sorghum-millet zone. Portères (1950: 490–492, 1962: 197–199; this volume) demonstrates that African rice, which derives from a wild and weedy annual species (*O. barthii* A. Chev. and Roehr. = *O. breviligulata* A. Chev. and Roehr.) native to the semiarid interior from Cape Verde to east of Lake Chad, has a primary center of variation in the area of the upper Gambia and Casamance Rivers. He postulates that it was initially taken into cultivation as "floating" rice in the area of the inland delta and subsequently spread by way of the valleys of the upper Niger and Senegal to the secondary center of variation where "non-floating" races were selected and techniques of cultivating rice in brackish water evolved. At the same time the dispersal of cultivated forms to other areas, including the Guinea Highlands, led to the selection of "upland" races adapted to dry cultivation. Portères further suggests (1950: 49; this volume) that rice cultivation supported the "megalithic civilization" of Senegambia which, from indirect archaeological evidence, is claimed to have flourished between 1500 and 800 B.C., and that, accordingly, the origins of rice cultivation in the inland delta of the Niger date back at least to 1500 B.C.

By the beginning of the Colonial period the cultivation of "wet" rice had spread eastward through the coastal swamps towards the Bandama River, and "dry" upland rice was being extensively cultivated in the interior. Thus, when Asiatic rice was introduced, it was accepted in the rice zone, where techniques appropriate to its cultivation had already been developed, but generally rejected in the vegecultural zone where maize, which was well suited to mounding and other aspects of root crop cultivation, found readier acceptance (Portères 1950: 492).

There is little direct evidence concerning the nature of the earliest food-producing systems of the rice zone, but it is possible to hypothesize from knowledge of existing traditional systems. The semiaquatic habitat of the floating rice, from which cultivated African rice is apparently derived, implies that this rice was first cultivated by hydraulic techniques, and the traditional system under which the seasonal flood regime of the Niger is still exploited for growing rice in the area of the inland delta provides a model for this earliest phase. Indeed, the existing system of *crue* and *décrue* cultivation in this area may be essentially unchanged from the earliest period of rice exploitation, partly as a consequence — as Portères points out (1950: 491) — of the genetic stability characteristic of a primary center of variation. Thus, techniques for the floodwater cultivation of rice were probably first developed in this area and subsequently extended, on a smaller scale, to other valleys subject to seasonal flooding. Likewise it appears probable that the first development of rice cultivation in tidal swamps and inlets took place in Senegambia, and that this practice later spread to appropriate parts of the southwestern coast.

But the process that brought about the most extensive spread of rice cultivation and gave shape to the rice zone as a whole was probably the selection of dry varieties and their incorporation into swidden systems of production. The transition from small-scale, stable systems of hydraulic cultivation in lowland areas to an extensive, mobile pattern of rice cultivation in upland and lowland forests marks a major step in the agricultural transformation of this part of West Africa; but it also raises the question of what, if any, food-producing systems were already established in the areas penetrated by rice-swidden cultivation. It is possible that, prior to the arrival of rice, large areas were occupied only by foragers who practiced no cultivation, although this seems improbable if arguments for the antiquity of protocultivation in the adjacent vegecultural zone are accepted. It is more likely that at least the proto-cultivation in domestic plots of plants native to the forest was already under way and that, once introduced, rice-swidden attained dominance as a more effective food-producing system. It is also possible that rice replaced other cereal crops which had reached the coast earlier from the interior, for there is some evidence that Guinea corn sorghums and possibly certain millets which exist as relict species in the southern Ivory Coast first gave way to African rice and were later almost eclipsed by the invasion of Asiatic rice (Portères 1950: 492).

The Sorghum-Millet Zone

It is clear from Table 2 that traditional agriculture in the sorghum-millet zone depends primarily on crops of African origin and that Asian and American species make only a minor contribution. The only non-African additions to the complex of cereals on which traditional agriculture in the zone is based are wheats and barley, which are thought to derive originally from southwestern Asia. They are only grown as minor crops, chiefly along the southern margin of the Sahara. They were probably introduced early in prehistoric times, but failed to spread ex-tensively because they were ill adapted to local regimes of day-length, temperature, and precipitation. Early in the prehistoric period, onions and shallots, both probably of west Asian origin, may also have reached the northern part of the zone where they are mainly grown today under small-scale irrigation.

Colonial additions include: the South American groundnut, which was probably introduced to the coast by the Portuguese and is now an important item in both subsistence and commercial agriculture in the interior; another tropical American pulse, the jackbean, which probably reached West Africa early in the Colonial period; chili or bird pepper, which, like its close relative the sweet chili, also derives from tropical America; and the mango from south Asia, which is valued for its fruit and widely planted along roadsides in the interior. However, none of these introduced crops has fundamentally altered traditional agriculture in the sorghum-millet zone which remains today essentially African.

As the question of the origins of the cereal crops which dominate this zone is the subject of specialist contributions to this volume, it is only touched upon here. Harlan, Stemler, and de Wet (this volume) and de Wet and Harlan (1971) conclude that sorghum may have been first domesticated south of the Sahara in the savanna zone which stretches eastward from Lake Chad. Climatically, this lies within the long dry-season zone which experiences seven and a half to ten arid months (Figure 5). If this conclusion is correct, it implies that sorghum first came under cultivation outside West Africa and that it later spread to, and was widely adopted in, the semiarid and subhumid lands west of Lake Chad. On the other hand, the millets which are traditionally grown in West Africa appear, with the exception of finger millet, to have been domesticated within the region (Figure 5). The probable Ethiopian and East African origin of the latter accords with its eastern distribution as a traditional crop in West Africa (Figure 4). It is valued principally as a beer grain and was probably diffused westward in historic times from the area of the upper Nile along the semiarid zone as far as Lake Chad (Portères 1950: 498, 1955a: 479, 1962: 204–205; this volume).

Pearl millet, which is the most widely cultivated millet in West Africa, has two conspicuous areas of interaction between the wild, weedy, and cultivated races (Harlan 1971: 471). The western of these two areas (Figure 5), which occupies part of Senegal and southern Mauritania, is probably the main source area of the pearl millet cultivated in West Africa; and within it, at sites along the Tichitt escarpment in south-central Mauritania, Munson (1968, 1970; this volume) has recovered evidence, in the form of impressions in pottery, of the collection and cultivation of *Pennisetum*. In the lower levels excavated, *Pennisetum* occurs very sparsely in association with other grasses presumed to be wild or semiwild; but it increases to 61 percent of all impressions in the phase dated by radiocarbon to between 1000 and 900 B.C. — when many of the specimens have definite characteristics of domesticated grain — and by the succeeding phase, between about 900 and 700 B.C., accounts for 82 percent of all impressions (Munson, this volume). This can be interpreted as evidence for a transition from a foraging economy in which subsistence was based partly on the gathering of wild grasses to one in which the cultivation of millet became important, but whether it indicates local domestication or the introduction and adoption of already domesticated *Pennisetum* cannot yet be determined.

The only other millet that is widely cultivated in West Africa is fonio. It is grown from Cape Verde to Lake Chad, but principally in uplands within the sorghum-millet zone (Figure 4). Its greatest varietal diversity occurs today in the region of the Fouta Djallon plateau and the valleys of the upper Senegal and Niger, and Portères (1955a: 479–

480) suggests that prior to the tenth century A.D. it may have been cultivated mainly in the area of the inland delta of the Niger where it was probably first domesticated (Portères, this volume). Black fonio, on the other hand, has an extremely restricted distribution, being cultivated at present only in the Atacora Mountains of Dahomey and on the Jos Plateau. It is grown mainly as a beer grain and may have originated as a cultivated plant in the Aïr region of the southern Sahara, subsequently spreading south and finally retreating in the Colonial period to its present residual areas as a result of unsuccessful competition with introduced maize (Portères 1950: 499). The remaining millet cultivated in West Africa is *Brachiaria deflexa*. It normally occurs wild but is also grown to a limited extent in Guinea (Harlan 1971: 471). Like the fonio millets, it may have been more widely cultivated in the past and subsequently displaced by more productive cereals. It is drought-tolerant, and its presence as a minor food item at the Tichitt sites from about 1100 to 400 B.C. (Munson, this volume) suggests that it may have a long history as a semiwild or cultivated species in the drier parts of the sorghum-millet zone.

In addition to the cereals, the crop complement of the zone includes a distinctive group of nutritionally valuable pulses thought to be of African origin. Little is known of their areas of origin and time of first cultivation in West Africa, but, of the four pulses listed in Table 2 as African in origin, only the two groundnuts appear to be probably native to West Africa. They have been found wild in the area of the Nigeria-Cameroon boundary (Hepper 1963), and this may be where they were first domesticated (Figure 5), although wild populations of the Bambara groundnut have also been reported from elsewhere in tropical Africa (Doku and Karikari 1971: 255–256). The cowpea has probably been long cultivated in West Africa; remains of it have been recovered from deposits in a rock shelter near Kintampo in Ghana which date to about 1400 B.C. (Flight, this volume). There are also existing wild forms of it which are gathered (Stanton 1962: 256–257), but where within tropical Africa it may have originated as a crop is unknown. Still less is known of the origin of the pigeon pea which, although thought to be native to Africa, has its greatest diversity of cultivars in India (Purseglove 1968: 236–237). Likewise sesame, which is widely cultivated in West Africa for its oil-yielding and edible seeds, may have been first domesticated in either Africa or India (Nayer and Mehra 1970); whereas black beniseed almost certainly originated in West Africa, which is the only region in which it is cultivated (Dalziel 1937: 26; Portères 1950: 501).

Little can be said with assurance about the origins of food-producing systems in the sorghum-millet zone, but a few speculations may be offered. On the basis of the present exiguous evidence it appears likely that pearl millet and possibly some of the other millets such as fonio and *Brachiaria deflexa* were among the first plants to be cultivated in prehistoric times. Perhaps their cultivation was begun by simple hydraulic techniques such as floodwater farming in river- and lake-side situations or as dry-farmed crops associated with flood-farmed rice. The suggestion that the early cultivation of fonio may have taken place largely in the area of the inland delta of the Niger and that black fonio may have been first cultivated in the Aïr region of the Sahara lends support to this view. The extensive diffusion of millets was probably delayed until they came to be cultivated by swidden methods; once this occurred, their spread throughout the zone and even into the more humid coastal areas became possible. The assumed introduction of sorghum from east of Lake Chad may well have hastened this process, especially in the less arid areas where it is dominant today; finger millet intruded into the eastern part of the zone probably at a much later time within the historic period.

When and how the African pulses and oil-seed plants were incorporated into food-producing systems remains unknown; but they are commonly grown by swidden methods, and some, such as bambara groundnut, are notably drought-tolerant. At least some of them may well have been components of the earliest swidden systems to evolve in the drier parts of the zone. When small-scale irrigation began also remains unknown, but it is probably ancient along the southern margin of the Sahara where its development may have been associated with the early introduction of west Asian crops across the desert.

THE ECOLOGICAL RELATIONSHIPS OF SWIDDEN SYSTEMS

It is clear from the foregoing discussion of traditional systems of plant food production that in West Africa swidden is practiced more widely than any other system, even though in areas of dense population long fallow cycles have long since given way to more intensive systems of cultivation. In the past, swidden techniques were practiced over a still greater proportion of the total cultivated area, being spatially dominant in all three of the major crop zones. It is therefore likely that closer examination of the ecological relationships that exist between different swidden systems will make a valuable — if only indirect—contribution to the understanding of agricultural origins in West Africa. In the last part of this study, therefore, these relationships are briefly examined as a prelude to a summary of the general hypothesis.

In the swidden systems of West Africa the major ecological contrast is between those systems in which seed crops predominate and those in which vegetatively reproduced crops do so. If the crops introduced in historic times are disregarded, the former systems include those based primarily on millets, sorghum, and African rice, whereas the latter comprise the yam-based systems of the vegecultural zone. The ecological differences between these two types of swidden include structural, edaphic, and nutritional contrasts. In vegecultural swidden plots, as has already been indicated, species diversity tends to be greater than in seed-cultural plots, plant stratification more intricate, and the canopy of vegetation more nearly closed. Recent introductions have added to crop diversity, but even in prehistoric times it was probably greater within the vegecultural zone than elsewhere; certainly life-form diversity would have been greater there, stratification more complex, and ground cover more complete. Compared to seed-cultural plots, vegecultural plots possess greater ecological stability in the sense that their plant and animal populations are less liable to major fluctuations (Preston 1969). This tendency is accentuated by the fact that opportunities for soil erosion are reduced by the more complete and seasonally persistent ground cover and by the practice of mounding which is much more usual in areas of vegeculture than in areas of seed culture.

The two types of swidden also appear to make contrasted demands on soil fertility. Vegecultural systems are dominated by carbohydrate-rich root and tree crops which tend to make smaller demands on plant nutrients than the more protein-rich cereals which dominate seed-cultural systems (Table 3). At harvest the seed-crop cultivator is likely to remove a greater fraction of fertility for consumption than is the vegeculturalist when he digs up his tubers, corms, or rhizomes. This may be one of the reasons for the tendency of vegecultural swidden plots to be cultivated for longer periods without excessive decline of yields than seed-cultural plots. Another reason is that the latter, with their open-canopy structure, are more liable to weed invasion and soil erosion. Thus structural and edaphic factors may combine to make seed-cultural swidden less durable and more prone to relatively rapid shifts from one temporary clearing to another. Other things being equal one may infer therefore that seed-culture will exhibit a greater tendency than vegeculture to expand into new areas.

This inference is strengthened if the nutritional effectiveness of the

Table 3.   Food values of selected crops indigenous or introduced in pre-Colonial times to West Africa (Sources: Coursey 1967; Latham 1965; Purseglove 1968, 1972)

	Calories (per 100 g. edible)	Protein (percent)	Carbo-hydrate (percent)	Fat (percent)
	THE VEGECULTURAL ZONE			
Yam (*D. rotundata*)	120	1.5	23.0	0.1
Cocoyam (taro)	111	0.5	27.0	—
Plantain	128	1.0	31.0	0.2
Oil palm oil	900	—	—	100.0
Kola (*C. nitida*)		9.0	74.0	2.0
Coffee (*C. arabica*)		13.0	9.0	12.0
	THE RICE AND SORGHUM-MILLET ZONES			
Rice (*O. sativa*)	354	8.0	77.0	1.5
Sorghum	355	10.4	71.0	3.4
Pearl millet	363	11.0	69.0	5.0
Bambara groundnut	367	18.0	60.0	6.0
Cowpea	340	22.0	60.0	1.5
Pigeon pea	328	20.0	58.0	2.0
Average: cereals and pulses	351	14.9	65.8	3.2
Sesame seeds	592	20.0	16.0	50.0

two types of swidden is also compared. As Table 3 indicates, the average protein content of the staple cereal and pulse crops is 14.9 percent, whereas that of the African yams is only 1.5 percent. However, yam consumption is often so high in the vegecultural zone — commonly one kilogram per head per day — that yams alone contribute appreciable amounts of such necessary dietary requirements as calcium, vitamin C, iron, and even protein, although the value of the protein contribution is limited by its low content of essential amino acids (Coursey 1967: 168–169). Thus, eaten in quantity, yams provide more than just a high caloric intake. Nevertheless, they and the associated root crops represent far less adequately balanced food sources than the combined cereals and pulses of the seed-cultural zones, and deficiency diseases, particularly kwashiorkor, are now prevalent in the vegecultural zone. Whether this manifestation of protein deficiency is a recent phenomenon associated with increased populations in the zone is uncertain. Coursey (1967: 169) suggests that the spread of kwashiorkor may be related to the displacement of yams by manioc which is more easily grown but contains still less protein (0.7 to 1.0 percent). In the past it is probable that vegeculturalists in West Africa obtained a larger supply of protein from fish and from wild terrestrial and aquatic animals than they do now and that fishing and hunting long remained important subsistence activities, as they do among many South American vegeculturalists today (Harris 1971: 478; Steward and Faron 1959: 291–298).

Table 4 summarizes data from the late 1940's on the relative contribution of vegetatively reproduced crops, seed crops, and animal foods to the caloric intake of three population groups in Nigeria. A strikingly clear contrast emerges between the northern seed farmers, who obtain 85.7 percent of their calories from guinea corn and pearl millet, and the southern vegeculturalists, who obtain 75.5 percent of their calories from manioc and yams; but of still greater interest are the southern vegeculturalist-fishermen who obtain 20 percent of their calories from fish. Although these three sample groups are not representative of traditional dietary patterns throughout West Africa, they do epitomize the major nutritional contrast between the seed-cultural and vegecultural zones; and, within the latter, the Soragbemi fishermen may represent a formerly more widespread strategy for securing a better balanced food supply between animal protein and vegetable carbohydrates. In the vegecultural zone some protein is also secured from the seeds of

Table 4.   Caloric contribution of different foods to the diets of three population groups in Nigeria (Source: Johnston 1958: 193–6)

Kontagora seed farmers		Illu vegeculturalists		Soragbemi vege-culturalist-fishermen	
(N. Nigeria)		(S. Nigeria)		(S. Nigeria)	
Average daily caloric intake	2,431	2,252		2,191	
Percent of caloric intake					
Guinea corn sorghum	74.4	Manioc	48.3	Manioc	54.3
Pearl millet	11.3	Yams	27.2	Yams	3.4
Total sorghum and millet	85.7			Cocoyams	0.6
Maize	5.9			Sweet potatoes	1.2
Total cereals	91.6	Total roots	75.5	Total roots	59.5
Other seed crops	5.9	Plantain	0.6	Plantain	0.7
Sweet potatoes	0.7	Sugarcane	0.1	Sugarcane	0.1
Manioc	0.3	Oil palm	13.5	Oil palm	13.1
Beef, milk and butter	0.8	Other seed crops	3.1	Other seed crops	6.1
Fish	0.1	Fish and monkey	3.6	Fish	20.0
Unmeasured items	0.6	Unmeasured items	3.6	Unmeasured items	0.5
Total	100.0	Total	100.0	Total	100.0

wild or semiwild tree crops such as the stimulants coffee and kola (Table 3), and palm oil not only provides essential fat for cooking but is also the principal source of vitamin A. A considerable measure of dependence on wild animals, fish, and wild or semiwild tree crops for protein and other nutritional needs sets limits to the ecological adaptability of vegecultural swidden and makes the occupation of habitats in which these resources are available advantageous; in the case of dependence on wild animals and fish, this is likely to enhance the adaptive advantages to vegeculturalists of riparian, coastal, and swamp- and savanna-edge habitats. Conversely, seed culture provides a better balanced and more self-sufficient vegetable diet which does not demand the same level of protein supplementation from wild sources. Its adoption thus frees communities from major dependence on fishing, hunting, and collecting, and makes possible expansion into habitats where protein from wild plants and animals is less readily available.

Consideration of these structural, edaphic, and nutritional contrasts between vegecultural and seed-cultural swidden systems suggests that the former tend to be relatively stable, whereas the latter are inherently more mobile and liable to spatial expansion. One might therefore predict, on the basis of ecological inferences alone, that in a region such as West Africa, where seed culture and vegeculture coexist, seed-cultural swidden should gradually gain spatial ascendancy over vegecultural swidden. This ecological inference adds significance to the indirect evidence which has already been noted for the spread of seed culture, and it is incorporated as an explanatory postulate in the general hypothesis on West African agricultural origins which can now be recapitulated.

THE ORIGINS OF AGRICULTURE IN WEST AFRICA: A SUMMARY HYPOTHESIS

It is suggested that within West Africa two broadly contrasted traditions of plant cultivation have evolved over a period of several millennia. In the southern, subhumid zone an essentially vegecultural system of food production emerged gradually out of an ancient substratum of proto-cultivation in which the collection and casual replanting of yams and other tuberous plants was an important subsistence activity. Forager populations living along forest margins and in streamside locations were the progenitors of yam domestication, and the beginnings of the process date back to Paleolithic times. The origin of yam-based vegeculture as the predominant system of food production is more recent, and the catalytic factor in the shift from casual harvesting to deliberate cultivation may have been contact with seed-crop cultivators from the dry interior. It is equally possible that the transition occurred independently of external influence as a result of accentuated pressure on wild food resources, perhaps as a consequence of population increase. The exploitation and spread of the oil palm accelerated the emergence of yam-based vegeculture as a dominant system of food production because palm oil provides both fat and vitamin A to supplement the carbohydrates derived from the root crops. In view of its nutritional significance and its relatively good chance of preservation, archaeological search for early evidence of the oil palm could make an important contribution to knowledge of agricultural origins in West Africa.

The earliest sites of yam-based vegeculture were small domestic plots in which other food-producing plants of different life form, including perhaps such plants as oil palm, kola, coffee, roselle, okra, and fluted gourd, were also raised. Cultivation by swidden methods was a later development as yams and other plants became established as staple crops. The system as a whole long remained partially dependent on wild food sources, especially for protein, and it retained a large measure of stability. It evolved to a high level of ecological, social, and ceremonial complexity within the vegecultural zone, extending into the more humid forest areas but failing to spread beyond the zone into other environmentally appropriate regions of Africa.

In the arid and semiarid zones of the interior, seed-cultural systems based on the cultivation of indigenous cereals and pulses gradually replaced preexisting patterns of foraging which relied substantially on gathered wild grasses and other seeds. The earliest domestication of African rice, and possibly of some of the indigenous millets, was achieved under conditions of simple floodwater cultivation, probably in the area of the inland delta of the Niger. Such hydraulic cultivation remained stable and localized in appropriate riparian and lacustrine situations, and it was not until varieties of dry rice were selected and cultivated by swidden methods that the large-scale spread of the crop into the rice zone occurred. A further, more specialized development of wet rice cultivation in tidal swamps took place in Senegambia and later spread on a small scale south and east down the coast.

Pearl millet, the fonio millets, and *Brachiaria deflexa* were also cultivated early by swidden methods and spread extensively in both the sorghum-millet zone and the rice zone, in the latter probably before rice itself. They, together with rice, are relatively nutrient-demanding, and their cultivation as swidden crops is associated with progressive degradation of vegetation cover and with soil erosion. At an early stage, but probably after pearl millet had been domesticated locally, sorghum was incorporated into the developing pattern of seed-crop production. It reached the area from east of Lake Chad and subsequently became the preferred staple in the more humid parts of the interior. Similarly, finger millet reached the area from farther east, but only in historic times; and it failed to spread far beyond Lake Chad.

One can thus envisage the early emergence of two essentially indigenous traditions of cultivation in West Africa: one ecologically stable and adapted to subhumid and humid woodlands and forests in the south, and the other unstable and expanding — perhaps in successive crop waves — from its areas of origin in the dry interior towards the coast. At present so little is known about the relative antiquity of these two traditions that the problem of dating must be left in abeyance, but it is clear that some form of seed-crop cultivation was underway in the interior at least by the second millennium B.C. The question of whether seed culture or the impetus towards it was first transmitted across the Sahara is also incapable of solution at present, although the strongly indigenous character of West African seed-crop associations argues against external origins. An attempt to recover and date early evidence of wheat, barley, sorghum, and millets at southern Saharan sites would help to resolve the question.

If the ecological thesis of expansive seed culture and stable vegeculture as ancient and contrasted traditions of food production in West Africa is acceptable, one should go on to consider what socioeconomic factors may have underlain the postulated spread of seed-crop systems. Such a question is, however, beyond the scope of this study, although one important factor may have been the different response of the two traditions to increases in population.

The hypothesis summarized here thus remains an invitation to enquiry. It is at least partly capable of direct archaeological testing, and it points towards the potential significance for detailed study of certain areas and problems. It is hoped that it may also stimulate questioning comparisons with other parts of Africa, such as Ethiopia (Harlan 1969), where traditional seed-cultural and vegecultural systems coexist.

REFERENCES

ALEXANDER, J., D. G. COURSEY
1969 "The origins of yam cultivation," in *The domestication and exploitation of plants and animals*. Edited by P. J. Ucko and G. W. Dimbleby, 405–425. London: Duckworth.

BAKER, H. G.
1962 Comments on the thesis that there was a major centre of plant domestication near the headwaters of the River Niger. *Journal of African History* 3:229–233.

BOSERUP, E.
1965 *The conditions of agricultural growth*. London: Allen and Unwin.

BUCHANAN, K. M., J. C. PUGH
1955 *Land and people in Nigeria*. London: University of London Press.

BURKILL, I. H.
1938 The contact of the Portuguese with African food plants which gave words such as "yam" to European languages. *Proc. Linn. Soc. London* 150:84–95.

CHEVALIER, A.
1936 Contribution à l'étude de quelques espèces africaines du genre *Dioscorea. Bull. du Mus. Nat. de l'Hist. Nat.* 2è serie, 8:520–551.

CONKLIN, H. C.
1963 *The study of shifting cultivation*. Panamerican Union Studies and Monographs 6. Washington, D.C.

COURSEY, D. G.
1967 *Yams*. London: Longmans.

COURSEY, D. C., C. K. COURSEY
1967 *Yams*. London: Longmans.

DALZIEL, J. M.
1937 *The useful plants of west tropical Africa*. London: Crown Agents for the Colonies.

DAVIES, O.
1960 The neolithic revolution in tropical Africa. *Transactions of the Historical Society of Ghana* 4:14–20.
1967 *West Africa before the Europeans: archaeology and prehistory*. London: Methuen.
1968 The origins of agriculture in West Africa. *Current Anthropology* 9:479–482.

DE WET, J. M. J., J. R. HARLAN
1971 The origin and domestication of *Sorghum bicolor. Economic Botany* 25:128–135.

DOKU, E. V., S. K. KARIKARI
1971 Bambarra groundnut. *Economic Botany* 25:255–262.

DRESCH, J.
1949 La riziculture en Afrique occidentale. *Annales de Géographie* 58:294–312.

FLIGHT, C.
1970 Excavations at Kintampo. *West African Archaeological Newsletter* 12:71–73.

FLOYD, B.
1964 Terrace agriculture in Eastern Nigeria: the case of the Maku. *Nigerian Geographical Journal* 7:91–108.
1969 *Eastern Nigeria.* London: Macmillan.

HARLAN, J. R.
1969 Ethiopia: a center of diversity. *Economic Botany* 23:309–314.
1971 Agricultural origins: centers and noncenters. *Science* 174:468–474.

HARLAN, J. R., J. PASQUEREAU
1969 Décrue agriculture in Mali. *Economic Botany* 23:70–74.

HARRIS, D. R.
1969 "Agricultural systems, ecosystems and the origins of agriculture," in *The domestication and exploitation of plants and animals.* Edited by P. J. Ucko and G. W. Dimbleby, 3–15. London: Duckworth.
1971 The ecology of swidden cultivation in the upper Orinoco rain forest, Venezuela. *Geographical Review* 61:475–495.
1972a "Swidden systems and settlement," in *Man, settlement and urbanism.* Edited by P. J. Ucko, R. Tringham and G. W. Dimbleby, 245–262. London: Duckworth.
1972b The origins of agriculture in the tropics. *American Scientist* 60: 180–193.
1973 "The prehistory of tropical agriculture: an ethnoecological model," in *The explanation of culture change: models in prehistory.* Edited by C. Renfrew, 391–417. London: Duckworth.

HARTLEY, C. W. S.
1967 *The oil palm.* London: Longmans.

HEISER, C. B., JR.
1969 Some considerations of early plant domestication. *BioScience* 19: 228–231.

HEPPER, F. N.
1963 Plants of the 1957–58 West African Expedition, part two. The Bambara groundnut (*Voandzeia subterranea*) and Kersting's groundnut (*Kerstingiella geocarpa*) wild in West Africa. *Kew Bulletin* 16:395–407.

IRVINE, F. R.
1961 *Woody plants of Ghana.* London: Oxford University Press.

JEFFREYS, M. D. W.
1957 The origin of the Portuguese word zaburro as their name for maize. *Bull. de l'I.F.A.N.* 29(B):111–136.
1963 How ancient is West African maize? *Africa* 33:115–131.
1971 Maize and the Mande myth. *Current Anthropology* 12:291–320.

JOHNSTON, B. F.
1958 *The staple food economies of western tropical Africa.* Stanford: Stanford University Press.

JONES, W. O.
1953 A map of manioc in Africa. *Geographical Review* 43:112–114.
1959 *Manioc in Africa.* Stanford: Stanford University Press.

KEAY, R. W. J.
 1959   *Vegetation map of Africa south of the Tropic of Cancer.* London:
        Oxford University Press.

LATHAM, M.
 1965   *Human nutrition in tropical Africa.* Rome: F.A.O.

MC MASTER, D. N.
 1962   Speculations on the coming of the banana to Uganda. *Journal of
        Tropical Geography* 16:57–69.

MIÈGE, J.
 1954   Les cultures vivrières en Afrique Occidentale. *Les Cahiers
        d'Outre-Mer* (January–March):25–50.

MIRACLE, M. P.
 1963   Interpretation of evidence on the introduction of maize into West
        Africa. *Africa* 33:132–135.
 1965   The introduction and spread of maize in Africa. *Journal of Afri-
        can History* 6:39–55.
 1966   *Maize in tropical Africa.* Madison: University of Wisconsin Press.

MOHR, B.
 1969   *Die Reiskultur in Westafrika.* Munich: Weltforum.

MUNSON, P. J.
 1968   Recent archaeological research in the Dhar Tichitt region of
        south-central Mauritania. *West African Archaeological Newsletter*
        10:6–13.
 1970   Corrections and additional comments concerning the "Tichitt
        Tradition." *West African Archaeological Newsletter* 12:47–48.

NAYER, N. M., K. L. MEHRA
 1970   Sesame: its uses, botany, cytogenetics, and origin. *Economic Bo-
        tany* 24:20–31.

NETTING, R. MC C.
 1968   *Hill farmers of Nigeria: cultural ecology of the Kofyar of the Jos
        Plateau.* Seattle: University of Washington Press.

PAULME, D.
 1954   *Les gens du riz: Kissi de Haute-Guinée Française.* Paris: Libraire
        Plon.

PORTÈRES, R.
 1950   Vieilles agricultures de l'Afrique intertropicale. *L'Agronomie Tro-
        picale* 5:489–507.
 1955a Les céréales mineures du genre *Digitaria* en Afrique et en Eu-
        rope, III: Ecologie générale et agriccle. *J. d'Agric. Trop. et de
        Bot. Appliquée.* 2(10–11):477–510.
 1955b L'introduction du maïs en Afrique. *J. d'Agric. Trop. et de Bot.
        Appliquée* 2(5–6):221–231.
 1962   Berceaux agricoles primaires sur le continent africain. *Journal of
        African History* 3:195–210.

PRESTON, F. W.
 1969   "Diversity and stability in the biological world," in *Diversity and
        stability in ecological systems.* Edited by G. M. Woodwell and H.

H. Smith, 1–12. Upton, New York: Brookhaven National Laboratory.

PURSEGLOVE, J. W.
1968   *Tropical crops Dicotyledons*, two volumes. London: Longmans.
1972   *Tropical crops Monocotyledons*, two volumes. London: Longmans.

SAUER, C. O.
1952   *Agricultural origins and dispersals*. New York: American Geographical Society.

SCHNELL, R.
1957   *Plantes alimentaires et vie agricole de l'Afrique noire*. Paris: Editions Larose.

SIMMONDS, N. W.
1962   *The evolution of the bananas*. London: Longmans.

STANTON, W. R.
1962   The analysis of the present distribution of varietal variation in maize, sorghum, and cowpea in Nigeria as an aid to the study of tribal movement. *Journal of African History* 3:251–262.

STEWARD, J. H., L. C. FARON
1959   *Native peoples of South America*. New York: McGraw-Hill.

TROLL, C., KH. PAFFEN
1963   "Map 5: seasonal climates of the earth," in *Weltkarten zur Klimakunde*. By H. C. Landsberg, et al. Heidelberg: Springer.

VERMEER, D. E.
1970   Population pressure and crop rotational changes among the Tiv of Nigeria. *Annals of the Association of American Geographers* 60:299–314.

WHITE, S.
1941   The agricultural economy of the hill pagans of Dikwa Emirate, Cameroons (British Mandate). *Empire J. of Exper. Agric.* 9:65–72.

WILLETT, F.
1962   The introduction of maize into West Africa: an assessment of recent evidence. *Africa* 32:1–13.

Social Anthropology and the Reconstruction of Prehistoric Land Use Systems in Tropical Africa: A Cautionary Case Study from Zambia

THAYER SCUDDER

As a social anthropologist-cultural ecologist, my closest affinity to the topic of this conference is my interest in the dynamics and complexity of contemporary systems of land use among African farmers. I use the words "dynamics and complexity" intentionally for they provide the theme for my contribution. While I share the fascination of my colleagues with origins and marvel at their ability to reconstruct so much from so little, I would like to flash a warning signal based on some of the results of recent research among woodland savanna cultivators in Central Africa. The warning is not for those who attempt to reconstruct the origins and dispersals of specific plant domesticates, but rather for those who attempt to use information from studies in plant genetics, ecology, and anthropology to reconstruct former systems of land use, and to speculate on ethnic affiliations and associated patterns of social organization.

For the past sixteen years Elizabeth Colson and I have been carrying out a long-term study of continuity and change among the Gwembe Tonga in the upper or Gwembe portion of the middle Zambezi Valley. Of a total population of approximately 85,000 Tonga living in the valley in 1956, 56,000 were relocated over the following two years in connection with the

Through 1963 this research was sponsored by the Rhodes-Livingstone Institute (now the Institute for African Studies of the University of Zambia). While the Institute has continued to provide us with substantial assistance until the present, financial support since 1965 has come from the Social Science Research Council, the American Council of Learned Societies, the Food and Agriculture Organization of the United Nations, the University of California (Berkeley), the California Institute of Technology, and the National Science Foundation. I wish to thank my colleagues Elizabeth Colson, Brian Fagan, C. S. Lancaster, and Stuart Marks for reading and commending on this article.

construction of the Kariba Dam. We are primarily interested in assessing the impact of resettlement and national development on these people, and especially on the 31,000 who were relocated on the Zambian (formerly Northern Rhodesian) side of the lake. Our approach was to make a detailed baseline study of selected communities prior to resettlement and then to follow them up in their new homes after their removal. The twelve month baseline study was completed in September, 1957, with one or both of us involved in revisits during 1960, 1962–1963, 1965, 1967, 1968, 1970, 1971, 1972, and 1973.

Because of an insufficiency of land around the lake shore margin, approximately 6,000 north bank Tonga from Chipepo Chieftaincy were resettled below the dam in the Lusitu area (Map 1). The majority were moved during the latter part of 1958. Throughout 1959 they suffered from inadequate water supplies with the result that the government decided to install an elaborate reticulation system with water pumped from the Zambezi to a number of storage tanks from which redistribution to the villages of the relocatees would occur. A repumping station, with associated tanks, was located on a high point near the Lusitu River approximately three miles from its confluence with the Zambezi. After excavations began, rich archaeological finds were uncovered, archaeologists were called in, and salvage operations were carried out during 1960, 1961, and 1962, with further work undertaken in 1968. Named Ingomble Ilede, the site is considered one of the more important Iron Age settlements in Africa, with the earliest occupation dated by Carbon 14 to the seventh century A.D. By coincidence, it is located within 100 yards of one of the six relocated villages that Colson and I have been studying over the past sixteen years. Called Mazulu, this village, prior to relocation, was located approximately 100 miles upriver from its present site and hence from Ingombe Ilede.

In a series of informative publications on Ingombe Ilede (see Fagan, et al. 1969; Fagan 1972), Fagan has utilized contemporary information collected by the ethnographer Reynolds and by Colson and myself. To gain insight into the economy of his Ingombe Ilede peoples, he has drawn heavily on my *Ecology of the Gwembe Tonga* (1962), which in turn drew heavily on field data collected in Mazulu Village prior to relocation in 1958. "Such a procedure is valid," he argues, "because there is no indication that the climate of the Gwembe has changed since the occupation of Ingombe Ilede and the peoples of the valley are unlikely to have changed their economic practices without impelling reasons to do so" (1969: 90). He goes on to state that, "In many respects the economy practiced by the inhabitants of the Ingombe Ilede was similar to that of the modern

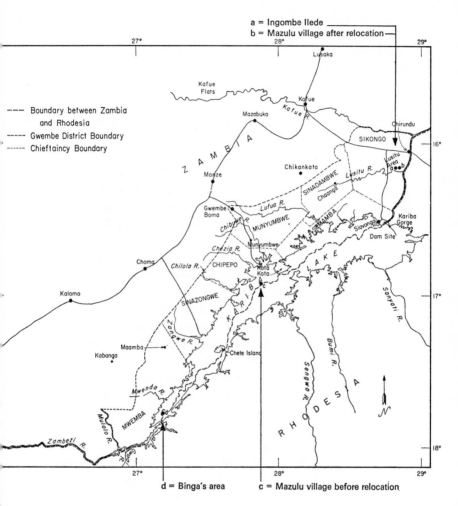

Map. 1

Gwembe Tonga. In an area such as the middle Zambezi where the environment is harsh, the incentives for economic change are small, and it is
hardly surprising to find similarities" (1969: 91). In a more recent
publication Fagan goes further when he writes, "In all probability the
inhabitants of Ingombe Ilede practiced an economy which bore marked
similarity to that of the modern inhabitants of the Gwembe," (1972: 25)
and "One is struck by the extraordinary continuity between modern life
in the middle Zambezi and the material culture and economy of the prehistoric inhabitants of the Lusitu area" (1972: 21).

While I have the greatest respect for Fagan's work as an archaeologist,
in his attempt to reconstruct the economy of the Ingombe Ilede peoples
through the use of historical and contemporary sources, he has over-
stressed aspects of continuity to the extent that variations in economic
patterns along with their possible explanations are played down. As
Fagan states, the Gwembe is a harsh environment for subsistence farmers;
and the people are unlikely to change their economic practices without
impelling reasons to do so. On the other hand, in studying human
societies within the context of a wider ecosystem consisting of the
physical, biotic, and sociocultural environments in which people act out
their lives, we are dealing with complex and dynamic systems. In the
Gwembe compelling reasons for change are not restricted to climatic
variations. As I hope to show, they also include variations in the distribution, structure, and density of settled human populations and in the
distribution and density of tsetse flies. And they include the appearance of
new peoples.

In the sections that follow, my intention is not to present an alternate
reconstruction. Rather, I wish to illustrate the type of major change which
has occurred in the economic and social life of the inhabitants of the
middle Zambezi Valley during the past one hundred years, and which
may have occurred in the past. The first section will deal with change in the
land-use system of those Gwembe Tonga with whom Colson and I are most
familiar. This will be followed by a brief consideration of apparent discontinuities between the final and the preceding levels of occupation at
Ingombe Ilede itself. I will also query the relevance of using our Tonga
data at all for reconstruction purposes by referring to Marks' research
among the Bisa of the neighboring Luangwa Valley and to Lancaster's
research among the Goba — a people who have inhabited the area
around Ingombe Ilede for centuries. Not only do these peoples belong to
different linguistic communities than the Tonga, but they also vary considerably in other aspects of their cultures.

My purpose is to emphasize the need for caution when attempting to

reconstruct agricultural systems, along with the need for a greater awareness of the dynamics involved in social change. While it is true, as Fagan
states, that there is continuity in the sense that the Ingombe Ilede economy, like those of the nineteenth and twentieth centuries, was based on a
combination of mixed farming, gathering, and hunting, within that context there is tremendous room for major variations in economic and social
behavior. There is no single Gwembe economy which has persisted
through time as an immutable entity. Rather, there has been a variety of
economies which reflect the people's backgrounds and their adjustment
to changes in the total ecosystem in which they have lived. In other geographical areas scholars should be on the lookout for similar variation.

The middle Zambezi Valley contains the Zambezi River for a distance
of approximately 500 miles between Victoria Falls and Mozambique's
Cabora Bassa Gorge. Located several thousand feet below the Central
African Plateau, the valley varies in width from less than a mile in gorge
areas at either end to over seventy miles at its widest point. The climate is
hot throughout most of the year, with the annual mean maximum temperature hovering close to 90° Fahrenheit. Though there is considerable
variation from year to year, and between different areas of the valley
within the same year, rainfall averages 25 inches with a pronounced dry
season lasting from April until November, or even December.

The vegetation of the valley is woodland savanna. Ecologically speaking,
it is complex. Not only is there considerable species diversity, but the
valley also contains a greater number of distinct vegetative associations
than do the more extensive plateaux to the north and south. Where these
have been modified by bush fallow systems of agriculture, even more
diversity has been introduced with a variety of plants and animals
associated with the different stages of the cultivation cycle. Immediately
after fallowing, for example, a variety of annual and perennial grasses
take over from cultivated crops. Not only do they provide for the local
inhabitants an annual source of food in the form of wild grasses, but
plant successions following cultivation also provide a preferred habitat
for two species of small antelope (duiker and steenbok) which provide an
additional source of protein. According to Marks (1973, personal communication), the same probably applies to the small rodents which still
figure prominently in the diet of contemporary Gwembe Tonga in March,
April, and May.

Although somewhat simplified in recent decades owing to the introduction of ox plows in the 1930's and the more recent cash cropping of early
maturing sorghum and cotton, ecologically the agriculture of the Gwembe Tonga is also relatively complex (Harris 1972: 182). During 1956 and

1957 I focused my study of Tonga agriculture on Mazulu — the Chipepo village that was subsequently relocated close to the site of Ingombe Ilede. At that time the nucleated population of the village numbered 120, with the village itself sited on infertile soils within 200 yards of the Zambezi. Within the village people lived in socially discrete households, the goal of each household head being to maximize his control over wives, other dependents, livestock, and land. In the latter case, access was sought to a variety of garden types, of which the most important were *jelele, kuti, unda*, and *temwa* (Figure 1). *Jelele* were riverbank gardens which could be

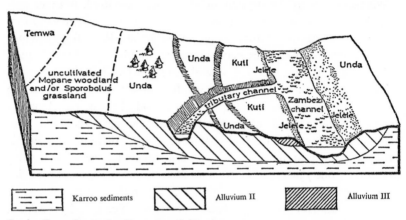

Garden Types Supporting Permanent Cultivation
Jelele: Zambezi river bank gardens cultivated primarily during the dry season.
Kuti: Annually inundated floodplain gardens cultivated during both the rains and
          the dry season.
Garden Types Supporting Land Rotation Cultivation
Unda: Rain gardens cultivated on rarely inundated Zambesi and tributary alluvia or
          on adjacent Karroo sediments.
Temwa: Rain gardens cultivated on Karroo sediments farther removed from the river
          system and more often than not separated from *unda* and associated villages by
          an uncultivated area of infertile land.

Figure 1.   Major middle river garden types (from Scudder 1962)

cultivated during the dry season after the peak flood of the Zambezi in March–April had passed. As the river receded from narrow flood plains back into its primary channel, the people interplanted maize, legumes, cucurbits, and tobacco along the riverbank. These crops were harvested as they matured throughout the dry season. *Kuti* gardens occupied the fertile and flat alluvial flood plains just back from the primary channels of the Zambezi and the lower reaches of its tributaries. In Tonga eyes they were the most valued gardens since they could be cropped twice annually. Just after the advent of the rains, maize was interplanted with a variety of vegetables including legumes, cucurbits, okra, sesame, and *Cleome gynandra* — the seeds of the last three being broadcast sown. These crops were harvested toward the end of the rains, with the fields then replanted in maize, legumes, curcurbits, and tobacco immediately after the recession of tributary or Zambezi floodwaters. Like riverbank (*jelele*) gardens, these floodplain gardens were recultivated year after year without fallowing and without a major reduction in crop yields.

Unda gardens tended to cluster around villages which in turn were sited on infertile soils as close to the river system as possible. *Unda* were of two types, both of which could only be cultivated during the rainy season. The first type consisted of older alluvial soils which rarely if ever were inundated during the annual flood. They lay between villages and the more fertile riverbank and floodplain gardens. The second type were of colluvial or Karroo origin and extended inland from village sites. Though varying greatly in fertility, they were never cultivated on a permanent basis. Like alluvial *unda*, they supported a bush fallow-system, with the period of fallowing, at best, equaling in duration the period of cultivation. While *unda* were interplanted like the previous two garden types, sorghum replaced maize on the heavier soils, and bulrush millet, sometimes interplanted with sorghum, replaced maize on the lighter soils. As for *temwa*, these were bush gardens well inland from villages and frequently separated from *unda* by areas of uncultivable bush. The Tonga verb, *ikutema*, means to fell trees, *temwa* being slash and burn gardens which were fallowed once rainy season yields began to drop.

Though most household heads desired access to all garden types, in 1956 per capita acreage, both within the large majority of households and within Mazulu village as whole, closely approximated one acre of land cultivated during the annual cycle. As Allan (1965: 55–59) has shown, this figure occurs with considerable frequency in a variety of land-use systems in African woodland savanna. Its recurrence is presumably based on the observation that during most years this amount of land produces sufficient grain (approximately 400 pounds) to last one person until the next rainy season's harvest. While yields of grain obviously vary from one year to another according to the crop planted, soil fertility, moisture, heat, and a variety of other factors including time of planting, neither the Valley Tonga nor myself are aware of significant differences in the yields of the three major cereals under local conditions. In 1956 Mazulu villagers practiced what I call ecological fragmentation. They covered their bets by planting a variety of crops in a variety of garden types at different times. If sorghum and millet failed because of drought in *unda* and *temwa* gardens, perhaps maize yields would be adequate in floodplain gardens where the water table was higher. And if the Zambezi flooded early, sweeping away crops in the flood plains, perhaps the inland gardens would provide an adequate return.

In describing the different garden types and their crops, I have purposely refrained from commenting on their relative importance in terms of food production. This has varied since Livingstone traveled up the Zambezi and then returned downriver in 1860, and the variation has important implications for both economic and social organization. In his journal Livingstone (1866: 252) commented on how he walked for hours close to the Zambezi between the Kafue and Zongwe confluences through continuous fields of sorghum. These would have been *unda* gardens according to the Gwembe Tonga classification. Fifty-four years later, Hemans (1935: 123) described hiking through garden land for two miles after leaving the Zambezi at Binga's village and walking inland over older alluvial deposits which are more extensive in this area because of the meandering course of the Zambezi. Though his crop reference is to "corn," the gardens were *unda* so that the reference undoubtedly is to sorghum as opposed to maize. Though Hemans and Livingstone also refer to dry season gardens, there is no mention of *temwa*, the inference being that sorghum planted in *unda* was the most important crop. Certainly this was the view of Mazulu farmers, several of whom independently told me in 1956 that long ago sorghum gardens extended without a break on either side of their village until they merged with similar gardens of their neighbors, the entire area of unbroken rainy season *unda* covering at least four miles.

Such was not the case in 1956–1957. By then bulrush millet was the staple the people relied on to carry them from one rainy season harvest to the next. The changeover appeared to have occurred during the previous ten years and was a response to the accelerated degradation of alluvial and Karroo *unda* because of overcultivation, which in turn was a response to increasing land scarcity arising from population increase. Though accurate demographic information is lacking, available evidence indicates that the Gwembe Tonga population has been on the increase throughout the present century. This time period starts with the cessation of slaving and inter- and intratribal warfare after the imposition of British rule and coincides with a gradual improvement in nutrition and medical care. The first reported degradation of *unda* gardens was mentioned by Trapnell and Clothier (1937: 54–55) after a 1932 trip through the Gwembe. By the middle 1950's Childe (personal communication) reported that in Binga's area the overcultivation and overgrazing of alluvial *unda* was correlated with a switch from perennial grasses to annual grasses and weeds. At the same time large areas of alluvial *unda* had been fallowed along the north bank of the Zambezi simply because reduced yields no longer justified the effort of cultivation. On either side of Mazulu village, for example, there was no longer an unbroken stretch of sorghum growing in alluvial *unda*. Rather a number of gardens had been placed under indefinite fallow.

Since the 1930's the Gwembe Tonga have responded to an increasing scarcity of cultivable land close to the Zambezi and its major tributaries in two major ways. The first was to migrate, moving as families and clusters of kin to pioneer new land. In Chipepo Chieftaincy most of the land available along the Zambezi was already under cultivation by the 1930's so that the people moved inland to unpopulated areas at the base of the escarpment or on the plateau. This was an ancient response — one that people had developed as a means to cope with the periodic food shortages that have plagued the Gwembe in recent centuries. Migration to the Zambian Plateau was especially common, so that by the time Colson began earlier fieldwork among the Plateau Tonga in the 1940's, many of them derived their origin from the Gwembe Valley. A more recent variant to the migration of whole families was labor migrancy, whereby younger men sought wage labor on the plateaux, using part of their income to purchase food for their village families, thereby partially offsetting the smaller yields resulting from reduced per capita acreages. Where land pressure was greatest, labor migration rates went up with more men spending more time absent from their rural homes. The most extreme case was in Mwemba Chieftaincy where novel social institutions were developed to cope with the prolonged absence of husbands as a source of labor and as the progenitors of children (Colson 1960:116).

By the late 1940's land scarcity on the adjacent plateau had also become a problem so that the out-migration of whole families from the Gwembe fell off sharply. It is probably no accident that at about this time the Gwembe Tonga developed a new system of agriculture. (See Scudder [1962: 54–61] for a detailed analysis of *temwa* development and of why *temwa* gardens did not develop at an earlier date.) This was based on the cultivation of *temwa* gardens in which bulrush millet was the dominant cereal. During the mid-1950's *temwa* harvests in Chipepo were a major reason for the reduced frequency of annual food shortages. In Mazulu village the average village adult cultivated 2.25 acres during the rainy season (dry season holdings were only one-tenth as large), with *temwa* comprising approximately two-thirds of the total. Bulrush millet was far more important in their diet than sorghum.

The principal garden type throughout most of the Gwembe by 1956, *temwa* was already beginning to have an impact on settlement patterns.

Because of their distance from the villages and their greater susceptibility to destruction by elephants, antelope, bush pigs and wart hogs, vervet monkeys and baboons, and grain-eating birds, many Tonga slept near their *temwa* during the harvest season. A minority had actually moved out of the villages to establish permanent but isolated homesteads close to their *temwa*. The development of this new garden type also was having a profound effect on the distribution of wealth and influence within the valley. To attract and keep dependents, household heads must have access to land. Before the opening up of *temwa* gardens, the better lands were not only claimed, but their distribution among men and women favored some lineages (and hence household heads) over others, as well as older over younger people. Since land in the more populated areas was primarily acquired through inheritance within the matrilineal lineage, and to a lesser extent through gifts, status "was determined to a large extent by position through birth within the kinship system rather than by individual effort. A landowner with ambition and personality could expect to influence those around him, whereas an equally ambitious and talented man without land was at a disadvantage" (Scudder 1962: 61). The number of rich landholders was limited. Largely senior elders, they were the ones who accumulated the most wives, other dependents, livestock, and influence. The opening up of *temwa* gardens changed all this by allowing ambitious smallholders of all ages to acquire wealth and influence by clearing large bush gardens in areas where agriculture had not occurred in the past. As a result, the proportion of "big men" in each community increased as did the competition between them for dependents. At the same time, the dependence of hard-working younger men on their elders was reduced. In a paper on Gwembe land law and holdings, Colson discusses in more detail how the distribution of land rights and the patterns of landholdings have varied on a number of occasions during the past half century, even though the same rules of land tenure have continued. Though once again the stress is on both continuity and change, what changes have occurred have had profound implications for relationships between husband and wife and between different age categories (see Colson 1966).

Bearing in mind that the relative availability and the distribution among the population of different garden types can have important implications for economic and social behavior, let us now turn to a consideration of Ingombe Ilede. The presence of sorghum and the location of the site itself indicates that these Iron Age farmers cultivated *unda* gardens. It is unlikely that they cultivated *temwa* and possible that they did not cultivate either *jelele* or *kuti* during the dry season. Except for the cowpea and certain cucurbits, the principal dry season crops in the 1950's were all New World imports. According to Clark (1965), the earliest evidence for maize in the middle Zambezi Valley comes from the eighteenth century, while the uppermost level (Level 7) at Ingombe Ilede is dated to the fifteenth century. In all probability it was the Portuguese who introduced these crops; perhaps they also introduced their cultivation in dry season gardens.[1] If this is correct (and we have no way of knowing at the moment), then the inhabitants of Ingombe Ilede cultivated only during the rains, and then primarily in *unda* gardens within a mile of their villages in which event they would not have been in sight of the Zambezi. Such a situation would have been very different from that of the majority of Gwembe Tonga prior to relocation. Not only did they cultivate a wider range of garden types during both the rains and the dry season, but they also considered themselves people of the Zambezi, with villages often deserted during the height of the dry season, since households had temporarily shifted their residence to their river gardens where they could enjoy life near the Zambezi.

There is considerable evidence for hunting at Ingombe Ilede. Though no wild food plants were recovered at the site, Fagan assumes that gathering also was important during food shortages, partly because of the presence of small grindstones and pounders and partly because of the fact that the Gwembe Tonga utilize a wide variety of wild produce today (see Appendix). Unfortunately, just as it is impossible to reconstruct the agricultural system of the Ingombe Ilede inhabitants on the basis of current information, so also is it impossible to assess the relative importance of hunting versus gathering. Though most scholars (including Fagan and myself) have frequently emphasized the harshness of the Gwembe Valley in comparison to other parts of Central Africa for mixed farmers, our comments really are based on observations of the present population of subsistence farmers. It cannot be generalized into the future or back into time. Through the combined use of modern medicine and irrigation, the Gwembe could become a garden paradise, as a number of successful commercial farmers are already learning today. Looking backward, I suspect that I have underemphasized the importance of periodic increases in population density in my analysis of the causes of food shortages and famine in the Gwembe Valley during the nineteenth and twentieth centuries. In my 1962 analysis (215–241) I dealt only indirectly with popula-

---

[1]   Though I am indebted to Lancaster (see 1973: 8) for continually reminding me of this point, we both agree that dry season gardens within the Gwembe may have preceded the Portuguese.

tion increase under the heading of "Degradation and Subdivision of Alluvial Holdings," with considerably more stress given to irregular rainfall, flooding, and plant and animal pests — all variables that were easier to handle analytically.

Taken as a whole, Gwembe District was lightly populated in 1956 with only about eight people per square mile in the large administrative district (also called Gwembe) that coincides with the distribution of the Gwembe Tonga on the north bank of the Zambezi. On the south bank densities were still lower. Such figures, however, are relatively meaningless. Because of water scarcity inland from the Zambezi and its major tributaries (most Karroo sediments drain rapidly and are poor aquifers), prehistoric and historic settlements have been within a mile of the river system. There, Gwembe Tonga have preferred to cultivate the better alluvial soils for as long as they can remember with the result that their number has been influenced by the availability of such soils. In 1956 population densities exceeded 100 per square mile along much of the north bank Zambezi frontage, a density that is high by Central African standards even if it is relatively low in comparison to the better woodland savanna soils of West Africa.

But this large population density could be a relatively recent phenomenon, correlated with the introduction of New World food crops and of dry season cultivation. Because of their high fertility, the more extensive areas of alluvia would stimulate population growth until either the carrying capacity of a given area was exceeded under the system of agriculture or a combination of factors (including drought, flood, and locust devastation) precipitated famine through a drastic reduction in yields. Under such conditions, one response of large Tonga villages was to gather wild food produce, a response which was encouraged by the diversity of vegetation within the Gwembe. Not only did the Gwembe Tonga utilize a larger number of wild food plants than did any other African population of either farmers or gatherer-hunters on which we have information, but they also elaborately processed a larger number of toxic plants than reported elsewhere. (See Scudder [1971] for a detailed analysis of food gathering among the Gwembe Tonga.)

I have often puzzled over why gathering should be so much more important among the Gwembe Tonga than among other farming populations. Though the difference may be more apparent than real simply because so few ethnobotanical studies have been carried out among African farmers, it might be due to the interplay of a rather unique series of factors including the Gwembe Tonga orientation toward fertile alluvia, the introduction of new crops and garden types by the Portuguese, population increase, and the availability of a very diversified and nutritious wild flora.

If this reasoning is correct, then we are not justified in projecting a major emphasis on gathering back into the past. Nor are we justified in assuming the Gwembe to be such a harsh habitat. If the population at Ingombe Ilede was relatively small (say below twenty-five per square mile), the local economy may have been much more focused on hunting and the extensive cultivation of sorghum — even though one is slightly suspicious of this conclusion since it corresponds so nicely with the preserved remains of all but the top level at Ingombe Ilede. Yet just such a situation has been reported by Marks (1971) for the Valley Bisa of the Luangwa Valley during the present century. Though food shortages also periodically occurred among the Bisa, my impression from reading Marks' manuscript is that they were less severe than among the Gwembe Tonga. This is logical simply because the population density was lighter, so that when grain crops failed the per capita availability of both game and wild food plants would be greater among the Valley Bisa than among the Valley Tonga. Indeed, by 1956, game was scarce in the more populated Gwembe neighborhoods, having been forced back into inland areas by heavy hunting pressure and the Tonga system of land clearance which removed all woody plants from cultivated areas except isolated trees and shrubs which were retained because they provided shade, edible products, or a valued source of timber. Between 1956 and the present, hunting and fishing have been the least important source of mealtime side dishes, following gathering, agriculture, and domestic animals in that order. In way of contrast, during 1966–1967 game alone was the most important side dish in three Valley Bisa villages during the August through October period, and in two of the three villages during May–July (agriculture being the most important source in the third).[2]

While stressing variations in land use among the Gwembe Tonga, we have been treating Ingombe Ilede as if its prehistoric inhabitants utilized a single economic system throughout the occupation of the site. Actually, there is no justification for such an assumption. Ingombe Ilede is characterized by two periods of occupation. The first began during the seventh century A.D. and lasted for several hundred years, after which the site remained unoccupied for several more centuries. It was then reoccupied for a relatively short period during the fifteenth century but before the

---

[2] This information is contained in an unnumbered table in Marks' 1971 manuscript. Since Marks emphasizes that game was more common during the time of his study than in the past, it is possible that wild food plants were proportionately more important at an earlier date.

arrival of the Portuguese (Fagan 1972: 13). About all we can say for the first period of occupation is that the people grew sorghum and hunted. While they also had small stock (all excavation levels) and cattle (upper levels only — Fagan, personal communication), the bones of domestic animals amount to less than 30 percent of the total animal remains. The situation today throughout most of the Gwembe would be the exact opposite, with the bones of cattle, goats, and sheep proportionately far more important than those of game. If there are appropriate contemporary analogies, they are not with the Gwembe Tonga but with the Valley Bisa of the Luangwa, and perhaps the Lusitu Goba (see following section on Goba) prior to the influx of Chipepo Tonga following relocation. And a critical variable could be the relative abundance of the tsetse species *Glossina morsitans*, and the prevalence of bovine and human trypanosomiasis. As with the Luangwa and most of the Rhodesian portion of the Gwembe, I suspect that the Lusitu was a fly area during most of the first millennium A.D., with the result that the keeping of cattle was difficult. Small stock may also have been adversely affected, while the apparent desertion of the site may have been correlated with the increasing fly densities and the presence of human as well as bovine sleeping sickness.[3] While little is known about long-term fluctuations in tsetse fly populations, we do know that the fly has a history of expansion and contraction within both the Gwembe and Luangwa Valleys. And in certain locales, human sleeping sickness has suddenly burst forth for unaccountable reasons with epidemics reported in both the Zambian and Rhodesian sections of the Gwembe during the present century (in the former case the outbreak was less than fifty miles down the Zambezi from the Lusitu).

Regardless of the validity of the sleeping sickness hypothesis, during the first few centuries of the present millennium, Ingombe Ilede was unoccupied, nor is there any evidence of occupation elsewhere in the Lusitu at that time. Reoccupation occurred for a short time period around A.D. 1400, with Fagan's descriptions of the associated finds giving me an impression of considerable change as opposed to continuity. For one thing, the proportion of bones of small stock and cattle now equals (in fact slightly exceeds) those of wild animals. This suggests a temporary recession of tsetse fly, and this in turn suggests fairly extensive cultivation since bush clearing and human settlement are still the most effective way to

---

[3]   During the entire Ingombe Ilede sequence, however, cattle were represented only by: "Four fragmentary ox mandibles, together with a maxilla, teeth, and a horn core" (Fagan 1969:84). Small stock mandibles numbered thirty.

keep the tsetse at bay in the valley. Increased population density is also suggested by two burial areas, one of which contains mainly women and children without ornamentation and other grave goods, while the second contains the richly decorated remains of eleven adults. Associated objects include gold beads and bracelets, iron and copper bangles, copper crosses, glass beads and conus shells; in sum a display of wealth that has yet to be seen elsewhere in the Gwembe. Indeed, Fagan (1972:14) describes the Ingombe Ilede gold burials as "among the most spectacular archaeological discoveries ever made in Africa."

Up until this point I have been writing as if the inhabitants of Ingombe Ilede during both periods of occupation were early or proto-Gwembe Tonga. While I do not deny this possibility, it is even more difficult to assess ethnic identities and to reconstruct social organization than it is to specify with any accuracy the land-use systems of prehistoric populations in Africa. This is especially the case with Ingombe Ilede. While Gwembe Tonga from Chipepo Chieftaincy were living close by at the time of its excavation, their presence was the recent result of compulsory relocation in connection with the Kariba Dam scheme. As far as they were concerned, they were forcibly settled in an unknown area of bad reputation and among a foreign people. These were the Goba who spoke not Tonga but a dialect of Shona, a language centered on the Rhodesian Plateau. Though these Goba saw themselves as a people in the process of becoming Tonga, the Chipepo relocatees saw them as Rhodesian immigrants speaking a foreign language and practicing alien customs. Both perceptions contain much truth. According to Lancaster, who is the main authority on the Goba, they may have arrived in the Lusitu area as Shona refugees as early as the fifteenth century (Lancaster 1970, 1971, 1973). This is tantalizingly close to the later occupation of Ingombe Ilede. In analyzing the grave goods associated with the rich burials, Fagan points out that many of the items are imports either from the adjacent plateaux or from India and the East. The eleven dead elite he sees as the leaders of a simple subsistence economy who lived at an important crossroad in the pre-Colonial long-distance trade of Central Africa. One tie, in Fagan's opinion, was with the Karanga peoples of the Rhodesian Plateau. Ancestral to the present day Shona, and associated with Zimbabwe, the peak of their power coincided roughly with the second occupation of Ingombe Ilede. Dominating the uplands between the Limpopo and Zambezi Rivers, their control included the Urungwe area. Southeast of the Lusitu, Urungwe mines (in Fagan's opinion) produced the copper and gold which eventually showed up at Ingombe Ilede. A possible access route was down the Sanyati to and across the Zambezi, and then around the Kariba Hills to the Lusitu. Another tie stretched downriver and was the route by which fine Indian cloth, conus shells, and glass beads passed up the Zambezi. Both routes continued to be utilized during early historic times. On traveling up the Zambezi, Livingstone wrote in his journal that villagers on both sides of the Kariba Hills were familiar with recent events in Mashonaland as a result of news traveling between valley and plateau along the Sanyati route.

As far as trade was concerned, the main resources of the Gwembe were ivory and salt, both of which were common along the Lusitu. Cotton cloth also may have been a trade item since the Gwembe is considered one of the best cotton growing areas in contemporary Central Africa. Be this as it may, both heavy cotton cloth and spindles were found in the Ingombe Ilede burials. And while there is little evidence as to when a trade in people began, by the 1870's slaves were being exported from the Gwembe. Egalitarian, and living in discrete and independent neighborhoods which seldom numbered as many as 2,000 people, the Gwembe Tonga and their Goba neighbors do not have the type of centralized political organization that would be necessary for repelling the attacks of well-organized outsiders.

Returning to the identity of the latter-day settlers at Ingombe Ilede, there are several possibilities, none of which present a very strong case on the basis of present evidence. One is that the people were early Gwembe Tonga. This is quite possible but hardly certain, since the Lusitu is an area where Tonga overlap with Goba among others. A second possibility is that the elite were itinerant traders, perhaps from downriver, who super-imposed themselves upon the local peoples. While Fagan rejects this option, seeing all the people as part of one ethnic population, his analysis nonetheless emphasizes a form of social stratification which has not been observed in the Gwembe until recently — and then as a result of wealth and status differentials arising through the process of national develop-ment whereby a minority of local villagers have become relatively wealthy cash croppers and shopkeepers who seek the company of government civil servants (teachers, agricultural agents, and so on) rather than of their fellow villagers. A similar process of social and economic differentiation may or may not have occurred as a result of other conditions in the past.

A third alternative is that the latter-day settlers were Karanga and even the predecessors of the contemporary Goba, a view which both the Goba and Lancaster encourage.[4] According to this hypothesis, Karanga settlers

---

[4] In a 1973 personal communication, Lancaster persuasively argues that those at-tempting to reconstruct the nature of the Ingombe Ilede economies should pay more attention to the land-use system of the Goba, especially prior to the tsetse eradication

occupied Ingombe Ilede around 1400 in connection with the long-distance trade of the Karanga State. The people flourished for a while, but then they dispersed, perhaps because of temporary soil exhaustion or because of a resurgence of tsetse fly[5] which killed off their stock and perhaps even some of the people, with the remainder scattering to smaller settlements. In time they re-emerged as the Goba whose former heritage as itinerant traders is still reflected in their high labor migration rate (much higher than among the Gwembe Tonga) and their aptitude for trading and shop-keeping when they remain in the valley (see Lancaster 1970).

   Though he wisely avoids dating the process, Lancaster has presented a convincing case (1971: 449) on how the contemporary Goba developed their present system of bride-service and uxorilocal residence while retaining the patrilineal inheritance of titles and positions. Among the patrilineal and patrilocal Shona of the plateau, from whom the Goba are derived, cattle are the common bride-price. But there is an alternative for poor Shona who do not have the cattle to obtain both a bride and another resident for their father's homestead. This is bride-service, whereby the groom moves to the residence of his in-laws and, as one of their dependents, works out his marriage payments. The Goba, or Valley Shona, Lancaster sees as Shona refugees who migrated to the valley where they lost their cattle and were not able to replenish their herds because of tsetse and bovine trypanosomiasis. In attempting to cope with new ecological conditions, they did not adopt new social forms. Rather, they utlized the low prestige pattern of bride-service and uxorilo-cal residence as a mechanism to deal with a world without cattle. Lancaster's analysis makes sense to me in part because it fits a theory that I am developing to explain the processes whereby forcibly relocated populations, and perhaps refugees and migrants also, adjust to a new habitat (Scudder 1973). Worded simply, they change no more than they have to in order to coninue doing what they have always done in the past. When the Chipepo Tonga were moved to the Lusitu, they utilized two old sets of institutions to adjust, on the one hand, to the Lusitu physical and biotic environment, and on the other, to the host population — in this case,

program associated with the Kariba resettlement of Chipepo Tonga. While I agree, the complex ethnicity of the Lusitu area makes the task of reconstruction difficult since the land-use system of the Goba presumably also has changed through time. Furthermore, there is little justification for correlating the Goba or their ancestors with the first and more extended occupation of Ingombe Ilede.

[5]   According to Lancaster (1973, personal communication), local tradition among the Goba suggests that there were no cattle in the Lusitu during the eighteenth and nine-teenth centuries. On the other hand, he would attribute the final desertion of Ingombe Ilede more to temporary soil exhaustion than to tsetse encroachment since the Goba, like some Gwembe Tonga, alternate between a number of known sites.

Goba (Scudder 1968: 172–174). In the adaptive process, changes occurred simply because the context was different, so that today I am aware of both continuity and change. This is what I miss in reading Fagan's interpretations of the Ingombe Ilede site. The continuity is there but at too high a level of generalization. An awareness of the type of changes that can occur as a result of migration, for example, of people with different backgrounds, and of variations in tsetse fly prevalence and human population densities is not made explicit.

While I suspect social anthropologists like myself will always be frustrated by the results of attempts at historical reconstruction, I am not saying that the attempts should not be made. Certainly they should. But at the same time more attention should be paid to what we already know about the dynamics of continuity and change in human behavior. Because the ecological frame of reference within which any population exists is continually changing, so too economic and social behavior is constantly undergoing adjustive changes which through incremental buildup over the years can make the behavior of a subsequent generation seem radically different from that of their predecessors. And yet, while major changes have occurred, the continuity is there also. Hopefully, future reconstructions of African systems of land use will pay more attention to the dynamics of both continuity and change.

APPENDIX (from Scudder 1971)

Latin name	Tonga name	Part used	Date used
VEGETABLE RELISHES			
Adansonia digitata	mubuyu	leaves[3]	Oct.–Dec.
Aerva lanata	insoboyo	leaves[3]	Dec.
Albizzia anthelmintica[P]	mukazibea (chundwe)	young leaves	Sept.–Oct.
Aloe (?) *zebrina*	kanembe	buds[2]	
Alternanthera nodiflora	chamudonga	leaves[2]	Nov., June–July
Amaranthus angustifolius	ibonko	leaves[1]	Dec.–Jan.; March
Amaranthus spinosus	sibongwe; iboa (DBF); bonko (BR); bongo (DBF)	leaves[3]	Aug.–Sept.
Amaranthus thunbergii	ibonko; iboa (BF)	leaves	Dec.–May
Amaranthus (?) *dubius* or *hybridus*	ibowa	young flowers	Dec.–March
Ammocharis tinneana	galamukoko	flowers and (?) leaves	Dec.
Argemone mexicana	mulyangombe (DBF)	leaves	
Bauhinia tomentosa	mukambo	young leaves	Nov.–Dec.

Latin name	Tonga name	Part used	Date used
Cassia obtusifolia	mucaca (BR)	leaves	
Celosia trigyna	isunku	leaves[1]	Jan.–March
*Ceratotheca sesamoides**	lunkomba (lilumia DBF and BR)	leaves[1]	year around
Chlorophytum kymatodes	kalubabwanga	leaves and[3] "female" flowers	Nov.–Dec.
Chrozophora plicata	muneneotuba (BR)		
Cissampelos mucronata	tendemulumi (BR)[4]		
*Cissus integrifolia**	debelebe; tebelebe (BR)	leaves[1]	Nov.–Dec.
Cleome gynandra	isungwa; also lioni, mulangazuba and mutukwani (last three DBF)	leaves and stem[1]	Dec.–April
Cleome monophylla	kanunubwi	shoots, flowers, leaves[3]	Jan.
Cocculus hirsutus	itende, tende (BR)	leaves[1]	June–July (?) also dried and stored
*Commelina diffusa**	nkwasia	leaves[1]	Nov.–Dec., May–Sept.
*Corchorus olitorius**	dyozu; (DBF notes kakonkwa, sia-magwia and teshi)	leaves[1]	Nov.–July
Corchorus tridens	kakonkwa, tielele (BR)	leaves	
Corchorus trilocularis	siachibwiiyi	leaves[3]	dry season and Dec.
*Corchorus sp.**	lunkwankwa	leaves[1]	Dec.–April
Corrigiola litoralis	injima; njina (BR), and kiuyu (BR)	leaves[2]	June–Aug.
Cucumis anguria/metuliferus	kashi (DBF)	leaves	
Cucumis ficifolius	tongalusunku	leaves	
Dicliptera verticillata	kiulu (BR)		
Dipcadi magnum	kakoba	leaves	
(?) *Disperma crenatum*	tubwani (BR)[4]		
Erythrococca menyharthii	impoko	leaves[3]	Dec.
Glinus oppositifolius	fodio (DBF)	leaves	
Haemanthus multiflorus[P]	galamukoko	(?) leaves	
Heliotropium ovalifolium	baba (BR)[4]	(?) leaves	
Hibiscus sp.	mupwepwe	pods[2]	Feb.–March
Hibiscus mechowi/meeusei	lukuku (DBF)	leaves	
Hyphaene ventricosa	malala	heart[3]	Jan.
Lactua (?) capensis	sani (BR)		
Loranthus menyharthii	jenyengwa (DCHP)	leaves	
Luffa cylindrica[P]	munganganga	young fruit	
Moringa oleifera[1]*	zakalanda	leaves and flowers	
Momordica foetida	munganganga (DBF)	young leaves	
Pollichia campestris	kafuakanswi (BR)	whole plant except root (DBF)	
Polygonum plebeium	kafuakanswi, kafua-wakanswi (DBF)	leaves	

Latin name	Tonga name	Part used	Date used
Polygonum senagalense	sibololozi; bololonzia (BR)	leaves	May–Aug.
Portulaca oleracea	masanze; mbelebele	leaves and[2] stems	June–Sept.
*Pterocarpus antunesi**	mukambo	leaves and[3] buds	Nov.–Dec.
Sesbania sesban[P]*	mbelebele; musebebe (BR and DBF)	dried leaves and flowers	Aug.–Nov.
Sida alba	chiwiyangongo	leaves	June–Aug.
Solanum nigrum[P]	mutuntulwa (?)	(?) leaves (DBF)[4]	
Sonchus oleraceus	kalulwe and sane (DBF)	leaves	
Sphaeranthus humilis or *S. incisus*	cimbwelele (BR)	(?) leaves	
Talinum crispatulum	chikonka or masanze	leaves	
Talinum portulacifolium	nyelele (DBF)	leaves	
Tetratelia tenuifolis	kanunubwi or kasukuboa	leaves, stem[2] and flowers	Dec.–Feb.
Trichodesma xeylanicum	deyu; nampwisa (BR)	leaves (also boiled with small rodents as flavoring)	
*Triplochiton zambesiacus**	mukonzo (the tree); mundioli; mutumbululwe (BR) and siankende (BR)	dried leaves[1]	May–Nov.
Turbina holubi	chivavani (DBF)	leaves	
Vellozia equisetoides	muswi, musuri	flowers[3]	Nov.
Ziziphus abyssinica[P]	muchecheche	leaves	
undet.; prob. an *Amaranthus**	shahipa (EC); siyahipa	leaves[3]	Dec.–Jan.

FRUITS AND NUTS

Latin name	Tonga name	Part used	Date used
Acacia albida[P]	muunga (tree); musangu (seeds); mujagwe (BR)	famine food:[1] seeds	Aug.–Oct.
Adansonia digitata	mubuyu	fruit: pulp[1] around seeds and porridge	April–Nov. and stored
Antidesma venosum	munkunyu	fruit: fresh	(?) April
Artabotrys (?) *brachypetalus*	mariagnombe	fruit: fresh	March
Azanza garckeana	muneko	fruit: pulp around seeds and porridge	April–July
Baphia massaiensis	munyunyumeenda (BR)	fruit: fresh[4]	
Bauhinia petersiana	mupondo	seeds: raw and apparently roasted	July
Berchemia discolor	mwii (tree); inji (fruit); mwinjii (BR)	fruit: fresh;[1] dried cakes, and porridge	March and stored

Latin name	Tonga name	Part used	Date used
Bridelia cathartica	mucendewabasokwe (BR)	fruit: fresh	
(?) *Capparis rosea*	mulolo (EC)	fruit	
Cleistochlamys kirkii	mupombolo (BR)	fruit: fresh	
Coccinia adoensis	mufufwe; maziula	fruit: fresh	March
Combretum mossambicense	maminambelele (BR)	fruit: fresh[4]	
Cordia ovalis	mukonyabusenga; mujelabatumbu (BR)	fruit: fresh (juice sucked)	May
Cordyla africana	mutondo	fruit: fresh and cooked; seeds (BR): roasted	(?) Nov.–Dec.
Croton gratissimus	mungae (BR)	fruit: fresh[4]	
Cucumis anguria/metuliferus	kashi (DBF)	fruit: fresh and cooked (DBF)	
Diospyros kirkii	mukula (tree); mucenje (fruit); mujenje (BR)	fruit: fresh[1]	Aug.–Sept.
Diospyros mespiliformis	mukula (tree); mucenji (fruit); mujenje (BR)	fruit: fresh[1]	July–Sept.
Feretia aeruginescens	munyasiankula (BR)	fruit: fresh	
Ficus capensis	mukuyu	fruit: fresh	Sept.–Oct.
Ficus sycomorus	mukuyu	fruit: fresh	Sept.–Oct.
Flacourtia indica	mutumbulwa	fruit: dried, boiled and eaten (BR)	
Garcinia livingstonei	mukonongo (BR); mutungwa (BR)	fruit: boiled and eaten with porridge	
Grewia bicolor	mwingili; musongonono (BR)	fruit: fresh	April
Grewia flavescens	mukunyukunyu (mugunyugunyu)	fruit: fresh; as a drink (BR)	
Grewia herbacea	mugunyugunyu (BR)	fruit: drink (BR)	
Grewia pachycalyx	mutumbululwe (BR)	fruit: fresh (BR)	
Hyphaene ventricosa	malala; kunka (fruit)	fruit: raw	June
Lannea discolor	mung'ongwa (BR)	nuts only	
Lannea stuhlmannii	mubumbu; mung'ogo (BR); mung'ongwa (BR)	fruit: fresh; nuts (BR)	(?) Nov.–Dec. (?) Nov.–Dec.
Lecaniodiscus flaxinifolius	mutalala (BR)	fruit: fresh	
Lonchocarpus capassa[P]	mukololo	famine food: seeds after prolonged boiling	Aug.–Oct.
Maerua glauca[P]	musoswe; muswezu; muswezio (BR)	famine food: fruit and seeds after prolonged boiling	(?) Aug.–Oct.
Manilkara mochisia	mupusio (BR)	fruit: fresh	

Latin name	Tonga name	Part used	Date used
Olax dissitiflora	boyabwansia; mucholiansimba	fruit: fresh	Nov.
Parinari (?) *curatellifolia*	mbula	fruit: fresh	(?) Aug.–Sept.
Piliostigma thonningii	musekese	seed pods (BR)[4]	
Popowia obovata	mucinga; mujinga (BR); mujingajinga (BR)	fruit: fresh	
Pseudocadia zambesiaca	munonge	fruit: fresh and a milk-curdling agent[1]	June
Rhus sp.	munoniamanzi (BR)	fruit: fresh (BR)	
Sclerocarya caffra	munhongwa; munongo (?)	nuts (seed kernels) and fruits: raw	Oct.–Nov.
Strychnos innocua[P]	muteme; mwabo (BR)	fruit pulp: fresh	Nov.–Dec.
*Tamarindus indica**	musika; insongwa (seed) (EC)	fruit pulp: fresh[1] and cooked; famine food: seeds after prolonged boiling	Aug.–Jan.
Trichilia emetica	musikili	fruit: cooked[4]	Dec.–Jan.
Vangueria infausta	mububu	fruit: fresh	March–April
Vangueriopsis lanciflora	muhumu	fruit: fresh and perhaps stored	rainy season
Xeroderris stuhlmannii	mutundulu	famine food: seeds after prolonged boiling	Aug.–Oct.
Ximenia americana[P]	muchovwa; muconvwa (BR) convwapati (BR)	fruit: fresh;[2] seed kernel: raw	Oct.–March
Ximenia spp.	mangombia (EC)	fruit: pulp and seeds	Dec.
Ziziphus abyssinica[P]	muchecheche; mwijejete (BR)	fruit: fresh	(?) May–June
Ziziphus mauritiana[1]	musao; musaua (BR)	fruit: fresh and[3] dried	

EDIBLE GRASS

Latin name	Tonga name	Part used	Date used
Brachiaria deflexa	chipungachidenene	grain :boiled	Feb.
Craspedorhachis uniflora	kanziennzie[2]	grain: boiled	Feb.
Dactyloctenium giganteum	sonkwe	grain: boiled	Feb.
Echinochloa colona	inzibaiba[2]	grain: boiled	Feb.
Panicum maximum	chamuzenene	grain: boiled	Feb.
Panicum novemnerve	mukaseza[2]	grain: boiled	Feb.
Rottboellia exaltata	mulungwe	grain: boiled	Feb.
Sorghum halepense	musonde[2]	grain :boiled	Feb.
Urochloa mossambicensis	impunga; inkutu[1]	grain: boiled; and stored	Feb.

Latin name	Tonga name	Part used	Date used
TUBERS			
Amorphophallus abyssinicus[P]	inkona	famine food: tuber with leaves and upper green part of stalk eaten after prolonged boiling (DBF and TS)	
Boscia (?) *albitrunca*	muwombwi (mubite) (GR)	tuber a famine food: stamped sections boiled (GR)	
Ceropegia tentaculata	shalipopo (shalipawpaw)[3]	tuber eaten raw or cooked	Dec., April; (?) probably year around
Coccinia adoensis	mufufwe; maziula	tuber a famine food	rainy season
Commiphora (?) *africana* and *pyracanthoides*	mubwabwa	tuber chewed raw[1]	year around
Crinum harmsi/pedicellatum	busimbisimbi (DBF)	tuber a famine food	
Cyperus fulgens	insiu	bulb eaten raw,[3] roasted or boiled after stamping	Oct.–Dec. (GR and TS)
Ipomoea shirambensis	lukuli	tuber chewed; also[1] a famine food: eaten after boiling	Nov.–Dec.
Neorautanenia (?) *mitis*[P]	(?) muntili, intindili	famine food (?)[4]	
Nymphaea and/or *N. caerulea*	inquibu	rootstock (raw or cooked); buds; and seeds	March
Plectranthus esculentus	luseze (GR); also lwidi (?)	tuber boiled[3]	year around and esp. dry season
Pteleopsis myrtifolia	muliabalombe (BR)	beverage (BR)	
Scilla sp.	inqwaqwa	skinned bulbs boiled with ashes	Nov.
undetermined	bonga (GR); mashyabe (EC)	bulb (raw)	
undetermined	bumpububu	famine food	
undetermined	kabombwe	famine food: roots eaten after prolonged boiling	
undetermined	kanagwelebe (EC)	root (raw)	Jan.
MUSHROOMS			
several undetermined species	bowa[1]		Nov.–Jan. and stored

KEY

* Consumption common in season either before resettlement, after resettlement or both (for any one month designated plant provides at least 5 percent of wild plants consumed at recorded meals).

P Plant contains a toxin. In the case of nuts, fruits and tubers special preparation (usually lengthy boiling) required before consumption.

I Introduced (*Moringa* is grown in Mwemba villages; *Ziziphus* apparently introduced in Sikongo by the Chikunda).

¹ Consumption documented both before and after relocation by Elizabeth Colson and/or Thayer Scudder.

² Consumption documented by Colson and/or Scudder prior to relocation only.

³ Consumption documented by Colson and/or Scudder after relocation only.

⁴ Use as a food plant needs further checking.

Note. Consumption data not included for fruits and nuts, most of which provide fresh snacks annually for those in the general vicinity.

Initials of other authorities are included only where the species in question was not collected by Thayer Scudder or where an alternate Tonga name was given:

EC   : Elizabeth Colson
DBF   : D. B. Fanshawe
DCHP: D. C. H. Plowes
GR   : Gordon Read
BR   : Barrie Reynolds

REFERENCES

ALLAN, W.
 1965   *The African husbandman.* Edinburgh: Oliver and Boyd.
CLARK, J. DESMOND
 1965   The Portuguese settlement at Feira. *Northern Rhodesia Journal* 6: 275–229.
COLSON, E.
 1960   *The social organization of the Gwembe Tonga.* Manchester: Manchester University Press.
 1966   Land law and land holdings among the Valley Tonga of Zambia. *Southwestern Journal of Anthropology* 22(1):1–8.
FAGAN, B. M.
 1972   *Ingombe Ilede: early trade in south Central Africa.* Reading, Massachusetts: Addison-Wesley Modular Publications.
FAGAN, B. M., D. W. PHILLIPSON, S. G. H. DANIELS
 1969   *Iron Age cultures in Zambia (Dambwa, Ingombe Ilede, and the Tonga),* volume two. London: Chatto and Windus.
HARRIS, D. R.
 1972   The origins of agriculture in the tropics. *American Scientist* 60:180–193.
HEMANS, H. N.
 1935   *The log of a native commissioner.* London: Witherby.
LANCASTER, C. S.
 1970   "Economics, behavior, and the relevance of economic anthropology:

a case study among the Goba or central Zambia." Unpublished doctoral dissertation.

1971 The economics of social organization in an ethnic border zone: the Goba (northern Shona) of the Zambezi Valley. *Ethnology* (4):445–465.

1973 "Ethnic identity in the middle Zambezi Valley." Unpublished manuscript.

LIVINGSTONE, D., C. LIVINGSTONE

1866 *Narrative of an expedition to the Zambezi and its tributaries.* New York: Harper and Brothers.

MARKS, S. A.

1971 "Large mammals and a brave people: a study of hunting among the Valley Bisa of Zambia." Unpublished manuscript.

REYNOLDS, B.

1968 *The material culture of the peoples of the Gwembe Valley.* New York: Praeger.

SCUDDER, T.

1962 *The ecology of the Gwembe Tonga.* Manchester: Manchester University Press.

1968 Social anthropology, man-made lakes and population relocation in Africa. *Anthropological Quarterly* 41:168–176.

1971 *Gathering among African woodland savannah cultivators – a case study: the Gwembe Tonga.* Zambian Papers 5. Manchester: Manchester University Press for the Institute for African Studies.

1973 "The human ecology of big projects: river basin development and resettlement," in *Annual review of anthropology,* volume 2. Edited by B. Siegel, 45–55. Palo Alto: Annual Reviews.

TRAPNELL, C. G., J. N. CLOTHIER

1937 *The soils, vegetation, and agricultural systems of North-Western Rhodesia.* Report of the Ecological Survey. Lusaka: Government Printer.

The Origins and Domestication of Yams in Africa

D. G. COURSEY

Although yams are among the most important of African plant domesticates, the origin of the edible yam in Africa and, indeed, elsewhere is a much misunderstood subject. Numerous misconceptions
have appeared recently in the writings of Africanists and others concerned with the history of early agriculture, although as early as the
publication of Watt (1890) it was recognized that the practice of yam
cultivation was indigenous to Africa as well as to Asia and tropical
America. This concept was also tacitly accepted in various writings of
Burkill (1921, 1939, 1960) and in some of the earliest writing of
Chevalier (1909). It has even been implied in otherwise responsible
works (Dumont 1966) that yams were introduced in cultivation to
Africa from America along with cassava and other crops. The view, expressed in some detail by Murdock (1959), that yam cultivation developed in West Africa only as part of the "Malaysian plant complex"
(of yams, aroids, sugar cane, and bananas) reaching West Africa later
than 2000 B.P., has gained wide acceptance, in spite of the above-
mentioned works of Burkill and Chevalier, those of Davies (1960,
1967, 1968), and the writer's own more recent publications on the
subject (Coursey 1967; Coursey and Alexander 1968; Alexander and
Coursey 1969). A recent review on the subject of the history of West
African agriculture (Havinden 1970) makes no substantial reference to
indigenous yam cultivation and appears uncritically to accept Murdock's Malaysian hypothesis of the origin of yam cultivation in the
continent. Proper understanding of the subject has been further complicated by differences in the taxonomic systems used for West African
yams, there being a consistent difference in this matter between Franco-

phone and Anglophone authors.

In considering the origins of the yams as domestic plants, it is necessary to realize that while some yams were brought into cultivation in
the African continent, other species of yams were domesticated at other
places in the world; today, yams of Asiatic origin are grown to a substantial degree in most parts of tropical Africa. In the Caribbean area,
where African yams are extensively cultivated, these same Asiatic
species are also grown. Yams are thus at the same time both African
and non-African domesticates. The domestication of the yam has been
described from a global point of view in a previous publication
(Alexander and Coursey 1969) where it is shown that different species
of *Dioscorea* were brought into cultivation independently in three areas
of the world: (1) in Southeast Asia, (2) in West Africa, (3) in pre-
Columbian tropical America. Different species were involved in these
three areas and thus no single Center of Origin of domestication, in
the Vavilovian sense, can be ascribed to the yams.

In view of the complexity of the situation, it may be useful briefly to
discuss the botany and taxonomy of the yams before proceeding to
the main theme.

BOTANY AND TAXONOMY

The yams we are concerned with here are members of the genus
Dioscorea. This is the type genus, and also by far the largest genus, of
the family Dioscoreaceae. It contains several hundred species which
occur throughout the tropics, with a few members in temperate and
montane regions. The Dioscoreaceae are themselves the principal
family of the order Dioscoreales, recently reestablished by Ayensu
(1972), although they were formerly (Burkill 1960; Coursey 1967)
classified with the Liliales (Table 1). The Dioscoreales are monocotyledons (although they show many features normally associated with
dicotyledons, and some species have a nonemergent second cotyledon)
which exhibit a number of primitive features compared with most of
the angiosperms, for example their inconspicuous flowers.

The Dioscoreales may well have been among the earliest angiosperms to have evolved, and their original appearance may thus have
been in what is now Southeast Asia as early as the late Triassic or early
Jurassic, the location and time regarded by Axelrod (1970) as that of
the origin of the angiosperms. Origin in this area, though at a rather
later date (early Cretaceous) is suggested by Burkill (1960). Though no

Table 1   Classification within the order Dioscoreales (after Ayensu 1972)

Order	Family	Genus
Dioscoreales	Dioscoreaceae	*Avetra*
		Dioscorea
		Rajania
		Stenomeris
		Tamus
	Trichopodiaceae	*Trichopus*
	Roxburghiaceae	*Croomia*
		Stemona
		Stichoneuron

fossil records of the genus are available prior to the Eocene, indirect evidence indicates that ancestral forms of *Dioscorea* had achieved pantropic, if not worldwide, distribution before the end of the Cretaceous. In any case they are widely distributed, especially in the tropical regions of the world, and achieved that distribution long before the advent of man. Fairly early in their evolution in geological time, they were subjected to ecological pressures which resulted in the development of an organ of dormancy (usually a tuber, but a rhizome in some of the more primitive species) and a climbing vine which is almost always of an annual nature.

The plant exists entirely as the dormant subterranean organ through the inclement period of the year which, in the tropics, is equated with the dry season. The substantial reserves of food and water contained in the organ of dormancy predispose the plant to attack by both animals and man. For this reason, most species of *Dioscorea* have some form of protection for their tubers which may take the form of alkaloidal or steroidal toxins, spinous development of the stems or even of the roots, or the habit of burying the organ of dormancy deeply in the ground so as to be inaccessible to rooting animals. For more detailed botanical information reference may be made to Waitt (1963), Coursey (1967), Coursey and Martin (1970), Burkill (1960), and Ayensu (1972).

The genus *Dioscorea* occurs today throughout the tropical regions of the world. There are substantial differences related to separation early in the evolutionary history between the New and Old World species. Within the Old World there are also differences between Africa and Asia; but these are considerably less, reflecting the much more recent evolutionary separation of the species of these two continental areas which is believed to have occurred in the Miocene when desiccation of what is now southwestern Asia was occurring. Old World species, apart from a few aberrant exceptions, have chromosome numbers based on ten, whereas the *Dioscorea* of the New World have chromosome numbers based on nine.

The yams which are of economic importance as food crops today, whether Asian, African, or American, have the following general characteristics: The plant grows during the rainy season as a twining vine which extends often for many meters through trees or undergrowth. In cultivation the vines are usually trained on stakes, strings, or wires. These vines, which are annual, bear racemes of inconspicuous white, greenish, or yellowish flowers; the male and female flowers are always separate and nearly always occur on separate plants. The female flowers are followed by dehiscent trilocular capsules, each loculus containing two seeds which are winged for dispersal by wind. At the end of the season of active growth, i.e. the rains, the vine dies down and the plant persists through the dry season in the form of dormant tubers. It is these tubers, the natural storage organs of the plant which enable it to survive the dry season, that are economically useful to man. In all the edible yams these tubers are annually renewed organs. In other species of *Dioscorea* which have not been used by man as food, the tuber is perennial and becomes larger and progressively more lignified from year to year while, as already mentioned, some primitive *Dioscorea* have rhizomatous organs of dormancy. In modern agricultural practice throughout the world, edible yams are propagated vegetatively by means of tuber cuttings or sets which are either small tubers or fragments of tubers. Millennia of vegetative propagation in cultivation have reduced the sexual fertility of many of the cultivars so that they flower comparatively seldom and set fertile seed even less frequently.

In Table 2 are listed the principal species that have been brought into cultivation by man in the three main areas of the world where yams are cultivated. Numerous other *Dioscorea* have occasionally been utilized as food by man in various parts of the world, but are of much less importance: most of these are discussed to some extent by Coursey (1967).

COURSES TOWARDS DOMESTICATION IN ASIA AND AMERICA

Before considering the processes by which domesticates of the genus *Dioscorea* arose in Africa, it may be well to review what is known from other parts of the world, especially Southeast Asia, a region which has

Table 2. Major food yam species (after Coursey 1967; Alexander and Coursey 1969)

	Africa	Asia	America
Major economic spp.	*D. rotundata* Poir [a b] *D. cayenensis* Lam. [b]	*D. alata* L. [a] *D. esculenta* (Lour.) Burk.	*D. trifida* L. f.
Secondary spp.	*D. bulbifera* L. [c] *D. preussii* Pax. *D. praehensilis* Benth. *D. sansibarensis* Pax. *D. dumetorum* (Knuth) Pax.	*D. bulbifera* L. [c] *D. hispida* Dennst. *D. pentaphylla* L. *D. nummularia* Lam. *D. opposita* Thunb. [d] *D. japonica* Thunb. [d]	*D. convolvulacea* Cham. et Schlecht. *Rajania cordata* L.

[a] These species are true cultigens, unknown in the wild.
[b] Some authors regard *D. rotundata* as only a subspecies of *D. cayenensis* (Note 2).
[c] *D. bulbifera* is the only species common to both Africa and Asia. The African form is, however, quite distinct and is sometimes regarded as a separate species, *D. latifolia* Benth.
[d] These are often together known as *D. batatas* Decne and are temperate species native to China and Japan.

been fairly intensively studied. This area has been regarded by several ethnobotanists since Sauer (1952) as a most important area of plant domestication. It is also the area in which some of the *Dioscorea* species now grown in Africa originated.

The principal species of yam of importance in tropical Southeast Asia and those areas, such as Indonesia and the Pacific, which have acquired their agricultural heritage from Asia are *D. alata* and *D. esculenta*. The origins of these species in cultivation have been discussed in considerable detail by Burkill (1924, 1951). Geographically, the ideas put forward are entirely acceptable, but the comparatively recent chronology, suggesting the beginnings of systematic cultivation little more than 2000 B.P., needs considerable revision: the writer did not appreciate the extreme antiquity of vegetative agriculture in Southeast Asia. Recent archaeological evidence (Chang 1967, 1970; Chang and Stuiver 1966; Gorman 1969) has indicated that non-grain-using Mesolithic cultures, which were related to the Hoabinhian ceramic traditions and possessed some knowledge of cultivation, existed in the region of domestication of these *Dioscorea* species at dates around 10,000 B.P. Harrison (1963) has suggested even greater antiquity for Stone Age cultures which had some form of systematic crop utilization in the area.

The most important of the Asiatic yams, *D. alata*, is a true cultigen, unknown in the wild state. It is believed (Burkill 1924, 1951) to have been derived by human selection from wild forms of common origin with *D. hamiltonii* Hook. and *D. persimilis* Prain et Burk., species whose natural ranges overlap in the northern-central parts of the Malaysian peninsula. As has been pointed out by this author, the yams likely to be most useful to man as food will be those native to regions with a fairly prolonged dry season as these will tend to have the largest tubers — tubers which become dormant most deeply and for the longest period and therefore have the greatest suitability for storage. In comparison, because of their almost continuous period of growth, equatorial *Dioscorea* species have little dormancy and, therefore, have much less tuberous development. In a more recent publication the same author (Burkill 1960) follows Haudricourt and Hedin (1943) and Sauer (1952) in supposing that the original cultivation of vegetatively propagated root crops in this area was undertaken by littoral peoples whose staple economy depended on fishing. This may perhaps be true of the Araceae, such as *Colocasia*, which are adapted to cultivation under extremely moist conditions; but as has been pointed out by Barrau (1965a), the vegecultural civilizations which are based on the Southeast Asian development of cultivation contrast fundamentally the production of such aroid crops under littoral or other moist conditions with the production of yams which are associated more with dry land conditions. The introduction of crops, whether vegetatively propagated or otherwise, into cultivation on such a basis has also been criticized by Heiser (1969). In view of this, and also in view of the facts indicated by Burkill (1924, 1951) that yam cultivation in Southeast Asia tends to be associated with upland rather than littoral or riverine peoples, it could be suggested that yam domestication was originally brought about inland, rather than at waterside areas. However, Chang (1970) considers that the cord-marked Hoabinhian ceramics indicate the association of these cultures with littoral or riverine habitats, and the distribution of archaeological material is certainly suggestive of this.

In a more recent publication, Barrau (1970) draws attention to the observation made by Burkill (1953) of the significance of the ritual protection which is afforded to certain *Dioscorea* by the Andaman Islanders — people who within the ethnographic present were without any conventional form of agriculture. On the basis of this and observations of other practices recorded among preagricultural peoples in the Southeast Asian area and among the Australian aborigines, it was suggested that the cultivation of crops such as yams derived initially from ritual protection afforded by gatherers to wild food plants.

After having been brought into cultivation, this species of yam was carried by man far out into the Pacific by the Polynesian migration, which probably originated in southern China and Indochina about 3500 B.P. (Suggs 1960), and later, around 2000 B.P. or more recently, to Madagascar and the East African littoral.[1] As we have indicated elsewhere (Coursey and Alexander 1968; Alexander and Coursey 1969), there is no reason to suppose that this species traveled across Africa in cultivation, contrary to the opinion expressed by Murdock and others. Its distribution in Africa has been mapped by Prain and Burkill (1939) showing that there are substantial areas in the central parts of the continent where it is not known. It was, however, carried in cultivation to West Africa by the Portuguese at an early date after the paleo-Colonial expansion into the Indian Ocean, as there are definite records of it from São Tomé by approximately the end of the sixteenth century (Burkill 1938).

The other principal Asiatic species, *D. esculenta*, appears to have followed roughly the same path to domestication and, subsequently, in cultivation. However, most varieties being less adapted for storage than *D. alata*, it was not so much favored by sea-going people; though it

[1] So little is known of the prehistory of Madagascar that it is virtually impossible to make any useful statement about the origins of agriculture on the island, whether in connection with yams or other crop plants.

It is generally assumed that the island was uninhabited at the time of the Malaysian colonization ca. 2000 to 1500 B.P. It is clearly established that these settlers carried *D. alata* with them as one of their principal food plants. It was an important crop there in 1516 and in 1638 according to historical evidence and until living memory, although now it is largely displaced by cassava (Burkill 1951). It is likely that *D. esculenta* and the Asiatic form of *D. bulbifera* were also brought to Madagascar from Asia.

The indigenous flora of Madagascar is in many ways distinct from that of continental Africa. In particular, the genus *Dioscorea* in Madagascar contains a substantial number of species unknown elsewhere (Jumelle 1922; Jumelle and Perrier de la Bathie 1910; Perrier de la Bathie 1925), and many were formerly used as food. Although some were highly esteemed, none appears to have been greatly ennobled in cultivation, and most retain deeply burying tuber forms. As in mainland Africa, many species are toxic but can be rendered edible by maceration and soaking.

Some of the most important indigenous species are: *D. analalavensis* Jum. et Perr.; *D. antaly* Jum. et Perr.; *D. bemandry* Jum. et Perr.; *D. mamillata* Jum. et Perr; *D. ovinala* Baker; *D. soso* Jum. et Perr. The last two of these were formerly most favored, being nontoxic and of good flavor. The island is also within the range of the African form of *D. bulbifera*.

possibly reached Madagascar at an early date with *D. alata*, it was not introduced in substantial quantities to Africa until late in the Colonial era (Miège 1948).

Various other species of yams of lesser importance in Asia have been considered by Barrau (1965a, 1965b, 1970) and by Haudricourt (1962, 1964).

Although the genus is more widely speciated in tropical America than in any part of the Old World, few of the American *Dioscorea* attained any great importance as crop plants in pre-Columbian America. However, a number of species (notably *D. trifida*) were utilized by Amerindians (Chevalier 1946). This comparative neglect of the genus as sources of food by the Amerindians is probably associated with the abundance of alternative root and tuber crops in the New World (Hawkes 1970), especially cassava and sweet potatoes which are more ecologically flexible and less seasonally yielding than most of the *Dioscorea*. Most of the yams cultivated in tropical America today are of Asiatic or West African origin. Although *D. trifida* is still grown to some extent and is greatly favored, it is regarded more as a vegetable relish than as a staple.

As has been pointed out by Burkill (1960), there has been a general east-to-west movement of the yams in domestication. Thus, Asiatic yams have been transferred in cultivation to both Africa and the New World, African species also being taken to the New World; but there has been little movement in cultivation in the reverse direction. The statement that the American *D. convolvulacea* has been taken in cultivation to West Africa (Dalziel 1937) has not been substantiated. It is believed that *D. trifida* has been grown on a small scale in Ceylon (Waitt 1963), but this is comparatively insignificant. African and American yams have recently been cultivated to a limited extent in New Caledonia and the New Hebrides (Bourret 1972).

COURSES TOWARDS DOMESTICATION IN AFRICA

The Indigenous Origin of the Domesticates

It has already been indicated that the genus *Dioscorea* was of pantropic distribution long before the advent of man, or even of the primates, and that by the Miocene, at the latest, the African members of the genus were isolated genetically from those of the New World and Asia — the desert areas of Arabia and southwestern Asia forming as effective a barrier as the Atlantic Ocean (Burkill 1960).

The majority of the yams grown in Africa today are improved or selected forms of recognizable African species which are known in the wild state in that continent and nowhere else. Asiatic species, mainly *D. alata*, but also to a lesser extent the Asiatic form of *D. bulbifera* and to a much lesser degree *D. esculenta*, are grown, but there is no evidence to suggest that these reached East Africa before the Indo-Malaysian contacts around 2000 B.P. or West Africa prior to paleo-Colonial Iberian contacts later than 500 B.P. This, in spite of such statements as those of Chevalier (1909) that "elle parait cultivée en Afrique depuis une très haute antiquité," or, more recently (1936), "les Noirs, lors de leur migration vers le continent Africain, apportaient avec eux . . . les Ignames de cette espèce" referring to *D. alata*. The range of cultivars of these species found in Africa is extremely limited, compared with what is known in Southeast Asia or the Pacific. The only African cultivated yam unknown in the wild except as an escape is *D. rotundata*, which is a true cultigen, and even this is closely related to known wild African species. It is clearly of African affinity, being so close to *D. cayenensis* that it is sometimes regarded as a subspecies.[2] Yam domes-

---

[2]   A word is needed here on the taxonomic history of the main West African yams, *D. rotundata* and *D. cayenensis*. Confusion initially arose from the unfortunate coincidence that both species were originally described botanically from cultivated material being grown in tropical America, that is, in locations and ecologies remote from their natural habitats. The former species was rather incompletely described by Poiret from Jamaican material in 1813 and the latter from material in Guiana (the specific is derived from the town of Cayenne) by Lamarck in 1789. Subsequently, in 1864, *D. rotundata* was reduced by Grisebach to subspecific status within *D. cayenensis*. This reduction was accepted by Prain and Burkill (1919) and has subsequently been maintained by Francophone writers such as Chevalier (1936) and Miège (1952, 1969). French authors, when referring to *D. cayenensis*, may thus often be discussing material that Anglophone authors would know as *D. rotundata*. In another publication (Burkill 1921), *D. rotundata* was restored to specific status and its identity with the white Guinea yam established, the taxon *D. cayenensis* being restricted to the yellow yam, on the basis of examinations of material in experimental cultivation in Singapore. In his major (1939) study of the African *Dioscorea*, Burkill discusses the species under the general heading of *D. cayenensis* although in his final major work (1960) he again refers to it as a separate species. This separation has also been adopted by Dalziel (1937) and has been fairly generally accepted by Anglophone workers in West Africa. It should be pointed out however that a distinction based merely on the color of the tuber flesh is not reliable as some yellow-fleshed forms of *D. rotundata* and some almost white-fleshed forms of *D. cayenensis* exist. The entire spectrum of cultivated forms as grown in the West Indies has been grouped under *D. occidentalis* Knuth, but this taxon is not valid. Recently, Ayensu (1970) has shown that there are differences in the vascular anatomy of cultivated material of the two types and considers that this warrants a formal separation. Biochemical differences involving the nature of the polyphenolics present in cultivated forms have also been pointed out by Bate-Smith (1968).

   Although *D. cayenensis sensu strictu* is widespread in the wild state in West Africa and other parts of the continent, *D. rotundata* appears to be a true cultigen,

tication in Africa depended, therefore, upon indigenous yam species and not upon plant introduction. Similarly, in view of what is now accepted as to the history of man in Africa (G. Clark 1969; J. Clark 1970; Shinnie 1971), it need not initially have depended upon external cultural contacts, although ideas derived from the grain-based agriculture of southwestern Asia influenced the later stages of its progress (J. Clark 1962; Alexander and Coursey 1969). To quote from Burkill (1939) "To the African himself is entirely due the invention of *D. cayenensis* as a crop plant."

Geographical Centers of African Yam Domestication

Wild African *Dioscorea* which are botanically close to the modern cultivated forms are widely distributed in the continent between the Sahara and the arid zones of southern Africa. Maps of the distribution of some of the principal species are given by Burkill (1960). Apart from some differentiation between high-rainfall-adapted forest species and others adapted to drier conditions, there is no very great localization within this very large area.

─────────────

unknown in the wild state like the Asiatic *Dioscorea alata* which it closely resembles. Similarly, it must be presumed to be of hybrid origin. The great similarity in tuber form between some cultivars of *D. alata* and some cultivars of *D. rotundata* has been a further cause of confusion (the growing plants can be readily distinguished by the alate stems of the former and the spinous stems of the latter) as has the fact that both are often referred to simply as "white yam."

Attention needs to be paid to an early and frequently overlooked work of Chevalier (1909) in which a relationship between cultivated yams of the *D. rotundata* type of the West African savanna and the wild species *D. praehensilis* is indicated. In his major African (1939) work Burkill also indicates the probability of *D. rotundata* being a hybrid form between *D. cayenensis* and *D. praehensilis* or perhaps *D. abyssinica* Hochst.

Today, *D. rotundata* is by far the most important of the African food yams, and it exists in a profusion of cultivars, most of which have never been properly documented. However, a substantial number of Nigerian cultivars have been described by Waitt (1965) and some others from the Ivory Coast by Miège (1952). In situations such as this where a large number of vegetatively propagated clonal cultivars exist which have arisen by spontaneous processes in cultivation, it is questionable whether strict Linnaean concepts of taxonomy can be applied. The classificatory approaches adopted for two other food crops which are of high antiquity in vegetative cultivation — that of Simmonds (1966) for the banana or the statistical taximetric approach used by Rogers (1967) for cassava — may well be appropriate. On this philosophy perhaps the most satisfactory way of considering the cultivated forms of the Guinea yams is to regard them simply as members of the *rotundata/cayenensis* group without commitment as to whether this currently represents one or two species, but acknowledging that at least two wild species have contributed

Nevertheless, at the present time, within the ethnographic present, and within the few hundred years that written history has existed in most of Africa, the use of cultivated yams as the principal food crop has been restricted to a comparatively limited part of Africa. This is the area of West Africa between the Bandama River of the central Ivory Coast in the west and the Cameroun mountains in the east, and from the sea, or the coastal lagoons or swamps in the south to the northern climatic limit of yam cultivation (roughly, the 800 millimeter isohyet). This is the ethnobotanical domain originally described by Miège (1954) as "la civilization de l'igname" in contrast to "la civilization du riz" to the west where the upland rice *Oryza glaberrima* Stapf. was traditionally the main nutritional basis of the diet. The concept of the "yam zone" has been investigated further by the present author (Coursey 1965, 1966, 1967; Alexander and Coursey 1969; Coursey and Coursey 1971; Ayensu and Coursey 1972), as has the association of the zone with ethnic boundaries, with the area occupied by people speaking languages of the eastern Kwa linguistic group (Murdock 1959), and with the highest indigenous cultures of the forest areas of Africa, such as the Akan states, Ife, Benin, and Igbo Ukwu (see Map 1). Today, this comparatively limited area of Africa produces more than ninety percent of the yams grown in the continent. This may in part be a reflection of the high population densities in much of the yam zone which, in turn, may well be associated with a long tradition of yam-based agriculture (Shaw, this volume). The fact remains that outside the yam zone, yams are proportionately quite minor crops.

On the basis of present-day distribution of cultivation, the writer has earlier (Coursey 1967) suggested a Center of Origin of yam cultivation, in the Vavilovian sense, "on the fringe of the West African forest belt, either within the savannah, or possibly in the Dahomey gap" and that there "may have been a subsidiary centre nearer or in the Congo basin." The first and more important of these would at least approximately

---

to their ancestry. The contributions of the two (or more) wild species vary from one cultivar to another so that the whole corpus of cultivated material represents in fact a spectrum of forms ranging at one extreme from selected forms of *D. cayenensis* sensu strictu to something approaching pure, but again selected, *D. praehensilis* at the other extreme. The more that the former species has contributed to the ancestry of a particular cultivar, the more it is adapted to forest rather than savanna conditions, that is, to a short dry season and a longer period of vegetative growth; the converse is also true. Further experimental work on this hypothesis is needed, however, in the form of chemotaxonomic studies on a large number of the cultivated forms, preferably in conjunction with work on the photoperiodic response of the same cultivars which may be indicative of their latitude of origin (Ayensu and Coursey 1972).

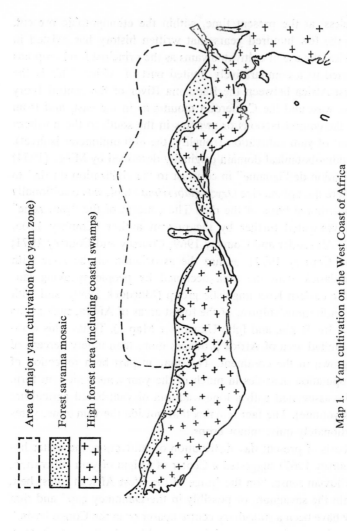

Area of major yam cultivation (the yam zone)

Forest savanna mosaic

High forest area (including coastal swamps)

Map 1.   Yam cultivation on the West Coast of Africa

coincide with the West African center proposed for various other African crops (Murdock 1959; Wrigley 1960; Portères 1962; Morgan 1962). No comment on the geographical Centers of Origin of yam cultivation in Africa had been made by either Vavilov or de Candolle.

It has been proposed recently (Harlan 1971) that the concept of a geographically compact Center of Origin is only applicable to grain-crop and similar domesticates of the temperate or subtropical regions and that the vegetatively-propagated crop plants of the humid tropical or equatorial regions were domesticated over much larger, diffuse areas or "noncenters." The African yams, on the basis of this concept, originated in cultivation merely somewhere within the African "noncenter."

The use of yams as food is, to a limited extent, certainly a feature of most of the area covered by Harlan's African "noncenter," but the intense concentration of the cultivation of yams, especially of the *rotundata/cayenensis* group, in the West African yam zone needs some further explanation. The use of the more highly ennobled cultivars towards the *rotundata* end of the hybrid spectrum (cf. Note 2) is largely confined to this part of Africa. These yams, in common with other members of the section Enantiophyllum of *Dioscorea*, are nontoxic; the wild forms have tubers which penetrate deeply into the ground and also often have spinous stems, which protect the plants from attack by rooting animals. Most of the yams commonly used in other parts of Africa (apart from recent non-African introductions) belong to other sections — for example *D. dumetorum*, Lasiophyton; *D. preussii*, Macrocarpeae; *D. bulbifera*, Opsophyton; and *D. sansibarensis*, Macroura — which secrete alkaloidal or steroidal toxins to a greater or lesser extent. Such toxins are comparatively simply removed by extraction of water — usually the running water of a stream, after some form of grating, shredding, or slicing — but nevertheless need the conscious application of a detoxification process. It may well be that there is a contrast between separate courses towards domestication that were followed more widely by the toxic yams and the nontoxic Enantiophyllum yams in a more restricted area.

In the case of the *rotundata/cayenensis* group of yams, although it may be incorrect to define a strictly Vavilovian Center of Origin of cultivation, progress towards domestication, the formation and ennoblement of clonal vegetative cultivars, and the emergence of cultigens appear to have taken place in a fairly limited area. If it is accepted that the yams of this group are of hybrid origin, with both forest species (*D. cayenensis* sensu strictu) and savanna species (*D. praehensilis* and/or *D. abyssinica*) contributing to their ancestry, they could only have arisen at the ecotone between forest and savanna, along with what could be termed as "Axis of Origin" generally running in an east to west direction, but dipping southward in the Dahomey Gap.[3]

The use of other species of yam is fairly well diffused over the whole of the African "noncenter," but nowhere else are they of such importance. It has been suggested on linguistic grounds that the cultivation of yams was formerly more widespread, at least in East Africa, and that they have been displaced by other crops, but the evidence is by no means clear (Posnansky 1968; Coursey 1969). It is certain, however, that in times of famine even the most highly toxic yams are used as emergency foods in many parts of Africa, even where yams are not normally cultivated today (Burkill 1939; Coursey 1967). The importance of yams in African cultural history appears, however, to be greatest in West Africa, and most of the discussion here refers to this area.

The Antiquity of Yam Domestication in Africa

Most of what can be said chronologically concerning the domestication of yams in Africa is necessarily highly speculative in view of the limited archaeological data that are available in the relevant parts of Africa, especially with regard to pre-Iron Age times. Not only has comparatively little systematic excavation been undertaken, but both soil and climate are unfavorable to the preservation of archaeological material; and neither parts of yam plants themselves, nor the wooden digging sticks that even today are often used in their cultivation, are likely to be preserved (Alexander 1970; Posnansky 1969).

Until recently, a general impression existed that all African agriculture was fairly recent and was derived largely from external influence.

---

[3] Shaw has suggested (this volume) that the dense populations in the southeastern parts of the yam zone — approximately the present-day Igbo-speaking areas — are associated with a high antiquity of controlled yam and oil palm exploitation in those areas. Further, there are some rather tenuous indications that at the other end of the zone the western limit of intensive yam cultivation has been moving further westward in comparatively recent times (less than 1000 B.P.) into the area where rice is the dominant staple. It has been pointed out by Harris (1972) that vegecultural systems do not normally expand at the expense of grain-based cultures.

Taken together, these considerations would be consistent with the concept that the earliest domestication of yams occurred at the eastern end of the forest-savanna axis of West Africa rather than elsewhere. It must be emphasized, however, that this is highly speculative and is contrary to the ideas on population movements in West Africa put forward by Flight (this volume).

It has been suggested that penetration of the forest zone for permanent settlement was impossible before the introduction of iron tools (J. Clark 1962), and even that modern human populations reached the coastal areas of West Africa only within the last millennium (Ward 1969). It is now becoming established, however, that there is some continuity of cultural tradition in the forest areas of West Africa extending back at least to the Mesolithic (Willett 1971; Ozanne 1971), the introduction of iron around 2500 to 2000 B.P. merely rendering the process of forest clearing more efficacious. It has been established (Gray 1962) that African Neolithic stone axes are quite effective tools for felling moderate-sized trees, while larger areas could be cleared by firing. Evidence from other parts of the humid tropics, such as New Guinea (Powell 1970), shows that forests were cleared effectively by people with only stone tools and fire at least 5000 B.P. Yam cultivation on a systematic basis obviously antedates the historic period on the West African coast. One of the earliest Iberian explorers (Pacheco Pereira 1505) mentions not only the cultivation of yams at various points, but an established trade in yams between Bonny in the eastern Niger delta and yam-growing areas "hundred of leagues" inland at the time of his visits, nearly 500 B.P. From then on there are frequent references to yams by European visitors to West Africa, many of whom emphasize the importance of the crop. The prohibition on the use of iron tools at certain rituals associated with yam cultivation is at least suggestive that it antedates the introduction of iron, but as the West African Iron Age is little more than 2,000 years old, this suggestion provides no indication of a very high antiquity of yam domestication. Indeed, it has been suggested (Baker 1962) that the yams "need not be assumed to have any great antiquity as cultivated plants." A conventional approach based on the views of J. Clark (1962, 1964) is that cultural diffusion from southwestern Asia via Egypt and the Sudan introduced grain-crop agriculture to the West African savanna, sorghum and millet replacing the wheat and barley of Asia and Egypt. The concept of agriculture was then transmitted to hunter-gatherers already inhabiting the northern fringes of the forest, who adopted yams and other tubers (such as *Solenostemon (Coleus), Anchomanes,* and *Sphenostylis*) into cultivation rather than grains. This contact would be dated around 5000 to 4000 B.P.

There is little doubt that such culture contacts and the introduction of iron tools two or three thousand years later played a major part in the development of yam cultivation in West Africa to its present level of sophistication. Somewhat comparable cultural interactions appear to have taken place in all three main areas of the world where yams are cultivated, at approximately the same time, 5000 to 4000 B.P. (Alexander and Coursey 1969).

These interactions can be regarded, of course, as taking place between the differing cultures of Harlan's "noncenters" with their corresponding centers. It has already been seen that in the Southeast Asian "noncenter" there is direct archaeological evidence for Mesolithic cultures based on some systematically controlled exploitation of economic plants. Thus, prior to cultural interactions with grain-crop agriculturalists, the inhabitants of the "noncenter" had progressed substantially beyond the basic hunter-gatherer level towards a symbiotic relationship with their food plants. Even in the absence of archaeological evidence, this is a more satisfactory hypothesis than one based on contact between relatively advanced agriculturalists and primitive hunter-gatherers. Most historic experience of such contacts indicates that they are associated with such severe cultural shock as to lead to the destruction or near destruction of the latter groups or to their assimilation almost without trace, whereas, in fact, in both Asia and Africa high cultures based on vegeculture have emerged (Coursey 1972). Although there is, at present, no clear evidence in Africa of Mesolithic horticultural civilizations comparable to those discussed by Chang (1970) in Asia, similar considerations may well apply, and African yam cultivation can be accepted as having its origins in a culture that developed initially without significant contacts from outside the "noncenter."

In the case of Southeast Asia, Barrau (1970) relates the emergence of symbiotic relationships between man and plant to religiously-sanctioned concepts of protection of edible wild plants, citing Burkill's discussion (1953) of the Andamanese ritual control of the collection of their main food yam, *D. glabra* Roxb., and other important vegetable foods from the wild. These ritual sanctions served to encode culturally the empirically acquired knowledge of the factors necessary to ensure the survival of the food plant species, while continuing to utilize it as a source of human food.

We have used an approach which is virtually identical, even in making reference to Burkill's concepts (1953), in an analysis of the West African New Yam Festival (Coursey and Coursey 1971). This festival is, or was within living memory, the major socioreligious event in the year in the West African yam zone, being the equivalent at once of the New Year and the Harvest Festival in the grain-crop-oriented cultures of temperate western Eurasia. It was held to mark the time when yams of the new crop could first be eaten, that is, the end of the period of ritual prohibition of their consumption, that period which corresponds to the phase of active growth of the yam plant during which it is highly susceptible to damage and, at the same time, would give only a very small yield of tubers. We have suggested that it is a social survival from extremely remote times when the inhabitants of the area were at the gathering stage of development but were beginning to develop some concept of protecting their wild food resources by ritual sanctions comparable to those of the Southeast Asian region (Barrau 1970; Coursey and Coursey 1971). It was also suggested that this concept of protection as a first phase of domestication might date back as far as the end of the terminal Pleistocene, when the contraction of the habitable environment, caused by the expansion of the Sahara, was placing a strain on the reserves of wild vegetable foods — of which yams would have been a most important element.[4]

There is, to date, no rigorous archaeological proof for this hypothesis, but what evidence is available is not inconsistent. Through much of the Congo basin and West Africa, artifacts are found which are described as hoes and as being suitable for the digging of yams and similar subterranean plant materials (Davies 1960, 1967, 1968) deriving from the paleolithic Sangoan and Lupemban cultures, dating from 40,000 B.P. or even earlier.

Evidence is now beginning to appear (Willett 1971) for the development of microlithic industries within the yam zone at dates around 10,000 B.P. — industries which are indicative of an increasing degree of cultural sophistication. Most of the artifactual material found so far is associated with hunting rather than plant-food-collecting activities, but the same applies to the material possessions of hunter-gatherer cultures within historic times, even though such people usually derive a substantial part of their nutrition from vegetable foods.

The Process of Domestication of Yams in Africa

In discussing the antiquity of yam utilization in Africa, we have already

---

[4] The concepts put forward here were originally developed on the basis of the assumption that the initial stimulus towards domestication of yams in West Africa was provided by the increasing desiccation of the environment at the close of a pluvial period, and the corresponding southward shift of the desert-savanna and savanna-forest ecotones. However, it should be pointed out that not dissimilar pressures on human populations could alternatively have arisen from the northward spread of the forest into the previously inhabited savanna at the onset of a pluvial. Recently developed ideas on the pluvial history of West Africa (van Zinderen Bakker, this volume) need to be considered in this content. The rest of the thesis presented here, however, remains unchanged by this alternative concept.

given some indication of the processes involved in the early stages of domestication. As has been indicated by Harris (1967, 1969, 1972), the domestication of vegetatively propagated crops such as yams should not be regarded as a sudden cultural change comparable to the "Neolithic Revolution" of Southwest Asia (Childe 1951, 1952), but rather as a gradual evolutionary process.[5] More detailed examination of this process indicates that it can be divided into the following phases:

1.   Hunter-gatherer man from the earliest times, or at least after he had established the controlled use of fire (before 60,000 B.P.), utilized yams of many species collected from the wild in those parts of Africa where they grow.

2.   In the period of the Sangoan and Lupemban paleolithic industries (45,000 to 15,000 B.P.), large stone hoes or picks were developed, apparently especially for the excavation of hypogeous plant foods including yams.

3.   During this period the first concepts of protecting wild food resources by ritual or other sanctions started to develop. It should be noted that even preagricultural peoples, such as the present-day Bushmen (Schapera 1930), have concepts of protection of wild plant food resources, some of which are systematized in magico-religious concepts. Further, it is established (Campbell 1966) that even Neanderthal man had begun to sublimate individual demands to the needs of the community, again using ritual sanctions as regulators of individual behavior.

4.   Beginning around 11,000 B.P., the evidence from Lake Chad (van

---

[5]   In the case of the cereal crops the first major step in the domestication process can simply be identified with a genetic factor – the appearance of th nonshattering rachis. No such simple distinction can be made in the case of the yams. It must also be borne in mind that the domestication process must be much more gradual than with the seed propagated crops, as sexual reproduction is only involved in the initial stages when the plant is still close to the wild form. Once a particular yam has been taken into domestication, it is propagated entirely clonally, and the opportunity for sexual recombination rarely if ever takes place. All plants of a single yam clone are essentially isolated fragments of the same individual plant and should therefore be genetically identical. It is well known, however, that yams are extremely plastic in cultivation, and it is possible that somatic mutation plays a part in this. The only criteria of domestication that can so far be suggested for the yams are: (1) the partial or complete loss of the natural defence mechanisms — toxicity, spinous development of stem or root, or deep-burying habit in the tuber; (2) loss of sexual fertility; and (3) a high degree of polyploidy. None of these, however, are entirely satisfactory. The degree of ploidy has not yet been studied in a sufficient variety of cultivated forms for definitive statements to be made with confidence, although very high polyploids are known. The loss of sexual fertility may be at least in part associated with the juvenility of form that is artifically maintained by the practice of continuous vegetative propagation from small tuber fragments.

Zinderen Bakker, this volume) suggests that there may have been a contraction of the West African forest and savanna environments which favored both man and yams. At about the same time the diffusion of more modern types of man (the proto-Negro) of the Kanjeran genetic stock into the West African savanna began (Brothwell 1963). These new human types were associated with the appearance of microlithic industries which may be regarded as indicative of the emergence of a more sophisticated level of interaction between man and his environment (but see Note 4).

5.   From the human point of view this process of interaction involved the increasing regularization of the exploitation of plant food resources. At the same time, man was modifying the natural ecosystem and thereby creating new ecological niches, prominent among which would have been middens and the cleared areas around habitations — situations comparable to the "dump-heaps" proposed by Anderson (1952) as the sites of many early plant domestications. In these artifactual environments and, especially, subject to the interest and protection of man, spontaneous hybrid or mutant plant forms were able to survive which would have been eliminated by natural selection processes in the undisturbed natural environment. This was of special relevance in the case of the nontoxic Enantiophyllum yams, ancestral to the yams cultivated today in West Africa. The human populations using wild or semi-wild yams originally lived mainly on the savanna between the forest and the Sahara; as this environment contracted and, at the same time, the human populations increased, they increasingly penetrated the forest fringes. Such clearings provided suitable locations for interspecific crossing between savanna species — *D. praehensilis* and *D. abyssinica* — and the forest *D. cayenensis* and for the survival, under protection, of forms superior to both as food plants but less adapted to survival in the wild — the ancestral *D. rotundata*. A parallel exists between this concept of a major step towards domestication occurring as part of human penetration of a nonoptimal environment and the Flannery-Binford model that has been used (Wright 1971) in connection with cereal domestication in southwestern Asia (Shaw, this volume).

6.   As the greater control of food resources permitted the further expansion of human populations and, simultaneously, as the move into the less congenial forest environment encouraged closer association for mutual protection within a human group, individual human settlements tended to increase in size. This generated further needs for regular food supplies concentrated into limited localities, and the domestication process moved forward from the simple, ritual protection of natural

"stands" of food plants (some of which were already in man-created ecological niches such as middens and disturbed ground) to the removal of wild plants to more convenient, accessible, or advantageous locations in or near settlements. Such an operation has actually been observed within the ethnographic present (Chevalier 1936) with *D. dumetorum* in the Ubangui-Shari: plants were collected for food from the wild, and those not immediately required were replanted near the settlements. This process was described as "protoculture."

7.   With increasing regularization of production, yams, by now of partially ennobled forms, became capable of supplying needs sometimes in excess of immediate requirements. The yam tuber, as the dormant phase of the entire plant, is inherently well adapted for storage, and tubers could therefore be reserved for future use. Once the concept of planting had been developed in connection with removal of wild plants to better locations, the idea of replanting a stored tuber, which had begun to sprout at the end of the endogenous period of dormancy, would not be a difficult one to develop.

8.   By 5000 to 4000 B.P., after an intervening pluvial period, another period of desiccation occurred causing further population movements out of the Sahara belt. These were now Neolithic grain-crop agriculturalists, already influenced by Southwest Asian cultural patterns. Interaction between these peoples and the yam "protoculturalists," who were fairly sophisticated by now, was possible on a basis of approximate equality, and cross-fertilization of ideas took place leading eventually to the development of a yam-based agriculture in something approaching the present form.

9.   With the introduction of iron-working into West Africa around 2500 B.P., penetration deeper into the forest was facilitated. As this human penetration into increasingly humid areas progressed, yams were increasingly favored ecologically at the expense of grain crops. The yam-using ethnic groups were thus able to evolve to higher cultural levels as they had a more adequate, reliable, and generally superior nutritional basis. The more complex societies thus developing, with varying degrees of socioeconomic specialization within a culture, gave opportunities for: increased conscious development of yam-growing practices; the elaboration of associated philosophical notions, enriching the nonmaterial culture; further ennoblement of cultivars; and the exchange of cultivars between groups, facilitating the spread of optimal forms.

SYNTHESIS

The domestication of the yam in Africa may thus be viewed as an essentially indigenous process based on wild African species. Only in its later stages was it influenced by external factors through cultural interactions — Southwest Asian Neolithic culture, the use of iron tools, and the introduction of non-African genetic material.

The initial moves towards domestication did not consist of any traumatic changes comparable to the "Neolithic Revolution" of Southwest Asia but rather of the gradual evolution of a symbiotic relationship between man and yam. At the same time this involved a realization of the physiological nature of the yam plant as needing protection from exploitation at certain stages of its growth cycle and an increasing communalization of control over plant food resources, subordinating immediate individual needs to long-term social ones. These two factors were eventually encoded into a complex of ritual socioreligious sanctions which regulated the behavior of man towards the yam plant in such a way as to facilitate the emergence of stable cultivars and cultigens. A "protocultural" system was elaborated capable of assimilating major external cultural influences when these occurred. The consequence was a complete agricultural complex.

These crucial processes occurred along an axis at the forest-savanna ecotone in the eastern part of West Africa corresponding to the present day "yam zone." It is suggested that the emergence of this symbiotic relationship is chronologically associated with the appearance of microlithic industries in a dry phase ca. 10,000 B.P. This crucial stage in the interrelationship of man and yam could thus be linked with the beginnings of the evolution and diversification of the ancestors of the Negro races.

REFERENCES

ALEXANDER, J.
  1970   "The domestication of yams: a multidisciplinary approach," in *Science and archaeology*. Edited by D. R. Brothwell and E. Higgs. London: Thames and Hudson.
ALEXANDER, J., D. G. COURSEY
  1969   "The domestication of the yams," in *The domestication and exploitation of plants and animals*. Edited by P. J. Ucko and G. W. Dimbleby. London: Duckworth.
ANDERSON, E.
  1952   *Plants, man and life*. Boston: Little, Brown.

AXELROD, D. I.
   1970   Mesozoic paleogeography and early angiosperm history. *Botanical Review* 36(3):277–319.
AYENSU, E. S.
   1970   Comparative anatomy of *Dioscorea rotundata* Poir and *Dioscorea cayenensis* Lamk. *Biol. J. Linn. Soc.*, supplement one, 63:127–136. 136.
   1972   *Anatomy of the Monocotyledons*, volume six: *Dioscoreales*. Edited by C. R. Metcalfe. Oxford: Clarendon Press.
AYENSU, E. S., D. G. COURSEY
   1972   Guinea yams. *Economic Botany* 26(4):301–318.
BAKER, H. G.
   1962   Comments on the thesis that there was a major centre of plant domestication near the headwaters of the River Niger. *Journal of African History* 3(2):229–233.
BARRAU, J.
   1965a   L'humide et le sec. *J. Polynesian Soc.* 74(3):329–346.
   1965b   Histoire et préhistoire horticoles de l'Océanie tropicale. *J. Soc. Océanistes* 21(21):55–78.
   1970   La région indo-pacifique comme centre de mise en culture et de domestication des végétaux. *J. Agric. Trop. Bot. Appl.* 17(12):487–504.
BATE-SMITH, E. C.
   1968   The phenolic constituents of plants and heir taxonomic significance. *J. Linn. Soc. (Bot.)* 60(383):325–356.
BOURRET, DOMINIQUE
   1972   Private communication from ORSTOM, New Caledonia.
BROTHWELL, D. R.
   1963   Evidence of early population change in central and southern Africa: doubts and problems. *Man* 63(132):101–104.
BURKILL, I. H.
   1921   The correct botanic names for the white and yellow Guinea yams. *Gdn's Bull., Straits Settl.* 2(12):438–441.
   1924   A list of oriental vernacular names of the genus *Dioscorea*. *Gdn's Bull. Straits Settl.* 3(4/6):121–244.
   1938   The contact of the Portuguese with African food plants which gave words such as "yam" to European languages. *Proc. Linn. Soc.*, London 150(2):84–95.
   1939   Notes on the genus *Dioscorea* in the Belgian Congo. *Bull. Jard. bot. Etat. Brux.* 15(4):345–392.
   1951   The rise and decline of the greater yam in the service of man. *Advmt. Sci.*, London 7(28):443–448.
   1953   Habits of man and the history of cultivated plants in the Old World. *Proc. Linn. Soc.*, London 164(1):12–42.
   1960   The organography and the evolution of the Dioscoreaceae, the family of the yams. *J. Linn. Soc. (Bot.)* 56(367):319–412.
CAMPBELL, B. G.
   1966   *Human evolution: an introduction to man's adaptations*. Chicago: Aldine Press.

CHANG, K-C.
1967 The Yale expedition to Taiwan and the South-East Asian horticultural evolution. *Discovery* 2(2):3–10.
1970 The beginnings of agriculture in the Far East. *Antiquity* 44:175–185.

CHANG, K-C., M. STUIVER
1966 Recent advances in the prehistoric archaeology of Formosa. *Proc. Natn. Acad. Sci. USA* 55:539–543.

CHEVALIER, A.
1909 Sur les Dioscoréas cultivés en Afrique tropicale et sur un cas de sélection naturelle relatif à une espècce spontanée dans la forêt vierge. *C.r. Hebd. Acad. Sci., Paris* 149(15):610–612.
1936 Contrbiution à l'étude de quelques espèces africains du genre *Dioscoréa. Bull. Mus. Natn. Hist. Nat. Paris*, second series 8(6): 520–551.
1946 Nouvelles recherches sur les ignames ccultivées. *Revue Int. Bot. Appl. Agric. Trop.* 26(279–280):26–31.

CHILDE, V. G.
1951 *Man makes himself*. New York: Mentor Books.
1952 *New light on the most ancient East*. London: Routledge and Kegan Paul.

CLARK, G.
1969 *World prehistory: a new outline*. Cambridge: Cambridge University Press.

CLARK, J. D.
1962 The spread of food production in sub-Saharan Africa. *Journal of African History* 3(2):211–228.
1964 The prehistoric origins of African agriculture. *Journal of African History* 5(2):161–183.
1970 *The prehistory of Africa*. London: Thames and Hudson.

COURSEY, D. G.
1965 The role of yams in West African food economies. *World Crops* 17(2):74–82.
1966 The cultivation and use of yams in West Africa. *Ghana Notes and Queries* (9):45–54.
1967 *Yams*. London: Longmans Green.
1969 Yams in East Africa. *Uganda Journal* 3(1):86.
1972 The civilizations of the yams. *Archeol. Phys. Anthropol., Oceania* 7(3):215–233.

COURSEY, D. G., J. ALEXANDER
1968 African agricultural patterns and the sickle cell. *Science* 160 (3835):1474–1475.

COURSEY, D. G., CECILIA K. COURSEY
1971 The New Yam Festivals of West Africa. *Anthropos* 66:444–484.

COURSEY, D. G., F. W. MARTIN
1970 The past and future of yams as crop plants. *Proc. 2nd. Int. Symp. Trop. Root Crops, Hawaii* 1:87–93, 99–101.

DALZIEL, J. M.
1937 *The useful plants of West Tropical Africa*. London: Crown Agents.

DAVIES, O.
  1960   The neolithic revolution in tropical Africa. *Trans. Hist. Soc., Ghana* 4(2):14–20.
  1967   *West Africa before the Europeans.* London: Methuen.
  1968   The origins of agriculture in West Africa. *Current Anthropology* 9(5):479–482.
DUMONT, R.
  1966   *False start in Africa.* London: Deutsch.
GORMAN, C. F.
  1969   Hoabinhian: a pebble-tool complex with early plant associations in South East Asia. *Science* 163(3868):671–673.
GRAY, R.
  1962   A report on the conference. *Journal of African History* 3(2):195–209.
HARLAN, J.
  1971   Agricultural origins: centers and noncenters. *Science* 154(4008):468–474.
HARRIS, D. R.
  1967   New light on plant domestication and the origins of agriculture. *Geogrl. Rev.* 57(1):90–107.
  1969   "Agricultural systems, ecosystems and the origins of agriculture," in *The domestication and exploitation of plants and animals.* Edited by P. J. Ucko and G. W. Dimbleby. London: Duckworth.
  1972   The origins of agriculture in the tropics. *American Scientist* 60(2):180–193.
HARRISON, T.
  1963   100,000 years of Stone-Age culture in Borneo. *J. Roy. Soc. Arts* 112(5091):174–191.
HAUDRICOURT, A. G.
  1962   Domestication des animaux, culture des plantes et civilization d'autrui. *L'Homme* 2:40–50.
  1964   Nature et culture dans la civilization de l'igname, origine des clones et des clans. *L'Homme* 4:93–104.
HAUDRICOURT, A. G., L. HEDIN
  1943   *L'Homme et les plantes cultivées.* Paris: Libraire Gallimead.
HAVINDEN, M. A.
  1970   The history of crop cultivation in West Africa. *Econ. Hist. Rev.* 23(3):532–555.
HAWKES, J. G.
  1970   The origin of agriculture. *Econ. Bot.* 24(2):131–133.
HEISER, C. B.
  1969   Some considerations on early plant domestication. *BioScience* 19(3):228–231.
JUMELLE, H.
  1922   Ignames sauvages et ignames cultivées à Madagascar. *Revue Int. Bot. Appl. Agric. Trop.* 2(9):193–197.
JUMELLE, H., H. PERRIER DE LA BATHIE
  1910   Fragments biologiques de la flore de Madagascar. *Ann. Mus. Colon. Marseille*, second series 8:373–468.

MIÈGE, J.
1948   Le *Dioscoréa esculenta* Burkill en Côte d'Ivoire. *Revue Int. Bot. Appl. Agric. Trop.* 28(313–314):509–514.
1952   L'importancce économique des ignames en Côte d'Ivoire. *Revue Int. Bot. Appl. Agric. trop.* 32(353–354):144–155.
1954   Les cultures vivrières en Afrique occidentale. *Cahiers d'Outre-Mer* 7(25):25–50.
1969   "Dioscoreaceae," in *Flora of west tropical Africa* 3(1):144–154. First edition edited by J. Hutchinson and J. M. Dalziel, revised second edition edited by F. N. Hepper.

MORGAN, W. B.
1962   The forest and agriculture in West Africa. *Journal of African History* 3(2):235–239.

MURDOCK, G. P.
1959   *Africa — its peoples and their culture history.* New York: McGraw-Hill.

OZANNE, P.
1971   "Ghana," in *The African Iron Age.* Edited by P. L. Shinnie. Oxford: Clarendon Press.

PACHECO PEREIRA, D.
1505   *Esmeraldo de situ orbis.* Lisbon. (Translated into English and published by the Hakluyt Society, London, 1937.)

PERRIER DE LA BATHIE, H.
1925   Ignames cultivées et sauvages de Madagascar. *Revue Bot. Appl. Agric. Trop.* 5(46):417–428.

PORTÈRES, R.
1962   Berceaux agricoles primaires sur le continent africain. *Journal of African History* 3(2):195–210.

POSNANSKY, M.
1968   Yams. *Uganda Journal* 32(2):231–232.
1969   Yams and the origins of West African agriculture. *Odu — A Journal of West Africans Studies* 1(1):101–111.

POWELL, JOCELYN M.
1970   The history of agriculture in the New Guinea highlands. *Search* 1(5):199–200.

PRAIN, D., I. H. BURKILL
1919   Dioscorea sativa. *Bull. Misc. Inf. R. Bot. Gdns, Kew* (9):339–375.
1939   An account of the genus *Dioscorea*, part two: Species which turn to the right. *Ann. R. Bot. Gdn., Calcutta* 14:211–528.

ROGERS, D. J.
1967   A computer-aided morphological classification of *Manihot esculenta* Cranz. *Proc. 1st Int. Symp. Trop. Root Crops, Trinidad* 1(1):57–80.

SAUER, C. O.
1952   *Agricultural origins and dispersals.* New York: The American Geographical Society.

SCHAPERA, I.
1930   *The Khoisan peoples of South Africa.* London: Routledge. Research.

SHINNIE, P. L.
  1971   *The African Iron Age.* Oxford: Clarendon Press.
SIMMONDS, N. W.
  1966   *Bananas.* London: Longmans, Green.
SUGGS, R. C.
  1960   *The island civilization of Polynesia.* New York: Mentor Books.
UCKO, P. J., G. W. DIMBLEBY, *editors*
  1969   *The domestication and exploitation of plants and animals.* London: Duckworth.
WAITT, A. W.
  1963   Yams, *Dioscorea* species. *Field Crop Abstr.* 16(3):145–157.
  1965   "A key to some Nigerian variations of yam (*Dioscorea spp.*)." Memorandum 60. Ibadan: Federal Department of Agricultural
WARD, W. E. F.
  1969   *A history of Ghana.* London: Allen and Unwin.
WATT, G.
  1890   *A dictionary of the economic products of India*, volume three, 115–136. London: Allen.
WILLETT, F.
  1971   "Nigeria," in *The African Iron Age.* Edited by P. L. Shinnie. Oxford: Clarendon Press.
WRIGHT, G. A.
  1971   Origin of food production in South Western Asia: a survey of ideas. *Current Anthropology* 12(4/5):447–477.
WRIGLEY, C.
  1960   Speculations on the economic prehistory of Africa. *Journal of African History* 1(2):189–203.

African Cereals: Eleusine, Fonio, Black Fonio, Teff, Brachiaria, paspalum, Pennisetum, and African Rice

ROLAND PORTÈRES

FINGER MILLET (*Eleusine coracana* Gaertner)

Eleusine coracana Gaertner 1788 is a domesticated cereal which is widely cultivated both in the Indian peninsula and in Ceylon, in Abyssinia, and on the mountainous regions of the Congo-Nile watershed.

Presumed Ancestry — (E. indica)

Since Hooker (1897) it is accepted that Eleusine derives from the wild species *Eleusine indica* Gaertner. However, certain important differences separate the two species. The cereal is more robust, taller, and rich in culms; its leaves are wide and long; the inflorescence has thick ears which are generally upright initially, then curved in toward the interior, arranged in a closed or half-open umbel; in general, there is no supernumerary ear beneath the umbel. The axis of the spikelet (rachis) does not disarticulate above the glumes at maturity; the spikelet does not fall off by itself for natural dispersal; the glumes and the lodicules have a different morphology. The achenes (caryopses) are globulo-ovoid, delicately covered with lines of fine striae, and emerge from their envelopes with difficulty.

In the case of *E. indica*, there are opposite characteristics; the achenes are trigonal, rough on the surface, and emerge from their envelopes easily. The chromosomal numbers are $2n = 36$ for the cereal and $2n = 18$ for the wild species. *E. indica* grows in cool regions of human habitation in the entire intertropical zone of Africa and Asia, from sea level up to an altitude of 2,800 meters (Himalayan). It is not a plant restricted particularly to high altitudes.

Variation in E. coracana

A large number of agrarian varieties of *E. coracana* are more or less well known. The existence of several subspecies has also been considered: (1) *E. coracana* Gaertner 1788 (*sensu stricto*) of Ceylon, (2) *E. stricta* Roxburgh 1832 of India, (3) *E. tocusso* Fresenius 1827 of Abyssinia, and (4) *E. luco* Welwitsch 1859 of Angola. They all derive from a Linnean type *E. coracana* Gaertner 1788 (*Cynosurus coracanus* Linnaeus 1753).

All of the species of eleusine are gathered during periods of famine in India and Africa. The grain of *E. indica*, in particular, is picked continuously in the regions around Lake Chad (Chevalier 1922; Dalziel 1937; Creac'h 1941), and in South Africa among the southern Sothos. On the Indian peninsula the grain of all species of eleusine is picked by indigent inhabitants (Royle 1839).

E. indica is a semiruderal commonly found along roadsides, in meadows, and in cultivated fields. De Candolle (1855) thought that since it has no Sanskrit name, it might be a plant of modern origin in India. In Africa, it is also a semiruderal.

Eleusine is raised especially at high altitudes, and the tendency is to believe that this cereal originated as such in mountainous regions, for example, the Abyssinian plateaux and the Himalayan foothills. However the plant can be cultivated just as well at very low altitudes.

In India, as in Abyssinia, barley (*Hordeum*) stops at approximately 1,600 meters. Rice in India grows at 900 meters with difficulty, with rare varieties being cultivated slightly higher (Nepal, Kashmir). In every case, eleusine is grown at succeeding altitudes, whenever the combination of soil and climate is not favorable to wheat (*Triticum*).

On the high plateaux of Abyssinia, eleusine reaches an altitude of 2,300 to 2,400 meters (in the Wuina Dega). In the eastern Himalayas and in Kashmir, it is normally grown up to 1,600 meters and sometimes up to 2,700 meters. In Uganda and in northern Malawi (Nyasaland), it does not go beyond 1,600 meters; among the Wachagas of Kilimanjaro, its cultivation is spread out between 1,200 and 1,800 meters; in western Kenya, among the Suks, it is grown between 1,500 and 2,500 meters.

The ecological adaptations of this cereal enable it to flourish in regions which limit the possibilities of exploitation of other cereals. It is also the only cereal which can adapt to very steep slopes, and it is commonly planted in such locations, most varieties being unable to tolerate stagnant humidity (Portères 1951a: 37–38).

In the hills and mountains of India, it is especially the types with more or less closed inflorescences (multiple ears curved in toward the center) which are cultivated; on low-lying and alluvial plains, it is especially the types with digitate inflorescences with straight ears (Roxburgh 1832). In Africa the types which have closed inflorescences are generally cultivated at high altitudes.

Geographic Origin: India or Abyssinia?

William Roxburgh (1832) suggested an Indian origin, clearly distinguishing between *E. indica, E. stricta, E. coracana,* and other species in India. He found the latter two only in the cultivated state.

E. coracana corresponded to Twaithes' Singhalese type, recognized by Gaertner, with umbels of curved ears resembling a loosely-closed fist. This type is cultivated especially on hills; it is hardy and precocious, drought-resistant, and not very productive.

E. stricta Roxburgh is very similar to *E. indica* in its umbels of widely spread and more numerous ears and its preference for rich, light soils. This is the type most cultivated throughout India; it is very productive, it has a longer vegetative cycle, and it produces fatter grains. In rocky and sandy soils, this type resembles *E. indica* (Watt 1908: 518). *E. stricta* has not been found in Africa.

For De Candolle (1883) the Sanskrit name (*Rajika*), the diversity of appellations in India (a sign of antiquity), and botanical probabilities all concur to show an Indian origin of *E. coracana.* At the same time, he points out the existence in Abyssinia of a closely related species, *E. tocussa* Fresenius, "an almost unknown plant of African origin."

There are many Sanskrit terms (*Rajika, Ragi*) which date, however, only from the eighth century of the Christian era (Bower Manuscript). Mention of a *Ragi* beer that Emperor Baber of Punjab drank in 1525 is made in his memoirs (Watt 1908). *Rajika* is the "red-colored" grain, and is compared to *Korakan*, the "dark grain" of Ceylon (Portères 1958).

In 1950, we took up this question again, concluding that the problem of the geographic origin of *E. coracana* still remained unresolved, although arguing in part for an Indian origin. In an exhaustive study particularly concerning this cereal (1951a), we were more favorably inclined toward this Asian origin.

In southern India, two sites have delivered grains of *Eleusine coracana*: (1) Hallur, on the western coast, dating from 1800 B.C., according to Dr. Nagaraja Rao; and (2) Paiyampali, on the eastern coast, according to Shri S. R. Rao (Allchin 1969).

Vavilov (1926), however, considered the high plateaux of Abyssinia the possible center of origin. His conclusion is based on the varietal diversification encountered there and on the importance given locally to this plant in cereal agriculture. But these facts are just as much in evidence all along the Congo-Nile dorsal, as far as Zululand and Angola, and likewise in India.

In a later study of the different appellations of this plant throughout the world (Portères 1958), we were inclined, however, without affirming or proving it, to indicate instead an African origin.

But the evidence that many varieties exist in Abyssinia and East Africa, and that their number decreases very rapidly toward the West, stopping in Chad and Bauchi, on the one hand, and in Angola, on the other, does not provide sufficient arguments to give an Indian origin to the Abyssinian center. Moreover, the two remote regions of eleusine cultivation mentioned above are recent (Lopez 1591), and probably only date from the middle of the sixteenth century. The Indian peninsula also concentrates a large number of varieties in Asia, but the surrounding regions (except for Ceylon) hardly have any at all. We have, then, at our disposal two large centers of varietal diversification without, however, being able to affirm that one derives from the other, or vice versa.

Expansion of Eleusine Within Africa

Among the Washagas of Tanzania (Kilimanjaro) who are the greatest and most advanced growers of eleusine in Africa, with systems and techniques highly adapted to diverse local conditions, eleusine is called m-Pégé, m-Bégé (Holst 1895). In Kenya around Lake Victoria and Mount Elgon, eleusine is known in Elgumi as Baga, in Nandi as Paiyna (languages of the Nilo-equatorial, ex-Nilo-Hamitic group).

The Nandis and the Suks are great cultivators of eleusine. They are sedentary peoples of a particular eastern Hamitic type, less pure, however, than those Masai who are of the eastern Hamitic type of the Ethiopian form. Among the Masai, the word Pagh means, as the case may be, "cereal, sorghum, or any other edible grain" (Beech 1911). The eastern Fulas also have as picked and gathered cereals: Pegge-ri, Pegam-ri, Paghi-ri. If one goes further south, one finds ro-Poko, ra-Poko, ri-Poko, u-Poko, and u-Poka in southern Rhodesia and in Natal;

these become *lu-Phoko* among the Kaffirs of Swaziland, among whom a Wajaja dialect yields *Luku*. This last vocable is the one which has passed into the southern Congo (Kasai) and Angola: *Luko, Lüko, Lüku, Luho, Luhe* (Welwitsch, etc. . . .).[1]

The migration of eleusine can be followed according to names from north of Lake Victoria to Natal and Angola. There is, then, the probability of an expansion starting from a northern point of arrival and following the route of the upper White Nile.

Thus, we may already suggest that all of East Africa, from Kenya and Uganda as far as Natal, on one hand, and from the Zambezi to Angola, on the other, has proceeded in the cultivation of eleusine from a migration of the cereal starting from two points of origin: (1) Lake Victoria and its eastern edge, and (2) the southeastern coast.

In his study of Bantu expansion, based on frequencies of general linguistic radicals and on radiocarbon dating in the whole area occupied by the Bantus, Oliver (1966) revealed four stages of expansion. The first encompasses the base of departure in the sparse Congo-Zambezi forests; the second is an extension reaching the coast of Mozambique and Gabon (the first half of the first current millennium, or A.D. 0 to 500); the third stretches the original nucleus close to the upper Zambezi in the south, and in the north to Lake Albert and to the west of Lake Victoria (the second half of the first current millennium, or A.D. 500 to 1000); and the fourth expands the Bantu domain as far as Mount Cameroon and Angola, on one hand, and to the entire western coast up to a meridian extended from Lake Victoria as far as Natal (the first half of the second current millennium, or 1000 to 1500 A.D.).

The mid-sixteenth century account of Lopez, which indicates the recent arrival of eleusine in Angola, coming from Lake Victoria, and the appellations given above are geographically encompassed in the fourth stage. The Bantus of the East and the South could have known eleusine only from the tenth to the sixteenth centuries. It is possible that it is at Lake Victoria, at the limit of the current domain of the Bantus, that one must look for an origin of cultivation of eleusine south of the equator.

---

[1] Lopez clearly distinguishes in Angola among three species of millet: (1) *Luco*, (2) *Mazza di Congo* or *Grano di Congo*, which is sorghum, and (3) *Mazza Manputo* '*grano de Portogallo*', still called *Manputo Portogallo*, which is '*Maiz*'. Welwitsch (1899) Ficalho, and others are positive about this — *Luco* is indeed eleusine. One must, then, reject Caspar Bauhini, 1623 (Pinax), for whom *Lucum* is the *Frumentum indicum* or *Milium indicum* of Pliny, corresponding to sorghum, as well as rejecting Linnaeus (1753) who gives synonymously both *Mazzo di Congo* and *Luco* to his '*Holcus saccharatus*' (sweet sorghum).

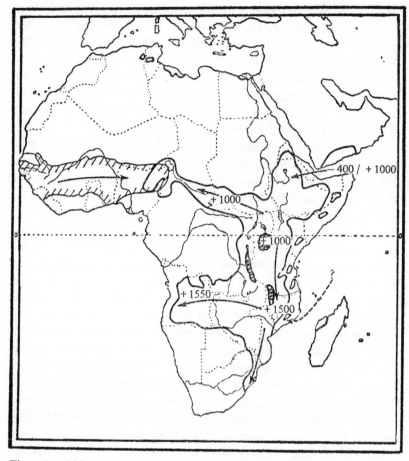

Figure 1:   African areas of cultivated millets — historical dates and movements of eleusine.
Key:

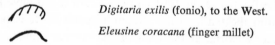

Digitaria exilis (fonio), to the West.

Eleusine coracana (finger millet)

It is possible that there was a second introduction through the south-eastern coast. On Zanzibar, eleusine is *Uimbi*, or *Uimbe*, and it is found in Kenya in Nianza and other Bantu dialects as *Wimbi* (Shantz 1920) and *Uwimbi*. In Mozambique *Naxenim* (Ficalho) is found, and in Zambia, *Mitchinim* (Kirk); on the coast of Coromandel and Malabar, the following appellations are found: Hindustani *Natcheene, Natchini, Nachani, Natchanee* (Ainslie 1813; de Orta 1913), Deccani Konkan

Nanchano (Nadkarni 1955), *Natchnee* (Graham n.d.; Birdwood 1862; etc.). *Natchini* is one of the two appellations (along with *Rajika*) known in Sanskrit for eleusine (de Orta 1913). Ficalho (1884) also believed in this Indian origin. In actual practice, these vocables only concern the western coast of India.

This is reconfirmed by the Shona appellation *Ragi*. In southwestern India this is the term for *E. coracana* in southern Hindi, among all the Dravidians, in Deccani, in Kanarese, and in Gujarati. It explains the Sanskrit *raji, rajika,* and *rajikan*. It is the "red" grain, dark red in color, thus an original meaning. *Rajika* is also, therefore, black mustard (*Sinapsis nigra* L.) in Sanskrit; the latter is a grain of the North, eleusine, a grain of the South.

As the terms of Indian origin (*Naxenim* and *Ragi*) did not penetrate deeply into the interior, nor to all the Shonas, one must suppose that the other ancient appellations were already well established. Thus, the second introduction on the coasts of Mozambique and from the mouth of the Zambezi was slightly later, but in the sixteenth century at the latest.

Geographically balancing the extension of the range of eleusine cultivation in Zambezi-Angola, there is a Nilo-Chadian extension of eleusine cultivation. The Bantus of the Northwest and those to the west of Lake Victoria currently grow eleusine in the Nilo-Chadian region.

If eleusine had been grown in the Nilo-Chadian region during Oliver's third stage, it would have been widely distributed in the Bantu territory. Since eleusine is not widely grown by the Bantu, it is highly improbable that it was grown in the Nilo-Chadian region during Oliver's third stage times. The beginning of eleusine cultivation thus must have been after the period A.D. 500 to 1000, therefore, appearing to be more or less contemporaneous with the migration to the south from Lake Victoria or after the year 1000.

It is worth emphasizing that from Senegal to the Red Sea, apart from the sorghums and pennisetums which cover the entire Sudan coastal zone, there exist two complementary areas of other millets: (1) *Digitaria exilis* (fonio, fundi) from Senegal to Bauchi and Lake Chad, and (2) *Eleusine coracana* from the Red Sea to Lake Chad and Bauchi.

Towards the Chadian contact, the two species have no great cultural importance and are varietally poor. Why were not each of these two cereals exploited over the whole climatic band? The expansion of one collided with the expansion of the other, and *vice versa*. *Digitaria* came from the upper Senegal Niger, eleusine from Nubia.

At the Chadian junction, the two cereals are geographically mixed. How long ago did this contact and interpenetration take place? Did the two millets arrive there together at the same time in history? Or rather, did one recede before the other, and, if so, which one? Did *Digitaria* arrive too late to expand toward the upper Nile, eleusine being established beforehand? Did eleusine repel *Digitaria*? The West African origin of *Digitaria* is certain but we hesitate to give eleusine an East African origin.

From the points of view of agrarian ecology, dietetics, cooking habits, and use as a fermented beverage (only eleusine), there is no trait common to the two cereals. One cannot speak of competition.

In this Nilo-Chadian region, Abyssinian terms designating eleusine are not found directly, only appellations coming from the Nubian corridor, whether they be properly Nubian, Nilo-Cushitic, or Arab Semitic (Portères 1958).

There exists a certain unity of appellations on the Eritrean and Ethiopian plateaux which is not an indication of great antiquity. Thus, *Dagussa* and *Dagusha* are found in Eritrea (Ciferri and Ciglioni 1939; Castellani and Baldrati 1939); in Ethiopia: *Dagussa* (Braun 1848; Schimper 1895; de Ronciglione 1912; Vavilov 1926; Castellani and Baldrati 1939; Ciferri and Ciglioli 1939), *Dagooja* (Russel 1923), *Tocussa* (Fresenius 1827), and *Tocusso* (Schweinfurth 1875); more specifically: Amharic *Dagusa* and Kaffa *Daucho* (Mooney 1956). Going up the White Nile and a short way up the Bahr-el-Ghazal (the edge of the Chadian region), one finds Shangalla (Dar mitchega) *Tan-Kah* (Salt 1814) and *Tokshin* (Massey 1926).

We have shown that these terms were derived from Semitic *Durra* and *Dokhn*, which are themselves doublets and apply to all sorts of cereals (Portères 1958, 1959). Thus, these vocables run as far as Chad.

Dagussa (or eleusine) is much more esteemed by the Muslims of the Abyssinian and Eritrean plateaux, while teff is mainly a luxury cereal eaten only by Christians (Cifferi and Ciglioli 1939).

Vavilov's thesis of 1926 making the high Abyssinian plateaux the homeland of this millet, considerably influenced opinions which had formerly been more oriented toward India. More recently, Murdock (1959) thought that Cushitic groups had supplied the Bantus with the Ethiopian varieties of eleusine millet and sorghum. The Semites invaded the northern highlands of Ethiopia (Axum) between 1000 and 400 B.C., perhaps bringing eleusine millet and Durra sorghum with them. It is probable that the Cushitic peoples were already cultivating hard wheat (*Trit. durum*), teff (*Eragrostis abyssinica*), barley, flax, and in many places, nung (*Guizotia abyssinica*). Simoons (1970) hesitates to link the ancient Cushitics, of before the Semitic invasion, with the cultivation of finger millet. The Semitic invasion of 1000 to 400 B.C., if it brought eleusine, is more recent than the datings of grains of this cereal found in southwestern India, 1800 B.C. (Allchin 1969).

From these arguments, then, we conclude that at present, nothing indicates an Abyssinian creation of the finger millet. Many arguments favor an Indian origin of the cultigen.*

Summary

Eleusine, or finger millet, seems to come from the currently wild species *Eleusine indica* Gaertner. The cultivated Indian forms are closer to the kinds resembling this latter species (*E. stricta* Roxb.) than to others whose inflorescence is closed in on itself (*E. coracana* Gaertner *sensu stricto*) or the kinds analogous to those of India and Ceylon which are cultivated in Africa.

The origin of this cereal had formerly been believed to be Indian. In 1926, Vavilov situated its origin in Abyssinia. With the aid of vernacular appellations and datings of the Bantu expansion in Africa (Oliver 1970), it is shown here that, starting from the Nubian corridor, cultivation of eleusine millet in East Africa and in the Zambezi-Angola and Nilo-Chadian regions was established only between the years 1000 and 1500 of our era. The high plateau of Abyssinia could have known it only between 1000 and 400 B.C., at the earliest. On the other hand, the presence of seeds has been discovered in southwestern India, in an archaeological site dating from 1800 B.C. In conclusion, this millet was first formed in India and not in Africa.

FONIO OR FUNDI MILLET (*Digitaria exilis* Stapf)

History

This slender *Digitaria* (*Digitaria exilis* Stapf) is a cultigen unique to West Africa, cultivated from Cape Verde to Lake Chad, in nonwooded

---

* In his discussion, Professor Portères did not consider *E. africana*, a wild tetraploid that crosses freely with cultivated eleusine, and which is found in Africa but not in India. In the opinion of the editors, the evidence (especially the presence of the most probable wild progenitor in Africa) strongly suggests an African highland origin of the crop. — *Editors.*

regions. It is better known as fonio or *Fundi*. Each year its cultivation covers approximately 721,000 acres, and during the most difficult months it supplies food to three to four million people.

The first mentions made of fonio go back to Al Omari who, while carrying on investigations in Cairo (1342–1346), was told by Abou Said that the basic food in the kingdom of Melli — at that time still under the rule of the sovereign of Ghana — was sorghum, used also for feeding horses and beasts of burden. Also known there were rice (*Oryza glaberrima*) and "Fonio, which resembles a grain of mustard, only it is smaller and whiter; people wash it, grind it, make a paste of it, and eat it."

At the conclusion of his *Journey to Sudan* (1353–1354), Ibn Batuta reports that somewhere between Iwakaten (currently Oulata in Mauritania), and Mali (between Bamako and Siguiri): "When the traveler arrives at a village, the Negresses bring him *Anli* [pearl millet], milk, chickens, palm flour [dried dates], rice, and *Founi*. This last foodstuff resembles mustard seed, and they use it to make *Cosocou* [couscous]; the traveler buys from them as much as he needs; rice is harmful to white men, and *Founi* is better for them."

We must next wait for Father Labat (1728) to tell us about the Island of Bisseaux (Bissao of Portuguese Guinea): "They still harvest there abundant quantities of a small seed rather like millet, extraordinarily white in color, which is easily ground into flour, and from which they make a thick gruel which they eat after melting butter or fat into it; it is called *Fonde*."

It was in 1798 that the botanist Afzelius gathered this cereal in Sierra Leone, where it was widely cultivated by the Africans. Only in 1842 it was described by Kippist as *Paspalum exile*. In 1915 Stapf integrated the species into the genus *Digitaria*. Since then, the plant has attracted no particular attention, except on the botanical level (Newbold 1924; Henrard 1950), and in regard to the deterioration of soil caused by its cultivation (Sudres 1947; Portères 1949, 1952, etc.). An agronomical study was made of it in 1905 by Dumas and Renoux in the Upper Senegal Niger, and in 1955, we devoted a general monograph to this cereal.

Stapf (1915) claimed that *D. exilis* derived from *D. longiflora* Pers., both of which are classed in a section of *Verrucipilae* which is characterized by spikelets covered with fine verrucose down, even though fonio has glabrous spikelets. The two species have, however, many other affinities. *D. longiflora* Pers. is paleotropical: Africa, Madagascar, and Asia.

Henrard (1950) also brings the two species together in a section of the *Atrofuscae*, a classification which he himself admits as being rather artificial.

The cultigen state is obvious, with the ancestral species remaining doubtful. In the genus *Digitaria*, the basic chromosomal number seems to be nine. *D. exilis* would have $2n = 54$ (Hunter 1934) and would be hexaploid (somatic triploid).

Current Varietal Diversification

In studying the varieties of fonio (Portères 1955c), we specified that they are much more numerous (up to fifteen) in the Futa-Jalon and its surroundings, likewise around the upper basins of the Senegal and Niger Rivers; on the edges of the river basins and toward the east as far as Chad, their number decreases sharply (see Figure 2). It is important to take into consideration the geographical localization of the botanical varieties, remembering that each one possesses a certain number of agricultural varieties (varietal populations).

One can first distinguish primitive types, with pedicels grouped by threes (sometimes by twos or fours), spikelets in one to two rows along the racemes, and an inflorescence having two racemes, each with fifty to one hundred spikelets for every ten centimeters; these types mature early and have sparse, fine culms.

The most primitive group is represented by var. *gracilis* R. Portères, with rough pedicels and leaves whose margins are quite curled. The agrarian varieties (varietal populations) are concentrated in nodules in the region of Kankan (Guinea), slightly south of what was formerly Melli II.

A slightly more elaborate group, var. *stricta* R. Port., has smooth, glabrous pedicels, leaves with slightly curled margins, and widely spaced spikelets which are apparently in one row, except in the middle of the raceme; the varietal populations are multiple through Guinea, Mali, the Casamance, and Upper Volta.

The inflorescence carry three to four racemes (sometimes two or five), with ninety to one hundred twenty spikelets per ten centimeter length of the raceme, pedicels grouped by fours (seldom by threes and never by twos), and spikelets apparently in two to three rows along the racemes. These are robust, late-maturing races, and are distributed in var. *rustica* R. Port. and var. *mixta* R. Port. In var. *rustica* all organs are covered with coarse setulae. Subvar. *rubra* is rich in anthocyanic pigments, and has elongated spikelets with narrow tips. The varietal

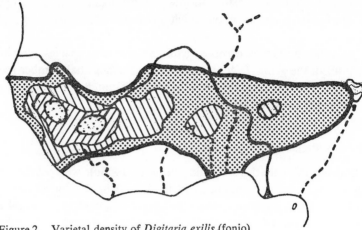

Figure 2.   Varietal density of *Digitaria exilis* (fonio)
   Key: Number of agrarian varieties:

   1 – 2 /–   ▨
   5 – 10 /–   ▨

   3 – 5 /–   ▨
   10 – 15 /–   ▨

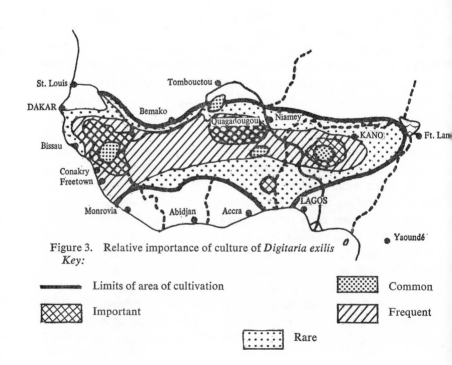

Figure 3.   Relative importance of culture of *Digitaria exilis*
   Key:

   ▬▬ Limits of area of cultivation   ▨ Common

   ▨ Important   ▨ Frequent

   ▨ Rare

populations are distributed especially in Guinea and Mali, extending toward Upper Volta and fingering out toward the Casamance. Subvar. *clara* has anthocyanic pigmentation absent or diffuse; short, convex spikelets; and white or rosy caryopses. These types are localized in the region of Kankan (vide var. *gracilis*), with some extensions into the Futa-Jalon and Bamako. Var. *mixta* R. Port. has generalized vegetative pigmentation and ellipsoidal convex spikelets; these types are more or less intermediate between subvar. *clara* and subvar. *rubra*, and are located only upstream of Kankan along the upper basin of the Niger.

Var. *densa* R. Port., a highly advanced type, possesses inflorescences of three to four racemes,* (seldom by threes, never by fours), and spikelets apparently in two to three rows on the racemes, which each carry 120 to 140 spikelets per ten centimeters of length. This racial grouping is strictly localized in the Togolese regions. They are tall, strong plants with a long vegetative cycle, and those of the Mossi country are seemingly derived from var. *rustica* subvar. *rubra*. The Lamba appellations *Sebre* and *Semre* come from the Western Fulani *Sereme* or *Serembe*, which mean "edible seed."

The geographical diagram (Figure 4) for the preceding botanical varieties, reports the degree to which they are widely cultivated. Against a general background (the entire area) populated by the varieties *stricta* and *rustica* subvar. *rubra*, one notices a precise localization of var. *gracilis* in the region of Kankan along the western upper Niger, but included within the area of var. *rustica* subvar. *clara*, which covers the whole basin of the Upper Niger as far as the central Nigerian delta. The concentration of var. *mixta* cuts across the subvarieties *clara* and *rubra*; it has been noted that var. *mixta* offers some characteristics of one or the other of the subvarieties mentioned above. Thus, the hybridogenous area would be ascertainable here. Finally, clearly detached, var. *densa* is localized in the region of Togo, but this variety derives from a form in Mossi country (Upper Volta) of var. *rustica* subvar. *rubra* (Portères 1955c: 499).

The geographical diagram clearly shows that the current center of discernible varietal diversification is situated on the upper basin of the Niger, from the river's source to the central delta. Historically, we are upon the domains of the old empires of Mali, developed in the twelfth and thirteenth centuries, following the decadence of the empire of Ghana (tenth through eleventh and up to the fourteenth centuries). It is no longer surprising that Abou Said and Ibn Batuta spoke a great

---

* There is an apparent omission in the text here, concerning grouping of the pedicels. — *Translator*.

deal of fonio or *Founi* in the middle of the fourteenth century as mentioned above. This millet was already widely cultivated as much in Mali as in more northern Ghana and, thus, elsewhere.

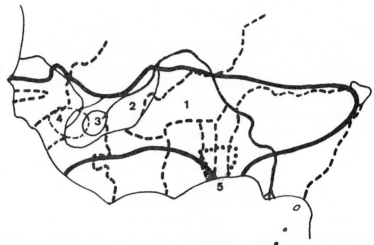

Figure 4.   Current geographical centers of varietal diversification of *Digitaria exilis*
Key: (1) Var. *stricta* + var. *rustica* subvar. *rubra*. (2) var. *rustica* subvar. *clara*.
(3) var. *gracilis*. (4) var. *mixta*. (5) var. *densa*

Ecology of the Center of Origin

The pluvio-climatic deterioration of the southern Sahara and ethnic migrations toward the south lead us to believe that the center of origin was probably located further to the north. The diverse species of *Digitaria* are not, on the whole, adapted to excessively dry conditions. The cultural limit of *D. exilis* is currently situated on the annual isohyet of 1,500 millimeters, while sorghums and pennisetums can be limited to the isohyet of 200 to 250 millimeters.

In these conditions, fonio can easily enter pluvial agricultural areas which may even have a critical insufficiency of rainfall. Precocious varieties are cultivated in dry conditions, and late varieties, in wet conditions; on the whole, this is a general rule in cultivation of fonio, as much geographically as in the heart of a region.

Heavy soils are rather ill-suited to the majority of cultivated varieties. But, in general, by working with a range of varieties, one can adapt the crop to all terrains and exposures, to fertile or unproductive conditions: sandy, limy, gravelly, or pebbly soils, slopes, plateaux and valleys, or riverbanks. In regard to this problem, we refer the reader to the examples and experiments given in 1955.

It is conceivable that domestication of fonio could have become established around the Nigerian central delta through accumulation of both types with a short vegetative cycle (varieties *gracilis* and *stricta*) and also much later, more robust, and more productive types (var. *rustica*). The river-fed waters of this "delta" formerly extended much further north.

The cultural importance of fonio in Hausa country allows us to presume the possible existence of a secondary center other than the one in Togo-Dahomey.

Appellations of Fonio

We previously made an important contribution to the knowledge of the appellations given to this millet in West Africa, approximately 100 generic terms and almost 400 vocables concerning varieties of culture.

By eliminating what is marginal in the general area of fonio and retaining only that which is in the present center of varietal diversification or its surroundings, it is perhaps possible to define the problem: that is, to have an idea of the human groups which were involved in the origin of the total domestication of a species which is clearly a cultigen.

This problem, already studied in 1959, can be summarized, in terms of the conditions set forth above, as follows: there exist only two vocables: *Fonio* (Fonyo) and *Fundi* (read *Fo-nyo* and *Fun' di*). *Fo* and *Fun'* are "thing, object"; *nyo* is a general term for millets, subsequently also including maize, and its original meaning of "food," "alimentary provision," or "that which is eaten"; *di* or *ndi* (nasalization before a dental) has the same meaning. *Fonio* and *Fundi* are "things to eat," "foods," edible grains. *Fonio* and variants come from the Mandingo linguistic group or from the Nigritic languages of the Middle Niger (Songhai, Djerma, Bozo). *Fundi* and variants are already quite marginal and concern the languages of the Senegalese group (Wolof, Fula), or Kissi, Mende, etc.

The use of *Nyo* (and not *di, ndi*) for an edible seed, linguistically connected to an entire Lybio-Berber group, is analogous in its designation of cereals. Were white racial groups the ones who "invented" fonio?

We conclude, therefore, that fonio millet, currently a cultigen, was born somewhere in the central Nigerian delta or in its surroundings, as is shown by the current geographic localization of the various racial nucleii ascertainable within the species, by the appellations, etc.

Summary

Fonio millet (*Digitaria exilis* Stapf) was mentioned in the fourteenth century by Arab travelers, from the basin of the Senegal River to the upper basin of the Niger. It is a true cultigen, engendered by culture. The closest wild species is *Digitaria longiflora*, which grows in all hot regions of Africa and Asia. Archaeologically, nothing is known about this cereal, which is confined to West Africa, from Cape Verde to Lake Chad. Jordanian botanical analysis reveals certain racial combinations in diffusion or in geographical localizations. This reveals the existence of four centers, three of which exhibit great interpenetration, the fourth being marginal (Togo) and representing a particular secondary center of diversification. All this taken together shows that there is a great probability that fonio was domesticated in the area around the central Nigerian delta. The vernacular appellations also seem to agree on this point.

BLACK FONIO (*Digitaria iburua* Stapf)

If fonio occurs in a continuous cultural area, there is another millet, quite close botanically, which occurs as a relict with two small geographical localizations quite distant from each other.

Digitaria iburua Stapf has been known to us only since 1911, when it was found by Dudgeon (1911: 149, 1922: 154) in northern Nigeria in the region of Zaria, growing in fields with pennisetum. In 1915 Lamb sent samples of it to the Royal Herbarium at Kew, noting that this graminaceous plant was sown in lines in the fields of the Hausa states. Stapf (1915: 381–386) gave use its botanical description.

In northern Nigeria the cultural sector covers the high plateaux of the Hausa country: Kano, Zaria, and Katsina. It is possible that it could include a small portion of the region of Zinder in Niger, as it is contiguous with the territory of Kano (Chevalier 1933: 831), but we are rather poorly informed on this subject.

The existence of another sector much further south has been indicated by Portères (1946: 389–392), strictly limited to the northern part of the secondary mountain chain of the Atakora and covering both a portion of Togo in the Atalotes and another in Dahomey, in the Somkarba part of Somba country, contiguous with the Birni-Natitingou district.

In all regions where *D. iburua* is cultivated, fonio *Digitaria exilis* is also cultivated. There is no competition between the two millets. In Hausa country, black fonio is also used to prepare a couscous locally called *Wusu-Wusu* (Dalziel 1937: 526). The same holds true in Dahomey. In Togo, the Lambas, who also raise fonio, dislike black fonio because of the difficulty in decortication with a pestle, and use it only to make a beer called *Tchapalo* (Portères 1946: 389–392).

Known vernacular appellations are obviously few in number: Zarian Hausa *Iburu* (Dudgeon 1911: 149, 1922: 154); Kano Hausa *Iburo* (Dalziel 1937: 526); Katsina Hausa *Ibura, Aburu, Ibiro, Alas, Makari* (Bargery 1934); Togolese Lamba *Afio-Warum*; and Dahomey Sompkarba *Ipoga* (Portères 1946: 389–392; 1955c: 359–363; 1958: 309), with *Afio* and *Ipo* for "fonio," *Warum* and *Ga* for "black," the spikelet being dark brown.

As it is a question of a cereal which, being cultivated between 400 and 1,300 meters, may be considered as a subalpine plant, we offered the hypothesis that it might have come from the Aïr Mountains, where it was known, if not domesticated, during a Neolithic Saharan age, subsequently disappearing from this center after the drying-up of the Sahara, carried further south by human migrations (Portères 1946: 389–392; 1955c: 359–363).

What is the possible ancestral species of black fonio? Stapf (1915: 381–386) linked it with *Digitaria ternata* Stapf, a species known throughout the hot regions of Africa and Asia. Later, Henrard (1950) contended that black fonio is close to the species *D. barbinodis* Henrard, a species endemic to Malian Sudan, and also close to *D. tricostulata* (Hackel) Henrard, which is known from Kenya to Natal.

Summary

Black fonio of West Africa (*Digitaria iburua* Stapf) is cultivated throughout the Hausa country of Nigeria. There is another small, separate area in the Atakora Mountains of Togo and Dahomey. The wild species which is botanically and geographically the closest to it would be *Digitaria barbinodis* Henrard, still present in Malian Sudan. It is possible that black fonio is a cereal born on the territory formerly occupied by the Hausas.

TEFF MILLET OF ABYSSINIA (*Eragrostis abyssinica* Link)

In 1773 the Scottish explorer James Bruce furnished the name and seed of a millet cultivated in Abyssinia to the Florentine botanist Zuccagni (1774), who made the cereal known under the name of *Poa Teff* Zucc. Jacquin, in 1781, then included this plant in the genus *Eragrostis*. Teff is now admitted in botanical nomenclature as *Eragrostis Tef* (Zucc.) Trotter 1938 (*E. abyssinica* [Jacq.] Link: = *Poa abyssinica* Bruce 1790).

The appellations *Taff* (Tigre), *Teff*, and *Tief* (Amharic), *Tafi* (Galla), etc. vary dialectically in Abyssinia: *Tef, Taf, Thaf, Ttheff, Tief, Ttraff, Tafi, Tifi, Dafi, Taftafo*, according to various authors (Portères 1958).

Teff etc. is a generic term which designates Graminaceae with inflorescences of loose flower clusters and fine pedicels, as with teff millet; these are generally species of the genera *Eragrostis* and *Sporobolus* (Portères 1958).

Unger (1886–1887) thought that he recognized teff millet in seeds found in the pyramid of Dassur, constructed around 2600 B.C. (Fourth Dynasty), and in the clay blocks of one structure in the ancient Jewish town of Ramses, dating from 1400 to 1300 B.C., built by Ramses II (Nineteenth Dynasty, beginning of the New Empire). Loret (1887) followed Unger on this point, but Koernicke (1885) thought that the seeds in question were rather *Eragrostis pilosa* P. B., a closely related species and a kind of direct or collateral ancestor of teff. For Schweinfurth (1867), they are probably *E. aegyptiaca* Del. Castellani and Baldrati (1939) follow Unger.

Haudricourt (1941), also tracing the history of teff, established that *Thaf* is a term of Semitic origin applied in Yemen to a picked cereal which is not necessarily *E. pilosa*; the Semites, arriving in Ethiopia, then applied this name to the cereal cultivated by the Hamites. Rozhevicz (1928) also connects the names *Thaf, Tef*, etc., to *E. pilosa*.

Extrapolating from the data we find in Harkavy's article (1870), we showed (1958) that the name *Tef* came from ancient Egyptian *T'ef* [food, nourishment]. The Egyptian word is probably the origin of Hebrew *Tzaf* [provision].

If the Semites had actually domesticated teff cereal, there is no doubt that it would also have been cultivated as far as Asia Minor and around the Persian Gulf, along East Africa. The plant did not leave Abyssinia, except at the end of the nineteenth century, and then as fodder for livestock.

Were the ancient Egyptians acquainted with it? It is clear that this cereal was born on the high Abyssinian plateaux, with the Cushitics;

it remained restricted to that area, without even crossing the mountains.

There are several varieties of teff millet in Abyssinia, described by Hochstetter (1848), Rozhevicz (1928), and Schimper (1895). Abyssinia seems to be, in fact, the ancient center of this culture (Rozhevicz 1928; Vavilov 1926), but no one knows how long ago it came into the hands of Cushitic cultivators.

THE "ANIMAL" MILLET OR "FONIO" OF FUTA-JALON
(Brachiaria deflexa C. E. Hubbard var. *sativa* R. Port.)

Many species of the genus *Brachiaria* are known in Africa as picked and gathered cereals. One need only cite them: *B. deflexa* C. E. Hubbard *(B. regularis* Stapf) in Mali (Chevalier 1933; Dalziel 1937) and at Lake Chad (Chevalier 1933; Dalziel 1937; Creac'h 1941); *B. distichophylla* Stapf in northern Nigeria (Holland 1922; Dalziel 1937) *(Brachiaria deflexa* C. E. Hubbard var. *sativa* R. Portères) and in Chad, Baguirmi Province (Chevalier 1933); *B. kotschyana* Stapf in Chad, Baguirmi (Chevalier 1933), an on the Ennedi plateau; *B. fulva* Stapf in northern Nigeria (Chevalier 1933; Holland 1922; Dalziel 1937); *B. obtusifolia* Stapf in eastern Sudan and from the Red Sea to the White Nile (Brown and Massey 1929); *B. pubifolia* Stapf around Lake Chad (Chevalier 1933; Creac'h 1941); *B. stigmatisata* Stapf in Mali, Bambara, and Khassonke countries (Chevalier 1933) and in the basin of the Logone where it is the most commonly harvested grain; and *B. xantholenea* Stapf in northern Nigeria (Dalziel 1937). Thus, the genus *Brachiaria* seems to be widely cultivated for its edible seeds.

We studied (1951b) a form grown in the Futa-Jalon, *B. deflexa* C. E. Hubbard var. *sativa* R. Port. which we collected in 1949 in the Futa-Jalon as: Fula *Funi Kuli* "animal fonio" or Dylon'ke *Fonio Kuli*. We have absolutely no knowledge about how old the cultivation of this millet is, having only a sample of seeds, with no number or indication other than: "Fonio, Upper Senegal-Niger." This administrative territory ceased to exist in 1919, being divided among Senegal, Malian Sudan, and Guinea. But the Futa-Jalon has never been part of it (Portères 1951b).

This millet is known only in the Futa-Jalon; it is cultivated in the regions of Labé, at an altitude of 1,000 meters, and Mali, at an altitude of 1,000 to 1,200 meters. In these regions fonio matures, according to the variety, ninety to one hundred thirty days after sowing; *Brachiaria* completes its entire cycle in seventy to seventy-five days. Because of its rapid vegetation, it is sown late (August), after the sowing of fonio (late May to late July). Grain yield is two to three times that of fonio.

The profitable fonio delivers whole kernels directly upon decortication, allowing the preparation of couscous; on the other hand, *Brachiaria* has very tender grains which are easily ground into a flour used in making biscuits and fritters. It can be eaten directly with rice, and also crushed with milk.

There is a common and rather curious practice of mixing cultures of *Digitaria* and *Brachiaria*; first, true fonio with its precocious variety *Fonie moriori* is sown, then, later, *Brachiaria*; everything arrives at maturity at the same time. First, the *Brachiaria* is harvested, and then the fonio. Some people grow *Brachiaria* separately on a plot in fonio fields. Others dislike it for tending to "invade" fields of fonio if both kinds are sown at the same time; this means that it takes up all the space because of its large, rapid development, hindering the growth of true fonio.

Otherwise, it is generally inserted into fonio culture on cleared land, following a fallow period of six to seven years (formerly, of twenty years).

Botanically, the species *Brachiaria deflexa* offers rather strong morphological variability. Stapf (1919) focused attention on the affinities among *B. deflexa* (as *B. regularis* Stapf), *B. ramosa* Stapf of West Africa, and *B. nidulans* Metz of Nubia and Eritrea. In the natural state there are also some glabrous forms and other villous ones.

B. deflexa var. *sativa* differs particularly from the standard species because of a totally glabrous state and a culm which is always branched. The panicle attains a length of twenty-five to twenty-eight centimeters; the glumes and lodicules are richer in nervation; the scutellum of the caryopsis covers one half to two thirds of the length of the grain; and the caryopses are plump.

Are we in the presence of a plant which is a cultural relict? It is currently known only in the Futa-Jalon highlands of Guinea near the upper basins of the Gambia and Senegal Rivers (the Bafing). We have seen above that this millet also was cultivated at the beginning of the twentieth century in the territory of the upper Senegal-Niger, which in no way included the Futa-Jalon.

This millet cannot be considered a cultigen; it is too close to the wild species which is, moreover, quite variable. On the other hand, we know of no decomposition of this plant into agricultural varieties, despite our own intensive research in the region of its culture in 1949,

1958, 1959, and 1961.

From these facts, it appears improbable that any connection could be established between the current cultivated type and impressions found on pottery of the peri-lacustrian Neolithic sites of Tichit in Mauritania, where it must be a question only of wild forms, or of wild forms appropriated by humans for grain production.

Summary

Brachiaria deflexa C. E. Hubbard is a wild cereal of the Sudan-Zambezi and Yemenite regions, widely exploited in the wild state. Many impressions of its seeds have been found on the pottery of the Neolithic sites of Tichit (Mauritania) (see Munson, this volume). One race of it has been cultivated on the "roof" of the Futa-Jalon (Guinea), at least since the beginning of the twentieth century; it differs relatively little from wild types, and has no agricultural varieties. It is improbable that it has been cultivated for very long.

AFRICAN "BASTARD MILLET GRASS"
(*Paspalum scrobiculatum* Linnaeus var. *polystachyum* Stapf)

The genus *Paspalum* Linnaeus includes cereal species which are either cultivated or picked in Africa and India. Var. *polystachyum* Stapf is one of the psychotropic cereals.

A common plant on plantations and in villages of the intertropical zone is the *Paspalum conjugatum* Bergius. Burkill (1935) reports that in the Botanical Garden of Singapore monkeys come onto the grass to gather and eat it, sliding the two spikes between their fingers to detach the grains; they do this before the harvesting of local cereals. It should be noted that it is certainly not a shortage of food which causes (or caused) this behavior in Singapore, and the motivation for eating it must be sought elsewhere, as will be suggested below.

As late as 1959, this cereal had not yet been mentioned as one of the cereals harvested by man. It is, however, sometimes gathered (this was especially true in the past) during periods of severe famine by the Kurankos of Guinea, near the Kissis of Guékédou. Its vernacular appellation in Kuranko, Malinke, Lele, and Toma is 'bird's fonio.' Its seeds are considered to be toxic, a fact which has not been noticed in other countries. Yet the farmer-growers of the Fula ethnic group of the Guirila of Beyla (Guinea) affirm that they are harmful during dry seasons when the equatorial winds blow (*Harmattan*). Using emulsion and picrosodic paper, we have found nothing more than a slight presence of free hydrocyanic acid and cyanogenetic glucosides (Portères 1959).

Paspalum commersonii Lamarck (*P. scrobiculatum* L. var. *commersonii* Stapf) is one of the best grains for picking for the Sarakolles from the area between the Niger and Senegal Rivers (Chevalier 1933). The use of its seeds as food has been noted in Sierra Leone, where this millet grows in the wild state in flooded rice fields; there, it is eaten in a mixture with rice (Dalziel 1937). Seeds are eaten in this way throughout West Africa. In Nigeria, the Hausas believe it causes digestive problems in asses.

In 1943 among the Kissis of Guinea, we saw it frequently being brought up from the bottom of rice paddies and planted out on the edges, in order that its seeds might be gathered when the rice is harvested. It seems that here again among the Mendes of Sierra Leone and the Kissis there is a particular motivation, perhaps analogous to that of the monkeys of Singapore.

Catherinet (personal communication, 1950) knows it to be harvested in the Logone basin (Chad) "when there is really nothing to eat."

In Sierra Leone among the Mendes, the Temnes, the Konos, the Kissis, the Dyaloukes, the Susus, and the Mandingos, the local appellations all translate as "bird's grass" (Dalziel 1937; Deighton 1957). According to Dalziel, the Sierra Leonean form comes from the form *parvispiculata* Stapf, "with little spikelets," at least in certain regions (which we believe to be forested or subforested).

Among the Kissis of Guinea, this species grows abundantly on rocky slopes where African rice *Sakili-fing*, coming from *Oryza glaberrima* Steudel var. *scoparia* R. Port. and var. *ebenicolorata* R. Port., is cultivated. When the rice is harvested, the wild millet is gathered at the same time; it is neither separated nor isolated; it is included in the gathering of bunches of rice and in winnowing and culinary preparation, the result being that it is always eaten with the rice.

The Kurankos go much farther than this. Here, *Paspalum* is the object of pseudo-cultivation, in that the hillsides are overgrown with this millet although the soils are quite impoverished and barely able to sustain the cultivation of rice, even African rice. When rice is harvested, it is above all the millet which is harvested. Everything is put into granaries, and the people actually eat a mixture composed of up to one-third *Paspalum* and two-thirds rice. Among the Kurankos and their neighbors, the Kissis of Guinea, the vernacular appellations always translate as "bird's grass" (Portères 1959).

Now, the question already posed, that of the motivation for this consumption, still remains to be answered.

Paspalum scrobiculatum L. var. *polystachyum* Stapf is a millet which did not attract attention until 1958, either. In all of West Africa, it accompanies the culture of African rice (*Oryza glaberrima*) as well as that of Asiatic rice (*O. sativa*) which has replaced African rice on some lands. It is harvested with the rice and accompanies the rice grains through all manipulations and transformations: storing, treading out, decortication, and winnowing. With a woven sieve it is very difficult to separate these grains from the rice; moreover, no attempt is made to do so.

Among the Susus of Guinea, it is called "black rice" because of the color of the spikelets as well as the whole plant which is dark brown when dried out. Among the Malinkes and Bambaras, the appellation yields "pull up — leave," which corresponds to the alternative: "Either you harvest it or you leave it in the field."

This millet is presented as having psychotropic properties, according to our terminology. In the region of Siguiri, there is a Malinke expression: "You can't do that, even if you eat a dish of borom'bia," which is the name of the plant. From different parts of Guinea, informants concur in attributing to the grain a psycho-physiological action manifested in trembling and "wide-open eyes" when a lot of it is eaten.

A Susu informant reports: "There are people who harvest it and eat it, prepared like rice. The great Marabouts (Muslim priests) in retreat eat (or ate) only that (not rice) so long as they haven't finished 'their work'. They don't go out for a week. They do it often, but not all of them do it; only 'those who are qualified'."

We are treating these wild or proto-cultivated millets of Africa at length because the same problems occur on the Indian subcontinent with a species cultivated as a cereal which also comes from the genus *Paspalum*.

The following questions then arise: (1) problems of motivation; and (2) the origin of the species cultivated in India: *Paspalum scrobiculatum* L. var. *frumentaceum* Stapf.

Paspalum scrobiculatum L. var. *frumentaceum* Stapf is the *Kodra* or *Kodo* millet of India. It is under this Latin binominal that Linnaeus designated the cultivated type. Lamarck called the wild type *P. commersonii*. Stapf treated these as a collective species: *P. scrobiculatum* L. var. *commersonii* Stapf.

In India seeds in certain seasons contain a narcotic poison. In the province of Gujarat they sell respectively toxic or nontoxic seeds under different names. Wet periods at the time of maturation and cultivation in wet soils allegedly develop the toxicity (Watt 1908).

When the fatty material is extracted, the toxic product is also removed; the residue, once defatted, is completely nontoxic. All research on glucosides and alkaloids has provided negative results. According to Hurst (after Webb 1948, 1949), certain forms are toxic and others are not, the toxic ones producing a delirium and vomiting.

Poisoning as it is known in Madras (Wisantham 1948) results in loss of appetite, a dazed state, tympanitis, vomiting, heavy perspiration, intense thirst, trembling, dizziness, stiffness, and difficulty in walking and speaking. There were no reported fatalities and the symptoms are said to disappear after twenty-four hours (Webb 1948). According to others, this poisoning results in death in both men and animals.

It has been reported that the seeds and plants are very toxic for elephants (Madras); that newly harvested seeds are quite narcotic, and that soaking in water diminishes toxicity; that seeds kept for several years lose this characteristic; that eaten with "whey" (acidity) they are acceptable; and that, perhaps, humans may acquire or possess a certain immunity to them.

We know of one toxic graminaceous plant, darnel (*Lolium temulentum* L.), which causes nervous phenomena, dizziness, intoxication, trembling, a dazed state, etc. The constant presence of mycelial fibers, especially in the pericarp, has been identified in the past (P. Guerin), and this symbiotic fungus is suspected of being one of the causes of darnel's toxicity. The same holds true for the seed of the graminaceous *Melica decumbens* Thunberg of South Africa.

An Indian Millet of African Origin?

Originally, for Linnaeus (1759) *P. scrobiculatum* L. included only the cereal species grown in India; *P. kora* Wildenow 1797 is the closest wild form in the same country, and it corresponds to *P. commersonii* Lamarck 1783. Stapf created a collective species *P. scrobiculatum* Linnaeus, including var. *frumentaceum* (the millet cultivated in India), var. *commersonii* (the wild form), and var. *polystachyum* (an African kind, from the Atlantic to eastern Sudan and East Africa). *P. commersonii* is thought of as being the origin of the Indian millet (Roxburgh 1832; Hooker 1897; Watt 1908).

Since *P. scr.* var. *frumentaceum* has many more affinities with *P.*

polystachyum (Brown 1814) than with *P. commersonii* Lamarck (1783) perhaps it is not in India that the origin of the "Kodra" millet should be sought. Between African protoculture and Indian and Singhalese agriculture of these millets, one may presume that a connection was probably established.

THE PROBLEM OF THE ORIGIN OF "CANDLE MILLET" *(Pennisetum)*[2]

Homelands

The "candle millet" (bulrush millet, pearl millet, etc.) has long been cultivated in all of intertropical Africa and as far as eastern India and its surroundings (especially Burma). At present, the times and places of the origin of its cultivation are still unknown (Africa? Middle Asia?).

It has long been an accepted belief that the origin of this cereal was in Africa. The arguments presented have great value. But it is a question of which region of Africa and which (current) botanical species were the points of departure for the transformation effected by man? These problems are not easily solved. In fact, we can offer only suggestions or interpretations.

All those who have studied pearl millet in India seem to agree on the fact that the subcontinent did not create this cereal. One starts from the fact that there is no known Sanskrit name for it; or, in a word, that "candle millet" cannot be found through any name in Sanskrit.

In a bas-relief of the Senacherib Palace at Koujoundjck (formerly Nineveh), now in the British Museum, reported by Layart as dating from circa 700 B.C., one can see soldiers fighting in a "field of cereals." Closer examination shows that this cereal can only be pearl millet.* Piedallu (1923) published an illustration of it in his work on sorghum. The document is very convincing, no confusion being possible with other cultivated plants, such as sorghums of the *Durra* or related types, or with reeds (Arundo). The appellation by which this cereal was known to the Assyrians is unknown (Piedallu 1923).

The Hindi term *Bajra* and other derivatives designating this millet

---

[2] See W. D. Clayton (1972) for recent classification of cultivated and weed pennisetums.

* The editors do not agree with Dr. Portères. The "field of cereals" is more probably a stand of reeds. — *Editors*.

seem to derive from eastern Arabic and from Persian (*buzir*, etc.) (Watson 1868), for "grains," "seeds."

The vocable *Bajra* and variants also apply to other cereals: *Setaria italica* (Gujarati, Bengali, Telinga), *Sorghum halepense* and sometimes *S. vulgare* (northwestern provinces), *Eleusine coracana* (Deccani), *Panicum frumentaceum*, and even maize (Iraq). It was introduced on the eastern coast of Africa, but Grant (in Speke 1863) found it in the region of the upper Nile applied to pearl millet.

Supposed Botanical Origins

Stapf (1934) believed that pearl millet or pennisetum millet probably derived from two ancestral species: (1) *Pennisetum purpureum* K. Schum. (or elephant grass) is given as the origin of the large-culmed millets of the subhumid tropical zone; and (2) small-culmed pennisetum would then derive from wild species, smaller than elephant grass, adapted to drier tropical zones, and distributed from the region of Senegal and Gambia to the Red Sea. Chevalier (1932) had already noted that some wild pennisetums of the dry tropical zone could have served to initiate some cultivated forms.

It is probable that *P. stenostachyum* Stapf and Hubbard, *P. perrottetii* K. Schum.,* of the Senegal-Gambian region, which is present in all fields of precocious millet, constitute the genetic basis of the sub-Linnaean cultivated species *P. gambiense* Stapf and Hubbard of the same West African region.

All cultivated pennisetums belong to a section (*Penicillaria* Stapf) of the genus *Pennisetum*, whose species have in common spikelets grouped in stemmed or unstemmed clusters, a shiny and leathery lower glume (lemma), the absence of glumella (lodicules), and anthers crowned with small tufts of hairs (penicillium). Some species are perennials due to their rhizomes, such as *P. purpureum*, which, in fact, is hardly to be considered as having served as a basis for cultivated millets. Most of the species are annuals.

P. mollissimum and *P. rogeri* do not seem to figure in the classification made by Stapf (1934). Under the influence of Leeke (1907), Stapf groups together (artificially?) cultivated species and those species which are weeds in fields or considered to be degenerate forms of plants that

---

* In current usage, *Pennisetum americanum* (L.) K. Schum. includes all cultivated pearl millets and their closest spontaneous relatives (annual diploids). All epithets used by Professor Portères are infraspecific taxa except *P. purpureum*, a distinct perennial tetraploid. — *Editors*.

were once cultivated. These semiwild species bear spikelets which fall off quickly and their narrow, pointed seeds are hidden by the husks. These species are numerous; and certain of them are considered to be progenitors or genetic associates of the cultivated millets, especially *P. violaceum, P. stenostachyum, P. perrottetii,* and *P. niloticum.*

This group presents a contrast with the other cultivated millets which have spikelets which do not fall off and fat seeds with enlarged tips. At maturity the seeds are generally visible between the half-opened husks. No wild species conforming morphologically to the cultivated types have ever been found.

The species of *Pennisetum* have flowers whose styles come out before the anthers, from the tip to the base of the false ear. In each hermaphrodite flower when the styles have dried, the anthers come out, beginning around the middle of the false ear. The result of this phenomenon of protogyny is that it allows cross-fertilization.

According to P. Leeke (1907), who described thirty-two forms of pennisetum millet, its origin is polyphyletic; he considers thirteen forms to be of primary status, derived from the following wild species: *P. gymnothrix* K. Schum., *P. perrottetii* K. Schum., *P. mollissimum* Hochst., *P. violaceum* C. L. Rich., and *P. versicolor* Schroder. These species are weeds of millet fields, and, in certain cases, seem to be hybrids. He distinguished four other secondary forms; the rest (fifteen) being forms considered to be tertiary, with one group having long awns and the other lacking them.

Chevalier (1934) believed that *P. stenostachyum* (given as *P. sampsoni* Stapf and Hubb.) which has branched culms and grows from Senegal to Nigeria, was only a recessive or hybrid form of the cultivated millet; it is always found in cultivated fields. *P. perrottetii* is found in Senegal in fallow lands where rice grass (Smilo) has been grown. The same holds true for *P. rogeri,* which grows in the same fields after harvest, and is considered by the local growers to be only a degenerate millet.

Stapf (1934), for his part, believes that pennisetum millet comes from the following ancestors: those with large culms, from the mesophytic species *Pennisetum purpureum* Schumacher (elephant grass); the others with small culms, growing in dry zones, from different species living along the edge of the Sahel and Sudan-Sahel regions, from Senegal and Gambia to the Red Sea.

Stapf and Hubbard (1934) distinguished eighteen cultivated races with corresponding binary names. Four are found in eastern Sudan and neighboring regions, eight in West Africa, and six in South and

East Africa and in India.

Geographical Distribution of Current Cultivated Types

In mapping the geographical distribution of cultivated pennisetum, the existence of botanico-geographical areas may be noted. We have shown this previously (Portères 1951c), but we have made some changes in this map (Figures 5, 6, 7, 8).

1.   Extreme West African area (group A, Figure 5) limited on the east by the lower Niger. It includes:

a.   *P. pycnostachyum*, restricted to the area between Senegal and Gambia and the upper Niger of Mali and Guinea, extending into Guinea and Sierra Leone.

b.   *P. gambiense*, from Senegal and Gambia to Ghana.

c.   *P. cinereum*, from the upper basins of the Senegal and Niger rivers as far as Ghana and Togo-Dahomey.

d.   *P. nigritarum*, very widely distributed from Senegal to beyond Lake Chad.

e.   *P. leonis*, in Sierra Leone and Guinea, limited in area and slightly marginal. Botanically, this species is separate from the preceding ones, which seem to have a common ancestor.

2.   Central West African area (group B, Figure 6) between the lower Niger and Lake Chad. It includes:

f.   *P. ancylochaete*, in the former Hausa states of northern Nigeria and Niger.

g.   *P. maiwa*, from its Hausa name, covering the plateaux of Bauchi, Bornu, and the area surrounding Lake Chad.

h.   *P. gibbosum*, around Lake Chad.

Note: These last three species seem quite dissimilar, probably coming from independant ancestors. On the other hand, *P. nigritarum*, which is closely linked to the varieties of far West Africa, has expanded as far as the regions around Lake Chad.

3.   Eastern Nile-Sudan area (group C, Figure 7) from Chad to the Red Sea and the Indian Ocean. It is characterized by primitive forms of culture. The spikelets fall off early, the seeds are well-hidden by the husks (glumes) which are not half-opened, and the culms tend to be hollow. Thus one finds here:

i.   *P. orthochaete*, in eastern Sudan.

j.   *P. perspeciosum*, in eastern Sudan, from Kordofan to the Blue Nile.

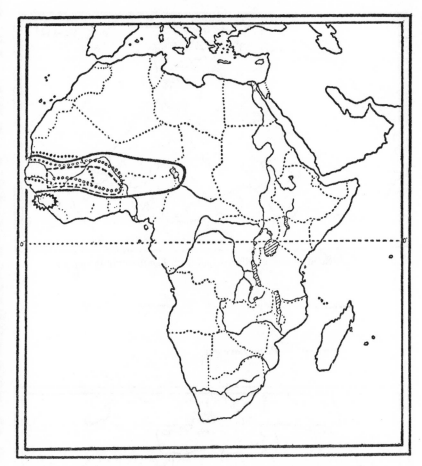

Figure 5.   West African cultivated species (gen. *Pennisetum*): (group A)

Key:

———	*P. pycnostachyum*	••••••••	*P. nigritarum*
– – – –	*P. gambiense*	◦•◦•◦◦◦•◦•	*P. cinereum*
	∿∿∿	*P. leonis*	

k.   *P. vulpinum*, in eastern Sudan, Abyssinia, and Eritrea.

l.   *P. niloticum*, more extensive, because it now ends at Lake Chad; but it could have been known further west, because some of it still remains in the region of Bakel (Senegal). It is also known throughout Egypt.

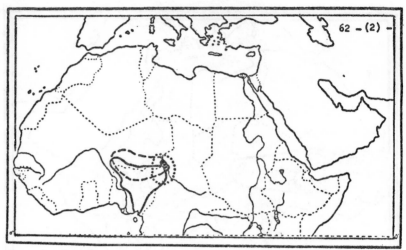

Figure 6. Cultivated species of Niger-Chad (gen. *Pennisetum*): (group B)

Key:

········· *P. maiwa* ━ ━ ━ ━ *P. gibbosum*

━━━ *P. ancylochaete*

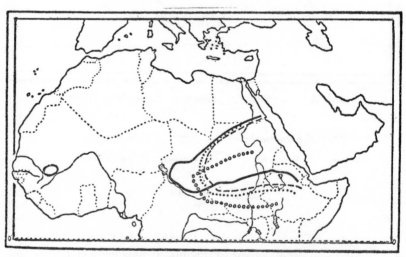

Figure 7. Cultivated species of the Nile (gen. *Pennisetum*): (group C)

Key:

━━━ *P. niloticum* ······· *P. perspeciosum*

━ ━ ━ *P. vulpinum* ooooooooo *P. orthochaete*

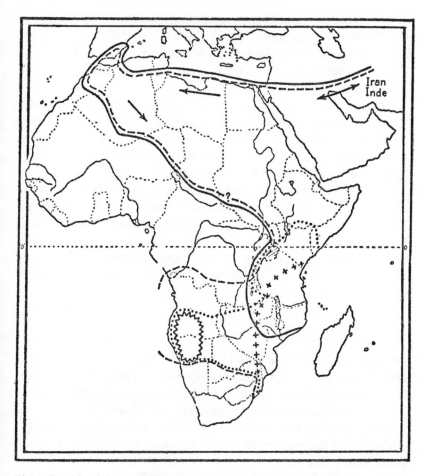

Figure 8.   Afro-Asian cultivated species (gen. *Pennisetum*): (group D)

Key:

——————   *P. spicatum*   ●●●●●●●●   *P. echinurus*

— — — —   *P. typhoides*   + + + +   *P. malacochaete*

ᴧᴧᴧᴧᴧ   *P. albicauda*

4.   East African and Angolan area (group D, Figure 8) extends from Kenya and Uganda to Natal, and from Tanzania to Angola. Found there are:

m.   *P. malacochaete*, of Tanzania and Mozambique.

n.   *P. echinurus*, from Uganda to Mozambique, then as far as Angola.

o.   *P. albicauda*, in southwestern Africa and Angola.

p.   *P. spicatum* Koernicke (*sensu stricto*), of Kenya and Uganda, of Tanzania and Mozambique, reappearing in North Africa and Spain, common in India.

q.   *P. typhoides* L. C. Rich. (*sensu stricto*), widespread from the lower Congo to Angola and southwestern Africa, then from Rhodesia to Natal, and throughout East Africa, known from eastern Sudan, Nubia, Abyssinia, and Eritrea, all the way to Egypt and North Africa, Arabia, Mesopotamia, and Iran. It is widely cultivated in India.

The last two species were the only ones known to botanists of the sixteenth and seventeenth centuries, some naming India as the homeland (C. Bauhini 1623, etc.), others referring to America (Clusius 1601); Bauhin distinguished *Panicum indicum* or *P. caeruleum* (with blue seeds, corresponding to *Pennisetum spicatum* Koern.), from *P. americanum sesquipedale* (corresponding to *Pennisetum typhoides* Stapf and C. E. Hubbard).

Summary

On the whole, pennisetum millet is found in limited areas within Africa. Only the last two species offer areas opening into Asia, near or distant, but all evidence proves that their original homeland is East Africa.

Moreover, these areas are grouped into four distinct centers (groups A, B, C, D), which are distributed over a like number of ancient cultural circles, and a like number of centers of human activity: (1) an ancient paleo-Nigritic region, divided into A and B; (2) a Nilotic-Cushitic region, C, with forms which are morphologically rather primitive; and (3) a Bantu region, D. In each region the human populations seem to have used the specific vegetal material of their own floristic basins.

Once again, everything seems to be just about in place: men, cultivated millets, and wild millets. Nevertheless, at present we have no knowledge of any picking or gathering of seed of the wild species of pennisetum, nor of those species considered to be "degenerates" of cultivated kinds.

In short, it is not easy to discern where domestication (including transformation) of pearl millet began, nor how the idea of domestication of other, botanically different species spread.

Perhaps a single botanical sort was domesticated somewhere. The forms of it which were obtained migrated along with humans and crossed with wild species to finally result in geographically independent racial nucleii. This is perhaps the most valid explanation and could also serve as the basis for understanding the origin of cultivated sorghums in the same way.

AFRICAN RICE (*Oryza glaberrima* Stapf)

Oryza glaberrima was named and succinctly described by Steudel (1855) who studied samples gathered by Jardin in the Los Islands in 1845–1848. Previously, this rice had been collected on the Cape Verde peninsula by M. Leprieur in 1826, but was confused with *O. sativa* (Portères 1955a).

This species has remained confined to West Africa up to the present. However, it must be remembered that in the past it was transported to America and continued to exist there, either in the sub-self-sown state (El Salvador), or in the cultivated state, in French Guiana and El Salvador (Portères, 1955b, 1960, 1966), as well as in Panama; all known types belong to varieties cultivated by the Susus of Guinea.

The cultivation of this rice currently extends from the shores of the Atlantic to the Sahel zone of Mauritania, from Senegal as far as Lake Chad and along the dorsal of the cretaceous uplift from the Bight of Benin to Lake Chad (Figure 9).

The closest wild species is *O. breviligulata*[3] A. Chevalier and O. Roerich 1914, which is self-sown in the area between Senegal and the basin of the Uele River (Figure 9).

In the type *O. glaberrima*, the specific epithet refers to the fact that the spikelets and the entire plant are free of down in contrast to type *O. sativa*, whose spikelets are downy. A hispid form of *O. glaberrima* found in marshy rice paddies was named *O. stapfii* by Rozhevicz (1931). (1931). It is now known that in the two species of cultivated rice there is one series of varieties with villous and another with glabrous spikelets.

In the wild species *O. breviligulata*, the forms have hispid spikelets, but certain (rare) forms with glabrous spikelets can be found.

O. stapfii Rozhevicz is a wild or pseudo-wild type ancestral to a part of the species *O. glaberrima* in its agro-botanical form var. *ebenicolorata* R. Portères *f. nigrohirtella* R. Port. (Portères 1956).

Primary and Secondary Centers of Variation

Study of the varieties of *O. glaberrima* cultivated in West Africa led us in 1945 to define, morphologically and with geographical localiza-

---

[3] *O. brevigulata = O. barthii*

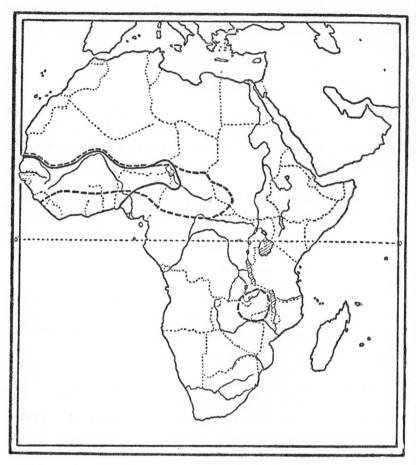

Figure 9.   West and southern African cultivated species (gen. *Oryza*)
   Key:

   $\subset\!\!\!-$ *Oryza barthii* A. Chev. 1911 (*O. breviligulata* A. Chev.)

   $\subset$ *Oryza glaberrima* Steudel

tions, three centers of varietal diversification:
1.   The original primary center of diversification is located in what is now the central Nigerian delta and its surroundings. It includes aquatic or subaquatic varieties, either floating or semi- or subfloating, which tend somewhat at times to branched culms. The panicles are very large, with thick axes and branches; they are erect and quite rigid, and not at all flexible, even at the tip. Spikelets are loosely attached to their pedicels and fall off easily at maturity and during handling. The caryopses have a reddish-brown pericarp, which is

generally quite pronounced; there are none known to have a white pericarp. Anthocyanic pigmenation is present in all varieties. All these characteristics are genetically dominant.

2. A secondary center of varietal diversification exists on both sides of the coastal Gambia River. The varieties have more delicate panicles than the ones discussed above; they are also erect, but the tip is rather flexible; the spikelets are firmly attached to their pedicels; the caryopses have white pericarps; anthocyanic pigmentation on the vegetal organs has disappeared, or is very faint; floral stigmas are light in color (white to pinkish), and the tips of the spikelets remain light in color. Its propensity for floating is in the process of disappearing. Under the local climatic conditions, all the kinds may be found in marshy rice paddies or swamps. Varietal populations of this type are quite distinct. All of the characteristics mentioned are of the recessive type in oryzicultural genetics.

3. A secondary center of varietal diversification which is in the process of acquiring independence is located on a part of the mountainous dorsal of Guinea, centered especially in the countries of the Kuranko and of the Toma (Macenta and Guéckédou in Guinea). The softening of the panicle is under way; the same holds true for depigmentation of the caryopses and of vegetal and floral organs; disarticulation of the spikelets has diminished to the point of non-existence.

Varietal separations have not yet been accomplished. These are diverse populations, each of which contains a mixture of individuals with dominant characteristics analogous to those of the central Nigerian delta, individuals with recessive characteristics of the same type as those individuals of Senegal and Gambia, and mixed individuals already marked by the recessive characteristics we have pointed out. It is within the very heart of these populations that the genetic change of the last group of individuals is taking shape. We find ourselves in the presence of a center where intense human selection is resulting in an increasing frequency of recessive traits because recessive traits are more desirable from the human point of view.

All of these kinds are raised locally, whether it be in pluvial culture (abundant rainfall) or in muddy swamps (Portères 1956).

The Senegal-Gambian and Guinean centers are far from the central Nigerian center and primary variation. No longer steeped in the "genetic juice" of genetic dominance, previously masked recessive traits are coming to light. The Guinean center shows that in very wet tropical conditions, the emergence of these recessive traits is in operation. (Current rainfall is 2,000 millimeters per year.)

As far as the Senegal-Gambian center is concerned, we must presume that the beginning of the change in gene frequencies took place in analogous conditions of wet tropical climate, that is, wetter than at present (1,100 to 1,200 millimeters of rainfall per year).

Ancient History of West African Rice Culture

In 1950 we advanced a hypothesis for the dating of the Senegal-Gambia center (Portères 1950, 1956, 1951c).

In the region where the races of the Senegal-Gambia center are located today, there is an important series of megalithic monuments, studied and clearly identified in the past by Dr. Jouenne, which line the *bolons*, or present distributaries, of the Gambia River. These *bolons* correspond to the old *arroyos* or brackish *marigots*, which were maintained by the ebb and flow of the tides, and which have now moved much further downstream as a result of the extension of the maritime deltas.

Senegal-Gambia rice culture in the Rip region must have been of the type currently practiced on the coast. The country is now occupied by the Mandingos, invaders from the twelfth and thirteenth centuries who pushed the rice growers toward the coast; it is possible that one of the current coastal population groups is descended from the one which possessed this advanced rice culture, which has been transmitted and diffused as far as Sierra Leone.

The megalithic monuments are arranged in figures of erect, oriented laterite steles (sun worship?). They could represent a terminus of that Lusitanian branch of the megalithic which descended to Morocco and even to Tripolitania. No bronze objects have been found in the few tombs there, only remains of pottery with ornamentation related to the current local type, and brass bracelets.

The civilization which came down to Senegal-Gambia does not seem to have received the evolutionary addition of bronze. It stopped at the megalithic stage, knowing the Aeneolithic only at a late date. Everything leads us to believe that the grouping which had received or brought this human culture disappeared suddenly after remaining in place for a rather long time.

We assume that the megalithic civilization which covered the provinces of Rip, Niani, and part of Saloum supported at the same time the Senegal-Gambia rice culture. By dating the first, we may date the second, and thus determine the approximate age of formation of this rice culture. It does not seem that one would be far from the truth in placing the developed phase of this civilization of erect, oriented stones between 1500 and 800 B.C., remembering also that the secondary Lusitanian megalithic center began around 2800 B.C. Radiocarbon dating of a stone circle provided a date of 800 B.C. (Portères 1970).*

Central Nigerian rice cultivation began probably around 1500 B.C., which would give it at least 3,500 years of existence, during which it has progressed but little; this stagnation is usual when an agriculture remains in the primary center of variation, its development hindered by dominant genes. On the other hand, indisputable progress has been made around its borders (the lake zone) and further away (Senegal-Gambia).

We have studied (1959) the African appellations for "rice" referring to the plant or the paddy and "rice," the food. As far as the terms in the rice-growing regions, properly speaking, of West Africa are concerned, they all center around *Malo/Maro/Mano* everywhere that Mandingo languages and dialects are found. However, we have linked them to Nigritic or even Bantu dialects, and we consider the Mandingos and proto-Mandingos to be only their heirs (Portères 1959).

Summary

Leaving aside Asiatic rice *O. sativa* L., introduced into Africa during the historical period (the Christian era), our attention is drawn to African rice *O. glaberrima* Steudel.

Analysis of about 1,500 varieties reveals the location of a center of origin of primary variation where only forms with genetically dominant characteristics are found; this center is located in the old central Nigerian delta. It probably dates from about the year 1500 B.C. or earlier. A secondary center of varietal diversification with genetically recessive characteristics is defined in Senegal-Gambia (Gambia). Finally, a third center of secondary diversification whose evolution, oriented in the direction of the Senegal-Gambian center, is found on the mountainous dorsal of Guinea (the forested region of Guinea). It is then suggested that the secondary Senegal-Gambian center could have been created along with the population groups which constructed the groupings of erect, oriented steles which line the *bolons* or arroyos where these rices are still marginally cultivated. Radiocarbon dating yields a date of 800 B.C.

* The radiocarbon date here referred to and discussions of the stone circles can be found in Fagan (1969) and Ozanne (1966a, 1966b). — *Editors.*

REFERENCES

AFZELIUS, ADAM
1967   *Sierra Leone journal 1795–1796.* Edited by Alexander Peter Kup. Uppsala Inst. för allm. och jämforande ethnografi.

AINSLIE, WHITELAW
1813   *Materia medica of Hindoostan,* two volumes. Madras: Longman.

ALLCHIN, F. R.
1969   "Early culivated plants in India and Pakistan," in *The domestication and exploitation of plants and animals.* Edited by P. J. Ucko and G. W. Dimbleby. London: Duckworth.

AL OMARI
1927   *Notebooks 1342–1346.* Translated by Demonbynes. Paris.

BARGERY, G. P.
1934   *Hausa-English dictionary and English-Hausa vocabulary.* Oxford.

BAUHINI, CASPAR
1623   *Pinax theatri botanici.* Basle: Jo. Rex.

BAUHINI, J.
1651   *Historai plantarum.* Ebroduni: Fr. Lud. Graffenried.

BEECH, MERVYN W. H.
1911   *The Suk, their language and folklore.* Oxford: Clarendon.

BIRDWOOD, G. C. M.
1862   *Catalogue of the economic products of the presidency of Bombay.* Bombay.

BRAUN, ALEXANDER
1848   Beitrag zur Kenntnis des abyssinischen Kulturpflanzen. *Flora* 6 (February): 89–98.

BROWN, A. F., R. E. MASSEY
1929   *Flora of the Sudan.* Sudan Government Printer.

BROWN, ROBERT
1826   Chapter 18 in *Voyages et découvertes dans le nord et dans les parties centrales de l'Afrique exécutés pendant les années 1822, 1823, et 1824,* three volumes. Edited by Dixon Denham and Hugh Clapperton. London: Murray.

BRUCE, J.
1790   *Travels to discover the source of the Nile,* five volumes. Edinburgh.

BURKILL, I. H.
1935   *A dictionary of economic products of the Malay Penninsula.* London: Crown Agents for the Colonies.

CASTELLANI, ETTORE, L. BALDRATI
1939   I — *Cereali dell'Africa orientale italiana. II — Teff (Eragrostis teff) cereale da panificazione dell'Africa orientale italiana montana.* Florence: Istituto Agricolo Coloniale Italiano.

CHEVALIER, A.
1922   Les petites céréales. *Revue Internationale de Botanique Appliquée et d'Agriculture Tropicale* 2:544–550.

1932 Resources végétales du Sahara et de ses confins nord et sud. *Revue Internationale de Botanique Appliquée et d'Agriculture Tropicale* 12(5).

1934 Etudes sur les prairies de l'ouest-africain. *Revue Internationale de Botanique Appliquée et d'Agriculture Tropicale* 14.

CHEVALIER, A., O. ROERICH
1914 Sur l'origine botanique des riz cultivés *C.R. Ac. Sc.* 159:560–562.

CIFFERI, R., G. R. CIGLIONI
1939 Cerealiculura in Etiopia. *Italia Agricola* 6:10–11.

CLAYTON, W. D.
1972 "Gramineae," in *Flora of West Tropical Africa.* Edited by J. Hutchinson and J. M. Dalziel (revised edition by F. N. Hepper), volume three, part two, 459–463. London: Crown Agents for the Overseas Governments.

CREAC'H, PAUL
1941 "Aliments et alimentation des indigènes du Moyen-Tchad." Thèse Faculté de Médecine de Marseille.

DALZIEL, J. M.
1937 *Useful plants of West Africa.* London.

DE CANDOLLE, A.
1855 *Géographie botanique.* Paris: V. Masson.
1883 *Origines de plantes cultivées* (second edition). Paris: G. Ballière.

DE CLUSIUS, CAROLUS
1601 *Rariorum plantarum historia.* Antwerp: Ex. Off. Plantiniana.

DE FICALHO, CONDE
1884 *Plantus uteis da Africa Portugueza,* volume one. Lisbon.

DEIGHTON, F. C.
1957 *Vernacular botanical vocabulary for Sierra Leone.* London.

DENHAM, DIXON, HUGH CLAPPERTON
1826 *Voyages et découvertes dans le nord et dans les parties centrales de l'Afrique exécutés pendant les années 1822, 1823, et 1824,* three volumes. London: Murray.

DE ORTA, GARCIA
1913 *Simples and drugs of India.* London: Sotheran.

DE RONCIGLIONE, P. ANGELO
1912 *Manuale Tigray-Italiano-Francese.* Rome.

DUDGEON, G.
1911 *The agricultural and forest products of British West Africa.* London: Murray.

DUMAS; RENOUX
1905 Culture du fonio dans les vallées du Sénégal et du Haut-Niger. *L'Agric. Prat. des Pays Chauds* 5(2):357–367. Nogent-sur-Marne.

FAGAN, B. M.
1969 Radiocarbon dates for sub-Saharan Africa. *Journal of African History* 10(1):150–151.

FRESENIUS, G.
1827 *Flore d'Abyssinie.* Museum Senckenbergianum in Frankfurt.
1837 *Beiträge zur Flora von Aegypten und Arabien.* Museum Senckenbergianum in Frankfurt.

GRAHAM
n.d.   *Catalogue of Bombay plants.* Bombay.
HARKAVY, M.
1870   Les mots Egyptiens dans le Bible. *Journal Asiatique* 15:161–186.
HAUDRICOURT, A.
1941   L'histoire du Tef. *Rev Int. Bot. Appl. Agric. Trop.* 21:128–130.
HENRARD, J. T.
1950   *Monograph of the genus Digitaria.* Leiden: Leiden University Press.
HOCHSTETTER
1848   In "Beiträge zur Kenntnis des abyssinischen Culturpflanzen," by A. Braun. *Flora* 6:89.98.
HOLLAND, J. H.
1922   The useful plants of Nigeria. *Bull. Misc. Inf. Kew Addit.*, series 9, Gramineae, part 4. London.
HOLST
1895   In *Die Gräser Ostafrikas und ihre Verwertung.* Edited by K. Schumann.
1895   In *Die Pflanzenwelt Ostafrikas und Nachbargebiete.* Edited by A. Engler. Berlin: Ebd.
HOOKER, J. D.
1897   *Flora of British India.* London: Macmillan.
HUNTER, A. W. S.
1934   A karyosystematic investigation in the Gramineae. *Canadian Journal of Research* 11:213–224.
IBN BATUTA
1843   *Voyage dans le pays des noirs,* volume five. Société Asiatique, five volumes. Guckin de Slane, Paris. Translated by C. F. Defrémery and R. B. Sanguinetti (1893). Paris: Imprimerie Nationale.
JARDIN, EDELESTAN
1850   Herborisations sur la côte occidentale d'Afrique pendant les années 1845, 1846, 1847, 1848. *Nouvelles Annales de la Marine et des Colonies* (July).
1875   Enumération des nouvelles plantes phanérogames et cryptogames découvertes dans l'ancien et le nouveau continent et recueillies par Edelestan Jardin. *Bull. Soc. Linnéenne de Normandie,* second series 9.
KIPPIST
1842   Paper in *Proceedings of the Royal Linnaean Society* 1.
1843   Paper in *Annals of Natural History* 11.
KOERNICKE, F.
1885   "Die Arten und Varietäten des Getreides," in *Handbuch des Getreidebaues,* two volumes. Edited by Koernicke and Werner. Bonn and Berlin.
LABAT, JEAN-BAPTISTE
1728   *Nouvelle relation de l'Afrique occidentale,* etc., five volumes.
LEEKE, P.
1907   *Untersuchung über Abstammung und Heimat der Negerhirse*

(Pennisetum americanum (*L.*) *K. Schum.*). Zeitschrift für Natur-wissenschaften 79.

LOPEZ, DUARTE
1961 *A report of the kingdom of Congo and the surrounding countries:* drawn out of the writings and discourses of the Portuguese, Duarte Lopez, by Filippo Pigafetta in Rome 1591. Translated from the Italian and edited with explanatory notes by Margarite Hutchinson (1881). New York: Negro University Press.

LORET, V.
1887 *La flore pharaonique.* Paris.

MARCHAL, A.
1950 Les pénicillaires cultivés au Niger. *L'Agronomie Tropicale,* 5(11, 12):582–592.

MASSEY, R. E.
1926 *Sudan grasses.* Publications Bot. Ser. Dept. Agric. and Forests. Khartoum (1).

MOONEY, H. F.
1956 *A preliminary list of Ethiopian plant names with their botanical equivalents.* Beirut.

MURDOCK, G. P.
1959 *Africa: its people and their culture history.* New York: McGraw-Hill.

NEWBOLD
1924 Notes on some foreign crab grasses. *Torreya* 24:9.

OLIVER, ROLAND A.
1970 "The problem of Bantu expansion," in *Papers on African prehistory.* Edited by J. D. Fage and R. A. Oliver, 140–156. Cambridge: Cambridge University Press.

OZANNE, PAUL
1966a The Anglo-Gambian Stone Circles Expedition. *West African Archaeological Newsletter* 4:8–12.
1966b *The Anglo-Gambian Stone Circles Expedition.* Bathurst: Government Printer.

PIDDINGTON, H.
1832 An English index to the plants of India. *For. Sec. Agr. and Hort. Soc.* Calcutta: Allen.

PIEDALLU, ANDRÉ
1923 *Le sorgho.* Paris: Société d'éditions géographiques, maritimes, et coloniales.

PORTÈRES, ROLAND
1945 Sur la ségrégation géographique des gènes de l'*Oryza glaberrima* Steudel dans l'Ouest-Africain et sur les centres de culture de cette espèce. *C.R. Ac. Sc.* 221:152–153.
1946 L'aire culturale du *Digitaria iburua* Stapf, céréale mineure de l'Ouest-Africain. *L'Agronomie Tropicale* 1(11, 12):389–392.
1949 Des plantes indicatrices du niveau de fertilité du complexe cultural édapho-climatique en Afrique tropicale. *Bull. Agric. Congo Belge* 40(1).
1950 Vieilles agricultures africaines avant le XVIe siècle. Berceaux

d'Agriculture et Centres de Variation. *L'Agronomie Tropicale* 5:489–507.

1951a *Eleusine coracana* Gaertner, céréale des humanités des pays tropicaux. *Bull. Inst. Français Afrique Noire* 12:1–78.

1951b Une céréale mineure cultivée dans l'Ouest-Africain (*Brachiaria deflexa* C. E. Hubbard, var. *Sativa* nov. var.). *L'Agronomie Tropicale* 6(1, 2):38–42.

1951c Géographie alimentaire. Berceaux agricoles et migrations des plantes cultivées en Afrique intertropicale. *C. R. Soc. Biogéographie* 239:16–21.

1952 Les successions linéaires dans les agricultures primitives de l'Afrique et leur signification. *Sols Africains* 2:14–26.

1955a Historique sur les premiers échantillons d'*Oryza glaberrima* St. recueillis en Afrique. *Journ. d'Agric. Trop. et de Bot. Appl.* 3:535–537.

1955b Présence ancienne d'une variété cultivée d'*Oryza glaberrima* St. *Journ. d'Agric. Trop. et de Bot. Appl.* 2.

1955c Les céréales mineures du genre Digitaria en Afriqque et Europe. *Journ. d'Agric. Trop. et de Bot. Appl.* 2.

1956 Taxonomie agrobotanique des riz cultivés, *O. sativa* L. et *O. glaberrima* St. *Journ. d'Agric. Trop. et de Bot. Appl.* 3.

1958–1959 Les appellations des céréales en Afrique. *Journ. d'Agric. Trop. et de Bot. Appl.* 5(1, 11) and 6(1, 7).

1960 Riz subspontanés et riz sauvages en El Salvador (Amérique Centrale). *Journ. d'Agric. Trop. et de Bot. Appl.* 7:441–446.

1966 Les noms des riz en Guinée. *Journ. d'Agric. et de Bot. Appl.* 13.

1970 "Berceaux agricoles primaires sur le continent africain," in *Papers in African prehistory*. Edited by J. D. Fage and R. A. Oliver, 43–58. Cambridge: Cambridge University Press.

ROZHEVICZ, R. J.
1928 A contribution to the knowledge of rice. *Bull. of Appl. Botany and Plant Breeding* 27:3–133. Leningrad.

ROXBURGH, WILLIAM
1832 *Flora Indica*. London.

ROYLE, J. FORBES
1839 *Illustrations of the botany and other branches of the natural history of the Himalayan Mountains*. London: Allen.

RUSSEL, FRED L.
1923 SPI Agric. Washington 57387. Sago, Western Abyssinia.

SALT, HENRY
1814 *A voyage to Abyssinia and travels to the interior*. London I: Rivington.

SCHIMPER, W.
1895 In *Die Gräser Ostafrikas und ihre Verwertung*. Edited by K. Schumann.

1895 In *Die Pflanzenwelt Ostafrikas und Nachbargebiete*. Edited by A. Engler. Berlin: Ebd.

SCHWEINFURTH, GEORG

1867 *Beiträge zur Pflora aethiopicus.* Berlin: Reimer. Loreau. Paris: Hachette.

1875 *Au coeur de l'Afrique 1868–1871. Voyages et découvertes dans les régions inexplorées de l'Afrique centrale.* Translated by H. Loreau. Paris: Hachette.

SHANTZ, H. L.

1920 SPI Agric. Washington 46844, 50001, 50060; 51498, 51942, 51943. Congo, Kenya, Uganda.

SIMOONS, FRED J.

1970 "Some questions on the economic prehistory of Ethiopia," in *Papers on African prehistory.* Edited by J. D. Fage and R. A. Oliver, 111–130. Cambridge: University of Cambridge Press.

SPEKE, J. H.

1863 *Journal of the discovery of the source of the Nile.* London: Blackwood.

STAPF, OTTO

1915 Iburu and Fondi, two cereals of Upper Guinea (*Digitaria iburua: D. exilis*). *Kew Bulletin* 8:381–386.

1919 "Gramineae: *Brachiaria regularis,*" in *Flora of tropical Asia,* volume nine. Edited by David Prain.

STAPF, OTTO, C. E. HUBBARD

1934 "Pennisetum," in *Flora of tropical Africa,* volume nine, part six: 954–1070. London: Crown Agents for the Colonies.

STEUDEL, E. T.

1855 *Synopsis plantarum graminaceum.* Stuttgart.

SUDRES, A.

1947 La dégradation des sols du Fouta-Djalon. *L'Agronomie Tropicale* 2(5, 6):227–246.

TROTTER, A.

1938 Di Attilio Zuccagni e della prima descrizione botanica del Tef etiopico. *Annali della Facoltà di Agraria della R. Università di Napoli,* series three, 9.

UNGER, A.

1886–1887 Die Pflanzen des alten Aegypten. Botanische Streifzüge auf dem Gebiete der Kulturgeschichte. *Sitzungsberichte Wissenschaft* 54, 55. Vienna.

VAVILOV, N. I.

1926 Studies of the origin of cultivated plants. *Bull. Appl. Bot. and Plant Breeding* 16(2):1–243. Leningrad.

VON LINNÉ, K.

1753 *Species plantarum.* Leipzig: Nauck.

1759 *Systema naturae.* Leiden.

WATSON, J. FORBES

1868 *Index to the native and scientific names of Indian and other eastern economic plants and products.* London: Trübner.

WATT, GEORGE

1908 *Dictionary of commercial products of India.* London: Murray.

WEBB, L. J.
1948, 1949   Article in *Comm. Science Indus., Research Austral. Bull.*
WELWITSCH
1899   *Catalogue of Welwitsch's African plants.* London.
WISANTHAM, G. R.
1948   Kirkkv Varaghu. Poisoning in man and animal in Madras presidency. *Proceedings of the 35th Industrial Science Congress Assoc.* Patna.
ZUCCAGNI, ATTILIO
1774   Dissertation.

Variability in Sorghum bicolor

J. M. J. DE WET, J. R. HARLAN, and E. G. PRICE

Sorghum bicolor (L.) Moench is large and variable. It includes cultivated sorghums as well as their closest spontaneous relatives (de Wet and Huckabay 1967). Subspecific variation among sorghums has been variously classified by taxonomists and plant breeders (Snowden 1936, 1955; Murty, Arundachalam, and Saxena 1967; Jakushevsky 1969; de Wet and Harlan 1971). Recently, Harlan and de Wet (1971) proposed that crop-weed/wild complexes are best treated as single species, with cultivated and spontaneous taxa included in separate subspecies. Cultivated sorghums were treated as subspecies *bicolor* and spontaneous taxa as subspecies *arundinaceum*. Both subspecies were further subdivided into races. The origin and evolution of these races are discussed (see Map 1).

TAXONOMY OF SORGHUM

Sorghum Moench is immensely variable, and was subdivided by Garber (1950) into sections *Chaetosorghum, Heterosorghum, Parasorghum, Sorghastrum, Sorghum (Eu-sorghum)*, and *Stiposorghum*. The affinities among these sections are poorly understood, but Celarier (1959) proposed that by excluding *Sorghastrum*, a more uniform genus *Sorghum* is constituted. *Sorghastrum* Nash differs from true sorghums in that the pedicellate spikelets are strongly reduced, often to the pedicel. *Parasorghum* and *Stipo-*

The research reported in this paper was supported financially by the Illinois Agricultural Experiment Station.

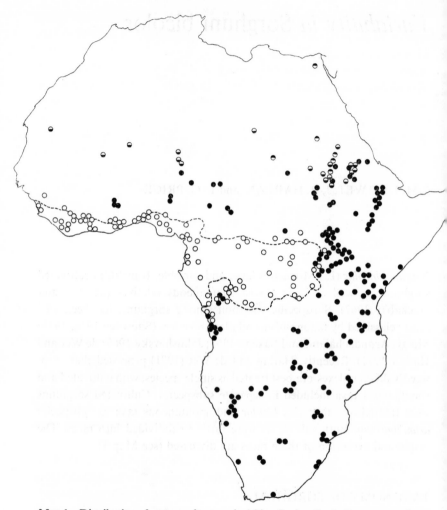

Map 1.   Distribution of ssp. *arundinaceum* in Africa. Broken line indicates approximate limit of forests; ○ race arundinaceum; ◑ race aethiopicum; ● race verticilliflorum; ◖ race virgatum

sorghum differ from the other subgeneric taxa by having extremely long awns, and the nodes are characterized by a distinct ring of hairs. *Sorghum, Heterosorghum,* and *Chaetosorghum* have glabrous or minutely pubescent nodes, with the pedicellate spikelets neuter or staminate in *Sorghum,* and reduced to the pedicel only in the other two sections. *Heterosorghum* has whorled panicle branches while those of *Chaetosorghum* are not whorled.

Section *Sorghum* remains extremely variable, but following Harlan and de Wet (1971, 1972), relatively simple to classify. It includes two species, *S. halepense* (L.) Pers. (to include *S. controversum* and *S. miliaceum*) and *S. bicolor* (L.) Moench. The latter species is divided into subspecies *bicolor* and subspecies *arundinaceum* (Desv.) de Wet and Harlan. Subspecies *bicolor* is recognized to include all cultivated grain sorghums and subspecies *arundinaceum* all related spontaneous sorghums.

CULTIVATED SORGHUMS

Cultivated species are frequently more variable than related wild species, and taxonomists often tend to overclassify cultigens (cf. Jeffrey 1968). Sorghum certainly is no exception. Snowden (1936) recognized twenty-eight cultivated species which he further subdivided into one hundred fifty-six varieties and numerous forms. These Snowdenian species were combined into five basic races and ten intermediate races by Harlan and de Wet (1972). Intermediate races resemble a basic race rather closely, but also incorporate characteristics of at least one other basic race in their spikelet morphology.

Bicolor is the least specialized of the basic races of cultivated sorghum and has the widest distribution. It has an open inflorescence, and the grain is somewhat elongated and usually covered by long glumes, resembling in these respects *arundinaceum* sorghums. Race bicolor (see Plate 1) is sporadically cultivated across the African savanna and in Asia from India to Japan and Indonesia. The morphological characteristics of this race can be reproduced by crossing any cultivated sorghum with any wild *arundinaceum* taxon, and backcrossing these hybrids with their cultivated parents. Primitive bicolors probably were the ancestors of the other basic cultivated races. The wide distribution of race bicolor in Asia, where possible wild progenitors are absent, suggests a relatively ancient origin and basic status for it among races of cultivated sorghum. It probably originated in the savanna somewhere between western Ethiopia and eastern Chad (Harlan 1971) from wild members of subspecies *arundinaceum*. The verticilliflorum-aethiopicum complex is still abundant in this region, is commonly harvested as human food, and provides excellent grazing for livestock of nomadic pastoralists.

Race guinea (see Plate 4) is widely grown in Africa, and is the commonly cultivated sorghum in parts of India, Burma, and Southeast Asia. It is the dominant sorghum in the broadleaf savanna of West Africa and the only sorghum grown in the tropical forest of the Guinea coast. Guinea sorghums probably originated in West Africa as selections out of primitive bicolors, for cultivation in high rainfall areas. The characteristic gaping glumes allow for rapid loss of moisture when the grain is mature. After ripening, the long glumes enclose the grain when the humidity is high, but open widely to expose the grain as soon as the air gets drier. East and West African guinea sorghums resemble each other in morphological detail, suggesting an eastward migration from their center of origin.

Race caudatum (see Plate 2) is an important sorghum in tropical Central Africa. It is extensively cultivated around Lake Victoria, extending northward to central Sudan and coastal Ethiopia, and westward across the savanna to Upper Volta. Caudatum differs from other cultivated sorghums in having plano-convex grains that bulge near the middle on the side of the embryo. It occupies essentially the area of first sorghum cultivation and must be a relatively old race. Carbonized grains from Daima near Lake Chad that date back to the ninth century A.D. (Connah 1967) have the characteristic turtle-back grains of present-day caudatum. However, it must have originated after the initial introduction of sorghum into Asia since it remained largely confined to its center of origin until historic times.

Race kafir (see Plate 5) is the dominant cultivated sorghum south of the equator. Like caudatum, it was an African sorghum until historic times. Kafir sorghums resemble race bicolor in spikelet morphology, except that the grains are usually quite exposed beyond the shorter glumes. Storage protein chemistry suggests that race kafir had an independent origin from wild verticilliflorum sorghums south of the equator (Schechter and de Wet 1972). This domestication could have taken place anywhere in the savanna. Wild sorghums are locally abundant, often harvested for food, and frequently gathered to flavor beer. Harlan and Stemler (this volume) propose that race kafir probably originated south of the ports from which cultivated sorghums were transported to Asia.

Race durra (see Plate 3) is the dominant sorghum in the Near East and parts of India. In Africa it is grown primarily along the southern fringes of the Sahara and the northeastern coastal regions. Distribution suggests an Indian or Near Eastern origin and later introduction into Africa. Durra sorghums probably originated as selections out of primitive bicolors for cultivation in dry areas. Inflorescences are frequently compact, but more open among kinds grown in wetter areas. Race durra can be recognized by its flattened and obovate grains, and glumes that are crinkled near the middle or with the tip of a different texture than the rest.

Racial differentiation in sorghum is associated with man and his agricultural activities. Race kafir is grown by the Bantu south of the equator, caudatum is confined to central tropical Africa, race guinea is basically a West African sorghum, and durra is associated in Africa with Islam. Character combinations identifying races are tightly linked, and true-breeding intermediate races can readily be produced by hybridization and selection for specific combinations of racial characteristics. Such intermediate races are frequently grown where two races become sympatric.

Races are extremely variable in respect to characteristics other than those used by de Wet and Harlan (1972) to identify them. These characters are associated with habitat adaptation and usage. Sorghum is a versatile crop; the stems are used as fodder, fuel, and building material. Stems are also chewed when young for the sweet sap produced, and the red color produced by some kinds is used as dye. The grains are eaten raw, boiled like rice, ground to produce flour, and used as medicine, to flavor beer, and to make malt. These numerous uses of sorghum are frequently mutually exclusive in the same village, and adjacent villages often grow different kinds of sorghum for similar uses. The different kinds are maintained by selection and isolation of seed stocks.

WILD SORGHUMS

Wild sorghums of *S. bicolor* are included in subspecies *arundinaceum*. These were divided by Snowden (1955) among several species. However, de Wet, Harlan, and Price (1970) demonstrated that hybridization among the four basic taxa *S. aethiopicum*, *S. arundinaceum*, *S. verticilliflorum*, and *S. virgatum* can give rise to all the variability described by Snowden. Since these taxa hybridize freely in nature wherever they are sympatric, and also cross readily with cultivated sorghums, they were included in *S. bicolor* by de Wet and Huckabay (1967). Following the classification of Harlan and de Wet (1972), they are treated as races rather than varieties of subspecies *arundinaceum*. The rhizomatous *S. propinquum* (cf. Snowden 1955) also crosses readily with members of *arundinaceum* and is included as a race in this subspecies.

Race propinquum is the only member of subspecies *arundinaceum* that occurs outside Africa. It is widely distributed in Southeast Asia, southern

China, southern India, and Ceylon. Propinquum differs from other *arundinaceum* sorghums in having well-developed rhizomes. In this respect it resembles *S. halepense*, but is diploid ($2n = 20$) rather than tetraploid. Celarier (1958) suggested that propinquum may have been one of the parents that contributed to the origin of tetraploid rhizomatous taxa. Nevertheless, propinquum is so closely allied to the African members of *arundinaceum* that hybrids between them are fully fertile. Propinquum is a forest grass, occupying wet, low-lying areas and streambanks. Habitat seems to exclude this race as a possible ancestor of cultivated Asian sorghums. It does, however, cross with cultivated taxa to produce fertile weedy complexes.

Race arundinaceum is widely distributed in the tropical forest of the Guinea coast and Congo. Its outstanding characteristics are large, broad leaves, and large, open inflorescences with long, pendulous branches. It occupies stream banks, alluvial soil, or the edges of paths in the forest, but is also found around villages and cultivated fields. Arundinaceum often hybridizes with race guinea to produce troublesome weeds. Its forest habitat seems to exclude arundinaceum as a possible direct ancestor of any cultivated race. However, Snowden (1955) suggested that it may have played a role in the evolution of West African cultivated sorghums. Introgression with early bicolor sorghums could have made possible the extension of cultivation into the tropical forest.

Race virgatum is confined to the drier regions of northeastern Africa. It is often abundant along stream banks and irrigation canals. Virgatum is characterized by long, narrow inflorescences with suberect branches that keep close to the central axis, and narrow leaves. Distribution excludes virgatum as a possible ancestor of cultivated sorghum. However, the seeds are relatively large and quite palatable and may have been harvested before the introduction of cultivated durra sorghums to Egypt and the drier areas of Sudan.

Race verticilliflorum extends across the African savanna. It resembles arundinaceum except that the inflorescence branches usually are not pendulous and are divided from near the base. Specimens from forest regions in East and South Africa are often difficult to classify with certainty into arundinaceum or verticilliflorum, and along the edge of the West African tropical forest these two races grade so completely into each other that classification becomes completely impossible. In Africa verticilliflorum sorghums are absent only from deserts, tropical forest, and areas with severe frost. It is often extremely abundant, covering several acres, and is frequently harvested for human consumption or to flavor beer. It could have been domesticated anywhere across the savanna. Harlan

Plates 1-4. Spikelet morphology of ssp. *bicolor*. Plate 1. race bicolor; Plate 2. race caudatum; Plate 3. race durra; Plate 4. race guinea

Plates 5-6.   Plate 5. race kafir; Plate 6. race drummondii

(1971) suggested that the most likely area is the central savanna between Ethiopia and Chad. Verticilliflorum crosses readily with cultivated sorghums. Derivatives of such crosses are often troublesome weeds in cultivated sorghum fields.

Race aethiopicum is widespread in the dry West African savanna. As recognized by us, it includes plants with narrow, relatively compact inflorescences and large, hairy spikelets. Typical specimens are highly cleistogamous while in others anthesis does take place. It readily intercrosses in nature with durra sorghums and is frequently found close to or in cultivated fields. However, aethiopicum also occurs in fertile soil close to streams and in wadi bottoms. These latter plants closely resemble verticilliflorum except for their larger spikelets. Phylogenetically they appear to be an extension of race verticilliflorum with larger grains, probably as an adaptation to dry habitats. Derivatives of introgression between verticilliflorum and durra sorghums can often not be distinguished from weed aethiopicums. Because of its distribution into the southern fringes of the Sahara, aethiopicum is retained as a distinct race. Snowden (1936), Portères (1962), and de Wet and Huckabay (1967) suggested that durra sorghums could have been derived from domestication of aethiopicum. Morphologically this seems quite possible. Furthermore, aethiopicum is locally very abundant in central Sudan, yields well, has large grains, and is quite palatable. However, distribution of durra sorghums and their association with Islam in Africa suggest an origin outside their present African range (Harlan and Stemler, this volume).

WEED SORGHUMS

Spontaneous sorghums associated with cultivation were classified in detail by Snowden (1936, 1955). Those that represent hybrids or hybrid derivatives between wild members of subspecies *arundinaceum* and cultivated sorghums (ssp. *bicolor*) will collectively be referred to as race drummondii (see Plate 6), in this discussion. As can be expected, this race includes a morphologically variable group of weeds. In Southeast Asia, propinquum crosses with bicolor and guinea sorghums and may have contributed towards the origin of Asian kaoliangs (included in race bicolor by Harlan and de Wet 1972). In Africa, members of arundinaceum and bicolor cross wherever they come together. Verticilliflorum is sympatric with all races of cultivated sorghums, arundinaceum is sympatric with races guinea and caudatum, aethiopicum is sympatric with caudatum and durra, and virgatum with race durra. Derivatives of hybridization between subspecies *arundinaceum* and subspecies *bicolor* are not always easy to distinguish on the basis of morphology from wild sorghums. Spikelet morphology is often of the wild type, and inflorescences of these hybrid derivatives frequently resemble those of their wild parents. However, they never occupy stable habitats, but are troublesome weeds in cultivated fields and other man-disturbed areas.

Hybrids, however, are not too frequently encountered, and they rarely develop into hybrid swarms. This is not surprising, because nature will favor segregants adapted to wild-type habitats, while the agricultural activities of man favor those with a weedy habitat. Successive backcrosses to either parent will rapidly result in recovery of parental types, often without any obvious transfer of traits from the other parent. Wild-type genes, however, can be transferred to cultivated sorghums. Completely cultivated morphology, except for fragile rachis, is often encountered in sorghum fields, sometimes even where wild sorghums are absent. Such characteristics evidently were introduced with weed sorghums. Transfer of cultivated-type genes to wild populations is less obvious. However, an increase in branching of the inflorescence and larger grains may indicate introgression from cultivated into related wild sorghums.

Cultivated sorghums also cross with tetraploid *S. halepense* ($2n = 40$) wherever these taxa are grown in the vicinity of each other. Such triploid hybrids, when backcrossed with *S. halepense*, can give rise to tetraploid offspring with one basic genome of cultivated sorghum. These tetraploids are aggressive weeds and commonly encountered in western and southern India. In America the widely distributed roadside weed, Johnson grass, probably originated from an early Mediterranean introduction of *S. halepense* and introduced African cultivated sorghums.

SORGHUM DOMESTICATION

Cultivated sorghums were derived from subspecies *arundinaceum* through domestication which initially took place in Africa. The wild races aethiopicum, arundinaceum, verticilliflorum, and virgatum cross readily with all races of cultivated sorghum, and any one or all of the races could have been domesticated at different places, and even different times. Snowden (1936) proposed that race arundinaceum gave rise to guinea sorghums, verticilliflorum to kafir sorghums, and race aethiopicum to both durra and bicolor sorghums. This proposed scheme of phylogenetic affinities between wild and cultivated taxa of *S. bicolor* was accepted by Portères (1962). However, de Wet and Huckabay (1967) demonstrated that there is no conclusive morphological or genetical basis for these assumptions. Archaeological data (cf. Doggett 1965) also provide no conclusive answer as to the ancestor of cultivated sorghum.

Distribution seems to exclude races virgatum and arundinaceum as possible direct progenitors of cultivated races. Arundinaceum is a forest grass and virgatum is a desert grass, both falling outside the primary area of sorghum cultivation across the savanna. Race durra is adapted to dry areas and guinea is grown in tropical forest, but both seem to be secondary adaptations from a primitive savanna cultivated sorghum. Thus, races aethiopicum and verticilliflorum remain as the most likely progenitors of subspecies *bicolor*. Phylogenetically, aethiopicum is nothing more than the extension of verticilliflorum into the southern fringes of the Sahara, and across the northern savanna it is impossible to distinguish consistently between them. They probably were domesticated as a complex, giving rise to a primitive bicolor sorghum.

The basic bicolor must have differed from the aethiopicum-verticilliflorum complex only in having tough, rather than fragile racemes, and possibly in having larger grains. Harlan, de Wet, and Price (1973) demonstrated that planting will automatically result in a change from articulating to nonarticulating spikelets and larger grains.

Wild sorghums have probably been harvested by man for food millennia before they became domesticated. Harvesting, by itself, will not lead to domestication of a cereal. It is the grains that were not harvested that contribute to the next generation, and wild-type characteristics are therefore maintained in natural stands. With planting, however, it is harvested grains that are planted season after season. A completely new set of adaptations now become advantageous. Pressures for increase in the percentage of seed recovered will automatically lead to selection for tough rachises and more determinate growth. Selection pressures for an increase in seedling vigor to compete with weeds will automatically lead to an increase in seed size. Once the wild progenitor becomes adapted to the manmade habitat and does not articulate its spikelets naturally, the cereal is domesticated.

Cultivated sorghums may all have been derived from a primitive domesticated bicolor-like race. This certainly seems to have been the case with guinea, caudatum, and durra sorghums. Race kafir, being more or less isolated from the other races until relatively recently (cf. Harlan and Stemler, this volume), may have been domesticated independently from race verticilliflorum somewhere south of the equator. Protein chemistry of grains seems to support such a conclusion (Schechter and de Wet 1972). However, the wide distribution of bicolor sorghums in southern Africa suggests that race kafir could also have been derived from the original central African domesticated race.

REFERENCES

CELARIER, R. P.
  1958 Cytotaxonomic notes on the subsection *halepense* of the genus *Sorghum*. *Bulletin Torrey Botanical Club* 85:49–62.
  1959 Cytotaxonomy of the Andropogoneae. III. Subtribe Sorgheae, genus *Sorghum*. *Cytologia* 23:395–418.
CONNAH, G.
  1967 Progress report on archaeological work in Bornu 1964–1966. North Hist. Res. Scheme, 2nd International Report, Zaria.
DE WET, J. M. J., J. R. HARLAN
  1971 The origin and domestication of *Sorghum bicolor*. *Economic Botany* 25:128–135.
DE WET, J. M. J., J. R. HARLAN, E. G. PRICE
  1970 Origin of variability in the spontanea complex of *Sorghum bicolor*. *American Journal of Botany* 57:704–707.
DE WET, J. M. J., J. P. HUCKABAY
  1967 The origin of *Sorghum bicolor*. II. Distribution and domestication. *Evolution* 21:787–802.
DOGGETT, H.
  1965 "The development of cultivated sorghums," in *Crop plant evolution*. Edited by Sir Joseph Hutchinson, 50–69. London: Cambridge University Press.
GARBER, E. D.
  1950 Cytotaxonomic studies in the genus *Sorghum*. *Univ. Calif. Publ. Bot.* 23:283–361.
HARLAN, J. R.
  1971 Agricultural origins: centers and noncenters. *Science* 174:468–474.
HARLAN, J. R., J. M. J. DE WET
  1971 Towards a rational classification of cultivated plants. *Taxon* 20:509–517.
  1972 A simplified classification of sorghum. *Crop Science* 12:172–176.
HARLAN, J. R., J. M. J. DE WET, E. G. PRICE
  1973 Comparative evolution of cereals. *Evolution* 27:311–325.
JAKUSHEVSKY, E. S.
  1969 Varietal composition of sorghum and its uses for breeding. *Bull. Appl. Bot. Genet. Plt. Br.* 41:148–178.
JEFFREY, C.
  1968 Systematic categories for cultivated plants. *Taxon* 17:109–114.
MURTY, B. R., V. ARUNDACHALAM, M. B. L. SAXENA
  1967 Classification and catalogue of a world collection of cultivated sorghums and pennisetums. *Indian J. Genet. Plt. Br.* 27 (Suppl.): 1–74.

PORTÈRES, R.
  1962 Berceaux agricoles primaires sur le continent africain. *Journal of African History* 3(2):195–210.
SHECHTER, Y., J. M. J. DE WET
  1972 Comparative electrophoresis of proteins and isozyme analysis of cultivated races of *Sorghum bicolor* var. *bicolor*. *Proceedings of the Symposium on Chemistry in Evolution and Systematics*. Strasbourg.
SNOWDEN, J. D.
  1936 *The cultivated races of* Sorghum. London: Allard and Son.
  1955 The wild fodder sorghums of the section *Eusorghum. J. Linn. Soc. London* 55:191–260.

The Races of Sorghum in Africa

JACK R. HARLAN and ANN STEMLER

From the world point of view, sorghum is the most important of the African domesticates. Many millions of people in Africa and Asia depend on it as a source of food. It has become a major feed grain of the United States and is being used more and more in Latin America, replacing maize in the drier regions. Sorghum is much more drought-resistant than maize and has proved to be one of the really great cereals that feeds the world.

The Crop Evolution Laboratory, University of Illinois, has been conducting studies on the origin and evolution of sorghum for several years. The extensive collection of cultivated sorghums at Kew has been carefully analyzed. Other herbaria with useful materials are Paris, Brussels, Florence, Nairobi, and Praetoria. In addition to these, some twenty-five small herbaria have been visited across Africa. Approximately ten thousand head samples have been obtained from the world sorghum collection for study and analysis. Professors de Wet and Harlan have made extensive field studies in most of the sorghum-growing countries of Africa.

We found in our studies that it was necessary to devise a new and simplified classification for the cultivated sorghums. The system developed by Snowden is basically sound, but we found it too difficult when thousands of samples were being studied. A simplified classification has been published (Harlan and de Wet 1972) and will not be treated in detail here. When a large number of sorghum samples was classified by the new method and plotted on a map of Africa, it became apparent that the distribution patterns were remarkably precise and clear. We feel these distributions to be so consistent that they must be based upon some historical sequence of events. This paper is an attempt to interpret the distributions of the races of sorghum in Africa.

THE RACES

The classification adopted involves five basic races: bicolor, guinea, kafir, caudatum, and durra; and ten intermediate races consisting of all combinations of the five basic races taken two at a time (Table 1).

Table 1.   The races of sorghum according to Harlan and de Wet

Basic races:		
Race (1)	bicolor	(B)
Race (2)	guinea	(G)
Race (3)	caudatum	(C)
Race (4)	kafir	(K)
Race (5)	durra	(D)
Intermediate races: (all combinations of basic races)		
Race (6)	guinea-bicolor	(GB)
Race (7)	caudatum-bicolor	(CB)
Race (8)	kafir-bicolor	(KB)
Race (9)	durra-bicolor	(DB)
Race (10)	guinea-caudatum	(GC)
Race (11)	guinea-kafir	(GK)
Race (12)	guinea-durra	(GD)
Race (13)	kafir-caudatum	(KC)
Race (14)	durra-caudatum	(DC)
Race (15)	kafir-durra	(KD)

The bicolor race is the most primitive and least specialized of the major races. It has an open head, somewhat resembling the wild sorghums; the spikelets have long glumes; the seed is elongate, more or less symmetrical dorsoventrally, and usually covered by the glumes. All of these characteristics are considered primitive in comparison to the highly specialized spikelets of the other four races.

Bicolor is found on a minor scale almost everywhere that sorghum is grown in Africa; consequently, we have not shown the distribution on maps. In India and the Far East it is relatively more important. While the race has primitive morphological features, some of the bicolor materials are recent evolutionary products. Bicolor morphology can be recovered from hybrids between wild sorghum and almost any cultivated race. Such derivates have been detected in Nigeria, Chad, Sudan, Ethiopia, Uganda, and South Africa and are widespread elsewhere in Africa. In Asia there seems to be little interaction between wild and cultivated sorghum except in Burma, Thailand, and the Indo-China region.

The guinea race also has an open head with relatively long glumes. However, the spikelets are highly specialized, and there is nothing like them in any of the wild races of sorghum. They are distinguished at maturity by widely gaping glumes that roll inward, and the seed is twisted almost 90 degrees between them.

The kafir race is distinguished by small, roundish, well exposed seeds, more or less symmetrical dorsoventrally, although the glumes are of variable length. The head is usually semicompact.

The caudatum race is characterized by asymmetrical seeds which are flattened on the lower side. In extreme cases the lower side may be even somewhat concave and the upper side rounded and bulging, producing a sort of beak at the tip. The seeds are well exposed and the head type is extremely variable ranging from loose, open heads to semicompact types.

Durra is perhaps the most specialized race of all. The head types are frequently very tight, forming a nearly round ball. The spikelets are highly specialized; the seed is obovate, widest slightly above the middle, very large and rounded above, and wedge-shaped below. The glumes often have a transverse crease.

DISTRIBUTION

The distributions of the principal races in Africa are shown in Maps 1 through 4. Each dot represents one to several collections either in herbaria or from the world collection. It is impossible, of course, to show all of the collections on the maps, but the number of specimens is substantial. Map 1, for instance, dealing with the guinea race and its intermediate forms, was based on over 1,000 collections available to us. Our sampling, however, is far from uniform. Some of the countries in Africa are very poorly collected, and others are well represented.

It will be noted from the maps that guinea is primarily a West African sorghum. It is the dominant race and occurs in its purest form there. It also occurs in East Africa where it is often modified by hybridization with other races. The guinea race also occurs in India on some scale. The caudatum race is primarily a race of Central Africa and occurs in its purest form in Chad and Sudan. Kafir is entirely a race of southern Africa. We have no authentic collection

AFRICA No. 206

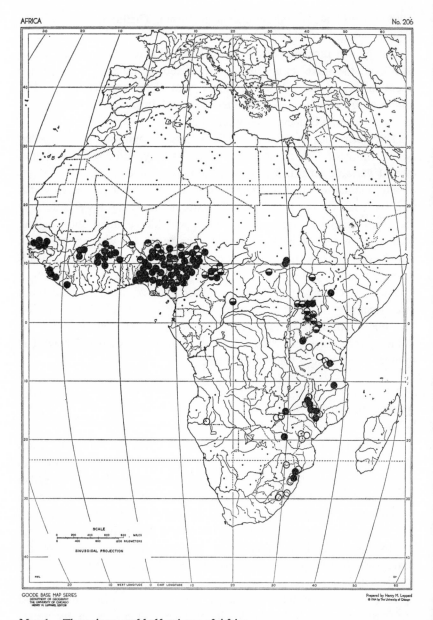

GOODE BASE MAP SERIES
DEPARTMENT OF GEOGRAPHY
THE UNIVERSITY OF CHICAGO
HENRY M. LEPPARD, EDITOR

Prepared by Henry M. Leppard
© 1954 by The University of Chicago

Map 1.   The guineas and half-guineas of Africa

   Key: Solid circles: guinea
            Open circles: guinea-kafir
            Solid bottoms: guinea-caudatum
            Solid tops: guinea-durra

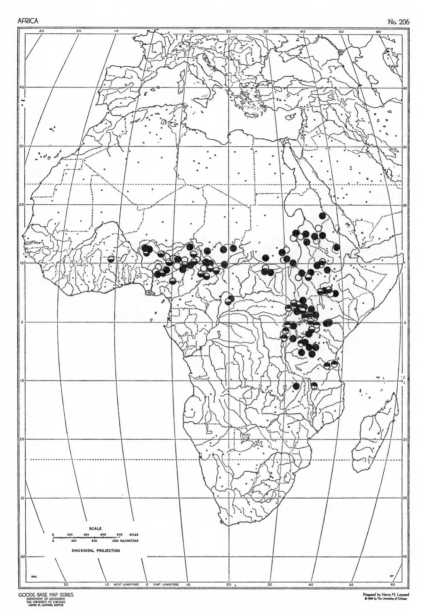

Map 2. The caudatums and half-caudatums of Africa

Key: Solid circles: caudatum
Open circles: durra-caudatum
Solid bottoms: guinea-caudatum
Solid tops: kafir-caudatum

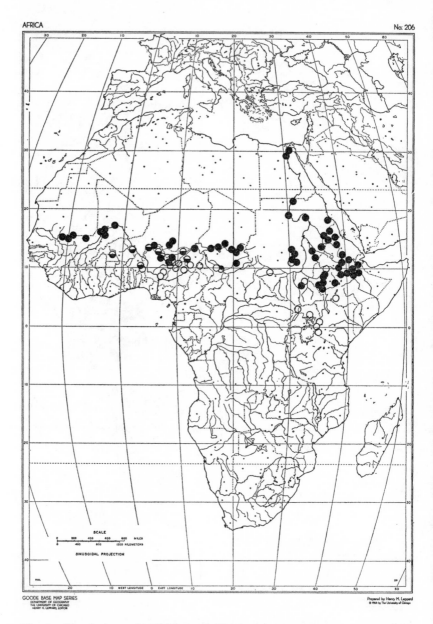

Map 3.   The durras and half-durras of Africa

   Key: Solid circles: durra
            Open circles: durra-caudatum
            Solid bottoms: durra-guinea

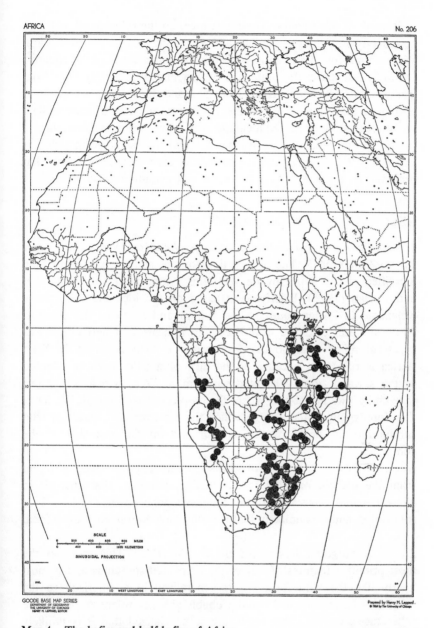

Map 4.   The kafirs and half-kafirs of Africa

Key: Solid circles: kafir
Open circles: guinea-kafir
Solid bottoms: kafir-caudatum

of it north of the equator. The durra race, on the other hand, is found abundantly in Ethiopia, Sudan, and along the fringes of the Sahara. We have not found authentic collections of durra south of the equator. Durra is essentially the only race of sorghum in the Near East from Turkey through Syria, Iran, Pakistan, and into India where it is estimated that four-fifths of the sorghums are durra. Intermediate races occur at the expected locations where two major races overlap.

The distributions are so precise in detail that some explanation is called for. We shall attempt to reconstruct the sequence of events that probably took place during the origin and evolution of sorghum.

RECONSTRUCTION OF EVENTS

1. *Sorghum was First Domesticated in the Area Designated "Early Bicolor" on Map 5.* The justification for this statement is more fully amplified in the paper by de Wet (this symposium) and in de Wet and Harlan (1971). Briefly, it is based on the idea that agriculture originated in Africa south of the Sahara and north of the equator. Archaeological evidence would seem to indicate that agriculture was practiced much later south of the equator than north of it. West Africa is ruled out because of the lack of a wild sorghum adapted to the savanna zone. The wild sorghum of West Africa is a forest race and grows in habitats where the crop is not well suited. We have, therefore, outlined the area in which the most massive stands of wild sorghum occur north of the equator and on the east side of the continent.
Negative: Past distributions of wild sorghums may have been different from the present ones. It is our feeling, however, that changes in climate would have shifted the indicated zone either northward or southward, and it is unlikely that it would have moved to West Africa.

2. *Early Sorghum Resembled the Bicolor Race.* This race has the most primitive features of any of the cultivated sorghums and is most nearly like the wild forms. It is generalized in comparison to the other four basic races and could probably give rise to any of them. The other races, on the other hand, are so specialized that it is unlikely that one could produce another.
Negative: We see no argument against this statement.

3. *Early Bicolor was Distributed at an Early Date to West Africa Where the Guinea Race Evolved.* We consider the guinea race the

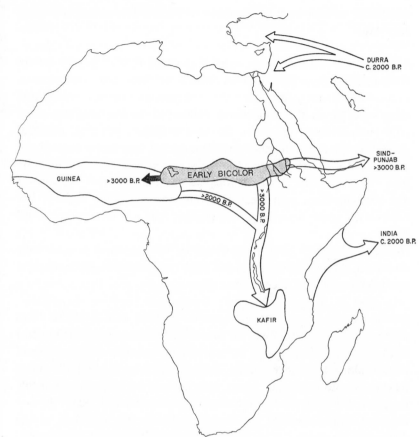

Map 5.   Early movements of sorghum
         Initial domestication in shaded area

earliest of the specialized races because of its distribution not only in
West Africa, but also in East Africa and India. No other race except
the generalized bicolor has so broad a distribution. Guinea is the
dominant and most characteristic sorghum of West Africa and almost
certainly evolved there. Elsewhere it appears in slightly modified
forms.

Negative: The only other alternative that we see would be an independent domestication in West Africa. We consider this unlikely
for reasons given above. It is true that the guinea race is better suited
to high rainfall than any of the other races of sorghum, and it is
possible that this adaptation was introduced from the forest arundinaceum race. We do not consider it likely, however, that arundinaceum

was the progenitor of guinea because of their differences in ecological amplitudes.

4. *Early Bicolor was Distributed to the Sind-Punjab Region Before 1000 B.C.* At some time sorghum became an important food plant in India. We do not know when the first introduction was made. Archaeologically, in the excavations conducted so far, sorghum dates only from Roman times. We do have evidence, however, of other African crops at about 1000 B.C. Pearl millet and finger millet have been found in Rangpur and Hallur respectively (Rao 1963; Nagaraja Rao 1967). If other African crops were being imported, we assume that sorghum came with them. Sorghum was apparently not very important for some time, however, because there is no Sanskrit word for it.
Negative: The only alternative would be for the durra race to have evolved in Africa and later to have been transported to India where it became the dominant race of the region.

5. *The Durra Race Evolved in India.* The distribution of the durra race in Africa suggests that it is intrusive. It is found abundantly east of the plateau in Ethiopia, in parts of Sudan, and only as an occasional culture along the fringes of the Sahara to the west. In India durra reaches its most extreme forms with creases on both glumes, while in Africa it is often modified through hybridization with other races.
Negative: An alternative explanation would be the evolution of the durra race in eastern Ethiopia from whence it was later transported to India, or perhaps even more likely, an evolution in both India and eastern Ethiopia with sea transport exchanging germ plasm over a long period of time.

6. *Early Bicolor was Distributed to Southern East Africa Where the Kafir Race Evolved.* Kafir is the characteristic race of southern Africa and is not found elsewhere. It seems most likely to have evolved in the region indicated in Map 5.
Negative: The only alternative would be an independent domestication in southern Africa from local populations of the wild verticilliflorum race.

7. *Guinea Moved Out of West Africa and Down the East African Savanna to South Africa.* Guinea is found up and down the agricultural zones of eastern Africa but is seldom a major race there. In

Malawi and Swaziland, however, there are local areas in which it is dominant. The guineas of East Africa are somewhat different morphologically from those of West Africa and, in general, tend to resemble guinea-kafirs in morphology.

Negative: There is no question that guinea reached eastern Africa, but there may have been alternative routes and times other than those indicated.

8. *The Guinea Race was Introduced Directly to India by Sea Trade Across the Indian Ocean.* There is no trace of guinea between southern Ethiopia and India. The race is not well suited to arid agriculture, and the most likely means of distribution seems to be transport from the East African ports to the Malabar Coast of India. This sea trade was flourishing at least 2,000 years ago. Apparently the kafir race was not taken to India. Therefore, it would seem most likely that northern ports such as Mombasa and Zanzibar were used.

Negative: There is no question that the guinea race reached India, but the time and route may not be as indicated. The lack of kafir in India might be due to its lack of adaptation on the Malabar Coast, while guinea is better suited to the higher rainfall of the Western Ghats. It may also be that the kafir race is very recent and had not evolved at the time that guinea sorghum was transported by ocean to India.

9. *The Caudatum Race Evolved in or near the Region of Initial Domestication.* Caudatum is important in eastern Nigeria, Chad, Sudan, and Uganda, and it is a minor race in Ethiopia. Caudatum has never spread much beyond this limited distribution, and, therefore, we suppose it to be a relatively new race. It has produced intermediate races with durra, guinea, and kafir. The occurrence of durra-caudatum in Uganda would indicate materials introduced from the north since durra has not been detected in Uganda. Intermediates with the kafir race are found to the south as expected.

Negative: We find no argument against this statement.

10. *The Durra Race Returned to Africa.* If our interpretation of an Indian evolution of durra is correct, then durra returned to Ethiopia and Sudan and spread westward along the fringes of the Sahara. The fact that sorghum is mentioned by Greek and Roman writers as having come from India would suggest that durra was introduced into Africa approximately 2,000 years ago. It is probable, however, that the distribution to the west was accomplished in Arab times.

476   JACK R. HARLAN, ANN STEMLER

Negative: An alternative evolution of durra has been suggested above.

11. *The Kafir Race Expanded Throughout Southern Africa.* We presume that the distribution of kafir is closely associated with the migrations and movements of Bantu agriculturalists.

12. *Meanwhile, Early Bicolors Spread Eastward to Burma and Indonesia and Northward into China Where the Kaoliangs Evolved.* Archaeological finds of sorghum have been reported in China dating to early or middle first millennium B.C. A word for sorghum does not appear in Chinese literature, however, until the fourth century A.D., and the crop was not important until after the Mongol conquest. The Chinese word *shu-shu* indicates "a millet from Szechuan." It has been suggested, therefore, that it was introduced originally from India by an overland route. The kaoliangs are morphologically related to bicolor and appear to represent a Chinese variant of some early bicolor race.

We realize that our reconstruction may extend beyond the safe limits of our evidence. The consistency of the distribution patterns, however, demands an explanation which cannot deviate very much from the one offered.

It has been our observation that the races of sorghum are intimately associated with the cultivators who grow them. At the edge of the Konso tribal area in southern Ethiopia, one may find two villages side by side with a completely different array of sorghums. A Konso village will grow sorghums peculiar to Konsoland, and the neighboring Galla village will grow an assortment of durras. In western Ethiopia enclaves of caudatum are grown by immigrants from Sudan. From Ethiopia westward to the Atlantic the same pattern holds. Particular peoples have an affinity for particular races or subraces of sorghum.

Perhaps, as a result, there is a crude general correspondence between the distribution of the basic races of sorghum and the distribution of the major language groups of indigenous Africans. Guinea is a sorghum of the Niger-Congo family, kafir a Bantu sorghum. Durra follows the Afro-Asian family fairly closely, and caudatum seems to be associated with the Chari-Nile family of languages. The correspondence is far from precise, but a more detailed study of minor variation in sorghums may prove revealing with respect to human history.

In addition to the broad regional patterns of the basic races, we can detect small areas with rather unusual assemblages of sorghums. One such region is in southern Ethiopia (shown in black on Map 6). The region has not been sampled adequately for us to draw any real con-

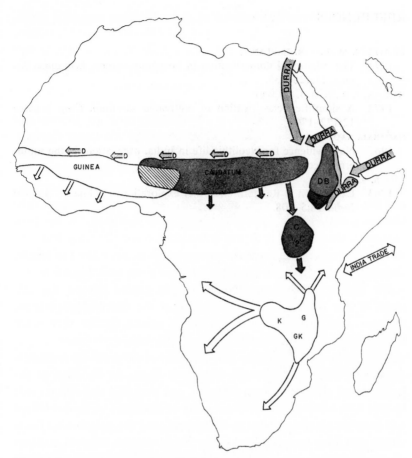

Map 6.   Later movements of sorghum

clusions, but we feel that the complexity of the sorghum array is associated with ethnographic complexities. A similar situation may exist in northern Cameroon, but we have not yet studied the materials in detail.

So far, our studies are really preliminary in nature, but they do suggest that a thorough analysis of crop variation could reveal a great deal about the people of Africa and that thorough ethnographic studies might help agronomists understand African crops. A closer cooperation between various specialists should be of great benefit to all who are interested in African plant domesticates.

REFERENCES

DE WET, J. M. J., J. R. HARLAN
1971   The origin and domestication of *Sorghum bicolor*. *Economic Botany* 25:128–135.
HARLAN, J. R., J. M. J. DE WET
1972   A simplified classification of cultivated sorghum. *Crop Science* 12:172–176.
NAGARAJA RAO, M. S.
1967   New evidence for Neolithic life in India: excavations in the southern Deccan. *Archaeology* 20:28-35.
RAO, S. R.
1963   Excavation at Rangpur and other explorations in Gujarat. *Ancient India* 18:5–208.

Biographical Notes

J. DESMOND CLARK was born in England in 1916. He received his B.A. and Ph.D. in Archaeology from Cambridge University in 1937 and 1950. He served during the war in Africa and was Director of the Rhodes-Livingstone Museum in Zambia from 1937 to 1961. Since then he has been Professor of Anthropology at the University of California at Berkeley. His archaeological fieldwork has been extensive; he has worked in most parts of central and southern Africa, Angola, Syria, the Sahara (Niger), and the Sudan. A Fellow of the British Academy and of the American Academy of Arts and Sciences, he is also a Member of the Permanent Committee of the Pan-African Congress on Prehistory and Quaternary Studies and, in 1971–1972, was a Guggenheim Fellow. Some 200 papers by Dr. Clark on archaeological subjects have been published in scientific journals in Africa, Britain, and the U.S.A. Books include: *The Kalambo Falls prehistoric site*, *The prehistory of Africa*, *The atlas of African prehistory* (compiler), *Background to evolution in Africa* (edited with W. W. Bishop), and volumes on the prehistory of Zambia, the Horn, Angola, and southern Africa. Dr. Clark is currently editor of the first volume of the *Cambridge history of Africa*.

D. G. COURSEY (1929–) was born and studied in London. He joined the Colonial Agricultural Service and worked in Nigeria (1951–1964), most of his research being concerned with yams and cassava. His work was continued at the University of Ghana (1964–1966). where he extended his interests in root crops from the purely agricultural to the socio-logical and prehistorical aspects. In 1966 he returned to England, where he now works for the Ministry of Overseas Development and is mainly concerned with agricultural advisory work in the developing world. He is author of the standard monograph on the yam and of about sixty other papers.

NICHOLAS DAVID (1937–   ) was born in Cambridge, where he received first degree (B.A., 1960) before doing graduate work at Harvard (M.A., 1962; Ph.D., 1966). He has taught at the University of Pennsylvania and at University College, London, and became Professor of Archaeology at the University of Ibadan in September 1974. He has done archaeological and ethnographic research on central African culture history and man-land relationships from the early Holocene period to the present day.

JOHANNES M. J. DE WET (1927–   ) is Professor of Cytogenetics with the Crop Evolution Laboratory, Department of Agronomy, at the University of Illinois. He received a B.Sc. with majors in Botany and Zoology from the University of Pretoria in South Africa (1949) and a Ph.D. in Genetics from the University of California at Berkeley (1952). His numerous publications deal with biosystematic research on tropical African plants and the origin and evolution of cereals. He has traveled widely in Africa, Southeast Asia, Australia, and Latin America. He did ethobotanical research in southern Africa during 1969 as a Guggenheim Memorial Fellow.

COLIN FLIGHT (1943–   ) was born in London and received his B.A. in Archaeology from the University of Cambridge in 1964. Between 1965 and 1969 he held a Lectureship in the Department of Archaeology, University of Ghana. He is now Lecturer in African Archaeology at the Centre of West African Studies, University of Birmingham, specializing in the later prehistory of Africa.

JACK R. HARLAN (1917–   ), born in Washington, D.C., received his B.S. from George Washington University in Botany (1938) and his Ph.D. from the University of California, Berkeley, in Genetics (1942). He has been engaged in plant breeding and genetics since 1942, working with forage grasses and cereal crops. Since 1966, he has been Professor of Plant Genetics with the Crop Evolution Laboratory, Agronomy Department, University of Illinois. His primary field of interest is the origin and evolution of cereal crops. He has published extensively on this subject as well as on cytogenetics and biosystematics of several genera of grasses. He has participated in archeaological expeditions in the Near East and has done extensive fieldwork in Africa and Asia. He is a Member of the National Academy of Sciences.

DAVID R. HARRIS (1930–) was educated at the University of Oxford and the University of California, Berkeley. His major fields of study are geography and ecology with research interests focusing on human modification of terrestrial ecosystems in prehistoric and historic time, with particular reference to the tropics. He has conducted fieldwork principally in the Caribbean and northern South America, in the southwestern United States, in North Africa and Greece, and in Papua New Guinea and the Cape York Peninsula, Australia. Some of his principal publications are: *Plants, animals, and man in the outer Leeward Islands, West Indies. An ecological study of Antigua, Barbuda, and Anguilla* (Berkeley and Los Angeles: University of California Press; 1965), "Ecosystems, agricultural systems and the origins of agriculture" (in *The domestication and exploitation of plants and animals*. Edited by Peter J. Ucko and G.W. Dimbleby, 3–15. London: Duckworth; 1969), "Swidden systems and settlement" (in *Man, settlement and urbanism*. Edited by Peter J. Ucko, Ruth Tringham and G.W. Dimbleby 245–262. London: Duckworth; 1972), "The origins of agriculture in the tropics" (*American Scientist* 60:180–193; 1972), and "The prehistory of tropical agriculture: an ethnoecological model "(in *The explanation of culture change: models in prehistory*. Edited by Colin Renfrew, 391–417. London: Duckworth; 1973). His present address is: Department of Geography, University College London, Gower Street, London WC1e 6BT, England.

E. S. HIGGS (1908–) is Director of Research in the Faculty of Archaeology and Anthropology, Cambridge University, and Director of the British Academy's Major Research Project "The Early History of Agriculture." He is primarily concerned with behavioral studies of prehistoric peoples and in the integration of archaeological and scientific theory, especially with regarad to the long-term prehistoric record.

PATRICK J. MUNSON (1940–), Associate Professor of Anthropology, Indiana University, received his Ph.D. in Anthropology from the University of Illinois in 1971. His primary research interests are the prehistory of eastern North America and the later prehistory of West Africa and the southwestern Sahara, with particular emphasis on subsistence ecology and the origins of food production in those areas.

JOHN PFEIFFER (1914–) received his B.A. from Yale in 1936. He is a science writer, former Science Director of the Columbia Broadcasting System, member of the editorial board of Scientific American, and Adjunct Professor of Anthropology at Livingston College, Rutgers University. He has published several hundred articles and book reviews as well as ten books, seven of them as a free-lance writer with the aid of grants from the Wenner-Gren Foundation for Anthropological Research, the Fulbright Commission, the Guggenheim Foundation, and the Carnegie Corporation of New York. His most recent publication is *The emergence of man* (1969; second edition 1972). He is currently completing a study of the origins of agriculture and the first cities.

ROLAND PORTÈRES (1906–1974) was born in Paris. He received his degree from the Ecole Agronomique of the University of Paris and worked with the Colonial Agricultural Service and Agricultural Research from 1928 to 1947 in West Africa. He was Laboratory Director at the Institut Nat. d'Agronomie Tropicale, Nogent-sur-Marne, Professor at the Museum Nat. Hist. Nat. Paris (Labor. Ethnobotanique from 1947), and Professor of Ethnobotany, University of Paris-Sorbonne (1969–1972). Beginning in 1947, he did fieldwork in Africa, Madagascar, and Central America. Dr. Portères wrote more than 200 publications concerned with tropical plants (wild and domesticated), applied botany, systematics, physiology, ethnobotany, agronomy rural economy, agricultural planification, pedology, pastures, etc. Plants particularly treated in his works include: coffee, vanilla, cinchona, oryza, digitaria, zea, colocasia, and pot herbs.

E. GLEN PRICE (1944–   ) was reared in farmland where grain and forage sorghums are major crops. He received his B.S. (1967) and M.S. (1968) from Oklahoma State University, Stillwater, and his Ph.D. (1973) in Agronomy from the University of Illinois, Urbana. He is currently self-employed at farming and agribusiness in west-central Oklahoma.

JOHN W. PURSEGLOVE (1912–   ), C.M.G., B.Sc., A.I.C.T.A., F.L.S., F.I.Biol., studied at Manchester and Cambridge Universities and the Imperial College of Tropical Agriculture, Trinidad. He has worked for over thirty years as an agriculturist and botanist in the tropics of Africa, the Far East and the New World. He was Professor of Botany at the University of the West Indies, Trinidad, 1957–1967, where he was the first Dean of the Faculty of Agriculture. He is at present Advisor on Tropical Crops for the Ministry of Overseas Development stationed at the East Malling Research Station, Kent. He is the author of four volumes on *Tropical crops.*

ROMUALD SCHILD (1936–   ) was born in Lwów. He recieved his M.A. from Warsaw University in 1957, a Ph.D. in Prehistoric Archaeology from the Institute for the History of Material Culture, Polish Academy of Sciences, in 1962. He took his habilitation at the same Institute in 1967. He has been with the Institute for the History of Material Culture since 1958 (Senior Researcher, *Dozent*, since 1968). His special interests include paleolithic and mesolithic archaeology of Central and Eastern Europe, and of northeastern and eastern Africa. He has done field-work in Poland, Sudan, Syria, Egypt, and Ethiopia.

THAYER SCUDDER (1930–) attended Harvard College and Harvard University, receiving his Ph. D. in Anthropology in 1960. Currently he is Professor of Anthropology at the California Institute of Technology where he has been on the faculty since 1964. His principal interests include long-term studies in the social sciences, river basin development, cultural ecology, and the responses of people to compulsory relocation. His fieldwork has been primarily in Zambia and Egypt, although he has consulted extensively for United Nations agencies.

THURSTAN SHAW (1914–) was born in Plymouth, England. He studied archaeology and anthropology at Cambridge University, where he received his B.A. (1936), M.A. (1941), and Ph.D. (by assessment of published work; 1968). He was Curator of the Achimota College Anthropology Museum, Gold Coast (Ghana) 1937–1945, in which post he conducted excavations and initiated the scientific archaeology of the country and made the collections which formed the nucleus of the Ghana National Museum. He worked in England (1945–1963), with three expeditions to West Africa and was Professor of Archaeology, University of Ibadan, Nigeria, 1963–1974. He has published: *Excavation at Dawu* (1961) and *Igbo-Ukwu: an account of archaeological discoveries in eastern Nigeria* (two volumes, 1970) and about eighty journal articles on various topics of African archaeology, especially concerning the Late Stone Age, the analysis of West African bronzes, the beginnings and spread of African food production, etc. Founder and Editor of the *West African Journal of Archaeology* (1971), Vice-President of the Pan-African Congress on Prehistory and the Study of the Quaternary (C.B.E. 1971), he is currently Visiting Research Professor, Ahmadu Bello University, Nigeria, and Lecturer in the Department of Archaeology, University of Cambridge.

PHILIP E. L. SMITH (1927–) was born in Newfoundland and educated at Acadia University (B.A., 1948), the Université de Bordeaux, and Harvard University (Ph. D., 1962). He has taught at the University of

Toronto and is now Professor of Anthropology at the Université de Montréal. His specialities in prehistoric archaeology are the Paleolithic of Europe and the Middle East, on which he has done fieldwork in France, Egypt, Iraq, and Iran; and the early food-producing societies, which he has been investigating in Iran since 1967. His principal publication is *Le Solutréen en France* (1966).

ANN STEMLER (1945–   ) is presently a Research Assistant at the University of Illinois. She was born in Chicago, Illinois, received the B.S. and M.S. degrees in Biological Science from the University of Illinois, Urbana, in 1967 and 1970, respectively, and received a Ph.D. in Botany at the University of Illinois in 1975. Her recent work is concerned with one of the staple grains of Africa, *Sorghum bicolor* (Linn.) Moench, its origin, history, and biochemical variation.

EDUARD M. VAN ZINDEREN BAKKER, SR. (1907–   ) was born in the Netherlands and studied at the Municipal University of Amsterdam where he received his Phil. Nat. D. in 1935 on the physiology of parasitic fungi. He settled in South Africa in 1947 where he became Professor and Head of the Department of Botany. Since 1973 he has been Director of the Institute for Environmental Sciences. His main interest is in the plant ecology of southern Africa and the sub-Antarctic and in the palynology of Africa, a study which he initiated in this continent. He has edited eight volumes of *Palaeoecology of Africa* and the monograph on the scientific expedition to Marion and Prince Edward Islands and has written five books and published sixty-eight articles. He is a member of various international committees on palynology and polar research.

FRED WENDORF (1924–   ) is Henderson-Morrison Professor of Anthropology at the Southern Methodist University in Dallas, Texas. He received his B.A. from the University of Arizona in 1948 and his Ph.D. in Anthropology from Harvard in 1953. In recent years he has been primarily interested in the prehistory of Northeast Africa (*The prehistory of Nubia*, 1968; *A Middle Stone Age sequence from the Ventral Rift Valley, Ethiopia*, 1974). He has also been concerned with the problems of the preservation of our archaeological heritage (*Pipeline archaeology*, 1956; *A guide to salvage archaeology*, 1959). He is Member of the Committee for Recovery of Archaeological Remains and is Treasurer of the Society for American Archaeology.

Index of Names

Abdel Aleem, Anwar, 280
Abou Said, 418, 421
Adams, Robert McC., 162
Adrian, Jean, 201
Afzelius, Adam, 418
Ainslee, Whitelaw, 414
Albritton, Claude C., 275
Alexander, John, 108, 130, 334, 337, 383, 384, 387, 389, 392, 393, 396, 398
Alexandre, P., 243
Alexandre-Pyre, S., 56
Alimen, H., 234
Allan, W., 128, 363
Allchin, F. R., 124, 200, 412, 417
Allison, P. A., 131, 132
Al Omari, 418
Ames, O., 134
Anderson, E., 124, 134, 253, 401
Anderson, Edgar, 188
Anderson, J. E., 73, 77
Arkell, A. J., 76, 79, 82, 94, 108, 113, 118, 119, 134, 136, 171
Armstrong, Robert G., 130, 136
Armstrong, R. L., 45
Arundachalam, V., 453
Assemien, P., 112
Aubreville, A., 232
Axelrod, D. I., 384
Ayensu, E. S., 384, 385, 391, 393
Aymonin, G., 53
Ayrton, Edward R., 113, 119

Bailloud, Gérald, 158, 176
Bakari, Ardo, 238

Baker, H. G., 124, 132, 133–135, 136, 188, 257, 299, 329, 397
Baldrati, L., 416, 426
Balout, Lionel, 109, 158, 171, 174
Bargery, G. P., 425
Barrau, J., 388, 390, 398
Bartell, Frank, 233–234, 235
Barth, H., 77, 231, 244, 245, 249, 250, 251, 252, 254, 257
Bassoro, M. H., 238
Bate-Smith, E. C., 391
Bauhini, Caspar, 413, 440
Baumgartel, Elise J., 113
Beech, Mervyn W. H., 412
Bernus, E., 77, 80
Berry, A. C., 72
Berry, R. J., 32
Billard, P.: *Essai de géographie physique*, 223
Binford, Lewis R., 130, 161, 198–199
Birdwood, G. C. M., 415
Bishop, W. W., 211
Blaeuw, Guiljelmo, 291
Blakney, C. P., 138
Bohannan, P., 89
Bond, G., 56
Bonnefille, R., 112
Boserup, Ester, 84, 85, 91, 92, 163, 321
Bourret, Dominique, 390
Braidwood, Linda, 159
Braidwood, Robert J., 157, 159, 176, 189, 269
Braun, Alexander, 416
Bronckers, F., 112

Brothwell, D. R., 401
Brown, A. F., 427
Brown, Jean, 116, 122
Brown, Robert, 432–433
Bruce, James, 426
Buchanan, K. M., 324
Buisson, E. M., 233
Burke, K., 51
Burkill, I. H., 124, 129, 130, 251, 291, 297, 298, 333, 383, 384, 385, 387, 388, 389, 390, 391, 392, 396, 398, 399, 429
Burnham, Philip C., 223, 243, 253
Burton-Page, J., 132
Busson, F., 88, 129
Buth, G. M., 134, 299
Butzer, Karl W., 48, 49, 50, 75, 116, 170, 278, 279

Cabot, J., 249
Callen, E. O., 32
Calvet, A., 171
Calvocoressi, D., 216, 218, 232, 236
Campbell, B. G., 400
Camps, Gabriel, 72, 73, 74, 75, 79, 112, 119, 158, 171, 172, 176, 201, 286
Camps-Farber, H., 72, 157
Cargo, Douglas B., 67
Carneiro, Robert L., 127
Carr-Saunders, A. M., 34
Carter, P. L., 75, 87, 215, 217
Castellani, Ettore, 416, 426
Caton-Thompson, Gertrude, 112, 169, 284
Celarier, R. P., 453, 458
Chamla, M. C., 81
Chang, Kwang-Chin, 109, 110, 130, 387, 388, 398
Chapelle, Jean, 76, 77, 191
Chevalier, A., 5, 13, 187, 254–255, 297, 335, 383, 390, 391, 392, 402, 410, 424, 427, 430, 434, 435
Childe, V. Gordon, 3, 109, 177, 198, 364, 400
Chmiekwska, Maria, 283, 285
Chowdhury, K. A., 134, 299
Churcher, C. S., 70
Ciferri, R., 416
Ciglioni, G. R., 416
Clark, Grahame, 109, 392
Clark, J. Desmond, 13, 18, 67–105, 107, 112, 113, 122, 123, 125, 130, 155, 161, 170, 171, 172, 174, 188, 211, 214, 257, 367, 392, 397
Clark, J. G. D., 68

Clarke, D. L., 219
Clausen, H., 45, 52
Clayton, W. D., 433
Clothier, J. N., 364
Clusius, Carolus, 440
Coetzee, J. A., 44, 45, 47, 48, 54, 57, 112
Cohen, J., 53
Colson, Elizabeth, 67, 357–358, 360, 365, 366, 380
Conklin, H. C., 314
Connah, Graham, 87, 114, 198, 232–233, 234–235, 456
Conrad, G., 74
Contenson, Henri de, 160
Cooke, C. K., 95
Cooke, H. B. S., 46
Coursey, Celia K., 334, 335, 337, 393, 398, 399
Coursey, D. G., 13, 15, 128, 129, 130, 131, 245, 250, 257, 298, 329, 334, 335, 337, 348, 383–408
Creac'h, Paul, 410, 427
Curwen, E. Cecil, 277
Cuyler, T., Jr., 160, 161, 163

Dabrowski, M. J., 281–282
Daly, P., 34
Dalziel, J. M., 88, 125, 128, 129, 132, 136, 137, 138, 206, 250, 252, 327, 328, 337, 341, 345, 390, 391, 410, 425, 427, 430
Dancette, C., 12
Dandelot, P., 88
Daniels, S. G. H., 197
Dansgaard, W., 45, 52
Darlington, C. D., 117
Darwin, Charles, 23
David, Nicholas, 127, 223–267
Davies, Oliver, 80, 87, 107, 117, 122, 129, 132, 197, 211, 212, 214–215, 335, 383, 399
De Candolle, A., 124, 395, 410, 411
Deveey, Edward S., 108, 113
De Ficalho, Conde, 413, 414, 415
De Garine, I., 239, 240, 241
Deighton, F. C., 430
Denham, D., 231, 244, 249, 250, 255
Denton, G. H., 45
De Orta, Garcia, 414, 415
De Ronciglione, P. Angelo, 416
Deschamps, M., 137
De Wet, J. M. J., 3–19, 84, 86, 111, 124, 136, 235, 245, 293, 297, 329, 343–344, 453–463, 465–466, 472
Diziain, R., 231

Doggett, H., 124–125, 200, 245, 293, 461
Doku, E. V., 345
Dombrowski, Joanne, 94, 133, 215
Dorst, J., 88
Dresch, J., 341
Drouhin, M. G., 195
Dudgeon, G., 424, 425
Dugast, R., 251
Dumas, Renoux, 418
Dumont, R., 383
Dupire, M., 82
Durotoye, A. B., 51
Dutil, P., 53

Ehret, C., 95
Ehrlich, P. R., 33
Eldridge, Mohammadou, 242, 243
Emiliani, C., 46
Evans-Pritchard, E. E., 84

Fagan, Brian M., 87, 112, 114, 115, 128,
    203, 234, 357, 358–360, 361, 367, 370–
    371, 372, 374, 445
Fagg, B. E. B., 115, 117, 126
Fanshawe, D. B., 380
Faris, D. G., 134
Faron, L. C., 349
Faure, H., 74
Filipowiak, W., 114
Flannery, Kent V., 110, 130, 156, 159,
    160, 161, 162, 165
Flight, Colin, 87, 115, 197, 211–221, 235,
    338, 345, 396
Flint, R. F., 44, 46, 56
Flohn, H., 43–44
Floyd, B., 324
Forde, Daryll, 129
Fouché, Leo, 115
Fresenius, G., 416
Friedel, M. C., 132
Furtado, C. X., 300

Gabel, Creighton, 95, 108, 111
Gaherty, Geoffrey, 126
Gama, Vasco da, 295, 300
Gardner, E. W., 112, 128, 169, 284
Gast, Marceau, 77, 201
Gauthier, J. G., 236
Gorman, Chester F., 109, 387
Gould, P. R., 219
Gray, Richard, 127, 129, 131, 397
Grébénart, D., 174
Greenberg, J. H., 126, 170, 238, 239, 241,
    243, 258

Greenway, P. J., 292, 295
Griaule, N., 235, 239
Grindley, J. R., 95
Grove, A. T., 80
Grundeman, Tulli, 125, 128
Guers, J., 112
Guilaine, J., 171
Guinet, Ph., 53, 112
Gulliver, P. H., 85
Guthrie, Malcolm, 126, 127, 258

Hagedorn, H., 74
Haggett, P., 219
Hamilton, A. C., 44, 47, 54
Han, Mark, 235
Hansen, C. L., 75, 278, 279
Harkavy, M., 426
Harlan, Jack R., 3–19, 67, 81, 86, 87, 96,
    107, 111, 117, 124, 136, 174, 177, 195,
    245, 251, 252, 293, 294, 297, 328, 329,
    336, 337, 343–344, 345, 352, 395, 398,
    453–463, 465–478
Harper, G., 58
Harris, David R., 17, 35, 85, 111, 130,
    168, 174, 264, 311–356, 361, 396, 400
Harrison, T., 388
Hartley, C. W. S., 132, 338
Hata, N., 249
Haudricourt, A. G., 388, 390, 426
Havinden, M. A., 383
Hawkes, J. G., 166, 390
Hays, T. R., 76
Hedberg, O., 47
Hedin, L., 388
Heiser, C. B., Jr., 340, 388
Helbaek, H., 33, 113
Hemans, H. N., 364
Hemardinquer, Jean-Jacques, 124
Henrard, J. T., 418, 419, 425
Hepper, F. N., 134, 345
Hervieu, J., 228, 233
Hester, James J., 81, 118, 167, 174, 202,
    203
Hiernaux, Jean, 127
Higgs, Eric S., 4, 17, 29–39, 72, 78, 87,
    109, 110, 156, 159, 169, 259
Ho, P. T., 130
Hobler, Philip M., 81, 118, 167, 174,
    202, 203
Hochstetter., 427
Hole, F., 160
Holland, J. H., 427
Holtz, F., 412
Home, Henry (Lord Kames), 161

Hooker, J. D., 409, 432; *Flora Nigritia*, 244
Horowitz, A., 50
Horowitz, M. M., 93
Howe, Bruce, 157
Hubbard, C. E., 297, 435
Huckabay, J. P., 124, 453, 457, 459, 460–461
Huffman, Thomas N., 127
Hugot, H. J., 75, 77, 109, 112, 113, 115, 122, 132, 172, 174, 201
Hunter, A. W. S., 419
Hurault, J., 51, 228–230

Ibn Batuta: *Journey to Sudan*, 418, 421
Ibn Hawqal, 239
Idris Alooma, 240
Imperato, P. J., 92
Irvine, F. R., 329
Irwin, H. T., 70
Irwin, L. F., 70
Isaac, G. Ll., 48, 67, 75, 94

Jackson, G., 132
Jackson, George, 223, 235
Jacques-Félix, H., 77, 191, 244, 251
Jakel, D., 74
Jakushevsky, E. S., 453
Jardin, Claude, 9
Jardin, Edelestan, 441
Jarman, H. N., 32–33
Jarman, M. R., 31, 32, 35, 37, 109, 110, 112, 159
Jauze, J. B., 234
Jeffrey, C., 455
Jeffreys, M. D. W., 334
Johannes, L. W., 17
Johnsen, S. J., 45, 52
Johnson, D. L., 78, 82
Johnston, B. F., 316, 319, 349
Johnston, H. H., 127, 258
Jones, W. O., 301, 333
Juillerat, B., 249
Jumelle, H., 389

Kaiser, W., 119
Kames, Lord. *See* Home, Henry
Kantor, Helene J., 69, 285
Kaplan, L., 301
Karikari, S. K., 345
Keay, R. W. J., 317
Kendall, R. L., 50, 55, 75, 112
Kennedy-O'Byrne, J., 124
Kirk-Greene, A. H. M., 242

Kitson, A. E., 211
Klein, Richard H., 67, 95
Koernicke, F., 426
Kroeber, Alfred L., 244

Labat, Jean-Baptiste, 418
Lal, B. B., 113
Lamarck, J. B., 391, 431
Lancaster, C. S., 357, 360, 367, 371, 372–373
Langway, C. C., Jr., 45, 52
Latham, M., 348
Laughlin, W. S., 88
Laurent-Tackholm, V., 136
Lawn, Barbara, 235
Lawrence, B., 30
Lawton, J. R. S., 129
Lawton, R. M., 55, 56
Layard, A. H., 433
Leakey, L. S. B., 115
Leakey, M. D., 115, 132
Le Berre, S., 250, 254
Lebeuf, A. M. D., 126
Lebeuf, J.-P., 232, 235, 236, 239, 240, 242; *Carte archéologique des abords du Lac Tchad*, 234; *Civilisation du Tchad, La* (with Masson-Detourbet), 234
Lecoq, P., 234
Lee, R. B., 25, 82, 88
Leeke, P., 434, 435
Legge, A. J., 32
Lembezat, B., 240, 241, 243
Leprieur, M., 441
Lestringant, J., 231, 241–242
Letouzey, R., 223–224, 227, 230–231, 259; *Étude phytogéographique*, 224
Lévi-Strauss, Claude, 165
Lhote, Henri, 76, 78, 156, 172, 201
Ligers, Z., 84, 92, 93
Linares de Sapir, Olga, 135
Linnaeus, Carolus, 413, 431, 432
Livingstone, D. A., 47, 96, 112, 131
Livingstone, David, 364, 372
Loat, W. L. S., 113, 119
Lobreau, D., 112
Lopez, Duarte, 412, 413
Loret, V., 426

McBurney, C. B. M., 119, 123, 156, 169, 171
McMaster, D. N., 334
MacNeish, R. S., 109
Maistre, C., 238, 252
Maley, J., 46, 50, 74, 77, 112

Marks, S., 271
Marks, Stuart A., 67, 82, 87, 88, 90, 357, 360, 361, 369
Marliac, A., 228, 233
Marshall, J., 124
Marshall, L., 81
Martin, F. W., 385
Martínez, C., 112
Mason, R. J., 115
Massey, R. E., 416, 427
Masson-Detourbet, A., 239, 240; *La civilisation du Tchad* (with Lebeuf), 234
Mathewson, R. D., 214
Mauny, Raymond, 76, 107, 138, 171, 189, 203
Meek, C. K., 238–239, 242, 250
Mehra, K. L., 124, 297, 345
Meighan, C. W., 108
Mellart, J., 169
Meunier, J., 12, 132
Miège, J., 112, 321, 390, 391, 392, 393
Miracle, M. P., 250, 301, 334
Mohr, B., 341
Monod, Théodore, 156, 164
Mooney, H. F., 416
Moreau, R. E., 56
Morgan, W. B., 129, 218, 395
Mori, Fabrizio, 75, 78, 176
Moss, R. P., 218
Movius, H. L., 269
Munson, Patrick J., 13, 50, 67, 75, 77, 112, 114, 172, 177, 187–209, 218, 344, 345, 429
Murdock, George P., 5, 111, 126, 129, 133–134, 187–188, 197, 244, 250, 254, 257, 258, 383, 389, 393, 395, 416
Murty, B. R., 453

Nachtigal, G., 244, 251
Nagaraja Rao, M. S., 411–412, 474
Nakao, S., 249
Nash, T. A. M., 91
Nayer, N. M., 345
Neely, J. A., 160
Netting, R. McC., 324
Neustupny, Evzen, 109
Newman, J. L., 89
Nicholson, G. E., 299
Nicolaisen, Johannes, 76, 77, 83, 201–202
Niklewski, J., 75
Noy, T., 168
Nunoo, R. B., 213
Okiy, G. E. C., 130

Olderogge, D. A., 257
Oliver, Roland A., 95, 126, 129, 258, 413, 415, 417
Olsson, Ingrid U., 109
Onwuejeogwu, M. A., 131
Owen, J., 132
Ozanne, Paul, 397, 445

Pacheco Pereira, D., 397
Paffen, Kh., 336
Pairault, C., 92, 244
Palmer, H. R.: *Sudanese memoirs*, 238
Pasquereau, Jean, 15, 195, 328
Passarge, S., 251–252
Paulme, D., 322
Peet, T. Eric, 113
Pelé, J., 250, 254
Perkins, Dexter, 33, 34, 156, 168
Perrier de la Bathie, H., 389
Perrot, Jean, 169–170
Pervès, M., 234
Pfeiffer, John E., 4, 17, 23–28
Phillips, J., 278
Phillipson, D. W., 115, 123, 128
Pias, J., 228
Pidoplichko, I. G., 29, 34
Piedallu, André, 433
Pliny, 413
Plowes, D. C. H., 380
Pons, A., 201
Portères, Roland, 5, 10, 124, 125, 127, 129, 134, 135, 136, 171, 187, 193, 200, 250, 251, 252, 257, 300, 319, 329, 334, 337, 341–345, 395, 409–452, 459, 460
Posnansky, M., 126, 128, 130, 396
Poulain, J. F., 12
Powell, Jocelyn M., 397
Prain, D., 389, 391
Preston, F. W., 347
Price, E. G., 86, 293, 453–463
Pugh, J. C., 324
Pullan, R. A., 228
Purseglove, J. W., 17, 114, 129, 245, 291–309, 329, 337, 341, 345, 348

Quézel, P., 112, 201

Rachie, K. O., 125
Rahtz, Philip A., 216
Ralph, E. K., 235
Rao, S. R., 412, 478
Raven, P. H., 33
Raymond, W. D., 132
Read, Gordon, 380

Redhead, J. F., 132
Reed, Charles A., 70, 109, 156, 278
Renfrew, Jane H., 168, 171
Reynolds, B., 358
Reynolds, Barrie, 380
Richardson, A. E., 55
Richardson, J. L., 48, 55
Robinson, K. R., 114, 116, 122
Rodden, Robert, 67
Rogers, D. J., 392
Rognon, P., 43
Rosenfeld, A., 234
Rossignol, M., 74
Roubet, Colette, 67, 73, 175
Roxburgh, William, 411, 432
Royle, J. Forbes, 410
Rozhevicz, R. J., 426, 427, 441
Russel, Fred L., 416

Said, Rushdi, 283, 284
Salt, Henry, 416
Sandelowsky, B., 122
Sassoon, Hamo, 114, 122, 123, 125
Sauer, Carl Ortwin, 4, 137, 337, 387, 388
Saxena, M. B. L., 453
Schalke, H. K. W. G., 45
Schapera, I., 400
Schechter, Y., 456, 461
Schiegl, W. E., 50
Schild, Romuald, 13, 18, 71, 269–288
Schimper, W., 416, 427
Schmidt, Peter, 216
Schneider, J.-L., 228
Schnell, R., 88, 329
Schubert, Claus, 241
Schultz, E., 53
Schweinfurth, George, 416, 426
Scudder, Thayer, 357–381; *Ecology of the Gwembe Tonga*, 358
Seddon, David, 108, 111, 112
Segalen, P., 223
Semenov, S. A., 277
Servant, M., 44, 53, 74, 170, 228, 229
Servant, S., 44, 53, 228
Servant-Vildary, S., 229
Seuss, Hans E., 109
Shack, William A., 136
Shantz, H. L., 414
Shaw, Thurstan, 17, 67, 86, 87, 107–153, 220, 393, 396, 401
Shiner, J. L., 82
Shinnie, P. L., 392
Sillans, R., 230, 231–232, 257
Simmonds, N. W., 136, 137, 295, 334, 392

Simoons, Frederick J., 94, 133, 136, 200, 417
Singh, Gurdip, 30
Slotkin, J. S., 161
Smith, A. B., 75, 78, 81, 83
Smith, Andrew, 67, 83
Smith, F. G., 112
Smith, H. S., 71
Smith, M. G., 70, 82
Smith, Philip E. L., 17, 67, 68, 70, 155–183
Smith, S. E., 84
Snowden, J. D., 200, 453, 455, 457, 458, 459
Solheim, Wilhelm G., II, 109
Sowunmi, M. A., 112
Speke, John H., 291, 434
Stanton, W. R., 345
Stapf, Otto, 297, 418, 424, 425, 428, 431, 432, 434–435
Stemler, Ann, 3–19, 96, 245, 293, 294, 343–344, 456, 459, 461, 465–478
Stenning, D. J., 231
Steudel, E. T., 441
Steward, J. H., 349
Streel, M., 55
Struever, Stuart, 112, 217
Stuiver, M., 45, 109, 387
Sudres, A., 418
Suggs, R. C., 389
Summers, R., 114, 115, 128
Suttles, Wayne, 166
Swart, E. R., 132
Swift, Jonathan, 291
Szumowski, G., 190

Tessman, G., 253
Thronwaite, C. W., 316
Thurnwald, R., 78
Tisserant, R. P. Ch., 250, 251, 252, 254
Toupet, Ch., 194
Trapnell, C. G., 55, 364
Trigger, B. G., 69, 72, 170
Troll, C., 336
Turnbull, C. M., 88, 90
Turnbull, Priscilla F., 191

Ucko, P. J., 108, 113, 119
Unger, A., 426
Urvoy, Y., 254

Vaillant, A., 249
Van Campo, M., 53, 112
Van der Hammen, T., 52

Van der Merwe, N. J., 115, 123
Van Loon, Maurits, 167
Van Meer, P. P. C., 132
Van Noten, Francis, 119, 122, 125
Vansina, J., 127
Van Zeist, W., 75, 159
Van Zinderen Bakker, E. M., 13, 43–63, 112, 170, 174, 228, 229, 293, 399, 400–401
Vaufrey, Raymond, 158, 171, 174, 190
Vavilov, N. I., 4, 111, 124, 133, 136, 172, 200, 291, 292, 384, 393, 395, 412, 416, 417, 427
Verin, P., 137
Vermeer, D. E., 323
Vermeersch, P., 71, 284
Vidal, P., 237, 253
Vignard, Edmond, 167
Vignier, P., 187
Vishnu-Mittre, 124, 125
Vita-Finzi, C., 87, 169
Vogel, Joseph O., 114, 122, 123, 128
Vuilleumier, B. S., 54

Waitt, A. W., 384, 390, 392
Ward, W. E. F., 397
Warren, A., 80
Washbourn-Kamay, C., 48
Washburn, S. L., 163
Watson, J. Forbes, 433–434
Watt, George, 124, 383, 411, 432
Webb, L. J., 432
Wehrmann, J., 17
Weiss, E. A., 298
Welwitsch, F. M. J., 413

Wendorf, Fred, 13, 18, 44–45, 67, 70, 71, 112, 116, 118, 119, 167, 169, 174, 202, 269–288
Wendt, W. E., 71, 283–284
Werth, E., 124
West, R. G., 123
Wheat, J. B., 70
White, F., 69
White, Leslie A., 198
White, S., 249, 324
Whiteman, A. J., 51
Wickens, Gerald E., 67, 83
Wieckowska, Hanna, 283, 285
Wiesenfeld, Stephen L., 131
Wilkinson, P. F., 32, 35
Willett, F., 216, 237, 334, 397, 399
Williams, M. A. J., 74
Williamson, Kay, 138
Wilson, Monica, 67
Wisantham, G. R., 432
Woodburn, J., 88
Wright, Gary A., 110, 159, 161, 401
Wright, H. E., 75
Wrigley, Christopher, 127, 188, 200, 395
Wymstra, T. A., 52

Yarnell, Richard A., 111
Young, T., 160, 161, 163

Zagwyn, W. H., 52
Zhukovsky, P. M., 4
Zohary, Daniel, 168, 169, 172
Zubrow, Ezra B., 175
Zuccagni, Attilio, 426

Index of Subjects

Abelmoschus (*Hibiscus*) *esculentus*, 254
Acacia, 11, 224
Acacia, 12, 17, 52, 53, 54, 227; *A. albida*. 12, 226; *A. ataxacantha*, 231; *A. nilotica*, 80–81
Acalypha, 54, 122–123
Adansonia, 11; *A. digitata*, 132, 226
Addax, 195
Aframomum melegueta, 138, 293–294
African breadfruit (rice) tree, 132
African elm, 115
Akee tree, 15, 135, 293, 326
Allanblackia floribunda, 132
Allium, 254; *A. cepa*, 138, 250
American Council of Learned Societies, 357
Anchomanes, 397
Andropogon, 227; *A. schirensis*, 226
Anogeissus leiocarpus, 227
Araceae, 388
Arachis hypogaea, 138, 252, 296
Aristida, 77
Artemisia, 53
Atili, 115
Atlas du Cameroun, 223–224
Atrofuscae, 419
Avena barbata, 10
Avocado, 340–341

Balanites, 83
Banana, 14, 94, 132, 137, 138, 254, 295, 313, 334, 383, 392. *See also* Ensete; Plaintain
Baobab tree, 11, 132, 245

Barley, 10, 30, 33, 69, 71, 86, 94, 112, 113 116–117, 119, 124, 133, 135, 139–140' 159, 162, 168, 169, 170, 171, 172, 177' 200, 201, 250, 269–271, 282, 284, 286, 292, 293, 343, 352, 397, 410, 416
Bastard millet grass, 429–433
Bean: common, 296, 301; geocarpa, 252, 256
Beniseed, black, 345
Bitterleaf, 138
Blighia sapida, 135, 293
Bloemfontein Centre for Palynology, 44
Borassus aethiopicum, 132
Boswellia, 227; *B. odorata*, 227
Brachiaria, 10, 76–77, 113, 427–429; *B. brizantha*, 77; *B. deflexa*, 10, 14, 113, 192–194, 195, 204, 293, 345, 346, 351–352, 427–429; *B. deflexa* var. *sativa*, 426, 428; *B. distichophylla*, 426; *B. kotschyana*, 427; *B. nidulans*, 428; *B. obtusifolia,* 427; *B. pubifolia*, 427; *B. ramosa*, 428; *B. regularis*, 427, 428; *B. stigmatisata*, 427; *B. xantholenea*, 427
Brachystegia, 55, 91
Brown University, 216
Bur grass, 113
Butyrospermum, 11; *B. paradoxum*, 14, 132, 293; *B. parkii* (*paradoxum*), 134

Cacao, 313, 325, 333
Cajanus cajan, 294, 297
Calabash, 115–116
California Institute of Technology, 357

Canarium schweinfurthii, 115, 217
Cannabis indica, 95
Capsicum annuum, 254, 296, 301; *C. frutescens*, 254, 296, 301
Carica papaya, 254
Carte archéologique des abords du Lac Tchad (Lebeuf), 234
Carte géologique de Cameroun, 224
Cassava, 14, 128, 137–138, 250, 251, 296, 301, 315, 318, 320, 321, 322, 323, 348, 349, 383, 389, 390, 392
Castor, 113, 252, 294, 298
Catha edulis, 14, 293
Ceiba pentandra: var. *caribaea*, 299; var. *guineensis*, 299; var. *pentandra*, 124, 293, 299
Celtis, 54, 77, 80–81, 83, 115, 172, 193, 216, 217; *C. integrifolia*, 191, 226
Cenchrus, 77; *C. biflorus*, 80, 113, 191, 192–194, 204
Ceratotheca sesamoides, 254
Cercis, 53
Chat (khat), 14, 293
Chenopodiaceae, 53
Chickpea, 86, 133
Chili pepper, 296, 301, 343
Chloris pycnothrix, 227
Chlorophera excelsa, 254
Cicer arietinum, 133
Citrullus, 114–115; *C. lanatus*, 14, 254, 294; *C. vulgaris*, 114, 134
Citrus, 295, 241
Citrus aurantifolia, 138, 254; *C. aurantium*, 138
Civilisation du Tchad, La (Lebeuf and Masson-Detourbet), 234
Cleome gynandra, 363
Cocoa, 296
Coconut, 138, 295, 296, 300, 334
Cocos nucifera, 138, 300
Cocoyam (dasheen), 128, 137, 138, 300, 315, 318, 320, 322, 333
Coffea arabica, 299; *C. canephora*, 294, 299; *C. excelsa*, 293; *C. liberica*, 293; *C. stenophylla*, 293
Coffee, 15, 293, 326, 339, 349–350, 351; arabica, 295, 299; robusta, 294, 299
Cola, 15, 293; *C. acuminata*, 132, 135, 138; *C. nitida*, 132, 135, 138
Coleus dazo, 134, 135, 351; *C. dysentericus*, 134, 135, 251
Colocasia, 128–129, 388; *C. esculenta*, 251; *C. esculenta* var. *esculenta*, 300; *C. esculentum*, 137, 138

Combretaceae, 53
Combretun, 227
Commiphora, 52, 54
Corchorus olitorius, 254
Cotton, 14, 84–85, 133–134, 136, 187, 200, 254–255, 296, 299, 372
Cowpea, 5, 14, 87, 114, 115, 134, 197, 217–218, 252, 294, 295, 297, 345, 366–367
Cram-cram (kram-kram), 80, 191
Cucumeropsis edulis, 134; *C. mannu*, 134
Cucumis melo, 294
Cucurbits, 117, 296, 318, 363, 366–367
Cynosurus coracanus, 410
Cyperus articulatus, 252; *C. esculentus*, 252

Dacryodes edulis, 132
Dactyloctenium, 187
Daniella oliveri, 227
Darnel, 432
Dasheen. *See* Cocoyam
Digitaria, 10, 92, 189, 415–416, 418, 419, 428; *D. barbinodis*, 425; *D. exilis*, 14, 125, 134, 135, 136, 187, 249, 293, 297, 415, 417–424, 425; *D. exilis* var. *densa*, 421; *D. exilis* var. *fonie moriori*, 428; *D. exilis* var. *gracilis*, 419, 421; *D. exilis* var. *mixta*, 419, 421; *D. exilis* var. *rustica*, 419; *D. exilis* var. *rustica* subvar. *clara*, 421; *D. exilis* var. *rustica* subvar. *rubra*, 419, 421; *D. exilis* var. *stricta*, 419, 421; *D. iburua*, 14, 125, 293, 424–425; *D. longiflora*, 134, 136, 418, 424; *D. ternata*, 425; *D. tricostulata*, 425
Dioscorea, 14, 135, 231, 298, 383–403; *D. abyssinica*, 250, 392, 395, 401; *D. alata*, 129, 137, 138, 250, 295, 298, 387, 388, 389–390, 391–392; *D. analalavensis*, 389; *D. antaly*, 389; *D. bemandry*, 389; *D. bulbifera*, 135, 250, 389, 391, 395; *D. cayenensis*, 129, 135, 138, 250, 293, 298, 391–393, 395–396, 401; *D. convolvulacea*, 390; *D. dumetorum*, 129, 135, 250–251, 395, 402; *D. esculanta*, 129, 387, 389–390, 391; *D. glabra*, 398; *D. "gribinguiensis,"* 251; *D. hamiltonii*, 388; *D. lecardi*, 251; *D. liebrechtiana* (= *cayenensis?*), 251; *D. mamillata*, 389; *D. minutiflora*, 250; *D. occidentalis*, 391; *D. ovinala*, 389; *D. persimilis*, 388; *D. praehensilis*, 251, 393–393, 395, 401; *D. preussii*, 395;

D. rotundata, 129, 135, 138, 250, 293, 298, 391–393, 395, 401; *D. sansibarensis* (= *D. macroura*), 251, 256, 395; *D. soso*, 389; *D. trifida*, 390
Dioscoreaceae, 250, 384
Dioscoreales, 384–385

Earthpea, 252, 255, 257
Echinochloa, 71, 77, 80, 187, 189; *E. colona*, 250; *E. pyramidalis*, 224; *E. stagnina*, 77, 250
Ecology of the Gwembe Tonga (Scudder), 358
Eggplant, 334
Egyptian Geological Survey, 269
Elaeis guineensis, 12–13, 14, 80–81, 113, 115, 135, 138, 197, 217, 293, 298; *E. madagascariensis*, 298
Eleusine, 116, 124–125, 126–127, 140, 187, 236, 409–417; *E. africana*, 297, 417; *E. coracana*, 14, 114, 124, 133, 135, 200, 249, 294, 297, 409–417, 434; *E. igna*, 86; *E. indica*, 409, 410, 411, 417; *E. luco*, 410; *E. stricta*, 410, 411, 417; *E. tocussa*, 410, 411
Ensete (false banana), 5, 8, 14, 93–94, 124, 135–136, 293
Ensete edule, 94; *E. edulis*, 135; *E. ventricosa*, 14, 293
Ephedra, 53
Eragrostis, 71, 77, 80, 426; *E. abyssinica*, 124, 133, 135, 300, 416, 426–427; *E. aegyptiaca*, 426; *E. pilosa*, 94, 426; *E. tef*, 14, 94, 293, 426
Essai de géographie physique (Billard), 223
Étude phytogéographique du Cameroun (Letouzey), 224

Fat hen, 35
Ficus, 226, 227
Fig, 254
Fimbrystylis, 235
Flax, 112, 416
Flora Nigritia (Hooker), 244
Fonio (fundi; hungry rice), 5, 14, 16, 92–93, 125, 134, 136, 187, 249, 293, 297, 344–345, 346, 351–352, 414, 415, 417–424, 425, 427–429
Fonio, black, 14, 345, 346, 424–425
Ford Foundation, 223
Frumentum indicum, 413

Garlic, 119
Gold of pleasure, 35

Gossypium, 254–255; *G. herbaceum*, 14, 133–134, 299
Gourd, 254, 294, 296, 298–299, 340
Grains of paradise. *See* Pepper, Melegueta
Graminaceae, 426
Gramineae, 112, 271, 278, 292
Grewia, 80–81, 114–115
Groundnut, 114, 117, 134, 138, 252, 293, 296, 297–298, 321, 324, 343, 345, 346
Guizotia abyssinica, 14, 293, 417

Hackberry, 191, 192, 216
Henna, 255
Hibiscus, 254; *H. cannabinus*, 134, 254, 294; *H. esculentus*, 133, 134, 138, 294; *H. sabdariffa*, 14, 133–134, 254, 293
Holcus saccharatus, 413
Hordeum, 112, 410; *H. spontaneum*, 172; *H. vulgare*, 250, 293
Hyparrhenia, 227; *H. rufa*, 224, 226, 227

Illinois Agricultural Experiment Station, 453
Illustrated London News, 232–233
Indigo, 254–255
Indigofera arrecta, 254–255
Institut Fondamental d'Afrique Noire, 189
Ipomoea batatas, 251, 296, 301
Irvingia, 132
Isoberlinia doka, 226, 227

Jackbean, 343
Jatropha curcas, 252
Jerboa, 195
Jew's mallow, 254
Journal of African History, 235
Journey to Sudan (Ibn Batuta), 418
Jujube, 187
Julbernardia, 55
Juniperus, 53

Kaffir melon, 114
Kaoliang, 459, 476
Kapok tree, 124, 293, 299
Karité (shea butter) tree, 11, 14, 132, 134
Kenaf, 294
Kerstingiella geocarpa, 134, 135, 252, 293, 298; *K. tisserantii*, 252
Kola, 132, 138, 293, 325, 326, 339, 340, 349–350, 351
"Kruis bessie," 114–115

Lagenaria, 86; *L. siceraria*, 134, 254, 294, 296, 298–299; *L. vulgaris*, 115–116
Lawsonia inermis, 255
Lemon, 295, 341
Lime, 138, 254, 341
Linum, 112
Locust bean tree, 293, 326
Lolium temulentum, 432
Lophira lanceolata, 227
Loudetia acuminata, 226
Luco, 413
Lucum, 413

Maize, 14, 30, 32, 115, 122, 137–138, 250, 254, 292, 296, 300–301, 315, 318, 320, 322, 334, 345, 363–364, 367, 413, 434, 465
Mango, 12, 132, 295, 343
Manihot esculenta, 138, 251, 296, 301
Manioc. *See* Cassava
Man the Hunger (Wenner-Gren symposium), 24
"Marula" (wild nut), 114–115
Mazza (Grano) di Congo, 413
Mazza Manputo (Grano de Portogallo), 413
Melica decumbens, 432
Milium indicum, 413
Millet, 27, 30, 76–77, 82, 83, 84, 89, 91–92, 97, 117, 123–127, 171, 172, 174, 177, 200, 203, 249, 296, 315, 320–321, 322, 324, 327–328, 341, 343–346, 347, 351–352, 363, 397, 413–414, 429–433
Millet, bulrush, 87, 112, 187, 191, 200, 201, 249, 255, 293, 294–295, 297, 363, 364, 365, 433–441
Millet, candle, 433–441
Millet, finger, 5, 14, 87, 114, 200, 249, 255, 294–295, 297, 344, 346, 352, 409–417, 474
Millet, floating, 250
Millet, foxtail, 32, 35
Millet, great, 114
Millet, Guinea, 10, 14
Millet, pearl, 5, 6, 7, 10–11, 14, 15, 112, 249, 328, 344, 346, 349, 351–352, 418, 433–441, 474
Monotes kerstingii, 227
Moringa, 11
Musa, 137, 295; *M. ensete (Ensete edulis)*, 135; *M. paradisiaca*, 254; *M. paradisiaca* var. *sapientum*, 254; *M. sapientum*, 137, 138; *M. sapientum* var. *paradisiaca*, 137, 138

Mustard, black, 415
Myrtus, 53

Nettle tree, 115, 245
Nicotiana tabacum, 296, 302
Niger seed, 293
Noog, 5, 14
Northwestern University, 216
Nung, 417

Oats, Ethiopian, 7, 10
Okra, 133, 138, 254, 294, 318, 340, 351, 363
Oleaceae, 53
Onion, 138, 250, 343
Orange, 138, 295, 341
Oryza barthii, 15, 80, 224, 442; *O. breviligulata*, 249, 341, 441; *O glaberrima*, 10, 14, 81, 129, 134, 135, 187, 249, 294, 341, 393, 418, 430–431, 441–445; *O. glaberrima* var. *ebenicolorata*, 430, 441; *O glaberrima* var. *scoparia*, 430; *O. sativa*, 138, 295, 341, 431, 441, 445; *O. stapfii*, 10, 441
Osaka Prefectural University, Japan, 249

Palaeoecology of Africa (journal), 56
Palm: date, 187, 245, 254; fan, 132; oil, 5, 12–13, 14, 80–81, 87, 113, 130, 131–132, 135, 138, 140, 197, 217, 218, 219, 293, 298, 313, 325–326, 334, 338, 339, 340, 349–350, 351, 396; raffia, 138
Panicum, 27, 77, 80, 84, 187; *P. caeruleum*, 440; *P. frumentaceum*, 434; *P. indicum*, 440; *P. laetum*, 113, 192, 193, 204; *P. miliaceum*, 171; *P. phragmitoides*, 227; *P. turgidum*, 114, 118, 195
Parkia, 12, 14; *P. clapertomiana*, 132; *P. filicoidea*, 293
Paspalum, 429–433; *P. commersonii*, 430, 431, 432–433; *P. conjugatum*, 429; *P. exile*, 418; *P. polystachyum*, 432–433; *P. scrobiculatum*, 9–10, 432; *P. scrobiculatum* var. *commersonii*, 430, 431, 432; *P. scrobiculatum* var. *frumentaceum*, 431, 432–433; *P. scrobiculatum* var. *parvispiculata*, 430; *P. scrobiculatum* var. *polystachyum*, 429–433
Pawpaw, 254
Pea, 295, 299–300
Peanut, 114
Pear, 132
Pennisetum, 76–77, 81, 83, 86, 88–89, 112, 113–114, 116–118, 124–125, 126,

135, 140, 172, 189, 191–194, 195, 196, 197, 201, 202, 203–204, 205, 215, 343, 433–441; *P. albicauda*, 439, 440; *P. americanum*, 14, 81, 249, 293, 297, 434; *P. americanum sesquipedale*, 440; *P. ancylochaete*, 436, 438; *P. cinereum*, 135, 436, 437; *P. echinurus*, 439, 440; *P. gambiense*, 434, 436, 437; *P. gibbosum*, 436, 438; *P. gymnothrix*, 435; *P. leonia*, 436, 437; *P. maiwa*, 436, 438; *P. malacochaete*, 439; *P. mil des Peules*, 6; *P. mollissimum*, 434, 435; *P. nigritarum*, 436, 437; *P. niloticum*, 435, 437, 438; *P. orthochaete*, 438; *P. perrottetii*, 435; *P. perspeciosum*, 438; *P. purpurpeum*, 434, 435; *P. pycnostachyum*, 436, 437; *P. rogeri*, 434, 435; *P. spicatum*, 133, 439, 440; *P. stenostachyum*, 434, 435; *P. typhoides*, 114, 439, 440, *P. typhoideum*, 134, 187; *P. versicolor*, 435; *P. violaceum*, 6, 435; *P. vulpinum*, 437, 438

Pepper: capsicum, 254; chili, 296, 301, 343; Melegueta (grains of paradise), 138, 293–294

Persicaria, pale, 35

Phaseolus lunatus, 301; *P. vulgaris*, 296, 301

Phoenix dactylifera, 254

Physic nut, 252

Piasa, 337

Pigeon pea, 294, 295, 297, 345

Pine, bristle-cone, 108–109

Pinus, 53

Pisum arvense, 299–300; *P. sativum*, 299–300

Plantain, 137, 138, 254, 315, 318, 320, 325, 333–334

Plectranthus, 129; *P. esculentus* (*Coleus dysentricus, Coleus dazo*), 14, 129, 251, 293

Poa abyssinica, 426; *P. teff*, 426

Podocarpus, 54

Polish Academy of Sciences, 269, 281–282

Pomegranate, 295

Potato: Hausa, 14, 129, 251, 293, 337; Kafir, 129

Prosopis, 227; *P. africana*, 227

Pseudocadia zambesiaca, 114–115

Pumpkin, 126, 134, 135, 296

Quercus, 53

Raphia hookerii, 138

Rhytachne, 77

Rice: African, 5, 10, 14, 15, 16, 81, 82, 97, 129, 134–135, 187, 249, 294, 315, 318, 320, 321–322, 327–328, 340–343, 346, 347, 351–352, 393, 396, 418, 403–431, 441–445; Asian, 10, 30, 130, 138, 295, 322, 341, 342, 343, 410

Rice, hungry. *See* Fonio

Ricinus communis, 113, 114, 133, 252, 294, 298

Rizga, 251

Roselle, 14, 133–134, 293, 340, 351

Rubber, 313, 325

Saccharum, 300

Salvadoraceae, 53

Sclerocarpa caffra, 114–115

Sclerocarya birrea, 227

Sedge, 235

Sesame, 14, 133–134, 252, 294, 295, 298, 345, 363

Sesamum, 135; *S. indicum*, 14, 133–134, 252, 294, 298; *S. radiatum*, 252

Setaria, 236; *S. italica*, 434; *S. pallidifusca*, 250

Shallot, 343

Shea butter (karité) tree, 11, 14, 132, 134, 293, 326

Sinapsis nigra, 415

Sisal, 296

Social Science Research Council, 357

Solanum, 8; *S. incanum*, 254

Solenostemon (*Coleus*), 397

Sorphum, 5, 7, 8, 14, 15, 77, 82, 83, 84–85, 87, 89, 91–92, 96, 97, 113, 114–115, 123–125, 135, 172, 174, 177, 187, 194, 195, 198, 200, 201, 203, 218, 234, 245–249, 250, 255, 292, 293, 294–295, 296, 297, 315, 320–321, 324, 327–328, 338, 341, 343–346, 347, 352, 363, 364, 365, 366, 369, 370, 397, 412, 413, 416, 418, 453–462, 464–477; aethiopicum, 459, 460–461; arundinaceum, 458, 460–461; bicolar, 459, 460, 466–467, 472–474, 476; caudatum, 86, 234, 245, 255, 456, 466, 467, 469, 475, 476; drummondii, 459; durra, 77, 135, 226, 238, 245, 249, 328, 416, 433, 456–459, 460–461, 466, 467, 470, 472, 474–476; guinea, 245, 249, 255, 328, 343, 349, 456, 459, 460–461, 466, 467, 468–469, 472–476; kafir, 96, 456, 457, 460, 461–462, 466, 467, 471, 472, 474, 475, 476; propinquum,

457, 459; verticilliflorum, 456, 458–459, 460–461; virgatum, 80, 458, 460–461
Sorghum, 77, 81, 83, 86, 88–89, 114–115, 116, 124–125, 133, 140, 189, 202, 204, 236, 453–462, 464–467; *S. aethiopicum*, 457; *S. arundinaceum*, 347, 457; *S. bicolar*, 14, 81, 86, 114, 245–249, 255–256, 297, 453–462; *S. bicolar arundinaceum*, 453, 457–458, 459–460; *S. bicolor bicolor*, 435, 459–461; *S. bicolor* var. *colorans*, 249; *S. controversum*, 435; *S. gambicum*, 135, 455; *S. halepense*, 434, 460; *S. mellitum*, 245–249; *S. miliaceum*, 435; *S. propinquum*, 457; *S. verticilliflorum*, 457; *S. vulgare*, 134, 187, 434
Sorrel, Guinea, 254
Southern Methodist University, 269
Sphenostylis, 397; *S. stenocarpa*, 14, 129, 134, 293
Sporobolus, 426; *S. pyramidalis*, 227
Squash, 114
Sterculia setigera, 227
Sudanese memoirs (Palmer), 238
Sugarcane, 295, 300, 334, 383
Sweet potato, 26, 128, 251, 296, 301, 333, 390

Tamarind, 245, 294
Tamarindus, 12; *T. indica*, 134, 294
Tamarix, 53
Tannia, 333
Taro, 128, 251, 333
Tef (teff), 5, 14, 16, 93–94, 124, 135, 200, 293, 416, 426–427
Telfairia occidentalis, 126, 134, 135
Terminalia, 227
Tiger nuts, 252
Tobacco, 254, 296, 302, 363
Tomato, bitter, 254
Treculia africana, 132
Triticum, 112, 250, 410; *T. compactum*, 113; *T. dicoccum*, 112, 293; *T. durum*, 293, 416; *T. vulgare*, 113

Uapaca togoensis, 227
United Nations, Food and Agricultural Organization, 357
United States: National Science Foundation, 223, 269, 357; Smithsonian Institution, 269

University of California, Berkeley, 357
University of California, Santa Barbara, 234
University of Ibadan, 235
University of Illinois, 465
University of Pennsylvania, 223, 235
University of Zambia, 357
Upper Benue Basin Archaeological Project (UBBAP), 223, 233–235
Urelytrum thyrsioides, 227
Urticaceae, 54

Vernonia amygdalina, 138; *V. colorata*, 138
Verrucipilae, 418
Vetiveria nigritana, 224
Vigna, 86, 197; *V. unguiculata* (*V. sinensis*), 14, 114–115, 116, 133, 134, 217, 252, 294, 297
Voandzeia, 5, 14
Voandzeia, 86; *V. subterranea*, 14, 114, 134, 135, 252, 293, 297–298
Volga Basin Research Project, 214

Waterlily, 80–81
Watermelon, 14, 254, 294
Wenner-Gren Foundation for Anthropological Research: *Man the Hunter* (symposium), 24
Wheat, 30, 94, 112, 113, 116–117, 124, 133, 135, 139–140, 159, 162, 164, 169, 170, 171, 172, 177, 200, 201, 202, 203, 250, 269–271, 278, 284, 292, 293, 343, 352, 397, 410; club, 113; durum, 293, 416; einkorn, 168; emmer, 10, 69, 112, 113, 124, 168–169, 172, 293

Xanthosoma, 128; *X. sagittifolium*, 251, 300

Yam, 5, 6, 8, 13, 14, 15, 27, 88–89, 91, 117, 129–131, 133, 135, 136, 137, 138, 140, 218, 219, 250–251, 255, 257, 293, 295, 296, 298, 315, 318, 320, 322, 323, 333–338, 339, 340, 347, 348, 349, 350–351, 383–403
Yan bean, 129, 293
Yampea, 14, 337
Yautia, 251

Zea mays, 115, 138, 250, 296, 300–301
Zizyphus, 77, 187